Instructor's Manual
with Test Item File and Video Guide

ESSENTIALS OF ENTREPRENEURSHIP AND SMALL BUSINESS MANAGEMENT

Instructor's Manual
with Test Item File and Video Guide

ESSENTIALS
OF ENTREPRENEURSHIP
AND SMALL BUSINESS
MANAGEMENT

Fourth Edition

Thomas W. Zimmerer
Norman M. Scarborough

David E. Tooch
University of New Hampshire

Judy Dietert
Southwest Texas State University

PEARSON
Prentice Hall

Upper Saddle River, New Jersey 07458

VP/Editorial Director: Jeff Shelstad
Acquisitions Editor: David Parker
Associate Editor: Melissa Yu
Manager, Print Production: Christy Mahon
Production Editor & Buyer: Carol O'Rourke
Printer/Binder: Technical Communication Services

10 9 8 7 6 5 4 3 2 1
ISBN 0-13-144043-8

CONTENTS

Essentials of Entrepreneurship and Small Business Management
16-Week Course Outline/Syllabus

Professor: Phone:
Office Location: E-mail:
Office Hours:

Meeting Time/Date
Bldg./Room#:

Text: Essentials of Entrepreneurship and Small Business Management
Zimmerer/Scarborough, Fourth Edition, Prentice Hall, 2005

Course Outcomes:

Evaluate the necessary qualities and characteristics of the successful entrepreneurial profile.

Recognize and determine the steps necessary to open and operate a small business enterprise.

Critique the basic forms of small business ownership.

Identify the marketing, financial, leadership and other competencies needed by an entrepreneur.

Use information, projections, logic and critical thinking to recognize an opportunity and solve small business problems in a multicultural, ethical and legal environment.

Develop a Business Plan.

Plan for Management Succession

Grading:

Components	
Quizzes (6 @ 25 pts. each)	150
Business Plan (100 + 50)	100
Participation/Exercises	100
Total Points	**400**

Participation/Business Plan/Student Conduct:

Students will be required to develop a business plan.
Additional research or in-class exercises may be assigned to help guide you in the development of an individual or group business plan.

Plagiarism is passing off someone else's work or idea as your own. Academic Dishonesty also includes failure on your part to keep your current and past assignments out of the hands of other students who may misrepresent their origins. To receive credit for quantitative assignments, please show all calculations. It is also suggested that you keep a record and/or rough drafts of written or other work until you have received your final grade.

Tentative Class Schedule

The course outline is only a suggested schedule and subject to change at the discretion of the instructor

Week

		Introductions
1	Chapter 1	The Foundations of Entrepreneurship
2	Chapter 2	Inside the Entrepreneurial Mind: From Ideas to Reality
3	Chapter 3	Strategic Management and the Entrepreneur
4	Chapter 4	Forms of Ownership and Franchising
5	Chapter 5	Buying an Existing Business
6	Chapter 6	Building a Powerful Marketing Plan
7	Chapter 7	E-Commerce and the Entrepreneur
8	Chapter 8	Integrated Marketing Communication and Pricing Strategies
9	Chapter 9	Managing Cash Flow
10	Chapter 10	Creating a Successful Financial Plan
11	Chapter 11	Crafting a Winning Business Plan
12	Chapter 12	Sources of Funds: Equity and Debt
13	Chapter 13	Choosing the Right Location and Layout
14	Chapter 14	Global Aspects of Entrepreneurship
15	Chapter 15	Leading the Growing Company and Planning for Management Succession
16	**Business Plans Due**	

Section I - The Challenges of Entrepreneurship

Chapter 1
The Foundations of Entrepreneurship **(PPT 1.1)**

Part One: Learning Objectives

1.   Define the role of the entrepreneur in business in the United States and around the world.

2.   Describe the entrepreneurial profile and evaluate your potential as an entrepreneur.

3.   Describe the benefits and drawbacks of entrepreneurship.

4.   Explain the forces that drive the growth in entrepreneurship.

5.   Explain the cultural diversity of entrepreneurship.

6.   Describe the important role small business plays in our nation's economy.

7.   Describe the ten deadly mistakes of entrepreneurship and how to avoid them.

8.   Put "failure" into the proper perspective.

9.   Explain how entrepreneurs can avoid becoming another failure statistic.

Part Two: Lesson Plan

I.   This is truly the era of the entrepreneur! The past two decades have seen record numbers of entrepreneurs launching new businesses. **(PPT 1.2, 1.3)**

II.   What is an entrepreneur?

An entrepreneur is one who creates a new business in the face of risk and uncertainty for the purpose of achieving profit and growth opportunities and assembles the necessary resources to capitalize on those opportunities. **(PPT 1.4)**

While we may not be able to teach entrepreneurship, we can teach the skills of small business management. This is an important distinction to make to students.

David McClelland the noted psychologist, characterized high achievers/entrepreneurs as having: **(PPT 1.5)**

A.   Desire for responsibility
B.   Preference for moderate risk
C.   Confidence in their ability to succeed
D.   Desire for immediate feedback

E. High level of energy
F. Vision for the future
G. Skill in organization
H. Value of achievement over money

Other characteristics of entrepreneurs

A. High degree of commitment
B. Willingness to accept risk, work hard and take action
C. Flexibility

Emphasize to your students that these are traits of entrepreneurs. Entrepreneurs are not cut from the same mold, and no one set of characteristics can predict entrepreneurial tendencies or success. **(PPT 1.6)**

YOU BE THE CONSULTANT SUMMARY – A Pigskin Revolution

Ed Sabol, a once unhappy coat salesman, had a passion for filming his son's high school football games and other activities. Word of Ed's filming abilities soon got around and he found himself working a number of local high school games. This led to Ed's successful bid ($3,000) to film the 1962 NFL championship game. Then commissioner Pete Rozelle was so impressed with the work that he agreed to Ed's proposal to create a new entity known as NFL Films that would both preserve the history of the game and promote it to the nation's sports fans. NFL Films' creative approach to the game has resulted in 82 Emmy Awards to date.

Ed retired in 1987, turning the reins over to his son Steve who has taken the company to new heights thanks in part to his empowering leadership style and product innovation. The company now has a 200,000 square foot state-of-the-art facility.

Q1. Identify the entrepreneurial traits that Ed Sabol and his son Steve exhibit?
Q2. How would you characterize the Sabol's philosophy, beliefs, and values to a small business as it grows?
Q3. What factors have led to NFL Films' success?

A1. Ed and Steve exhibit great confidence in their own abilities, a vision for current and future markets, high energy and commitment.
A2. The Sabol's put their philosophy and values to work by delegating responsibilities and empowering employees which has resulted in the growth of the business that is also their passion and joy.
A3. Those factors include creativity and innovation, resulting in a product that has distinguished itself in the marketplace.

III. The Benefits of Entrepreneurship **(PPT 1.7)**

A. Opportunity to create your own destiny
B. Opportunity to make a difference
C. Opportunity to reach your full potential
D. Opportunity to generate impressive profits
E. Opportunity to contribute to society and be recognized for your efforts
F. Opportunity to do what you enjoy and have fun at it

IV.   The Potential Drawbacks of Entrepreneurship **(PPT 1.8 thru 1.12)**

A.   Uncertainty of income -"The entrepreneur is the last one to be paid."
B.   Risk of losing your entire investment
C.   Long hours and hard work
D.   Lower quality of life until the business gets established
E.   High levels of stress
F.   Complete responsibility
G.   Discouragement

V.   Behind the Boom: What's Feeding the Entrepreneurial Fire **(PPT 1.13 thru 1.15)**

A.   Entrepreneurs as heroes
B.   Entrepreneurial education
C.   Demographic and economic factors
D.   Shift to a service economy
E.   Technological advancements
F.   Independent lifestyles
G.   E-Commerce and The World Wide Web
H.   International opportunities

VI.   The Cultural Diversity in Entrepreneurship **(PPT 1.16, 1.17)**

A.   Young Entrepreneurs
B.   Women Entrepreneurs
C.   Minority Enterprises
D.   Immigrant Entrepreneurs
E.   Part-time Entrepreneurs
F.   Home-Based Businesses
G.   Family Businesses
H.   Copreneurs
I.   Corporate Castoffs
J.   Corporate Dropouts

YOU BE THE CONSULTANT SUMMARY – Never Too Young

Erica Gluck had a desire to earn her own money at the age of seven. She convinced a local pasta shop to allow her to sell their products off site on weekends. Erica never looked back as she went on to start her own pasta company, expand its product lines, hire her parents and give a portion of her profits back to the community.

Adam Witty, a college student, observed his father repeatedly giving up (season) tickets to Orlando Magic games that often went unused because of last minute business commitments. That sparked the idea for a Web-based company that allows buyers to securely purchase tickets to events that normally would not be available. Adam started the company from his dorm room, was able to utilize the facilities of his school and expanded his product lines to include a wide variety of sporting events.

The University of Maryland created a forum that allows about 100 student entrepreneurs to live and work together. That environment has inspired about twenty of those students to start their own business.

Q1. In addition to the normal obstacles of starting a business, what other barriers do young entrepreneurs face?

Q2. What advantages do young entrepreneurs have when launching a business?

Q3. What advice would you offer a fellow college student about to start a business?

Q4. Work with a team of your classmates to develop ideas about what your college or university could do to create a culture of entrepreneurship on your campus or in your community.

A1. Young entrepreneurs may not be taken seriously, may have a more difficult time raising capital and have far less practical experience.

A2. Young entrepreneurs have no fear, may have little or nothing to lose and a high level of energy.

A3. College students should take advantage of the facilities, professors, programs and opportunities that their school offers (all of which they pay for).

VII.   The Power of "Small" Business (PPT 1.18)

Because big business is more visible than small business, most people underestimate the role of the small firm in the U.S. economy.

A. Definition of a Small Business

1.   One which is independently owned and operated and not dominant in its field.
2.   Eligibility requirements based on industry.
   a)   <u>Retailing</u> - annual sales/receipts not exceeding $3.5 to $13.5 million, depending on the industry.
   b)   <u>Services</u> - annual receipts not exceeding $2.5 to $14.5 million, depending on the industry.
   c)   <u>Wholesaling</u> - yearly sales must not be over $9.5 to $22 million, depending on the industry.
   d)   <u>Agriculture</u> - annual receipts not exceeding $1.0 to $3.5 million, depending on the industry.
   e)   <u>Construction</u> - General construction - annual receipts not exceeding $17 million.
   f)   <u>Special Trade Construction</u> - annual receipts not exceeding $7 million.
   g)   <u>Manufacturing</u> - maximum number of employees may range from 500 to 1,500 depending on the industry.

B. White House Conference on Small Business definition: A firm employing 500 people or fewer. The most commonly used measure is the number of employees on a firm's payroll. (PPT 1.19 thru 1.21)

C. The Committee for Economic Development states that a small business must meet two of four criteria:

1. Management is independent.
2. Capital is supplied and ownership is held by an individual or a small group.
3. Area of operation is mainly local; markets need not be local.
4. Size is small when compared to the biggest unit in the field.

YOU BE THE CONSULTANT – A Chilly Idea

Willis Carrier invented the air conditioner in 1902 to solve a variety of problems that manufacturers were experiencing with their raw materials. The Carrier Engineering Company, formed in 1915, went on to develop products that would air condition large spaces including those outside of the manufacturing area. That feature became an effective marketing tool for retailers and eventually spread to practically every form of space occupied by humans in every country of the world.

Willis Carrier may not have ever imagined the impact that his entrepreneurial and small business spirit and actions would have on the way that we all work and live.

Q1. Was launching a business any easier in Willis Carrier's day than it is today? Explain.
Q2. Explain how Willis Carrier exhibits the entrepreneurial spirit?
Q3. Develop a list of other entrepreneurs whose products, services, or businesses changed the world. Select one that interests you and prepare a short report on him or her.

A1. While none of us are in position to know what it was really like 100 years ago, we clearly live today in a world of unlimited business opportunity.
A2. Willis Carrier had the imagination and skill of an inventor, the desire and commitment of an entrepreneur, and the willingness to work with people from all walks of life.

VIII. The Ten Deadly Mistakes of Entrepreneurship **(PPT 1.22, 1.23)**

Causes of Small Business Failure

1. Management mistakes
2. Lack of experience
3. Poor financial control
4. Weak marketing efforts
5. Failure to develop a strategic plan
6. Uncontrolled growth
7. Poor location
8. Improper inventory control
9. Incorrect pricing
10. Inability to make the "entrepreneurial transition "

IX . Putting Failure into Perspective **(PPT 1.24)**

- There are no such things as failures, only results.
- Always look to turn a negative situation into a positive opportunity.
- Have no fear of failure and be sure to have a contingency plan.
- The only people who never fail are those who never do anything or never attempt anything new.

The successful entrepreneur understands the meaning of these clichés and knows how to deal with adversity in a proactive and positive manner.

X. How to Avoid the Pitfalls **(PPT 1.25)**

1. Know your business in depth.
2. Develop a solid business plan in writing.
3. Manage financial resources.
4. Understand financial statements.
5. Learn to manage people effectively.
6. Keep in tune with yourself.

YOU BE THE CONSULTANT SUMMARY - If At First You Don't Succeed, So What?

The textbook case and the world are full of stories of now famous and successful business people that experienced bankruptcy and/or business failure a number of times prior to achieving the success that we are all familiar with.

Q1. Do those entrepreneurs exhibit the entrepreneurial spirit? If so, how?
Q2. How do these entrepreneurs view failure? Is their view typical of most entrepreneurs?

A1. Those entrepreneurs all had the proper perspective, a contingency plan and the desire to succeed.
A2. Failure is simply the unacceptable result of an action. Failure is a lesson and an experience that can lead to success. This is clearly the perspective of most entrepreneurs.

Part Three: Suggested Answers to Chapter Discussion Questions

1. What forces have led to the boom in entrepreneurship in the United States and around the globe?

- The dream of owning and operating a business
- The effect of downsizing
- The belief that small is beautiful
- The opportunity to enter profitable niche markets
- The growing international and e-commerce markets

2.   What is an entrepreneur? Give a brief description of the entrepreneurial profile.

An entrepreneur is one who creates a new business in the face of risk and uncertainty for the purpose of achieving profits and growth by identifying opportunities and assembling the necessary resources to capitalize on them.

3. Inc. Magazine claims, "Entrepreneurship is more mundane than it's sometimes portrayed... you don't need to be a person of mythical proportions to be very, very successful in building a company." Do you agree? Explain.

Anyone can become an entrepreneur. There are no limitations on this form of economic expression. The skills of entrepreneurship and innovation can be learned.

4. What are the major benefits of business ownership?

- Opportunity to gain control over your own destiny
- Opportunity to make a difference
- Opportunity to reach your full potential
- Opportunity to reap unlimited profits
- Opportunity to contribute to society and be recognized for your efforts
- Opportunity to do what you enjoy

5. Which of the potential drawbacks to business ownership are most crucial?

- Uncertainty of income
- Risk of losing invested capital
- Long hours and hard work
- Quality of life until the business gets established
- High levels of stress
- Complete responsibility

6. Briefly describe the role of the following groups in entrepreneurship: women, minorities, immigrants, part-timers, home-based business owners, family business owners, copreneurs, corporate castoffs and corporate dropouts.

Women often face discrimination in the workplace. Entrepreneurship offers women opportunities for economic growth. *Minorities* also face discrimination in the workplace and can benefit from entrepreneurship. *Immigrant* entrepreneurs arrive with more education and experience. Their dedication and desire to succeed enables them to achieve their dreams. *Part-timers* have the best of both worlds and can ease into a business without sacrificing a steady paycheck and benefits. *Home-based* businesses are booming. Technology and this "Homecoming" support nearly 44 percent of US households with some form of home office activity. *Family* businesses are an integral part of our economy. 90 percent of U.S businesses are family owned. *Copreneurs* are entrepreneurial couples that work together. They represent the fastest growing business sector. *Corporate Castoffs* have extensive on-the-job experience and are dislocated workers due primarily to corporate downsizing. *Corporate Dropouts* leave organizations to pursue a better way of life spearheaded by the "trust gap" over job security.

7. What is a small business? What contributions do they make to our economy?

"One which is independently owned and operated and not dominant in its field of operation."

- Small businesses employ more than 50% of the nation's private sector workforce.
- Almost 90% of all businesses employ fewer than 20 workers.
- Small companies have created 66% of all new jobs since the early 1970s.

- Small businesses produce 48% of the nation's GDP and account for 53% of all sales.
- The current growth rate is 800,000 to 900,000 new ventures each year.

8.   Describe the small business failure rate.

Because of limited resources, inexperienced management and lack of financial stability, small businesses suffer a mortality rate significantly higher than that of larger, established businesses.

9.   Outline the causes of small business failures. Which problems cause most business failures?

- <u>Poor operations management</u> - The manager lacks the ability to operate a small business.
- <u>Lack of experience</u> - Many owners start businesses in industries that they have no experience in.
- <u>Poor financial management</u>- Many owners start with too little money and with little or no understanding of financial spreadsheet applications.
- <u>Over-investing in fixed assets</u> - Owners who over-invest in fixed assets sometimes find themselves with no access to funds for working capital or expansion.
- <u>Poor credit practices</u> - Owners often sell on credit to meet (or beat) the competition and find that they lack the additional working capital required or the ability to collect on accounts.
- <u>Failure to plan</u> – The lack of a strategic plan to guide the business in the long run.
- <u>Unplanned and uncontrolled growth</u> - Growth is natural and healthy, but unplanned growth can be fatal to a business.
- <u>Inappropriate location</u> - Owners who choose a business location without proper analysis, investigation, and planning often fail. Too often, owners seek "cheap" sites and locate themselves straight into failure.
- <u>Lack of inventory control</u> - Although inventory is typically the largest investment for the owner, inventory control is one of the most neglected duties.
- <u>Inability to make the "Entrepreneurial Transition"</u> - Can we learn to empower others to make decisions and act independently?

10.   How does the typical entrepreneur view the possibility of business failure?

Although failure is a possibility, it is never a deterrent. Failures are the unacceptable results of actions taken that provide a valuable lesson for the future.

11.   How can the small business owner avoid the common pitfalls that lead to business failure?

- Know your business in depth
- Develop a solid business plan
- Manage financial resources
- Understand financial statements
- Learn to manage people effectively

12.   Why is it important to study the small business failure rate and the causes of small business failures?

It is important to know what the major causes of small business failures are so that the prospective entrepreneur can avoid those pitfalls.

13.   Explain the typical entrepreneurs attitude toward risk.

Risk is inherent to all future actions. Entrepreneurs are not necessarily high-risk takers; they prefer and willingly accept and manage low-to-moderate risk situations.

14.   Are you interested in launching a small business? If so, when?
What kind of business? Describe it. What can you do to ensure its success?

General discussion with students in your class

Part Four: Lecture or Critical Thinking Case Studies - Not Found In Student Text

THREE WOMEN WHO MADE IT
ENTREPRENEURIAL COLLAGE
SOMETIMES YOU WIN-SOMETIMES YOU LOSE

THREE WOMEN WHO MADE IT

When Janet Jones picks up passengers in her taxi, they are not the usual type; in fact, they are furry and four-legged. Jones's cab service, Pet-Mobile, is reserved for pets-- dogs, cats, rabbits, small livestock, and birds. Her cab service shuttles animals to grooming appointments, veterinary checkups, boarding, and other destinations. "My service is designed to help people who don't have transportation, folks with busy work schedules, and those who would rather stay in bed on a Saturday morning," she says.
Jones typically charges $20 to $30 for a round-trip, although rates vary depending on the number of pets, their size, and the distance traveled. Her truck, distinctively painted with the name of her business, is fully equipped with leashes, carrying crates and harnesses to ensure pet safety in transit.

Joanne Marlowe began her entrepreneurial career at age thirteen. In the ten years that followed, she launched several companies in the garment industry. During June, 1988, Marlowe discovered that a co-founder had embezzled thousands of dollars from her company, Double Sharp Garments. "I was pretty depressed, and one of my friends pointed out that I lived across the street from the beach but had never gone. Never had time," she recalls. "It was a beautiful Lake Michigan day," Marlowe says. "I laid out my towel. To pamper myself, I spent a lot of time putting on suntan oil. Just as I stretched out, a gust of wind picked up the towel and covered me in sand. I hit the roof. My friend said, `Joanne, instead of getting angry, why don't you figure out a fix?'" Marlowe figured that a weighted beach towel would be relatively inexpensive to produce, and that it could be telemarketed. "So instead of relaxing at the beach, I spent the day coming up with a prototype and had the product developed within five weeks. I had it to market within eight weeks," she remembers. The workload was terrific. "I was sleeping about three hours a day from July to October. I wasn't very healthy, but it worked," remembers Marlowe. It *did* work, The company that Marlowe started with just $750 now sells more than $8 million worth of the towels each year.

Celia Tejada always dreamed of becoming a clothing designer so she could translate the secret vision of her Spanish homeland into fashionable clothing. Born in a tiny village in northern Spain, Tejada studied at an internationally known design school in Bilbao before coming to the United States in 1979. While working for an interior designer, Tejada came up with a sweatshirt combining a tic-tac-toe design and the Italian phrase for "kiss me." The department store I. Magnin purchased the design for a Valentine's Day promotion.

In 1986, Tejada decided that "I knew enough to start my own business, and I took the plunge." She spent the next six months working feverishly on market research, determining costs and prices, forecasting cash flow, and designing her logo. She based her product line on the Spanish attitude toward leisure time. "In Spain, we have a saying: `The mornings are for sport, the afternoons are for relaxation, and the nights are for parties,'" she jokes. She first introduced a line of sportswear called Tejada Deporte. In 1988, she added a line of dressier, higher-priced clothing with heavier Spanish design elements called Signature Sportswear. "When starting a company from scratch," she says, it's not easy to find people willing to wear many hats. In the beginning, I handled all the marketing, design, and production and a customer-service person doubled as secretary." Today, more than three hundred specialty shops nationwide and three upscale California department stores carry her lines.

1. What particular barriers do women face in launching businesses?
2. What advantages does entrepreneurship offer women over working for someone else?
3. What disadvantages do women face as entrepreneurs?

Sources: Adapted From Marcia Pear, "Clothes That Say Ole!" *Nation's Business*, April 1990, pp. 14-15. Copyright 1991. U.S. Chamber of Commerce: "Poodle Taxi: Share a Pet-Mobile Service," *Your Own Business*; "Marlowe's Ghosts," *Inc.*, November 1989. pp.66-67.

ENTREPRENEURIAL COLLAGE

Entrepreneurs are as varied and unique as their business ideas. They come in all shapes, sizes, ages, and colors. Consider the following collage of entrepreneurs:

- Ten-year-old Brandon Bozek started his business, Bloomin' Express, when he noticed that the flowers customers bought from the local supermarket wilted after just a day or two. Brandon's fresh-flower subscription service rings up sales of $150 per month, and most of the $75 in profit goes into savings. He telephones his order to a local flower market every Tuesday morning. On Thursdays, with the help of his "steering wheel consultants" (his parents), Brandon delivers the floral orders to his customers.
- Gerald Levinson's radio was stolen from his car three times despite the car alarm and stereo lock he used. So Levinson found a better way: He designed a "stolen radio facade" that fits over a radio to make it look as if it has already been stolen. The unit is very convincing-complete with loose wires and cracked plastic.
- Mary Anne Jackson, a former executive at Beatrice Foods, went out on her own to start the first prepackaged food company aiming its products at kids. Her company, My Own Meals, generates more than $5 million in sales. "All I had when I started was an idea for a product and a prayer," she says.
- Michael Williams saw an opportunity in an unexploited ethic niche, a black comedy club. With $1,000 of his savings, Williams rented a hall and placed an ad in a magazine for black stand-up comedians. Eight local comics performed. The show was a hit and the Comedy Act Theater was born. Today, the club grosses $600,000 annually, and Williams has opened a second club with plans to open twenty-four more.

- If you are around kids, chances are that you have heard about the Teenage Mutant Ninja Turtles. The Turtles' creators, Kevin Eastman and Peter Laird, were struggling artists swapping drawings in their living room in 1983. Eastman sketched a masked upright turtle armed with an oriental weapon. "It was a spontaneous thing. I did it to make Peter laugh," Eastman says. Within minutes, the two had created one of the most recognizable sets of heroes in kid-dom. Eastman and Laird launched their own comic book publishing company, and their first black-and-white comics sold rapidly. Soon after, the artists signed a licensing agreement with Playmate Toys for a variety of children's products. The reptilian heroes Leonardo, Donatello, Raphael, and Michelangelo were once the hottest non-electronic toys on the market since Cabbage Patch dolls. Their action toys, movies, cartoons, comic books, and other products generate between $5 million and $15 million in revenues for the two creators. "I'm now a businessman instead of an artist," observes Eastman. Cowabunga!

1. What common factors do you see in these entrepreneurs' stories?
2. What contributions do small businesses like these make to the U.S. economy?

Sources: Adapted From "Kids in Business," *Changing Times*, March 1990, pp.96-97; Terri Thompson, "How Tykes Can Be Tycoons," *US News & World Report*, February 19, 1990, pp. 68-69; "Fooling the Fools," *Entrepreneur*, December 1989, p. 118; Christine Forbes and Erika Kotite, "Entrepreneurs Across America," *Entrepreneur*, June 1990 p 96; Wayne Lionel Aponte "Have You Heard the One About the Comedy Club," *Wall Street Journal*, October 31, 1990, p. B2; Christopher Geehern, "Cowabunga Dude," *Entrepreneur*, March 1991, pp. 76-81.

SOMETIMES YOU WIN - SOMETIMES YOU LOSE

The greatest glory is not in never failing but in rising up every time we fall.
    -*Confucius*

Philip J. Romano, founder of Fuddruckers, a nationwide gourmet hamburger chain, truly is a restaurant entrepreneur. Romano has experienced the taste of failure on more than one occasion. Yet he realizes that success in the volatile restaurant business requires trying creative new concepts that may fail. Failure is common in the restaurant industry; eating and drinking establishments top the list of businesses with the greatest failure rates.

Much of Romano's success is attributable to his ability to anticipate dining trends and to develop effective restaurant promotions. He caught on to the salad-bar trend early in his first restaurant, the Nag's Head Bar in West Palm Beach. He captured customers' interest with another venture after his grand- opening; he padlocked the door and sent keys to select customers. The gimmick created an informal cadre of salespeople touting the restaurant by word of mouth. When meat prices pushed up prices 30 percent at his Friends of Edinburgh Scottish Pub, Romano had new menus printed. But he issued the old menus to regular customers, who continued to pay the old prices as long as they brought their old menus. The gimmick at his lunch-oriented First National Bar & Grill was for customers to punch time clocks and pay by the minute.

The gimmicks didn't always work, and Romano's instincts about diners' preferences weren't always correct. His Pasta Palace, a combination art-deco movie house and pasta restaurant, opened in 1975, well before art-deco or pasta became chic in Florida. It closed quickly.

In 1985, Romano thought he was catching the wave for lighter fare with his health-oriented Stix Eating Spa in San Antonio. But the upscale restaurant appealed to only a very small customer base, and sales fell well below expectations. "It was the right restaurant in the wrong place," he claimed after the restaurant closed.

Even Fuddruckers, which for a time was one of the hottest food chains around, began to slide. Romano overestimated the public's willingness to pay $5 for a burger. The restaurant failed to adapt its menu and its prices in time and incurred a huge loss. Romano sold Fuddruckers the next year.

His current venture, Romano's Macaroni Grill, is highly successful. Modeled after his memories of his grandfather's warm Italian kitchen, the restaurant draws crowds on traditionally slow nights. Romano offers free meals on Monday or Tuesday each month. The catch: customers never know which Monday or Tuesday!

Romano's newest restaurant idea presents yet another challenge for him: convincing New Yorkers to indulge their palates with hearty Tex-Mex fare. The competition will be stiff; there are some twelve thousand competing restaurants in Manhattan, and overhead expenses are outrageously high.
The real test of success or failure will be told on the tables of the Texas Tortilla Bakery.

1.   Describe the small business failure rate.
2.   What factors cause most small business failures?
3.   Is failure among entrepreneurs necessarily bad? Why or why not?

Sources: Adapted From Marj Charlier, "Romano Varies Menu to Cook Up Another Restaurant," reprinted by permission of *Wall Street Journal*, April 11, 1990. p. B1. _ 1990. Dow Jones & Company, Inc. All rights reserved worldwide.

Part Five: Supplemental Readings

"The Essence of Entrepreneurial Success," Richard L. Osborne, Management Design, Nov. 15, 1995, Vol. 33, No. 7.

"The Dark Side of the Entrepreneur," S.D. McKenna, Leadership and Organizational Development Journal, Nov. 1996, Vol. 17, No. 6.

"Clarifying the Entrepreneurial Orientation Construct and Linking it to Performance," G.T. Lumpkin and Gregory G. Dess, Academy of Management Review, Jan. 1996, Vol. 21, No. 1.

"Go Ahead-Jump! There's Never Been a Better Time to Chuck the Corporate Grind," Andy Kessler, Forbes, Feb. 26, 1996, Vol. 157, No. 4.

"Wanted: Entrepreneurial Skills, Employers Seek Candidates Who Have Run Their Own Businesses," Terrence L. Johnson, Black Enterprise, April 1996, Vol. 26, No. 9.

"Entrepreneurs Who Excel," Michael Barrier, Nation's Business, August 1996, Vol. 84, No. 8.

Chapter 2
Inside the Entrepreneurial Mind: From Ideas to Reality **(PPT 2.1)**

Part One: Teaching Objectives

1.   Explain the differences among creativity, innovation and entrepreneurship.

2.   Describe why creativity and innovation are such an integral part of entrepreneurship.

3.   Understand how the two hemispheres of the human brain function and what role they play in creativity.

4.   Explain the ten "mental locks" that limit individual creativity.

5.   Understand how entrepreneurs can enhance the creativity of their employees as well as their own creativity.

6.   Describe the steps in the creative process.

7.   Discuss techniques for improving the creative process.

8.   Describe the protection of intellectual property involving patents, trademarks, and copyrights.

Part Two: Lesson Plan

One of the tenants of entrepreneurship is the ability to create new and useful ideas that solve the problems and challenges that people face every day.

I.   Creativity, Innovation, and Entrepreneurship **(PPT 2.2, 2.3)**

Creativity is the ability to develop new ideas and discover new ways of looking at problems and opportunities.
Innovation is the ability to apply creative solutions to problems and opportunities that enhance or enrich peoples' lives.

One entrepreneur explains, "Creativity is only useful if it is channeled and directed."

Leadership expert Warren Bennis says, "Today's successful companies live and die according to the quality of their ideas." **(PPT 2.4)**

Entrepreneurship is the result of a disciplined, systematic process of applying creativity and innovation to needs and opportunities in the marketplace.

Innovation must be a constant process because most ideas don't work and most innovations fail.

13

II.   Creativity—A Necessity for Survival **(PPT 2.5)**

Creativity is an important source for building a competitive advantage and for survival.

Making the inferential leap from what has worked in the past to what will work today (or in the future) requires entrepreneurs to cast off their limiting assumptions, beliefs, and behaviors and to develop new insights into the relationship among resources, needs, and values.

A *Paradigm* is a preconceived idea of what the world is, what it should be like, and how it should operate. These ideas become so deeply rooted in our minds that they become blocks to creative thinking, even though they may be outdated, obsolete, and no longer relevant.

Can creativity be taught? Research shows that anyone can learn to be creative. Author Joyce Wycoff believes everyone can learn techniques and behaviors that generate ideas.

Word game in table format– Figure 2.1 How Creative Are You? **(PPT 2.6, 2.7)**

III.   Creative Thinking

Research into the operation of the human brain shows that each hemisphere of the brain processes information differently and that one side of the brain tends to be dominant over the other.

The human brain develops asymmetrically, and each hemisphere tends to specialize in certain functions. The left brain handles language, logic and symbols. The right brain takes care of the body's emotional, intuitive, and spatial functions.

Right-brained lateral thinking is somewhat unconventional, unsystematic, and relies on kaleidoscope/lateral thinking (considering a problem from all sides and jumping into it at different points). **(PPT 2.8 thru 2.10)**

Left-brained vertical thinking is narrowly focused and systematic, proceeding in a highly logical fashion from one point to the next. It is guided by linear, vertical thinking (from one logical conclusion to the next).

Those who have learned to develop their right-brained thinking skills tend to:
> -challenge custom, routine, and tradition
> -realize there is more than one "right answer"
> -have "helicopter skills" to rise above daily routine
> -ask the question, "Is there a better way?"

Entrepreneurs can learn to tap their innate creativity by breaking down the barriers to creativity that most of us have.

Entrepreneurship requires both left- and right-brained thinking. Have students test their skills with the Perception and Creativity Exercises (Figure 2-2 What Do You See?).

YOU BE THE CONSULTANT SUMMARY – The Spirit of Entrepreneurship in the Olympics

Throughout history, Olympic athletes have pushed back the frontiers of their sports by developing new techniques, improved training methods, and innovative solutions to existing problems. Two of the best examples of applying creativity to their sports are figure skater Sonja Henie and high jumper Dick Fosbury.

Before Sonja Henie came along, figure skaters performed a series of precise, routine moves that emphasized accuracy and control. Henie transformed the sport into the graceful combination of motion, music, and muscle that it is today. Even her costumes proved to be an exciting innovation. Trained in both dance and ballet as a child, Henie cast aside the existing paradigms of what ice-skating was as she recognized the possibilities of transferring dance movements onto the ice. Today, other skaters like Nancy Kerrigan and Katarina Witt continue her legacy of creativity and change by injecting elements of gymnastics and performing triple jumps and axels.

In the 1968 Olympics in Mexico City, Dick Foley forever changed the sport of high jumping. He approached the bar at a different angle and then curved his body over the bar face up, kicking his legs over the end of the jump. "Fosbury Flop," as the style became known, transfers the weight of the jumper over the bar in stages. He broke the world's high jumping record by 6cm, but also had the satisfaction of creating a new style used by athletes all over the world today.

Q1. What is a paradigm? How does a paradigm stifle creativity?
Q2. Work with a small group of your classmates to identify a local business that is bound by a paradigm.
Q3. What impact is this paradigm having on the business? Identify the paradigm and then generate as many creative suggestions as you can in 20 minutes that would change the paradigm.
Q4. What can entrepreneurs do to throw off existing paradigms?

A1. A paradigm is a preconceived idea of what the world is, what it should be like, and how it should operate. They are deeply rooted in our minds and become blocks to creative thinking.
A2. & 3. Students will provide a range of examples.
A4. Think with an open mind, allow yourself to be creative, don't allow yourself to become rule driven, and avoid mental blocks.

IV.   Barriers to Creativity (**PPT 2.11, 2.12**)

There are many barriers to creativity-- time pressures, unsupportive management, pessimistic coworkers, overly rigid company policies, and countless others.

The most difficult hurdles to overcome are those that individuals impose upon themselves. In his book, *A Whack on the Side of the Head*, Roger von Oech identifies ten "mental blocks" that limit individual creativity. They are as follows:

1. *Searching for just one right answer*
2. *Focusing on being logical*
3. *Blindly following rules*
4. *Constantly being practical*
5. *Viewing play as frivolous*
6. *Becoming overly specialized*
7. *Avoiding ambiguity*

15

8. *Fearing looking foolish*
9. *Fearing mistakes and failure*
10. *Believing that "I'm not creative"*

Questions to Spur the Imagination Table 2.1 **(PPT 2.13 thru 2.15)**

1. Is there a new way to do it?
2. Can you borrow or adapt it?
3. Can you give it a new twist?
4. Do you merely need more of the same?
5. Less of the same?
6. Is there a substitute?
7. Can you rearrange the parts?
8. What if you do just the opposite?
9. Can you combine ideas?
10. Can you put it to other uses?
11. What else could we make from this?
12. Are there other markets for it?
13. Can you reverse it?
14. What idea seems impossible, but if executed, would revolutionize your business?

V.   How to Enhance Creativity

New ideas are fragile creations, but the right organizational environment can encourage people to develop and cultivate them.

Ensuring that workers have the freedom and the incentives to be creative is one of the best ways to achieve creativity.

Entrepreneurs can stimulate their own creativity and encourage it among workers by: **(PPT 2.16, 2.17)**

1. Embracing diversity
2. Expecting creativity
3. Expecting and tolerating failure
4. Encouraging curiosity
5. Viewing problems as challenges
6. Providing creativity training
7. Providing support
8. Developing a procedure for capturing ideas
9. Rewarding creativity
10. Modeling creative behavior

Enhancing Individual Creativity by using the following techniques: **(PPT 2.18, 2.19)**

1. Allow yourself to be creative
2. Give your mind fresh input every day
3. Recognize the creative power of mistakes

16

4. Keep a journal handy to record your thoughts and ideas
5. Listen to other people
6. Talk to a child
7. Keep a toy box in your office
8. Read books on stimulating creativity or take a class on creativity
9. Take some time off

YOU BE THE CONSULTANT SUMMARY – The Creative Side of Entrepreneurship

When St. Petersburg, one of the most splendid, harmonious cites in Europe, was being laid out early in the eighteenth century, many large boulders brought by a glacier had to be removed. One particularly large rock was in the path of one of the principle avenues that had been planned. Submitted bids to remove the rock were very high since no modern equipment existed. While the officials pondered what to do, a peasant presented himself and offered to get rid of the rock for a much lower price. The next morning the peasant showed up with a crowd of other peasants carrying shovels. They propped the rock up, dug a large hole and pushed the rock in. This was an early example of creative thinking.

Managers at the Cleveland Museum used a similar kind of creative thinking to ensure the success of a dazzling exhibit of ancient Egyptian treasures. Taking a different approach to marketing, managers held a free private showing to the town's taxi drivers. Impress the cab drivers, they reasoned, and the "cabbies" would recommend the new exhibit to their tourist. That's exactly what happened. During the exhibit's run in Cleveland, the museum enjoyed shoulder-to-shoulder attendance, thanks to the talkative cab drivers and creative museum managers.

The Principle of an Oregon middle school solved a maintenance problem (girls putting lipstick on and pressing their lips to the mirrors) by having the janitor demonstrate to a group of girls how difficult it was to clean the mirrors (by dipping a long-handled squeegee in the toilet and cleaning one of the mirrors).

Q1. Contact a local small business owner and ask him/her about a problem his/her company is having. Work with a small team of your classmates and use the type of creative thinking described above to generate potential solutions to the problem. Remember to think creatively.

A1. Students will provide a range of solutions.

VI.   The Creative Process **(PPT 2.20 thru 2.32)**

Although new ideas may appear to strike like a bolt of lightning, they are actually the result of the creative process, which involves seven steps:

1. Preparation
2. Investigation
3. Transformation
4. Incubation
5. Illumination
6. Verification
7. Implementation

Brian Le Gette and Ron Wilson, engineers and students of business, have a passion for modifying or redesigning already existing every day products to create new and successful markets that make money and improve the comfort level of their customers.

This is a classic story of two student entrepreneurs who first charged $7,500 worth of materials on their credit cards, created their first product (modified earmuffs) at home, and sold it on the street. Their initial success led to an appearance on the QVC channel, where they sold 5,000 additional units in just eight-and-one-half minutes. Three years later, the partners had sold 600,000 more units.

Next came the raising of $2 million of capital that allowed them to hire employees and to modify and redesign a number of other every day products (self-inflating stadium seats, pop-open beach mats and so on). Big Bang Products went on to generate annual sales of more than $35 million and continues to grow.

"Innovation is the easy part," says Le Gette. "The difficult part is choosing the right innovation."

Q1. What is Big Bang Products' competitive edge in the marketplace?
Q2. Try the company's approach yourself. Work with a team of your classmates to select an every day product and brainstorm ways in which it could be improved.
Q3. How would you determine the market potential of your new and improved design?

A1. The old business term "product differentiation" best describes their competitive edge. Each of the partner's products is more comfortable, more practical, and just different enough from the competitions'. It is also produced in a manner that lends itself to competitive pricing in large volumes.
A2. Students will generate many good ideas. Entrepreneurs should be encouraged to move forward with their best idea.

A3. Potential new products could be test marketed locally in the same manner as the partners in this case. New products could become legally protected and then shopped around to existing manufacturers and marketers. Students could also create a business plan for their newly designed products.

VII.   Techniques for improving the Creative Process (**PPT 2.33**)

Brainstorming is a process in which a small group of people interact, with very little structure, with the goal of producing a large quantity of novel and imaginative ideas. For a brainstorming session to be successful, an entrepreneur should follow these guidelines:

1. keep the group small—five to eight members
2. company rank and department affiliation are irrelevant
3. have a well-defined problem to address
4. limit the session to 40 to 60 minutes
5. appoint someone the job of recorder
6. use a seating pattern that encourages communication
7. encourage all ideas from the team, even wild and extreme ones
8. establish a goal of quantity of ideas rather than quality
9. forbid evaluation or criticism
10. encourage "idea hitch-hiking"

Mind-mapping is an extension of brainstorming. It is a graphical technique that encourages thinking on both sides of the brain, visually displays the various relationships between ideas, and improves the ability to view the problem from many sides. It relates to the way the brain actually works. Rather than throwing out ideas in a linear fashion, the brain jumps from one idea to another. In many creative sessions, ideas are rushing out so fast that many are lost if a person attempts to shove them into a linear outline.

The Mind-mapping Process works this way:
1. sketch a picture symbolizing the problem
2. write down every idea that comes to your mind – use key words and symbols
3. when idea flow starts to trickle, stop
4. allow your mind to rest a few minutes

Rapid Prototyping transforms ideas into actual models that point out flaws and lead to improvements. The three principles of rapid prototyping are "The Three R's": *rough, rapid, and right*.

YOU BE THE CONSULTANT SUMMARY – Evaluating Ideas for Their Market Potential

In 1989, Charles H. Duell, US Commissioner of Patents, advised President McKinley to close the US Patent Office because, "Everything that can be invented has been invented." He was of course way off the mark.

This case encourages students to test their new product ideas using a number of screening techniques. The following questions can help an entrepreneur or inventor assess the profit potential of an idea:

1. What benefits does the product or service offer? Is the need real?
2. Has the problem been pinpointed? What problems or difficulties will it cause?
3. On a scale of 1 to 10, how difficult is it to execute?
4. Can customers afford it? Does it have a natural sales appeal?
5. What existing product/services will compete?
6. On a scale of 1 to 10, how easily can its benefits be understood?
7. How complex is the product? Can you develop the prototype yourself?
8. On a scale of 1 to 10, how difficult will it be to get product into the customer's hand?
9. How unique is the product and how easily can it be copied?
10. How much will it cost to produce?

Michael Michalko, the author of *Cracking Creativity: The Secrets of Creative Geniuses*, suggests using the (PMI) Plus, Minus, Interesting Technique to calculate a score that gives the entrepreneur some sense of an idea's market potential. "First list all the positives (plus) aspects of the idea," he says. "Then list all the negative (minus) aspects. List everything that's interesting about it, but not sure if it's a plus or minus. Evaluating an idea in this way will lead to one of three results. You'll decide it's a bad idea, a good idea, or you'll recycle it into something else."

Students should try their hands at evaluating an idea.

19

Q1. Use the resources on the World Wide Web and your library to explore the prospects for Randi Altschul's product (the disposable cell phone).

Q2. Use the information you collect to answer as many of the questions listed above as possible. Conduct a (PMI) plus, minus, interesting analysis for Randi's idea.

A1. & A2. Comparisons should be made between the content and quality of student research responses.

VIII. Protecting Your Ideas **(PPT 2.34, 2.35)**

Entrepreneurs must understand how to put patents, copyrights and trademarks to work for them.

- *Patents* – a grant from the federal government's Patent and Trademark Office (PTO), to the inventor, giving the exclusive right to use or sell the invention in this country for 20 years from the date of the patent application.
- Inventors who develop a new plant can obtain a *plant patent* (by grafting or cross-breeding not planting seeds).
- Most patents are granted for new product inventions, but design patents, which extend beyond the date the patent is issued, are given to inventors who make new original and ornamental changes in the designs of existing products that enhance their sales.
- A device cannot be patented if it has been in print anywhere in the world.
- Before beginning the lengthy process of applying for a patent, it is best to seek the advice of a patent agent or attorney. A list of registered professionals can be found at: http://www.uspto.gov/web/offices/dcom/olia/oed/roster/

The patent process: **(PPT 2.36)**

1. Establish the inventions novelty
2. Document the device
3. Search existing patents
4. Study search results
5. Submit the patent application
6. Prosecute the patent application

A *Trademark* is any distinctive word, phrase, symbol, design, name, logo, slogan or trade dress that a company uses to identify the origin of a product or to distinguish it from other goods in the market. A *Service Mark* is the same as a trademark, except that it identifies and distinguishes the source of a service rather than a product. **(PPT 2.37, 2.38)**

A *Copyright* is an exclusive right that protects the creators of original works of authorship such as literary, dramatic, musical, and artistic works. This includes motion pictures, software, choreography, books, and recordings. **(PPT 2.39)**

Protecting Intellectual Property is imperative in the marketplace today. Unfortunately, not every businessperson respects the rights of ownership to products, processes, names, and works. The primary weapon is efficient use of the legal system. Before bringing a lawsuit, an entrepreneur must consider the following issues:

1. Can the opponent afford to pay if you win?
2. Will you get enough from the suit to cover the costs of hiring an attorney?

3   Can you afford the loss of time and privacy from the ensuing lawsuit?

Part Three: Suggested Answers to Chapter Discussion Questions

1. Explain the differences among creativity, innovation, and entrepreneurship.

    Creativity is the ability to develop new ideas and to discover new ways of looking at problems and opportunities. Innovation is the ability to apply creative solutions to those problems and opportunities to enhance or enrich people's lives. Entrepreneurship is the ability of the entrepreneur to succeed by doing things in an innovative way.

2. How are creativity, innovation, and entrepreneurship related?

    Creativity has become a core business skill, and entrepreneurs lead the way in developing and applying that skill. Successful entrepreneurs come up with creative ideas and then find ways to make them work to solve a problem or fill a need. In an ever-changing world, creativity and innovation are vital to a company's success and survival.

3. Why are creativity and innovation so important to the survival and success of a business?

    Sometimes creativity involves generating something from nothing. When small business owners cannot outspend their larger rivals, they can create powerful competitive advantages by "out creating" and "out innovating" their larger rivals. Today's successful businesses live and die according to the quality of their ideas.

4. One entrepreneur claims, "Creativity unrelated to a business plan has no value." What does he mean? Do you agree?

    Yes, creativity is only useful if it is channeled and directed.

5. What is a paradigm? What impact do paradigms have on creativity?

    A paradigm is a preconceived idea of what the world is, what it should be like, and how it should operate. They are deeply rooted in our minds and become immovable blocks to creative thinking.

6. Can creativity be taught or is it an inherent trait? Explain.

    It can be taught. Research indicates that anyone can be creative. Each person can be taught techniques and behaviors that can help them generate more ideas.

7. How does the human brain function? What operation does each hemisphere specialize in? What hemisphere is the "seat" of creativity?

    Each hemisphere of the human brain processes information differently and one side of the brain tends to be dominant over the other. The left brain is guided by linear, vertical thinking and handles language, logic and symbols. The right brain takes care of the body's emotional, intuitive, and spatial functions, relying heavily on images.

8. Briefly outline the "ten mental locks" that can limit individual creativity. Give an example of a situation in which you subjected yourself to one of these mental locks.

    Searching for the one right answer
    Focusing on being logical
    Blindly following the rules
    Constantly being practical
    Viewing play as frivolous
    Becoming overly specialized
    Avoiding ambiguity
    Fearing looking foolish
    Fearing mistakes and failure
    Believing that "I'm not creative"

    Each student will have a different "mental lock" experience.

9. What can entrepreneurs do to stimulate their own creativity and to encourage it among workers?

    Enhancing individual creativity:

    Allow yourself to be creative
    Give your mind daily input
    Keep a journal
    Read books that stimulate creativity
    Take a class on creativity
    Take some time off

    Ways to enhance creativity:

    Expect it
    Tolerate and expect failure
    Encourage curiosity
    View problems as challenges
    Provide creativity training
    Provide support
    Reward creativity
    Model creative behavior

10. Explain the steps of the creative process. What can an entrepreneur do to enhance each step?

    1. Preparation
    2. Investigation
    3. Transformation
    4. Incubation
    5. Illumination
    6. Verification
    7. Implementation

Techniques for improving the creative process include brainstorming, mind-mapping, and rapid prototyping.

11. Explain the difference among a patent, a trademark, and a copyright. What form of intellectual property does each protect?

A patent is a grant from the federal government's Patent and Trademark Office (PTO) to the inventor of a product, giving the exclusive right to make, use, or sell the invention in this country for 20 years from the date of filing the patent application. A Trademark is any distinctive word, phrase, symbol, design, name, logo, slogan, or trade dress that a company uses to identify the origin of a product or to distinguish it from other goods in the marketplace. A copyright is an exclusive right that protects the creators of original works of authorship such as literary, dramatic, musical, and artistic works (e.g., video games, software, sculptures, motion pictures, choreography and others).

Part Four: Lecture/Critical Thinking Case Studies-Not Found In Student Text

SHOOTING THE ENTREPRENEURIAL RAPIDS
THE LITTLE BAKERY THAT TED AND JOYCE BUILT

SHOOTING THE ENTREPRENEURIAL RAPIDS

Bill Masters, founder of Perception, Inc., the world's leading kayak manufacturer, learned the value of hard work early on. Having worked all but three months of his life since he was ten, Masters quickly gained the small-town equivalent of "street smarts" growing up in Liberty, South Carolina. He learned how to fix practically anything and discovered his aptitude for math. Coming from a very modest economic background, Masters dismissed the possibility of attending college as too expensive. Instead, he followed the technical track in high school and after graduating, went to work in a local plant.

Recognizing the value of a solid education, Masters enrolled in night classes at a local technical school. Later, he transferred to Clemson University, where he majored in electrical engineering. While there, some friends invited him on a July 4 kayak trip on the Chatooga River. It was his first river trip in a kayak but he was hooked! "I just went crazy for it," he recalls. He bought a used kayak and taught himself to repair fiberglass.

By the time he graduated in 1974, Masters had started a small business, Marbaglass, in his backyard. The company manufactured fiberglass molds for the synthetic marble industry, and with the leftover fiberglass resin, Masters made kayaks for a few paying customers who were mostly friends. But when the OPEC oil embargo struck, Masters's supply of fiberglass resin dried up, and he was forced to put his business on hold.

In 1976, Masters decided to get back into business. He sold everything he had and borrowed $10,000 from a local bank to start Perception, Inc. As the company grew, moving first into an old mortuary and then into an old laundromat Masters realized he needed more capital. With the help of a few close business advisers, Masters decided to form a corporation and sell stock to raise the money he needed. He quickly discovered that he still had a lot to learn about running a business, "I walked into our first board meeting and ... said, `Hi, guys. What are we going to do?' Well, they let me know right away that their time was more valuable than that."

Over the next few years, Masters attended every seminar that the Small Business Administration offered and read every book he could find on small business management. He then began to apply the business principles and financial controls he had learned.

Masters soon developed an innovative rotational molding machine to produce superior, one-piece, molded polyethylene kayak hulls. To build the machine, Perception, Inc. had to go deeply into debt. "We hocked everything we owned but the cocker spaniel," he recalls.

Customers began to recognize the benefits of Perception's unihull design, and by 1981, the company's luck began to improve. Masters wanted to regain total control of his company's future, so he bought out his stockholders and "took the company private." As sales in the United States climbed, Masters saw an opportunity to expand into international markets. Perception, Inc. moved first into Great Britain and then into New Zealand, countries where today it controls 30 percent of the kayak market. Soon the company cracked the Japanese market. Today, Perception, Inc. has more than 50 percent of the kayak market in Japan and a similar market share in the United States.

Bill Masters is a creative entrepreneur with a sense of vision; ideas are his specialty, and he has plenty of them. His goal is to launch five successful companies before he retires. He already has two up and running (the second one is Perception Systems, Inc., which is developing a computerized desktop manufacturing system) and a third is in the incubator stage. "You can't be normal and mainstream to be creative, you've got to be a little off," he jokes. Being "off" certainly has paid off for Bill Masters.

1. Which benefits of entrepreneurship has Bill Masters reaped?
2. What factors have led to Masters's success in business?
3. What part has innovation and creativity played in Bill's success?

Source: Adapted From Margaret Pridgen, "He Takes Fun Seriously," Clemson World, Spring 1991, pp.16-19.

THE LITTLE BAKERY THAT TED AND JOYCE BUILT

In 1981, Ted and Joyce Rice decided to forgo job security and start their own business. They considered a number of alternatives - carpentry, a delicatessen, and charter sailing before deciding on cinnamon rolls. "This was not a situation where Joyce made the world's best cinnamon rolls and somebody said, `Why don't you sell these commercially?'" recalls Ted. Joyce began experimenting at home until she came up with just the right recipe. The copreneurs believed their business idea would work "if we could add showmanship, letting our customers see the people who are handling their food, and the equipment it's being made in."

Their first venture was a custom-made, twenty-foot trailer rigged as a mobile bakery. During the summer of 1983, the Rices were selling their cinnamon rolls at cattle shows and state fairs. Everywhere they went, Ted recalls, "We had a lot of people asking us, `where's your permanent bakery?'" In January 1985, the Rices opened a bakery, T.J. Cinnamons, in a Kansas City shopping mall between two escalators to catch shoppers "coming and going." They put a glass roof on the bakery so shoppers could see the rolls being made. Sales soared.

The couple soon flooded with requests for franchising information. "It was at that point that we went to our lawyers and said, `We think we have something that's a little more than a one-bakery operation,'" says Joyce. The Rices knew their idea would be copied, so they created a new company, Signature Foods, with two business associates, to start franchising. They opened the first franchised T.J.

Cinnamons bakery in late 1985. Since then, the bakery has expanded its product line to include fifty different items. Today, the little business that Ted and Joyce built is the leading bakery franchise in the nation, with annual revenues exceeding $50 million.

1. What special problems do copreneurs face when building and running their businesses?
2. What suggestions would you offer a couple about to launch a business together?
3. What advice would you give them on how to prevent their special way of operating from being copied?

Sources: Adapted From Sharon Nelton, "Partners in Entrepreneurship," *Nation's Business*, March 1989, pp. 38-39; Michael Barrier, "Rolling in Dough," *Nation's Business*, February 1990, pp.15-16. Copyright 1990. U.S. Chamber of Commerce.

Part Five: Chapter 2 Exercise

TEST YOUR ENTREPRENEURIAL I.Q.

Respond by circling True or False to the following statements.

1. As a child you, looked for ways of making or earning money instead of relying on an allowance.
   True   False

2. I am responsible for my own fate. People who rely on luck are irresponsible.
   True   False

3. Just because a product can be sold cheaply doesn't mean everyone in that market will buy it.
   True   False

4. I can handle having incomplete information before venturing into a new project.
   True   False

5. Statistics support the fact that entrepreneurs who have had family members venture into successful small business ownership before them are more likely to be successful.
   True   False

6. When I am passionate about something, I can work on it for days on end, sometimes sacrificing getting the proper rest.
   True   False

7. Hard work and a successful financial backing will not ensure the success of a small business.
   True   False

8. You should advertise and focus the sale of your product or service to meet the needs of as many people as possible.
   True   False

9. When you have an idea you feel will be successful, you rarely let anyone talk you out of it, even if they speak with the voice of reason.
   True   False

10. I am not afraid of taking a calculated risk.
    True   False

The ENTREPRENEURIAL I.Q. Test and the following responses can be used to stimulate classroom discussion on the entrepreneurial profile and related topics introduced in subsequent chapters of the text, or it can be given simply as a handout for self-study with the suggested answers attached.
Score 1 point for each TRUE answer. This number represents your entrepreneurial I.Q.

9-10   Very good, keeping pace with successful small business strategies in the twenty-first century will be crucial to successful business survival.

7-8   Satisfactory, however today's fast-paced small business environment won't always let you get away with a few mistakes.

5-6   Or below-you could lose the farm!

SUGGESTED ANSWERS TO THE ENTREPRENEURIAL I. Q. TEST

1. TRUE-Innovation is essential to the entrepreneur and often starts at a very young age.

2. TRUE-Most entrepreneurs are driven by what has been termed an internal locus of control, whereby they take responsibility for all their successes as well as disappointments. Good or bad, they prefer not to rely on luck or make excuses for their various circumstances. As such, they may view people who blame others as weak or unrealistic. These people are seen to have what has been termed as an external locus of control.

3. TRUE-Successful entrepreneurs know that cutting prices is easily copied by a larger store or corporate chain. Establishing a creative competitive edge is what allows the small business owner to compete for *loyal, repeat customers* who don't jump to competitors each time a price is lowered a few cents.

4. TRUE-An ability to handle a little ambiguity is imperative to the entrepreneurial psyche. Operating in the real world where everything is not always under his/her control is a daily requirement.

5. TRUE-Just as in most things, having a mentor or someone who understands your current challenges can act as a positive catalyst.

6. TRUE-Successful entrepreneurs are driven with an internal excitement that motivates them when others might be overwhelmed.

7. TRUE-Many hard working, motivated entrepreneurs have lost their shirts and Aunt Jenny's nest egg by simply failing to clearly establish whether or not a justifiable need existed within the community for their product/service. Sooner or later start-up cash runs out and customers have to start buying.

8. TRUE-Beating the competition these days requires attracting the right customer with that special innovative flair. Trying to satisfy everybody spreads expertise and advertising dollars too thin.

9. TRUE-If every entrepreneur allowed someone to talk them out of something simply because it appeared the reasonable thing to do, most inventions would never reach maturity or distribution. Rumor has it that Bill Gates's first Business Plan was not accepted as a feasible idea by his college instructor.

10. TRUE-A strong trait in the innovative spirit of the American Entrepreneurs is his/her ability to take on risk.

Part Six: Supplemental Readings

Carlye Adler, Maria Atanasov, John S. DeMott, Joel Dryfuss, Anne Field, Anne Ashby Gilbert, Sheryl Nance-Nash, and Michael Scully, "More Hot Ideas," *Your Company*, May/June 1999, pp. 34-49.

Jennifer Katz, "The Creative Touch," *Nation's Business*, March 1990 p. 43.

Warren Bennis, "Cultivating Creative Collaboration," *Industry Week*, August 18, 1997, p. 86.

Peter Carbonara, "30 Great Small Business Ideas," *Your Company*, August/September 1998, pp. 32-58.

Carla Goodman, "Sparking Your Imagination," *Entrepreneur*, September 1997, p. 32.

Joanne Cleaver, "The 30 Day Launch," *Success*, February 1999, pp. 24-25.

Betty Edwards, *Drawing on the Right Side of the Brain*, (Los Angeles: J.P. Tarcher, Inc., 1979), p. 32.

Karen Axelton, "Imagine That," *Entrepreneur*, April 1998, p. 96; "Thomas Edison Biography," http://edison-ford-estate.com/ed_bio.htm

Joseph Schumpeter, "The Creative Response in Economic History," *Journal of Economic History*, November 1947, pp. 149-159.

Epstein, "How to Get a Great Idea," p. 102.

Stephanie Barlow, "Turn It On," *Entrepreneur*, May 1993, p, 52.

Mark Henricks, "Good Thinking," *Entrepreneur*, May 1996, p.70.

Roy Rowan, "Those Hunches Are More Than Blind Faith," *Fortune*, April 23, 1979, p. 112.

Goodman, "Sparking Your Imagination," pp. 32-36.

Janean Chun, "Theory of Creativity," *Entrepreneur*, October 1997, p. 130.

Paul Bagne, "When to Follow a Hunch," *Reader's Digest*, May 1994, p. 77.

Ed Brown, "A Day at Innovation U." *Fortune*, April 12, 1999, pp. 163-165.

General Information Concerning Patents (Washington, D.C.: U.S. Patent and Trademark Office, 1997), p. 15; Tomima Edmark, "Bright Idea," *Entrepreneur*, April 1997, p. 98; Tomima Edmark, "What Price Protection?" Entrepreneur, September 1998, pp. 109-110; U.S. Patent and Trademark Office, "Attorneys and Agents," http://www.uspto.gov/web/offices/pac/doc/general/attorney.html

Chapter 3
Strategic Management and The Entrepreneur **(PPT 3.1, 3.2)**

Part One: Learning Objectives

1. Understand the importance of strategic management to a small business.

2. Explain why and how a small business must create a competitive advantage in the market.

3. Develop a strategic plan for a business using the nine steps in the strategic planning process.

4. Discuss the characteristics of three basic strategies: low cost, differentiation, and focus, and know when to employ them.

5. Understand the importance of controls such as the balanced scorecard in the planning process.

Part Two: Lesson Plan

I.   Building a Competitive Advantage **(PPT 3.3 thru 3.5)**

Developing a strategic plan allows a company to create a competitive advantage-- an aggregation of factors that sets a company apart from its competitors and gives it a unique position in the market. No business can be everything to everyone. Creating a strategic plan prevents a small business from failing to differentiate itself from its competitors.

Another avenue for a small business seeking a competitive advantage is customer intimacy, focusing on the goods and services that customer's want and value. When it comes to developing a strategic plan, small companies have a variety of natural advantages over their larger competitors: fewer product lines, a better defined customer base, a specific geographical area, and closer customer contact.

No business can be everything to everyone. The goal of developing a strategic plan is to create a competitive advantage for the small business-- the aggregation of factors that sets the small business apart from its competitors and gives it a unique position in the market.

Strategic Management includes developing a game plan to guide a company as it strives to accomplish its vision, goals, and objectives and to keep it from straying off its course.

Strategic Planning should include:

- Both a short- and long-term planning horizon
- Company goals and objectives
- Complete industry and other relevant information
- Customer and employee input
- Customer focus

II.   The Strategic Management Process **(PPT 3.6, 3.7)**

Strategic planning is a continuous process that consists of nine steps:

- Step 1: Develop a clear vision and translate it into a meaningful mission statement **(PPT 3.8 thru 3.10)**

    A vision is the entrepreneur's dream of something that does not yet exist. It provides direction, a basis for decision-making and a source of motivation. A company's vision statement incorporates the values of its owner and is about more than just making money. A clearly defined vision leads to a company's mission statement that includes a description of the business, its products, its markets and customers, its competitive distinction and its effects on the community at large.

- Step 2: Assess the company's strengths and weaknesses **(PPT 3.11)**

    Strengths are positive internal factors that a company can use to accomplish its mission. Weaknesses are potentially negative factors that could inhibit those efforts. This on-paper analysis allows the entrepreneur to have a better perspective of the overall venture, to establish a foundation to build on (strengths) and to meet and remove the challenges and obstacles standing in the way of success (weaknesses).

- Step 3: Scan the environment for significant opportunities and threats facing the business **(PPT 3.12, 3.13)**

    With the internal inventory complete, the firm now searches for external opportunities such as specific market niches that match up well with internal resources. The key to success is to take action and to stay a step ahead of the competition. External threats may come from competitors, government agencies, rising interest rates and so on. The firm must have a plan for shielding itself from those threats.

YOU BE THE CONSULTANT – Something New, Something Blue

While the airline industry has always been accustomed to change, the recent events of terrorism, war and recession have created the most challenging of times for executives who must have a solid strategic plan in place in order to succeed.

David Neeleman, a former Southwest Airlines executive, formed JetBlue in the year 2000. Neeleman devised a strategic plan somewhat similar to Southwest's in that his planes fly only point-to-point as opposed to the traditional hub-and-spoke system used by its larger rivals. Neelman uses only one type of jet to minimize training and maintenance costs, flies longer than average routes, and has a non-union workforce that cooperates with one another, focuses on customer service and has a stake in the company through employee stock options. A number of other cost-cutting and revenue-enhancing features are built into the company's operations that combine to distinguish the JetBlue brand from others.

Neeleman and JetBlue face a number of longer-term challenges (labor, aircraft cost and maintenance and so on) that require never-ending attention to strategic management issues.

Q1. Go online to the JetBlue Website or to business magazine websites to learn more about JetBlue. Prepare an analysis of the company's strengths, weaknesses, opportunities, and threats.
Q2. Identify the sources of JetBlue's competitive advantages. Are these sources sustainable?
Q3. What strategic advice can you offer David Neeleman to ensure JetBlue's future success?

A1 & A2 & A3. Students should connect the strategic management concept and steps presented in the text with the specific circumstances surrounding JetBlue.

- Step 4: Identify the Key Factors for Success in the Business **(PPT 3.14, 3.15)**

Every business has a certain degree of control over key variables such as production capabilities, market opportunities, its labor force, access to raw materials, inventory and so on. Success comes from the ability to recognize and to capitalize on those opportunities, and to maximize revenues and/or minimize costs accordingly.

- Step 5: Analyze the Competition **(PPT 3.16 thru 3.20)**

Analyzing all forms of competition must be a never-ending process for all companies. Markets and competitors come and go very quickly. Reaction time is often relatively slow, so the entrepreneur must have the ability to anticipate changes in the marketplace. There is an abundance of information available through many sources (public information, websites, market researchers). Knowledge management is the process of collecting information, analyzing it, and taking action in an effective manner.

YOU BE THE CONSULTANT – Snow and Soda: A Profitable Mix

There is an unlimited amount of useful knowledge and information to gain from any company in any industry. The Crowley family has proved that many times over by borrowing techniques used in their bottling plant (Polar Beverages), applying those to their ski area (Wachusett Mountain) and vice-versa.

A key factor for the success of both operations is filling unused capacity. An hour of unused or inefficient production time in the bottling plant has the same effect as an hour of unused or inefficient time on the ski slopes. The ski area was able to fill its idle capacity by targeting a number of diversified markets that use the slopes at different times of the day and week. The bottling plant was able to fill its idle capacity by reshaping the size of its bottles to better pack trucks.

On the surface, companies in different industries may appear to have little in common. The entrepreneur recognizes the opportunities of technology transfer-- applying the lessons learned in one business and applying those same principles to assorted others.

Q1. Explain the core competencies that Wachusett Mountain has built. What is the source of its core competencies?
Q2. Identify Wachusett Mountain's strengths, weaknesses, opportunities, and threats.
Q3. Explain how Wachusett Mountain uses knowledge management to build a competitive advantage. What other steps would you suggest the company take in this area?

A1. Core competencies are primarily in the areas of production and marketing. The source is top management's vision and ability to take actions that enhance revenues and cut costs.
A2. Students will generate a wide-ranging list in each category of their SWOT analysis.
A3. The process of knowledge management is a way of life for the mangers of both companies. Both have

an active program of constantly gathering and assessing information that could be applied to either operation. Students will again generate many ways in which both companies can expand their base of knowledge.

- Step 6: Create company goals and objectives **(PPT 3.21)**

A company (or person for that matter) with no goals wanders aimlessly into the future. Setting goals provides focus and direction for a company and its people. Objectives are the specific targets of performance required to achieve goals, such as production, marketing, financing and profit standards. Goals and objectives should be measurable, reachable, and in writing.

- Step 7: Formulate Strategic Options and Select the Appropriate Strategies **(PPT 3.22 thru 3.26)**

A strategy is a road map of the actions an entrepreneur draws up to a company's mission, goals, and objectives. A strategy is the master plan that incorporates all of the parts (marketing, finance, personnel, operations) to make up the whole.

- Step 8: Translate Strategic Plans into Action Plans **(PPT 3.27)**

Entrepreneurs must convert strategic plans into operating (tactical) plans that guide their companies on a daily basis. Involving and empowering employees throughout the entire process is often a key to successful outcomes. If an organizations people have a vision for the future direction and goals of a company, and if they are given a stake in the company, they are more likely to work in unison to achieve those goals.

YOU BE THE CONSULTANT – One-of-a-Kind Chip Maker

The story of entrepreneurs Mark and Stacey Andrus is similar to many others in that they started small (with a pushcart selling hot dogs, then pita-wrapped sandwiches), discovered a unique market niche (turning day old bread into pita chips), and finally established and grew their company from rags to riches.

Their major strategy for success is in the cost control area. Even as sales grew from $25,000 to $450,000, Mark and Stacey kept their operation simple, low cost and self-sufficient. Their inclination is always to find the cheapest and most practical way to produce and sell a high quality product with a strong market base.

The couple also recognized the need for outside capital in order to grow their company and implemented their strategy by preparing a sound and professional business plan that allowed them to secure financing and turn their dreams into reality.

Q1. Which of the three basic strategies described in this chapter are Mark and Stacy Andrus using? Explain. How effective is it?
Q2. When it comes to implementing their strategy, how do the Andruses use their size to their advantage? How would you rate the level of creativity they exhibit in managing their business?
Q3. What suggestions would you offer the Andruses to improve the company's future?

A1. The Andruses implemented the cost leadership strategy by working to become the lowest cost producer within their industry. Their no-frills, do-it-yourself, second-hand/modified equipment strategies have worked well.

A2. Their relatively low-cost, high-volume production and sales techniques, along with their high level of creativity are key contributors to their success.

A3. Students will generate many good ideas for future growth.

- Step 9: Establish Accurate Controls **(PPT 3.28 thru 3.31)**

With a vision, mission statement, strategic and tactical plan now in place, managers must constantly measure and assess the actual production, sales, costs and other performances of their departments and people, and effect any changes necessary to stay on schedule and on budget.

III. Conclusion

The strategic planning process is never-ending. It provides structure and discipline and requires the entrepreneur to pay close attention to the details of both the internal and external factors that determine success.

Part Three: Suggested Answers to Discussion Questions

1. Why is strategic planning important to a small company?

Firms must continually strive for strategic and operational excellence. Failing to think strategically about a business is inviting disaster. Strategic planning creates a blueprint for business owners to follow to achieve specific objectives.

2. What is a competitive advantage? Why is it important for a small company to establish one?

A competitive advantage is an aggregation of factors that sets a company apart from its competitors and that gives it a unique position in the market. No business can be everything to everyone. Developing a strategic plan helps the small business differentiate itself from other companies -- a common pitfall for many small firms. Smaller firms have an advantage over larger firms because they are well suited to concentrate on niche markets. Developing a strategic plan allows the small company to meet the customers' needs today, while looking one step ahead to what they will need tomorrow.

3. What are the nine steps in the strategic management process?

   Step 1. Develop a clear vision and translate it into a meaningful mission statement.
   Step 2. Assess the company's strengths and weaknesses.
   Step 3. Scan the environment for significant opportunities and threats facing the business.
   Step 4. Identify the key factors for success in the business.
   Step 5. Analyze the competition.
   Step 6. Create company goals and objectives.
   Step 7. Formulate strategic options and select the appropriate strategies.
   Step 8. Translate strategic plans into action plans.
   Step 9. Establish accurate controls.

4. "Our customers don't just like our ice cream," write Ben Cohen and Jerry Greenfield, co-founders of Ben and Jerry's Homemade Inc. "They like what our company stands for. They like how doing

business with us makes them feel." What do they mean?

Ben & Jerry's mission statement expresses the firm's character, identity and scope of operations. The organization and its employees live it each day and translate it each time they come into contact with their customers. It has become a true natural part of the organization, embodied in the minds, habits, attitudes and decisions of everyone in the company every day.

5. What are strengths, weaknesses, opportunities and threats? Give an example of each.

    Strengths: positive internal factors that contribute to a company's ability to achieve its mission, goals, and objectives. Examples include: a committed workforce and quality products.
    Weaknesses: negative internal factors that inhibit a company's ability to achieve its mission, goals, and objectives. Examples include: high rates of employee turnover and poor customer service.
    Opportunities: positive external options that a business could exploit to accomplish its mission, goals, and objectives. Examples include: expanding global markets and changes in customer tastes.
    Threats: negative external forces that inhibit a business' ability to accomplish its mission, goals, and objectives. Examples include: expanding global markets and changes in customer tastes.

6. Explain the characteristics of effective objectives. Why is setting objectives important?

    Characteristics of effective objectives include:
    They are specific: quantifiable and precise.
    They are measurable: well-defined reference point from which to start and use as a measuring point.
    They are attainable: does not mean easy to accomplish, but difficult enough to require motivation to achieve.
    They are realistic and challenging: must be within the organization's reach. The higher the objectives, the higher performance will be.
    They are timely: must specify not only what is to be accomplished, but when it is to be achieved as well.
    They are written down: makes objectives more concrete, less abstract.

    Setting objectives is important because it gives the entire organization "specifics" on what target(s) it is moving toward. Objectives of a small business are the directions which guide the business to its destination.

7. What are business strategies?

    Business strategies are road maps of the tactics and actions an entrepreneur draws up to fulfill the firm's mission, goals, and objectives. The firm's mission, goals, and objectives define the ends the company wants to achieve, and the strategy is the means for reaching them.

8. Describe the three basic strategies available to small companies. Under what conditions is each successful?

    Three strategies available to small companies include:
    1. Cost leadership: strive to be the low-cost leader. The most successful conditions are when buyers are sensitive to price changes, competing firms sell the same commodity products, and companies can benefit from economies of scale.
    2. Differentiation: seeks to build customer loyalty by positioning goods or services in a unique or different fashion. Key concept is to be special at something important to the customer.

3. <u>Focus</u>: select one (or more) segments(s), identify customers' special needs, wants, and interests, and approach them with a product or service specifically designed to excel in meeting these needs, wants, and interests. Key concept is to create the perception of *value* in the customer's eyes.

9. Explain how a company can gain a competitive advantage using each of the three strategies described in this chapter: cost leadership, differentiation, and focus. Give an example of a company that is using each strategy.

   1. <u>Cost leadership</u>: by containing costs, lower prices will net sufficient profit margins. Example: Wal-Mart
   2. <u>Differentiation</u>: positioning one's product or service apart from the competition builds loyal customers that are not easily pulled away by the competition. Example: Mercedes Benz, Cadillac.
   3. <u>Focus</u>: select one (or more) segments(s), identify customers' special needs, wants, and interests, and approach them with a good or service specifically designed to excel in meeting those needs, wants, and interests. Examples: Exercise equipment, tall men's clothing, Television Networks such as (BET) Black Entertainment.

10. How is the controlling process related to the planning process?

    Most often, the actual results of a small business will deviate from the company's plan. Thus, controlling procedures must be established to measure performance and make corrections as changes occur.

11. What is a balanced scorecard? What value does it offer entrepreneurs who are evaluating the success of their current strategies?

    A set of measurements unique to a company that includes both financial and operational measures and gives a manager a quick yet comprehensive picture of the company's total performance. Rather than sticking solely to the traditional financial measures of a company's performance, the scorecard gives a manager a view from both a financial and operational perspective. The complexity of managing a business demands that an entrepreneur is able to see performance measures in several areas simultaneously.

Part Four: Lecture or Critical Thinking Case Studies-Not In Student Text

SEGMENT, CONCENTRATE, AND DOMINATE
SUCCESS IN THE LOW END OF THE MARKET

SEGMENT, CONCENTRATE AND DOMINATE

Tyson Foods, Inc. is the nation's leading poultry producer, processing 635,000 birds per hour and offering some two thousand chicken-based products. CEO Don Tyson explains, "You just don't want to be number two. I've tried both sides, and number one's the only place to be." Tyson's father, John, founded the company to raise chickens during the Great Depression. In the 1950s, he built the company's first processing plant and brought son Don into the business. In 1963, Tyson Foods went public.

Don Tyson took over the company in 1967 after his father's death. Tyson began pouring millions into expanding the company, primarily by making acquisitions. Along the way, he learned a valuable lesson about selling chicken: You can get higher prices by differentiating your products and adding value to them. After watching the price of generic chicken bounce up and down for a decade, Tyson decided to try something different: feeding a small whole chicken so that its meat is juicier and then selling it in an individual plastic bag. The "Rock Cornish game hen," as Tyson called the product, caught on so well that the company could charge a higher price.

Tyson knew a good thing when he saw it. He began to create a flock of other specialty chicken products, differentiating them from the usual commodity chickens and adding value in a variety of ways—de-boning, skinning, breading, bite sizing, and so forth. In 1976, Tyson's Ozark Fry became the first mass-marketed chicken breast patty. In 1980, the company revolutionized the fast-food industry with the Chicken Mc Nugget, now a staple in McDonald's menu. By the end of 1980, Tyson Foods was selling two dozen different chicken products while most of its competitors were still selling just one—old fashioned processed chickens. The company's marketing theme became segment, concentrate, and dominate.

Not all of Tyson's differentiation ideas were high-flying successes. A giblet burger made from surplus gizzards was a major flop several years ago. Even the Arkansas prison system wouldn't buy giblet burgers for its inmates. Tyson's entries into the turkey market haven't fared very well either.

But more often than not, Tyson's differentiated products have proved to be huge successes. As Americans have quadrupled their consumption of chicken over the past decade, Tyson has continued to churn out new products--from precooked chickens to those ethnically prepared --to keep up with changing lifestyles and tastes. The company has responded to the growing number of Americans leaving the kitchen and going out to eat, by diversifying into the foodservice segment--restaurants, hotels, schools, and hospitals. Tyson sells chicken to eighty of the one hundred largest fast-food chains, and in poultry food service, Tyson commands 77 percent of the market.

Don Tyson, who graces *Forbes's* list of the four hundred richest Americans, wears standard-issue khaki work clothes with "Don" embroidered on the breast pocket. His dress is indicative of the company's laid-back corporate culture. Employees own 20 percent of Tyson Foods stock through an employee stock ownership plan (ESOP). Yet Don Tyson's plain appearance hides his business acumen. "Don Tyson sees the bigger picture," says a long-time counselor. "He's concerned with what happens five years from now, ten years from now." That long-term view led Tyson to buy out rival Holly Farms Corporation in 1990. It also gave him the vision to see the opportunities in differentiating what most people see as a commodity.

1. How has Tyson Foods differentiated its chicken products?
2. Has Tyson's strategy been successful? Under what conditions does a differentiation strategy work best?
3. What are the risks and rewards of pursuing such a strategy?

Source: Adapted from Dick Anderson, "Don Tyson Rules the Roost," *Southpoint*, March 1990, pp. 16-20.

SUCCESS IN THE LOW END OF THE MARKET

Many business advisers claim that low-cost strategies are outdated. Customers, they say, want more than just low prices; service, quality, and other sources of value are more important. These days, price may be one of the least effective weapons in a company's competitive arsenal, but for some businesses, price competition is a way of life. To compete successfully on price, companies must be smart, tough, and consistent. The decision to be a low-price competitor must drive every other strategic decision the company makes.

Jan Bell Marketing, Inc., a jewelry manufacturer and distributor, is one of the best players in the low-price game. Low prices and cost control are essential to Jan Bell's success, given its primary customer base--most of the nation's wholesale clubs. The company manages to sell gold chains and earrings, tennis bracelets, and rings to these wholesalers for about one third of what other manufacturers charge.

How does Jan Bell do it? There's no one big secret. Instead, at every step of the manufacturing and distribution process, the company does at least one little thing to keep costs down. For instance, when buying raw materials, Jan Bell purchases in bulk directly from the source. The company bypasses middle people to minimize the prices of gold, silver, diamonds, and other precious stones. In addition, Jan Bell always pays cash for its purchases. "If you don't ask your suppliers to be your banker, they will be willing to shave somewhere between 3 percent and 5 percent off the purchase price," says cofounder Isaac Arguetty.

Jan Bell also spreads its purchases throughout the year, unlike most jewelers, which concentrate their purchases in August or September in anticipation of the Christmas holiday season. We're probably able to save 10 percent or 15 percent by being in the market year round," says cofounder Alan H. Lipton.

The company also strives to minimize its inventory costs by manufacturing jewelry that will sell quickly and not just at Christmas. There are no one-of-a-kind items sitting in inventory pumping up carrying costs. "We're going for tonnage," says Lipton. That decision rules out much of the jewelry market, so Jan Bell concentrates on high-volume consumers. Sam's Club, Pace Membership Warehouse, and other wholesale clubs make up 80 percent of the company's sales.

Jan Bell also strives to keep overhead costs low. The business contracts out about 92 percent of its assembly work. "By doing some of the work ourselves, we know what it costs to produce the product," says Arguerry. "This way we know exactly what outside contractors should be charging us." In addition, the company maintains no trucking fleets. Finished goods from contractors are logged in, inspected, and shipped out by Federal Express within forty-eight hours of their arrival. Any raw materials that pile up are sold quickly to other jewelry makers at cost plus 15 percent.

Although a low-cost strategy leaves little room for error, Jan Bell makes it work--extremely well. The six year-old company has seen its sales and profits climb each year. By allowing price to govern every aspect of its strategy, Jan Bell has found success in the low end of the market.

1. What factors allow Jan Bell to keep its costs far below those of competitors?
2. Under what conditions does a low-cost strategy work best?
3. What are the advantages of pursuing a successful low-cost strategy? What are the disadvantages?

Source Adapted From Paul B. Brown, "How to Compete on Price," *Inc.*, May 1990, pp.105-107.

Part Five: Chapter 3 Exercise

COMPANY MISSION STATEMENT EXERCISE

This exercise may be used as an in-class group discussion exercise or as a take-home self-study handout with suggested examples. (Refer to Table 3.1)

1. Individual students or small groups should begin by selecting a particular business or industry type. For example: An individual or group could develop two different mission statements for firms in

the infant and toddler day care industry. One would focus on an innovative day care center in an upscale neighborhood, while the other could focus on a community day care center in an inner city neighborhood. The idea is to search for the correct words that provide an image or vision, and make each business distinctly different. This could also be done for other industries such as lawn care & maintenance (one could use only environmentally friendly products), espresso stands (one on a college campus compared to one at the airport) or retail outlets etc...

2. Students should use words that convey a sustainable image or vision that accurately reflects the firm's competitive advantage. Read aloud, without identifying the specific firm or industry, it should still provide a clear idea of what business the firm is in, who its customers are, and its purpose.

3. Once the students have completed their mission statements read them out loud without mentioning the industry or company name. An accurate mission statement will provide a clear idea of the type of business and its purpose. It should not, however, be a complete business description.

SUGGESTED EXAMPLES AND COMMENTS

Correct Upscale Day Care Center Example
The mission of the Hollywood Day Care Center is to provide an innovative, creative, learning environment for infants and toddlers in a secured environment away from home. Our staff is highly qualified and focused on meeting your child's every need.

Correct Inner City Day Care Example
The mission of the Neighborhood Daycare Center is to provide a friendly warm environment for infants and toddlers. Our multicultural staff prides itself on meeting the needs of the communities working parents while providing an affordable secure environment for the communities precious children.

Incorrect Upscale Day Care Center Example 1
The mission of the Hollywood day care center is to care for infants and toddlers in a very special environment with a choice of different language classes, artistic expressions and anything else you want to pay for. Our hours are from 5:30 AM to midnight Monday through Friday and from 6 to 9 PM on Saturday and Sunday. We also have a nurse and special sick rooms for those times when your child is ill. At any time, you can tune in to your child's day by signing onto the Internet with your special parent's password.

Incorrect Upscale Day Care Center Example 2
Our mission is to provide an innovative environment with a number of different choices to meet your every need. Our high tech computers will provide you with a sense of security when your loved ones are away from home. Your every need will be met.

Note: "To make a profit." Although a mission statement of this type has worked for famous companies like Coca-Cola, because quality and attention to customer preferences are implied, it is not normally enough to provide vision and direction to most small business ventures.

Part Six: Supplement Readings

Chaneski, Wayne S. "Recognizing and responding to threats in your industry." *Modern Machine Shop.* July 1996 v69 n2 p.46(2).

Bird, Anat. "Keys to corporate culture: vision, flexibility, consistency." *American Banker*. July 10, 1996 v161 n130 p.17(1).

Payne, Blackbourn, Hamilton, and David W. Cox. "Make a vision statement work for you." *The Journal for Quality and Participation*. Dec. 1994 v17 n7 p.52(2).

Shepard, James F. "Renewing the corporation." *Canadian Business Review*. Autumn 1996 v23 n3 p.25(3).

Chapter 4
Forms of Business Ownership and Franchising **(PPT 4.1 thru 4.6)**

Part One: Learning Objectives

1.   Explain the advantages and the disadvantages of the three major forms of ownership: the sole proprietorship, the partnership, and the corporation.

2.   Discuss the advantages and the disadvantages of the S corporation, the Limited Liability Company, the professional corporation, and the joint venture.

3.   Describe the three types of franchising: trade name, product distribution, and pure.

4.   Explain the benefits and the drawbacks of buying a franchise.

5.   Understand the laws covering franchise purchases.

6.   Discuss the right way to buy a franchise.

7.   Outline the major trends shaping franchising.

Part Two: Lesson Plan

I.   The Sole Proprietorship **(PPT 4.7, 4.8)**

The sole proprietorship is the most popular type of ownership, defined as business owned and managed by one individual.

A.   Advantages
1.   Simple to create
2.   Least costly form of ownership to begin
3.   Profit incentive
4.   Total decision-making authority
5.   No special legal restrictions
6.   Easy to discontinue

B.   Disadvantages
1.   Unlimited personal liability
2.   Limited skills and capabilities
3.   Feelings of isolation
4.   Limited access to capital
5.   Lack of continuity for the business

YOU BE THE CONSULTANT - Where do Small Business Owners Turn for Advice...It's All in the Family

A national survey revealed that small business owners tend to seek advice from family members.

Q1. Who else could provide a business owner with objective advice?
Q2. Is who you ask for advice a source of potential problems? Explain.

A1. A partial list includes: bankers, suppliers, attorneys, accountants, employees and other business owners.
A2. Anyone's advice is a source of potential problems since no one can predict the future. The astute business owner seeks advice from a variety and wide range of people in order to gather a full perspective on the given situation.

II.   The Partnership **(PPT 4.9 thru 4.12)**

A partnership is an association of two or more people who co-own a business for the purpose of making a profit.

- A.   The partnership agreement
- B.   The Uniform Partnership Act (UPA)
- C.   Advantages
    1.   Easy to establish
    2.   Complementary skills
    3.   Division of profits
    4.   Larger pool of capital
    5.   Ability to attract limited partners
    6.   Little governmental regulation
    7.   Flexibility
    8.   Taxation
- D.   Disadvantages
    1.   Unlimited liability of at least one partner
    2.   Capital accumulation
    3.   Difficulty in disposing of partnership interest without dissolving the partnership
    4.   Lack of continuity
    5.   Potential for personality and authority conflicts
- E.   Types of partnership
    1.   Limited Partnership
    2.   Limited Liability Partnership
    3.   Master Limited Partnership

YOU BE THE CONSULTANT – How Will the Assets of the Business be Valued for Dissolution?

Partnerships, Death and Feuds

The death of a partner often results in conflict among family members as to the disposition of assets.

Q1. What provisions of a partnership agreement could eliminate this and other problems?

A1. All partnerships should establish legally binding agreements that strive to answer every possible "what-if" question (what if-- someone dies, someone wants to sell, we do not agree, and so on).

YOU BE THE CONSULTANT – Rosabeth Moss Kanter on Partnerships

The Howard Professor and Chairholder offers six guidelines for partners to consider.

Q1. If you were asked to add a "seventh rule," what would it be?
A1. Students will generate ideas as they think about the best and most solid partnership agreement.

III.   Corporations **(PPT 4.13 thru 4.15)**

The corporation is a separate entity apart from its owners, and may engage in business, make contracts, sue and be sued, and pay taxes. It is the most complex form of business ownership.

A.   "C Corporations" are creations of the state.
   1.   Domestic corporation
   2.   Foreign corporation
   3.   Alien corporation
B.   Incorporation
   1.   Certificate of Incorporation
   2.   Bylaws
C.   Advantages
   1.   Limited liability of stockholders
   2.   Ability to attract capital
   3.   Ability to continue indefinitely
   4.   Transferable ownership
D.   Disadvantages
   1.   Cost and time involved in the incorporation process
   2.   Double taxation
   3.   Potential for diminished managerial incentives
   4.   Legal requirements and regulatory red tape
   5.   Potential loss of control by the founder(s)

IV.   Other Forms of Ownership **(PPT 4.16, 4.17)**

A.   "S" Corporation: An "S" corporation is the same as any other corporation, except that a distinction is made for federal income tax purposes.
   1.   Criteria for businesses seeking "S" status
   2.   Advantages
      a.   Retains all of the advantages of regular corporations
      b.   Passes all profits/losses through to individual shareholders
      c.   Avoids double taxation
      d.   Avoids taxes paid on assets that have appreciated in value and are sold
   3.   Disadvantages
      a.   Increase in individual tax rates above maximum corporate tax rate

41

b. Many fringe benefits cannot be deductible business expenses
4.   Choosing an "S" Corporation wisely

B.   <u>The Limited Liability Company (LLC)</u>: The limited liability company is a cross between a partnership and a corporation, but is not subject to many of the restrictions incurred by "S" Corporations.
1.   Articles of organization
2.   Operating agreement
3.   Limited to no more than two of the following corporate concepts:
      a.   Limited liability
      b.   Continuity of life
      c.   Free transferability of interest
      d.   Centralized management

C.   <u>The Professional Corporation</u>: Professional corporations are designed to offer professional - lawyers, doctors, dentists, accountants, and others - the advantages of the corporate form of ownership.

D.   <u>The Joint Venture</u>: A joint venture is much like a partnership, except it is formed for a specific, limited purpose.

YOU BE THE CONSULTANT SUMMARY – Which Form Is Best?

Watoma Kinsey and her daughter Katrina are about to launch a business that specializes in children's parties. The Kinseys have leased a large building and have renovated it to include many features designed to appeal to kids.

Watoma and Katrina have invested $45,000 each, developed a business plan and have negotiated a $40,000 bank loan. The Kinseys want to minimize their exposure to potential legal and financial problems so a large portion of their startup costs went to purchase a liability insurance policy to cover the Kinseys in case a child is injured at a party. If their business plan is accurate, the Kinseys will earn a small profit in their first year (about $1,500), and a more attractive profit of $16,000 in their second year of operation. Within five years, they expect their company to generate as much as 50,000 in profits. The Kinseys have agreed to split the profits and the workload equally.

The Kinseys believe their business will be successful and eventually want to franchise their company. For now, they want to perfect their business system and prove that it can be profitable before they try to duplicate it in the form of franchises. As they move closer to the launch date for their business, the Kinseys are reviewing the different forms of ownership.

Q1. Which form(s) of ownership would you recommend to the Kinseys? Explain.
Q2. Which form(s) of ownership would you recommend the Kinseys *avoid*? Explain.
Q3. What factors should the Kinseys consider as they try to choose the form of ownership that is best for them?

A1. Due to the Kinsey's desire to minimize their exposure to potential legal and financial problems, their choice of ownership should be a corporation.
A2. Any form of partnership should be avoided due to the issue of liability. Students should discuss the issue of liability.
A3. Students should list and briefly discuss the factors that every entrepreneur should consider prior to making a final decision on the form of ownership (taxes, liability, capital, business goals, management succession and so on).

Louise Tallman spent much of her childhood playing and working in her mother and aunt's antique shop. Her interest, involvement and love of antiques led her to attend a school of art and design. Upon graduation, Louise decided to start her own antique shop and is in the process of completing her business plan.

Q1. What are the questions that you would pose to Louise in order to help her select the form of ownership for her antique shop? Please explain the relevance of each question and answer, to determination of the suggested form of ownership.

A1. Louise's current financial (asset) position and her short- and long-term personal and business goals must be known in order to properly answer the question. Students should be encouraged to make assumptions that will position them to offer good advice.

V.   Franchising **(PPT 4.18)**

        In franchising, semi-independent business owners (franchisees) pay fees and royalties to a parent company (franchiser) in return for the right to become identified with its trademark, to sell its products or services, and often to use its business format and system.

VI.   Types of Franchises **(PPT 4.19)**

        A.   Tradename franchising
        B.   Product distribution franchising
        C.   Pure (or comprehensive or business format) franchising

VII.   The Benefits of Buying a Franchise **(PPT 4.20, 21)**

        A.   Management training and support
        B.   Brand name appeal
        C.   Standardized quality of goods and services
        D.   National advertising programs
        E.   Financial assistance
        F.   Proven products and business formats
        G.   Centralized Buying Power
        H.   Site Selection and Territorial Protection
        I.   Greater chance for success

VIII.   The Drawbacks of Buying a Franchise **(PPT 4.22 thru 4.25)**

        A.   Franchise fees and profit sharing
        B.   Strict adherence to standardized operations
        C.   Restrictions on purchasing
        D.   Limited product line
        E.   Unsatisfactory training programs
        F.   Market saturation
        G.   Less freedom

IX.   Franchising and the Law **(PPT 4.26, 4.27)**

In response to problems that occurred in the 1950's to the franchising boom and the associated franchisers who defrauded their franchisees, laws have been enacted to prevent such behavior.

Uniform Franchise Offering Circular (UFOC): franchisers must register a UFOC and deliver a copy to the prospective franchisees before any offer or sale of a franchise. It establishes full disclosure and guidelines for the franchising company. It contains 23 rules, the franchise agreement, and any contracts accompanying it.

Trade Regulation Rule: enacted by the Federal Trade Commission (FTC) requiring all franchisers to disclose detailed information on their operations at the first personal meeting or at least ten days before a franchise contract is signed, or before any money is paid. In this section, the twenty-three major topics required by the Trade Regulation Rule are discussed as well.

X.   The Right Way to Buy a Franchise **(PPT 4.28)**

A.   Evaluate yourself
B.   Research your market
C.   Consider your franchise options
D.   Get a copy of the franchiser's UFOC
E.   Talk to existing franchisees
F.   Ask the franchiser some tough questions
G.   Make your choice

(PPT 4.29)

YOU BE THE CONSULTANT SUMMARY – The Opportunity of a Lifetime

Joe Willingham, a 51 year-old victim of downsizing is overly excited and anxious to spend all of his available cash on a franchise that he knows very little about. He is being pressured by both the salesman (who claims to have another buyer in waiting) and his soon to end severance package.

Q1. What advice would you offer Joe about investing in this franchise?
Q2. Map out a plan for Joe to use in finding the right franchise for him. What can Joe do to protect himself from making a bad franchise investment?
Q3. Summarize the advantages and disadvantages Joe can expect if he buys a franchise.

A1. Joe is in no position to invest in this franchise-- he needs to take a step back and properly assess the opportunity.
A2. Joe should begin with a "self-assessment" analysis in order to determine what he really wants to do with his future. If a franchise is the answer, Joe needs to learn all that he can about franchises in general and then compare and contrast his options through the business planning process.
A3. Students should list and discuss the list of advantages and disadvantages presented in the text.

XI.   Trends Shaping Franchising **(PPT 4.30)**

A.   The changing face of franchisees
B.   International Opportunities
C.   Smaller, non-traditional locations

D. Conversion franchising
E. Multiple-unit franchising
F. Master franchising
G. Piggybacking

Part Three: Suggested Answers to Discussion Questions

1. What factors should an entrepreneur consider before choosing a form of ownership?

   Factors to be considered before choosing a form of ownership include:
   - Tax considerations – calculate the firm's tax bill under each form of ownership.
   - Liability exposure - how much personal liability is involved in the ownership form?
   - Start-up capital required - how much capital does the entrepreneur have and how much will he need?
   - Control - how much control is involved for each type of business organization? How much is the entrepreneur willing to give up?
   - Business goals - how large and profitable does the entrepreneur expect the business to be?
   - Management succession plans - consider smooth transition when passing company to the next generation of buyers.
   - Cost of formation - some forms are more costly to create.

2. Why are sole proprietorships so popular as a form of ownership?

   Sole proprietorships are a popular form of ownership for several reasons. First, they are simple to create. Anyone wanting to start a business can do so by obtaining the necessary licenses from state, county, and/or local governments. Also, this form is normally the least expensive. In addition, the owner has the total decision making-authority, can keep all profits remaining after expenses are paid, and may discontinue the sole proprietorship fairly easily if he wishes.

3. How does personal conflict affect partnerships?

   The success/failure of a partnership depends on the cohesiveness of its partners. In the beginning, there is an "emotional high" when the startup of the business begins. Partners are so busy creating strategies and focusing on the new business, that they often do not consider the idea of future conflict with other partners. If this conflict does occur, the partnership may suffer. The mutual goals and general business philosophies may not be shared among the partners at this time. Thus, the demise of many partnerships can often be traced to interpersonal conflict if there are no procedures in place to resolve these problems.

4. What issues should the articles of partnership address? Why are the articles important to a successful partnership?

   The major provisions of a partnership agreement include the following:
   a. The name of the partnership
   b. The purpose of the business
   c. The domicile of the business
   d. The duration of the partnership
   e. The partners and their legal addresses
   f. The contribution of each partner to the business
   g. An agreement on how the profits (or losses) of the partnership will be distributed

h.   An agreement on salaries or drawing rights against profits for each partner
i.   The procedure to be followed in the event that the partnership wishes to expand through the addition of a new partner
j.   How assets of the partnership will be distributed if the partners voluntarily dissolve the partnership
k.   Sale of partnership interest
l.   Absence or disability of one of the partners
m.   Provisions for alteration or modification of the partnership agreement

5.   Can one partner commit another to a business deal without the other's consent? Why?

Yes, if the partner was exercising good faith and reasonable care in the performance of his duties, the law of agency holds that the actions of a general partner binds the other partners to a business deal made in the name of the partnership, without the other's consent.

6.   What issues should the Certificate of Incorporation cover?

A Certificate of Incorporation normally will include the following:
a.   The name of the corporation
b.   A statement of the purpose of the corporation
c.   The time horizon of the corporation
d.   The names and addresses of the corporation
e.   Place of business
f.   Capital stock authorization
g.   Capital required at the time of incorporation
h.   Provisions for preemptive rights
i.   Restrictions on transferring shares
j.   Names and addresses of the initial officers
k.   The bylaws by which the corporation will operate

7.   How does an S Corporation differ from a regular corporation?

An S Corporation offers many of the same advantages of a corporation--limited liability, capital formation, and others--while being taxed as a partnership. Thus, the S Corporation avoids the corporate disadvantage of double taxation.

8.   What role do limited partners play in a partnership? What happens if a partner takes an active role in managing the business?

The limited partner is treated, under the law, exactly as in a general partnership. The limited partner(s) is treated more as an investor in the business venture; limited partners have limited liability, and can only lose the amount invested in the business. If the limited partner does take an active part in managing the business, a limited partner may actually forfeit limited liability, taking on the liability status of a general partner.

9.   What advantages does a Limited Liability Company offer over an S Corporation? A partnership?

An LLC eliminates many restrictions imposed by an S corporation such as: a maximum of thirty-five shareholders, none of whom can be foreigners or corporations; a limitation to one class of stock; restriction on members' ability to become involved in managing the company; and limited personal liability with imposed requirements. The LLC is not subject to such restrictions.

There are two advantages an LLC has over a C corporation. First, an LLC offers limited liability and a C corporation does not. Also, an LLC does not pay income tax and avoids the double taxation of C corporations.

10.   How is an LLC created? What criteria must an LLC meet to avoid double taxation?

Creating an LLC is much like creating a corporation. Two documents are required to be filed: the articles of organization and the operating agreement. The articles of organization establish the company's name, its method of management, its duration, and the names and addresses of each organizer. The operating agreement outlines the provisions governing the business' conduct.

11.   Briefly outline the advantages and disadvantages of the major forms of ownership.

Sole proprietorship – least costly to start, total control, typically favorable tax considerations.
Partnership – typically favorable tax considerations, however, unlimited liability for general partner(s). Several other forms which may be costly to establish but limit liability.
Corporation – least favorable tax considerations, costly to establish, however, limited liability for owners.
Sub-S corporation and LLC's combine the more favorable characteristics of both a sole proprietorship and corporation.

12.   What is franchising?

In franchising, semi-independent business owners (franchisees) pay fees and royalties to a parent company (franchiser) in return for the right to sell its products or services and often to use its business format and system.

13.   Describe the three types of franchising and give an example of each.

Trade name franchising-- involves franchising only a brand name like True-Value Hardware or Western Auto.
Product distribution franchising-- involves a franchiser licensing a franchisee to sell specific products under the franchiser's brand name and trademark through a selective, limited distribution network, e.g., Exxon, Chevrolet, and Pepsi Cola.
Pure franchising-- involves providing the franchisee with a complete business format, e.g., Burger King.

14.   Discuss the advantages and the limitations of franchising for the franchisee.

The Benefits of Buying a Franchise include:

- *Management training and support*--Franchisers provide training programs for franchisees in an attempt to reduce failures due to incompetent management.
- *Brand name appeal*--Franchisee has the ability to identify his business with a widely recognized product or service, giving the firm immediate drawing power.
- *Standardized quality of goods and services*--Since the quality of the product or service sold determines the franchiser's reputation, he maintains uniform quality standards.
- *National advertising programs*--Franchisers design mass advertising programs that accomplish

47

more than the franchisees could achieve individually.

- *Financial assistance*--Often, entrepreneurs can purchase franchises for less money requirements than what it costs to start businesses from scratch, and some franchisers offer financial help.
- *Proven products and business formats*--Franchisees can depend on an established product and business system.
- *Territorial protection*--Franchisees are guaranteed territorial protection in some cases; they have the right to exclusive distribution of the product/service in this territory.
- *Greater chance for success*--The failure rate for franchisees is substantially lower than that of independent businesses.

The Drawbacks of Buying a Franchise include:

- *Franchise fees and profit sharing*--Franchisees are required to pay initial franchise fees plus a share of gross receipts throughout the life of franchise arrangement.
- *Strict adherence to standardized operations*--The franchisee may be restricted in his freedom to make decisions about business operations.
- *Restrictions on purchasing*--Franchisees frequently are required to purchase goods or services from approved vendors.
- *Limited product line*--Franchise agreements normally require franchisees to sell only approved products and services from the outlet.
- *Unsatisfactory training programs*--Some franchisers do not deliver all they promise in a "franchisee training program."
- *Market saturation*--Some franchisers do not offer franchisees territorial protection and the market becomes over-saturated.
- *Less freedom*--When a franchisee signs a contract, he is agreeing to sell the franchiser's product or service following its prescribed formula. In essence, there is a lack of independence.

15. Why might an independent entrepreneur be dissatisfied with a franchising arrangement?

Franchisees automatically surrender a certain degree of autonomy upon signing a franchise agreement. Many entrepreneurs feel stifled by the controls imposed on them by franchisers, and they resist them. In many cases, the franchisee becomes an "employee" or a "junior partner."

16. What kinds of clues should tip off a prospective franchisee that he/she is dealing with a disreputable franchiser?

The following clues should tip off a prospective franchisee that he is dealing with a disreputable franchiser:

* Claims that the franchise contract is a standard one that "you don't need to read."
* A franchiser who fails to give you a copy of the required disclosure document at your first face-to-face meeting.
* A marginally successful prototype store or no prototype at all.
* A poorly prepared operations manual outlining the franchise system or no manual at all.
* Oral promises of future earnings without written documentation.
* A high franchisee turnover rate or a high termination rate.
* Attempts to discourage you from allowing an attorney to evaluate the agreement.
* No written documentation to support claims and promises.

* A high-pressure sale - sign contract now or lose the opportunity.
* Claiming to be exempt from federal laws requiring complete disclosure of franchise details.
* "Get-rich-quick schemes"; promises of huge profits with only minimum effort.
* Reluctance to provide a list of present franchisees for you to interview.
* Evasive, vague answers to your questions about the franchise and its operations.

17. What steps should a potential franchisee take before investing in a franchise?

The following steps will help you make the right choice:

a. *Evaluate yourself*--an entrepreneur should first know his own traits, goals, experience, likes, dislikes, risk-orientation, and other characteristics.
b. *Research your market*--know the market in the area you plan to serve.
c. *Consider your franchise options*--read trade journals such as *Franchise Opportunities Guide*, published by the International Franchise Association. Also, many magazines such as *Entrepreneur, Inc., and Success* offer information about franchising.
d. *Obtain a copy of franchiser's UFOC*--this document summarizes the details that will govern the franchise agreement. It outlines exactly the rights and obligations of the franchisee.
e. *Talk to existing franchisees*--one of the best ways to evaluate the reputation of a franchiser.
f. *Ask the franchiser some tough questions*--gather as much information regarding the franchise beforehand.

18. What is the FTC's Trade Regulation Rule? Outline the protection the Trade Regulation Rule gives all prospective franchisees.

The Trade Regulation Rule requires all franchisers to disclose detailed information on their operations at the first personal meeting or at least ten days before the franchise contract is signed, or before any money is paid. Its purpose is to help potential franchisee's investigate the franchise deal and to introduce consistency into the franchiser's disclosure statements. It does not verify the accuracy of the data, thus no protection is provided. This information should be used as a starting point for investigation.

19. Describe the current trends in franchising.

Current trends in franchising include:

* *International Opportunities*--Franchising is becoming a major export industry for the U.S. About 11% of U.S. franchisers have outlets in other countries, and another 28% expect to go abroad by the year 2000.
* *Smaller, non-traditional locations*--Due to high costs of building full-scale violations, franchises are putting scaled-down outlets directly in the path of customers in places such as college campuses, grocery stores, gas stations, theaters, and airports.
* *Conversion franchising*--Owners of independent businesses become franchisees to gain the advantage of name recognition.
* *Multiple-unit franchising*--A franchisee opens more than one unit in a broad territory within a specific time period. "Franchisers are finding it's far more efficient in the long run to have one well-trained franchisee operate a number of units than to train many franchises."

49

- *Master franchising*--A franchisee is given the right to create a semi-independent organization in a particular territory to recruit, sell, and support other franchisees.
- *Piggybacking (or combination franchising)*--Franchisers team up with other franchisers selling complimentary products or services by combining two or more franchises under one roof.

20.   One franchisee says, "Franchising is helpful because it gives you somebody [the franchiser] to get you going, nurture you and push you along a little. But, the franchiser won't make you successful. That depends on what you bring to the business, how hard you are prepared to work, and how committed you are to finding the right franchise for you." Do you agree? Explain.

It is true that franchising allows a franchisee to begin with a given structure, and establishes rules and guidelines for the business. While these "givens" do help, they will not make the franchisee successful. The franchisee must contribute to the business. Characteristics such as enthusiasm and commitment are not embedded in the plan "given" to the franchisee by the franchiser. These things must come from within the franchisee and be communicated throughout the organization in order for it to be successful.

Part Four: Lecture or Critical Thinking Case Studies-Not In Student Text

PARTNERSHIPS INCORPORATED
STAYING IN BOUNDS

PARTNERSHIPS INCORPORATED

Bob Sober's first experience in a partnership left him with painful memories. In their fledgling architectural firm, the six partners "were all for one and one for all," he recalls. But the euphoric feeling soon wore off. Before long, Sober explained, "there was a growing feeling that some people were contributing lots and others little, and that those who were doing little should do more."

The resentment grew. Ultimately, it took one full year for the partners to dissolve the business. Bob Sober and David Broach ended up buying out the other four partners. The two soon joined forces with Bob Workman and set about building another business. This time, however, they vowed not to repeat the mistakes of the past.

The trio formed a corporation called BSW Group, Inc. As the company grew, the corporation's owners invited architects to become partners, not with them, but with the corporation itself. In essence, the firm consisted of a collection of partnerships between BSW Group and individual architects rather than a single large partnership.

Although every partnership is separate from the others, the BSW Group is one of the two partners in each one. Broach, Sober, and Workman are general partners, and the individual architects are operating partners. This arrangement offers several distinct advantages. The profits that each operating partner earns are unaffected by the profits generated by the other operating partners. The operating partners are compensated solely on the basis of the work they produce. Because each partner has an easy-to-judge bottom line, performance appraisals are automatic. From the BSW Group, partners get management and support service (accounting, payroll, insurance. etc.) and marketing clout unavailable in smaller firms.

The operating partners own at least one studio, a work group of five to seven people, and their equipment. Each studio works for one client, and the partners don't compete with one another for new clients, because the general partners attract new business and feed it to the various studios.

Operating partner Janet Merk thinks the partnership arrangement is ideal. After working for eighteen months in someone's studio, she accepted a partnership invitation. BSW Group contributed a $70,000 line of credit, and Merk put up a $17,500 certificate of deposit, or 25 percent of $70,000, which is her share of the partnership's profits. Her ownership can grow to 50 percent over time. "Friends don't understand why I gave 75 percent of my profits away," says Merk. "But I have more resources here than I'd ever have on my own. In the end, I'm going to make more money." One veteran operating partner echoes Merk's enthusiasm, "I enjoy being the owner of a company. It says something about me."

The arrangement has created a company full of motivated entrepreneurs. "We allow people to satisfy their ambitions with our organization," says Sober.

1. How does the BSW Group partnership arrangement differ from a traditional partnership?
2. What advantages does this structure offer the BSW Group and its operating partners?
3. What potential problems do you see with this arrangement? ·

Source: Adapted from Torn Richman. "Making Partnerships Work," *Inc.*, October 1990, pp.168-184.

STAYING IN BOUNDS

Franchising offers franchisees a multitude of advantages--from instant name recognition and a coordinated advertising program to financial assistance and a complete management system. For many franchises, this structure spells success, but for some, especially true entrepreneurs, the structure is overly restrictive. One franchise consultant observed, "A franchise usually works best when people follow a proven system. An entrepreneur, on the other hand, is not a mechanical type but a risk-taker. There is a built-in conflict right there."

Becoming a franchisee does mean you will have to give up some degree of control and independence in your business. But does signing on as a franchisee mean there's no room for innovation and creativity? Not at all. Indeed, innovation and creativity are critical ingredients in any business success story, and Fastframe franchisee Nicholas Ialenti has proved there is room in franchising for both concepts. In the first four months of business, Ialenti pushed his frame-shop franchise into the ten top-selling Fastframe locations in the country.

By putting his entrepreneurial spirit to work within the franchise framework, Ialenti has achieved incredible success. He created an Artist of the Month program to display local artists' work in his store. The Art Walk, as Ialenti calls the window display, has been a tremendous boon to business. "People come by in droves just to browse," he says. Many of those browsers end up becoming customers.

Whereas Nicholas Ialenti has turned his store into an attraction for customers with his Art Walk, Women's Workout World franchisee Sandy Sass has added some special touches to set apart her exercise club from her rivals. In addition to the normal huff-and-puff activities, Sass offers a manicure service, a training salon, body-fat testing, and nutritional advice. Sass "wanted to make a woman's trip to the club as enjoyable and beneficial as possible. Women today are very busy," she says. "They are squeezing in a job, they're busy being `Mom's taxi,' or whatever. This way, they can kill two birds with one stone." Business is booming, and Sass's customers make the most of the extra services.

Both Ialenti and Sass have managed to add unique services and a touch of creativity to their franchise outlets without violating any of their franchisers' rules. Another innovative franchisee claims that franchising "allows more than it doesn't allow. There's lots of room for variation." Franchising coupled with a healthy dose of the entrepreneurial spirit can create an incredibly successful combination.

1. Why do most franchisers, especially well-established ones, tend to discourage innovation among franchisees?
2. Do you think there is room for innovation and creativity in franchising? Why?
3. How can franchisers encourage franchisees to be creative yet remain within the business system?

Sources: Adapted from Ellie Winninghoff, "The Entrepreneurial Mindset," *Entrepreneur*, April 1990, pp.155-158: Frances Huffman. "Breaking the Mold." *Entrepreneur*, January 1990, pp.84-91 Reprinted by permission from *Entrepreneur* magazine.

Part Five: Supplemental Readings

Crump, James G. "Strategic Alliances fit pattern of industry motivation." *The Oil and Gas Journal*. March 31, 1997 v95 n13 p.59(3).

Tahir, Liz. "The advantages of strategic planning." *WWD*. March 4, 1997 v173 n42 p.S103(2).

"Strategic alliances: the partnership paradox; top execs explore today's retailer-vendor relationships." *Daily News Record*. Feb. 24, 1997 v27 n24 p.15(1).

"The ABC's of strategic alliances: Kurt Salmon Associates offers a blueprint for planning a merchant/vendor partnership. *WWD*. Feb. 24, 1997 v173 n36 p.114(2).

Friedrich, Craig W. "Treasury announces delay in proposed effective date of proposal making conversion of "large" C corporations to S corporations and further extends proposal." *Journal of Corporate Taxation*. Autumn 1996 23 n3 p.288-290.

Burton, Hughlene A. "S corporation current developments: S corporation eligibility, elections and terminations; operations; reorganizations; and proposed legislative changes." *The Tax Adviser*. Oct. 1995 26 n10 p590(10).

Shook, Carrie. "Learning by Doing." *Forbes*. April 7, 1997 v159 n7 p78(3).

Tannenbaum, Jeffrey. "Franchisers push local marketing efforts by franchisees." *The Wall Street Journal*. April 1, 1997 pB2(W) pB2(E) col 3 (10 col in).

Chapter 5
Buying an Existing Business **(PPT 5.1 thru 5.3)**

Part One: Learning Objectives

1.   Understand the advantages and disadvantages of buying an existing business.

2.   Define the steps involved in the *right* way to buy a business.

3.   Explain the process of evaluating an existing business.

4.   Describe the various techniques for determining the value of a business.

5.   Understand the seller's side of the buyout decision and how to structure the deal.

6.   Understand how the negotiation process works and identify the factors that affect the negotiation process.

Part Two: Lesson Plan

I.   Buying an Existing Business **(PPT 5.4 thru 5.9)**

      A.   Advantages
- A successful existing business may continue to be successful.
- An existing business may already have the best location.
- Employees and suppliers are established.
- Equipment is installed and productive capacity is known.
- Inventory is in place and trade credit is established.
- The new business owner hits the ground running.
- The new owner can use the experience of the previous owner.
- Easier financing.
- It's a bargain (maybe).

      B.   Disadvantages
- It's a loser (maybe).
- The previous owner may have created ill will.
- Employees inherited with the business may not be suitable.
- The business location may have become/is unsatisfactory.
- Equipment and facilities may be obsolete or inefficient.
- Change and innovation are difficult to implement.
- Inventory may be outdated or obsolete.
- Accounts receivable may be worth less than face value.
- The business may be overpriced.

II.   Steps in Acquiring a Business **(PPT 5.10)**
- Analyze your skills, abilities.
- Prepare a list of potential candidates.
- Investigate and evaluate candidate businesses and evaluate the best one.
- Explore financing options.

- Ensure a smooth transition.

YOU BE THE CONSULTANT- Is This Any Way to Buy a Business?

David Clausen's eagerness to buy a business got the best of him as he clearly "leaped before he looked." He was lucky to purchase the business for a very low price from the obviously disinterested and ill-advised family of the deceased former owner. Clausen persevered through a rough and slow start, updated his equipment to gain a competitive edge and turned the company into a success story. It is still unclear as to whether Clausen has a passion for the mapmaking business.

Q1. Evaluate the way in which David Clausen went about finding a business to buy, assessing it, and searching for financing. What did he do right? What did he do wrong?

Q2. What should Clausen have done differently?

A1. Using a broker was a good start, as was determining his own business value (apart from the owner's asking price). Clausen gave no thought as to the kind of business that would be compatible with his experience or personality. He also had no systematic approach in gathering information nor did he conduct research. An appraisal was not conducted to determine the fair market value of business assets.

A2. Clausen should have first analyzed his own skills and interests, and then proceeded to prepare a list of potential candidates, investigate and evaluate each, explore financing options and ensure a smooth transition through the building of a formal business plan.

III.   Evaluating an Existing Business – The Due Diligence Process (PPT 5.11)

A potential buyer should explore a business opportunity by examining five critical areas.

1.   Why does the owner want to sell?
2.   Assess the condition of the business:
   - The physical plant
   - Accounts receivable
   - Lease arrangements
   - Business records
   - Intangible assets
   - Location and appearance
3.   What is the potential for the company's products or services?
   - Customer characteristics and composition
   - Competitor analysis
4.   What legal aspects should you consider? (PPT 5.12 thru 5.16)
   - Liens
   - Bulk transfers
   - Contract assignments
   - Covenants not to compete
   - Ongoing legal liabilities
5.   Is the business financially sound?
   - Income statements and balance sheets for past 3-5 years
   - Income tax returns for the past 3-5 years
   - Owner's compensation (relatives, skimming)
   - Cash flow

The Lusby's began their search for a new business venture in the correct manner. They took the time to consider both their personal and lifestyle goals. They then proceeded to take a close look at their major category options and limit those to one. This was followed by a nationwide search for the retail establishment with living quarters that they were after.

Their search unfortunately ended too soon. They failed to properly assess the past, present and future outlook of the business, its markets, products and finances. Those oversights caused problems that could have been avoided. Their initial search for their best business match did come back to bless them as they rode out the storm and now enjoy their new life.

Q1. Suppose that the Lusbys came to you for advice on buying their business. What would you have told them?
Q2. Should the Lusbys have done anything differently in their quest to buy a business? Explain.

A1. & A2. The Lusbys should have completed the steps and the process of buying a business. They identified the kind of business and lifestyle that they wanted, but did not properly assess the marketing, operational and financial condition and potential of the business.

IV.   Methods for Determining the Value of a Business **(PPT 5.17)**

Business valuation is partly an art and partly a science. Establishing a price for a privately held business may be difficult due to the nature of the business itself.

A.   There are a few rules for establishing the value of a business:
- There is no single best method to determine a business's worth. The best way is to compute the value using different methods and choose the best one.
- Both parties, buyer and seller, must be satisfied with the deal.
- Both the buyer and seller should have access to business records.
- Valuations should be based on facts, not fiction.
- Both parties should deal with one another honestly and in good faith.

B.   Business valuation techniques
1.   The Basic Balance Sheet Methods **(PPT 5.18)**
    a.   The Balance Sheet Technique
    b.   Adjusted Balance Sheet Technique
2.   Earnings approach **(PPT 5.19 thru 5.29)**
    a.   Variation 1: Excess Earnings Method
    b.   Variation 2: Capitalized Earnings Approach
    c.   Variation 3: Discounted Future Earnings Approach
    d.   Market Approach

V.   Understanding the Seller's Side **(PPT 5.30 thru 5.33)**

A.   *Structuring the Deal*: This is one of the most important decisions a seller can make. Tax implications can be significant; therefore, a skilled tax planner can help.

B.   *Exit Strategy Options*:

- *Straight business sale
- *Form a family limited partnership
- *Sell a controlling interest
- *Restructure the company
- *Sell to an international buyer
- *Use a two-step sale
- *Establish an employee stock ownership plan (ESOP)

YOU BE THE CONSULTANT – A Seller's Tale

The owner of the magazine Dive Travel made the decision to sell his business. That was the easy part. It took more than a year to locate a serious and qualified buyer and another six months to finalize the deal. After a sometimes-heated negotiation process, a short- and long-term agreement was reached to the satisfaction of both parties.

Q1. Why is the process of valuing a business so difficult for the entrepreneur who founded it?

Q2. Which method(s) of valuing a business do you think would be most appropriate in placing a realistic value on Dive Travel? Explain.

Q3. Evaluate the final deal the parties struck from both the buyer's and the seller's perspectives. Do you think the deal was "fair"?

A1. It is relatively easy to place a value on the physical plant assets of a business. Placing a value on the name, reputation and standing of the business (goodwill) is much more difficult. The seller will often have a much higher value in mind than the buyer.

A2. Buyers should always run as many pricing models and pro-forma spreadsheets on a business as possible in order to collectively and carefully determine a fair price.

A3. The buyer and seller were both satisfied with the deal in the end.

VI.   Negotiating the Deal **(PPT 5.34)**

  A.   Factors Affecting the Negotiation Process
         - How strong is the seller's desire to sell?
         - Is seller willing to finance part of purchase price?
         - Must the seller close the deal quickly?
         - What deal structure fits your needs?
         - What are tax consequences for both parties?
         - Is seller willing to stay on as a consultant?
         - What general economic conditions exist in the industry?

  B.   The Negotiation Process

         - Refer to figure 5.6

Part Three: Suggested Answers to Discussion Questions

  1.   What advantages can an entrepreneur who buys a business gain over one who starts a business "from scratch"?

The advantages of buying an existing business may include:

a. *A Successful Existing Business May Continue to be Successful*: Buying a thriving business increases the likelihood of success. Former owners have already established a customer base, built supplier relationships, and set up a business system. With these in place, the new owner has an advantage over one who is starting from scratch.

b. *An Existing Business May Already Have the Best Location*: If the location of a business is critical to its success, it may be wise to purchase a business that is already strategically located.

c. *Equipment is Installed and Productive Capacity is Known*: The buyer does not have to invest in equipment, and the previous owner may have established an efficient production operation. Thus, the new owner can use these savings in time and money to improve and expand the existing equipment and procedures.

d. *Inventory is in Place and Trade Credit is Established*: Establishing the right amount of inventory can be costly. If there is too little inventory, customer demand cannot be satisfied. If too much is available, excessive capital is tied up, costs are increased, and profits decrease. There is a tremendous advantage if previous owners have established a balance in inventory. In addition, a proven track record gives the new owner leverage in negotiating credit concessions.

e. *Experience of Previous Owner*: If the previous owner is around, the new owner can benefit from his/her expertise. Even if the owner is not present, business records can guide the new owner.

f. *It's a Bargain*: If the owner needs to sell on short notice, wants a substantial down payment in cash, or the business requires special skills, the number of buyers will be small, which may lead the owner to sell at a lower price.

2. How would you go about determining the value of the assets of a business if you were unfamiliar with them?

When evaluating an existing business, a potential buyer should assemble a team of specialists to help in determining the potential business opportunity. The team is usually composed of a banker, an accountant familiar with the industry, an attorney, and perhaps a small business consultant or business broker. Company records, interviews with management, and particularly financial statements will help the potential owner and the team of specialists to identify the assets. Once the assets are identified, it may be necessary to hire a professional to assess value to the major components of the building -- structure, plumbing, heating and cooling system, as well as inventory.

3. Why do so many entrepreneurs run into trouble when they buy an existing business? Outline the steps involved in the right way to buy a business.

Buying an existing business can be risky if approached haphazardly. To avoid costly mistakes, an entrepreneur should follow a logical, methodical approach:

- *Analyze your skills, abilities and interests*: Consider what business activities you enjoy most, what kind of business you want to buy, what you expect from the business and how much time and energy you have to invest.
- *Prepare a list of potential candidates*: Examine businesses for sale, as well as those that may be in the "hidden market."
- *Investigate and evaluate candidate businesses and choose the best one*: Investigate potential candidates in more detail. Perform a SWOT analysis on each. Examine company financial statements.
- *Explore financing options*: Consider the options for financing. Often, financing for an

existing business is easier than for a new one. Although many traditional lenders shy away from deals involving purchases of existing business and others only lend a portion of the assets, most buyers still have access to a ready source of financing-- the seller. Many times, the seller will finance anywhere from 30 to 80 percent of the purchase.

- *Ensure a smooth transition*: To avoid a bumpy transition, the business buyer should: concentrate on communicating with employees, be frank, open, and honest with employees, listen to employees-- they have knowledge of the business, consider asking the seller to serve as a consultant until the transition is complete.

4. When evaluating an existing business that is for sale, what areas should an entrepreneur consider? Briefly summarize the key elements of each area.

When evaluating an existing business, a potential buyer should explore a business opportunity by Answering these five critical questions.
1. *Why does the owner want to sell?* Every prospective business buyer should investigate the <u>real</u> reason the owner wants to sell.
2. *What is the physical condition of the business?*
3. *What is the potential for the company's products or services?*
4. *What legal aspects should you consider?*
5. *Is the business financially sound?*

5. How should a buyer evaluate a business's goodwill?

Goodwill is a financial term for the reputation of the business and its ability to attract customers based on that reputation. Goodwill has a value, but it is very difficult to determine in a precise manner. The earnings approach to the valuation of a firm offers some help on valuing goodwill. One measure of goodwill is the difference between a reasonable expected return on investment and what you purchase the business for. Another measure if the difference between the value of the assets of the business and what you pay for it.

6. What is a restrictive covenant? Is it fair to ask the seller of a travel agency located in a small town to sign a restrictive covenant for one year covering a twenty-square-mile area? Explain.

Under a restrictive covenant, the seller agrees not to open a new competing store within a specific time period and geographic area. The covenant must be negotiated with the owner and not the corporation to bind the owner. The covenant must be part of a business sale and must be reasonable in scope in order to be enforceable. As for the restrictive covenant of a travel agency in a small town, the answer depends on several factors. If this is the only travel agency, it appears that restricting a new one would create a monopoly, thus, the covenant probably would not be reasonable. In addition, while the term of one-year seems to be reasonable, the term of the twenty-square-mile area may or may not be reasonable depending on the size of the town, and the possibilities of a new travel agency being built in the next town.

7. How much negative information can you expect the seller to give you about the business? How can a prospective buyer find out such information?

Although the seller cannot lie about the facts or mislead the seller, do not expect the seller to disclose anything negative about the business. The sale of a business is based on the old concept of "buyer beware." Two key steps a potential buyer should take in order to find out such "negative" information are reviewing business records and interviewing/questioning management, legal council and others.

8. Why is it so difficult for buyers and sellers to agree on a price for a business?

The negotiation process between the buyer and seller appears to be adversarial. The selling party usually wants the "maximum" financial gain from his business; on the other hand, while the buyer wants to buy a good business, he wants to pay the "minimum." These two forces pull against one another.

9. Which method of valuing a business is best? Why?

There is no "best" method for determining the value of a business; each method has advantages and disadvantages and some are more appropriate than others under different circumstances. All available methods should be considered as an aid to determining a truly fair price.

10. Outline the different exit strategy options available to a seller.

Existing strategy options include:
<u>Straight Business Sale</u>: selling a business outright.
<u>Form a Family Limited Partnership</u>: entrepreneur takes the role of general partner with the children becoming limited partners in the business.
<u>Sell a Controlling Interest</u>: sell majority interest in companies to investors, competitors, suppliers, or large companies with an agreement they will stay on after the sale as managers or consultants.
<u>Restructure the Company</u>: replace the existing corporation with a new one, formed with other investors.
<u>Sell to an International Buyer</u>: sell to foreign buyer(s).
<u>Use a Two-Step Sale</u>: allows the buyer to purchase the business in two phases -- getting 20%-70% today and agreeing to buy the remainder within a specific time period. Until the final transaction takes place, the entrepreneur retains at least partial control of the company.
<u>Establish an Employee Stock Ownership Plan</u>: a plan in which a trust is created for employees to purchase their employers' stock.

11. Explain the 5 Ps of a successful negotiation process. What tips would you offer someone about to enter into negotiations to buy a business?

The 5 *P*'s of a successful negotiation process include:
1. *Poise*
2. *Patience*
3. *Persuasiveness*
4. *Preparation*
5. *Persistence*

12. One entrepreneur who recently purchased a business advises buyers to expect some surprises in the deal no matter how well prepared they may be. He says that every potential buyer must build some "wiggle room" into their plans to buy a company. What steps can a buyer take to ensure that he has sufficient "wiggle room"?

If the 5 P's of negotiations are addressed, there should be enough room to negotiate and resolve concerns in the buyer's favor since planning and sufficient time have been given.

DETERMINING THE VALUE OF A SERVICE BUSINESS

DETERMINING THE VALUE OF A SERVICE BUSINESS

Art McDonald was a pioneer of the prisons-for-profit concept. His company, Eclectic Communications, Inc., was one of the first to enter into the private prison industry, housing and feeding prisoners in California.

McDonald had never been a financial wizard, and he knew he needed help when a competitor, Corrections Corporation of America, offered to buy his company for $10.5 million. McDonald wondered what his company was worth. Clouding the valuation issue was the fact that Eclectic is a service business with few tangible assets. Most of its worth lies in hard-to-value intangibles such as managerial talent, quality services, and reputation. So McDonald called in Bonnie Niten Baha, a business valuation expert, who established a value for Eclectic using three different approaches: market, cost, and income.

The market approach uses the value of a comparable public company as a model for determining the worth of a business. Baha found three public companies in the private prison business, but didn't consider them comparable; too much of their revenues came from non-prison operations. She did, however, have the value that Corrections Corporation of America placed on Eclectic-- their $10.5 million offer two years earlier. That offer was 1.37 times Eclectic's sales revenue and 61 times its net profit. Applying those figures to Eclectic's current sales and profits, Baha found: Sales revenue of $11 million x 1.37 = $15.1 million and Net profit of $181,550 x 61 = $11.1 million.

The cost approach values a business at what it would cost to duplicate it. When Baha applied this method, it produced the lowest value for Eclectic.

The income-approach views a business as an income-generating entity. Its value is determined by the profits that it will produce in the future, discounted back to their present value. First, McDonald, his accountant, and Baha forecast every item on Eclectic's income statement for the next five years. Then they came up with a discount rate that accurately reflected the risks and returns associated with running the company.

Baha calculated that Eclectic's rate of return on equity was 17.41 percent. She considered it to be an extremely well managed, established company, but to reflect the risks of running a business, she raised the discount rate to 18 percent. Putting that figure into perspective, Baha says, "I've used discount rates that are as high as 40 or 50 percent," when valuing some small businesses. The resulting discounted future value was $10,755.534. Her pricing model, however, assumed only minority ownership in the business. She adjusted the value to reflect majority ownership of Eclectic--called a control premium. To find it, she evaluated two studies of company sales involving control premiums; one showed an average premium of 38.3 percent, and the other reported 58.6 percent. Baha pinned a 35 percent premium on Eclectic, making the total estimated value $14,519,971.

What did McDonald learn about the value of his company? Baha's final report included an estimated range of $11 million and $15 million. That was good enough for McDonald, who has decided

60

to keep Eclectic for now. "If I can continue to have fun and make the business grow rapidly," he says, "we can sell it for a tremendous amount in the future."

1. Why didn't Baha use any of the balance sheet techniques to value Eclectic Communications, Inc.?
2. Find examples in this case that illustrate the statement "Business valuation is partly art and partly science"?
3. Do you agree with the methods that Baha used to value the company? Why did she use more than one method?

Source: Adapted from Ellya E. Spragins, "Locking Up Good Value," Inc., November 1989, pp. 157-158.

Part Five: Supplemental Readings

Stern, and Wilma Randle. "The best way to start a business...may to be buy one." *Working Woman.* March 1996 v21 n3 p33(3).

Price, Courtney. "The pros and cons of buying a business." *Black Enterprise.* Nov. 1994 v25 n4 p143(6).

Harrison, Chris. "Timing and tenacity in a business sale." *The Financial Times.* Feb. 3, 1997 pFTS4(2).

Miracle, Barbara. "Buy a business, buy a job." *Florida Trend.* Jan. 1997 v39 n9 p30.

"Quality supplants "bid-and-buy" tradition." *Industrial Distribution.* Oct. 1996 v85 n10 pF10(3).

Narva, R., and Ira Bryck. "Case study: keep the firm in the family?" *Nation's Business.* May 1996 v84 n5 p60(1).

Chapter 6
Building a Powerful Marketing Plan **(PPT 6.1)**

Part One: Learning Objectives

1. Describe the principles of building a guerrilla marketing plan and explain the benefits of preparing one.

2. Explain how small businesses can pinpoint their target markets.

3. Discuss the role of market research in building a guerrilla marketing plan and outline the market research process.

4. Describe how a small business can build a competitive edge in the marketplace using guerrilla-marketing strategies: customer focus, quality, convenience, innovation, service, and speed.

5. Discuss the marketing opportunities the World Wide Web (WWW) offers entrepreneurs and how to best take advantage of them.

6. Discuss the "four Ps" of marketing--product, place, price, and promotion--and their role in building a successful marketing strategy.

Part Two: Lesson Plan (PPT 6.2, 6.3)

I. Building a Guerrilla Marketing Plan

Marketing is the process of creating and delivering desired goods and services to customers and involves all of the activities associated with winning loyal customers.

Guerilla marketing strategies are unconventional, low cost, creative techniques-small companies can get more "bang" from their marketing bucks.

Guerilla Marketing Principles

1. Find a niche and fill it
2. Don't just sell, entertain
3. Strive to be unique
4. Create an identity for your business
5. Connect with customers on an emotional level

A Guerilla marketing plan should accomplish four objectives:

1. It should determine customer needs and wants through market research.
2. It should pinpoint the specific target markets the company will serve.

3. It should analyze the firm's competitive advantages and build a marketing strategy around them.
4. It should help create a marketing mix that meets customer needs and wants.

II.   Pinpointing the Target Market **(PPT 6.4)**

Target markets are the specific groups of customers at whom the company aims its goods or services.

III.   Determining Customer Needs and Wants Through Market Research

Demographics are the characteristics and trends of a population including age, income, gender (composition), education, household size, race and ethnicity.

A.   The Value of Market Research **(PPT 6.5)**

Market research serves as the foundation for the marketing plan. Its objective is to learn how to improve the level of satisfaction for existing customers and to find ways to attract new customers. By performing some basic market research, small business owners can detect key demographic and market trends. Market research does not have to be time consuming, complex, or expensive to be useful.

Faith Popcorn, a marketing consultant, offers tips to help spot significant trends:

i.   Read as many current publications as possible
ii.   Watch the top ten TV shows
iii.   See the top ten movies
iv.   Talk to at least 150 customers a year about what they're buying and why
v.   Talk with the 10 smartest people you know
vi.   Listen to your children

B.   How to Conduct Market Research **(PPT 6.6 thru 6.8)**

Step 1: Define the objective
Step 2: Collect the data
Step 3: Analyze and interpret data
Step 4: Draw conclusions and act

YOU BE THE CONSULTANT – Data Mining: A Sure Bet for Harrah's

Harrah's Entertainment, the parent company to 26 gambling casinos in 13 states, experienced a significant increase in market share and profitability through their collection, analysis and use of statistical data.

Former Harvard Professor Gary Loveman, once a consultant to Harrah's, devised a system that allows the company to really know its customers and to market accordingly. "This is the replacement of intuition and hunch with science," says Loveman.

Q1. Work with a group of your classmates in a brainstorming session to identify other industries that could benefit from a data collection and mining system like the one Harrah's uses so effectively. In what ways could those businesses use data to become more effective marketers?

Q2. Discuss the ethical issues that Harrah's faces as a result of its data collection and mining efforts.

Q3. What benefits does Harrah's gain from its efforts? What benefits do Harrah's customers gain?

A1. Students will identify many different businesses that would benefit from market research and should clearly connect and convert the information to marketing efforts that address customer's wants and needs.

A2. Gambling can become a serious addiction that adversely affects the lives of people.

A3. Harrah's is able to use their knowledge to offer their customers exactly what they want in terms of gambling, entertainment and accommodations-- much to the delight and satisfaction of both parties.

(PPT 6.9 thru 6.12)

YOU BE THE CONSULTANT – "What Would Tommy Wear?

A group of entrepreneurs living on Florida's Gulf Coast created an imaginary figure named Tommy Bahama. Tommy's handsome, successful and stylish image was transformed into a line of apparel aimed at 35 to 65 year-old men.

The partners experienced a few years of frustration with unsuccessful and changing market strategies and financial challenges until they finally opened their own model store in Naples, Florida that featured a combination restaurant and clothing outlet. That successful venture led to the opening of 17 more "restaurant-retail compounds."

The partners are pursuing international sales opportunities and the prospect of opening a hotel and golf resort. And it all began with the question, "What Would Tommy Wear."

Q1. Work with a group of your classmates in a brainstorming session to identify brands whose names have faded.

Q2. Use the resources of your library and the World Wide Web to research one of the brands you identified. What went wrong? What caused the brand to lose its popularity?

Q3. What lessons from the Tommy Bahama success story should the managers of the brand you identified have used to avoid problems?

Q4. What advice would you offer the partners about keeping the Tommy Bahama brand going strong?

A1. Students will think of and learn a valuable lesson from several now defunct companies.

A2. Student's responses should focus on the connection between customers specific needs and wants and their selected companies failures to offer and market the "right" products or services.

A3. Student's answers should address both the marketing and entrepreneurial flexibility and perseverance of the partners.

A4. Students will offer a variety of marketing strategies for the partners to consider.

IV. Plotting a Guerrilla Marketing Strategy: How to Build a Competitive Edge **(PPT 6.13 thru 6.28)**

1. Focus on the Customer

   Every business depends on customer satisfaction. If you can't take care of your customers, someone else will.

2. Devotion to Quality

   Quality goods and services are a prerequisite for survival. Today quality is more than just a slogan. Businesses buy into strategies like *Total Quality Management (TQM)*-- where quality is in the product or service and in every other aspect and component of the business as well.

3. Attention to Convenience

   Customers want convenience. Studies show that customers rank convenience at the top of their purchasing criteria. Successful companies must show that it is easy for customers to do business with them.

4. Concentration on Innovation

   In order to keep up with changing markets, small businesses must be innovative. Small businesses are frequently leaders in innovation even though they do not have the resources that larger businesses do.

5. Dedication to Service and Customer Satisfaction

   Steps to achieving stellar customer service and satisfaction:

   1. Listen to customers
   2. Define superior service
   3. Set standards and measure performance
   4. Satisfied customers exhibit one of the following:
      i. Loyalty
      ii. Increased purchases
      iii. Resistance to rivals' attempt to lure them away with lower prices
   5. Examine your company's service cycle
   6. Hire the right employees
   7. Train employees to deliver superior service
   8. Empower employees to offer superior service

9. Use technology to provide improved service
10. Reward superior service
11. Get top managers' support
12. View customer service as an investment, not an expense

<u>Emphasis on Speed</u>

To be competitive, companies must reduce the time it takes to develop, design, manufacture, and distribute a product, which results in reduced costs, increased quality, and increased market share.

YOU BE THE CONSULTANT – The Power of the Little Blue-and-White Boxes

Jiffy baking products (the little blue-and-white boxes), once a sideline operation of the Chelsea Milling Company commands over 50% of its market. The company seems to defy modern day business practices by remaining privately held and by not advertising.

That strategy has paid off handsomely by allowing the company to maintain a low overhead and a small management team that can make decisions and take actions efficiently. The result is a high quality product with strong demand and a price that no one can beat.

The third generation family business owner has upgraded the company's manufacturing facilities and general business practices and now has the company exploring a variety of new markets (exporting, institutional markets and food service).

Q1. What is the basis for Chelsea Milling's marketing strategy? How effective is it?
Q2. How easily could a competitor duplicate Chelsea's marketing strategy for Jiffy?
Q3. How successful do you think a company launching a product such as Jiffy today would be if it never advertised?
Q4. How would you evaluate the opportunities Chelsea Milling faces for Jiffy products?

A1. The basis for the company's marketing strategy is cost efficiency. It is very effective because many of its customers are price-sensitive shoppers.
A2. Under the right business conditions, a competitor could start locally with the same strategy and grow it over time. Students should be encouraged to present and defend their options.
A3 and A4: Same answer as above.

V.   Marketing on the World Wide Web (WWW) **(PPT 6.29 thru 6.31)**

The Internet is a vast network that links computers around the globe via the WWW. By establishing a *Web site*, a small business can sell its products electronically around the world. It is a phenomenal commercial opportunity that offers businesses a worldwide marketing and distribution system. It is the "Great Equalizer" in a world of larger competitors.

Today's business students and entrepreneurs are on the frontier of an industry and market that will likely see tremendous growth in the next few years. The opportunity is now.

VI.   The Marketing Mix (PPT 6.32 thru 6.39)

        1.   Product
        2.   Place
        3.   Price
        4.   Promotion

Part Three: Suggested Answers to Discussion Questions

1.   Define the marketing plan. What lies at its center?

        The marketing plan focuses the company's attention on the *customer* and recognizes that satisfying the customer is the foundation of every business. Its purpose is to build a strategy for success with a focus on the customer.

2.   What objectives should a marketing plan accomplish?

        The marketing plan has four objectives:
        •   Determining customer needs and wants through market research
        •   Pinpointing specific target markets the small company will serve
        •   Analyzing the firm's competitive advantages and building a marketing strategy around them
        •   Helping to create a marketing mix that meets customer need and wants

3.   How can market research benefit a small business owner? List some possible sources of market information.

        Market research provides the foundation for the marketing plan. By performing basic market research, small business owners can identify key demographic and market trends.

        Possible sources of market information include:
        •   Current publications
        •   Top ten shows
        •   Top ten movies
        •   Customers
        •   Smart people you know
        •   Children

4.   Does market research have to be expensive and sophisticated to be valuable? Explain.

        No, market research does not have to be expensive and sophisticated to be valuable. For example, for most business owners, information is often *floating* around. It is a matter of collecting and organizing the data to make it valuable.

5.   Describe several market trends and their impact on small business.

        •   *Increasing population diversity* offers special challenges to business owners.
        •   *Changing family patterns* will force marketers to rethink their strategies.

- *Greater environmental and health concerns* have consumers more focused on the environmental impact of the products and services they buy.
- *Emergence of "premium" and "discount" niches* – an increasing number of lower income households force more buyers to become bargain shoppers.
- *Surge in "baby boomers" and the elderly* results in changing needs for those consumers.
- *Greater emphasis on social responsibility* has a growing number of consumers buying products associated with a cause they care about.
- *Slower growing markets and shorter product life cycles* require businesses to focus on narrow niches, understand customer needs and wants, and give them value.

6. Why is it important for small business owners to define their target markets as part of their marketing strategies?

Small businesses must be more focused on the types of customers they want to target. Small firms are ideally suited to reach market segments that their larger rivals overlook or consider too small to be profitable. A clear, concise target market allows a small business to be profitable.

7. What is a competitive advantage? Why is it important for a small business owner to create a plan for establishing one?

A competitive advantage is an aggregation of factors that sets a company apart from its competitors. Developing a strategic plan allows a small business to differentiate itself from other companies. Developing a strategic plan allows the small company to meet the customer's needs of today, while looking one step ahead to what they will need tomorrow.

8. Describe how a small business owner could use the following sources of a competitive advantage:

1. Focusing on a niche: target a specific segment of the population that your business can efficiently serve-- senior citizens.
2. Entertaining: offer a service that customers enjoy and actively seek out-- gambling.
3. Striving to be unique: the latest craze in body piercing and tattoos.
4. Creating an identity for the business: a name or a song that everyone associates with your product.
5. Connecting with customers on an emotional level: environmentally safe products.
6. Focusing on the customer: specialized exercise equipment for disabled people.
7. Focusing on the customer: health and beauty aids—hair coloring.
8. Devotion to quality: specialty food products.
9. Attention to convenience: business location.
10. Concentration on innovation: battery powered blenders.
11. Dedication to service: installation and maintenance of product lines.

9. One manager says, "When a company provides great service, its reputation benefits from a stronger emotional connection with its customers, as well as from increased confidence that it will stand behind its products". Do you agree? Explain. If so, describe a positive service experience you have had with a company and your impressions of that business. What are the implications of a company providing poor customer service? Describe a negative service experience you have had with a company and your impressions of that business. How likely are you to do business with that company again?

It is true in most cases that a great service experience creates a bond, confidence in the product or service and the desire to be a repeat customer. Students will share their positive and negative service experiences and comment on the business implications of each.

10. What marketing potential does the World Wide Web offer small businesses? What does it take for a company to market successfully using the Web?

The WWW is a vast network connecting the world's computers and information sources. With its ability to display colorful graphics, sound, animation, video and text, the web allows small business companies to equal and even surpass their larger rival's web presence. It offers businesses a worldwide marketing and distribution system. Successful companies must have a marketing strategy that will get them a high volume of web attention and recognition and a line of products and services that people want to buy.

11. Explain the concept of the marketing mix. What are the four P's?

Applying the concept of the marketing mix requires a company to conduct useful market research and to develop and market each of the four P's—Product, Price, Place and Promotion.

12. List and explain the stages in the product life cycle. How can a small firm extend its product's cycle?

The stages include: the introductory stage, the growth stage, maturity, market saturation and decline. A focus on product innovation and change, as well as the development of more stable products, versus fad merchandise, can extend the product life cycle.

13. With a 70 percent customer retention rate (average for most U.S. firms, according to the American Management Association), every $1 million of business in 2000 will grow to more than $4 million by the year 2010. If you retain 80 percent of your customers, the $1 million will grow to a little over $6 million. If you can keep 90 percent of your customers, that $1 million will grow to more than $9.5 million. What can the typical small business do to increase its customer retention rate?

Practice the company philosophy of dedication to service, customer satisfaction, and customer astonishment.

ARE WE MAKING THE GRADE?

ARE WE MAKING THE GRADE?

On the surface, Granite Rock Company looks like any other small, family-owned construction material supplier. But a closer examination reveals a highly sophisticated, quality-conscious, customer-oriented industry leader in what is ordinarily considered a commodity business.

Granite Rock quarries produce concrete, asphalt, sand, and gravel; they sell brick, drywall, cinder block, and masonry tools. On average, Granite Rock customers pay a 6 percent premium over competitors' prices. How, then, does Granite Rock maintain its leadership position in such a cutthroat industry? "Our competitors tend to see price as the main wedge," says general manager Wes Clark. "We are not low price, but we are high value."

Selling value can be a successful marketing strategy if customers recognize and are willing to pay for it. Granite Rock concentrates on understanding exactly how its customers define such nebulous terms as value, quality, and service. The company also regularly monitors its performance (from the customer's perspective) and feeds all of this information directly to its workforce.

Here's how Granite Rock's customer satisfaction system works:

Every three or four years, the company conducts an extensive survey of its customers to determine their needs and wants and what factors are most important to them when choosing a supplier. Every year, Granite Rock sends a report card to customers, asking them to grade their top three suppliers on these factors. The factors include various measures of product quality and customer service, and the grades range from A ("The Best") to F ("Terrible"), with a "No Opinion" option.

Granite Rock then combines the results of the survey with those from the report cards to generate a Customer Service Graph. The graph has two axes: the importance axis and the performance axis. The importance axis depends on the results of the extensive customer survey. (In its most recent survey, Granite Rock found that on-time delivery and product quality were most important to customers, whereas credit terms and salespeople's skills were least important.) The performance axis plots the results of the report card. The company's grade is determined by adding the number of A's and B's it gets.

1. What benefits does Granite Rock's customer satisfaction system offer to its customers and to the company itself?
2. Which areas of the Customer Service Graph would be most and least important to Granite Rock? Why?

Source: Adapted from Edward O. Welles, "How're We Doing?" *Inc.*, May 1991, pp.80-83.

Selecting a Voice That Lends Credibility to Your Plan

In developing your business plan, you must keep the reader in mind as you select the type of voice you will be addressing your readers with. There are (3) basic voices used in developing a business plan.

- **First Person - (I) or (We) in the plural**

  First person voice is most effectively used when trying to convey a more personal image or tone.

  For example, a personal trainer, cosmetologist or artist are very much a part of the product or service they provide. A day care center for seniors appears more caring as shown in the following statement: "We provide home cooked meals and pay individual attention to the personal dietary needs of each of our valued guests."

- **Second Person - (You) - The opening paragraph of this handout is written in second person.**

  This voice has often been used by motivational speakers and self-help book authors, and is most effective when trying to initiate action from the reader. For example, "All you need to do is pick up the phone and call 1 800 CARLOAN and you're on your way to driving the car of your dreams." It is also used successfully in writing training manuals and when giving directions.

- **Third Person - (They or The Firm) - The Organization.** This voice is often used by professional organizations and smaller firms who wish to promote a more professional image. Carefully done, it can lend a more professional image to the sole proprietor, writing her own small business plan. For example, "The proprietor, Hella-Ilona Johnson, has established the business in a prime location to better serve the needs of Kitsap County."

1. Individually, or as a group exercise, write a few lines about how the entrepreneurial project you are involved with became a business venture. Re-write the statements using all three voice styles and determine which style contributes best to the credibility of the venture. Once you determine which voice lends the most credibility to your business plan, be sure you use with the same voice throughout the entire document.

6.2 Group Plan Description

Plan/Project Description

Business Topic: _____
or Name

Each Group Member's Name:
(print in alphabetical order)

```
_____    _____
_____    _____
_____    _____
_____    _____
_____    _____
_____    _____
_____    _____
_____    _____
_____    _____
```

Group   Coordinator:

_____
(if individual plan name here)

Description of Project/Plan:

Comments:

6.3 Project/Group Feedback Sheet Meeting# ____ Date ____

Group Member Name: _____
Area(s) of Responsibility-Specific Performance Target for Next Meeting Date

_____

Group Member Name: _____
Area(s) of Responsibility-Specific Performance Target for Next Meeting Date

_____

Group Member Name: _____
Area(s) of Responsibility-Specific Performance Target for Next Meeting Date

_____

Group Member Name: _____
Area(s) of Responsibility-Specific Performance Target for Next Meeting Date

_____

Group Member Name: _____
Area(s) of Responsibility-Specific Performance Target for Next Meeting Date

_____

Group Member Name: _____
Area(s) of Responsibility-Specific Performance Target for Next Meeting Date

_____

Part Six: Supplemental Readings

Hacker, Robert C. "7 steps to a successful business plan." *Target Marketing*. Feb. 1997, v20 n2 p33(2).

Hayes, John R. "Ya gotta give 'em what they want." *Forbes*. Jan. 27, 1997 v159 n2 p62(1).

Jensen, Jeff. "Picabo Street wins starring role in Nike game plan." *Advertising Age*. Nov. 11, 1996 v67 n46 p3(2).

Reilly, Brian. "DMA puts focus on Web marketing." *Business Marketing*. Nov. 1996, v81 n9 p2(2).

Cornillie, Tim. "Add maneuverability to your marketing plan." *Mediaweek*. Oct. 21, 1996 v6 n40 pS15(2).

Section III – Building a Business Plan

Chapter 7
E-Commerce and the Entrepreneur **(PPT 7.1)**

Part One: Teaching Objectives

1. Describe the benefits of selling on the World Wide Web.

2. Understand the factors an entrepreneur should consider before launching into e-commerce.

3. Explain the twelve myths of e-commerce and how to avoid falling victim to them.

4. Discuss the five basic approaches available to entrepreneurs wanting to launch an e-commerce effort.

5. Explain the basic strategies entrepreneurs should follow to achieve success in their e-commerce efforts.

6. Learn the techniques of designing a killer Web site.

7. Explain how companies track the results from their Web sites.

8. Describe how e-businesses ensure the privacy and security of the information they collect and store from the Web.

9. Learn how to evaluate the effectiveness of a company's Web site.

Part Two: Lesson Plan (PPT 7.2 thru 7.5)

Students of today are fortunate to be witness to the early stages of e-business. It is important for students to incorporate e-business in order to remain current in the marketplace. E-commerce has removed the obstacle of size for many small business entrepreneurs, replacing that with speed.

I. Benefits of Selling on the Web

- The opportunity to increase revenues
- The ability to expand their reach into global markets
- The ability to remain open 24/7
- The capacity to use the Web's interactive nature
- The power to educate and inform
- The ability to lower the cost of doing business
- The ability to spot and capitalize on new business opportunities
- The ability to grow faster
- The power to track sales results

II.   Factors to Consider before Launching into E-Commerce **(PPT 7.6 thru 7.9)**

As with any proposed change or new venture, business owners must consider the variables and challenges facing them:

- Is the product or service conducive to e-business?
- Can the business afford not to add e-business to its mix?
- Will customers use the web to buy?
- How and where to best start a Web site?
- What are the specific goals and objectives of the Web site?
- What affects would a Web site have on customer relations, channels of distribution, financial condition of the business and so on?

III.   Twelve Myths of E-Commerce **(PPT 7.10 thru 7.20)**

E-Commerce already has many stories of success and failure. Make sure that you do not fall victim to one of the following e-commerce myths:

1. Setting up a business on the Web is easy and inexpensive.
2. If I launch a site, customers will flock to it.
3. Making money on the Web is easy.
4. Privacy is not an important issue on the Web.
5. The most important part of any e-commerce effort is technology.
6. "Strategy? I don't need a strategy to sell on the Web! Just give me a Web site, and the rest will take care of itself."
7. On the Web, customer service is not as important as it is in a traditional retail store.
8. Flash makes a Web site better.
9. It's what's up front that counts.
10. E-commerce will cause brick-and-mortar retail stores to disappear.
11. The greatest opportunities for e-commerce lie in the retail sector.
12. It's too late to get on the Web.

YOU BE THE CONSULTANT – Changing the Rules of the Game

Entrepreneur Andrew Field bought a print shop and used his selling skills to boost sales to about $1 million annually. The high fixed cost structure of his business resulted in only a break-even situation however and Field saw no hope for improvement given his relatively small local markets.

The idea for a website finally struck. Field devised an interactive Web site system to fill his idle capacity. Customers design and submit their orders through a simple program. The company then e-mails a project number and link to a proof of the order, and once approved by the customer, a production, shipping and delivery date are established.

Field filled his idle capacity and then took his company to the next level by soliciting more work and sub-contracting that to competitor companies. Word of the ease and reliability of Field's system has spread, and the company now averages about 7,000 visitors to its site each day, generating sales of $8 to $9 million.

Q1. Would Field's strategy for handling excess capacity be feasible without the Web? Explain.
Q2. In what ways does the Web enable Field's strategy to be successful?
Q3. Visit the Printingforless.com Web site. Does the site accomplish its goal of making the process simple for customers? Explain. Can you make any suggestions for improving the site's design?

A1. Field's strategy would not be successful because of the limitations of the size of his local markets. The Web is Field's link to a far greater volume of customers.
A2. The Web enables Field's strategy to be successful by providing access to the production capacity of other companies, by providing access to customers outside of his geographic area, and through a user-friendly system of designing, ordering and processing jobs.
A3. Students will offer a variety of ideas and options.

IV.   Approaches to E-Commerce **(PPT 7.21 thru 7.26)**

The short- and long-term goals of a company along with its target markets and budgetary constraints help to define the best approach to an e-business venture. Entrepreneurs have five basic choices:

1. On-line shopping malls
2. Storefront-building services
3. Internet Service Providers and Application Service Providers
4. Hiring a Professional to Design a Custom Site
5. Building a Web site In-House

V.   Strategies for E-Success **(PPT 7.27, 7.28)**

- Consider focusing on a niche in the market.
- Develop a community.
- Attract visitors by giving away "freebies."
- Make creative use of e-mail, but avoid becoming a "spammer."
- Make sure your Web site says "credibility."
- Consider forming strategic alliances.
- Make the most of the Web's global reach.
- Promote your Web site on-line and off-line.

YOU BE THE CONSULTANT – Two Companies That Get It Right

Chris Warner, mountain climber and outdoorsman extraordinaire, created Earth Treks, a web-based company that takes its on-line visitors to the peaks of the highest mountains and to the great volcanoes of the world through the photographs and journals created by the expedition leaders themselves. The site has created a community of dedicated climbers whose numbers continue to grow.

The company's next generation market is also being developed through an educational program aimed at six-to-eighteen year-old students who learn about the different climates, countries and cultures of the world, along with leadership and team skills. The program also hosts birthday parties and provides training for kids on its indoor climbing walls.

Spencer Chesman developed iGourmet, a web-based company aimed at food enthusiasts from around the world. Customers learn about foods and related products through the photos and narrative on the site, and place orders that come with a 100 percent guaranteed return policy. iGourmet also developed a special foam-lined shipping chest that keeps its perishable items cool for up to 48 hours. That feature has contributed to the company's 75% repeat business rate.

Q1. Which of the strategies for e-success described in this chapter are these two companies using? Explain.

Q2. Although Earth Treks and iGourmet are in very different businesses, what similarities do you see in their approaches to e-commerce?

Q3. Visit the Web sites for these two companies. Select a local business that has a significant Web presence and, in a brainstorming session with several of your classmates, develop a set of strategies for e-success based on what you have learned.

A1. Both companies have focused on very specific niche markets. Earth Treks has also been successful in developing a community among its site visitors. iGourmet's credibility is enhanced through its 100 percent guaranteed return policy.

A2. Both companies developed relatively low-cost sites that are customer friendly and that reach prospects from around the world.

A3. Students will identify a local company and will apply some of the same strategies used by the two businesses in this case.

VI.   Designing a Killer Web Site (**PPT 7.29 thru 7.32**)

Web users demand fast and reliable sites, have little patience, and currently buy from a relatively low number of the e-businesses that they visit. While there is no sure-fire formula for success, the following suggestions will help:

- Understand your target customer.
- Select a domain name that is consistent with the image you want to create for your company and register it.
- Be easy to find.
- Give customers what they want.
- Build loyalty by giving online customers a reason to return to your Web site.
- Establish hyperlinks with other businesses, preferably those selling products or services that complement yours.
- Include an e-mail option and a telephone number in your site.
- Give shoppers the ability to track their orders on-line.
- Offer Web shoppers a special all their own.
- Assure customers that their on-line transactions are secure.
- Post shipping and handling charges up front.
- Keep your site updated.
- Consider hiring a professional to design your site.

YOU BE THE CONSULTANT – The Amazon.com of the Pool and Spa Industry

Dan Harrison, founder of Poolandspa.com is an early pioneer and success story of e-commerce. The Long Island, New York based business started in Harrison's basement in 1980, moved to a retail store, expanded to include service and accessories in response to the recession of the early 1990's and in 1994, explored something new he had heard about-- the Internet.

Harrison also created a Hot Tub Newsletter that was first mailed to the company's 2,000 local customers. That number quickly grew to 20,000 as the result of the company's 150-page Web site developed in 1995. The quality of Harrison's newsletter and the presence and contributions of his Moose the Hot Tub Dog contributed greatly to the company's popularity and success.

Harrison also embarked on an aggressive search engine marketing strategy. While that application comes with a high cost, it is carefully tracked through statistical data and analysis. Harrison's company now generates more than $7 million in annual revenues and has a goal of becoming the Amazon.com of the pool and spa industry.

Q1. Why is search engine marketing so important to online businesses?
Q2. Conduct a Web search to develop a list of at least five techniques that small companies can use to optimize their use of search engines.
Q3. What advice would you offer a business owner who has just launched an e-commerce company about driving traffic to the company's Web site?

A1. Search engine marketing is the means to attracting very large numbers of customers from around the world.
A2. Students will recommend techniques that should make both marketing and financial sense for their selected small businesses.
A3. Same answer as above.

VII.   Tracking Web Results (PPT 7.33, 7.34)

Firms using Web sites must closely track the benefits of increased sales against increased costs. Web analytics are software tools that measure a site's ability to attract customers, generate sales and keep customers coming back. Other tracking methods include: clustering, collaborative filtering, profiling systems and artificial intelligence. The art and science of quantifying the return on investment from e-commerce continues to develop.

VIII.   Ensuring Web Privacy and Security (PPT 7.35, 7.36)

The Web's ability to track the behavior of its customer raises concerns and issues over the privacy of that information. Companies are encouraged to take the following steps to ensure that the information they collect is being used in a legal and ethical manner:

- Take an inventory of the customer data collected.
- Develop a company privacy policy for the information you collect.
- Post your company's privacy policy prominently on you Web site and follow it.
- Consult with an attorney.

Security is another unresolved and developing Web site issue. Hackers, viruses, credit card fraud and unauthorized users continue to adversely affect companies, customers, and the growth of e-commerce. Virus and intrusion detection software and firewalls may help to wad off attacks from hackers.

Part Three: Suggested Answers to Chapter Discussion Questions

1. In what ways have the Internet and e-commerce changed the ways companies do business?

The Internet and e-commerce continue to revolutionize the business world. Small businesses now have markets that span the globe that include both customers and competitor companies who may cooperate as sub-contractors.

2. Explain the benefits a company earns by selling on the Web.

Selling on the Web can provide relatively low cost access to increased sales and profits. A Web business can be run from a student's dorm room or from an entrepreneur's home.

3. Discuss the factors entrepreneurs should consider before launching an e-commerce site.

Entrepreneurs should consider the following:

- How to exploit the Web's interconnectivity and relationship building opportunities with customers
- How to develop a plan that fits within the company's overall strategy
- How to generate the highest percentage of repeat business
- How to create and maintain a meaningful and exciting Web presence
- How to measure success

4. What are the 12 myths of e-commerce? What can an entrepreneur do to avoid them?

1. Setting up a business on the Web is easy and inexpensive-- careful planning, execution and follow-up analysis are a must.
2. If I launch a site, customers will flock to it-- assuming that the entrepreneur has a clear and attractive site positioned within the right search engine.
3. Making money on the Web is easy-- making money is almost never easy.
4. Privacy is not an important issue on the Web-- the world wide access of the web has also created worldwide access to hackers and other unwanted intruders.
5. The most important part of any e-commerce effort is technology-- technology represents just one of the components required for success.
6. A strategy is not necessary, just develop a site and the rest will take care of itself--a strategy will result in an action plan that can help a company achieve its goals.
7. Customer service on the web is not as important as it is in a traditional retail store-- customer service is a major key to repeat business and referrals.
8. Flash makes a Web site better-- only if that flash is part of a well thought out marketing plan.
9. It's what up front that counts-- what's up front counts in part, but the rest of the system must be solidly in place as well.
10. E-commerce will cause brick-and-mortar retail stores to disappear-- e-commerce represents just one component of the marketplace and just one part of a firm's target market mix.
11. The greatest opportunities lie in the retail sector-- manufacturing and service-based companies will continue to be prominent worldwide players.
12. It's too late to get on the web-- e-commerce is currently in the early growth stages of the product life cycle.

5. Explain the five basic approaches available to entrepreneurs for launching an e-commerce effort. What are the advantages, the disadvantages, and the costs associated with each one?

1. On-line shopping malls (for products) offer the easiest and least expensive entry. Lack of prominence and control are limitations of this option.
2. Storefront-building services also offer easy and low cost entry. It may be difficult to distinguish one company from the next.
3. Internet Service Providers and Application Service Providers offer a low cost means to create an on-line store. Fees are often tied to volume that provides a correlation cost (to volume) structure.
4. Hiring Professionals to Design a Custom Site costs more but may provide far greater returns; this may not be a feasible option for a start-up venture.
5. Building a Web site In-House provides the owner with complete control but costs more.

6. What strategic advice would you offer an entrepreneur about to start an e-company?

An entrepreneur should use the same approach as starting any business venture-- a business plan. Special emphasis must be placed on both the non-personal and "personal" marketing efforts.

7. What design characteristics make for a successful Web page?

Successful design characteristics are very customer-connected and may include: a strong connection to the target customer, the proper and desired company image, be easy to find, be easy to use, provide access to the firm's staff, provide the ability to track orders, and offer security, privacy and reliability.

8. Explain the characteristics of an ideal domain name.

The ideal domain name will clearly depict and communicate the nature of products and services offered.

9. Describe the techniques that are available to e-companies for tracking results from their Web sites. What advantages does each offer?

A variety of software exists and is being further developed that allows a company to count and track inquiries in great detail, to monitor customer behavior, to analyze correlations from those behaviors and to calculate return on investment. These and other upcoming features will allow a business to quantify and improve on the effectiveness of e-business ventures.

10. What steps should e-businesses take to ensure the privacy of the information they collect and store from the web?

E-businesses should establish, post and follow a privacy policy in order for it to be meaningful and effective.

11. What techniques can e-companies use to protect their banks of information and their customers' transaction data from hackers?

E-companies should analyze and adopt virus and intrusion detection software and also consider a firewall that only allows company employees to have access to a company's network and programs.

12. Why does evaluating the effectiveness of a Web site pose a problem for on-line entrepreneurs?

As with all statistical models, some information is hard or impossible to quantify. In addition, many of the traditional models do not fit well with e-commerce business and are currently in the development stages.

Chapter 8
Integrated Marketing Communications and Pricing Strategies **(PPT 8.1)**

Part One: Learning Objectives

1. Describe the basis of a marketing communications plan.

2. Describe the operational elements of a marketing communications plan.

3. Describe the advantages and disadvantages of the various advertising media.

4. Identify four basic methods for preparing an advertising budget.

5. Explain practical methods for stretching the small business owner's advertising budget.

6. Describe effective pricing techniques for both introducing new products or services and for existing ones.

7. Explain the pricing methods and strategies for retailers, manufacturers, and service firms.

8. Describe the impact of credit on pricing.

Part Two: Lesson Plan

I.   The Basis of A Marketing Communication Plan **(PPT 8.2 thru 8.4)**

1. Define the purpose of the company's marketing communications program by creating specific and realistic measurable objectives.
2. Analyze the firm and its target audience. A small business owner should address the following questions:

- What business am I in?
- What image do I want to project?
- Who are my target customers and what are their characteristics?
- Through which medium can they be reached?
- What do my customers really purchase from me?
- What benefits can the customer derive from my goods or services?
- How can I prove those benefits to my target customers?
- What sets my company, products, or services apart from the competition?
- How do I want to position my company in the market?
- What advertising approach do my competitors take?

3. Design an advertising message and choose the best media for transmitting it. Entrepreneurs should build their ads around a unique selling proposition (USP).

II.   The Operational Elements of a Marketing Communications Plan **(PPT 8.5 thru 8.7)**

The *marketing communication plan* is made operational through ensuring that all elements of the plan achieve a consistent message based on the firm's USP.

1. *Advertising* is any sales presentation that is non-personal in nature and is paid for by an identified sponsor.
2. *Promotion* is any form of persuasive communication designed to inform consumers about a product or service and to influence them to purchase those goods or services.

III.   Publicity or Public Relations **(PPT 8.8 thru 8.12)**

1.   *Publicity or public relations* is a thoughtful process of gaining positive recognition about the business or its products/services through writing interesting and newsworthy articles about what the business is doing or plans to do.

The following tactics can help any small business owner stimulate publicity:

a.   Write an article that will interest your customers or potential customers.
b.   Sponsor an offbeat event designed to attract attention.
c.   Involve celebrities "on the cheap."
d.   Contact local TV and radio stations and ask for an interview.
e.   Publish a newsletter.
f.   Contact local business and civic organizations and offer to speak to them.
g.   Offer or sponsor a seminar.
h.   Write news releases and fax or e-mail them to the media.
i.   Volunteer to serve on community and industry boards and committees.
j.   Sponsor a community project or support a non-profit organization or charity.
k.   Promote a cause.

2. *Personal selling* is the personal contact between sales people and potential customers resulting from sales efforts. **(PPT 8.13 thru 8.16)**

The selling process:

1.   Approach – establish rapport
2.   Interview – identify needs and preferences
3.   Demonstrate – make and match claims with needs
4.   Validate – prove the claims
5.   Negotiate – work out and overcome objections
6.   Close – as soon and as often as possible

IV.   Selecting Advertising Media **(PPT 8.17, 8.18)**

A. Key advertising concepts:
1.   How large is my firm's trading area?
2.   Who are my target customers and what are their characteristics?
3.   Which media are my target customers most likely to watch, listen to, or read?
4.   What budget limitations do I face?
5.   What media do my competitors use?
6.   How important is repetition and continuity of my advertising message?
7.   How does each medium compare with others in its audience, its reach, and its frequency?
8.   What does the advertising medium cost?

B. Traditional media options: **(PPT 8.19 thru 8.38)**
1.   Word-of-mouth advertising and endorsements
2.   Newspapers
3.   Radio
4.   Television
5.   Magazines
5.   Direct Mail
6.   High-Tech Mail and The World Wide Web
7.   Outdoor Advertising
8.   Transit Advertising
9.   Directories
10.   Trade Shows
11.   Specialty Advertising
12.   Point-of-Purchase Ads

YOU BE THE CONSULTANT - Fat Free But Not Famous-- Yet

Candice Vanice obtained a patent for her fat-free fries and started Marvel LLC. She quickly learned that breaking into the retail food business is difficult-- food brokers favor nationally recognized and advertised brands.

Candice had faith in her product and turned next to a more localized strategy of giving out free samples and collecting customer surveys at several markets in her hometown of Kansas City. Customer feedback was overwhelmingly positive.

With practically no money available for advertising, Marvel LLC must find a way to convince food brokers and supermarkets to carry her product

Q1. Work with a team of your classmates to develop a creative advertising and promotional plan for Marvel LLC. What unique selling proposition should Vanice use?
Q2. How should Vanice use publicity to draw attention to her 8th Wonder Fat Free Fries?
Q3. According to one marketing expert, "A product can be copied or imitated but a brand cannot." What can entrepreneurs such as Candace Vanice do to build brand name recognition when they do not have the

advertising budgets large companies have?

A1. It will be difficult for students to propose a solid plan without conducting extensive market research on the food business, its distribution networks and its geographic buying patterns. Given the information in this case, students must select low- and/or no-cost techniques that focus on the unique and positive health benefits of the product.

A2. Feature stories in local newspapers and magazines, community events such as school and health fairs and other low cost publicity will help Vanice develop an audience for her product.

A3. Using the methods described above, on a regular basis, will serve to "put and keep the name of the product under the consumer's nose."

V.   Preparing an Advertising Budget **(PPT 8.39)**

Four methods of determining an advertising budget:

1.   *What is affordable?*
2.   *Match the expenditures of competitors.*
3.   *Use the percentage of sales method.*
4.   *Use the Objective-and-task method.*

VI.   Advertise Big on a Small Budget **(PPT 8.40, 8.41)**

Cooperative advertising -- a manufacturing company shares the cost of advertising with a small retailer if the retailer features the company's products in the ads.

Shared advertising -- a group of similar businesses forms a syndicate to produce generic ads that allow the individual businesses to dub in local information.

Other cost-saving suggestions for advertising expenditures:
- Repeating ads that have been successful
- Using identical ads in different media
- Hiring the services of independent copywriters, graphic designers, photographers, and other media specialists
- Advertising when customers are most likely to buy

Public relations -- Many businesses rely on the media for attention.

VII.   Pricing: Communicating Image and Value **(PPT 8.42)**

Setting prices for products and services is complex and difficult and requires that a number of factors be carefully considered. Price conveys an image that must match the company's target markets. The firm must also consider its place among the competition.

The factors that small business owners must consider when determining price for goods and services includes:
- Product/service costs
- Market factors - supply and demand
- Sales volume
- Competitors' prices
- The company's competitive advantage

- Economic conditions
- Business location
- Seasonal fluctuations
- Psychological factors
- Credit terms and purchase discounts
- Customers' price sensitivity
- Desired image

VIII. Pricing Strategies and Tactics **(PPT 8.43, 8.44)**

    A.   When introducing a new product, the owner should try to satisfy three objectives:

        1.   Getting the product accepted
        2.   Maintaining market share as competition grows
        3.   Earning a profit

    B.   When introducing a new product, firms may choose from three basic strategies:

        1.   *Market Penetration*: set prices below competitors to gain market entry.
        2.   *Skimming*: set higher prices for new products and for markets with little or no competition.
        3.   *Sliding-Down-the-Demand-Curve*: set higher prices initially and slide down as technology improves and/or one step ahead of competitors.

    C.   Pricing established goods and services offers the following techniques:

- Odd pricing
- Price lining
- Leader pricing
- Geographical pricing
- Opportunistic pricing
- Discounts
- Multiple unit pricing
- Suggested retail prices

IX. Pricing Strategies and Methods for Retailers **(PPT 8.45)**

    1.   Markup
    2.   Follow-the-leader pricing
    3.   Below-market pricing
    4.   Adjustable or dynamic pricing

X. Pricing Concepts for Manufacturers **(PPT 8.46, 8.47)**

Cost-plus pricing is the most common used pricing technique for manufactures.

Direct costing and price formulation:
        a.   *Absorption costing*: all manufacturing and overhead costs are absorbed

87

into the finished product's total cost.

    b.   *Variable (direct) costing*: the costs of the product include only those costs that vary directly with the quantity produced.

XI.   Pricing Strategies and Methods for Service Firms **(PPT 8.48)**

Most service firms set prices based on hourly rates and materials that include a margin for both overhead and profit.

YOU BE THE CONSULTANT SUMMARY - Pricing Web Services

Kerry Pinella discovered her passion while working as a Web site developer, and soon thereafter left that firm to form her own company with two partners. The quality and reliability of their work helped to establish and grow a solid clientele in a relatively short time.

While on a retreat midway through their second year of operation, the partners came to realize that their target profits were not being met. They wondered if their price of $45 per hour was the cause. Kerry and her partners need help in answering that question.

Q1. Help Kerry answer the question she has posed.
Q2. What factors should Kerry and her partners consider when determining their final price?
Q3. Is the company's current price too low? If so, what signals could have alerted Kerry and her partners?

A1. & A2. Kerry and her partners should take a close look at the prices that their competitors offer for similar services. They should also look closely at their own overhead to see if costs can be reduced. The partners should also evaluate their current client base and promotional mix to determine if their target market mix is on target and if they are reaching their desired prospects.
A3. The above analysis will help to determine if their price is too low. Their high rate of successful bidding may have been a clue.

XII.   The Impact of Credit on Pricing **(PPT 8.49)**

- Credit cards
- Installment credit
- Trade credit

Part Three: Suggested Answers to Discussion Questions

1.   What are the elements of promotion? How do they support one another?

Promotion -- any form of persuasive communication designed to inform consumers about a product or service and to influence them to purchase those goods and services.

    a.   *Publicity* -- any commercial news covered by the media that boosts sales and for which the small business does not pay.
    b.   *Personal selling* -- the personal contact between sales people and potential customers resulting from sales efforts.
    c.   *Advertising* -- any sales presentation that is non-personal in nature and is paid for by an

identified sponsor.

All are concerned with reaching out to the consumers, whether the business is paying for it or not.

2.   Briefly outline the steps in creating an advertising plan. What principles should the small business owner follow when creating an effective advertisement?

The first step in creating an advertising plan is to develop specific, measurable objectives for the program. The owner must then analyze the firm and its customers to focus on specific advertising targets. The owner then designs an advertising message and chooses the media for transmitting it.

Generally, an ad should conform to certain principles. It should:

1.   Be easily recognized
2.   Advertise products/services that customers perceive as being valuable
3.   Have a simple layout
4.   Have a message easy to understand
5.   Be built around a central theme
6.   Contain illustrations that complement the good or service
7.   Identify the store clearly
8.   Include a price or price range
9.   Be honest, believable, and in good taste

3.   What factors should a small business manager consider when selecting advertising media?

Factors a small business manager should consider when selecting advertising media include:

1.   How large is my firm's trading area?
2.   Who are my target customers and what are their characteristics?
3.   Which media are my target customers most likely to watch, listen to, or read?
4.   What budget limitations do I face?
5.   What media do my competitors use?
6.   How important are repetition and continuity of my advertising message?
7.   What does the advertising medium cost?

4. Create a table to summarize the advantages and disadvantages of the following advertising media:

Advertising Mediums	Advantages	Disadvantages
Newspapers	*selected geographical coverage *flexibility *timeliness *communication potential *prompt responses	*wasted readership *reproduction limitations *lack of prominence *short ad life
Radio	*universal infiltration *market segmentation *flexibility and timeliness *friendliness	*poor listening *need for repetition *limited message
Television	*broad coverage *visual advantage *flexibility *design and assistance	*brief exposure *costs
Magazines	*long life spans *multiple readership *target marketing *ad quality	*costs *long closing time *lack of prominence
Specialty Adv.	*reaches select audiences *personalized nature *versatility	*potential for waste *costs
Direct Mail	*selectivity *flexibility *reader attention *rapid feedback	*inaccurate mailing lists *high relative costs *high throwaway costs
Outdoor Adv.	*high exposure *broad reach *flexibility *cost efficiency	*brief exposure *legal restrictions *lack of prominence
Transit Adv.	*wide coverage *repeat exposure *low cost *flexibility	*generality *limited appeal *brief message
Directories	*prime prospects *long life	*increasing costs *wasted effort
Trade Shows	*a natural market *preselected market *new customer market	*fails to reach new customers

5. What are fixed spots, preemptive spots, and floating spots in radio advertising?

Radio ads are usually sold in 10-, 20-, 30-, and 60- second spots. Fixed spots are guaranteed to be broadcast during specific contracted times. Preemptible spots are less expensive, but they are "preempted" by fixed spots purchased by other advertisers. Floating spots are the least expensive, but the station chooses their broadcast times, using them as fillers.

6. Describe the characteristics of an effective outdoor advertisement.

Outdoor ads are a unique advertising medium; they remain stationary and the viewer is in motion. To be effective, an outdoor ad should be short, simple, and clear. Big layout and type sizes using bright contrasting colors provide maximum readability. The owner should consider these questions:

- Is the key lettering and visual large enough?
- Could the message contain fewer or simpler words?
- Does the design hold together as a single unit?
- Will it register quickly from a distance?

7. Describe the common methods of establishing an advertising budget. Which method is most often used? Which technique is most often recommended?

1. *What is affordable* -- Management spends whatever it can afford on advertising.
2. *Matching competitors* -- The approach is to match the advertising expenditures of the firm's competitors either in a flat dollar amount or as a percentage of sales.
3. *Percentage of sales* – The most commonly used method. Relates advertising expenditures to actual sales results.
4. *Objective-and-task* – The most difficult and least used technique. Advertising expenditures are linked to specific objectives.

The percentage of sales is most often used because of its simplicity. The objective and task is the most recommended because it relates the advertising budget to the specific objectives established for the ad program.

8. How does pricing affect a small firm's image?

A company's pricing policy offers important information about its overall image. Thus, when developing a marketing approach to pricing, a small business manager must establish prices that are compatible with what its customers expect and are willing to pay. Understanding the firm's target market allows the small business to set prices properly.

9. What competitive factors must the small firm consider when establishing prices?

Factors that small business owners must consider when determining final price include:

- Product/service costs
- Market factors - supply and demand
- Sales volume

- Competitors' prices
- The company's competitive advantage
- Economic conditions
- Business location
- Seasonal fluctuations
- Psychological factors
- Credit terms and purchase discounts
- Customers' price sensitivity
- Desired image

10. Describe the strategies a small business could use in setting the price of a new product. What objectives should the strategy seek to achieve?

When introducing a new product, the owner should try to satisfy three objectives:
1. Getting the product accepted
2. Maintaining market share as competition grows
3. Earning a profit

Three basic strategies to choose from in establishing the new product's price include:

1. *Penetration*: set prices below competitors to establish a market and achieve sales volume.
2. *Skimming*: set a higher-than-normal price for a unique market with little or no competition.
3. *Sliding-Down-the-Demand-Curve*: set high prices initially and then lower based on competitor behavior and/or technological advancement.

11. Define the following pricing techniques:

1. *Odd pricing*: establish prices that end in odd numbers with the belief that merchandise selling with an odd ending number ($12.95) is cheaper than an item evenly priced ($13.00).
2. *Price lining*: manager stocks merchandise in several different price ranges, or price lines. Each category of merchandise contains items that are similar in appearance, quality, cost, performance, or other features.
3. *Leader pricing*: small retailer marks down the customary price of a popular item in an attempt to attract more customers.
4. *Geographical pricing:* small company sells merchandise at different prices to customers located in different territories.
5. *Discounts*: reduction in the price of stale, outdated, damaged, or slow-moving merchandise.

12. Why do so many small businesses use the manufacturer's suggested retail price? What are the disadvantages of this technique?

Small business owners frequently use suggested retail prices because this eliminates the need for a pricing decision. Suggested retail prices are easy to use.

13. What is a markup? How is it used to determine individual price?

Markup is the difference between the cost of a good or service and its selling price. It can also be expressed as a percentage of either cost or selling price.

14.   What is a standard markup? A flexible markup?

A standard markup is a technique that is usually used in retail stores. It applies a standard percentage markup to all merchandise.
A flexible markup is usually more practical, and involves assigning various markup percentages to different types of products.

15.   What is cost-plus pricing? Why do so many manufacturers use it? What are the disadvantages of using it?

Cost-plus pricing establishes prices using the costs of the direct materials, direct labor, factory overhead, selling and administrative costs required to produce a product plus a reasonable profit margin. Cost-plus pricing is very popular, primarily because of its simplicity. Also, since a profit is added onto the firm's cost, the manufacturer is guaranteed a profit. But, cost-plus pricing does not encourage the manufacturer to focus on efficient use of his resources since a profit is added onto costs. Also, manufacturers' cost structures vary significantly and cost-plus pricing may not be competitive.

16.   Explain the difference between full-absorption costing and direct costing. How does absorption costing help a manufacturer determine a reasonable price?

Full absorption costing is the traditional method of product costing. It "absorbs" the cost of direct materials, direct labor, plus a portion of fixed and variable factory overhead into each unit manufactured. It is not very helpful in setting prices because it confuses the true relationships among price, volume, and costs by including fixed expenses in unit-cost computations.

Direct costing includes only those costs of production that vary directly with the volume of production. Fixed overhead expenses are considered to be expenses of the period. The result is a clear picture of the price-costs-volume relationship.

17.   Explain the technique for a small service firm setting an hourly price.

Most service firms base their fees on the actual numbers of hours required to perform the service. The first step is to estimate the actual number of hours of producing the service and the total costs incurred. Then, the owner must compute the total cost per productive hour. Next, the owner should determine his desired profit to compute the final price.

18.   What benefits does a small business get by offering customers credit? What costs does it incur?

When small businesses offer customers credit, they receive several benefits such as: increased probability, speed, and magnitude of customer spending; customers give higher service ratings; in some cases, the business retains the title of the merchandise until it is paid in full; the interest received on the loans is often greater than the original amount paid for the item.

However, there are costs incurred as well. The main cost when issuing credit to customers is that credit cards are not free to businesses. Typically, small businesses must pay one to six percent of the total credit card charges for the use of the system.

Part Four: Lecture or Critical Thinking Case Studies-Not In Student Text

THE PRICE OF SERVICE
PRICING: ART OR SCIENCE?... OR BOTH?

THE PRICE OF SERVICE

Most companies charge their customers the same price for a product-- even if it costs more to satisfy some of them. Some customers require no after-sale service; others demand a tremendous amount of hand-holding, support, and service. To David and Linda ("Charlie") West, owners of the San Luis Sourdough Company, it didn't make sense to charge everyone the same price. So the Wests designed a system that sets prices for their sourdough bread based on how much service their customers--local supermarkets and specialty food shops--require.

Here's how the pricing strategy works: if a customer chooses Level 1 service--having San Luis Sourdough deliver the bread to its back door--the wholesale price is 97 cents per loaf. If the store also wants to be able to return day-old bread for a full credit--Level 2 service--the cost of a loaf is $1.02. If the customer wants the convenience of returns plus the service of having San Luis Sourdough put the bread on the shelf and price it by sticking a bar code label on each bag and another on the shelf (Level 3 service), the price is $1.05 per loaf.

The Wests' prices are not arbitrary; they simply cover the cost of the extra service. The 5 cents premium per loaf for the privilege of returning day-old loaves covers the cost of the bread and handling the returns. Similarly, the 8 cents per loaf charge for stocking, pricing, and accepting returns pays for the Level 3 service. Studies show it takes a driver 30 minutes to stock and price a shelf, and drivers earn $8 per hour (salary and benefits). The average customer order is 100 loaves, producing a cost of 8 cents per loaf. "We don't care which pricing option you choose," says Dave. "They're all the same to us." About 60 percent of San Luis Sourdough's customers choose Level 2 service; the remainder are evenly divided between Levels 1 and 3. In essence, San Luis Sourdough is passing on the cost of service to its customers. Rather than absorb the extra 5 cents to 8 cents per loaf to charge everyone the same price, the Wests let their customers pay for it. How can they get away with it? After all, Sourdough's customers typically require their other bread suppliers to charge one price--whatever the level of service. The Wests cite three reasons. First, their big customers recognize that Sourdough is a small business, and they're willing to give the little guy a break. Second, the Wests bake a superior loaf of bread. Their customers recognize Sourdough's higher-quality product and are willing to be more flexible in order to stock it. Third, the Wests are honest when dealing with their customers. "What we've told all our customers--and it's true--is that we just don't have the resources of a huge bread company," says Charlie. "We have to compete on the quality of our product, not our level of service."

Very few customers ever complain. Costco Wholesale, Inc., a national supermarket chain touting its reputation for the lowest prices, has no problem paying the 8 cents premium for Level 3 service. "I'm happy," explains the buyer. "We don't have the manpower here to stock the shelves, price, and handle returns. As long as I'm still able to offer the lowest price on their bread, it's a very workable arrangement."

Charlie and David West offer these rules for keeping customers happy while asking them to pay for extra service:

Don't gouge. Charge exactly what the service costs. Don't add a surcharge; it only alienates customers.
Don't play favorites. If customers choose to get extra service, they will pay for it. "If we started providing Level 3 service to one company for the price of Level 2 or even Level 1, pretty soon we'd have to do it for everybody," says Dave. "By handling every customer in the same way, we don't run the risk of alienating anyone."
Give them a reason to go along. Unless your product is unique, it's difficult to convince customers to pay a premium for service.
Let them establish the level of service they want. Don't force service on customers; let them tell you what service they want. You'll both be better off.

1.   What are the advantages and disadvantages of Sourdough's pay-for-service policy'?
2.   Would such a policy work for every small business? Why or why not?
3.   What must a small business do to make such a policy succeed?

Adapted from Paul B. Brown, "You Get What You Pay For," *Inc.*, October 1990, pp. 155-156.

PRICING: ART OR SCIENCE?... OR BOTH?

The law of demand states that the quantity of a product demanded decreases when the price of that product increases, other things being equal. So when the Fleischman Division of Nabisco, Inc., raised the price of a fifth of gin by 22 percent over a two-year period, sales should have dropped off. Right? Not exactly. "The strategy helped incredibly," exclaims the company's manager. "Sales were deteriorating; now they're coming up. Sales are considerably above last year's." Smirnoff vodka, a moderately priced domestic brand, has been fighting higher-priced imported rivals, including Stolichnoya, Finlandia, Icy, and Tanqueray Sterling, to maintain its dominant market share. To keep sales from slipping, Smirnoff actually raised its prices in an effort to take on a more upscale look.

A growing number of middle-price brands are under attack from competing products in both the luxury and the discount markets. As the demographic profile of the U.S. population changes, customers are moving away from middle-of-the-road products they perceive as just average in favor of either premium products or those offering the lowest prices. Elegant stores such as Neiman-Marcus and discount retailers such as Wal-Mart are prospering while bread-and-butter Sears struggles. Super premium ice cream such as Ben & Jerry's Homemade are thriving-as are supermarkets' inexpensive private label brands-while basic brands such us Sealtest are fighting to hold their share. "The mainstream brands of old are increasingly under pressure from both ends of the spectrum," says one Harvard professor of marketing.
"It's hard for middle-segment (products) to compete either on elegance or on price," adds a business executive.

These days, choosing the right price is even more important than it was in the past. Although much has been written on the science of pricing products, the fact is that in many cases, pricing remains an art. Of course, production costs and factory overhead figure into a product's price, but many other less tangible, less measurable factors also influence a pricing decision. Lower prices are preferred for most products, but there are exceptions. According to Gerald Katz, vice-president of a pricing consulting firm, "The higher you price certain products like a Mercedes Benz, the more desirable they become."

Pricing is a function subject to much criticism. One consumer advocate claims. "Everybody thinks people go about pricing scientifically, but very often the process is incredibly arbitrary." Companies consider costs, competitors' prices on similar items, or image "and then take a good guess," as one apparel manufacturer explains. Psychology also play's a role in pricing. Cowden Manufacturing sells jeans at $9.86 in its outlet stores. According to sales manager James McAskill, "When people see $9.99 they say, 'That's $10.' But $9.86 isn't $10, it's just psychological."

Another psychological factor is the link between price and quality. Most consumers associate high quality with high prices. But the link is questionable. One researcher attempted to relate the prices of a broad range of packaged foods to their quality ratings and found that "the correlation ... is near zero." Still, image plays an important role in setting prices. For example, the ingredients of a bottle of perfume retailing for $100 may cost only $20, but the $100 creates an air of mystique and sophistication. "Women are buying atmosphere, and hope, and the feeling they are something special," says a major perfume manufacturer.

Consumers consider more than price alone when making purchase decisions. Quality, reliability, service support, ease of operation, and other intangibles rank high on a customer's list of buying criteria. For some, price is not a consideration at all. When Ferrari recently introduced its F40, a 475-horsepower twin-turbo engine model with a top speed of 201 mph, wealthy car enthusiasts quickly purchased the 1,000 cars manufactured. The sticker price was $350,000 (air conditioning and a radio not included). Because demand was so high and the supply of the F40 so limited, eager buyers quickly bid the price to over $1 million! Similarly, when Jaguar released 350 XJ220s at the highest sticker price ever for a new car-$500,000-the model sold out in just ten days! Tom Monoghan, founder of Domino's Pizza, who is awaiting his Ferrari F40, concedes that he doesn't know how much he's paying. "I never talk price," he says. "I don't buy cars for that reason." One marketing manager echoes that sentiment, "There is a segment of the market that wants to buy the best despite the cost."

1.   Why are some companies raising the prices of their products to make them more attractive?
2.   What factors other than price enter into a buyer's purchase decision?
3.   How could a small business use knowledge of the factors listed in your answer to Question 2 to support its pricing strategy?

Sources: Adapted from "Pricing of Products Is Still an Art, Often Having tittle Link to Costs," *Wall Street Journal*, November 25,1981, p 49, with permission of the *Wall Street Journal*. DowJones & Company, In 1981;

Carrie Dolan, "Well, would You Expect 475 Horses to Sell for Peanuts?" *Wall Street Journal*. February 15, 1990, p. A1;

Kathleen Deveny, "Middle Price Brands Come Under Siege," *Wall Street Journal*, April 2, 1990, p. B1.

Part Five: Chapter 7 Exercises

ENTREPRENEURIAL
GENERAL PRICING APPROACHES

When offering an undifferentiated product or service that is viewed by your target market as similar to the competition, a penetration pricing strategy may be effective if it is not matched by the competition or initiates a pricing war. A new or differentiated product/service may command a skimming price if it is viewed as unique or distinctly different from the competition. Free delivery, extended warranties, repeat customer discounts and follow-up customer service programs are augmented parts of your product/service that set you apart from the competition. These strategies allow you to compete on product and service features as opposed to lowest cost strategy because your target market is less price sensitive.

I.   COST PLUS PRICING EXAMPLE

This particular pricing approach requires accurate knowledge of current product/service costs. Information can be obtained from suppliers, industry standards, past experience or business records. When using any type of historical record, be sure to stay updated with current supplier costs.

> **Example (1):**
> - A contractor knows that a certain project will cost $1500 per day and will require 8 days to complete. If he requires a gross profit margin of 28%, how much should he bid for the project?
>
>> First, find total project cost:
>>
>> $$\$1500 \text{ X } 8 \text{ days } = \$12,000$$
>>
>> Second, find total cost (%):
>>
>> $$100\% - 28\% = 72\%$$
>>
>> Finally, find bid price:
>>
>> $$\frac{\text{Total Project Cost}}{\text{Total Cost (\%)}} = \frac{\$12,000}{.72} = \$16,667$$
>>
>> To check your figures:
>>
>> $$\frac{\text{Profit} = \$4667}{\text{Bid} \quad \$16,667} = 28\%$$

II. BREAK EVEN PRICING EXAMPLE

There are several variations on breakeven pricing. This example utilized per unit selling price and per unit costs. All forms of breakeven pricing provide the entrepreneur with valuable information relative to his/her individual pricing structures. For example, pricing decisions must consider constraints. The upper limitations to pricing are generally set by the consumer, while the lower limits are defined by the firm's cost structure. A Break Even Analysis can help us determine our minimum level of production. Anything in line with projected sales above this figure can be allocated to profit.

Example (2):
- If yearly fixed costs to run the factory are $200,000 and each widget costs $10 to make and can be sold for $15, how many widgets must we make to break even?

$$\frac{\text{Fixed Costs}}{\text{Sales Price - Variable Costs}} = \frac{\$200,000}{\$15 - \$10} = 40,000 \text{ widgets}$$

Determine the Break Even number of widgets in sales dollars we need to sell to realize a profit of $50,000, assuming our costs remain the same as above:

$$\frac{\$200,000 + \$50,000}{\$15 - \$5} = 50,000 \text{ widgets}$$

(multiply this by $15) = $750,000 in sales

Example (3):
- If sales are projected at 100,000 widgets, determine the Break Even Price per widget given the following information:

Direct Labor	$6
Direct materials	$3
Misc.	$1
Total Cost per widget	$10

Manufacturing Overhead	$150,000
Misc. Expenses	$ 25,000
Administration	$ 25,000

First, find total costs for production of 100,000 widgets:

	100,000 widgets X $10	= $1,000,000
plus	($150,000+25,000+25,000)	= $ 200,000
		$1,200,000

Now find Break Even Price per widget:

$$\frac{\$1,200,000 \text{ (total costs)}}{100,000 \text{ (\#of widgets)}} = \$12 \text{ per widget}$$

Example (4):
- **Find Break Even Price for a service business projecting sales demand of 5000 service hours with 2.5 employees @ 40 hours per week (-2 weeks vacation).**

Given the following information:.

Number of employees = 2 full time = 40 hours/week and 1 @ 20 hours
Service hours projected = (50 weeks x 2 1/2 employees x 40 hrs/week)
= 5000 possible working hours
Labor cost per hour = $12
Equip maintenance = $2,300
Rent & Utilities = $8,000
Misc. Overhead = $4,500

First, determine total costs:

5000 labor hours X $12 = $60,000 (labor)

plus ($2,300+8,000+4.500) = $14,800
For A Total Cost of = $74,000

Now find break even price per hour:

$$\frac{\text{Total Costs}}{\text{Projected Labor hours}} = \frac{\$74,000}{5000} = \$14.80/hr$$

This firm needs to collect $14.80 for each hour worked per employee-just to break even.

III. INITIAL MARKUP (%) PRICING

This particular pricing approach is often used by retailers. All product/service dollar figures in the following examples are based on retail selling price, and relate to a specific product/service or merchandise category.

Example (5):
- **If a certain retailer wants to make $5 on a widget that costs him $15, his general markup (%) would be:**

$$\frac{\$5 \text{ profit}}{\$20 \text{ selling price}} = 25\%$$

Example (6):

- To obtain a more accurate percentage, we must consider markdowns and inventory theft, operating expenses and anticipated profit. Solve for the Initial Markup Percentage:

Estimated Projections:

Sales	$100,000
Operating Expenses	$35,000
Markdowns & Theft	$ 5,000
Anticipated Profit	$ 6,000

Initial Markup (%)   = $\dfrac{\text{Operating Expenses + Markdowns \& Theft + Profit}}{\text{Net Sales + Markdowns \& Theft}}$

$$= \frac{\$35,000 + \$5,000 + \$6,000}{\$100,000 + \$5,000} = 43.8\%$$

Example (7):

- If a retailer sells several types of merchandise categories, the overall or average markup percentage may be found by considering the percentage of net sales that each merchandise category contributes. The estimate for calculating the Average Initial Markup for various merchandise categories follows:

	Initial Markup (%)		(%) of Total Retailer Sales	
Widgets	43.8%	X	50%	= 21.5%
Thing-ama-jigs	38%	X	25%	= 9.5%
Dilly-bobs	50%	X	25%	= 12.5%
			Average Initial Markup (%)	= 43.5%

1. Experiment with several entrepreneurial pricing approaches to find the most accurate way to determine your venture's breakeven price, initial markup, bid price, or average initial markup percentage.

Part Six: Supplement Readings

Rust, Roland. "Determining the optimal return on investment for an advertising campaign." *European Journal of Operational Research*. Dec. 20, 1996 v95 n3 p511(11).

Pollack, Judann. "Minute Maid ad budget will triple boost brand: $50 mil program aims to change perception of its orange juice." *Advertising Age*. Nov. 25, 1996 v67 n48 p29(1).

Fairhurst, Ann. "Determining advertising budgets for service enterprises." *The Journal of Services Marketing*. Nov-Dec 1996 v10 n6 p18(15).

Kim, Ji Soo and Jin Wook. "A breakeven analysis procedures for a multi-period project." *View Engineering Economist*. Wntr 1996 v41 n2 p95(10).

Newman, R., and Mark D. Hanna. "Including equipment flexibility in break-even analysis: two examples." *Production & Inventory Management Journal*. Wntr 1994 v35 n1 p48(5).

Dennis, Michael. "What credit manages should know about break-even analysis." *Business Credit*. Feb. 1995 v97 n2 p6(1).

Section III - Building the Business Plan: Marketing and Financial Considerations

Chapter 9
Managing Cash Flow (PPT 9.1)

Part One: Learning Objectives

1. Explain the importance of cash management to a small company's success.

2. Differentiate between cash and profits.

3. Understand the five steps in creating a cash budget and use them to create a cash budget.

4. Describe fundamental principles involved in managing the "Big Three" of cash management: accounts receivable, accounts payable, and inventory.

5. Explain the techniques for avoiding a cash crunch in a small company.

Part Two: Lesson Plan

    I.   Cash Management (PPT 9.2 thru 9.5)

        Cash is the most important yet least productive asset that a small business owns. Businesses must have enough cash to meet their obligations or run the risk of declaring bankruptcy. It is entirely possible for a business to earn a profit and still go out of business by running out of cash. Small and growing companies are like "sponges," soaking up every available dollar to fund growth and sales.

        The first step in managing cash more effectively is to understand the company's *cash flow cycle* - the time lag between paying suppliers for merchandise or materials and receiving payment from customers for the product or service. Business owners should calculate their cash conversion cycle whenever they prepare their financial statements. On a daily basis, business owners should generate reports showing the following: total cash on hand, bank balances, "summary of day" sales, "summary of the day" cash receipts, and a summary of accounts receivables collections.

        The next step in effective cash management is to shorten the length of the cash flow cycle.

    II.   Cash and Profits Are Not the Same

        Profit (or net income) is the difference between a company's total revenues and total expenses. It measures how efficiently the business is operating. *Cash flow* measures a company's liquidity and its ability to pay its bill and other financial obligations on time by tracking the flow of cash into and out of the business over a period of time. Profitability does not guarantee liquidity. Cash is the money that flows through a business in a continuous cycle without being tied up in any other asset.

III.   The Cash Budget **(PPT 9.6)**

The need for a cash budget arises because the uneven flow of cash in a business cycle creates surpluses and shortages. It is based on the cash method of accounting. Credit sales to customers are not recorded until the customer actually pays, and purchases made on credit are not recorded until the owner pays them. Depreciation, bad debt expense, and other non-cash items that do not involve cash transfers are omitted entirely from the cash budget. A cash budget is nothing more than a "cash map." It shows the amount and timing of cash receipts and cash disbursements day-by-day, week-by-week, or month-by-month and is used to predict the amount of cash the firm will need to operate smoothly over a specific period of time.

IV.   Preparing a Cash Budget **(PPT 9.7 thru 9.16)**

Five basic steps to preparing a cash budget include:

1.   Determining an adequate minimum cash balance – the most reliable method is based on past experience. For example, past operating records may indicate that it is desirable to maintain a cash balance equal to five days' sales.
2.   Forecasting sales – sales forecasts are the heart of the cash budget and are based partially on past patterns. Financial analysts suggest creating three estimates— optimistic, pessimistic and most likely.
3.   Forecasting cash receipts – the budget must account for the delay between the sale and the actual collection of the proceeds. It is vital to act promptly once an account becomes past due.
4.   Forecasting cash disbursements – many cash payments are fixed amounts due on specified dates. Others are standard like: the purchase of inventory, salary and wages, overhead, selling expenses and so on. Financial analysts suggest that new owners add an additional 10 to 25 percent to estimate disbursement totals as a cushion.
5.   Determining the end-of-month cash balance – the cash balance at the end of the month becomes the beginning balance for the following month. Anticipate cash shortages and surpluses; this can reduce lending expenses and time.

YOU BE THE CONSULTANT SUMMARY - In Search of a Cash Flow Forecast

Douglas Martinez, owner of a plumbing supply company must prepare a cash budget as part of his loan application package. Douglas has a monthly sales forecast and credit collection history to go along with his current cash balance that provides the basis for the preparation of his cash budget.

Q1. Assume the role of Douglas' SBDC consultant and help him put together a cash budget for the six months beginning in October.
Q2. What conclusions can you draw about Douglas's business from this cash budget?
Q3. What suggestion can you make to help Martinez improve his company's cash flow?

A1. Students should prepare a cash budget, by month, for the period of October through March. Students may be directed to run the numbers on all three sales forecast scenarios and/or by some weighted average.

See below.

A2. & A3. Students should first assess the current situation and then proceed to make recommendations that may include shortening the receivables period, lengthening the payables period, buying more efficiently and other cost cutting or revenue enhancing applications that would affect cash flow.

Overall his business has a very positive cash flow. Questions could be raised about the annual expense of $6,600 for advertising while other expenses seem very reasonable. Sales reflect a normal cycle. Focus on (both) increasing revenues and negotiating a high discount on purchases as sales increase.

Current cash balance	$8,750
Sales pattern	71% on credit and 29% in cash
Collections of credit sales	68% in 1 to 30 days;
	19% in 31 to 60 days;
	7% in 61 to 90 days;
	6% never collected (bad debts).

Sales forecasts:

	Pessimistic	Most Likely	Optimistic
July (actual)	--	$18,750	--
August (actual)	--	$19,200	--
September (actual)	--	$17, 840	--
October	$15,000	$17,500	$19,750
November	$14,000	$16,500	$18,500
December	$11,200	$13,000	$14,000
January	$ 9,900	$12,500	$14,900
February	$10,500	$13,800	$15,800
March	$13,500	$17,500	$19,900

Utilities expenses	$800 per month.
Rent	$1,200 per month
Truck loan	$317 per month

The company's wages and salaries (including payroll taxes) estimates are:

October	$2,050
November	$1,825
December	$1,725
January	$1,725
February	$1,950
March	$2,425

The company pays 63 percent of the sales price for the inventory it purchases, an amount that it actually pays in the following month. (Martinez has negotiated "net 30" credit terms with his suppliers.) Other expenses include:

Insurance premiums	$1,200 payable in August and February.
Office supplies	$95 per month
Maintenance	$75 per month
Computer supplies	$75 per month
Advertising	$550 per month
Legal and accounting fees	$250 per month
Miscellaneous expenses	$60 per month

A tax payment of $1,400 is due in December.
Martinez has established a minimum cash balance of $2,000.

"Well, what do you think?" Douglas asked the consultant.

1. Assume the role of the SBDC consultant and help Douglas put together a cash budget for the six months beginning in October.

Assumptions:

Current cash balance   = $8,750.00
minimum cash balance   = $2,000.00
sales are 71% credit and 29% cash
credit sales are collected in the following manner:

★   68% in 1-30 days
★   19% in 31-60 days
★   7% in 61-90 days
★   6% bad debts

Sales forecasts are as follows:

	Most Likely	Pessimistic	Optimistic
July (actual)	$18,750		
August (actual)	$19,200		
September (actual)	$17,840		
October	$17,500	$15,000	$19,750
November	$16,500	$14,000	$18,500
December	$13,000	$11,200	$14,000
January	$12,500	$9,900	$14,900
February	$13,800	$10,500	$15,800
March	$17,500	$13,500	$19,900

The company pays 63% of the sale price for the inventory it purchases - an account that it actually pays in the following month.

Rent	$1,200/month
Truck Loan	$317/month
Utilities	$800/month
Insurance Premiums	$1,200 payable in August & February
Office Supplies	$95/month
Maintenance	$75/month
Computer Supplies	$75/month
Advertising	$550/month
Legal & Accounting fees	$250/month
Miscellaneous expenses	$60/month
Tax Payment	$1,400 due in December
Wages and Salaries	
October	$2,040
November	$1,825
December	$1,725
January	$1,725
February	$1,950
March	$2,425

The authors suggest that the sales forecast be weighted to include both the optimistic and pessimistic sales outcomes. To accomplish this, sales for the cash budget will be weighted as follows:

Most Likely	60%
Optimistic	20%
Pessimistic	20%
	100%

You may want your students to prepare three separate cash projects or base it on the most likely forecast.

	Cash Budget					
	Oct.	Nov.	Dec.	Jan.	Feb.	March
Sales	$17,450	$16,400	$13,840	$12,460	$13,540	$17,180
Credit Sales	$12,390	11,644	9,826	8,847	9,613	12,198
Collections						
68% - 1 mo. After	12,131	11,866	11,152	9,411	8,473	9,207
19% - 2 mo. After	3,648	3,390	3,316	3,116	2,630	2,367
7% - 3 mo. After	1,313	1,344	1,249	1,222	1,148	969
Cash Sales (29%)	5,061	4,756	4,014	3,613	3,927	4,982
Total Cash Receipts	$22,153	$21,356	$19,731	$17,362	$16,178	$17,525
Cash Disbursements						
Inventory	$11,239	$10,994	$10,332	$8,719	$7,850	$8,530
Rent	1,200	1,200	1,200	1,200	1,200	1,200
Truck Loan	317	317	317	317	317	317
Utilities	800	800	800	800	800	800
Office Supplies	95	95	95	95	95	95
Maintenance	75	75	75	75	75	75
Computer Supplies	75	75	75	75	75	75
Advertising	550	550	550	550	550	550
Legal & Acct.	250	250	250	250	250	250
Misc. Expenses	60	60	60	60	60	60
Insurance					1,200	
Taxes			1,400			
Wages & Salaries	2,040	1,825	1,725	1,725	1,950	2,425
Total Cash Disbursements	$16,701	$16,241	$16,879	$13,866	$14,422	$14,377
End of Month Balance Cash (beginning)	$8,750	$14,202	$19,317	$22,169	$25,665	$27,421
+ Cash Receipts	22,153	21,356	19.731	17,362	16,178	17,525
- Cash Receipts	16,701	16,241	16,879	13,866	14,422	14,377
Cash Ending	14,202	19,317	22,169	25,665	27,421	30,569
Borrowing	0	0	0	0	0	0

V.   The "Big Three" of Cash Management **(PPT 9.17 thru 9.25)**

Accounts Receivable-- extending credit to customers. A firm should always try to accelerate the collection of its receivables. If possible, a firm should also work to reduce or even eliminate credit sales.

How to establish a credit and collection policy
*   Screen customers carefully by developing a detailed credit application. Know when to walk away from an order—why make the sale if you won't get paid?
*   Establish a written credit policy and let every customer know the company's credit terms in advance.
*   Send invoices promptly (cycle billing).
*   Take immediate actions when an account becomes overdue.

Steps to encourage prompt payment of invoices:
*   Ensure that invoices are clear, accurate and timely.
*   Make sure that invoice prices agree with the quotations on purchase orders or contracts.
*   Highlight the terms of the sale (2/10/net30, net 30).
*   Include a telephone number and contact person in your organization in case the customer has a question or concern.
*   Work with company owners or representatives in a positive and collaborative fashion to reduce and eliminate their overdue accounts.
*   As a last resort, consult with your attorney and/or turn the account over to a collection attorney.

Accounts Payable – suppliers and others extend credit to you. Take advantage of and never abuse those opportunities.

Inventory – is the #1 expense for all retail and manufacturing businesses.

Few owners use any formal method for managing inventory, so a small business typically has either too much or the wrong type of inventory. This ties up cash and is very expensive to the firm. A typical manufacturing company pays 25-30 percent of the value of its inventory in handling and finance costs; however, retailers carrying too little inventory experience stock outs and lost sales.

VI.   Avoiding the Cash Crunch **(PPT 9.26, 9.27)**

Tools that allow small business managers to get the maximum benefit from their companies' pool of cash include:
Bartering: the exchange of goods and services for other goods and services rather than for cash is an effective way to conserve cash.
Trimming Overhead Costs: high overhead expenses can strain a small firm's cash supply. Ways to trim overhead costs include:
1.   Periodically evaluate expenses
2.   When practical, lease instead of buy

3. Avoid nonessential outlays
4. Negotiate fixed loan payments to coincide with your company's cash flow cycle
5. Buy used or reconditioned equipment, especially if it is "behind-the-scenes" machinery
6. Hire part-time employees and freelance specialists whenever possible
7. Control employee advances and loans
8. Establish an internal security and control system
9. Develop a system to battle check fraud
10. Change your shipping terms
11. Switch to zero-based budgeting

Be on the lookout for employee theft.
Keep your business plan current.
Investing Surplus Cash.

YOU BE THE CONSULTANT – The Trusted Employee

Lloyd and Jim Graff own and operate Graff-Pinkert, a company founded by their father. The mid-western based operation generates sales of $8 to $10 million and employs eighteen people. The Graff's have always considered the operation "a family affair" and wouldn't want it any other way.

The "family" situation came crashing down one day when the Graff's discovered that their bookkeeper, a long-time employee, had embezzled more than $200,000 from the firm through a check altering scheme. The bookkeeper was fired and subsequently served a term in prison.

The Graff's now say that "we're more skeptical but not cynical. We still approach it as a family business. If we couldn't run it that way, we'd hang it up."

Q1. Identify some of the factors that led Graff-Pinkert to become a victim of embezzlement. What impact does this crime have on a company's cash flow?
Q2. What recommendations would you make to the Graff's about protecting their business from embezzlement in the future?
Q3. Working with several of your classmates, use the resources of the Web to develop a list of steps entrepreneurs should take to prevent their business from becoming victims of employee theft and embezzlement?

A1. The company made the mistake of placing all financial transactions in the hands of one person with no system of checks and balances. The owner's were also naïve in thinking of their employees as one big happy family. Any unscheduled or unknown drainage of funds will adversely affect a firm's cash flow.
A2. The Graff's need a system of checks and balances involving two or more people that also includes a clear and regularly audited paper trail of transactions.
A3. Students will discover many resources that address employee theft.

Part Three: Suggested Answers to Discussion Questions

1. Why must entrepreneurs concentrate on effective cash management?

Cash is the lifeblood of any business. It is the most important yet least productive asset a business owns. Proper cash management enables the owner to meet cash demands, to avoid keeping unnecessary cash balances and to maximize the profit-generating power of each sales dollar. More businesses fail for lack of cash than for lack of profit.

2.   Explain the difference between cash and profit.

Profit and cash are not the same. Profit is the net increase over a period of time in capital cycled through the business, indicating how effectively the firm is being managed. Cash is the money that flows through the business in a continuous cycle. A business cannot spend profits--only cash.

3.   Outline the steps involved in developing a cash budget.

There are five basic steps to preparing a cash budget:
1.   Determining an appropriate minimum cash balance
2.   Forecast sales
3.   Forecast cash receipts
4.   Forecast cash disbursements
5.   Determine end-of-month cash balances and needs

4.   How can an entrepreneur launching a new business forecast sales?

For an established business, a sales forecast can be derived from past experience and past sales data. The founder of a new business must rely on published statistics, market surveys, the opinions of outside experts and his/her own judgment to create a sales forecast.

5.   What are the "Big Three" of cash management? What effect do they have on a company's cash flow?

6.   Outline the basic principles of managing a small firm's receivables, payables, and inventory.

The answers to questions 5 & 6 are combined:

The "Big Three" of Cash Management are:

> *1. Accounts Receivable* -- extending credit to customers. Cash flow is greatly affected due to the time lag between the sale and the actual collection of cash. The related principles of managing include:
> - Screen customers carefully by establishing a detailed credit application. Know when to walk away from an order.
> - Establish a firm written credit policy and let every customer know the company's credit terms in advance.
> - Send invoices promptly.
> - Take immediate action when an account becomes overdue.
> - Ensure that all invoices are clear, accurate, and timely.
> - State clearly a description of the goods or services purchased and an account number, if possible.

110

- Make sure that prices on invoices agree with the price quotations on purchase orders or contracts.
- Highlight the terms of sale (e.g. "net 30") on all invoices and reinforce them, if necessary.
- Include a telephone number and a contact person in your organization in case the customer has a question or a dispute.

2. Accounts Payable – suppliers and others extend credit to you. This can have a very favorable affect on a firm's cash flow as inventory may be purchased using the supplier and/or bank funds. The basic principles of management revolve around ordering merchandise that will turn over and be paid for in a timely fashion.

3. Inventory – is the number one expense for all retail and manufacturing businesses. Inventory affects cash flow because the cash is locked in place until sold. The major principle of management is maximizing inventory turnover.

7. How can bartering improve a company's cash position?

Bartering-- the exchange of goods and services for other goods and services, can be an effective method of conserving cash. The owner receives goods and services without having to spend cash. In addition, the owner may be able to collect uncorrectable accounts.

8. What steps can entrepreneurs take to conserve cash within their companies?

Tools that allow small business managers to get maximum benefit from their companies' pools of cash include:

1. *Bartering*
2. *Trimming Overhead Costs*
3. *Keeping your business plan current*
4. *Investing Surplus Cash*

9. What should a small business owner's primary concern when investing surplus cash be?

The primary concerns for investing surplus cash should be safety and liquidity.

Part Four: Lecture or Critical Thinking Case Studies-Not Found In Student Text

THE EVILS OF INVENTORY
CASH, CASH, WHO'S GOT THE CASH?

THE EVILS OF INVENTORY

When Howard Skolnik bought a small company that manufactured steel drums for use in storing hazardous chemicals, "no one...understood how the costs associated with excessive inventory and

111

warehousing were hurting profits," he says. Growing small businesses typically tie up more unnecessary cash in inventory than in any other asset. "If you can free up the cash from inventory, you can spend it on growth instead," Skolnik philosophizes.

Skolnik has put his philosophy into practice at his company, Skolnik Industries. It is a progressive $10 million a year business. The company maintains one of the leanest inventories in the industry, yet its inventory control system facilitates shipments to customers within twenty-four to forty-eight hours. The heart of the system is a computerized inventory-tracking operation that continuously updates warehousing records on a product-by-product basis. That information feeds into a financial reporting system that tracks trends in five key areas that Skolnik has identified in his company. The result is an early-warning system for inventory problems, a common source of cash flow dangers.

The reporting system tracks the following for Skolnik's:

Gross margin return on investment. Subtracting the cost of goods sold (labor, materials, and overhead) from sales revenue and then dividing the result by sales revenue is how Skolnik calculates this ratio. According to one of Skolnik's financial advisers, manufacturers should be able to produce a 15 percent to 25 percent rate of return on each product line by this measure. "Some of my biggest selling lines were not profitable," admits Skolnik. "So I eliminated some and looked for ways to reduce costs on others." For example, he reduced the number of shades of blue he offered from fifteen to two.

Inventory turnover. The inventory turnover ratio tells Skolnik how rapidly inventory is moving through his business. He shoots for a turnover rate of eight times per year. A business that turns its inventory just four times a year--half that of Skolnik Industries--ties up twice as much cash as Skolnik does, at a cost of whatever interest that money could have earned had it been invested elsewhere.

Percentage of orders shipped on time. The downside of high inventory turnover is the ever-present danger of failing to fill customer orders promptly. Inventories that are too lean mean that customer service levels may fall. To avoid these, Skolnik tracks the percentage of orders shipped on time. If this ratio drops below the mid-nineties, it's a sign that inventory levels need to be pumped up.

Length of time to fill back orders. Another way to destroy customer service is to allow the time required to fill back orders to slip. "Watch the number of days it takes to fill back orders, and make it a major goal not to tolerate any type of worsening, because it will ultimately hurt sales," Skolnik advises.

Proportion of customer complaints to shipped orders. Although any number of problems can cause customer complaints, Skolnik believes this ratio (complaints divided by total orders shipped) is an early warning signal of inventory and warehouse problems. Skolnik considers a customer complaint ratio above 2 percent to be unacceptable. At that point, analyzing individual complaints reveals underlying problems in the company's basic operations.

"It all ties together," says Skolnik. "When your inventory is well maintained, you can keep your customers happy and still afford to pay for your growth."

1.   Why is managing inventory properly such an important part of cash flow management?

2. What are the dangers of carrying excessive inventory? Insufficient inventory?
3. Evaluate Skolnik Industries' method of tracking its inventory.

Source: Jill Andresky Fraser, "Hidden Cash," *Inc.*, February 1991, pp.81-83.

CASH, CASH, WHO'S GOT THE CASH?

Most entrepreneurs find it extremely easy to forget about cash flow management; it's not very exciting, and there are a million day-to-day pressures driving cash management out of the owner's schedule. In reality, however, cash flow analysis is one of the building blocks of a successful enterprise. The risks of ignoring cash flow management are high, especially for entrepreneurial companies. Too often, fledgling businesses show paper profits but cannot pay their bills because they run out of cash. The faster a company grows, the more likely it is to experience cash flow complications.

When it came to managing cash flow, John Brandon, founder of Via Systems, Inc., a Colorado Springs computer software venture, was the typical entrepreneur. He thought cash flow analysis belonged only in textbooks on small business management. "To me," he recalled, "cash flow meant that if I looked at my checkbook and had enough money, I was OK." A decade earlier, Brandon had watched a growing business fail, and he was determined to avoid that happening again. With annual sales approaching $1 million and with Via systems poised for rapid growth, Brandon realized he was managing his company's most valuable asset by the seat of his pants. "I had developed enormous anxieties that we were going to run out of cash and not be able to pay for the expansion I wanted to take on," he noted.

In its sixth year, Via Sitemaps was facing a challenge. I was a one-product company, and rather than "wait for the product to run out its life," Brandon decided "it was time to change direction." But that would take cash, and Brandon realized he "couldn't think about diversifying product lines, expanding staff, adding new locations, or acquiring new divisions. In essence, when a company's cash outflows are about to climb significantly, it's time to pay special attention to cash management.

Brandon and his wife, Kathie, the company's bookkeeper, decided to bring in an expert to help them set up a cash management system. They turned to Paul Parish, a senior consultant at the firm that handled Via Systems' accounting. The Brandons wanted to answer two questions: First, was there any basis for their fear of running out of cash, and second, would they have enough cash to add new software products?

To answer these questions, parish helped the Brandons prepare a cash budget, forecasting detailed cash flows eighteen months into the future, with broader estimates for a three-to-five year span. "It was hard work, pouring over financial records and trying to figure out exactly what happens to every single sales dollar that we generate," he remembered.

Parish explained cash flow analysis to the Brandons in this way: "Cash flow is a cycle. Once a company makes a sale, cash passes through various stages from billing to disbursements and so on. The more efficiently it passes along, the less cash any company, big or small, needs during any particular month to keep its operations going smoothly." To track that cycle, Parish analyzed six phases of Via Systems' cash flow:

1. Cash receipts: how the company invoiced customers, collected accounts receivable, and tracked

113

late payers.

2.   Cash concentration: the speed and efficiency with which cash receipts were put to work for the company.

3.   Cash disbursements: the way Via Systems timed bill payments.

4.   Forecasting: the accuracy of the Brandon's projections regarding the amount and timing of cash flows.

5.   Inventory: how much cash the company has tied up in raw materials and unsold goods.

6.   Bank relations: the flow of money among the company's various bank accounts and the details of its borrowing capacity.

The analysis showed several weaknesses in Via Systems' cash flow cycle, including poorly timed disbursements and lack of a bank credit line.

The hard work paid off handsomely. "We worked up a set of projections that showed us going from a positive cash flow of more than $8,000 in February to a negative cash flow totaling about $45,000 in March and April, when we started bringing new products to market," says Brandon. Their forecasts were on target. "When I went negative for those two months, it didn't worry me because I had faith in our long-term assumptions," he added. By May, Via Systems' cash balance climbed to $5,500 and has climbed steadily since.

"Before the analysis, I didn't know which steps I could take," admits Brandon. "Now I've introduced four new products to the market, and we've done beautifully...My cash flow plan is a living, breathing document."

1.   Why should fast-growth companies worry most about cash flow crises?
2.   Why do the typical entrepreneurs fail to manage their company's cash properly?
3.   What benefits does proper cash management offer any business owner?

Adapted from Jill Andresky Fraser, "A Confidence Game," *Inc.*, December 1989, pp.175-178.

Part Five: Chapter 8 Exercises

8.1 To Figure Depreciation Expense

In completing your monthly Income Statements you must consider all business expenses. *Depreciation* represents the cost of using equipment that were purchased for use in the business. Each one becomes worn or obsolete over a period of time known as the *useful life* of the asset. The IRS publishes tables listing the useful life of assets by particular industry type.

As a business uses these assets, a portion of their cost is recuperated or expensed. This kind of expense is called *depreciation*. Land is not a depreciable asset. Items that do not represent a significant cost to the business may be expensed in the month they are purchased. For instance, an iron purchased by a dry cleaner would be written off as an expense in the month purchased; however, a dry cleaning machine worth thousands would be expensed on a monthly basis.

Calculating the depreciation expense for a machine value of $12,000 is as follows:

Purchase Cost	$12,000 (includes delivery & installation costs)
Useful Life	3 Years
Yearly Depreciation Amount	$12,000/3 Years = $4,000
Monthly Expense	$4,000/12 = $333.33

As you depreciate business assets over their useful life, the assets' *book value* also changes on the company's Balance Sheets. Notice how the dry cleaning machine's value changes from its Jan. 1 purchase date to its end of the year value of $8,000 on ANY OLE" DRY CLEANERS Balance Sheets. The $8,000 end of the year value is the result of expensing $333.33 per month on ANY OLE's Profit & Loss Statements (not shown) for 12 months.

ANY OLE' DRY CLEANERS
BALANCE SHEET
FOR THE PERIOD ENDING

	Jan. 1, 2001	Dec. 31, 2001
ASSETS		
Current		
Cash	0	0
Accounts Receivable	0	0
Inventory	0	0
Fixed		
Cleaning Machine	12,000	8,000
Bldg.	100,000	90,000
Land	25,000	25,000
TOTAL ASSETS	137,000	123,000
LIABILITIES		
Current		
Accounts Payable	0	0
Short Term Debt	0	0
Long term		
Bank Loan	0	0
TOTAL LIABILITIES	0	0
OWNER EQUITY		
John's Capital Account	137,000	123,000
[Drawing Account]		
TOTAL LIABILITIES&O.E.	137,000	123,000

If we make the assumption that no other business activity occurred during the year, notice what effect the depreciation expense has on Owner's Equity (Net Worth). Also notice that at all times, the accounting equation remains balanced. Assets = Liabilities + Owners Equity

Can you determine what the assets value would be after two full years of being depreciated? If you determined the value to be $4,000, you are correct.

8.2 Figuring the Current and Long-Term Portion of Debt

One of the three major balance sheet components is Liabilities--the creditor's claims against the company's assets. Liabilities are classified as either current or long-term depending on their definition. Current liabilities are those debts that must be paid within one year or within the normal operating cycle of the business—or whichever is longer. Long-term liabilities are those that come due after one year. Bank loans to finance long-term assets over their useful life are typically classified as long-term liabilities; however, the portion of debt that is due within the current year should be listed under current liabilities. The current and long-term portion of debt is calculated as follows:

Given:

XYZ Loan amount	$120,000
Contracted interest rate	10% stated as .10
Negotiated monthly payment	$2,000

First find yearly interest due:

$$\begin{array}{r} \$120,000 \\ \underline{x \quad .10} \\ \$\ 12,000 \end{array}$$

Next calculate total yearly payments:

$ 2,000	per month
x 12	months
$24,000	

Next find the year's reduction in principle:

Year payment total	$24,000
Year Interest due	<12,000>
Applied to principle	$12,000

Finally, determine current and long-term portion of the $120,000 debt:

Loan Amount	$120,000
Amount applied to principle this year	-12,000
(remainder after interest is deducted from payments)	
Principal amount left for repayment after this year	$108,000

In summary, with a negotiated monthly payment of $2,000 per month, on a principal loan amount of $120,000, the interest due will claim $12,000 of our total monthly payment amount. The remaining $12,000 will be applied to our $120,000 loan in the first year. This results in the remaining portion of long-term debt-- $108,000. The balance sheet will reflect the following account numbers:

LIABILITIES
Current Liabilities
Current portion of (XYZ LOAN) $12,000

Long-term liabilities
Long-term portion of (XYZ Loan) $108,000

Given the following information, calculate the current and long-term portion of debt for the following set of business circumstances.

Given:

ABC Loan amount	$60,000
Contracted interest rate	10% stated as .10
Negotiated monthly payment	$1,000

Answer:	ABC Current portion	= $6,000
	ABC Long-term portion	= $54,000

Part Six: Supplement Readings

"Cash vs. Profits: The Differences is Critical for Small Business." *PR Newsire*. March 25, 1997 p325SFTU035.

Nigel, Healey. "The Billion Dollar Swop Shop." *Management Today*. April 1994, p50(5).

Melvin, Mary Kay. "Budgeting, cash, ticket controls: Virginia panel covers the ABCs." *Amusement Business*. Jan. 13, 1997 v109 n2 p22(1).

LaFemina, Lorraine. "Taking control of company cash." *LI Business News*. March 13, 1995 n11 p3(1).

Ecker, Donald. "Managing cash flow to increase bottom line." *San Diego Business Journal*. Jan. 16, 1995 v16 n3 p18(2).

Brown, Ann. "Managing your cash flow: should you have a controller?" *Black Enterprise*. May 1995, v25 n10 p38(1).

Chapter 10
Creating a Successful Financial Plan **(PPT 10.1)**

Part One: Learning Objectives

1.   Understand the importance of preparing a financial plan.

2.   Describe how to prepare the basic financial statements and use them to manage to a small business.

3.   Create projected (pro forma) financial statements.

4.   Understand the basic financial statements through ratio analysis.

5.   Explain how to interpret financial ratios.

6.   Conduct a breakeven analysis for a small company.

Part Two: Lesson Plan

I.   Basic Financial Statements **(PPT 10.2)**

A.   *The balance sheet*-- takes a "snapshot" of a business at a given date, providing owners with an estimate of its value in terms of assets, liabilities and equity.

B.   *The income statement*-- also called a profit and loss (P&L) statement, compares expenses against revenues for a certain period of time to indicate profits or losses.

C.   *The statement of cash flows*-- shows the actual flow of cash into and out of a business for a certain time period.

II.   Creating Projected Financial Statements

A.   The determination of funds needed for starting and sustaining a business for the initial growth period-- the entrepreneur typically relies on data collection through extensive market and field research and on published statistics summarizing the performance of similar companies.

B.   Develop Pro Forma Statements

Pro Forma Statements (projected) help the small business owner transform goals into reality by estimating the profitability and overall financial condition of the business for the initial one- to three-year period.

1.   Always start with the sales forecast and work down.
a.   *The pro forma income statement* begins with the sales forecast and estimates the corresponding expenses required to generate those sales dollars. Banks typically require two- to three-year projections.
b.   *The pro forma balance sheet* starts with the beginning balances of cash, inventories, assets and liabilities. Banks typically require a year-

119

one and year-two balance sheet projection.

    c.   *The pro-forma cash flow statement* charts cash flow, by month, (typically) for the first two years of operation. It is often one of the major criteria for lending decisions by creditors.

III.   Ratio Analysis **(PPT 10.3 thru 10.15)**

Ratio Analysis expresses the relationship between two selected accounting elements and is one technique used in conducting a financial analysis.

The twelve key ratios include:

A.   <u>Liquidity Ratios</u> indicate whether the business will be able to meet its short-term financial obligations as they come due.
1. *Current ratio*-- measures solvency through the relationship between current assets and current liabilities.
2. *Quick ratio*-- focuses even more on liquidity by removing inventory from the current ratio calculation.

B.   <u>Leverage Ratios</u> measure the relationships between financing supplied by a firm's owners and by its creditors.
3. *Debt ratio*-- measures total debt against total assets-- the extent or percentage of total assets owned by creditors
4. *Debt-to-net-worth ratio*-- indicates the degree of leveraging by measuring capital contributions from creditors against those by the owners (debt-to-equity).
5. *Times interest earned*-- a measure of the firm's ability to make the interest payments on its debt.
6. *Average inventory-turnover ratio*--measures the average number of times inventory is "turned over" during the year.
7. *Average collection period ratio*--measures the average number of days it takes to collect receivables.
8. *Average payable period ratio*-- indicates the average number of days it takes a company to pay its accounts payable.
9. *Net Sales to Total Assets ratio*-- the measure of a firm's ability to generate sales in relation to its assets.
10. *Net Sales to Working Capital ratio*-- measures the sales that a business generates for every dollar of working capital.
11. *Net profit on sales ratio*—measures a firm's profit per dollar of sales.
12. *Net profit to equity ratio*—measures an owner's rate of return on investment.

YOU BE THE CONSULTANT - Yes, But Are Those Profits Real?

Desperate companies and dishonest people have unfortunately taken to manipulating financial statements in an attempt to fool stockholders, creditors, suppliers and others, and to buy time. It is relatively easy to deceive outsiders by "doctoring" statements (reported phony revenues and gross profits, inflating inventories, misreporting expenses and so on).

Q1. Refer to the balance sheet and income statement for Sam's Appliance Shop (fig. 10.1 and 10.2) and do some "creative accounting" of your own. Inflate the inventory values by a significant amount and see what happens to net worth and profits.

Q2. Recalculate the twelve key ratios for Sam's Appliance Shop. Compare the results. Which version would look better to a banker? Why?

Q3. Who loses when managers of a company commit inventory fraud? What are the ethical implications of such practices?

Q4. What dangers does the practice of "earnings management" hold for companies and their investors?

A1. & A2. Students should be led to realize how easy it is to recreate the financial standing of a company by manipulating numbers that influence profitability and ratio analysis.

Answer: As an example: if inventory is increased from $455,455 by **50%** to $683,183, total assets would be increased by $227,727 to $1,075,382., and net worth to $495.382. Increasing inventory to 683,183 results in cost of goods sold changing to $1,062,389 and gross profit to $808,452. Net income rises to $288,357 (a dramatic increase from the original $60,629).

	New	Original
Current Ratio	2.49:1	1.87:1
Quick Ratio	.63:1	.63:1
Debt Ratio	.54:1	.68:1
Debt to Net Worth Ratio	2.20:1	2.20:1
Times Interest Turnover	1.43:1	2.05:1
Average Collection Period	50 days	50 days
Average Payable Period	59.3	59.3
Net Sales to Total Assets	1.74:1	2.21:1
Net Sales to Working Capital	3.42:1	5.86:1
Net Profit on Sales	3%	3%
Net Profit on Equity	22.6$	22.6%

A3. Many individuals both inside and outside of a company are adversely affected by fraud. Suppliers, stockholders, employees, creditors and even customers are affected. Any such unethical practice may permanently damage the reputation and existence of a company.

A4. Bankruptcy and prison time are the primary dangers of accounting fraud.

YOU BE THE CONSULTANT - All Is Not Paradise in Eden's Garden: Part 1

Joe and Kaitlin Eden, co-owners of Eden's Garden, a small nursery, lawn and garden supply business, received their year-end financial statements from accountant Shelley Edison. The Eden's are having trouble keeping up with their bills-- Edison has offered to show the Edens how to analyze financial statements and avoid such problems. Students are provided with balance sheet and income statement data.

Q1. Assume the role of Shelley Edison. Using the financial statements for Eden's Garden, calculate the 12 ratios covered in this chapter.
Q2. Do you see any ratios that, on the surface, look suspicious? Explain.

A1.

Current Ratio	$\frac{129,936}{87,622}$	=	1.48:1
Quick Ratio	$\frac{129,936-88,157}{87,622}$	=	.48:1
Debt Ratio	$\frac{87,622,+119,846}{280,843}$	=	74:1
Debt to Net Worth Ratio	$\frac{87,622,+119,846}{73,375}$	=	2.83:1
Time Interest Earned	$\frac{30,189,+21,978}{21,978}$	=	2.37:1
Average Inventory Turnover	$\frac{395,683}{78,271,+86,157\div2}$	=	4.8 times/yr.
Average Collection Period	$\frac{289,484}{25,952}$	=	11.15 times/yr
	$\frac{365}{11.15}$	=	32.7 days
Average Payable Period	$\frac{403,569}{54,258}$	=	7.44 times/yr.
	$\frac{365}{7.44}$	=	49 days
Net Sales to Net Assets	$\frac{689,247}{280,843}$	=	2.45:1
Net Sales to Working Capital	$\frac{689,247}{129,936-87,622}$	=	16.29:1
Net Profit on	$30,189$	=	4%

Sales	689,247		
Net Profit to Equity	$\frac{30,189}{73,375}$	=	41%

A2. Ask students to go to Robert Morris Associates Annual statement studies or Dun and Bradstreet's Key Business ratios and compare the 12 ratios calculated for Eden's Garden against businesses within this industry of a similar size (look under Nursery, and Lawn and Garden Supplies). Answers will vary depending on the year or edition used. Part 2 of this exercise will ask for additional analysis.

IV.   Interpreting Business Ratios-- Ratios are useful yardsticks when measuring a small firm's performance and can point out potential problems before they develop into a crisis. **(PPT 10.16 thru 10.27)**

    A.   Comparison of a firm's ratios to businesses within the same industry is a useful tool. A firm can also develop ratios unique to its operation. Several organizations compile and publish operating statistics including key ratios. This information may be found in the following sources:

        1.   Robert Morris Associates
        2.   Dun & Bradstreet, Inc.
        3.   Vest Pocket Guide to Financial Ratios
        4.   Industry Spotlight
        5.   Bank of America
        6.   Trade associations
        7.   Government agencies

    B.   What Do All of These Numbers Mean? Learning to interpret financial ratios just takes practice--students are presented with the twelve ratios from Sam's Appliance Shop along with a corresponding analysis from Robert Morris Associate's Annual Statement Studies.

YOU BE THE CONSULTANT - All Is Not Paradise in Eden's Garden: Part 2

Having now calculated and compared the ratios for Joe and Kaitlin Eden's business to the industry averages in the Robert Morris Associates database, it is time to meet with and help the clients.

Q1. Analyze the comparisons you have made of Eden's Garden's ratios with those from Robert Morris Associates. What "red flags" do you see?
Q2. What might be causing the deviations you have observed?
Q3. What recommendations can you make to the Edens to improve their company's financial performance?

A1. The average collection period and average payable period numbers are beyond industry norms. Profitability on sales is also below normal.
A2. Under-pricing and sluggish collection of receivables will adversely affect cash flow causing extended

payable periods and other problems.

A3. Students will offer a number of recommendations that should include pricing, cost control and expedited collections.

V. Breakeven Analysis (PPT 10.28 thru 10.31)

The *breakeven point* is the level of production and sales volume at which a company's revenues equal its expenses, resulting in a net income of zero.

A. Determining variable and fixed expenses.

    1. Fixed expenses--costs that do not vary with changes in the volume of sales or production.

    2. Variable expenses--costs that vary directly with changes in the volume of sales or production.

B. Steps in calculating the breakeven point

    Step 1: Determine the expenses a business can expect to incur.
    Step 2: Categorize those expenses as fixed or variable.
    Step 3: Calculate the percentage of variable expenses to net sales.
    Determine the percentage of contribution margin to sales.
    Step 4: Compute the breakeven point.

C. Include Desired Net Income into the Breakeven Analysis calculations.

D. Calculate the Breakeven Point and Desired Profit in both units and dollars.

E. How to use the Breakeven Analysis data.

YOU BE THE CONSULTANT - Where Do We Break Even?

Students are provided with the cost structure and data for Anita Dawson's existing business and for her proposed growth venture.

Q1. Calculate Anita's current breakeven point; include a break-even chart.

Q2. Calculate Anita's breakeven point under the proposed growth venture.

Q3. Would you recommend that Anita expand her business? Explain.

A1.

    <u>First</u> calculate the contribution margin:
    Variable costs = \$337,000 + \$42,750 = \$379,750
    Sales are given at \$495,000
    Variable costs as a percentage of sales = 379,750/495,000 = .77
    Contribution margin = 1.0 - .77 = .23

    <u>Then</u> calculate breakeven sales dollar amount

$$\frac{\text{Total Fixed Cost}}{\text{Contribution margin}} \quad = \quad \frac{\$78,100}{.23} \quad = \quad \$339,565$$

124

A2.   First calculate the contribution margin:

Given New Sales = $495,000 + $102,000 = $597,000
Cost of Goods Sold as a percentage of original sales ($337,000/$495,000) = .68
Variable costs = (.68)($597,000) + 42,750 + $22,400 = $471,110
Variable costs as a percentage of sales = $471,110/597,000 = .79
Contribution margin = 1.0 - .79 = .21

Then calculate breakeven sales dollar amount

$$\frac{\text{Total Fixed Cost}}{\text{Contribution margin}} = \frac{\$78,100 + 66,000}{.21} = \$686,190$$

A3.   No, assuming that her cost of goods remained constant at 68% of sales, the additional $22,400 in variable cost would reduce the contribution margin to 21%. With the additional $66,000 to fixed costs, breakeven rises from $339,565 to $686,190. An amount above the projected new sales amount of $597,000, (495,000+102.000).

At first glance, Anita should be discouraged from expanding. Students may note however that the contribution margin percent is very low, indicating low pricing, high cost of goods or both. An improvement in either area would lower the breakeven point significantly.

Part Three: Suggested Answers to Discussion Questions

1.   Why is developing a financial plan so important to an entrepreneur about to launch a business?

Developing a financial plan is one of the most important steps in launching a new business venture. Prospective investors will demand such a plan before putting their money into a startup company. A financial plan is a tool that helps entrepreneurs manage their businesses more effectively, steering their way around the pitfalls that cause failures.

2.   How should a small business use the 12 ratios discussed in this chapter?

Ratios help measure a firm's performance and can point out potential problems before they become more serious. One way to use ratios is to compare a business to others in the same industry. It is also helpful for the owner to analyze the firm's financial ratios and trends over time.

3.   Outline the key points of the twelve ratios discussed in this chapter. What signals does each give the manager?

1. Current ratio-- the firm's ability to pay current liabilities using current assets.
2. Quick ratio--extent to which firm's most liquid assets cover its current liabilities.
3. Debt ratio--measure the financing supplied by business owners and creditors.
4. Debt-to-net-worth ratio--compares what the business owes to what it owns.
5. Times interest earned--a measure of the firm's ability to make interest payments.

125

6. Average inventory turnover ratio--measures the number of times inventory is "turned over" per year.
7. Average collection period-- the average number of days to collect accounts receivables.
8. Average payable period-- the average number of days it takes to pay accounts payables.
9. Net sales to total assets ratio-- measures a firm's ability to generate sales in relation to its assets.
10. Net sales to working capital-- measures sales generated for every dollar of working capital.
11. Net profit on sales ratio-- measures a firm's profit per dollar of sales.
12. Net profit to equity ratio—measures an owner's rate of return on investment (ROI).

4. Describe the method for building a projected income statement and a projected balance sheet for a new business.

A projected income statement starts with a sales forecast that should based primarily on market research about the firm's competition and customer base. The sales forecast allows the income statement and balance sheet to be completed.

5. Why are pro forma financial statements important to the financial planning process?

No entrepreneur should launch a business without first creating a sound financial plan and attracting the capital to operate it. Pro forma statements are a vital element in such a plan, as they estimate the firm's future profitability and overall financial condition. These statements help the owner determine what funds are required to launch the business and sustain it through its initial growth period.

6. How can breakeven analysis help an entrepreneur launch a business?

Breakeven-analysis first lets an entrepreneur know the sales volume that must be generated to "break even." It also serves as a "reality check" in relation to the competition, the customer base, and the sales volume that must be generated in order to earn the desired profit.

Part Four: Lecture or Critical Thinking Case Studies-Not In Student Text

THE GREAT GAME OF BUSINESS
IT'S ALL IN THE NUMBERS

THE GREAT GAME OF BUSINESS

Accounting is just a necessary function that every small company must perform; it's nothing that can help the business compete, right? Wrong.

Managers and employees at Springfield Remanufacturing Company, a Missouri-based business that rebuilds engines, would argue that the accounting and financial functions can be a source for building a competitive edge. Indeed, SRC has developed a creative system that uses accounting as a strategic weapon.

When managers and employees bought SRC from International Harvester in a leveraged buy-out, the company was losing money fast, despite IH's best efforts to turn it around. Facing huge debts and a short time horizon, President Jack Stack created "the great game of business"--a plan for survival and growth. He began by teaching every employee how to read, analyze, and understand financial statements and other numbers of the business.

The game Stack created is to beat the numbers. According to Stack, "I think you need an invisible enemy to get your dander up. We set up this income statement as the enemy." Employees at SRC not only understand the numbers, they also act on them. Stack states, "We need our people to look at the labor; we need them to look at the overhead; and we need them to look at the material [costs]. We need them to make management decisions at virtually every operation at every time of the day." For example, some of the toughest jobs in the plan are in the maintenance department; when a machine or tool breaks down, the operator wants it fixed yesterday. Stack related the following story:

"One day, I went out to the maintenance foreman, and I asked him, 'Are you reading the statements? Are you getting any meaning out of the statements?' He said, 'Yeah.' 'How?' Stack asked. 'I go over the labor portion of that financial statement and I look for the departments that are not meeting their standards,' the foreman explained. 'Then I go to my people. Any department that is not meeting their standards and has a machine down, I send my maintenance people there first.' Stack responded, 'That's a phenomenal way of scheduling your manpower.' The foreman replied, 'If I can get these guys up to standard, then we're going to make more money.'

And so it goes at SRC. Employees actually use numbers to make business decisions that benefit the company and themselves. Stack claims, "What we have done here is break down, individually, each and everyone's responsibility and show how those results flow into a financial statement and how they actually contributed to the success or failure in that particular period of time." As a result, SRC employees have come to understand the importance of their jobs to the company. Stack continues, "Our people know exactly the profit and loss of every piece [of work] they perform, and how that piece fits into the whole."

Stack is convinced that SRC is in a stronger competitive position because its employees understand and use financial information creatively. The evidence is the dramatic increase in company sales--from $16 million to $43 million--in just three years. Jack Stack concludes, "We use numbers from the competitive side of things. We needed a game to unify everybody out in that factory. We needed something that was concrete. We needed something that they could believe in, and this game was absolutely perfect to play."

1. What financial summaries should small business owners prepare to improve their control over their business?
2. Why do some owners fail to prepare adequate financial summaries and reports?
3. What benefits does SRC gain form its approach to financial management?

Adapted from "Numbers," in Paul Hawken, "Growing a Business," KQED Video, 1988.

IT'S ALL IN THE NUMBERS

Although trained as a behavioral psychologist, Larry Stifler, founder of Health Management Resources Inc. (HMR), "is a numbers guy," says one employee. Stifler uses his "sixth sense"--an uncanny ability to see relationships in numerical terms--to manage his highly successful weight-control business. He showed a knack for numbers as a kid when he performed math tricks in his head on stage.

"I do everything by the numbers," he explained. That includes running his $60 million company, which combines medically supervised very low-calorie diets (VLCDs) with extensive behavior modification and support programs. HMR targets clinically obese individuals, not casual post-holiday dieters, and treats them as medical patients.

Rather than incur the high start-up and maintenance costs of freestanding diet clinics (and raising its break-even point to excessive levels), HMR invests between $25,000 and $30,000 to open clinics in existing hospitals and medical facilities. The weight-loss clinics belong to HMR, which shares a portion of gross revenues with hospitals. In other cases, HMR trainers show hospital professionals how to open and operate their own diet clinics and then offer ongoing, off-site training sessions for hospital staffers. The company also sells its liquid weight-loss supplement to non-HMR-affiliated clinics. All of this has pushed HMR into the number one spot in the nation's medically supervised VLCD market. "Larry has a commitment to health," observes one employee. "He lives it. He's not in business just to make money. But he believes in capitalism too. There's no conflicts between profitability and running a good program. Profitability and clinical effectiveness go hand in hand."

Although Stifler admits to being a numbers guy, he doesn't use numbers in the traditional sense to manage his companies. For instance, HMR has no budgets in place, and no one in the company plans in dollar amounts. Stifler despises the bean-counting philosophy on which businesses have traditionally relied, scrutinizing every budget line item for places to cut costs. Instead, Stifler relies almost exclusively on ratios to express relationships among the people, things, and events that are crucial to HMR's success. Once he understands those relationships, he builds mathematical models that capture the essence of those factors required for business success.

Stifler uses his ratios and models to make better business decisions. For instance, HMR spends almost nothing on consumer advertising. Why not? After looking at a few ratios, Stifler discovered that he didn't need to. Using company records, he noted that on average, every patient that moves from the VLCD phase into HMR's eighteen-month maintenance stage recommends 2.2 additional patients who enter the program. The number told him that to keep the program self-sustaining, HMR had to get 46 percent of all patients into the maintenance phase (because 46% x 2.2 = 100%). If more than 46 percent go into the maintenance stage, the program will grow automatically, and this means that every dollar spent offering top-quality patient care will produce $2.20 in additional revenue. "So," Stifler noted, "I said, 'Set up the business for quality care, and it will grow by itself.'"

Stifler uses these numerical relationships to allocate resources in the company without a budget. The key variable at HMR is the number of patients enrolled in the weight-loss program; everything is ultimately related to the number of patients enrolled. Stifler starts by determining a reasonable patient-staff ratio, say 50:1. He knows the cost of each employee in regard to compensation and benefits as well as the cost of office equipment and furniture to support each one. Then he builds a mathematical model incorporating these relationships. Employees simply track the number of patients enrolled and follow the model. "I never write a budget or proposals," marvels one employee. "I just work with patients, and in a year of working here, there's nothing we've wanted that we couldn't get. The model tells us."

Stifler also uses ratios to keep track of how well the system is working and to control the business. The first ratio he looks at every month measures productivity--net sales revenue divided by the number of full-time employees in the company. "This will tell me if there's something wrong. If productivity is the same or better from month-to-month, then we're OK."

The second relationship he studies tells him at a glance how the two parts of the business--products and service--are performing relative to each other. HMR generates a profit by selling its liquid diet supplement. Although it charges patients for the service it provides them, the service basically is a cost incurred to sell the supplement. To keep track of the cost of providing the service, Stifler keeps two checking accounts--one for product receipts and expenditures and one for service revenue and expenditures. Because HMR makes money on product sales and loses money on service, Stifler must write a check from the product account to cover the service deficit. The size of the check is not important; Stifler knows something is wrong only if the cost of service rises as a proportion of product revenue.

If the service/product ratio is out of balance, Stifler calculates eighteen different ratios covering a variety of cost categories; the denominator in every case is net revenue. "This may sound deceptively simple," he says, "but nobody has to shuffle 150 pieces of paper after four months to see what went wrong. I can do it at the end of the month in three minutes." If a ratio is off, Stifler knows exactly where the problem is and can begin doing something about it immediately. In essence, it's numbers--in the form of ratios--that enable Stifler to see the big picture at HMR and to be sure it's properly formed.

1. How important are budgets to HMR? Ratio analysis?
2. What is the key variable of interest to Stifler in monitoring HMR's financial performance? How might other businesses-- retailers, wholesalers and manufacturers translate this variable into something relevant to them?
3. Why do so few business owners actively manage their companies' financial affairs?

Source: Tom Richman, "The Language of Business," *Inc.*, February 1990, pp.41-50.

Part Five: Chapter 9 Exercises

9.1 Startup Expenses-Wish Lists and the Pro Forma Balance Sheet

Startup costs need be determined before developing a new firm's first balance sheet. Purchasing used equipment, utilizing leases and hiring temporary employees are ways to help a small business conserve needed cash in the opening stages of development. Although many firms startup without the necessary capital to see them through the first few years, it is not recommended. The basic rule-of-thumb is to open the doors with at least enough cash to see the business through three months worth of expenses or to use published industry standards throughout the year.

After determining the cash and inventory balances sufficient to meet industry standards (RMA Annual Statement Studies) entrepreneurs can use tools like the planning forms shown in figures 9.3 and 9.4 of the student text to determine other assets the firm will need to open its doors and operate its business. Once this "wish list" has been identified, the entrepreneur's contribution in either assets or cash is taken into consideration and the remaining amount needed to be financed is then determined.

In the example below, the owner will contribute $83,000 in either cash or assets, leaving an amount of $120,000 to be financed by outside sources.

Jazmine Johnson's Educational Toy Store
Jazmine Johnson has just developed a "wish list" of things she will need to start her new educational toy

store. Inventory and cash requirements were determined from industry averages found in *Dunn & Bradstreet's Costs of Doing Business* reports. (See your textbook under-The Pro Forma Balance Sheet). The other items and their costs were determined from actual estimates and research from the local business community.

To keep the accounting equation in balance, all items from the "wish list" must be accounted for on the balance sheet. Assets = Liabilities + Owners' Equity (Net worth). If anything new is added, the numbers will not balance unless the new items are identified on the "wish list" first. Then subtract the amount the owner can supply (equity infusion) to determine the amount needed to be financed.

Use the icons and various symbols in the example "Wish List" and First balance Sheet to keep track of specific items as they make their transition from the "Wish List" to balance sheet accounts.

The "Wish List" for Jazmine's Educational Toy Store is as follows:

Inventory	$100,000
Furniture and Fixtures	30,000
*Deposits	5,000
Prepaid Insurance	2,000
*Licenses	800
*Professional Fees	1,300
•Building Renovations	25,000
~Opening Cash Requirement	30,000
Opening Advertising	5,000
*Employee Training	2,000
*Miscellaneous	2,500
	203,600
° Owner's Equity Infusion	<83,600>
» Bank Loan	$120,000

FIRST BALANCE SHEET

ASSETS		LIABILITIES	
current		**current**	
Cash (~)	$30,000	Accounts Payable	0
Inventory	100,000	Current Portion Loan (»)	$12,000
Prepaid Insurance	2,000		
Prepaid Advertising	5,000	**long term**	
Prepaid Misc. (*)	11,600	L.T. Loan (»)	108,000
		Total Liabilities	120,000
fixed			
Furniture and Fixtures	30,000	**OWNER EQUITY**	
Leasehold Improvements(•)	25,000	John Doe Equity (°)	83,600
Total Assets	$203,600		
		Total Liabilities & Owners Equity	$203,600

130

Individually, or in a group setting, use your business plan idea to identify the "Wish List" and first balance sheet for a new business in the industry. To determine the cash requirement for this exercise use the rule-of-thumb of three months of operating expenses plus all costs to open the doors for the first time. This should include enough cash to cover your wage responsibilities, rent, utilities, employee training etc...If industry standards are unavailable at your institution, approximate your starting inventory and other expenses.

Part Six: Supplement Readings

Dennis, Michael C. "The limitations of financial statement analysis." *Business Credit.* Feb. 1995, v97 n2 p32(2).

Sack, Karen J. "Composite industry data." *Standard & Poor's Industry Surveys: Retailing.* Dec. 19, 1996 v164 n51 p25(2).

Reich, S. and Andre Shih. "Profit analysis crucial in asset-liability management." *American Banker.* Jan. 15, 1997 v162 n10 p22(1).

Artz, W. and Raymond Neihengen Jr. An analysis of finance company ratios in 1994." *Journal of Commercial Lending.* Sept 1995 v78 n1 p33(8).

Sudarsanam, P.S. and R.J. Taffler. "Financial ratio proportionality and inter-temporal stability: an empirical analysis." *Journal of Banking and Finance.* April 1995, v19 n1 p45(33).

Dahltedt, R., Salmi, T., Luoma, M. and Arto Laakkonen. "On the usefulness of standard industrial classifications in comparative financial statement analysis." *European Journal of Operational Research.* Dec. 8, 1994 v79 n2 p230(9).

Section III - Building The Business Plan: Marketing and Financial Considerations

Chapter 11
Crafting a Winning Business Plan **(PPT 11.1)**

Part One: Learning Objectives

1. Explain why every entrepreneur should create a business plan, as well as the benefits of a plan.

2. Describe the elements of a solid business plan.

3. Understand the keys to making an effective business plan presentation.

4. Explain the "5 Cs of Credit" and why they are important to potential lenders and investors reading business plans.

Part Two: Lesson Plan

I.   Why Develop a Business Plan? **(PPT 11.2 thru 11.5)**

The plan serves as an entrepreneur's road map to building a successful business. It describes the direction the company is taking, what its goals are, where it wants to be, and how it plans to get there. The Business Plan serves three essential functions-- it provides an operational guide for action and success, it attracts lenders, and it is a reflection of its creator.

II.   The Elements of a Business Plan **(PPT 11.6 thru 11.13)**

Every plan is unique. There are many resources available to use as a guide. The seemingly overwhelming task of building a business plan is easily broken down into workable parts that any student or entrepreneur can undertake. Plans may include the following:

A.   Executive Summary
B.   Mission Statement
C.   Company History
D.   Business and Industry Profile
E.   Objectives
F.   Business Strategy
G.   Description of Firm's Product/Service
H.   Marketing Strategy
I.   Documenting Market Claims
J.   Competitor Analysis
K.   Description of the Management Team
L.   Plan of Operation
M.   Forecasted Or Pro-Forma Financial Statements
N.   The Loan or Investment Proposal

YOU BE THE CONSULTANT – Are all Dot-Com Ventures Dead?

While the market shakeout among dot.com companies has produced some fear and skepticism, most agree that the industry is still in its infancy stages. The current norm for proposed dot.com business plans is to keep them short and more focused on a one- to two-year period. More emphasis must be placed on the exact description of the business and on the management team that will make it happen. The mechanism for attracting customers and for processing orders is another unique aspect that must clearly communicate the proposed firm's strategy for establishing its "product differentiation." The executive summary continues as the initial means for getting and keeping the attention of investors.

Q1. In what ways are a plan for a traditional business and one for an e-business similar? Different?

Q2. Suppose that a good friend comes to you and announces that he is going to launch an Internet business but needs financing to do it. You ask about his business plan. "I don't have the time to write a business plan," he says. What do you tell him?

Q3. Assume that you convince your friend that he should write a business plan. He asks your advice on how to write the plan. What advice do you offer?

A1. Similarities continue in the areas of the business description, its target markets and financial projections, the management team and operational procedures. Differences lie mostly in the ability to attract customers and process orders, the team that will be behind the scenes to make it happen and the strategy to be successful in a shorter than traditional time period.

A2. Any serious entrepreneur that needs or expects outside help must take the time to research and document the proposed venture.

A3. Start by following the guidelines of any of the many business plan-building resources. The initial draft will serve as a reality check and allow the entrepreneur to revise and present a viable and professional plan.

YOU BE THE CONSULTANT – The Presentation

Dick Bardow, a well-educated and experienced inventor and researcher in the medical equipment industry is seeking outside venture capital for his patent pending product. He is frustrated by the reaction to a presentation that he made to a Ms. Guinn and her staff of investors and analysts.

Bardow spent considerable time describing the power and potential of his new technology, while the group only seemed interested in hearing about market strategies and returns on investment.

Q1. Identify the possible problems with Dick Bardow's presentation of his business plan to Ms. Guinn.

Q2. Should potential lenders and investors evaluate new ventures that are based on cutting edge technology differently from other business ventures? Explain.

Q3. List at least five suggestions you would make to Dick Bardow to improve his business plan and his presentation of it.

A1. The major problem with Bardow's presentation is that it focused mostly on the technical side of the product and included too many unanswered questions from the business side.

A2. New ventures in cutting edge technology must be scrutinized more closely than others as they come with a higher degree of risk.

A3. Bardow should have conducted and included the results of extensive market research to show the investors that he already had "a long line of anxious and excited customers" waiting to buy his new product. His presentation should have included financial projections, ranging from conservative to optimistic scenarios, with each offering an acceptable return on investment. Finally, Bardow's plan would be complete with a description of the production and operational procedures needed to get the product to the customer in a timely and efficient manner.

III.   Making the Business Plan Presentation **(PPT 11.14, 11.15)**

Keys to making an effective business plan presentation:

A.   Demonstrate enthusiasm, but don't be too emotional.
B.   Know your audience.
C.   "Hook" investors quickly with an up-front explanation of the new venture, its opportunities, and the benefits to them.
D.   Keep it simple and to the point.
E.   Avoid the use of technological terms.
F.   Use visual aids.
G.   Close by reinforcing the nature of the opportunity and the related benefits to investors.
H.   Be prepared for questions.
I.   Follow up with every investor to whom you make a presentation.

YOU BE THE CONSULTANT - Battle of the Plans

Colleges across the country sponsor business plan competitions that often include start-up venture capital for the top finishers.

Q1. If your school does not already have a business plan competition, work with a team of your classmates in a brainstorming session to develop ideas for creating one. What would you offer as a prize? How would you finance the competition? Whom would you invite to judge it? How would you structure the competition?
Q2. Use the World Wide Web to research business plan competitions at other colleges and universities across the nation. Using the competitions at these schools as benchmarks and the ideas you generated in question #1, develop a format for a business plan competition at your school.
Q3. Assume that you are a member of a team of entrepreneurial students entered in a prestigious business plan competition. Outline your team's strategy for winning the competition.

A1. & A2. & A3. Answers and student responses will vary for all three questions

IV.   What Lenders and Investors Look For in a Business Plan **(PPT 11.16)**

Bankers and other lenders include the **five Cs of credit** as a part of their evaluation of the credit-worthiness of loan applications. The higher a business scores on these five Cs, the greater its chance will be of receiving a loan.

- Capital

- Capacity
- Collateral
- Character
- Conditions

V.   Concluding remarks-- the business plan perspective

VI.   Business Plan Format-- contents and sources

Part Three: Suggested Answers to Discussion Questions

1.   Why should an entrepreneur develop a business plan?

The reasons for a business plan are twofold-- it serves as a guide to company operations by charting a future course and strategy, and it attracts lenders and investors.

2.   Describe the major components of a business plan.

Although a business plan should be tailored to fit each specific situation and company, it typically includes: an executive summary, a mission statement, a business and industry profile, a description of the company's strategy, a profile of its products or services, its marketing strategy and competitor/customer base analysis, a management team profile, a plan of operation, financial data, and a loan or investment proposal.

3.   How can an entrepreneur seeking funds to launch a business convince potential lenders and investors that a market for the product or service really does exist?

Entrepreneurs can begin to convince lenders and investors that a market for their product or service exists by conducting a market analysis and answering the following questions:
   A.   Who are the prospective buyers (specifically) for your products or services?
   B.   What is their motivation to buy?
   C.   How many customers does the market contain?
   D.   What are the projected annual sales?
   E.   How will you outsmart the competition and capture market share?

4.   How would you prepare to make a formal presentation of your business plan to a venture capital forum?

As with all presentations, entrepreneurs should be informed and well-prepared before making business plan presentations. The following tips might also be helpful:
   A.   Demonstrate enthusiasm, but don't be overemotional.
   B.   "Hook" investors quickly with an up-front explanation of the new venture, its opportunities, and the anticipated benefits to them.
   C.   Use visual aids.
   D.   Hit the highlights, leave details to questions and later meetings.
   E.   Avoid the use of technological terms.
   F.   Close by reinforcing the nature of the opportunity and relate benefits to investors.
   G.   Be prepared for questions.
   H.   Follow up with every investor you make a presentation to.

5.   What are the five Cs of credit? How does a banker use them when evaluating a loan request?

The five Cs of credit include: capital, capacity, collateral, character, and conditions. Bankers score the small business in terms of the five Cs-- the greater the score, the higher probability that the small business will receive the loan.

Part Four: Lecture or Critical Thinking Case Studies-Not Found In Student Text
DON'T FORGET THE BUSINESS PLAN

DON'T FORGET THE BUSINESS PLAN

Ned Densmore, owner of the Village Book Store in Littleton, New Hampshire, is a firm believer in the power of a business plan. Before buying the small retail book store in 1975, Densmore wrote a detailed plan analyzing its strengths and weaknesses, customers, and growth potential. Given his years of experience working for other bookstores, it would have been easy for Densmore to skip creating a plan for the venture. "Even though book retailing seemed to be something I could do just by snapping my fingers," he says, "I felt I needed to sit down and see if the goals stated in my business plan matched the need for a bookstore in downtown Littleton. I also looked at the inventory and the site and put this information down on paper to help me understand what I was getting into."

Thanks to the guidance of Densmore's business plans, the Village Book Store is a thriving success, having expanded to more than seven thousand square feet and ten employees. The store has expanded its product line to include music cassettes, compact disks and toys. "A business plan allows you to be proactive rather than reactive, providing a great chance for success," according to Densmore.

Unfortunately, Densmore is the exception rather than the rule when it comes to preparing business plans. Too few small business owners take the time to develop well-thought-out plans that often leads to unpleasant surprises later on. "A business plan is just taking what people know and committing it to paper," observes one small business consultant. "When you see it written down, it helps you think things through and check off all the areas that need to be thought about in detail-- staffing, facilities, utilities, and so on."

Not only are business plans valuable tools for managing a small business, but they also are essential to obtaining financing. Borrowing money on a handshake and a promise has gone the way of the ten-cent candy bar, "Banks require sophisticated planning from small businesses," says Densmore. "No longer can you pass your local banker on the street and say `I need $25,000.' He or she will say, `Great, let me see the business plan.'"

Gordon Christie, owner of Touch of Class Catering and the Grand Affairs banquet hall of Virginia, also credits much of his success to a solid business plan. "At 27," he recalls, "I set a goal for myself: I wanted to own my own business by the time I was 30." At 19 he began by running the catering business out of a truck. Then, with a four-year timetable in mind, he created a thorough, well-researched business plan. The plan included all of the usual financial statements and projections as well as an architect's drawing of the proposed site and a detailed artist's rendering of the interior, depicting its color scheme, style, and character. With his plan in hand, Christie set up a meeting with a venture capitalist. The plan was so impressive that Christie got the financing he needed from the investor after that initial meeting. "I'd been dreaming about this for years," says Christie, "so I had a pretty good idea of what I wanted."

136

Lenders and investors look for entrepreneurs who know what they want to do and have a plan for doing it. "They need to convince me they know their business," says one banker. One consultant advises entrepreneurs drafting business plans to incorporate the five Ms: market, methodology, management, money, and menaces (Murphy's law). Another banker wants to know what assumptions the entrepreneur used to assemble the plan. "If you tell me the utilities are going to be $1,200 a month without showing me you contacted three lighting companies and you averaged the figures they gave you, the $1,200 is meaningless," he points out. "Prospective borrowers have to show they didn't just pick these numbers out of the sky but that they did their homework." Other business counselors suggest including the following in the plan:

- A clear statement of the business.
- A clear statement of the business status.
- A clear statement of the market.
- A clear statement of the competition.
- A clear statement of suppliers.
- An accurate description of the business financial condition.

The best business plan is the one that the entrepreneur actually uses to manage the business successfully. Updating and revising the plan annually, especially its financial projections, are essential. "If you don't, you're at the mercy of what's out there," says Densmore. "And if you fail, you have no one to blame but yourself."

1. Identify the two main purposes of a business plan. Is one more important than the other? Why or why not?
2. Why do so many small business owners fail to prepare business plans? What are the consequences?
3. What major elements should a small business owner incorporate into a comprehensive business plan?

Source: Wirt M. Cook, "Put It in Writing," Reprinted with permission from *Entrepreneur* magazine, June 1991, pp.40-42.

Part Five: Supplemental Readings

"Effective Business Planning," Thomas Zurowski, Saskatchewan Business, July-August 1996, Vol. 17, No. 4.

"Developing a Personal Business Plan," Stewart L. Stokes Jr., Information Systems Management, Spring 1997, Vol. 14, No. 2.

"Tips for Preparing a Business Plan," Linda Elkins, Nation's Business, June 1996, Vol. 84, No. 6.

"The Do's & Don't's of Writing a Winning Business Plan (A Flexible Plan Will Help in the Management of a Business)," Black Enterprise, April 1996, Vol. 26, No. 9.

"Make Your Case: How to Create a Business Plan that Sells," M. John Storey, Success, May 1995, Vol. 42, No. 4.

"Consider Creating a 'War Room' to Develop Your 1997 Business Plan," John Haskell, Los Angeles Business Journal, (Small Business Column) Sept. 30, 1996, Vol. 18, No. 40.

Chapter 12
Sources of Financing: Debt and Equity **(PPT 12.1 thru 12.3)**

Part One: Learning Objectives

1. Explain the differences in the three types of capital small businesses require: fixed, working, and growth.

2. Describe the differences in equity capital and debt capital and the advantages and disadvantages of each.

3. Describe the various sources of equity capital available to entrepreneurs, including personal savings, friends and relatives, angels, partners, corporations, venture capital, and public stock offerings.

4. Describe the process of "going public," as well as its advantages and disadvantages and the various simplified registrations and exemptions from registration available to small businesses wanting to sell securities to investors.

5. Describe the various sources of debt capital and the advantages and disadvantages of each: banks, asset-based lenders, vendors (trade credit), equipment suppliers, commercial finance companies, savings and loan associations, stock brokers, insurance companies, credit unions, bonds, private placements, Small Business Investment Companies (SBICs), and Small Business Lending Companies (SBLCs).

6. Identify the various federal loan programs aimed at small businesses.

7. Describe the various loan programs available from the Small Business Administration.

8. Discuss valuable methods of financing growth and expansion internally.

Part Two: Lesson Plan

I. Planning for Capital Needs **(PPT 12.4)**

Rather than relying on a single source of funds, entrepreneurs may need to piece together multiple sources, a method known as *layered financing*.
Capital is any form of wealth employed to produce more wealth. It exists in many forms in a business, including cash, inventory, plant, and equipment. Small businesses require three types of capital:

A. Fixed Capital - Capital needed to purchase the business's permanent or fixed assets.
B. Working Capital - Capital used to support the business's day-to-day operations.
C. Growth Capital - Capital requirements surface when an existing business is expanding or changing its primary direction.

II. Equity Capital vs. Debt Capital **(PPT 12.5, 12.6)**

Equity Capital represents the personal investment of the owner(s) in a business.
Debt Capital represents the financing that a small business owner has secured and must repay with interest.

III. Sources of Equity Financing **(PPT 12.7 thru 12.29)**

A. Personal Savings - The most common form of equity funds is the entrepreneur's pool of personal savings. Entrepreneurs should expect to provide between 20% - 50% of the required start-up funds.

B. Friends and Family Members

C. Angels - Angels are wealthy individuals, often entrepreneurs themselves, who invest in business start-ups in exchange for an equity stake.

D. Partners - Entrepreneurs can choose to take on a partner(s) to expand their capital.

E. Corporate Venture Capital – Some large corporations, both U.S. and foreign, finance and invest in small companies.

F. Venture Capital Companies - Venture capital companies are private, for profit organizations that purchase equity positions in young businesses with high growth and profit potential.

G. Public Stock Sale - One method of raising large capital is to sell shares of stock, known as "going public."

YOU BE THE CONSULTANT – Filled With Promise, But Low on Capital

After serving as consultants to some technology companies, Astro Teller and his friends launched BodyMedia, a company built around a device worn on the arm that measures, records and analyzes bodily functions and calorie burn-rates. The partners bounced from market to market due to financial and other constraints and are sorely in need of a second round of financing in order to sustain their operation.

Q1. What role do factors that are beyond entrepreneurs' control-- such as a faltering economy or a falling stock market-- have on their ability to attract the capital they need?
Q2. Explain why the following funding sources would or would not be appropriate for BodyMedia: family and friends, angel investors, an initial public offering, a traditional bank loan, asset-based borrowing, or one of the many federal or SBA loans.
Q3. Work with a team of your classmates to devise a workable strategy for raising the capital BodyMedia needs to market their product.

A1. The availability of capital and the degree of investor risk is directly affected by the economy, the stock market, interest rates and other factors beyond the entrepreneur's control.
A2. & A3. Students will offer the trade-offs and advantages and disadvantages of each of the funding sources, and will devise strategies for securing financing.

IV. The Nature of Debt Financing **(PPT 12.30 thru 12.39)**

Debt financing involves funds that small business owner's borrow and must repay with interest. Borrowed capital does allow entrepreneurs to maintain complete ownership.

A.   Sources of Debt Capital

- Commercial Banks
- Equipment Suppliers
- Commercial Finance Companies
- Savings and Loan Associations
- Stock Brokerage Houses
- Insurance Companies
- Credit Unions
- Bonds
- Private Placements
- Small Business Investment Companies (SBICs)
- Small Business Lending Companies (SBLCs)

V.   Federally Sponsored Programs

- Economic Development Administration (EDA)
- Department of Housing and Urban Development (HUD)
- U.S. Department of Agriculture's Rural Business-Cooperative Service
- Small Business Innovation Research (SBIR)
- The Small Business Technology Transfer Program

YOU BE THE CONSULTANT – Two Financing Puzzles

Lissa D'Aquanni, owner of The Chocolate Gecko, has been able to slowly grow her home-based company by raising funds in creative ways such as selling gift certificates and bartering for services. She now faces her biggest fundraising challenge-- the purchase and renovation of a commercial building.

John Acosta, owner of Jolly Technologies, faces the same fundraising challenge as Lissa, as he attempts to raise $100,000 to modify the production and enhance the marketing efforts for his garage door- opening device.

Q1. Describe the advantages and the disadvantages of both equity capital and debt capital for Lissa D'Aquanni and John Acosta.

Q2. Explain why the following funding sources would or would not be appropriate for these entrepreneurs: family and friends, angel investors, an initial public offering, a traditional bank loan, asset-based borrowing, or one of the many federal or SBA loans.

Q3. Work with a team of your classmates to brainstorm ways that Lissa D'Aquanni and John Acosta could attract the capital they need for their businesses. What steps would you recommend they take before they approach the potential sources of funding you have identified?

A1. Students will offer the general advantages and disadvantages of each form of capital, but should realize that neither principle has any equity at this time.

A2. Students will offer perspectives on each form of financing that is relevant to the principle's situations.

A3. Students should be encouraged to think outside of the box and to generate both traditional and creative ways in which the principles could acquire financing.

VI.   Small Business Administration (SBA) **(PPT 12.40 thru 12.43)**

The SBA has several programs designed to help finance both start-up and existing businesses that do not qualify for traditional loans. Programs include:

- 7(A) Loan Guaranty Program
- The CAPLine Program
- The Export Working Capital Program
- The International Trade Program
- Section 504 Certified Development Company Program
- Microloan Program
- Pre-qualification Loan Program
- Disaster Loans

VII.   State and Local Loan Development Programs **(PPT 12.44)**

These programs come in a variety of forms. They focus on developing small businesses that create the greatest number of jobs and economic benefits.

VIII. Internal Methods of Financing **(PPT 12.45)** ·

Bootstrap financing is a term used for internal methods of financing that include factoring, leasing rather than purchasing equipment, using credit cards, and managing the business frugally.

Part Three: Suggested Answers to Discussion Questions

1.   Why is it so difficult for most small business owners to raise the capital needed to start, operate, or expand their ventures?

The financial industry has been through difficult times, resulting in credit crunches. Banks have tightened their lending criteria, venture capitalists have become more conservative, private investors have grown more cautious, and the issuing of public stock remains viable for only select businesses with established track records.

2.   What is capital? List and describe the three types of capital a small business needs for its operations.

Capital is any form of wealth employed to produce more wealth. Fixed Capital is used to purchase a company's fixed assets. Working Capital is used to sustain day-to-day operations. Growth Capital is used to expand an existing business or to change its primary direction.

3.   Define equity financing. What advantages does it offer over debt financing?

Equity financing represents the personal investment of the owner(s) of the business. The primary advantage of this type of financing is that is does not have to be repaid with interest.

4.   What is the most common source of equity funds in a typical small business? If an owner lacks sufficient equity capital to invest in the firm, what options are available for raising it?

The owner's personal savings is the most common source of equity financing. Owners that lack sufficient funds may turn to family and friends, angels, partners, venture capital companies, corporations, and public stock offerings.

5.   What guidelines should an entrepreneur follow if friends and relatives choose to invest in her business?

Entrepreneurs should be honest and objective in their presentation of the investment opportunity and risks involved. It is also wise to establish a written agreement that addresses the many what-if questions that may arise.

6.   What is an "angel"? Assemble a brief profile of the typical private investor. How can entrepreneurs locate potential angels to invest in their businesses?

Angels are wealthy investors, often entrepreneurs themselves, who invest in business start-ups in exchange for an equity stake in the company. The typical angel is a 47-year-old white male with a college education earning $100,000 per year with a net worth of $1 million (excluding homes). Most have financial or business experience, and most are drawn to companies at the start-up or early growth stage. The typical angel invests in local companies. The primary way to locate angels is by networking through friends, attorneys, investment institutions, business associations, and other business owners.

7.   What advice would you offer an entrepreneur about to strike a deal with a private investor to avoid problems?

Entrepreneurs should be honest with private investors about their needs and expectations. They should realize that private investors are usually not looking for a quick return on investment. Entrepreneurs should keep in mind that angels typically expect a 35%-50% return on investment depending on risk. Private investors normally invest during the start-up or early growth stages. Eighty-two percent of angel investments are for $500,000 or less.

8.   What types of businesses are most likely to attract venture capital? What investment criteria do venture capitalists use when screening potential businesses? How do these compare to the typical angel's criteria?

Venture capital companies typically invest in high-tech industries such as computer software, medical care, biotechnology, and communications-- any company with extraordinary growth potential. Many venture capitalists seek to purchase 30%-40% of a business through common stock or convertible preferred stock. Although venture capitalists usually prefer to allow the founding team of managers to employ their skills to operate the business, they may join the boards of directors and/or send in some new management to protect their investment. Many are choosing to focus their investments in niche markets, rely heavily on their gut instincts and look for businesses that have competent management, a competitive edge, and presence in a growth industry.

9. How do venture capital firms operate? Describe their procedure for screening investment proposals.

   Venture capital companies are for-profit organizations that purchase equity positions in young businesses with high-growth and-profit potential, producing annual returns of 300-500 percent over five to seven year periods. The screening process of venture capital firms is extremely stringent and revolves around ownership, control, and investment preferences.

10. Summarize the major exemptions and simplified registrations available to small companies wanting to make public offerings of their stock.

    The SEC has established simplified registration statements and exemptions from the registration process: Regulation S-B, Regulation D (Rules 504,505,506), Private Placements, Interstate Offerings (Rule 147), Regulation A and Direct Stock Offerings (DPO).

11. What role do commercial banks play in providing debt financing to small businesses? Outline and briefly describe the major types of short-term, intermediate, and long-term loans commercial banks offer.

    Commercial banks provide the greatest number and variety of loans (almost 50%) to small businesses, offering commercial loans, lines of credit and floor planning.

12. What is trade credit? How important is it as a source of debt financing to small firms?

    Trade credit focuses on extending credit in the form of delayed payments, usually 30, 60, or 90 days interest free. It is an extremely important source of small business financing, especially when small businesses are seen as a bad risk by commercial banks.

13. What functions do SBICs serve? How does an SBIC operate? What methods of financing do SBICs rely on most heavily?

    SBICs are privately owned financial institutions that are licensed and regulated by the SBA. They use a combination of private and public funds to provide long-term capital to small businesses. The most common forms of SBIC financing are: loans with the option to buy stock, convertible debentures, straight loans and preferred stock.

14. Briefly describe the loan programs offered by the following:
    a. the Economic Development Administration
    b. the Department of Housing and Urban Development
    c. the Department of Agriculture's Rural Business-Cooperative
    d. local development companies

    (a) The Economic Development Administration (EDA) offers loan guarantees to create new business and to expand existing businesses in areas with below average income and high unemployment.
    (b) The Department of Housing and Urban Development (HUD) sponsors several loan programs to assist qualified entrepreneurs in raising capital. The Urban Development Action Grants are extended to cities and towns that, in turn, lend or grant money to entrepreneurs to start small businesses that will strengthen the local economy.

(c)   The Department of Agriculture's Rural Business-Cooperative Service loan program is open to all businesses and is designed to create non-farm employment opportunities in rural areas--those with population below 50,000 and not adjacent to a city where densities exceed 100 persons per square mile. The RBS does not make direct loans to small businesses, but it will guarantee as much as 90 percent of a bank's loan up to $25 million.

(d)   Local Development Committees (LDCs) are profit seeking or non-profit organizations that combine private funds and public funds to lend money to small businesses. Each LDC can qualify for up to $1 million per year in loans and guarantees from the SBA to assist in starting small businesses in the community.

15.   Explain the purpose and the methods of operation of the Small Business Innovation Research Program and the Small Business Technology Transfer Program.

The Federal government encourages local residents to organize and fund local development companies (LDC), on either a profit or not-for-profit basis. After raising initial capital by selling stock to at least 25 residents, the company seeks loans from banks and from the SBA.

16.   How can a firm employ bootstrap financing to stretch its current capital supply?

Firms generate internal financing through bootstrapping. Bootstrapping encompasses factoring, leasing rather than purchasing equipment, using credit cards, and managing the business frugally.

17.   What is a factor? How does the typical factor operate? Explain the advantages and the disadvantages of a factor.

Factors are financial institutions that buy 'accounts receivable' at a discount. The small business owner retains the responsibility for customers who fail to pay their accounts. Factoring is a more expensive type of financing, but for businesses that cannot qualify for those loans, factoring may be the only choice for a small business.

Part Four: Lecture or Critical Thinking Case Studies-Not Found In Student Text

THE GLOBAL SEARCH FOR CAPITAL
ARE YOU READY--REALLY READY--FOR START-UP FINANCING?

THE GLOBAL SEARCH FOR CAPITAL

During the 1990s, a growing number of American entrepreneurs turned to foreign sources of venture capital. A recent survey of venture capitalists found that 76 percent believe that foreign venture investments in the United States will increase, with Japan, the United Kingdom, and Germany leading the way. Another venture capital hot spot is the Pacific Rim, especially the countries known as the Little Dragons-South Korea, Taiwan, Singapore, and Hong Kong. Investors in these nations are eager to pump money into U.S. small businesses, and they have plenty of capital to invest. Traditionally, Japan has had a lock on foreign investments in the United States and still is the leader, funneling some $75 billion in U.S. investments each year. But the Little Dragons are coming on strong. Taiwan's investment in the United States has grown by 300 percent since 1986 to $700 million. Singapore's bankroll has swelled to

$1.3 billion per year, a 669 percent increase since 1986. Hong Kong's investments in the United States total $1.3 billion (up 115 percent), and South Korea stands at $900 million (up 235 percent).

These foreign venture capital dollars represent an important potential source of financing for U.S. entrepreneurs. Landing Pacific Rim venture financing requires a lot of legwork and an introduction from an insider. "You have to know somebody who has connections," says one U.S. entrepreneur who has raised $3 million in equity capital from Asian investors. Like venture capitalists worldwide, those in the Pacific Rim invest in people, not products or ideas. Before investing, they want to get to know the entrepreneur and the management team. For instance, Peter H. Hsieh, an immigrant from Taiwan, approached three Taiwanese companies to raise the capital he needed to expand his computer-chip manufacturing business. Five months later, Hsieh succeeded in raising $3.5 million from them. Once they got to know him, the investors analyzed his business plan in detail. "The process is not that different from getting money in the States," Hsieh explains.

Many entrepreneurs who have used Pacific Rim capital to launch their companies say that Little Dragon investors are not greedy. "They want the American management team to stay put," claims one. Like most venture capitalists, they work to protect their investments. When Peter Hsieh's company, Elite Microelectronics, began shipping its first computer chips, its foreign investors helped set up fifteen sales representatives across the globe. "They're interested in your problems and will work with you on solving them," he points out.

Pacific Rim venture capitalists and angels do not limit their investments to just high-tech industries; they look for well-managed companies and are willing to invest across the board. Robert Corey, president of Four Pi Systems Corporation, a maker of X-ray equipment, bypassed Wall Street and went straight to Taiwan and Singapore searching for the money to start his company. His efforts paid off. He found investors from both countries who put up the $5 million he was seeking. "The interest of Asians investors is just tremendous," he says.

The search for capital has no national boundaries; foreign investors are eager to funnel capital into start-ups. Peter Hsieh, an immigrant from Taiwan, turned to three Taiwanese companies to launch his computer-chip manufacturing business, Elite Microelectronics.

1. How is raising foreign venture capital different from obtaining equity capital from U.S. investors?
2. What are the similarities?
3. What barriers must an entrepreneur overcome when approaching foreign investors for equity capital?

Adapted from David J. Morrow, "An Asian Honeymoon," *International Business*, June 1991, pp. 28-32; "Business Bulletin," *Wall Street Journal*, March 22, 1990, p. A1.

ARE YOU READY--REALLY READY--FOR START-UP FINANCING?

Almost every entrepreneur has a start-up financing horror story - how the banker giggled while reviewing the business plan or when the venture capitalist stated, "Our interest in your business is lower than whale dung." Because of experiences such as these, entrepreneurs often assume that lenders and investors lack either money or the good sense to know a good deal when they see it. But the real reason that most entrepreneurs can't get financing for their new businesses is they're just not ready for the money. In other words, if they got the money today, most entrepreneurs would spend it without any long-term positive results. Being ready for start-up financing means having a plan for spending the money wisely and being able to prove to others that they will follow it. Failing to convince potential lenders and investors that they can add value to their business using these people's money is a surefire way to get rejected. Here are some of the reasons that entrepreneurs fail to get start-up money:

Poor communication
Potential lenders and investors are amazed at the number of requests for financing they get-without any description of what the business is. If you won't take the time to prepare a professional, concise business plan that explains in detail your business concept, don't expect to see much interest from outside investors and lenders. Neatness counts, too. Remember: The plan is a reflection of its creator.

Insufficient sales and marketing strategies
Too often, entrepreneurs pay insufficient attention to the marketing strategies they intend to employ. Remember the old adage: "Nothing in business happens until someone sells something." Investors like to see about 30 percent of a business plan devoted to marketing and selling.

Ignoring the negatives
Every business venture faces threats and problems. Investors get nervous if an entrepreneur cannot explain them or, worse, tries to cover them up.

Overuse of technical jargon
The safest route to use when presenting your idea is to assume the listener knows nothing about your industry or business and to explain it accordingly. Don't turn off potential investors by using technical jargon.

Overemphasis on the product or service
A common tendency of entrepreneurs is to fall in love with their goods or services. You know why yours is a better mousetrap, but will your target customers see the benefits it offers them? Spend time initially selling the entire business concept-not just a product or a service-to potential lenders and investors.

No assumptions for financial projections
Entrepreneurs who cannot explain where they got the numbers for their financial projections stand little chance of attracting financing. Making financial projections involves more than just pulling numbers out of the blue. Investors usually are more interested in the assumptions behind the projections than in the projections themselves.

Insufficient evidence of a market
If you say there is a market for your product or service, prove it. Offer evidence of market research, endorsements from prototype users, purchase orders, or other signs of interest from real live customers. Statements such as "This market is so huge that if we can get just one percent of it, we'll all be rich" don't carry much clout with potential investors.

Failing to know how much money you need
The correct answer to the question "How much money will you need?" is not "How much can I get?" This is a dead giveaway that the entrepreneur is not ready for financing.

<u>Failing to set yourself and your business apart from the rest</u>
Lenders and investors see thousands of entrepreneurs and business plans each year. Why should they invest in you? If you fail to show them how and why you and your business concept are superior, you'll never get the financing you need.

What can you do to prove you're ready for the financing you're seeking? Satisfy these criteria:

- Your business plan must explain the business-not just the product or service-and its competitive advantage.
- Your business plan must show that you understand the power of the bottom line, providing a way to pay back loans or produce an attractive return on your investment.
- You must have a clear strategy for marketing your product or service and know what it will cost to make or provide.
- You must show exactly how you will use the money to meet your company's goals.
- You must prove that the business concept will work-that customers will buy your good or service-before looking for money.

Before starting your search for financing, be sure you're really ready for it.

1. What mistakes do entrepreneurs searching for financing most often make?
2. What advice would you give an entrepreneur about to begin her search for start-up capital?

Adapted from Bruce J. Blechrnan, "Make No Mistake," Entrepreneur. December 1991, pp. 28-31; Bruce J. Blechman, "Ready or Not," Entrepreneur. August 1991, pp. 20-22. Reprinted with permission of Entrepreneur magazine.

Part Five: Supplement Readings

"Where the Money Is," Charlotte Taylor, <u>Executive Female</u>, March-April 1997, Vol. 20, No. 2.

"New Communications Technology Spawns a Venture Capital Feeding Frenzy," Michael Selz, <u>The Wall Street Journal</u>, Feb. 11, 1997.

"SBA Microloans Fuel Big Ideas," Susan Hodges, <u>Nation's Business</u>, Feb. 1997, Vol. 85, No. 2.

"SBA Loans: A Reliable Source of New Financing Opportunities," Nancy Passapera, <u>The Journal of Lending & Credit Risk Management</u>, Jan. 1997, Vol. 79, No. 5.

"How Are Small Firms Finances? Evidence from Small Business Investment Companies," Elijah Brewer III., Hesna Genay, William E. Jackson Jr., Paula R. Worthington, <u>Economic Perspectives</u>, Nov.-Dec. 1996, Vol. 20, No. 6.

"Capital Ideas for Financing," Sharon Nelton, <u>Nation's Business</u>, Sept. 1996, Vol. 48, No. 9.

Section IV - Putting the Plan to Work: Building a Competitive Edge

Chapter 13
Choosing the Right Location and Layout **(PPT 13.1)**

Part One: Learning Objectives

1.   Explain the stages in the location decision: choosing the region, the state, the city and the specific site.

2.   Describe the location criteria for retail and service businesses.

3.   Outline the location options for retail and service businesses: central business districts (CBDs), neighborhoods, shopping centers and malls, near competitors, outlying areas, and at home.

4.   Explain the site selection process for manufacturers.

5.   Describe the criteria used to analyze the layout and design considerations of a building, including the Americans with Disabilities Act.

6.   Explain the principles of effective layouts for retailers, service businesses, and manufacturers.

7.   Evaluate the advantages and disadvantages of building, buying, and leasing a building.

Part Two: Lesson Plan

   I.   Location: A Source of Competitive Advantage **(PPT 13.2 thru 13.8)**

   The location decision is very important to entrepreneurs and is based on a series of analyses of critical factors unique to each business. Tax rates, availability of qualified workers, the quality of the infrastructure, traffic patterns and other factors vary from one site to another and can influence the growth rate and ultimate success of a business.

   1. Choosing the Region
   2. Choosing the State
       - Proximity to Markets
       - Proximity to Raw Materials
       - Wage Rates
       - Labor Supply
       - Business Climate
       - Tax Rates
       - Internet Access
   3. Choosing the City
       - Population Trends

148

- Competition
- Clustering
- Compatibility with the Community
- Local Laws and Regulations
- Transportation Networks
- Police and Fire
- Utilities
- Quality of Life
4. Choosing the Site

II.   Location Criteria for Retailers and Service Businesses: **(PPT 13.9 thru 13.15)**

- Trade Area Size
- Retail Compatibility
- Degree of Competition
- Index of Retail Saturation
- Transportation Network
- Physical, Racial or Emotional Barriers
- Political Barriers
- Customer Traffic
- Adequate Parking
- Reputation
- Room for Expansion
- Visibility

III.   Location Options for Retail and Service Businesses

- Central Business District
- Neighborhood Locations
- Shopping Centers and Malls
- Near Competitors
- Outlying Areas
- Home-based Businesses

IV.   The Location Decision for Manufacturers **(PPT 13.16, 13.17)**

Suitable manufacturing plant sites are limited by zoning regulations, utility and transportation needs, proximity to raw materials and other special requirements.

- Foreign Trade Zones
- Empowerment Zones
- Business Incubators

149

YOU BE THE CONSULTANT - The "Cheers" of Bel Air

Entrepreneurs David and Jane Wolff sought to save and revitalize their downtown Bel Air, Maryland main street by establishing a coffee shop that offers unique design, product and service features. The Wolff's took advantage of a state-sponsored loan program and through their hard work have successfully created the "Cheers" of Bel Air "where everybody knows your name."

Q1. What advantages and disadvantages does choosing a downtown location offer an entrepreneur like David Wolff?

Q2. Assume the role of consultant. Suppose that officials in a town with which you are familiar approached you about revitalizing the central business district. What advice would you offer them?

Q3. What factors should entrepreneurs evaluate when comparing a downtown location against a location in a shopping center or mall?

A1. Central Business Districts may offer a charming atmosphere and historic character. The Wolffs were able to attract customers from the entire trading area of the city and benefit from customer traffic generated by the other stores. Disadvantages may include a higher crime rate, intense competition, traffic congestion, inadequate parking and higher rental rates.

A2. Make it safe and attractive and research and offer government and state grant and loan programs and other incentives to attract and assist prospective investors.

A3. Factors to evaluate include: costs, business and industry location norms, proximity to customers and suppliers, hours of operation, and complementary and competitive businesses.

Source: Adapted from Hilary Stout, "When Building Up a Business Means Turning Around a Town," *Wall Street Journal*, June 11, 2000 p. B1.

V.   Layout and Design Considerations **(PPT 13.18 thru 13.22)**

- Adequate Size
- External Appearance
- Entrances
- Conformity with The American With Disabilities Act
- Signs
- Building Interiors
- Ergonomics
- Lights and Fixtures

YOU BE THE CONSULTANT - Not Your Typical CPA Firm

Location and layout decisions are not limited to just retailers and manufacturers and need not follow traditional methods. That statement was proven true by the Lipschulz, Levin and Gray accounting firm that literally tore down their office walls and doors, put their furniture on wheels and transformed their once dismal work environment into a productive, profitable and fun place to be.

Q1. What impact does the space in which people work have on their ability to do their jobs effectively?

Q2. Use the resources in your library and on the World Wide Web to learn more about ergonomics and layout. Then, select a workspace (perhaps on your campus or in a local business) and spend some time watching how people work in it. Finally, develop a list of recommendations for improving the design of the space to enhance workers' ability to do their jobs.

A1. Layout is the logical, or sometimes "fun" arrangement of the physical facilities in a business that contributes to efficient operations, increased productivity and higher sales. Planning for the most effective and efficient layout in a business can produce dramatic improvements. Ergonomics helps adapt a work environment to employee and customer physical needs, and is an integral part of a successful design.

A2. Consider allowing students to work in groups and share their Internet research findings.

Source: Adapted from Nancy K. Austin, "Tear Down the Walls," *Inc.*, April 1999, pp. 66-7.

  VI. Layout: Maximizing Revenues, Increasing Efficiency or Reducing Cost **(PPT 13.23-13.28)**

    Layout for Retailers
- Grid layout
- Free-form layout
- Boutique layout

    Layout for Manufacturers
- Product layout
- Process layout
- Fixed position layout
- Functional layout

  VII. Build, Buy, or Lease?

An entrepreneur's decision on whether to build, buy, or lease a facility is largely dependent on access to capital and the ability to find the best site. Buying is always preferred as it can provide a good return on investment (in real estate) and helps to avoid unwanted surprises (leasing and rental terms). The advantages and disadvantages should be carefully considered.

Part Three: <u>Suggested Answers to Discussion Questions</u>

1. How do most small business owners choose a location? Is this wise?

   Most entrepreneurs fail to do their homework and fail to go beyond their own city or town in determining a location for their business. When entrepreneurs stay within their "comfort zones" and don't follow a specific process, they tend to overlook superior locations that could greatly benefit their firms.

2. What factors should a manager consider when evaluating a region in which to locate a business? Where are such data available?

Managers should follow a structured process that considers many factors including markets, labor, taxes, laws, the business climate, population trends, competition, transportation and so on. That data is available from market research, government statistics, local boards and organizations.

3. Outline the factors important when selecting a state in which to locate a business.

The factors listed in question two are also a part of the state selection process.

4. What factors should a seafood processing plant, a beauty shop, and an exclusive jewelry store consider in choosing a location? List factors for each type of business.

Seafood processing plant:	Consider access to raw materials, suppliers, labor, transportation, and customers.
Beauty Shop:	Consider access to customers, but realize that lower-rent properties are a viable option.
Jewelry Store:	Consider your business's access to customers.

5. What intangible factors might enter into the entrepreneur's location decision?

Reputation of the location
The number, size, and type of other stores presently located in or planned for the area
The nature of competing business
The character of the transportation network

6. What are zoning laws? How do they affect the location decision?

Zoning laws control the use of the land, buildings, and sites. Location decisions may be restricted by zoning laws and may also affect the flow and degree of commerce in that section of the city or town.

7. What is the trade area? What determines a small retailer's trade area?

Trading areas are regions from which a business can expect to draw customers. Variables include the scope of the trading area and the type and size of the operation.

8. Why is it important to discover more than just the number of passersby in a traffic count?

The numbers alone do not indicate the breakdown of the target market groups.

9. What types of information can the entrepreneur collect from census data?

Census data provides population and demographic information, and can be used to analyze trends.

10. Why may a "cheap location" not be the "best location"?

A "cheap location" may generate sales and profits that are well below those offered through other sites.

11. What is a foreign trade zone? An empowerment zone? A business incubator? What advantages and disadvantages does each one of those offer?

A foreign trade zone is a specifically designated area where international trade occurs with the primary purpose of limiting or removing barriers to trade. It allows resident companies to import materials and components from foreign countries, and to assemble, process, manufacture or package them and then ship the finished product while either reducing or eliminating tariffs and non-tariff barriers to free trade. A business incubator is a site that offers low-cost, flexible rental space with a multitude of support services (secretarial services, meeting rooms, fax machine, telephone systems) for its residents. The goal is to nurture young companies during the start-up period and to help them survive until they are strong enough to go out on their own.

12. Why is it costly for a small firm to choose a location that is too small?

Locations that are too small may lead to costly renovations and/or relocation.

13. What function does a small firm's sign serve? What are the characteristics of an effective business sign?

A sign tells potential customers who you are and what you are selling. An effective sign reaches the group of customers most likely to make actual purchases. Effective signs are large enough to read, contain a short, clear message, and are legible in daytime and night.

14. Explain the Americans with Disabilities Act. What businesses does it affect? What is its purpose?

The ADA requires practically all businesses to make their facilities accessible to physically challenged customers and employees. The law requires businesses with 15 or more employees to accommodate physically challenged people. The law requires business owners to remove architectural and communication barriers when "readily achievable." Although the law allows for a good deal of flexibility in retrofitting existing structures, buildings that are occupied after January 25, 1993, must comply with all aspects of the law.

15. What is ergonomics? Why should entrepreneurs utilize the principles of ergonomics in the design of their facilities?

Ergonomics is the science of adapting the physical plant for the comfort, safety and productivity of workers. An ergonomically designed workplace can improve workers' productivity and reduce the number of days lost to injuries and accidents.

16. Explain the statement: "Not every portion of a small store's interior space is of equal value in generating sales revenue." What areas are most valuable?

Some businesses calculate revenues per square foot of space. Some space will not generate revenues (such as traffic, break and display areas), but are equally valuable to the overall profit maximizing plan.

17. What are some of the key features that determine a good manufacturing layout?

Creating and maintaining an efficient workflow are of utmost concern to manufacturing firms. Raw material yield, production and safety are also key features.

18. Summarize the advantages and disadvantages of building, buying and leasing a building.

Decision to Build
Advantages: Constructing a new building allows the entrepreneur to design and build a facility that matches perfectly with his/her needs. New buildings create an image of a modern, efficient, and top quality business. New buildings can be constructed with the most modern features, in effect reducing total costs over time.
Disadvantages: The major disadvantage is the high initial outlay of capital, that must be weighed against the ability to generate additional sales revenue and reduce costs.

Decision to Buy
Advantages: Buying an existing building may cost less than constructing a new building. It may also be easier to estimate revenues and costs.
Disadvantages: The initial cost to purchase the existing building may deplete available finances.

Decision to Lease
Advantages: The major advantage of leasing is that it requires little or no initial investment. Firms short on cash may find leasing to be their best option.
Disadvantages: One major disadvantage is that the property owner may choose not to renew the lease. If the business is successful, relocating may be costly and may decrease the customer base. Another disadvantage is limited options on remodeling and that any modifications of the structure may become the property of the owner.

Part Four: Lecture or Critical Thinking Case Studies-Not Found In Student Text

SCINTILLATING SCENTS

SCINTILLATING SCENTS

Retailers are always looking for ways to boost sales of their products and services-- better window displays, flashier advertisements, more appealing layouts and color schemes and other tactics. The latest addition to their arsenal of tools is odor engineering- Alan Hirsch, director of the Smell and Taste Treatment and Research Foundation, Ltd., recently studied the effects of odors on customer behavior. His conclusion: Odors bring back strong memories and evokes certain feelings among many consumers, thereby giving aromas the potential to be powerful sales tools. Retailers can use odors in their stores to encourage customers to buy more and to buy certain products.

Hirsch found that women respond more favorably to scents than do men, and that smokers disliked most odors. The study also showed that women prefer floral scents, whereas men respond more positively to spicy scents. The one scent that customers tend to hate universally is fish. Knowing who their target customers are, retailers could then select the appropriate scent to appeal to them. "Lighting and sound have an impact on people's decision to buy," notes Hirsch, "but I think odors can have a much greater impact."

In Hirsch's study, thirty-five subjects examined a Nike gym shoe in two rooms identical in appearance but filled with different fragrances. One room was scented with a mixed floral scent; the other had no odor. A much higher percentage of customers-- 84 percent-- preferred the shoe when they viewed it in the florally scented room. Of that 84 percent, 10 percent said they would pay an average of $10.33 more than the subjects in the odor-free room said they would. Even those who disliked the floral odor said they would pay more.

Retailers aren't the only ones who can benefit from odor engineering. Researchers are discovering new relationships between scents in the workplace and employees' productivity and performance. Consequently, some companies are pumping various aromas into work areas to relax employees and boost their performances. One Japanese company claims to have cut computer entry errors by 21 percent when the office air was scented with lavender. When the air was scented with jasmine, errors dropped by 33 percent, and when it had a lemon fragrance, errors fell by 54 percent. The researchers' conclusions: Lavender scents reduce stress; jasmine relaxes; and lemon stimulates. Research on scents and their impact on customers and employees continue, but one day, scents may replace music in offices nationwide.

1.   How can retailers use scents to make their stores more appealing to customers?
2.   How can offices and manufacturing operations use scents to enhance their employees' work environment?
3.   What are the benefits of odor engineering? What are the ethical issues in odor engineering?

Adapted from Stephanie Barrow, "The Nose Knows," Reprinted with permission from *Entrepreneur* magazine, April 1991, p.38; "Get a Whiff of These Findings," *Communication Briefings*, February 1990, p.6.

Part Five: Supplemental Readings

"Place Matters," John Case, *Inc.*, May 15, 1996, Vol. 18, No. 7, pp. 94-96.

"A Growing Outlet for Small Firms," Roberta Maynard, *Nation's Business*, Aug. 1996, Vol. 84, No. 8, pp. 45-48.

"Retailers Bring Store from Malls to Shoppers' Neighborhoods," Alina Matas, *Knight-Ridder/Tribune Business News*, March 10, 1997.

"Airport Retailing Takes Off," Shelly M. Reese, *Stores*, Sept. 1996, Vol. 78, No. 9, pp. 74-76.

"Prime Retail Location: the World Wide Web," Michael Moeller, Norvin Leach, Jim Kerstetter, *PC Week*, May 13, 1996, Vol. 13, No. 19, pp. 1-2.

Section IV - Putting the Plan to Work: Building a Competitive Edge

Chapter 14
Global Aspects of Entrepreneurship **(PPT 14.1)**

Part One: Learning Objectives

1.   Explain why "going global" has become an integral part of many small companies' strategies.

2   Describe the principal strategies small businesses have for going global.

3.   Explain how to build a thriving export program.

4.   Discuss the major barriers to international trade and their impact on the global community.

5.   Describe the trade agreements that will have the greatest influence on foreign trade in the 21st century-- GATT and NAFTA.

Part Two: Lesson Plan

I.   Why Go Global? **(PPT 14.2)**

Today's business environment is very competitive and businesses can no longer consider themselves to be domestic companies if they truly want to compete.

Advantages of going global include:

- Offset sales declines in domestic markets
- Increase sales and profits
- Extend the product life cycle
- Lower manufacturing costs
- Improve competitive position
- Raise quality levels
- Become more customer-oriented

Questions to address:

- Are there profitable markets?
- Do we have the necessary resources?
- Do we understand the cultures, economic systems and other unique aspects of prospective trading nations?
- Are there viable exit strategies?
- Can we afford not to go global?

II.   Strategies for Going Global **(PPT 14.3 thru 14.10)**

- Employing a Presence on the World Wide Web
- Trade Intermediaries
  - Export Management Companies
  - Export Trading Companies
  - Agents
  - Resident Offices
  - Foreign Distributors
- Joint Ventures
- Foreign Licensing
- International Franchising
- Counter trading and Bartering

III.   The Exporting Process **(PPT 14.11 thru 14.16)**

Anyone can export. Start by developing an export business plan:

- Analyze your products and services.
- Analyze your commitment.
- Research markets and pick your target.
- Develop a distribution strategy.
- Secure financing.
- Develop a shipping strategy.
- Develop contracts to ensure collection of receivables.

YOU BE THE CONSULTANT – Opportunity or Risk?

Fareedom Hartoqa, a native of Jordan, now works in Saudi Arabia as a trade specialist. He is interested in establishing business relationships with U.S. firms that can supply much needed oil and gas production technology and equipment. He has visited and met with several Texas based companies to explore the possibilities.

Q1. If you were one of the undecided company CEO's involved with Mr. Hartoqa's visit, what questions would you raise?
Q2. What are the factors that you would evaluate in the determination of whether the opportunities outweigh the risk?

A1. The CEO would raise the same questions as with any prospective business partner. Those questions would focus on product specifications, quantities and price, financial terms, shipping, government regulations and others unique to the transaction.
A2. The standard benefit/cost analysis will determine the profitability and feasibility of the project. Other factors in this case might include security issues, insurance against government lockouts, and unique cultural factors about the country.

IV.   Barriers to International Trade **(PPT 14.17 thru 14.19)**

Many U.S. firms are simply ignorant about exporting opportunities. In addition, some governments use a variety of barriers that block free trade among nations in an attempt to protect their own industries. Foreign firms are restricted access into global markets and all consumers suffer and pay the price.

Barriers to international trade include:

- The "I'm too small to export" attitude
- Lack of Information
- Lack of Available Financing
- Tariffs
- Quotas
- Embargos
- Dumping
- Political Barriers
- Cultural Barriers

V.   International Trade Agreements **(PPT 14.20)**

In an attempt to boost world trade, several organizations and agreements between nations have been created. The most prominent include:

- The General Agreement on Tariffs and Trade (GATT) was designed to reduce tariffs among member nations and to facilitate trade across the globe. The World Trade Organization replaced GATT in 1995.

- The North American Free Trade Agreement (NAFTA) created a free trade area between Canada, Mexico, and the United States.

(PPT 14.21, 14.22)

YOU BE THE CONSULTANT – Safe Water Systems

Safe Water Systems developed a solar water pasteurizer that has been exported to more than 50 countries. The system uses the sun's rays and requires virtually no maintenance. In addition to the successful development of a profitable system, thousands of lives have been enhanced and saved thanks to a new and inexpensive source of clean water.

Q1. What additional steps can a small company like Safe Water Systems take to more effectively distribute its needed products in developing countries?
Q2. In your opinion, should the U.S. government intercede with governments of other countries to ask them to eliminate any barriers to the distribution of life-saving products?

A1. There are many expansion options for a company like Safe Water Systems to consider, including government partnerships and grants, joint ventures with other companies and countries, expanded or varied product lines to better suit new markets and so on.

A2. Students will provide a variety of ideas and options regarding government participation.

Part Three: <u>Suggested Answers to Discussion Questions</u>

1.   Why must entrepreneurs learn to think globally?

Today's business environment is very competitive and often forces domestic business owners to look beyond the traditional boundaries of the U.S. Global markets are growing and offer many market niche opportunities.

2.   What forces are driving small businesses into international markets?

Political, social, cultural, and economic forces are driving small businesses into international markets. Powerful technology and increased access to information make it easier for companies of all sizes to engage in international trade.

3.   What advantages does going global offer a small business owner? Risks?

Advantages include:
>   Offsetting sales declines in domestic markets
>   Increasing sales and profits
>   Extending product life cycles
>   Lowering manufacturing costs
>   Improving competitive position
>   Raising quality levels
>   Becoming more customer-oriented

Risks include:
>   Entrepreneur's unwillingness to commit adequate resources of time, people, and capital into global market
>   Possibility of not making money
>   Being insensitive to cultural differences
>   Not developing and maintaining global attitude

4.   Outline the eight strategies that small businesses can use to go global.
-       Launch a World Wide Web Site
-       Rely on trade intermediaries
-       Develop joint ventures
-       Consider foreign licensing
-       Consider international franchising
-       Use countertrading and bartering
-       Establish international locations
-       Develop an export business plan

5.   Describe the various types of trade intermediaries small business owners can use. What functions do they perform?

Export Management Companies (EMCs)-- are merchant intermediaries that provide small businesses with a low-cost, efficient, independent international marketing department. Their focus is on exporting and they typically do not handle competing firms.

Export Trading Companies (ETCs)-- are businesses that buy and sell products in a number of countries and offer a wide variety of services - exporting, importing, shipping, storing, and distributing - to their clients who may be competitors. They focus on long-term relationships.

Manufacturer's Export Agents (MEAs)-- are businesses that act as international sales representatives in a limited number of markets for various non-competing domestic companies. They are commissioned based and focus on short-term commitments.

Export Merchants--Export merchants are domestic wholesalers who buy goods from many domestic manufacturers and then market them in foreign markets. Most export merchants specialize in particular industries and often carry competing lines.

Resident Buying Offices--A government- or privately-owned operation established in a country for the purpose of buying goods from businesses there. The buying office handles all the details of exporting.

Foreign Distributors--Domestic small companies export their products to foreign distributors who handle all of the marketing, distribution, and service functions in the foreign country. They offer exporting small businesses the benefits of knowledge in their local markets, the ability to cover a given territory thoroughly, and prompt sales and service support.

6.   What is a domestic joint venture? A foreign joint venture? What advantages does taking on an international partner through a joint venture offer? Disadvantages?

Domestic joint venture--two or more U.S. small businesses form an alliance for the purpose of exporting their goods and services abroad.
Foreign joint venture--a domestic small business forms an alliance with a company in the target nation.

Advantages of international joint venture:
- Penetrate protected markets.
- Lower production costs.
- Share risks and high R&D costs.
- Gain access to marketing and distribution channels.

Disadvantages of international joint venture:
- Failure of the venture.
- Relationships that sour.
- Becoming overly dependent on the partner.

7. What mistakes are first-time exporters most likely to make? Outline the steps a small company should follow to establish a successful export program.

First-timer exporters often fall victim to 12 mistakes:

1. Failure to obtain qualified export counseling and to develop a master international marketing plan before starting an export business.
2. Insufficient commitment by top management to overcome the initial difficulties and financial requirements of exporting.
3. Insufficient care in selecting overseas distributors.
4. Chasing orders from around the world instead of establishing a basis for profitable operation and orderly growth.
5. Neglecting export business when the U.S. market booms.
6. Failure to treat international distributors on an equal basis with domestic counterparts.
7. Assuming that a given marketing technique and product will automatically be successful in all countries.
8. Unwillingness to modify products, meet regulations or cultural preferences of other countries.
9. Failure to print service, sale, and warranty messages in locally understood languages.
10. Failure to consider use of an export management company.
11. Failure to consider licensing or joint venture agreements.
12. Failure to provide readily available servicing for the product.

8. What are the benefits of establishing international locations? Disadvantages?

Benefits of establishing international locations include:
- Start-up costs are often lower in foreign countries.
- Foreign countries often have lower labor costs.
- Foreign markets offer attractive sales and profit possibilities.
- The company's competitive skills are strengthened and its reputation is enhanced.

Disadvantages of establishing international locations include:
- The substantial investment in establishing locations in foreign lands can be too draining on small businesses.
- It is often difficult to find the right person to manage an international office.
- Often times, foreign business infrastructures are in disrepair or are nonexistent.

9. Describe the barriers businesses face when trying to conduct business internationally. How can a small business owner overcome these obstacles?

Three major domestic barriers to international trade are common:

Attitude of "I'm too small to export"--The first step to building an export program is recognizing that the opportunity to export exists.

Lack of Information--Entrepreneurs should thoroughly research the possibility of going global and use every possible resource available to them such as government and private organizations' international exporting and marketing information, in order to make valid decisions. Companies must also be willing to make the necessary adjustments to their products and services, promotional campaigns, packaging, and sales techniques in foreign markets.

Lack of Available Financing--Many entrepreneurs cite lack of financing as a major barrier to international trade. Before embarking on an export program, entrepreneurs should have available financing lined up.

International barriers include tariffs, quotas, embargoes, dumping, political barriers, and cultural barriers. Entrepreneurs should be aware of and examine all international barriers *before* building their export programs. If the barriers are too cumbersome, the venture may not have a high probability of success.

10. What is a tariff? A quota? What impact do they have on international trade?

Tariffs are taxes or duties that a government imposes on goods and serves imported into that country. In essence, tariffs raise the price of imported goods making them less attractive to consumers, and serves to protect the makers of comparable domestic products and services.

A quota is a limit on the amount of a product imported into a country. Quotas help protect domestic markets by limiting quantities of foreign products.

11. What impact have the GATT, WTO, and NAFTA trade agreements had on small companies wanting to go global? What provisions are included in these trade agreements?

GATT was designed to reduce tariffs among member nations and to facilitate global trade. GATT has enabled small businesses to more easily enter the global market by lowering tariffs or trade barriers. The World Trade Organization was established to settle trade disputes among member nations.

NAFTA created a free trade area between Canada, Mexico, and the United States. All three countries agreed to knock down trade barriers, both tariff and non-tariff. NAFTA's provisions include: tariff reductions, the elimination of non-tariff barriers, simplified border processing, tougher health and safety standards, and increased protection of patents, copyrights, and trademarks.

12. What advice would you offer an entrepreneur interested in launching a global business effort?

Entrepreneurs should thoroughly investigate foreign markets. They should familiarize themselves with foreign customs, languages, and cultures. Learn to think and act globally and make sure employees are trained in the same manner. Above all, weigh the pros and cons of each foreign market. If you make the decision to go global, be willing to put all the necessary resources behind the venture to increase your probability of success.

Part Four: Lecture or Critical Thinking Case Studies-Not Found In Student Text

EXPORTING JUNK DOWN UNDER
THE TWELVE MOST COMMON EXPORT MISTAKES

EXPORTING JUNK DOWN UNDER

Bill Rucker never intended to get into the export business. In fact, he never even suspected that he could get into it. Rucker, founder and chief executive officer of Tracom, Inc., buys used diesel engines and parts and resells them to re-manufacturers. In short, his company operates a highly specialized junkyard, concentrating in big-truck engines, parts, and transmissions. What's even more unusual about Tracom is that 40 percent of its sales come from global markets. Each year, Rucker exports more than $1 million worth of old crankshafts, cylinder blocks, steering boxes, diesel injectors, and other junk. "If I can export," he says incredulously, "anyone can." Can you imagine going into a bank and asking to borrow $3 million to buy junk for export?"

Rucker succumbed to his entrepreneurial tendencies at age nineteen when he opened an auto repair shop, which after three years, he gave up to buy a gas station. Then he started a company to buy used school-bus transmissions from junkyards and resell them to re-manufacturers. To boost his business, Rucker put an ad in a local magazine offering transmissions for sale. Somehow that magazine found its way into the hands of Leon Will, a truck salvage dealer in Australia. "I got a call one day from Adelaide (Australia)," he recalls. "There was a lot of scratchiness on the phone. He said, `how you doin', mate?' I was very surprised. What was this guy calling me for? He needed some used Ford steering boxes, and I said I'd try to get them. I called up a guy I knew that had one hundred steering boxes and wanted $5 apiece for them. So I called Leon back and said I wanted $25 apiece. He said that was the greatest thing he'd ever heard. He sent me $2,500, and in the end we shipped him $10,000 worth of parts. I'd never done anything outside Fort Worth before. It was exciting. That's what made me want to do more exporting."

In his dealings with Leon Will, Rucker recognized that foreign customers generally are not as well off as Americans and that they tend to rebuild engines over and over again rather than buy new ones. Because he already had experience doing business in Australia, Rucker decided to actively seek orders there. Using an industry directory of truck dealers, he found Detco Australia, one of the largest re-builders and distributors of diesel engines in the world. When Rucker filled an order for $50,000 worth of diesel engines, he was officially in the export business.

The heart of Rucker's business is the intelligence network that enables him to find engines and engine pans, which usually are scattered in thousands of scrap yards and sheds across the land. "We've taken an industry that was disorganized and disjointed and brought a little organization to it," he explains. Half of Tracom's supply comes from salvage yards, trucking companies, and truck dealers. Another third of its supply comes from people offering Rucker their junk for sale. The balance of Tracom's supply comes from independent parts dealers-- junk bird dogs that search out needed parts, buy them on the spot, and resell them to businesses like Rucker's.

Recognizing the value of a comprehensive inventory database, Rucker developed a system, now computerized, to track his own parts inventory as well as the pans available in salvage yards across the country. The database contains more than 100,000 items, one third of which Rucker actually owns; the rest is extended inventory-items that other salvage yards have for sale. When a customer requests a specific part, Rucker lets his computer do the search. "It takes about four keystrokes," he says. The computer system essentially allows him to match supply with demand. He recently modified the system so that customers can tap directly into it to check on the availability of a particular part-- a valuable service for foreign customers.

Shortly after his first big sale to Detco Australia, Rucker packed his bags and headed down under to drum up more business. While there, he called on Detco's president and struck a deal to be its sole U.S. supplier of engines and components. A year later, he trekked to England with the same purpose and made similar deals with re-manufacturers there.

As successful as he was drumming up export business, Rucker had trouble back home-- getting export financing. Banks balked at such international deals, citing them as too risky. "I went to banks with letters of credit that were solid," he recalls. "Bankers looked at them and said, 'You've never done it' or 'You don't have enough hard assets.' I went to the biggest bank in Fort Worth. They said a letter of credit didn't guarantee that I would get the goods or ship them." Rucker financed his early deals by selling his domestic accounts receivable to factors, an expensive source of funds.

Then Rucker found Vijay Fozdar and Fred Waldkoetter, two entrepreneurs who had launched Bristol International, Ltd., a trade merchant bank specializing in financing foreign sales. "Very few banks have the international capability to help small companies," says Fozdar. "We wanted to be the training wheels for small companies [selling in international markets]." After his past experience with bankers, Rucker at first was dubious about Bristol International. Fozdar understood, "He had a need for financing, but he had reached all the dead ends and was frustrated," he says. Rucker approached Bristol with a $50,000 deal to ship engines to Australia. Bristol approved the deal and released the funds that same day before any papers had been signed. Finally, with a source of financing, Rucker could focus on building his export business. "I'd like to add one big foreign customer each year," he says.

Rucker has discovered many benefits in exporting other than increased profitability. "When you're dealing internationally," he says, "you're dealing with people a cut above. It tends to raise you to their level. You have to be as professional as the $500 million company you' re selling to. It's also helped me focus my business. It's made me much more aware of world issues and broadened my horizons."

1.   Why do small businesses neglect international markets?
2.   What is the principal barrier to export markets that Rucker faced?
3.   What suggestions can you offer small businesses wanting to break into foreign markets by exporting?

Sources: Stephen D. Solomon, "The Accidental Trader," *Inc.*, March 1990, pp. 84-89.

THE TWELVE MOST COMMON EXPORT MISTAKES

Exporting can be intimidating, especially for an inexperienced small business owner, and overcoming export barriers puts an extra burden on small companies that usually have thin resources. Patrick M. Williams, chairman of Stanley Industrial Corporation, a small maker of ventilating equipment, chooses not to export because of the problems his former employer had in foreign markets. "It's not worth the hassle," he explains.

When a small business runs into export trouble, it is usually because it fell victim to one or more of the twelve most common mistakes that exporters make:

1. *Not obtaining qualified export counseling and developing a master international marketing plan before starting an export business.* To be successful, a firm first must define its goals, objectives, and the problems it may encounter. Second, it must draw up a plan to achieve these objectives despite the problems involved. Unless the firm is fortunate enough to have a staff with considerable export expertise, it may not be able to take this crucial first step without qualified outside guidance.

2. *Not obtaining enough commitment by top management to overcome the initial difficulties and financial requirements of exporting.* Although the early delays and costs of exporting may seem difficult to justify when compared with established domestic trade, the exporter should take a long-range view and shepherd his international marketing efforts through these early difficulties. If a good foundation is laid for export business, the benefits derived should eventually outweigh the investment.

3. *Not taking sufficient care in selecting overseas distributors.* The choice of each foreign distributor is crucial. The complications of overseas communications and transportation require international distributors to act with greater independence than their domestic counterparts do. Also, because a new exporter's history, trademarks, and reputation are usually unknown in the foreign market, foreign customers may buy on the strength of a distributor's reputation. A firm should therefore carefully evaluate the personnel handling its account, the distributor's facilities, and the management methods employed.

4. *Chasing orders from around the world instead of establishing a basis for profitable operations aid orderly growth.* If exporters expect distributors to promote their accounts, the distributors must be trained, and their performance must be continually monitored. This requires a company to put a marketing executive in the distributor's geographical region. New exporters should concentrate on one or two geographical areas until there is sufficient business to support a company representative. Then, while this initial core area is expanding, the exporter can move into another geographical area.

5. *Neglecting export business when the U.S. market booms.* Too many companies turn to exporting when business falls off in the United States. Then when domestic business starts to boom again, they neglect their export trade or relegate it to a secondary place. Such neglect can seriously harm the business and motivation of their overseas representatives, strangle the U.S. company's own export trade, and leave the firm without recourse when domestic business falls off once more. Even if domestic business remains strong, the company may eventually realize that it has succeeded only in shutting off a valuable source of additional profits.

6. *Not treating international distributors on an equal basis with domestic counterparts.* Often companies have institutional advertising campaigns, special discount offers, sales incentive programs, special credit term programs, warrant offers, and the like in the U.S. market but fail to offer similar assistance to their international distributors. This is a mistake that can destroy the vitality of overseas marketing efforts.

7. *Assuming that a given market technique and product will automatically be successful in all countries.* What works in one market may not work in others, and so each market has to be treated separately.

8. *Not being willing to modify products to meet other countries' regulations or cultural*

166

preferences. Foreign distributors cannot ignore local safety and security codes and import restrictions. If necessary modifications are not made at the factory, the distributor must make them-usually at a greater cost and perhaps not as well. Also note that the resulting smaller profit margin makes the account less attractive.

9. *Not printing service, sales, and warranty messages in the local language.* Although a distributor's top management may speak English, it is unlikely that all sales personnel (let alone service personnel) have this capability. Without a clear understanding of sales messages or service instructions, these persons may be less effective in performing their functions.

10. *Not using an export management company.* If a firm decides that it cannot afford its own export department (or has tried one unsuccessfully), it should consider appointing an appropriate export management company (EMC).

11. *Not considering licensing or joint venture arrangements.* Import restrictions in some countries, insufficient personnel/financial resources, or a limited product line causes many companies to dismiss international marketing as unfeasible. Yet many products that can compete on a national basis in the United States can be successfully marketed in most other markets in the world. A licensing or joint venture arrangement may be the simple, profitable answer to any reservations. In general, all that is needed for success is flexibility in using the proper combination of marketing techniques.

12. *Not providing readily available servicing for the product.* A product without the necessary service support can acquire a bad reputation in a short period, potentially preventing further sales.

1. What steps can a small business owner beginning an export program take to avoid these twelve mistakes? Why do most small business owners shy away from exporting?

Sources: Martha E. Mangelsdorf, "Unfair Trade," Inc., April 1991, pp. 28-36; A Basic Guide to Exporting (Washington. DC: U.S. Department of Commerce) 1986), pp.85-86.

Part Five: Supplemental Readings

"Small Firms Going Global," Jim Ostroff. *WWD*, Feb. 28, 1997, Vol. 173, No. 40, p. S30.

"Firms with Global Goals Can Learn Exporting Basics at ITC," Leslie Rosewater. *Memphis Business Journal*, Sept. 23, 1996, Vol. 18, No. 20, p. 34.

"Think Big; The Net Gives Small Businesses a Reach They Once Only Dreamed Of," Jim Carlton. *The Wall Street Journal*, June 17, 1996, p. R27.

"A Global Reach For Small Firms," James Worsham. *Nation's Business*, Oct. 1995, Vol. 83, No. 10, p. 40.

Section IV - Putting the Plan to Work: Building a Competitive Edge

Chapter 15
Leading the Growing Company and Planning for Management Succession **(PPT 15.1)**

Part One: Learning Objectives

1. Explain the challenges involved in the entrepreneur's role as leader and what it takes to be a successful leader.

2. Describe the importance of hiring employees and how to avoid making hiring mistakes.

3. Explain how to build the kind of company culture and structure to support the entrepreneur's mission and goals and to motivate employees to achieve them.

4. Discuss the ways in which entrepreneurs can motivate their workers to higher levels of performance.

5. Describe the steps in developing a management succession plan for a growing business that will allow a smooth transition of leadership to the next generation.

Part Two: Lesson Plan

I. Leadership in the New Economy **(PPT 15.2 thru 15.6)**

Small business managers take on a wide range of roles and responsibilities, but the most important is the role of leader. *Leadership* is the process of influencing and inspiring others to work to achieve a common goal and then giving them the power and the freedom to achieve it. Management and leadership are not the same; yet both are essential to a small company's success. Leadership without management is unbridled; management without leadership is uninspired. Leadership gets a small business going; management keeps it going.

Effective leaders exhibit certain behaviors:
1. Create a set of values and beliefs for employees and passionately pursue them.
2. Define and then constantly reinforce the vision they have for the company.
3. Respect and support their employees.
4. Set the example for their employees.
5. Create a climate of trust in the organization.
6. Focus employees' efforts on challenging goals and on reaching those goals.
7. Provide the resources employees need to achieve their goals.
8. Communicate with their employees.
9. Value the diversity of their workers.
10. Celebrate their workers' successes.
11. Encourage creativity among their workers.
12. Maintain a sense of humor.
13. Create an environment of motivation, training, and freedom to achieve goals.
14. Become a catalyst for change when change is needed.
15. Keep their eyes on the horizon.

To become effective, a small business leader must perform four vital tasks:
- Hire the right employees and constantly improve their skills.
- Build an organizational culture and structure that allow both workers and the company to reach their potential.
- Motivate workers to higher levels of performance.
- Plan for "passing the torch" to the next generation of leadership.

II.   Hiring the Right Employees **(PPT 15.7 thru 15.18)**

Avoid hiring mistakes

Elevate recruiting to a strategic position in the company
- Look inside the company first
- Encourage employee referrals
- Make employment advertisements stand out
- Use the Internet as a recruiting tool
- Recruit on campus
- Forge relationships with schools and other sources of workers
- Recruit "retired" workers
- Offer what workers want

Create practical job descriptions and job specifications
- Conduct a job analysis
- Develop a job description
- Determine job specifications

Plan an effective interview by
- Developing a series of core questions and ask them of every candidate
- Ask open-ended questions rather than "yes" or "no" questions
- Create hypothetical situations candidates would likely encounter on the job and ask how they would handle them
- Probe for specific examples in the candidates' past work experience that demonstrate the necessary traits and characteristics
- Ask candidates to describe a recent success and a recent failure and how they dealt with them

Conduct the interview
- Breaking the ice
- Asking questions
- Selling the candidate on the company

Check references

YOU BE THE CONSULTANT - Last Resort Workers

Tim Rock, owner of an Iowa-based printing company turned to prisoners as a last resort to solve his labor shortage problem. Jerry Strahan, owner of a New Orleans-based hot dog vending business turned to

169

mission centers for the homeless and to street people as a last resort to staff his 22 hot dog push carts. Both men were able to make it work thanks to their patience and creativity.

Q1. Why must employers such as Tim Rock and Jerry Strahan resort to such extreme measures to find workers?
Q2. What techniques would you recommend for motivating workers such as those described in this case?
Q3. Are there other options for recruiting employees that you might suggest Rock and Strahan explore?

A1. Sustained periods of low unemployment, increased competition for workers and the changing attitudes of workers have resulted in a severe labor shortage in many areas of the country.
A2. Almost anyone can be motivated to work hard. The employer's job is to find out what each individual wants and needs from life-- their motivators For a prisoner, it may be the chance for freedom, for a homeless person, it may be finding a way to stop drinking.
A3. Students will offer many options and solutions to the employee shortage problem.

Sources: Adapted from Ann Harrington, "Does Anybody Here Want a Job?" *Fortune*, May 15, 2000, pp. 489-498; Leigh Buchanan, "The Taming of the Crew," *Inc.*, August 1999, pp. 27-40.

III.   Building the Right Organizational Culture and Structure **(PPT 15.19 thru 15.24)**

Company culture is the unwritten code of conduct that governs the behavior, attitudes, relationships and style of an organization. For a small company, having the right kind of structure and culture can lead to a competitive advantage. The most successful companies rely on some of the following principles:

- Respect for work and life balance
- A sense of purpose
- A sense of fun
- Diversity
- Integrity
- Participative management
- Learning environment

Managing Growth and a Changing Culture

Structure

- The Craftsman
- The Classic
- The Coordinator
- The Entrepreneur-plus-Employee Team
- The Small Partnership
- The Big-Team Venture

Making Teams Work

- Assigning teams inappropriate tasks
- Creating "make-nice" teams
- Failing to provide adequate training for team members and leaders
- Sabotaging teams with under-performers
- Switching to team responsibilities but keeping pay individually-oriented

- Make sure teams are appropriate for the company and the work
- Make sure that teams are appropriate for the task to be accomplished
- Form teams around the natural work flow and give them specific tasks to accomplish
- Provide adequate support and training for team members and leaders
- Involve team members in determining how their performances will be measured, what will be measured, and when it will be measured
- Make at least part of team members' pay dependent on team performance

IV. The Challenge of Motivating Workers (PPT 15.25 thru 15.38)

Motivation is the degree of effort an employee exerts to accomplish a task. In lots of ways, motivation reveals itself as excitement. Managers can motivate their employees by using a combination of many techniques.

- Empowerment
- Job Design
  - Job enlargement
  - Job rotation
  - Job enrichment
  - Flextime
  - Job sharing
  - Flexplace
- Rewards and Compensation
- Feedback
- Performance Appraisals

YOU BE THE CONSULTANT SUMMARY - The New Company Town

Competition for employees has become so fierce, that some companies now offer on-site fitness centers, valet services, day care, retail outlets, bank services and hair salons just to name a few. The goal is to free up time for workers by taking care of chores and mundane tasks. As one worker put it, "you never have to leave the place."

Q1. What are the benefits to companies and to workers of the services and facilities such as those described in the case? What potential disadvantages do you see with companies offering such services and facilities?
Q2. Would *you* want to work at such a company? Explain.

A1. The benefits described may attract workers and motivate them to work hard and stay on. The main disadvantage lies in the fact that tangible rewards such as money or products tend to lose their motivational impact after the initial hit. Workers come to expect what they are getting and need new sources of motivation.
A2. Students should be encouraged to think about what they want from a job beyond a paycheck, and most importantly, should think about what their future employees may need or want.

Source: Jerry Useem, "Welcome to the New Company Store," *Fortune*, January 10, 2000, pp. 62-70.

V.   Management Succession: Passing the Torch of Leadership (**PPT 15.39 thru 15.42**)

For growing businesses, it is almost inevitable that the leadership wand will have to be passed off to the next generation. 90% of all U.S. companies are family owned as are one-third of all fortune 500 companies.

How to Develop a Management Succession Plan:
    Step 1. Select the successor
    Step 2. Create a survival kit for the successor
    Step 3. Groom the successor
    Step 4. Promote an environment of trust and respect
    Step 5. Cope with the financial realities of estate and gift taxes

YOU BE THE CONSULTANT SUMMARY - Who's Next?

Dick Strossner is the second-generation owner-operator of a bakery started by his father. As he nears retirement, the issue of succession has now surfaced. Dick's son may or may not be next in line to run the business. Dick also has his long-time employees and some tax issues to consider.

Q1. What advice would you offer Dick Strossner concerning a management succession plan?
Q2. What steps should Strossner take to develop a management succession plan?
Q3. What tools would you suggest Strossner use for minimizing estate taxes?

A1. Dick should begin to work on a succession plan immediately. He should begin by objectively talking to his children, without making them feel guilty and then meet with an attorney that specializes in estate tax issues. Does he want the business to generate income for him for his remaining years? The exact nature of the trust will depend on current federal and state estate laws and associated tax regulations. His options could include: selling the business to several of the employees quite possibly through a buy/sell agreement, setting up an irrevocable trust if he is interested in lowering his estate taxes.
A2. The steps to developing a management succession plan include:
    Step 1. Make the decision and select the successor
    Step 2. Create a survival kit for the successor
    Step 3. Groom the successor
    Step 4. Promote an environment of trust and respect
    Step 5. Begin to cope with the financial realities of estate and gift taxes
A3. Strossner should consult with an attorney that specializes in estate planning.

Source: Adapted from Jenny Munro, "Bridging the Generation Gap," *Upstate Business*, October 8, 2000.

Part Three: Suggested Answers to Discussion Questions

1.   What is leadership? What is the difference between leadership and management?

Leadership is the process of influencing and inspiring others to work to achieve a common goal and then giving them the power and the freedom to achieve it. Management and leadership are not the same; yet both are essential to a small company's success. Leadership without management is unbridled; management without leadership is uninspired. Leadership gets asmall business going; management keeps it going.

2.   What behaviors do effective leaders exhibit?

Effective leaders exhibit many of the following characteristics:
1.   Create a set of values and beliefs for employees and passionately pursue them.
2.   Respect and support their employees.
3.   Set the example for their employees.
4.   Focus employees' on challenging goals and keep them driving toward those goals.
5.   Provide the resources needed to achieve goals.
6.   Communicate with their employees.
7.   Value the diversity of their workers.
8.   Celebrate their workers' successes.
9.   Encourage creativity among their workers.
10.   Maintain a sense of humor.
11.   Keep their eyes on the horizon.

3.   Why is it so important for small companies to hire the right employees? What can small business owners do to avoid making hiring mistakes?

Every "new hire" a business owner makes determines the heights to which the company can climb, or the depths to which it will plunge. To effectively hire employees, entrepreneurs should develop meaningful job descriptions and specifications; plan and conduct effective interviews; and check references on each employee before hiring them.

4.   What is a job description? A job specification? What functions do they serve in the hiring process?

Job descriptions are written statements of duties, responsibilities, reporting relationships, working conditions, and materials and equipment used in the position. Job specifications are written statements about the qualifications and characteristic needed for the job. Both items help small business owners prepare a "blue-print" of the position and the type of person who will be most successful in the job.

5.   Outline the procedure for conducting an effective interview.

An effective interview consists of three phases: breaking the ice, asking questions, and selling the candidate on the company. The first phase is used to set the candidate and the interviewer at ease. In the second phase, the interviewer asks questions and listens to the candidate's responses and body language. Effective interviewers spend about 25% of the time talking and 75% of the time listening.

6.   What is company culture? What role does it play in a small company's success? What threats does rapid growth pose for a company's culture?

Company culture is the unwritten code of conduct that governs the behavior, attitudes, relationships, and style of an organization. For a small company, having the right kind of structure and culture can lead to a competitive advantage. As companies grow, their culture may begin to change and break down.

7. Explain the six different management styles entrepreneurs rely on to guide their companies as they grow (craftsman, classic, coordinator, entrepreneur-plus-employee team, small partnership, and big-team venture).

The Craftsmen is responsible for all tasks and is in total control. It is a one-man or one-woman show. Most often, this management style occurs in the start-up and early growth stages.
The Classic begins to hire employees, but does not pass any significant authority to them. The owner still watches over everything. This style does provide more growth potential than the craftsmen, but there are still limits to growth while the owner remains in tight control.
The Coordinator operates by outsourcing a large portion of the work and then coordinates all of the activities from "headquarters."
The Entrepreneur-plus-Employee Team is the first shift into a team-based management approach. The entrepreneur delegates authority to key employees, but retains the final decision making power.
The Small Partnership owner realizes that there is an advantage in sharing responsibility for the company with others. This can be very advantageous, but the loss of total control is an issue.
The Big-Team Venture approach is the broadest-based management style and usually occurs when the company grows larger. When the firm outgrows the ability of its' partners time, ability, and energy, then the Big-Team Venture is appropriate.

8. What mistakes do companies make when switching to team-based management? What can they do to avoid these mistakes? Explain the four phases teams typically go through.

The most common reasons for team failure are indirectly correlated to the success factors.
   1. Assigning teams inappropriate tasks.
   2. Creating "make-nice" teams.
   3. Inadequate training for team members and leaders.
   4. Sabotaging teams with under performers.
   5. Switching to team responsibilities but keeping pay individually-oriented.

By avoiding these mistakes and keeping in mind the four stages of team development, most small businesses can form successful teams. The four stages that teams go through as they make their way to accomplishing tasks are: Startup, Reality Strikes, Realigning Expectations, and Performance.

9. What is empowerment? What benefits does it offer workers? The company? What must a small business manager do to make empowerment work in a company?

Empowerment involves giving all workers, at all levels, the freedom and responsibility to control their own work, to make decisions, and to take action to meet the company's objectives. Employees that are empowered have a sense of "enlightenment" within the organization. This leads to personal success for the employees, as well as organizational success.

10. Explain the difference among job simplification, job enlargement, job rotation, and job enrichment. What impact do these different job designs have on workers?

In job simplification, the work is broken down into its simplest form and then standardized into tasks. Job simplification evokes monotony and impersonal, unchallenging work.

In job enlargement, more tasks are added to a job in order to broaden its scope. The idea is to make the job more varied and to allow employees to perform a more complete unit of work.

Job rotation involves cross-training employees so that they can move from one job in the company to others. Job rotation provides variety to workers and increases skills and understanding.

Job enrichment builds motivators into a job by increasing the planning, decision-making, organizing, and controlling functions that workers perform. The idea is to make every employee a manager, at least for his or her own particular job.

11. Is money the "best" motivator? How do pay-for-performance compensation systems work? What other rewards are available to small business managers to use as motivators? How effective are they?

Money may not always be the "best" motivator because its effect as a motivator is usually only short-term and does not have a lasting effect on motivation. Small business managers can use praise, recognition, feedback, and inexpensive perks to motivate their employees for the long-term.

12. Suppose that a mail-order catalog company selling environmentally friendly products identifies its performance as a socially responsible company as a "critical number" in its success. Suggest some ways for the owner to measure this company's "socially responsibility index."

Business owners may measure social responsibility in any number of ways as long as the method meets two criteria-- validity and reliability. Validity is the extent to which a technique actually measures what it is intended to measure and how well it measures that factor. Reliability is the extent to which a measurement device produces consistent results over time. Managers should carefully define the measurements and the techniques that will be used.

13. What is performance appraisal? What are the most common mistakes managers make in performance appraisals? What should small business managers do to avoid making these mistakes?

During a performance appraisal, an employee's performance is evaluated against established performance standards. Many managers make the mistake of having performance appraisal only once a year, which limits feedback. Managers commonly make the mistake of forgetting the real purpose of performance appraisals-- to encourage and help employees improve their performance, by letting the meeting become an uncomfortable confrontation. Employers should provide clear objectives to employees, be aware of employee performance, be prepared, and be honest and sincere in appraisals.

14. Why is it so important for a small business owner to develop a management succession plan? Why is it so difficult for most business owners to develop such a plan? What are the steps that are involved in creating a succession plan?

With growing small businesses, any stumble or inability to implement necessary strategic actions can open up the market for competitors to gain market share. Entrepreneurs must maintain their aggressive postures while mastering new roles generated by company growth. This growth brings about many problems and challenges, that in some cases, owners cannot adjust to. It is at this point where succession comes to light. The entrepreneur must make a decision to either limit his/her company's growth by staying at the helm or bring in "professional" managers to guide the company through its growing pains. Planning for succession involves:

Step 1 Select the successor.
Step 2 Create a survival kit for the successor.
Step 3 Groom the successor.
Step 4 Promote an environment of trust and respect.
Step 5 Cope with the financial realities of estate taxes.

15. Briefly describe the options a small business owner wanting to pass the family business on to the next generation can take to minimize the impact of estate taxes.

There are several ways to reduce estate taxes: lifetime giving, trusts, Grantor-Retained Income Trusts (GRITs), estate freeze, Employee Stock Ownership Plans (ESOPs), and Buy/Sell Agreements.

Part Four: Lecture or Critical Thinking Case Studies-Not Found In Student Text

SELF-MANAGEMENT WORK TEAMS AND THEIR IMPACT ON PERFORMANCE
THE POWER OF FEEDBACK

SELF-MANAGEMENT WORK TEAMS AND THEIR IMPACT ON PERFORMANCE

A.E. Staley Company of Lafayette, Indiana, operates virtually without managers. The plant's 265 employees work in small teams with leaders of their own choosing-- they designate work assignments and do their own hiring and firing. "This movement away from hierarchical and authoritarian management to participative management has all the characteristics of a firestorm," observes the respected business quarterly National Productivity Review.

The A.E. Staley Company began this experiment in self-management in 1974. The plant employs salaried technicians who use computer-controlled machines to convert corn into high-fructose syrup. Employees are divided according to function and shift into sixteen teams of about fifteen persons each. Each team chooses two leaders from its ranks, one of them in charge of the actual work and the other in charge of training, discussion, and records.

It was three years before production at the plant began to justify the experiment. But since then, productivity has risen to extraordinary heights. Operating costs are below those of similar plants; absenteeism and turnover are under one percent; downtime in a 24-hour workday is less than one percent; and production is running at 115 percent of engineering specifications.

Any questions about who's in charge?

1. Why has it taken business so long to trust and respect employees enough to install self-managed work teams?
2. Describe the types of individuals and groups you feel are the best candidates for self-management.

176

Source: Adapted from Harry Bucas, "Who's in Charge Here?" *Inc.*, May 1985, pp.57-64, with permission of the publisher.

THE POWER OF FEEDBACK

Robert C. Dorn of the Center for Creative Leadership stresses that to help subordinates, "A manager must give them feedback about their performance. Feedback given in an atmosphere of openness, mutual respect, and support can improve performance. But when the executive's attitude is clearly one of 'you dummy' or worse, she succeeds in eroding the quality of relationships-usually without enhancing produce outcomes."

How can you give feedback? Here are some guidelines.

- Feedback should be helpful to the person receiving it.
- Be specific and accurate. State what is factual and observable.
- Feedback should be given in a way that communicates acceptance of the recipient as a worthwhile person.
- Encourage the employee to talk.
- Choose only one to three specific behaviors for an employee to work on.
- Let the employee know the consequences of not improving.

1. Why, in your opinion, is it so difficult to give employees feedback when their work performance is not up to expectations?
2. As a new manager, how would you deal with an employee who denies responsibility for a poor performance?

Source: Adapted from Sharon Nelton, "Feedback to Employees Can Nourish Your Business," *Nation's Business*, July 1985, pp. 62-63, with permission of the publisher. Copyright 1985, U.S. Chamber of Commerce.

Part Five: Supplemental Readings

"Getting a Handle on Fast Growth," Roberta Maynard, *Nation's Business*, March 1997. Vol. 85, No. 3, p. 33.

"How the '97 Outlook Shapes Up by Region," *Nation's Business*, Jan. 1997, Vol. 85, No. 1 pp. 18-20.

"Lawsuits: A Family Threat," Frank S. Schneider, *Denver Business Journal*, Feb. 14, 1997, Vol. 48, No. 23, p. 14A.

"Majority of Small Businesses Lack Succession Plans," *Best's Review - Life-Health Insurance Edition*, Aug. 1996, Vol. 97, No. 4, pp. 86-88.

"Forming a Family Firm? Go Into It with Eyes Open," James W. Lea, *Washington Business Journal*, Nov. 22, 1996, Vol. 15, No. 28, p. 38.

"A Secret About Secrecy," Drew S. Mendoza, Craig E. Aronoff, *Nation's Business*, Nov. 1996, Vol. 84, No. 11, pp. 56-58.

Chapter 1   The Foundations of Entrepreneurship

Multiple Choice Questions:

1. A recent study by Ernst and Young found that 78% of influential Americans believe that entrepreneurship will be the defining trend of this century. The entrepreneurial opportunity that topped their list was:
    a. the Internet
    b. globalization
    c. downsizing of corporate America
    d. None of the above.

    a., Medium, Page 2

2. Current competitive conditions favor:
    a. large companies with their hierarchies and layers of management.
    b. companies in industries that were once regulated by government but have recently been deregulated.
    c. small companies that can quickly move into and out of niche markets as they emerge and recede.
    d. Both A and B are correct.

    c., Medium, Page 2

3. Which of the following is NOT a characteristic of the typical entrepreneur?
    a. Confidence in his/her ability to succeed
    b. Value of money over achievement
    c. Desire for immediate feedback
    d. A future orientation

    b., Easy, Page 4

4. Which of the following is NOT a characteristic of the typical entrepreneur?
    a. Desire for responsibility
    b. High degree of commitment
    c. Low energy levels
    d. Confidence in his/her ability to succeed

    c., Easy, Page 4

5. Characteristics of entrepreneurs include all of the following EXCEPT:
    a. Tolerance for ambiguity
    b. Flexibility
    c. Skill at organizing
    d. Low degree of commitment

    d., Easy, Page 4

6. Entrepreneurs are characterized by:
   a. skill at organizing.
   b. desire for immediate feedback.
   c. high energy levels.
   d. All of the above.

   d., Easy, Page 4

7. Entrepreneurs who repeatedly start businesses and grow to a sustainable size before striking out again are known as _____ entrepreneurs.
   a. Opportunistic
   b. Persistent
   c. Serial
   d. None of the above.

   c., Easy, Page 4

8. Surveys show that owners of small businesses believe that they _____ than if they worked for a large company.
   a. work harder
   b. earn more money
   c. are happier
   d. All of the above.

   d., Medium, Page 6

9. In a large organization, an individual may be stifled and limited by a wide variety of factors. But, by owning one's own business, the only limits are one's own creativity, talent, and determination. In this sense, small business ownership offers the advantage of:
   a. the opportunity to reach one's full potential.
   b. the opportunity to reap unlimited profits.
   c. the chance to learn from others' mistakes.
   d. None of the above.

   a., Medium, Page 6

10. Which of the following is a benefit of entrepreneurship?
    a. The opportunity to gain control over your own destiny
    b. The opportunity to reach your full potential
    c. The opportunity to do what you enjoy
    d. All of the above.

    d., Easy, Page 6

11. The only boundaries imposed on an entrepreneur's success are those imposed by:
    a. society.
    b. his/her own creativity, enthusiasm, and vision.
    c. financial institutions.
    d. licensing agencies.

    b., Medium, Page 6

12. Which of the following is NOT a characteristic of the entrepreneurial experience?
    a. Uncertainty
    b. Ambiguity
    c. Guaranteed success
    d. Hard work

    c., Easy, Page 9

13. ____% of new businesses fail within two years, while ____% fail within six years.
    a. 35;64
    b. 51;64
    c. 35;80
    d. 64;80

    a., Difficult, Page 9

14. The majority of new business owners work:
    a. fewer than 40 hours per week.
    b. more than 40 hours per week.
    c. more than 70 hours per week.
    d. more than 80 hours per week.

    b., Medium, Page 10

15. Which of the following is a potential disadvantage of owning your own business?
    a. Uncertainty of income
    b. Risk of losing your entire investment
    c. High level of stress
    d. All of the above.

    d., Easy, Page 10

16. Which of the following forces is driving the entrepreneurial trend in our nation?
    a. Increased entrepreneurial educational opportunities
    b. E-commerce and the World Wide Web
    c. Technological advancements and modern business machinery
    d. All of the above.

    d., Easy, Page 11

17. Which of the following is NOT one of the forces driving the entrepreneurial trend in our country?
    a. Shift away from a service economy
    b. Independent lifestyle
    c. International opportunities
    d. E-commerce and the World Wide Web

a., Medium, Page 11

18. The service sector of the U.S. economy produces _____% of the jobs and _____% of the GDP in the country.
    a. 92; 85
    b. 76; 75
    c. 65; 66
    d. 50; 24

a., Difficult, Page 12

19. Most entrepreneurs launch their businesses between the ages of ____ and _____.
    a. 20; 34
    b. 25; 44
    c. 30; 44
    d. 35; 49

b., Difficult, Page 12

20. Which of the following statements concerning small businesses and international markets is FALSE?
    a. Although terrorism and global recession have slowed the growth of international trade somewhat, global opportunities for small businesses have a long-term positive outlook.
    b. Although the U.S. is an attractive market, approximately 95 percent of the world's population lives outside its borders.
    c. Because exporting is so complex and requires a company to have so many international experts on staff, exporting is not feasible for small businesses.
    d. Small companies comprise 97% of all businesses engaged in exporting, yet they account for only 30% of the nation's export sales.

c., Difficult, Page 13

21. Small companies that have expanded successfully into foreign markets tend to rely on all but which of the following strategies?
    a. Research foreign markets thoroughly
    b. Focus on many countries initially
    c. Utilize government resources designed to help small companies establish an international presence
    d. Forge alliances with local partners

b., Medium, Page 14

22. Which of the following statements is/are NOT true of Generation X?
    a. They are the most entrepreneurial generation in history.
    b. They are three times more likely to start businesses than other generations.
    c. They are responsible for approximately 80% of all business start-ups.
    d. All of the above are true.

d., Medium, Page 14

23. Which of the following statements about women-owned businesses is FALSE?
    a. The businesses women start tend to be smaller than those men start.
    b. Women own about 28% of all privately-held businesses in the U.S.
    c. The survival rate of women-owned businesses is much lower than that of U.S. businesses overall.
    d. Most women-owned companies are concentrated in retailing and services.

c., Difficult, Page 16

24. Women own about _____% of all privately-held businesses in the United States.
    a. 8
    b. 28
    c. 48
    d. 68

b., Difficult, Page 16

25. Women are opening businesses at a rate of approximately ____ times that of the national average.
    a. 1.5
    b. 2
    c. 3
    d. 4

b., Difficult, Page 16

26. Which of the following statements is NOT true regarding the diversity of entrepreneurs?
    a. Minority-owned businesses have come a long way in the past decade, and their success rate is climbing.
    b. Minority-owned businesses now account for approximately one-third of all businesses in the U.S.
    c. Immigrants with more education and experience than those of the past are coming to the U.S. and succeeding in entrepreneurial ventures.
    d. The numbers of part-time and home-based entrepreneurs are rising.

b., Medium, Page 16

27. _____% of all U.S. businesses are family-owned and managed.
a. 25
b. 50
c. 70
d. 90

d., Difficult, Page 19

28. Which of the following is NOT a characteristic of a successful working relationship between copreneurs?
a. A clear definition of one partner as "boss" and the other as "subordinate"
b. Compatible business and life goals
c. Complementary business skills
d. A clear division of roles and authority based on each partner's skills and abilities

a., Medium, Page 19

29. Which of the following is NOT a characteristic of copreneurs?
a. Mutual respect
b. Complementary business skills
c. A clear division of roles and authority
d. An understanding that one is the superior and the other is the subordinate

d., Easy, Page 19

30. Approximately _____% of corporate managers who are "cast off" as companies downsize become entrepreneurs.
a. 5
b. 15
c. 20
d. 45

c., Difficult, Page 20

31. Melinda and John Perez, both corporate attorneys in New York City, have grown tired of their lengthy daily commute, the stress of their jobs, and the overbearing policies of their employers. They have decided to leave their six-figure jobs and together open a guide service in Wyoming. Melinda and John are:
a. corporate castoffs
b. corporate dropouts
c. copreneurs
d. B and C are correct.

d., Medium, Page 20

32. The majority of small companies are concentrated in the _____ and _____ industries.
    a. manufacturing; retail
    b. manufacturing; service
    c. retail; service
    d. wholesale; retail

    c., Medium, Page 21

33. The nation's small businesses:
    a. employ more than 51% of the nation's private sector work force.
    b. create more jobs than do big businesses.
    c. account for 47% of business sales.
    d. All of the above.

    d., Medium, Page 21

34. What percentage of companies in the U.S. are considered "small"?
    a. 58
    b. 65
    c. 79
    d. 99

    d., Medium, Page 21

35. David Birch, president of the research firm Cognetics, suggests that three percent of small businesses created _____ percent of new jobs.
    a. 20
    b. 50
    c. 70
    d. 90

    c., Difficult, Page 21

36. Small companies:
    a. created fewer jobs than big companies in the last decade.
    b. are concentrated in the manufacturing and retail sectors.
    c. are the leaders in offering training and advancement opportunities to workers.
    d. account for approximately 10 percent of the nation's GDP and 25% of business sales.

    c., Medium, Page 21

37. Which of the following is NOT true regarding the research of David Birch, president of Cognetics?
    a. "Gazelles" grow 20% or more per year and have at least $100,000 in annual sales.
    b. "Mice" never grow much and don't create many new jobs.
    c. The largest businesses are "elephants," which have continued to shed jobs for several years.
    d. The majority of small companies are "gazelles."

d., Medium, Page 21

38. In terms of innovation and research, small businesses:
    a. create four times the innovations per research and development dollar than medium-sized firms and 24 times the innovations per research and development dollar than large companies.
    b. contribute 20% more innovations per employee than large companies.
    c. have created such important innovations as air conditioning, FM radio, the laser, the automatic transmission and the personal computer.
    d. All of the above.

d., Difficult, Page 22

39. Which of the following products was NOT invented by a small business?
    a. Air conditioning
    b. Camcorder
    c. FM radio
    d. Escalator

b., Easy, Page 22

40. John has come to you for advice on starting a business venture. He wants to know the best way to gain the experience he'll need. You suggest that he:
    a. read a small business book.
    b. seek experience in the field he wishes to enter by working for another firm for a while.
    c. determine his weaknesses and return to school for a term or two.
    d. just jump in and learn as he goes.

b., Medium, Page 23

41. The primary cause of small business failures is _____.
    a. lack of capital
    b. management mistakes
    c. poor location
    d. improper inventory control

b., Easy, Page 23

42. Entrepreneurs tend to be overly _____ and misjudge the _____ requirements of going into business.
    a. optimistic, personal
    b. optimistic, financial
    c. pessimistic, financial
    d. optimistic, professional

    b., Easy, Page 23

43. Which one of the following is one of the ten deadly mistakes entrepreneur's make?
    a. Weak marketing efforts
    b. Understanding financial statements
    c. Seeking help from experts
    d. Controlled growth

    a., Easy, Page 24

44. According to management expert Peter Drucker, startup companies can expect to outgrow their capital bases each time sales increase _____ percent.
    a. 5 to 10
    b. 20 to 30
    c. 40 to 50
    d. 70 to 80

    c., Medium, Page 25

45. All of the following are symptoms of ten deadly mistakes entrepreneurs make EXCEPT:
    a. believing a product will sell itself.
    b. figuring things out as they go.
    c. extending credit just to make a sale.
    d. tempering optimism with reality.

    d., Medium, Page 26

46. The only people who _____ are those who never do anything or never attempt anything new.
    a. succeed
    b. prosper
    c. profit
    d. fail

    d., Easy, Page 27

47. One hallmark of successful entrepreneurs is the ability to:
    a. be willing to gamble.
    b. fail intelligently.
    c. overlook past successes.
    d. repeat the same mistake.

    b., Medium, Page 27

48. Which of the following was NOT identified as one of the suggestions for small business success?
   a. Develop a business plan as you grow your business.
   b. Manage your financial resources and understand financial statements.
   c. Know your business in depth.
   d. Learn to manage people successfully.

   a., Easy, Page 29

49. Which of the following is/are true regarding business plans?
   a. Provide a pathway to success
   b. Allow entrepreneurs to replace faulty assumptions with facts before making the decision to go into business
   c. Create a benchmark against which entrepreneurs can measure actual company performance
   d. All of the above.

   d., Easy, Page 29

50. Most entrepreneurs believe that _____ is what matters most, but _____ is the most important financial resource for a small business owner.
   a. cash; profit
   b. profit; cash
   c. profit; inventory
   d. inventory; cash

   b., Medium, Page 29

True/False Questions:

51. Current competitive conditions favor large companies over smaller ones because of their ability to use their size to achieve efficiency and economies of scale.

   False, Easy, Page 2

52. Increased entrepreneurial activity is a phenomenon unique to the U.S.

   False, Easy, Page 2

53. The 21st century has seen record numbers of entrepreneurs launching businesses.

   True, Easy, Page 2

54. Members of Generation X no longer see launching a business as being a risky career path.

   True, Easy, Page 2

55. Seventy-eight percent of influential Americans believe that entrepreneurship will be the defining trend of this century.

    True, Medium, Page 2

56. Entrepreneurs are not willing to give up a steady paycheck.

    False, Medium, Page 3

57. Research has isolated a set of characteristics that can predict who will succeed as an entrepreneur.

    False, Medium, Page 3

58. An individual who possesses all of the characteristics of the typical entrepreneur is virtually guaranteed success in launching a small business.

    False, Medium, Page 3

59. Serial entrepreneurs repeatedly start businesses and grow them to a sustainable size before striking out again.

    True, Easy, Page 4

60. The typical entrepreneur values money over achievement.

    False, Easy, Page 5

61. The only boundaries imposed on an entrepreneur's success are those imposed by his or her own creativity, enthusiasm, and vision.

    True, Medium, Page 6

62. Surveys show that small business owners believe they work harder, earn more money, and are happier than if they worked for a large company.

    True, Medium, Page 6

63. The opportunity to reap impressive profits is the primary motivation for most entrepreneurs.

    False, Medium, Page 6

64. To most entrepreneurs, there is little difference between work and play; the two are synonymous.

    True, Medium, Page 6

65.   The majority of new business owners work fewer than 40 hours per week.

False, Medium, Page 10

66.   The majority of new business owners devote more than 40 hours per week to their companies.

True, Medium, Page 10

67.   One advantage of being your own boss and owning a small business is that work hours are very flexible and leisure time is abundant.

False, Easy, Page 10

68.   An important factor helping to drive the entrepreneurial trend in our economy is the favorable attitude Americans have towards entrepreneurs.

True, Easy, Page 11

69.   Most entrepreneurs start their business between the ages of 20 and 29.

False, Medium, Page 12

70.   Nearly two-thirds of entrepreneurs start their businesses between the ages of 25 and 44.

True, Difficult, Page 12

71.   The number of colleges and universities offering courses in small business management and entrepreneurship is declining.

False, Easy, Page 12

72.   Because of their low startup costs, service businesses are popular with entrepreneurs.

True, Medium, Page 12

73.   Modern technology and office machines enable one-person, home-based businesses to look much bigger than they are to their customers.

True, Easy, Page 13

74.   A recent small business Internet survey shows small businesses that use the web to market their products and services out-perform those that don't.

True, Medium, Page 13

75.   Approximately 95 percent of the world's population lives within the borders of the U.S.

False, Easy, Page 13

76. Small companies comprise 97% of all businesses engaged in exporting, yet they account for only 30% of the nation's export sales.

    True, Difficult, Page 14

77. There is concern over the future of entrepreneurship because so few high school and college students want to start their own companies.

    False, Easy, Page 14

78. Diversity may be considered a characteristic of entrepreneurs, as they don't fit any statistical norm.

    True, Easy, Page 14

79. Minority owned businesses have come a long way in the past decade, and their success rate is climbing.

    True, Medium, Page 16

80. Although their businesses grow more slowly than those owned by men, women-owned businesses have a higher survival rate than U.S. businesses overall.

    True, Medium, Page 16

81. Increasing numbers of women are discovering that the best way to break the "glass ceiling" that prevents them from rising to the top of many organizations is to start their own companies.

    True, Easy, Page 16

82. Although about 69% of women-owned companies are concentrated in the retailing and service sectors, female entrepreneurs are branching out rapidly into previously male-dominated industries.

    True, Medium, Page 16

83. Most home-based businesses are simple cottage industries such as crafts or sewing.

    False, Easy, Page 17

84. A major advantage of launching a business part-time is the lower risk it offers in case the business fails.

    True, Easy, Page 17

85. Successful "copreneurs" create a division of labor based on expertise.

    True, Easy, Page 19

86. Not all family-owned businesses are small; in fact, over one-third of the *Fortune* 500 companies are family businesses.

    True, Medium, Page 19

87. Most family businesses survive to the second and third generations.

    False, Medium, Page 19

88. Of the 25 million businesses in the U.S., about 40 percent are family-owned and managed.

    False, Difficult, Page 19

89. About 20 percent of downsized corporate managers have become entrepreneurs.

    True, Medium, Page 20

90. Because they have college degrees, a working knowledge of business, and years of management experience, both corporate castoffs and corporate dropouts who become entrepreneurs will most likely increase the small business survival rate.

    True, Easy, Page 20

91. Corporate downsizing has spawned a generation of entrepreneurs known as "corporate castoffs."

    True, Easy, Page 20

92. David Birch considers "gazelles" those businesses that grow at 20% or more per year and gross at least $100,000 in annual sales.

    True, Difficult, Page 21

93. Small companies have created two-thirds to three-fourths of the net new jobs in the U.S. economy.

    True, Medium, Page 21

94. Small businesses actually create more jobs than do big businesses.

    True, Easy, Page 21

95. About 75 percent of the businesses in the U.S. can be considered "small."

    False, Easy, Page 21

96. Large companies create significantly more innovations per research and development dollar spent than small firms.

    False, Medium, Page 22

97. Because of their size and limited resources, small businesses rarely create innovations that are important to the U.S. economy.

    False, Easy, Page 22

98. An often fatal error made by many small business owners is to open their businesses on a "shoestring," causing them to be undercapitalized.

    True, Easy, Page 23

99. The primary cause of small business failure is lack of capital.

    False, Easy, Page 23

100. About 24 percent of new businesses fail within six years.

    False, Difficult, Page 23

101. The faster a small company grows, the greater its appetite for cash.

    True, Easy, Page 24

102. To boost sales, small businesses, especially startups, should grant credit to anyone who wants to buy their products or services.

    False, Medium, Page 24

103. As an entrepreneur, you are always working for someone else – your customers.

    True, Easy, Page 24

104. The lifeblood of the small business—sales—is influenced heavily by choice of location.

    True, Easy, Page 25

105. Expanding a business usually requires no significant changes in structure or business practices.

    False, Easy, Page 25

106. Establishing prices that will generate the necessary profits means that business owners must understand how much it costs to make, market, and deliver their products and services.

    True, Easy, Page 25

107. Small business owners are more likely to underprice their products and services rather than overprice them.

    True, Medium, Page 25

108. If an entrepreneur has a good enough product or service to sell, a business plan is not really necessary since the product or service will sell itself.

    False, Easy, Page 29

109. Most entrepreneurs have a sound business plan.

    False, Easy, Page 29

110. Successful entrepreneurs recognize that their most valuable asset is their time, and they learn to manage it effectively to make themselves and their companies more productive; having passion about their businesses, products, and customers enables them to stay motivated.

    True, Easy, Page 30

Essay Questions:

111. What is an entrepreneur? Give a brief profile of a typical entrepreneur. What is the primary motivation for the typical entrepreneur?

    An entrepreneur is someone who creates a new business in the face of risk and uncertainty for the purpose of achieving profit and growth by identifying opportunities and assembling the necessary resources to capitalize on them.

    While entrepreneurs tend to exhibit no isolated set of required traits, an entrepreneurial profile contains the following characteristics:
    - Desire for Responsibility
    - Preference for Moderate Risk
    - Confidence in Their Ability to Succeed
    - Desire for Immediate Feedback
    - High Level of Energy
    - Future Orientation
    - Skill at Organizing

    Entrepreneurs are motivated most by a desire to control their own destiny, reach their own potential, make a difference, reap unlimited profits, and enjoy what they are doing. **Page 3**

112. Discuss the potential benefits and drawbacks of entrepreneurship.

    Entrepreneurs benefit by controlling their own destiny, reaching their own potential, making a difference, reaping impressive profits, contributing to society, and enjoying what they are doing.
    Potential drawbacks include: the uncertainty of income, risk of losing their entire investment, long hours and hard work, a somewhat lower quality of life until the business gets started, high levels of stress and absolute responsibility.

    Page 6

113. Describe the factors that are driving the current entrepreneurial trend in the U.S. economy.

    - A more positive attitude toward entrepreneurs
    - Higher levels and greater availability of entrepreneurial education
    - Demographic and economic factors, such as younger people starting businesses and greater opportunities for wealth
    - Shift to a service economy, which opens up opportunities for small business owners
    - Technological advancements make it easier for small businesses to compete on a more level playing field with larger companies
    - Independent lifestyle, allowing people more freedom to make choices about what they want to do
    - E-commerce and the World Wide Web provide an additional opportunity for a level playing field with larger companies
    - International opportunities are opening more doors than ever before for entrepreneurs

    Page 11

114. Discuss the role that the following groups are playing in leading the ongoing surge in entrepreneurial activity:
    - women
    - minorities
    - immigrants
    - part-time entrepreneurs
    - home-based entrepreneurs
    - family businesses
    - copreneurs
    - corporate castoffs
    - corporate dropouts

    Women often face discrimination in the workplace. Entrepreneurship offers women opportunities for economic growth.
    Like women, minorities also face discrimination in the workplace and can benefit through entrepreneurship.
    Immigrant entrepreneurs arrive with more education and experience. Their dedication and desire to succeed enable them to achieve their entrepreneurial dreams.
    Part-timers have the best of both worlds and can ease into a business without sacrificing a steady paycheck and benefits.

Home-based businesses are booming. Technology and this "Homecoming" support nearly 44 percent of U.S. households with some form of home office activity.
Family Businesses are an integral part of our economy. 90 percent of all the businesses in the U.S. are family owned.
Copreneurs are entrepreneurial couples who work together. They represent the fastest growing business sectors.
Corporate Castoffs have extensive on-the-job experience and are dislocated workers due to corporate downsizing.
Corporate Dropouts leave organizations to pursue a better way of life spearheaded by the "trust gap" over job security.
Page 16

115. Discuss the impact of small businesses on the U.S. economy, including sales, GDP, job creation, and innovation.

The resurgence of the entrepreneurial spirit is the most significant economic development in recent business history. Small businesses have introduced innovative products and services, pushed back technological frontiers, created new jobs, opened foreign markets, and in the process, sparked the U.S. economy into regaining its competitive advantage in the world.
Approximately 99 percent of all businesses in the U.S. are small businesses. They employ 51% of the nation's private sector workforce, created 2/3-3/4 of new jobs in the U.S. since the early 1990s, produce 51 percent of the country's private GDP, and account for 47 percent of business sales.
Page 21

116. Describe the ten deadly mistakes of entrepreneurship and how to avoid them.

A. Management Mistakes—Primary cause of business failure; may include lack of knowledge, leadership ability, etc.
B. Lack of Experience—In the field they want to enter (technical ability).
C. Poor Financial Control—Undercapitalization; lax customer credit policies; lack of understanding of financial aspects; lack of proper cash management techniques.
D. Weak Marketing Efforts—Building a strong customer base requires a sustained creative marketing effort. Keeping them coming back requires that you provide them with value, quality, convenience, service, and fun.
E. Failure to Develop a Strategic Plan—Failure to plan, however, usually results in failure to survive. Without a clearly defined strategy, a business has no sustainable basis for creating and maintaining a competitive edge in the marketplace. Building a strategic plan forces an entrepreneur to assess *realistically* a proposed business's potential.
F. Uncontrolled Growth--Expansion usually requires major changes in organizational structure, business practices such as inventory and financial control procedures, personnel assignments, and other areas. But the most important change occurs in managerial expertise.
G. Poor Location—The location question is much too critical to leave to chance. Especially for retailers, the lifeblood of the business – sales – is influenced heavily by choice of location.
H. Improper Inventory Control—Insufficient inventory levels may lead to dissatisfied customers; too much inventory leads to increased storage and handling costs.

Entrepreneurs must ensure that they not only have the correct amount of inventory, but also the correct items in inventory.

I. Incorrect Pricing—Establishing prices that will generate the necessary profits means that business owners must understand how much it costs to make, market, and deliver their products and services. They must ensure that they are not underpricing their products and services.

J. Inability to Make the Entrepreneurial Transition—After the start-up, growth usually requires a radically different style of management, one that requires delegation of authority.

Page 22

117. Describe the small business failure rate. What are the primary causes of business failures, and what steps can an entrepreneur take to avoid becoming a business failure statistic?

Because of their limited resources, inexperienced management, and lack of financial stability, small businesses suffer a mortality rate significantly higher than that of larger, established businesses.

Some steps to take to avoid failure include: achieving management competence, gaining experience, achieving financial control, developing a strategic plan, controlling growth, seeking out a good location, controlling inventory, knowing your business in depth, understanding financial statements, developing a solid business plan, learning to manage people effectively, and keeping in tune with yourself.

Page 27

Chapter 1
The Foundations of Entrepreneurship
Mini-Case

Case 1-1: Bill's Dilemma

Bill Hudson was a real craftsman when it came to being a machinist. Bill had learned almost all that he knew from Hugo Huffman, his first and only employer. Bill Hudson was married and had three young children. He was 33 years old and had worked for Hugo ever since he finished his tour in the army. In 12 years Bill had polished his skills under the watchful and critical eye of Hugo Huffman. Hugo was quick to recognize Bill's talent for the trade. Bill had a positive attitude about learning and displayed a drive for perfection that Hugo admired.

Hugo's Machine Shop was a successful small business. Its success was based mostly on the reputation for quality that had been established over its 42 years in operation. Hugh had come to this country with his new wife, Hilda, when he was in his late twenties. Now the business was a success, but Hugo remembered the early years when he and Hilda had to struggle. Hugo wanted the business to continue to produce the highest quality craftsman products possible. On a Friday evening, he called Bill into his office at closing time, poured him a cup of half-day-old coffee, and began to talk with him about the future.

"Bill, Hilda and I are getting old and I want to retire. It's been 42 years of fun but these old hands need a rest. In short, Hilda and I would like you to buy the business. We both feel that your heart is in this craft and that you would always retain the quality that we have stood for." Bill was taken back by the offer. He, of course, knew Hugo was getting older, but had no idea Hugo would retire. Bill and his wife, Anna, had only $4,200 in the bank. Most of Bill's salary went for the normal costs of rearing three children. Hugo knew Bill did not have the money to buy the business in cash, but he was willing to take a portion of the profits for the next 15 years and a modest initial investment from Bill.

Bill had, for the past four years, made most of the technical decisions in the shop. Bill knew the customers and was well respected by the employees. He had never been involved in the business side of the operation. He was a high a school graduate but had never taken business courses. Bill was told by Hugo that even after deducting the percentage of the profits he would owe under the sales agreement, he would be able to almost double his annual earnings. Bill would have to take on all the business functions himself because Anna had no business training either.

Questions

1. Which entrepreneurial characteristics does Bill have that may be important to his success? Which characteristic could lead to his failure?

This case requires the student to compare Bill's personality characteristics with those of the typical entrepreneur. Factors in Bill's favor include knowledge of the technical aspects of the business, a willingness to learn, a devotion to the business and its customers, and a favorable sales arrangement.

Factors working against Bill include his lack of business training and experience, a lack of personal assets, and possibly, insufficient management skills.

2. What steps should Bill take to avoid the pitfalls common to a small business?

Generally, it appears that Bill has a good chance of becoming a success if he can overcome the weaknesses mentioned above. The established business – and its reputation – that Bill is purchasing are important benefits.

3. If you were Hugo, would you sell Bill the business under the terms discussed in the case? Explain.

Yes. Both parties would benefit from the deal.

Chapter 2   Inside the Entrepreneurial Mind: From Ideas to Reality

Multiple Choice Questions:

1.   What is the entrepreneurial "secret" for creating value in the marketplace?
      a.   Applying Creativity and Innovation to Solve Problems
      b.   Creating New Products and Services
      c.   Learning by Doing
      d.   Applying Lessons Learned from History

      a., Difficult, Page 35

2.   The ability to develop new ideas and to discover new ways of looking at problems and opportunities is called:
      a.   entrepreneurship
      b.   innovation
      c.   creativity
      d.   creative thinking

      c., Easy, Page 35

3.   The ability to apply creative solutions to problems and opportunities to enhance or to enrich people's lives is called:
      a.   entrepreneurship
      b.   innovation
      c.   creativity
      d.   creative thinking

      b., Easy, Page 35

4.   Harvard's Theodore Levitt says that creativity is _____ new things, and innovation is _____ new things.
      a.   thinking; doing
      b.   doing; thinking
      c.   seeing; doing
      d.   thinking; applying

      a., Medium, Page 35

5.   Creativity often involves creating something from nothing. However, it is more likely to result in:
      a.   elaborating on the present.
      b.   putting old things together in new ways.
      c.   taking something away to create something simpler or better.
      d.   All of the above.

      d., Difficult, Page 36

6. Entrepreneurship is a constant process that relies on:
    a. creativity, innovation, and profit.
    b. the ability to win over the consumer.
    c. creativity, innovation, and application in the marketplace.
    d. intellectual property rights.

    c., Difficult, Page 35

7. When developing creative solutions to modern problems, entrepreneurs must:
    a. go beyond merely using whatever has worked in the past.
    b. limit the creative process to only profitable ventures.
    c. remember what has worked in the past.
    d. pay attention to limiting factors.

    a., Medium, Page 35

8. A(n)_____ is a preconceived idea of what the world is, what it should be like, and how it should operate.
    a. innovation
    b. entrepreneur
    c. paradigm
    d. profitable vision

    c., Easy, Page 37

9. Research shows that anyone can learn to be creative. The problem is:
    a. many organizations fail to foster an environment that encourages creativity.
    b. most people never tap into their pools of innate creativity.
    c. most people have never been taught to be creative.
    d. All of the above.

    d., Medium, Page 38

10. Research into the operation of the human brain shows that each hemisphere of the brain:
    a. develops symmetrically.
    b. controls similar functions.
    c. does not dominate the other hemisphere.
    d. processes information differently.

    d., Easy, Page 39

11. The left-brain is guided by:
    a. kaleidoscopic, lateral thinking.
    b. linear, vertical thinking.
    c. asymmetrical thinking.
    d. intuitive thinking.

    b., Easy, Page 39

12. The right brain is guided by:
    a. kaleidoscopic, lateral thinking.
    b. linear, vertical thinking.
    c. asymmetrical thinking.
    d. logical thinking.

    a., Easy, Page 39

13. Which hemisphere of the brain is responsible for language, logic, and symbols?
    a. Right Hemisphere
    b. Left Hemisphere
    c. Lateral Hemisphere
    d. Intuitive Hemisphere

    b., Easy, Page 39

14. Which hemisphere of the brain is responsible for the body's emotional, intuitive, and spatial functions?
    a. Right Hemisphere
    b. Left Hemisphere
    c. Vertical Hemisphere
    d. Logical Hemisphere

    a., Easy, Page 39

15. Which hemisphere of the brain processes information in a step-by-step fashion?
    a. Right Hemisphere
    b. Left Hemisphere
    c. Lateral Hemisphere
    d. Intuitive Hemisphere

    b., Easy, Page 39

16. Which hemisphere of the brain processes information all at once and by relying heavily on images?
    a. Right Hemisphere
    b. Left Hemisphere
    c. Vertical Hemisphere
    d. Logical Hemisphere

    a., Easy, Page 39

17. _____ vertical thinking is narrowly focused and systematic, proceeding in a highly logical fashion from one point to the next.
    a. Left-brained
    b. Right-brained
    c. Unconventional
    d. Intuitive

    a., Medium, Page 39

18. _____ lateral thinking is somewhat unconventional and unstructured.
    a. Left-brained
    b. Right-brained
    c. Systematic
    d. Logical

    b., Medium, Page 39

19. In his book <u>A Whack on the Side of the Head</u>, Roger von Oech views a "playful attitude"
    as:
    a. frivolous.
    b. fundamental to creative thinking.
    c. a mental block.
    d. limiting individual creativity.

    b., Easy, Page 42

20. All of the following represent barriers to creativity that entrepreneurs impose upon
    themselves except:
    a. focusing on being too logical.
    b. being too practical.
    c. blindly following rules.
    d. searching for more than one answer.

    d., Medium, Page 43

21. Roger von Oech believes that blindly following rules leads to:
    a. order, which stimulates creativity.
    b. a clearer vision and business venture.
    c. new ways of doing things.
    d. a mental block towards creativity.

    d., Medium, Page 42

22. Joseph Schumpeter wrote that entrepreneurs perform the vital function of:
    a. challenging accepted ways of doing things.
    b. creative destruction.
    c. revolutionizing current patterns of production.
    d. All of the above.

    d., Medium, Page 44

23. Entrepreneurs can stimulate their own creativity and encourage it among workers by:
    a. expecting and tolerating failure.
    b. avoiding problems.
    c. limiting rewards.
    d. not taking chances.

    a., Medium, Page 45

24. Which of the following is NOT one of the ways entrepreneurs can stimulate their own creativity and encourage it among their workers?
    a. Provide creativity training
    b. Encourage curiosity
    c. View challenges as problems
    d. Develop a corporate culture that both fosters and rewards creativity

    c., Difficult, Page 45

25. Employees must be given the tools and resources they need to be creative. One of the most valuable resources is:
    a. providing challenges.
    b. rules and guidelines.
    c. time.
    d. money.

    c., Difficult, Page 46

26. Hiring a diverse workforce:
    a. helps in enhancing organizational creativity.
    b. allows for different ideas and varying methods of problem solving.
    c. brings in people from different backgrounds, with different cultural experiences, hobbies, and interests.
    d. All of the above.

    d., Easy, Page 45

27. All of the following are enhancements to individual creativity except:
    a. keeping a journal to record thoughts and ideas.
    b. limiting your reading sources.
    c. taking time off.
    d. allowing yourself to be creative.

    b., Easy, Page 48

28. Which of the following is NOT an enhancement to individual creativity?
    a. Listening to other people.
    b. Recognizing the creative power of mistakes.
    c. Keeping a toy box in your office.
    d. Working without breaks until the project is complete or the problem is solved.

    d., Medium, Page 48

29. Which stage of the Creative Process includes on-the-job training?
    a. Implementation
    b. Preparation
    c. Illumination
    d. Verification

    b., Medium, Page 50

30. Which stage of the Creative Process requires one to develop a solid understanding of the problem or decision?
    a. Investigation
    b. Preparation
    c. Illumination
    d. Verification

    a., Medium, Page 51

31. Which stage of the Creative Process involves viewing the similarities and differences in the information collected?
    a. Transformation
    b. Incubation
    c. Illumination
    d. Verification

    a., Medium, Page 51

32. The ability to see the similarities and the connections among various data and events is called:
    a. Convergent thinking
    b. Divergent thinking
    c. Transformational thinking
    d. Illumination

    a., Easy, Page 51

33. The ability to see the differences among various data and events is called:
    a. Convergent thinking
    b. Divergent thinking
    c. Transformational thinking
    d. Illumination

    b., Easy, Page 51

34. _____ thinking is the ability to see similarities and _____ thinking is the ability to see differences among various data and events.
    a. Divergent; Convergent
    b. Convergent; Divergent
    c. Convergent; Transformational
    d. None of the above.

    b., Medium, Page 51

35. During the Incubation Phase of the Creative Process, the entrepreneur might do all of the following EXCEPT which one to let ideas "marinate" in his mind?
    a. Do something totally unrelated for awhile.
    b. Relax and play regularly.
    c. Work on the problem or opportunity in a different environment.
    d. Don't allow himself to daydream.

    d., Medium, Page 52

36. At which stage of the Creative Process does a spontaneous breakthrough occur, allowing all of the previous stages to come together to produce the "Eureka Factor" or the "light bulb goes on"?
    a. Implementation
    b. Preparation
    c. Illumination
    d. Verification

    c., Medium, Page 52

37. "Verification" refers to:
    a. validating the idea as accurate and useful.
    b. possibly conducting experiments, running simulations, test marketing a product or service.
    c. possibly asking questions such as "will it work?" and "is it really a better solution?"
    d. All of the above.

    d., Medium, Page 53

38. The focus of this step in the Creative Process is to transform the idea into reality.
    a. Implementation
    b. Preparation
    c. Illumination
    d. Verification

    a., Medium, Page 53

39. _____ is a process in which a small group of people interacts to produce a large quantity of imaginative ideas.
    a. Groupthink
    b. Mind-mapping
    c. Brainstorming
    d. Prototyping

    c., Easy, Page 55

40. Effective Brainstorming involves all of the following except:
    a. a small group of people
    b. an open uninhibited environment
    c. an effective method to evaluate ideas
    d. very little structure

c., Medium, Page 55

41. _____ is a graphical technique that encourages thinking on both sides of the brain, visually displays the various relationships among the ideas, and improves the ability to view a problem from many sides.
    a. Brainstorming
    b. Mind-mapping
    c. Prototyping
    d. Groupthink

b., Easy, Page 56

42. Mind-mapping is a useful tool for jump-starting creativity. It includes all of the following except:
    a. sketching a picture to symbolize the problem or area of focus in the center of a sheet of paper.
    b. writing down every idea that comes into your mind, connecting each idea to the central picture.
    c. allowing your mind to rest for a few minutes before integrating the ideas.
    d. forcing creativity when ideas start to trickle.

d., Medium, Page 56

43. The premise behind _____ is that transforming an idea into an actual model will lead to improvements in its design.
    a. Rapid Prototyping
    b. Mind-mapping
    c. Brainstorming
    d. Inventions

a., Medium, Page 56

44. The three principles (3 R's) of Rapid Prototyping are:
    a. develop a rough model, rapidly and for the right price.
    b. develop a complete model, rapidly and for the right problem.
    c. develop a rough model, rapidly and for the right problem.
    d. develop a right model, roughly, for the right price.

c., Medium, Page 56

45. Steps in the Patent Process include:
    a. establishing whether or not it is a novelty.
    b. documenting and verifying the date the idea was first conceived.
    c. searching existing patents.
    d. All of the above.

d., Medium, Page 58

46. To which governmental office must applications for patents be submitted?
    a. The U.S. Patent and Trademark Office
    b. The individual State Offices of Patent Development
    c. Both A and B are correct.
    d. None of the above.

a., Medium, Page 58

47. Any distinctive word, phrase, symbol, name or logo a firm uses to distinguish itself or its products is called a:
    a. trademark.
    b. patent.
    c. copyright.
    d. service mark.

a., Easy, Page 60

48. A _____ is an exclusive right that protects the creators of original works such as literary,
    dramatic, musical, and artistic works.
    a. Trademark
    b. Patent
    c. Copyright
    d. Service Mark

c., Easy, Page 61

49. Copyrights protect the creator of original works such as:
    a. software, choreography, and motion pictures.
    b. symbols, names and designs.
    c. Both A and B are correct.
    d. None of the above.

a., Medium, Page 61

50. Which of the following questions should you consider before entering a lawsuit to protect intellectual property?
    a. Can you afford the loss of time, money and privacy the lawsuit will bring?
    b. Can the opponent afford to pay if you win?
    c. Do you expect to get enough from the suit to pay for the costs of hiring an attorney?
    d. All of the above.

d., Medium, Page 62

True/False Questions:

51.	Creativity is the ability to apply creative solutions to problems and opportunities to enhance or enrich people's lives.

False, Easy, Page 35

52.	Innovation is the ability to develop new ideas and to discover new ways of looking at problems and opportunities.

False, Easy, Page 35

53.	Creativity is the ability to develop new ideas and to discover new ways of looking at problems and opportunities.

True, Easy, Page 35

54.	Innovation is the ability to apply creative solutions to problems and opportunities to enhance or enrich people's lives.

True, Easy, Page 35

55.	Successful entrepreneurs come up with ideas and then find ways to make them work to solve a problem or fill a need.

True, Medium, Page 35

56.	Creativity and innovation are the signature of large, entrepreneurial businesses.

False, Easy, Page 35

57.	Creativity and innovation are the signature of small, entrepreneurial businesses.

True, Easy, Page 35

58.	Although creativity sometimes involves generating something from nothing, it more likely results in elaborating on the present, putting old things together in new ways, or taking something away to create something simpler or better.

True, Medium, Page 36

59.	Innovation must be a constant process because most ideas don't work and most innovations fail.

True, Difficult, Page 36

60.	For every 3,000 new product ideas, four make it to the development stage, two are actually launched, and only one becomes successful in the market.

True, Difficult, Page 36

61. On average, new products account for 2/3 – 3/4 of companies' sales.

    False, Difficult, Page 36

62. Creativity is not only an important source for building a competitive advantage, but it also is necessary for survival.

    True, Medium, Page 37

63. History is always a reliable predictor of the future of business.

    False, Medium, Page 37

64. Entrepreneurs must embrace traditional assumptions and perspectives about how things ought to be because they support creativity.

    False, Medium, Page 37

65. A paradigm is a preconceived idea of what the world should be like.

    True, Easy, Page 37

66. Paradigms may become so deeply rooted in our minds that they become immovable blocks to creative thinking.

    True, Medium, Page 37

67. While most people see what they've always seen, entrepreneurs are able to see beyond preconceptions.

    True, Medium, Page 37

68. Successful entrepreneurs push technological and economic boundaries forward and sometimes make unconventional decisions.

    True, Medium, Page 37

69. The rapidly accelerating rate of change has created an environment in which staying in a leadership position requires constant creativity, innovation, and entrepreneurship.

    True, Medium, Page 38

70. Research shows that not everyone can be creative.

    False, Medium, Page 38

71. Businesses typically foster an environment that encourages creativity.

    False, Difficult, Page 38

72.   Research shows that each hemisphere of the human brain processes information differently and that one side of the brain tends to be dominant over the other.

True, Easy, Page 39

73.   The left brain is guided by linear, vertical thinking.

True, Easy, Page 39

74.   The right brain is guided by linear, vertical thinking.

False, Easy, Page 39

75.   The left-brain relies on kaleidoscopic, lateral thinking.

False, Easy, Page 39

76.   The right brain relies on kaleidoscopic, lateral thinking.

True, Easy, Page 39

77.   The left brain handles language, logic, and symbols.

True, Easy, Page 39

78.   The right brain takes care of the body's emotional, intuitive, and spatial functions.

True, Easy, Page 39

79.   The right brain processes information intuitively—all at once, relying heavily on images.

True, Easy, Page 39

80.   The left brain processes information in a step-by-step fashion.

True, Easy, Page 39

81.   The left brain processes information intuitively—all at once, relying heavily on images.

False, Easy, Page 39

82.   The right brain processes information in a step-by-step fashion.

False, Easy, Page 39

83.   Right-brained individuals tend to challenge tradition, custom, and routine.

True, Medium, Page 39

84. Left-brained individuals realize that there may be more than one right answer.

     False, Medium, Page 39

85. Entrepreneurship requires both left and right-brained thinking.

     True, Easy, Page 40

86. Right-brain thinking draws on the power of divergent reasoning, which is the ability to create a multitude of original, diverse ideas, while left-brain thinking counts on convergent reasoning, the ability to evaluate multiple ideas and choose the best solution to a given problem.

     True, Difficult, Page 40

87. Entrepreneurs need to rely on left-brain thinking to generate innovative product, service, or business ideas and use right-brain thinking to judge the market potential of the ideas they generate.

     False, Difficult, Page 40

88. Intuition is based on the accumulated knowledge and experiences a person encounters over the course of a lifetime and resides in the subconscious.

     True, Easy, Page 43

89. "Constantly Being Practical" is a mental block that can stifle creativity.

     True, Medium, Page 43

90. Viewing play as frivolous is a mental block, which stifles creativity.

     True, Medium, Page 43

91. Ambiguity tends to destroy creativity.

     False, Difficult, Page 44

92. Failure is an important part of the creative process, as it provides a chance to learn how to succeed.

     True, Medium, Page 45

93. Employees tend to rise—or fall—to the level of expectations entrepreneurs have of them.

     True, Medium, Page 45

94. Hiring a diverse work force makes it more difficult to achieve creativity in the workplace.

     False, Medium, Page 45

95. Entrepreneurs can encourage creative thinking in their employees by setting examples of creative behavior and rewarding creative behavior when exhibited by their employees.

    True, Medium, Page 47

96. "Divergent Thinking" is the ability to see similarities and connections among various data and events.

    False, Easy, Page 51

97. "Convergent Thinking" is the ability to see the differences among data and events.

    False, Easy, Page 51

98. It may appear in the Incubation Stage of the Creative Process that the entrepreneur is loafing, as he is taking time to reflect on the information collected.

    True, Medium, Page 52

99. The Illumination Stage of the Creative Process is often called the "Eureka Factor" and is characterized by a spontaneous breakthrough.

    True, Medium, Page 52

100. The typical entrepreneurial philosophy is "Ready, aim, aim, aim…"

    False, Medium, Page 53

101. When "Brainstorming," individuals should be encouraged to use "idea hitchhiking," or building new ideas on those already suggested.

    True, Medium, Page 56

102. During a brainstorming session, company rank and department affiliates are irrelevant.

    True, Medium, Page 55

103. Mind mapping is a graphical technique that encourages thinking on both sides of the brain, visually displays the various relationships among ideas, and improves the ability to view a problem from many sides.

    True, Medium, Page 56

104. Rapid prototyping, transforming an idea into an actual model, typically does not lead to improvements in design.

    False, Medium, Page 56

105. A patent gives the inventor the exclusive right to make, use, or sell an invention for 50 years.

    False, Medium, Page 58

106. One study reports that for the typical small business, obtaining a patent and maintaining it for 20 years costs about $10,000.

    True, Difficult, Page 58

107. Trademarks are distinctive words, symbols, designs, names, or logos used for company identification.

    True, Easy, Page 60

108. A patent protects the creator of original works of authorship such as for software.

    False, Medium, Page 60

109. The U.S. Copyright Office does not require registering the creative work because registering it does not give creators greater protection over their work.

    False, Medium, Page 61

110. The major problem with relying on the legal system to enforce ownership rights is the cost of infringement lawsuits, which can quickly exceed the budget of most small businesses.

    True, Medium, Page 62

<u>Essay Questions:</u>

111. What is the entrepreneurial "secret" for creating value in the marketplace?

    Creativity and Innovation should be used in combination to allow the entrepreneur to solve real world problems and to exploit opportunities and the profits that come with them. Creativity should always be directed and complement the business plan.
    Creativity is the ability to develop new ideas and to discover new ways of looking at problems and to exploit opportunities that people face everyday. Innovation is the ability to apply creative solutions to those problems and opportunities to enhance and enrich people's lives.
    Page 35

112. Explain the differences between the left and right sides of the brain.

    The left brain is guided by linear, vertical thinking, whereas the right brain relies on kaleidoscopic, lateral thinking. The left brain handles language, logic, and symbols, whereas the right brain takes care of the body's emotional, intuitive, and spatial functions. The left brain processes information in a step-by-step fashion, whereas the right brain processes it intuitively—all at once, relying heavily on images. Left-brained vertical

thinking is narrowly focused and systematic, whereas right-brained lateral thinking is somewhat unconventional, unsystematic, and unstructured.
Page 39

113. List five of the "mental locks" that limit individual creativity.

    The five should come from the following list:
    - Search for the one "right" answer.
    - Focus on "being logical."
    - Blindly follow the rules.
    - Constantly be practical.
    - View play as frivolous.
    - Become overly specialized.
    - Avoid ambiguity.
    - Fear looking foolish.
    - Fear mistakes and failure.
    - Believe that "I'm not creative."

    Page 42

114. List five ways entrepreneurs can stimulate their own creativity and encourage it among workers.

    The five should come from the following list:
    - Expect creativity.
    - Embrace diversity.
    - Expect and tolerate failure.
    - Encourage curiosity.
    - View problems as challenges.
    - Provide creativity training.
    - Provide support.
    - Reward creativity.
    - Model creative behavior.

    Page 45

115. List five ways individuals can enhance their own creativity.

    The five should come from the following list:
    - Allow yourself to be creative.
    - Give your mind fresh input every day.
    - Recognize the creative power of mistakes.
    - Keep a journal handy to record your thoughts and ideas.
    - Listen to other people.
    - Read books on stimulating creativity or take a class on creativity.
    - Talk to a child.
    - Keep a toy box in your office.
    - Take some time off.

    Page 48

116. List and briefly explain the seven steps in the Creative Process.

    a. Preparation – Get your mind ready for creative thinking through formal education, OJT, work experience, etc. This helps to build creativity and innovation.

    b. Investigation – Develop a solid understanding of the problem or decision.

    c. Transformation – View the similarities and differences in the information collected.

    d. Incubation – Take time to reflect on the information collected.

    e. Illumination – A spontaneous breakthrough occurs, causing the "light bulb to go on." All of the previous stages come together to produce the "Eureka factor."

    f. Verification – Validate the idea as accurate and useful. May include conducting experiments, running simulations, test marketing a product or service, etc., to verify that the new idea will work and is practical.

    g. Implementation – Transform the idea into reality.

Page 50

117. Explain "brainstorming" and list at least five of the guidelines for a successful brainstorming session.

Brainstorming is a process in which a small group of people interact with very little structure with the goal of producing a large quantity of novel and imaginative ideas. The goal is to create an open, uninhibited atmosphere that allows member of the group to "freewheel" ideas. Five guidelines should come from the following list:

- Keep the group small—five to eight members.
- Have a well-defined problem for the group to address, but don't reveal it ahead of time.
- Limit the session to 40-60 minutes.
- Appoint someone to be the recorder and write every idea on a flip chart.
- Use a seating pattern that encourages communication and interaction.
- Encourage all ideas from the team, even wild and extreme ones.
- Establish a goal of quantity of ideas rather than quality.
- Forbid evaluation or criticism of any idea during the session.
- Encourage participants to use "idea hitchhiking" or to "piggyback"/build new ideas on those already suggested.

Page 55

118. Why is it important for an entrepreneur to use techniques like Mind-mapping, which use both sides of the brain?

Mind-mapping, a graphical technique that encourages thinking on both sides of the brain, visually displays the various relationships among ideas, and improves the ability to view a problem from many sides. Since entrepreneurs themselves tend to be left or right-brained thinkers, techniques like Mind-mapping encourage them to look at problems and opportunities in a different way. Mind-mapping is also a useful tool that includes: sketching a picture symbolizing the problem, connecting each idea to the central picture or words with a line, and allowing your mind to rest for a few minutes before beginning to integrate the ideas.

Page 56

119. List the steps an entrepreneur should follow in order to enhance his/her chances of receiving a patent.

    a. Establish the invention's novelty.
    b. Document the device.
    c. Search existing patents.
    d. Study search results.
    e. Submit the patent application.
    f. Prosecute the patent application.

Page 58

Chapter 2
The Challenges of Entrepreneurship
Mini-Case

Case 2-1: Protecting Your Intellectual Property

Devo, Anthony, and Spencer were childhood friends who had always talked about starting a business together after college graduation. Devo had the financial background and startup capital to contribute and Spencer and Anthony had the technical knowledge they believed would give them the competitive advantage needed to become an industry leader.

During their early college years Anthony and Spencer developed a new and innovative way to manufacture computer components. When they shared their idea with Devo, he was able to draw up a detailed business plan to present to potential investors when the three were ready to launch their venture. They had been very careful not to disclose anything about their innovative idea to other colleagues or any of their friends and were anxious to get started.

After selecting the company name "Millennium Computers" the three friends come to you for advice on intellectual property rights.

Questions

120. To protect their innovative process for manufacturing computer components from unauthorized use, which type of intellectual property should the threesome apply for? Identify the office to which they should apply and outline the steps involved in the process.

- They should apply for a patent through the Patents and Trademark Office (PTO). To receive a patent, the inventor must follow these steps:
  - Establish the invention's novelty
  - Document the device or process
  - Search existing patents
  - Study search results
  - Submit the patent application
  - Prosecute the patent application

121. Should they consider protecting or registering their company name? Which intellectual property would cover this concern? Could they use the name without registering it?

Entrepreneurs do not have to register trademarks to establish their rights to use those marks; however, registering a mark with the (PTO) does give entrepreneurs greater power in protecting their marks.

122. Since the primary weapon to protect intellectual property is the legal system, what would you advise the friends if they have to protect intellectual property sometime in the future by threatening a lawsuit?

The major problem with relying on the legal system to enforce ownership rights is the cost of infringement lawsuits, which can quickly exceed the budget of most small firms. Before bringing a lawsuit, the entrepreneurs must consider the following issues:
- Can the opponent afford to pay them if they win?

- Will they expect to get enough from the suit to cover the costs of hiring an attorney and preparing a case?
- Can they afford the loss of time, money and privacy from the ensuing lawsuit?

Chapter 3   Strategic Management and The Entrepreneur

Multiple Choice Questions:

1. Which of the following is NOT one of the three components of intellectual capital?
    a. human
    b. structural
    c. competitor
    d. customer

    c., Medium, Page 68

2. _____ involves developing a game plan to guide a company as it strives to accomplish its mission, goals, and objectives to keep it on its desired course.
    a. Competitive advantage
    b. Mission
    c. Strategic management
    d. Market segmentation

    c., Easy, Page 69

3. The aggregation of factors that sets a company apart from its competitors and gives it a unique position in the market superior to its competition is its:
    a. mission statement.
    b. competitive advantage.
    c. competitive profile.
    d. strategic plan.

    b., Easy, Page 69

4. A strategic plan:
    a. serves as a blueprint for helping business owners to match their companies' strengths and weaknesses to the environment's opportunities and threats.
    b. is a company's game plan, helping it to accomplish its mission, goals, and objectives.
    c. is crucial to creating a company's competitive advantage that sets it apart from its competition and gives it a unique position in the market.
    d. All of the above.

    d., Medium, Page 69

5. Which of the following was NOT identified as a way for the typical small business to establish a competitive advantage?
    a. Lowering prices
    b. Providing higher quality goods or services
    c. Improving customer service
    d. Doing whatever the company does for its customers better than its competitors

    a., Medium, Page 69

6. _____ are a unique set of capabilities that a company develops in key operational areas (e.g., quality, service, innovation, and others) that allow it to vault past its competitors.
    a. Core competencies
    b. Opportunities
    c. Key success factors
    d. Mission statements

    a., Medium, Page 69

7. The relationship between core competencies and competitive advantage is best described by which statement?
    a. Strengthening a company's competitive advantage strengthens its core competencies.
    b. A company's core competencies become the nucleus of its competitive advantage.
    c. As a company's core competencies become stronger, its competitive advantage becomes weaker.
    d. There is no relationship between core competencies and competitive advantage.

    b., Difficult, Page 69

8. Which of the following is NOT a characteristic of the strategic management procedure for a small company?
    a. It should use a relatively short planning horizon—two years or less, typically.
    b. It should begin with an extensive objective-setting session.
    c. It should encourage the participation of employees and even outsiders to improve the reliability and creativity of the resulting plan.
    d. It should allow for flexibility and not be overly structured.

    b., Medium, Page 71

9. A clearly defined vision helps a company in which of the following ways?
    a. Provides direction
    b. Determines decisions
    c. Motivates people
    d. All of the above.

    d., Easy, Page 71

10. A small company's mission statement:
    a. establishes its purpose in writing.
    b. gives the business and everyone in it a sense of direction.
    c. defines what the company is, why it exists, and its reason for being.
    d. All of the above.

    d., Easy, Page 72

11. When developing a company's mission statement, an entrepreneur should remember to:
    a. write the statement alone without anyone else's interference.
    b. omit statements about her values because they may turn some stakeholders off.
    c. keep it short and simple.
    d. All of the above.

    c., Difficult, Page 74

12. _____ are positive internal factors that contribute toward accomplishing the company's mission, goals, and objectives, while _____ are negative internal factors that inhibit the accomplishment of a firm's mission, goals, and objectives.
    a. Strengths; Weaknesses
    b. Weaknesses; Strengths
    c. Opportunities; Threats
    d. Threats; Opportunities

    a., Easy, Page 75

13. Kevin Abt noticed that people were cooking meals in their homes less often but wanted to avoid the hassle of going out to eat. They wanted to "eat in" without cooking. Abt launched a company, Takeout Taxi, that delivers restaurant-prepared food to his customers' homes and businesses. Takeout Taxi is the result of a(n):
    a. strength.
    b. weakness.
    c. opportunity.
    d. threat.

    c., Medium, Page 75

14. Maria Sanchez is the owner of the Main Street Cafe. A new restaurant opens a few blocks away. To Maria, this new restaurant constitutes a(n):
    a. strength.
    b. weakness.
    c. threat.
    d. opportunity.

    c., Medium, Page 76

15. _____ are positive external factors a firm could exploit to accomplish its objectives, while _____ are negative external forces that inhibit a firm's ability to achieve its mission, goals, and objectives.
    a. Strengths; Weaknesses
    b. Weaknesses; Strengths
    c. Opportunities; Threats
    d. Threats; Opportunities

    c., Medium, Page 76

16. Every business is characterized by a set of controllable variables that determines the relative success (or lack of it) of market participants called:
    a. distinctive competencies.
    b. key success factors.
    c. opportunities and threats.
    d. competitive edge.

    b., Easy, Page 77

17. Your _____ competitors offer the same products and services, and customers often compare prices, features, and deals from these competitors as they shop.
    a. significant
    b. direct
    c. indirect
    d. All of the above.

    b., Easy, Page 79

18. Which of the following is an effective method of collecting information about competitors?
    a. Ask customers and suppliers what competitors are doing.
    b. Talk to employees, especially sales representatives and purchasing agents, about competitors.
    c. Attend trade shows and collect competitors' sales literature.
    d. All of the above

    d., Easy, Page 80

19. Which of the following is NOT a recommended method of collecting competitive intelligence?
    a. Attend trade shows and collect competitors' sales literature.
    b. Buy competitors' products or services and assess their quality and features, benchmarking their products and services against yours.
    c. Pay competitors' employees to become informants about their companies' strategies, markets, and trade secrets.
    d. Watch for employment ads from competitors to determine the types of workers they are hiring.

    c., Medium, Page 80

20. Which of the following is true about the information-gathering process in competitive analysis?
    a. It is an expensive process which only large companies can afford.
    b. It can be relatively inexpensive and easy for the small business owner to conduct.
    c. It is a process closely regulated by various federal laws which prohibit doing things like purchasing competitive products and analyzing them.
    d. It is a process that requires expert help and is relatively expensive.

    b., Difficult, Page 80

21. Purchasing rival companies' products, taking them apart, and analyzing them is:
    a. called industrial espionage.
    b. considered illegal due to federal regulation.
    c. benchmarking.
    d. cataloging.

c., Easy, Page 80

For Questions 22-26, consider the following competitive profile matrix:

Key Success Factors	Weight	Your Business		Competitor 1		Competitor 2	
		Rating	Weighted Score	Rating	Weighted Score	Rating	Weighted Score
Quality	.35	4	1.40	2	.70	1	.35
Service	.20	4	.80	2	.40	2	.40
Convenience	.15	2	.30	4	.60	1	.15
On-Time Delivery	.20	2	.40	4	.80	2	.40
Location	.10	3	.30	1	.10	2	.20
TOTAL	1.00		3.20		2.60		1.50

22. Which of the following statements is TRUE?
    a. Overall, Competitor 2 is the strongest of these three companies.
    b. Your company's most serious weakness is its poor quality.
    c. Your company's most vulnerable point against these two competitors is in the area of on-time delivery.
    d. The most important of the key success factors is location.

c., Medium, Page 81

23. Which company has the **strongest** competitive position?
    a. Your company
    b. Competitor 1
    c. Competitor 2
    d. Impossible to tell from the information given

a., Medium, Page 81

24. Which company has the **worst** location?
    a. Your company
    b. Competitor 1
    c. Competitor 2
    d. Impossible to tell from the information given

b., Medium, Page 81

25. In terms of quality, which company has the **weakest** competitive position?
    a. Your company
    b. Competitor 1
    c. Competitor 2
    d. Impossible to tell from the information given

    c., Medium, Page 81

26. Which key success factor does the entrepreneur who built this table believe is most important?
    a. Quality
    b. Service and on-time delivery
    c. Convenience
    d. Location

    a., Medium, Page 81

27. A competitive profile matrix:
    a. identifies a firm's core competencies.
    b. permits the small business owner to divide a mass market into smaller, more manageable segments.
    c. allows the small business owner to evaluate her firm against competitors on the key success factors for the industry.
    d. creates a road map of action for the entrepreneur in order to fulfill her company's mission, goals, and objectives.

    c., Difficult, Page 81

28. _____ are the broad, long range attributes the small business seeks to accomplish; _____ are the more specific targets for performance.
    a. Goals; objectives
    b. Goals; strategies
    c. Objectives; goals
    d. Strategies; goals

    a., Easy, Page 83

29. Which of the following is NOT a characteristic of a well-written objective?
    a. Realistic, yet challenging
    b. Measurable
    c. General
    d. Timely

    c., Medium, Page 83

30. The focal point of any company's strategy, whatever it may be, should be:
    a. its product or service.
    b. its competition.
    c. its customers.
    d. its strengths and weaknesses.

    c., Medium, Page 83

31. A _____ is a road map of the tactics and actions an entrepreneur draws up to fulfill the company's mission, goals, and objectives.
    a. mission
    b. strategy
    c. competitive edge
    d. core competency

    b., Easy, Page 83

32. _____ spell(s) out the "ends" an organization is to achieve; _____ define(s) the "means" for achieving the ends.
    a. Mission, goals, and objectives; strategy
    b. Key success factors; strategy
    c. Strategy; mission, goals, and objectives
    d. Strategy; vision

    a., Medium, Page 83

33. The relationship between a company's mission, goals, and objectives and its strategy is best described by which of the following statements?
    a. Developing a company's strategy lays the groundwork for creating its mission, goals, and objectives.
    b. The mission, goals, and objectives spell out the ends the company wants to achieve, and the strategy defines the means for reaching them.
    c. Although managers must change a company's mission, goals, and objectives as competitive conditions change, they should avoid adjusting the company's strategy to prevent the company from losing its focus and momentum.
    d. There is no real link between a company's mission, goals, and objectives and its strategy.

    b., Difficult, Page 83

34. A strategy should:
    a. be comprehensive and well integrated.
    b. focus on establishing for the firm the key success factors in the industry.
    c. identify how the firm will accomplish its mission, goals, and objectives.
    d. All of the above.

    d., Medium, Page 85

35.	A cost-leadership strategy works well when:
	a.	buyers are sensitive to price changes.
	b.	competing firms sell the same commodity products.
	c.	a company can reap savings from economies of scale.
	d.	All of the above.

	d., Medium, Page 85

36.	Small firms pursuing a cost-leadership strategy have an advantage in reaching customers whose primary purchase criterion is:
	a.	quality.
	b.	constant innovation.
	c.	price.
	d.	customer service.

	c., Easy, Page 85

37.	Which of the following statements concerning a cost-leadership strategy is **true**?
	a.	Companies pursuing this strategy concentrate on a niche within the overall market.
	b.	A cost-leadership strategy is built on differences among market segments.
	c.	A cost-leadership strategy works best when buyers' primary purchase criterion is price.
	d.	All of the above.

	c., Medium, Page 85

38.	The principle behind a _____ strategy is to select one or more market segments, identify customers' special needs, and approach them with a good or service designed to excel in meeting these needs.
	a.	cost-leadership
	b.	differentiation
	c.	focus
	d.	concentration

	c., Easy, Page 86

39.	Cost-leadership may have which of the following inherent dangers?
	a.	What is chosen to distinguish the product does not boost its performance.
	b.	An overfocus on the physical characteristics of the product.
	c.	The identified niche is not large enough to be profitable.
	d.	An overemphasis on costs to the elimination of other strategies.

	d., Difficult, Page 86

40. Which of the following statements concerning a differentiation strategy is **true**?
    a. A differentiation strategy seeks to build customer loyalty by positioning goods or services in a unique fashion.
    b. A differentiation strategy is built on a company's core competence.
    c. A differentiation strategy must create the perception of value in the customer's eyes.
    d. All of the above

d., Medium, Page 86

41. A small company following a _____ strategy seeks to build customer loyalty by positioning its goods and services in a unique fashion.
    a. differentiation
    b. cost-leadership
    c. focus
    d. niche

a., Easy, Page 86

42. A company that offers superior product quality, extra customer service, and fast delivery times is pursuing a:
    a. cost-leadership strategy.
    b. differentiation strategy.
    c. concentration strategy.
    d. strategic alliance.

b., Medium, Page 86

43. Which of the following is a danger in choosing a differentiation strategy?
    a. Focusing only on physical characteristics of a product or service and ignoring important psychological factors, such as status, prestige, image, and customer service.
    b. Choosing a market that is not large enough to be profitable.
    c. Misunderstanding the firm's true cost drivers.
    d. All of the above.

a., Difficult, Page 87

44. Shere Vincente operates a travel service that specializes in arranging trips for women, giving special attention to their needs and preferences, from security and comfort to activities and events designed to appeal to her target customers. Vincente is pursuing a _____ strategy.
    a. cost-leadership
    b. differentiation
    c. focus
    d. positioning

c., Medium, Page 88

45. Rather than attempting to serve the total market, the small firm pursuing a _____ strategy specializes in serving a specific target segment.
    a. cost-leadership
    b. differentiation
    c. focus
    d. head-to-head

c., Medium, Page 88

46. Small companies must develop strategies that exploit all of the competitive advantages of their size by:
    a. responding quickly to customers' needs.
    b. remaining flexible and willing to change.
    c. constantly innovating.
    d. All of the above.

d., Easy, Page 89

47. In order for the control process to work, the business owner must:
    a. make as few changes and modifications in the operational plans as possible.
    b. concentrate on competitive information.
    c. identify and track key performance indicators.
    d. maintain control and delegate as little authority and responsibility as possible.

c., Medium, Page 91

48. Which of the following is NOT one of the four important perspectives a balanced scorecard should look at a business from?
    a. Competitor perspective
    b. Internal business perspective
    c. Innovation and learning perspective
    d. Financial perspective

a., Difficult, Page 92

49. Skatell's, a small jewelry store with three locations, designs and manufactures much of its own jewelry while its competitors (many of them large department stores) sell standard, "off-the-shelf" jewelry. As a result, many customers see Skatell's as the place to go for unique pieces of jewelry. Skatell's reputation for selling unique and custom-designed jewelry is a(n):
    a. strength.
    b. weakness.
    c. opportunity.
    d. threat.

a., Medium, Page 74

50. Refer to the previous question. Skatell's business strategy would best be described as:
    a. low-cost.
    b. differentiation.
    c. focus.
    d. generic.

    b., Medium, Page 86

True/False Questions:

51. With the growth of the World Wide Web, globalization, and increased competition, the business environment has become more turbulent and challenging to business owners.

    True, Easy, Page 68

52. One of the biggest changes entrepreneurs face is the shift in the economy from a base of financial to intellectual capital.

    True, Medium, Page 68

53. The three components of intellectual capital are human, structural, and customer.

    True, Medium, Page 68

54. Narrower product lines, smaller customer bases and more limited geographic areas give small companies a natural advantage over large businesses when preparing a strategic plan.

    True, Medium, Page 68

55. The most effective way for a small business to establish a competitive advantage is by offering lower prices.

    False, Easy, Page 69

56. Small companies' core competencies are often the result of benefits such as agility, speed, closeness to customers, superior service, and innovative ability—all of which are size advantages that allow them to do things that their larger competitors cannot.

    True, Medium, Page 69

57. Although developing a strategic plan is important for large companies, it is not essential to managing a small company successfully because of its limited resources.

    False, Easy, Page 70

58. Large companies have a natural advantage over small firms when it comes to preparing a strategic plan.

     False, Medium, Page 70

59. The ideal strategic planning process for a small company should start with setting objectives.

     False, Medium, Page 71

60. The ideal strategic planning procedure for a small company should be formal and highly structured.

     False, Medium, Page 71

61. Ideally, strategic planning is not an outcome but an ongoing process.

     True, Easy, Page 71

62. The most effective way to communicate the values of a company to everyone it touches is to formulate an effective mission statement.

     True, Medium, Page 72

63. The mission statement addresses the first question of any business venture: "What business am I in?

     True, Easy, Page 72

64. A company's mission statement defines what it stands for, why it exists, and its reason for being.

     True, Easy, Page 72

65. As business and competitive conditions change, so should a small company's mission statement.

     True, Medium, Page 74

66. A company's mission statement should be lengthy and use fancy jargon to impress outsiders.

     False, Medium, Page 74

67. Strengths are positive internal factors that contribute towards accomplishing the company's mission, goals, and objectives.

     True, Easy, Page 74

68. Conducting a SWOT analysis for her own business and for her key competitors allows an entrepreneur to gain a competitive edge by matching her company's strengths against her competitors' weaknesses.

True, Easy, Page 74

69. To be effective, the small business owner should limit strategic analysis to only the two or three most significant opportunities facing the firm.

True, Medium, Page 75

70. Weaknesses are negative external forces that inhibit the firm's ability to achieve its mission, goals, and objectives.

False, Easy, Page 75

71. After a company's strengths and weaknesses are assessed, the strategic planning process should identify opportunities and threats facing the company and should isolate the key factors for success in business.

True, Medium, Page 75

72. Threats are negative external forces that inhibit a company's ability to achieve its mission, goals, and objectives.

True, Easy, Page 76

73. "Big Box Retailers" present an opportunity for many small business owners.

False, Medium, Page 76

74. A firm's strategy must focus on establishing for the firm the key success factors the entrepreneur has identified for the industry.

True, Medium, Page 77

75. A small business owner can collect a great deal of information about competitors through a number of low-cost competitive intelligence methods.

True, Easy, Page 80

76. Significant competitors are those that offer the same products and services your company offers, and customers often compare prices, features, and deals from these competitors as they shop.

False, Medium, Page 80

77. Conducting successful competitive intelligence on rivals' strategies and actions may include researching their websites, buying their products to assess their quality, and watching for employment ads to determine the type of employees they are hiring.

True, Easy, Page 80

78. Experts estimate that 70 to 90 percent of the competitive information a company needs already resides with employees who collect it in their daily dealings with suppliers, customers, and other industry contacts.

True, Difficult, Page 80

79. Performing competitive intelligence on rivals' strategies and actions does NOT mean that entrepreneurs must engage in unethical or illegal espionage activities.

True, Medium, Page 80

80. It is unwise for entrepreneurs to monitor competitors' strategies and actions because such activities require them to engage in illegal or unethical behavior.

False, Medium, Page 80

81. One of the goals of competitive analysis is to improve a firm's reaction time to competitor's actions.

True, Medium, Page 80

82. A competitor analysis should include an analysis of direct competitors as well as significant and indirect competitors.

True, Medium, Page 80

83. A competitive profile matrix analyzes how well a company and its rivals match the key success factors in the industry.

True, Medium, Page 81

84. "Improving the company's cash flow" is a good example of an effective objective.

False, Difficult, Page 83

85. The strategic planning process works best when employees are actively involved with managers in setting company goals and objectives.

True, Easy, Page 83

86. Setting seemingly impossible objectives, those outside of the likely reach of employees, helps managers to create and maintain a high motivation level.

    False, Medium, Page 83

87. "Increasing our market share from 8 percent to 10 percent by the end of the current fiscal year" is a good example of an effective objective.

    True, Medium, Page 83

88. Goals and objectives provide targets to aim for and a basis for evaluating a company's performance.

    True, Easy, Page 83

89. Objectives should be as general as possible to permit flexibility in the business.

    False, Medium, Page 83

90. Goals are the broad, long-range attributes that a business seeks to accomplish; objectives are more specific targets of performance.

    True, Easy, Page 83

91. A company's strategy spells out the ends the business wants to achieve, and its mission, goals, and objectives define the means for reaching them.

    False, Medium, Page 83

92. Before an entrepreneur can build a successful strategy, she must establish a clear mission, goals, and objectives in order to have appropriate targets at which to aim her strategy.

    True, Medium, Page 83

93. A strategy is a road map of action for fulfilling a firm's mission, goals, and objectives.

    True, Easy, Page 83

94. A company pursuing a cost-leadership strategy strives to be the lowest-cost producer relative to its competitors in the industry.

    True, Easy, Page 85

95. Small firms pursuing a cost-leadership strategy have an advantage in reaching customers whose primary purchase criterion is high quality.

    False, Medium, Page 85

96. A danger of cost-leadership is that a company may misunderstand what processes actually drive its true costs.

True, Medium, Page 85

97. The best way to build a cost-leadership competitive advantage is to focus entirely on manufacturing costs.

False, Easy, Page 85

98. One key to building a successful differentiation strategy is to be better than competitors at some characteristic that customers value.

True, Easy, Page 86

99. To be successful, a differentiation strategy must create the perception of value in the customer's eyes.

True, Medium, Page 86

100. One danger in choosing a differentiation strategy is trying to differentiate on the basis of something that the customer does not perceive as valuable.

True, Medium, Page 86

101. The key to a successful differentiation strategy is to build it on a core competency, something the company is uniquely good at doing in comparison to its competitors.

True, Easy, Page 86

102. A differentiation strategy frequently allows the company the opportunity to charge a higher price for its products or services.

True, Medium, Page 86

103. The focal point of the entire strategic plan and the competitive strategy chosen should be the customer.

True, Easy, Page 87

104. A small business following a focus strategy attempts to serve its narrow target markets more effectively and efficiently than competitors trying to appeal to the broad market.

True, Medium, Page 88

105. A focus strategy recognizes that not all markets are homogenous.

True, Medium, Page 88

106. Focus strategies build on differences among market segments.

     True, Medium, Page 88

107. The secret to good control is identifying and tracking key performance indicators.

     True, Medium, Page 91

108. To evaluate the effectiveness of their strategies, some companies are developing balanced score cards, a set of measurements unique to a company that includes both financial and operational measures and gives managers a quick, comprehensive picture of the company's total performance.

     True, Medium, Page 91

109. When creating a balanced scorecard for his or her company, an entrepreneur should establish goals for each critical indicator of company performance and create meaningful measures for each one.

     True, Medium, Page 91

110. A balanced scorecard should look at a business from four important perspectives: competitor, internal, innovation and learning, and financial.

     False, Difficult, Page 91

Essay Questions:

111. Assume that you are a consultant to a small independent hardware store in a town where a retail giant such as Wal-Mart, K-mart or Target is about to open. The large retailer sells many of the same items the small hardware store sells, but at lower prices. What advice would you offer the owner concerning the hardware store's strategy? Explain.

     To compete successfully against a larger competitor, the small business owner must develop a true competitive advantage and utilize those core competencies that set the small business apart from the giant conglomerates like Wal-Mart.

     Through the strategic management process, a concise plan could be developed. The typical small business has fewer product lines, a better-defined customer base and a specific geographical area. Valuable information can be obtained through close customer contacts and a more flexible approach to meeting customer needs.
     Page 69

112. What is strategic management? What role does a strategic plan play in a small company?

     Strategic management involves developing a game plan to guide a company as it strives to accomplish its vision, mission, goals and objectives and to keep it from straying off its desired course.

It gives owners a blueprint for matching their companies' strengths and weaknesses to the opportunities and threats in the environment.
Page 69

113. What advice would you offer an entrepreneur on how to create a mission statement for his or her company?

   Tips for writing a powerful mission statement include:
   Keep it short
   Keep it simple
   Get everyone in the company involved
   Keep it current
   Reflect your values and beliefs
   Reflect concern for future
   Keep tone positive and upbeat; use it to lay ethical foundation for company.
   Look at other companies' mission statements; make sure it's appropriate for company culture.
   Use it.
   Page 72

114. Define each of the following terms and give an example of each: strengths, weaknesses, opportunities, and threats.

   Strengths are positive internal factors that a company can use to accomplish its mission, goals and objectives
   (ex)
   special skills or knowledge
   positive public image
   experienced sales force

   Weaknesses are negative internal factors that inhibit the accomplishment of a company's mission, goals and objectives.
   (ex)
   lack of capital
   shortage of skilled labor
   inferior location

   Opportunities are positive external options that a firm can exploit to accomplish its mission, goals and objectives.
   (ex)
   proprietary technology
   emergence of potentially new target market(s)
   lower interest rates

   Threats are negative external forces that inhibit a company's ability to achieve its mission, goals and objectives
   (ex)
   new competitors

adverse legislation
economic recession
Page 74

115. Assume you own a small shoe store. Discuss the three different types of competition you might face and give examples of each.

    Direct competitors offer the same products and services, and customers often compare prices, features, and deals from these competitors as they shop. Other shoe stores would be direct competitors. Significant competitors offer some of the same products and services. Although their product or service lines may be somewhat different, there is competition with them in several key areas. Department stores and athletic stores would be examples of significant competitors. Indirect competitors offer the same or similar products or services only in a small number of areas, but their target customers seldom overlap yours. Discount stores and thrift stores may be examples of indirect competitors.
    Page 79

116. Assume you own a small print shop. Why is it important for you to monitor your competitors' activities? Describe at least five techniques you might use to monitor competitors' strategies and actions ethically and inexpensively.

    A recent survey identified the greatest small business challenge as competition. Other studies suggest that keeping tabs on rivals' movements through competitive intelligence programs is vital to strategic activity and survival.

    Specific techniques you might use include:

    Reading industry trade publications
    Asking customers and suppliers
    Talking to employees
    Attending trade shows
    Buying competitors products (benchmarking)
    Obtaining credit reports
    Checking library resources
    Using World Wide Web
    Visiting competing businesses
    Watching for employment ads from competitors
    Conducting patent searches for patents filed by competitors
    Page 80

117. What is strategy? Describe the three basic strategies small companies can choose from: cost-leadership, differentiation, and focus. Explain the conditions under which each works, its benefits, and its pitfalls.

    Strategy is a road map of the actions an entrepreneur draws up to a company's missions, goals and objectives. It is a master plan that covers all of the major organizational parts and ties them together.

    Cost leadership: strives to be the lowest cost producer.

Best when primary purchase criterion is price, and the power to set industry's floor price and economies of scale are available. Disadvantage is if cost drivers are unknown or other strategies are overlooked.

Differentiation: seeks to build customer loyalty by positioning its product/service in a unique different fashion.

Best when differentiation is in the form of a "true benefit" to the customer. Disadvantage is trying to differentiate on the basis of something that does not boost performance or lower cost.

Focus: select one or more customer(s)/market(s) to create a niche.

Best when creating real value for customer by differentiation or low cost in a narrow target segment.
Disadvantages include not being able to capture enough of a market share to be profitable.
Page 83

118. Assume you own a small camera shop that sells and repairs cameras and equipment. Discuss some of the methods you might select to allow you to successfully compete against the many large retailers that are nearby.

In most cases, small business owners will not be able to select a cost leadership strategy to meet the larger competitors who have a size advantage over them. Therefore, this small business owner will probably have a greater chance of success utilizing a focus and/or differentiation strategy.

He might use a focus strategy by concentrating on a specific market segment, identifying those consumers' special needs, wants, and interests, and approaching them with a mix of product offerings that excel in meeting those needs, wants, and interests.

He might use a differentiation strategy that would seek to build customer loyalty by positioning his goods and services in a unique or different way than the competition. For example, he may offer superior customer service, special product features, complete product lines, instantaneous parts availability, absolute product reliability, supreme product quality, and extensive product knowledge. He might also offer on-site repair of camera equipment.
Page 85

Chapter 3
Strategic Management and The Entrepreneur
Mini-Case

Case 3-1: Finding a Competitive Advantage

Copreneurs Ed and Yolanda recently opened a vintage used car lot called Cherry Lane. They sell antique and collectible cars on consignment for the owners at a fee of 30 percent of the selling price. The price is further reduced by 10% if a particular car is not sold within the first 30 days. One of the first customers convinced Yolanda that this was the only fair thing to do, and in an effort to provide something for "the cost conscious buyer," she provided what she thought was excellent customer service and implemented the idea.

Ed and Yolanda feel Cherry Lane has an ideal location. It is located adjacent to the city's baseball stadium, alongside the freeway in the center of all the other car dealerships. Although Cherry Lane has significant foot traffic, most people never make offers to buy.

In an effort to increase sales, Ed and Yolanda are working on a new marketing strategy that they believe should be quite different from the "shotgun" approach they had been using over the last few months.

Questions:

119. What is a competitive advantage? Does Cherry Lane have one? If so, what is it?

A competitive advantage is an aggregation of factors that sets a company apart from its competitors and gives it a unique position in the market. No business can be everything to everyone. Developing a strategic plan allows the small business to differentiate itself from other companies -- a common pitfall for many small firms. Cherry Lane has an advantage over regular car dealerships because they are well suited to concentrate on the collectible car enthusiast niche in their marketplace.

120. As Ed and Yolanda begin the strategic planning process, what steps should they take?

Step 1: Develop a clear vision and translate it into a meaningful mission statement..
Step 2: Assess the company's strengths and weaknesses.
Step 3: Scan the environment for significant opportunities and threats facing the business.
Step 4: Identify the key factors for success in the business.
Step 5: Analyze the competition.
Step 6: Create company goals and objectives.
Step 7: Formulate strategic options and select the appropriate strategies.
Step 8: Translate strategic plans into action plans.
Step 9: Establish accurate controls.

The strategic planning process does not end with these ten steps; rather, it is an ongoing process that an entrepreneur will repeat.

121. Considering the three basic small business strategies identified in your textbook, which one would work best for Cherry Lane? Why?

A Cost Leadership strategy would not complement the higher price image that these collectible cars usually have.

Some students may identify the appropriate strategy as Differentiation; however, the other car dealerships are not direct competitors, nor is their market the same.

The Focus strategy could be used to more successfully position Cherry Lane with its ability to meet the needs of a special customer base-collectible car buffs. Rather than attempting to serve the total market, the focusing firm specializes in serving a specific target segment or niche. Lowering prices with this special target market is not as important creating the perception of *value* in the customers' eyes.

Chapter 4 Forms of Business Ownership and Franchising

Multiple Choice Questions:

1. The key to choosing the right form of ownership is:
   a. forming an S-corporation because it is the best form of ownership.
   b. understanding the characteristics of each form and knowing how they affect your business and personal circumstances.
   c. forming either an S-corporation or a limited liability company since they are the only forms that offer owners liability protection.
   d. irrelevant since choosing a form of ownership is merely a technicality and has little impact on the business and its owner(s).

   b., Medium, Page 100

2. Which of the following issues would influence an entrepreneur's choice of a form of business ownership?
   a. tax considerations
   b. management succession plans
   c. liability exposure
   d. All of the above.

   d., Easy, Page 100

3. The most common form of business ownership that is also the simplest to create is the:
   a. sole proprietorship.
   b. partnership.
   c. corporation.
   d. S-corporation.

   a., Easy, Page 100

4. Marco is opening a new computer repair shop. He is owner and sole employee. He has paid the appropriate fees and licensing costs and begun his business. This is an example of a(n):
   a. S-corporation.
   b. partnership.
   c. corporation.
   d. sole proprietorship.

   d., Easy, Page 100

5. Which form of ownership generally has the **least** ability to accumulate capital?
   a. Partnership
   b. Sole proprietorship
   c. Corporation
   d. S-corporation

   b., Easy, Page 102

6. The most critical disadvantage of the sole proprietorship is:
   a. the owner's unlimited personal liability.
   b. limited access to capital.
   c. lack of continuity.
   d. limited skills and abilities of the owner.

   a., Difficult, Page 102

7. A partnership agreement defines how the partners will be compensated. Normally,
   a. partners are <u>not</u> entitled to salaries or wages, but are compensated by a share of the profits of the business.
   b. the general partner's salary is set at two times the salaries of the limited partners.
   c. both general and limited partners are permitted salaries, but all silent or dormant partners are compensated only by sharing in the profits.
   d. while the agreement establishes payout schedules, it does **not** spell out what constitutes profit.

   a., Difficult, Page 103

8. Which of the following issues would a typical partnership agreement address?
   a. The contributions of each partner to the business
   b. How the partnership profits (or losses) will be distributed
   c. How a partner can sell her ownership in the business
   d. All of the above.

   d., Easy, Page 103

9. Probably the most important reason to have a partnership agreement is that:
   a. it identifies the name of the partnership and protects that name from infringement by others.
   b. it states the location and the purpose of the business.
   c. it determines how the partnership and the partners will pay taxes.
   d. it resolves potential sources of conflict that, if not addressed in advance, could later result in partnership battles and dissolution of an otherwise successful business.

   d., Medium, Page 103

10. In a partnership, the _____ partner(s) has (have) unlimited liability for the partnership's debts.
    a. limited
    b. dormant
    c. nominal
    d. general

    d., Easy, Page 105

11. In a general partnership:
    a. each partner is held responsible for an agreement/decision made by any one of the partners.
    b. partners can be held responsible only for decisions they make personally.
    c. no partner can be held legally responsible for decisions since the partnership itself is a legal entity.
    d. no decision is binding unless all partners agree to it in writing.

    a., Difficult, Page 105

12. All of the following are advantages of a partnership **except**:
    a. partnerships are relatively easy and inexpensive to establish.
    b. partnerships avoid double taxation since the partnership itself is not subject to federal taxation.
    c. partnerships have the greatest ability to accumulate capital of all of the forms of ownership.
    d. partnerships offer the ability to combine the management and business skills of two or more people in a complementary and powerful fashion.

    c., Easy, Page 105

13. Which of the following is required to form a partnership?
    a. A general partner
    b. A limited partner
    c. A secret partner
    d. All of the above

    a., Easy, Page 105

14. Which of the following is NOT true of a limited liability partnership?
    a. All partners are limited partners.
    b. Most states restrict this form of ownership to certain types of professions such as attorneys, physicians, dentists, accountants, etc.
    c. Although LLPs have many of the characteristics of partnerships, they are taxed as a corporation.
    d. All of the above *are* actually true.

    c., Medium, Page 108

15. Acme Corporation is chartered in Delaware, but its primary area of operation is in South Carolina. In South Carolina, Acme would be considered a(n) _____ corporation.
    a. alien
    b. domestic
    c. foreign
    d. local

    c., Medium, Page 108

16. The "Das Spelunker" corporation, formed in Germany and conducting business in the U.S., is considered to be a(n) _____ corporation.
    a. alien
    b. domestic
    c. foreign
    d. distant

    a., Medium, Page 108

17. A corporation receives its charter from:
    a. the federal government.
    b. the state.
    c. the board of directors.
    d. the stockholders.

    b., Medium, Page 108

18. Which of the following is true regarding the corporate form of ownership?
    a. generally has the greatest ability to accumulate capital
    b. most complex form of ownership
    c. separate legal entity in the eyes of the law
    d. All of the above.

    d., Easy, Page 108

19. Which of the following generally is **not** required by a Certificate of Incorporation?
    a. The names and the addresses of the incorporators
    b. A statement of the corporation's purpose
    c. A statement of how stock proceeds will be used
    d. The corporation's bylaws

    c., Medium, Page 109

20. Which of the following statement(s) is/are true?
    a. Closely held corporations are owned by only a few shareholders, often family members.
    b. Most closely held corporations require shareholders interested in selling their stock to offer it first to the corporation. This is known as the right of first refusal.
    c. Shares of stock the corporation itself owns are called treasury stock.
    d. All of the above.

    d., Medium, Page 109

21. Which of the following is **not** an advantage of the corporate form of ownership?
    a. Limited liability for the owners
    b. It is the easiest and least expensive form of ownership to create.
    c. Easy transfer of ownership
    d. Perpetual life

    b., Easy, Page 109

22. Which of the following is a disadvantage of the corporation form of ownership?
    a. An inability to accumulate capital
    b. The unlimited liability to the members of the board
    c. Double taxation on profits
    d. The lack of continuity

    c., Easy, Page 110

23. In the _____ form of ownership, the business itself pays income taxes.
    a. proprietorship
    b. partnership
    c. corporation
    d. all of the above

    c., Easy, Page 110

24. Carlos founded the "Taco Factory" 20 years ago as a family-oriented restaurant. Over the years as they grew the business, he incorporated and sold stock to outside investors. Recently the stockholders voted to seek liquor licenses and to sell beer and hard liquor in the restaurants. Carlos opposed this, citing the history of the restaurant's "family" environment, but was voted down. Carlos has experienced which drawback of the corporate form of ownership?
    a. The inability to accumulate capital
    b. The potential for diminished managerial incentives
    c. Legal requirements and red tape
    d. The potential loss of control

    d., Medium, Page 111

25. An S-corporation form of ownership overcomes which disadvantage of the regular or C-corporation form of ownership?
    a. The double taxation issue
    b. The expense and difficulty of formation
    c. The amount of regulation and red tape involved in its operation
    d. The potential loss of control by the founder

    a., Medium, Page 112

26. Which of the following would be **most** likely to benefit from choosing S-corporation status?
    a. Startup companies anticipating net losses
    b. Corporations where net profits before any compensation to shareholders is less than $100,000 per year
    c. Highly profitable firms with substantial dividends to pay out to shareholders
    d. A and C only.

    d., Difficult, Page 112

27. Which of the following statements is NOT true regarding the liquidation of an S-corporation?
    a. The owners pay all taxes, debts, and creditors.
    b. The owners obtain the written approval of shareholders to dissolve the company.
    c. The owners file a statement of intent to dissolve with the secretary of state's office in each state they do business in.
    d. The owners distribute all assets of the corporation to the shareholders.

c., Medium, Page 113

28. A limited liability company:
    a. is similar to an S-corporation in that it is a cross between a partnership and a corporation.
    b. prevents owners who want to maintain their limited liability status from actively managing the company.
    c. can have a maximum of 50 owners.
    d. All of the above.

a., Difficult, Page 113

29. A limited liability company is most like a(n):
    a. general partnership.
    b. master partnership.
    c. sole proprietorship.
    d. S-corporation.

d., Medium, Page 113

30. Which of the following documents must an entrepreneur file to create a limited liability company?
    a. The articles of organization
    b. The articles of incorporation
    c. The operating agreement
    d. A and C only.

d., Medium, Page 113

31. Which of the following is NOT true regarding the limitations of professional corporations?
    a. Seventy-five percent of the shares of stock must be owned and held by individuals licensed in the profession of the corporation.
    b. At least one of the incorporators, one director, and one officer must be licensed in the profession.
    c. The Articles of Incorporation, in addition to all other requirements, must designate the professional services to be provided by the corporation.
    d. The professional corporation must obtain from the appropriate licensing board a certification that declares the shares of stock are owned by individuals who are duly licensed in the profession.

a., Difficult, Page 115

32. A joint venture is different from a partnership in that the joint venture:
    a. can be formed only by two individuals.
    b. is formed for a specific purpose.
    c. continues indefinitely.
    d. requires that profits be shared equally.

    b., Medium, Page 115

33. Income from a joint venture is taxed as the income from a(n):
    a. sole proprietorship.
    b. partnership.
    c. corporation.
    d. S-corporation.

    b., Medium, Page 115

34. McDonald's is an example of a _____ franchise.
    a. conversion forms
    b. trade name
    c. product distribution
    d. pure

    d., Easy, Page 118

35. _____ franchising involves providing the franchisee with a complete business system, an established name, the building layout and design, accounting systems, etc., while _____ franchising allows the franchisee to use the franchiser's trade name without distributing the products exclusively under the franchiser's name.
    a. Product distribution; trade name
    b. Trade name; pure
    c. Pure; trade name
    d. Pure; product distribution

    c., Easy, Page 118

36. Which of the following is NOT a potential advantage of franchising for the franchisee?
    a. Management training and assistance
    b. National advertising program
    c. Centralized buying power
    d. Limited product line

    d., Easy, Page 118

37. Franchisers generally do which of the following regarding financial assistance to franchisees?
    a. Provide direct financing
    b. Assist in finding financing and occasionally provide direct assistance in a specific area
    c. Waive royalty fees for franchisees not making an adequate profit
    d. Generally do nothing, as having or finding financing is a requirement for qualifying for a franchise.

    b., Medium, Page 120

38. The failure rate for franchises is:
    a. higher than the rate for all new businesses.
    b. no different from the rate for all new businesses.
    c. lower than the rate for all new businesses.
    d. indeterminable because of the Right to Privacy Act.

    c., Medium, Page 121

39. Franchise royalty fees typically range from _____ to _____ percent of a franchisee's continuing sales.
    a. 1; 3
    b. 5; 9
    c. 3; 7
    d. 7; 12

    c., Difficult, Page 122

40. When it comes to purchasing products, equipment, etc., the franchiser
    a. cannot require the franchisees to buy from the franchise company.
    b. can set prices franchisees pay for the products, etc., but cannot set the retail price the franchisees charge.
    c. is permitted to set the retail price for the franchisee.
    d. cannot require franchisees to buy from an "approved" supplier.

    b., Medium, Page 123

41. Which of the following is NOT a potential disadvantage of a franchise?
    a. Unsatisfactory training program
    b. Limited product line
    c. Less freedom
    d. Actually, all of the above ARE potential disadvantages of a franchise.

    d., Easy, Page 123

42. The FTC's philosophy regarding the UFOC focuses on:
    a. catching and prosecuting abusers of franchise laws.
    b. verifying the accuracy of UFOC information.
    c. providing information to prospective franchisees and helping them make wise decisions.
    d. licensing prospective franchisers.

    c., Difficult, Page 125

43. Which of the following is an indication of a dishonest franchiser?
    a. A high-pressure sale
    b. A "get-rich-quick" scheme
    c. Attempts to discourage you from getting an attorney to review the contract
    d. All of the above.

    d., Easy, Page 126

44. Which of the following should make a potential franchisee suspicious about a franchiser's honesty?
    a. Claims that the franchise contract is a standard one and that there's no need to read it or have an attorney look it over
    b. An offer of direct financing of a specific element of the franchise package
    c. Not providing detailed operational information until 10 days before signing the contract
    d. Requiring franchisees to spend a certain percentage of profits on advertising

    a., Medium, Page 126

45. In addition to reading the franchiser's UFOC, it would be wise for the potential franchisee to seek a franchise that offers which of the following?
    a. A unique concept or marketing approach
    b. A registered trademark
    c. A positive relationship with franchisees
    d. All of the above.

    d., Easy, Page 129

46. The primary market for U.S. franchisers is _____, followed by _____.
    a. Japan; Mexico, Canada, and Europe.
    b. Australia; Mexico, Canada, and Europe.
    c. Mexico; Canada, Europe, and Australia.
    d. Canada; Mexico, Japan, and Europe.

    d., Medium, Page 132

47. Chris Jaffe, the owner of a small independent doughnut shop, is worried that a large doughnut franchise will open an outlet near her location and take away much of her business. Taking a proactive approach, Jaffe contacts the franchise, and after a few months of negotiations, becomes a franchisee. Jaffe is an example of which trend in franchising?
    a. Piggyback
    b. Conversion
    c. Master
    d. Subfranchising

    b., Medium, Page 132

48. McDonald's recently set up several small franchises in non-traditional locations such as a hospital, a college campus, an airport, a subway station, and a sports arena. These locations are based on the principle of:
    a. conversion franchising.
    b. intercept marketing.
    c. multi-unit franchising
    d. piggyback franchising.

    b., Medium, Page 133

49. When the franchiser has the right to establish a semi-independent organization in a particular territory to recruit, sell, and support other franchises, you have a _____ franchise.
    a. multi-unit
    b. piggyback
    c. conversion
    d. master

d., Easy, Page 133

50. Establishing a Baskin-Robbins franchise inside a Blimpee's franchise is an example of _____ franchising.
    a. multi-unit
    b. master
    c. piggyback
    d. diversionary

c., Easy, Page 133

True/False Questions:

51. Entrepreneurs should not spend much time selecting a form of ownership for their businesses because making the choice is merely a technicality which has little impact on the business and its owner(s).

False, Easy, Page 100

52. For entrepreneurs launching their first businesses, the sole proprietorship is the best form of ownership.

False, Medium, Page 100

53. Changing from one form of ownership to another once a business is up and running can be difficult, expensive, and complicated.

True, Easy, Page 100

54. Some forms of ownership are much more costly and involved to create.

True, Easy, Page 100

55. Of all U.S. business firms, sole proprietorships are the most common, accounting for nearly 73 percent.

True, Easy, Page 100

56. The sole proprietorship is the easiest form of ownership to create, but once formed, it is subject to the greatest number of regulations.

False, Medium, Page 101

57. All the profits of a sole proprietorship are taxed as current income of the owner even if they are not withdrawn from the business.

   True, Medium, Page 101

58. If a sole proprietorship fails, the owner is not liable for its debts since the business is a separate legal entity.

   False, Easy, Page 101

59. In a sole proprietorship, the owner has limited liability.

   False, Easy, Page 101

60. The sole proprietorship is the form of ownership with the least ability to accumulate capital.

   True, Easy, Page 101

61. If a sole proprietor dies, retires, or becomes incapacitated, the business automatically terminates.

   True, Medium, Page 101

62. The most common form of business ownership in the United States is the partnership.

   False, Easy, Page 103

63. State law requires that individuals creating a partnership file the Articles of Partnership with the Secretary of State.

   False, Medium, Page 103

64. Although not required by law, a written partnership agreement that spells out the terms of operating the partnership and the status of each partner should be developed.

   True, Easy, Page 103

65. In a partnership, profits (and losses) must be shared according to the ratio of capital originally invested in the partnership.

   False, Medium, Page 103

66. Defining the duties, responsibilities, contributions, and roles of the partners in a partnership agreement is not necessary since the law covers these provisions automatically.

   False, Medium, Page 103

67. If a partnership agreement does not exist, the partnership will be governed by the Uniform Partnership Act.

   True, Medium, Page 104

68. There is no limit to the number of general partners a partnership may have, but it must have at least one general partner.

True, Medium, Page 105

69. A general partner is personally liable only for the amount of money he has invested in the partnership.

False, Easy, Page 105

70. Profits earned by a partnership are taxed in the same fashion as those earned by a sole proprietorship.

True, Easy, Page 105

71. The partnership, like the proprietorship, avoids the disadvantage of double taxation.

True, Easy, Page 105

72. One of the advantages of a partnership over a proprietorship is the increased sources of capital and credit it offers.

True, Easy, Page 105

73. In a partnership, the business itself is subject to federal income tax.

False, Easy, Page 105

74. One disadvantage of the partnership form of ownership is the great potential for personality and authority conflicts.

True, Easy, Page 106

75. A common denominator in many partnership disputes is the lack of a written agreement clearly spelling out the roles, rights and responsibilities of each partner.

True, Easy, Page 106

76. If a limited partner withdraws, sells his ownership in the partnership, or dies, the partnership is not forced into dissolution.

True, Medium, Page 106

77. A limited partner is personally liable only for the amount of money she has invested in the partnership.

True, Easy, Page 107

78. A limited partner is treated as an investor in a business venture and does not take an active role in managing it.

True, Easy, Page 107

79. Each partner in a limited liability partnership is a limited partner; there are no general partners.

True, Medium, Page 107

80. A corporation formed and chartered in Kansas is considered a domestic corporation when doing business in Kansas and a foreign corporation when doing business in Missouri.

True, Medium, Page 108

81. A corporation formed in Taiwan doing business in the United States is a foreign corporation.

False, Medium, Page 108

82. Stockholders in the corporation have the same kind of liability as do general partners in a partnership.

False, Medium, Page 108

83. Corporations must obtain a federal charter before they can conduct any business.

False, Medium, Page 108

84. When filing the corporate charter, a corporation must file in the state in which its headquarters are located.

False, Medium, Page 108

85. Most states do **not** require a Certificate of Incorporation or a charter to be filed for a new corporation.

False, Easy, Page 108

86. A business with more than five owners must be a corporation.

False, Medium, Page 108

87. "Double taxation" refers to the fact that corporations are required to pay both federal and state income taxes.

False, Medium, Page 110

88. "Double taxation" refers to the fact that the corporation itself must pay taxes on its net profits, and the stockholders must also pay taxes on the portion of those same profits distributed to them as dividends.

True, Easy, Page 110

89. Ownership of a corporation can easily be transferred through the sale of stock.

True, Easy, Page 110

90. Company founders can become minority stockholders in a corporation but can never lose their final authority or control over business decisions because they are the founders.

False, Medium, Page 111

91. An S-corporation maintains the advantages of the corporate form of ownership while having the ability to be taxed as a partnership.

True, Easy, Page 111

92. An S-corporation can issue both voting and non-voting common stock to its shareholders.

True, Medium, Page 111

93. Choosing S-corporation status is usually beneficial to startup companies anticipating net losses and to highly profitable firms with substantial dividends to pay out to shareholders.

True, Difficult, Page 112

94. A limited liability company must have at least two owners.

True, Medium, Page 113

95. The limited liability company, like an S-corporation, is a form of ownership that is a cross between a partnership and a corporation.

True, Medium, Page 113

96. As in a limited partnership, owners of a limited liability company who want to maintain their limited liability status cannot actively participate in the management of the company.

False, Medium, Page 113

97. To form a limited liability company, an entrepreneur must file both the articles of incorporation and the operating agreement with the Secretary of State.

True, Medium, Page 113

98. Like an S-corporation, a limited liability company does not pay income taxes; its income flows through to its owners, who pay taxes on their shares of the limited liability company's net income.

True, Medium, Page 113

99. A limited liability company cannot have any more than two of the following corporate characteristics: limited liability, continuity of life, free transferability of interest, and centralized management.

True, Medium, Page 114

100. In a professional corporation, all shares of stock must be owned and held by individuals licensed in the profession of the corporation.

True, Medium, Page 114

101. A professional corporation is created in the same way as a regular corporation, and exists to provide the advantages of corporate ownership, including limited liability, to professionals such as doctors and lawyers.

True, Medium, Page 114

102. A joint venture is much like a partnership except that it is formed for a specific limited purpose.

True, Easy, Page 115

103. A franchise is an arrangement in which semi-independent business owners pay fees and royalties to a parent company in return for the right to sell its products or services and often to use its business format and system.

True, Easy, Page 118

104. Before entering a franchise contract, a potential investor should ask, "What can a franchise do for me that I cannot do for myself?"

True, Easy, Page 118

105. Quality is so important in franchising that most franchisers retain the right to terminate the franchise contract and to repurchase the outlet if a franchisee fails to maintain quality standards.

True, Medium, Page 118

106. When a franchisee buys a franchise, she is purchasing the expertise and the business of the franchiser.

True, Easy, Page 118

107.Pure franchising involves the right to use all the elements of a fully integrated business operation.

True, Easy, Page 118

108.Most franchisers provide extensive financial help such as loans and low-rate financing for their franchises.

False, Medium, Page 120

109.The failure rate for franchises is below that for other types of new businesses.

True, Medium, Page 121

110.In addition to other fees, franchisees must also pay royalties but only on net profits; in other words, no profits, no royalties.

False, Medium, Page 122

111.By signing the franchise contract, a franchisee typically surrenders some freedom and autonomy in operating his business.

True, Easy, Page 122

112.A major advantage of a franchise contract is the national advertising campaign that most franchisers provide free of charge for their franchisees.

False, Medium, Page 122

113.It is illegal for a franchiser to require franchisees to purchase products only from "approved suppliers."

False, Medium, Page 123

114.Having an attorney review and evaluate a franchise contract is unnecessary since the FTC requires all franchisers to offer a "standard" franchise contract.

False, Medium, Page 124

115.The franchise contract defines the rights and the obligations of both parties and sets the guidelines which govern the franchise relationship.

True, Easy, Page 125

116.If a franchiser encourages you to sign without reading the agreement, or discourages you from "spending the money on an attorney," this is a warning sign that the franchiser might be dishonest.

True, Easy, Page 126

117. A good method for evaluating a franchiser's reputation is to interview existing franchise owners about the operation.

   True, Easy, Page 129

118. The primary market for U.S. franchisers is Mexico, with Japan and Europe next.

   False, Medium, Page 131

119. A master franchise gives a franchisee the right to create a semi-independent organization in a particular territory to recruit, sell, and support other franchisees.

   True, Easy, Page 133

120. A multi-unit franchise gives the franchisee the right to open more than one franchise outlet in a territory within a specific time frame.

   True, Easy, Page 133

Essay Questions:

121. What factors should an entrepreneur consider when choosing a form of ownership?

   Tax considerations
   Liability exposure
   Start-up capital requirements
   Control
   Business goals
   Management succession plans
   Cost of formation
   Page 100

122. What is a sole proprietorship? Explain the advantages and the disadvantages of a sole proprietorship.

   A business owned and managed by one (1) individual.

   Advantages:
   Simple to create
   Least costly form of ownership to begin
   Profit incentive
   Total authority
   No special legal restrictions
   Easy to discontinue

   Disadvantages:
   Unlimited personal liability
   Limited skills and capabilities
   Feeling of isolation
   Limited access to capital

Lack of continuity for the business
Page 100

123. What is a partnership? Explain the advantages and the disadvantages of a partnership.

An association of two or more people who co-own a business for the purpose of making a profit.

Advantages:
Easy to establish
Complementary skills
Division of profits
Larger capital pool
Ability to attract limited partners
Little governmental regulation
Flexibility
Taxation

Disadvantages:
Unlimited liability of the general partner(s)
Not effective in capital accumulation
Difficulty in disposing of partnership interest without dissolving partnership
Lack of continuity
Potential conflicts
Page 103

124. John and Bill are considering starting a partnership. Why is it important for them to develop a formal partnership agreement? List at least ten of the provisions their partnership agreement should include.

The partnership agreement is important because it states in writing all of the terms of operating the partnership and protects each partner involved.

The standard partnership agreement should include the following:

Name of partnership
Purpose of business
Domicile of the business
Duration
Partner names and addresses
Contributions of each partner
How profits/losses distributed
Agreement on salaries and draws
Procedure for expansion of new partners
How assets will be distributed
Sale
Salaries, draws and expense accounts
Partners' absence or disability
Dissolution
Alterations or modifications
Page 103

125. Outline the incorporation process.

A Certificate of Incorporation or charter must be filed with the Secretary of State. The Certificate of Incorporation includes such things as:

- The type and value of capital stock the corporation wants
- Time horizon (50 years, perpetuity)
- Restrictions, if any, on transferring shares
- Rules under which corporation will operate
- Statement of purpose
- Corporation name
- Name and address of incorporators

Page 108

126. What is a corporation? Explain the advantages and the disadvantages of a corporation.

A corporation is a separate legal entity apart from its owners that receives the right to exist from the state in which it is incorporated.

Advantages:
Limited liability of stockholders
Ability to attract capital
Ability to continue indefinitely
Transferable ownership

Disadvantages:
Cost and time of incorporation
Double taxation
Diminished managerial incentives
Regulatory red tape
Founder – loss of control potential

Page 108

127. What is an S-corporation? Explain the advantages and the disadvantages of an S-corporation.

A corporation that retains the legal characteristics of a regular (C) corporation but has the advantage of being taxed as a partnership if it meets certain criteria.

Advantages:

Continuity of existence
Transferability of ownership
Limited liability for owners
Income taxed once – at individual's rate
Avoids "C" corporation tax on assets
Owners can get year-end payouts
Can have "S" corporation subsidiaries

Disadvantages:

>   Lower rate than top individual tax rates
>   Many fringe benefits cannot be deducted
>   **Page 111**

128. What kinds of companies would benefit **most** from S-corporation status? Least?

    S-corporation status is usually beneficial to start-up companies anticipating net losses and to highly profitable firms with substantial dividends to pay out to shareholders. In these cases, owners can use the losses to offset other income. Also owners who plan to sell in the near future prefer "S" corporations because taxable gains on "S" corporations are lower.

    S-corporation status would be least beneficial for companies whose characteristics include:

    - Higher individual tax rates
    - Profitable service companies that pay out much of their profits to shareholders in the form of benefits
    - Fast growing companies that retain most of earnings to finance growth
    - When loss of fringe benefits exceeds tax savings
    - Sizeable net operating losses that cannot be used against "S" corporation earnings
    - Income before any compensation is less that $100,000 per year

    Page 111

129. What is a limited liability company? How is one formed? What benefits does an LLC offer?

    A relatively new form of ownership that, like an S corporation, is a cross between a partnership and a corporation; however, it is not subject to many of the restrictions imposed on S corporations.

    The process of creating a LLC is much like creating a corporation. The articles of organization actually create an LLC by establishing its name, address, method of management, its duration, and the names and addresses of each organizer. An operating agreement, similar to an organization's by laws, is also created. An LLC must have at least two owners (called members).

    Unlike an S corporation, it offers limited liability without imposing any ceilings on their numbers and does not restrict the partners from participating in day-to-day operations and management of the business. The LLC also avoids double taxation because its income flows through to its members who divide it as they see fit.
    Page 107

130. Compare and contrast the following forms of ownership: a corporation, an S-corporation, and a limited liability company.

    - All have limited liability.
    - The LLC and S corporation are both similar to a partnership in the way they see fit

to divide income. They both avoid double taxation.

- Both the C and S corporation have continuity of existence and transferability of ownership.
- The LLC is not subject to the same restrictions as an S-corporation. For example, an S- corporation cannot have more than 75 shareholders, no shareholders may be foreigners or corporations, and it may have only one class of stock. This is not the case with the LLC.
- Unlike the corporation, an LLC does not have perpetual life.

Page 111-114

131. Define franchising. Explain the three types of franchising. Which is the fastest-growing segment?

A system of distribution in which semi-independent business owners (franchisees) pay fees and royalties to a parent company (franchiser) in return for the right to become identified with its trademark, to sell its products or services, and often use its business format and system.

The three types of franchising are:

1. Tradename
2. Product distribution
3. Pure (Business Format)

Pure franchising outlets' sales are growing at a faster rate.
Page 116

132. Outline the benefits and drawbacks of buying a franchise.

Benefits:
Management and training support
Brandname appeal
Standardized quality of goods and services
National advertising programs
Financial assistance
Proven products and business formats
Centralized buying power
Site selection and territorial protection
Greater chance for success

Drawbacks:
Franchise fees and profit sharing
Strict adherence to standardized operations
Restrictions on purchasing
Limited product line
Unsatisfactory training programs
Market saturation
Less freedom
Page 118

133.   Outline the recommended procedure for buying a franchise.

Evaluate yourself
Research your market
Consider your franchise options
Get a copy of the franchiser's UFOC
Talk to existing franchisees
Ask the franchiser some tough questions
Make your choice
Page 118

134.   What is a Uniform Franchise Offering Circular? How can it help a potential franchisee?

The law requires franchisers to register and deliver a copy to perspective franchisees before any offer or sale of a franchise. The UFOC establishes full disclosure guidelines for any company selling franchises. It can help potential franchisees avoid being defrauded by requiring that the franchiser disclose detailed information on their operation at the first personal meeting, or at least ten days before a franchise contract is signed, or before any money is paid.
Page 125

135.   What are some indicators that a potential franchisee might be dealing with a dishonest franchise? What steps can a potential franchisee take to avoid becoming a victim of a dishonest franchise?

Indicators:

- Claims that contract is standard and "you don't need to read it"
- Failure to provide disclosure information
- Marginally successful or no prototype
- Oral promises of future earnings with no documentation
- High turnover rate
- Poor manual or none at all
- Unusual amount of litigation
- Attempt to discourage attorney advice
- High pressure sales
- Claiming to be exempt from federal laws
- Get-rich-quick schemes
- Reluctance to provide references
- Evasive or vague answers

Steps to take:

- Do your research
- Ask for UFOC
- Investigate thoroughly
- Preparation, common sense, and patience
Page 126

136. Explain the following franchise concepts and give an example of each: intercept marketing, conversion franchising, multi-unit franchising, and master franchising.

Intercept marketing is the principle of putting a franchise's products or services directly in the paths of potential customers, wherever they may be. Example: putting a scaled down version of a Subway sandwich shop in a gas station convenience store.

Conversion franchising is a trend in which owners of independent businesses become franchisees to gain the advantage of name recognition. Example: an Italian restaurant owner buys a franchise like the Olive Garden restaurant.

Multi-Unit franchising is a method whereby a franchisee opens more than one unit within a specific time frame. Example: an individual or family owning all the local McDonalds.

Master franchising a method of franchising that gives the franchisee the right to create a semi-independent organization in a particular territory to recruit, sell and support other franchisees. Example: an individual fluent in Spanish works to recruit as many franchisees as possible in Spain.
Page 132

137. Explain three trends currently shaping the franchising industry.

Three current trends can be included from the following list:

- Franchisees are better educated and more financially secure
- Internationalism of American franchise system
- Smaller non-traditional locations
- Conversion franchising
- Multiple-unit franchising
- Master franchising
- Serving aging baby boomers

Page 127

Chapter 4
Forms of Ownership and Franchising
Mini-Cases

Case 4.1: "Today, You Gotta' Be a Corporation"

Duke has been a successful used car dealer for 25 years in the same location, operating as a proprietorship. In those 25 years, he's expanded his operation and become the largest independent car dealer in a city of 85,000 people. Few people in town can boast of a business reputation better than Duke's. As he says, "I've always done business in a fair and honest fashion, and I've tried to give my customers an honest deal. The public has responded well, and last year the business revenue increased to an all-time high of $830,000."

As the business has grown, so have Duke's liabilities. On a given day, Duke will have cars worth from $350,000 to $450,000 as inventory on the lot. "Twenty years ago, if I'd asked the bank for a line of credit of $200,000, they'd have tossed me out the front door. There's no question today business is different."

Duke's only daughter recently married a garage mechanic who has worked in the area for the past three years. Though Duke thinks the boy is certainly nice enough, he doesn't believe he is very smart. "The kid sure knows how to fix a car, but that's as far as it goes," says Duke. "On my last visit to the accountant, he suggested I consider incorporating. I guess he knows what he's talking about. That's all you hear today - 'you gotta be a corporation.' I guess he's right. But, to tell you the truth, I don't know."

138. Should Duke incorporate or should he remain a proprietorship? Why?

139. Would you recommend Duke establish an S-corporation? What conditions would he have to meet?

140. Would a limited liability corporation be any better for Duke? Why or why not?

Duke's business looks as though it would qualify for S-corporation status, and, as the text describes, there are many tax advantages to this form of ownership. Given the volume of sales and the "good living" Duke makes, he should consider this form of ownership.

Case 4.2: Pipe Dreams

Ralph Emerson thought he'd been a librarian long enough, and when the opportunity arose to open a small tobacco, pipe and cigar shop in the newly renovated downtown business district, he was ready to act. Pipe Dreams is a franchiser of smoke shops, and was founded eight years ago by a noted tobacconist in New York City. The concept for the shops is simple, yet sophisticated. It is simple in the sense that the shops sell only tobacco-related products, but sophisticated in the breadth and quality of the inventory they carry. Each franchise, depending on size, is stocked with inventory selected by the company's founder. The franchiser finances the shop's initial inventory. The franchisee is expected to create a decor within predetermined standards that Pipe Dreams establishes. Each franchisee must attend a three-day workshop, outlining the fundamentals of tobacco blending, the merchandising of pipes and cigars, and the techniques of successful business operation.

The franchise contract requires the franchisee to contribute 1.5 percent of gross revenue to a national advertising campaign. According to the contract, Pipe Dreams will finance the required fixtures for the store for ten years. Also, the franchiser supplies all inventory at very favorable prices because it purchases in large quantities.

Ralph knows he can buy tobacco products from a variety of wholesalers. He also has some ideas on what would make a tobacco shop successful in this town. Ralph knows that Pipe Dreams franchisees have had a high success rate in the past.

141. Help Ralph make a decision by outlining the advantages and the disadvantages of a franchise arrangement.

142. Assuming that Ralph has adequate capital, would you recommend that he invest in the franchise or open his own tobacco shop? Why?

Chapter 4 outlines the advantages and disadvantages of franchise arrangements. The case suggests that the Pipe Dreams franchise (like many franchises) offers the entrepreneur a greater chance of success than "starting from scratch."

Given Ralph's lack of experience in business, generally, and in managing a tobacco shop, specifically, it probably is wise for him to take the franchise option. Once he learns the business and gets established, he could explore the possibility of terminating the franchise relationship.

Chapter 5   Buying an Existing Business

Multiple Choice Questions:

1. The due diligence process of analyzing and evaluating an existing business:
   a. may be just as time consuming as the development of a comprehensive business plan for a start-up.
   b. helps to determine if the company will generate sufficient cash to pay for itself and leave you with a suitable rate of return on your investment.
   c. helps to determine what the company's potential for success is.
   d. All of the above.

   d., Easy, Page 140

2. Advantages to buying an existing business that you don't have with a startup include:
   a. greater access to venture capital.
   b. the opportunity to participate in a national advertising campaign.
   c. inventory is in place and trade credit is established.
   d. easy implementation of innovations and changes from past policies.

   c., Medium, Page 141

3. Which of the following is a potential disadvantage of purchasing an existing business?
   a. The employees inherited with the business may not be suitable.
   b. The previous owner may have created ill will among the company's customers.
   c. Equipment and facilities may be obsolete or inefficient.
   d. All of the above.

   d., Easy, Page 142

4. An entrepreneur who is considering purchasing a business analyzed the company's accounts receivable. The following table summarizes her findings.

Age of Accounts	Amount	Probability of Collection
0 - 30 days	$12,000	.96
31 - 60 days	$ 4,000	.87
61 - 90 days	$ 2,500	.71
91 - 120 days	$ 1,400	.65
121 + days	$ 800	.24

   How much should this potential buyer be willing to pay for these accounts receivable?
   a. $0. A buyer should never purchase existing accounts receivable.
   b. $20700
   c. $17,877
   d. Not enough information given.

   c., Difficult, Page 143

5. The inventory in an existing business
   a. is always current and salable.
   b. usually appreciates over time, making the business a bargain.
   c. should be judged on the basis of its market value, not its book value.
   d. is usually stated honestly and does not need an independent audit.

   c., Medium, Page 143

6. When acquiring a business, the buyer should do which of the following?
   a. Conduct a self-analysis of skills, abilities, and interests.
   b. Prepare a list of potential candidates.
   c. Investigate potential candidates and carefully evaluate them.
   d. All of the above.

   d., Easy, Page 144

7. The first step an entrepreneur should take when buying an existing business is to:
   a. explore financing options.
   b. prepare a list of potential candidates.
   c. analyze her skills, abilities, and interests in an honest self-audit.
   d. contact existing business owners in the area and ask if their companies are for sale.

   c., Medium, Page 144

8. Which of the following is (are) a potential source for tapping into the hidden market of companies that might be for sale but are not advertised?
   a. Business brokers
   b. "Networking"
   c. Industry contacts
   d. All of the above.

   d., Easy, Page 145

9. Which of the following statements concerning financing the purchase of an existing business is **true**?
   a. It is usually more difficult than securing financing for a start-up business.
   b. Usually, the business seller is not a good source of financing.
   c. The buyer should be able to make the payments on the loans out of the company's cash flow.
   d. All of the above.

   c., Medium, Page 146

10. Which of the following statements concerning financing the purchase of an existing business is **not true**?
    a. The business seller usually is a good candidate for a source of financing.
    b. The deal should allow the buyer to make the loan payment out of the company's cash flow.
    c. The buyer should wait until late in the purchase process to arrange financing to avoid processing fees in case the deal falls through.
    d. All of the above.

    c., Medium, Page 146

11. Perhaps the ideal source of financing the purchase of an existing business is:
    a. a venture capitalist.
    b. the Small Business Administration.
    c. the seller of the business.
    d. an insurance company.

    c., Medium, Page 146

12. To ensure a smooth transition when buying an existing business, a buyer should:
    a. communicate with employees to reduce their uncertainty and anxiety.
    b. be honest with existing employees about upcoming changes and plans for the company's future.
    c. consider asking the seller to stay on and serve as a consultant until the transition is complete.
    d. All of the above.

    d., Easy, Page 146

13. The most common reasons owners of small- and medium-sized businesses give for selling their businesses are:
    a. need for money and low return on investment.
    b. boredom and burnout.
    c. low return on investment and burnout.
    d. greater opportunities working for someone else and low return on investment.

    b., Medium, Page 148

14. Which of the following is a criterion for a bulk transfer?
    a. The seller must give the buyer a signed, sworn list of existing creditors.
    b. The buyer and the seller must prepare a list of the property included in the sale.
    c. The buyer must give notice of the sale to each creditor at least ten days before he takes possession of the goods or pays for them.
    d. All of the above.

    d., Medium, Page 151

15. Laurette has entered into a contract with Jackson to purchase his retail music shop. Jackson's lease on the existing building (which is in an excellent location) has five years remaining. If Laurette wants the lease to be part of the business sale,
    a. she should include a clause in the sales contract in which Jackson agrees to assign to her his rights and obligations under that lease.
    b. she should notify the landlord of Jackson's assignment of the lease agreement to her.
    c. A and B are correct.
    d. None of the above. Because Jackson does not actually own the building, he can transfer no rights to it to Laurette.

    c., Difficult, Page 152

16. During the acquisition process, the potential buyer usually must sign a _____, which is an agreement to keep all conversations and information secret and legally binds the buyer from telling anyone any information the seller shares with her.
    a. covenant not to compete
    b. nondisclosure document
    c. letter of intent
    d. purchase agreement

    a., Medium, Page 152

17. Which of the following is required for the covenant not to compete to be enforceable?
    a. Part of a business sale
    b. Approved by a court of law
    c. Reasonable in scope
    d. Only A and C.

    d., Medium, Page 152

18. The three main sources of potential legal liabilities for the buyer of an existing business include all but which of the following?
    a. Problems with the physical premises, such as hazardous materials
    b. Product liability claims
    c. Labor problems and disputes
    d. Errors and omissions

    d., Medium, Page 152

19. A toy manufacturer is sued based on the claim of injuries caused by a product it makes. This is an example of a:
    a. product liability lawsuit.
    b. promissory estoppel lawsuit.
    c. restrictive covenant lawsuit.
    d. contingent liability lawsuit.

    a., Easy, Page 152

20. Generally, a seller of an existing business can assign any contractual right to the buyer unless:
    a. the contract specifically prohibits the assignment.
    b. the contract is personal in nature.
    c. A and B are correct.
    d. None of the above. Business sellers typically cannot assign any contractual rights to buyers.

    c., Medium, Page 152

21. When evaluating the financial position of a business he is considering buying, an entrepreneur should examine:
    a. its income statements and balance sheets from the past three to five years.
    b. its income tax returns for the past three to five years.
    c. the owner's compensation and that of relatives.
    d. All of the above.

    d., Medium, Page 153

22. In a business sale, a letter of intent:
    a. states that the buyer and the seller have reached a sufficient meeting of the minds to justify the time and expense of negotiating a final agreement.
    b. should contain a clause calling for "good faith negotiations" between the parties.
    c. addresses such issues as price, payment terms, a deadline for closing the deal, and others.
    d. All of the above.

    d., Easy, Page 155

23. During the acquisition process, the buyer and the seller sign a _____, which spells out the parties' final deal and represents the details of the agreement that are the result of the negotiation process.
    a. covenant not to compete
    b. nondisclosure document
    c. letter of intent
    d. purchase agreement

    d., Easy, Page 155

24. The main reason a buyer purchases an existing businesses is for:
    a. its future income and profits.
    b. its customer base.
    c. its tangible assets.
    d. its goodwill.

    a., Medium, Page 156

25. A valuation method that is more realistic than the balance sheet because it adjusts book value to reflect actual market value is the:
    a. excess earnings method.
    b. market approach.
    c. capitalization method.
    d. adjusted balance sheet method.

d., Medium, Page 156

26. When valuing inventory for a business sale, the most common methods used are:
    a. first-in-first-out (FIFO) and last-in-first-out (LIFO).
    b. first-in-first-out (FIFO) and average costing.
    c. cost of last purchase and replacement value of inventory.
    d. cost of last purchase and average costing.

c., Medium, Page 157

27. Which of the following statements about valuing a business is true?
    a. The balance sheet technique is the best way to value a business.
    b. Business valuation is partly art and partly science.
    c. Buyers should rely on the seller's industry expertise and years of experience to determine what his company is worth.
    d. None of the above.

b., Medium, Page 156

28. Business valuations based on balance sheet methods suffer certain disadvantages, including:
    a. they are extremely complex and are difficult to calculate.
    b. they do not consider the future earning potential of the business.
    c. they fail to take into account what is usually the largest asset a company owns: inventory.
    d. All of the above.

b., Difficult, Page 158

29. Which of the following valuation methods does **not** consider the future income-earning potential of a business?
    a. balance sheet technique
    b. excess-earnings method
    c. discounted future earnings approach
    d. market approach

a., Medium, Page 158

Use the following information to answer the Question # 30-32:

Baubles and Bells, a small business, is up for sale. The book value of its assets is $397,650, and its liabilities have a book value of $148,500. After adjusting for market value, total assets are worth $386,475, and total liabilities are $153,600. The business is considered to be a "normal risk" venture. The new owner (if he buys) plans to draw a salary of $28,000. Estimated earnings for the upcoming year are $88,400. Complete net earnings estimates for the next five years are:

	Pessimistic	Most Likely	Optimistic
Year 1	$82,000	$88,400	$90,500
Year 2	$85,000	$90,000	$93,000
Year 3	$88,000	$92,500	$95,500
Year 4	$91,000	$95,000	$97,000
Year 5	$94,000	$97,000	$98,500

30. Under the excess earnings method, what is the "extra earning power" of the business?
    a. $86,219
    b. $2,181
    c. $11,175
    d. Cannot be determined from the information given

    b., Difficult, Page 159

31. Using the adjusted balance sheet technique, what is the business worth?
    a. $397,650
    b. $386,475
    c. $249,150
    d. $232,875

    b., Difficult, Page 159

32. Using the excess earnings method, what is the company's "goodwill"?
    a. $6,543
    b. $33,525
    c. $15,267
    d. Cannot be determined from the information given

    a., Difficult, Page 159

33. The valuation approach that considers the value of goodwill is the:
    a. balance sheet technique.
    b. excess earnings method.
    c. discounted future earnings approach.
    d. market approach.

    b., Easy, Page 159

34. Which of the following is considered to be an opportunity cost of buying an existing business?
    a. The salary that could be earned working for someone else
    b. Dividends
    c. The owner's investment in the business
    d. A and C are correct.

    d., Medium, Page 159

35. The amount the seller of a business receives for "goodwill" is taxed as
    a. a long-term capital gain.
    b. regular income.
    c. superlative income.
    d. None of the above.

    b., Medium, Page 160

36. If a business buyer estimates that 20 percent is a reasonable rate of return for an existing business expected to produce a profit of $27,000, its capitalized value would be:
    a. $5,400.
    b. $32,400.
    c. $135,000.
    d. $540,000.

    c., Medium, Page 160

37. Which method of business valuation relies on three forecasts of future earnings: optimistic, pessimistic, and most likely?
    a. Balance sheet technique
    b. Excess-earnings method
    c. Discounted future earnings
    d. Market approach

    c., Medium, Page 160

38. The capitalized earnings approach determines the value of a business by capitalizing its expected profits using:
    a. the interest rate that could be earned on a similar risk investment.
    b. the prime interest rate.
    c. the normal rate of return.
    d. the prevailing return of inflation.

    a., Medium, Page 160

39. In the earnings methods of business valuation, the rate of return associated with a "normal risk" business is:
    a. 15 percent.
    b. 25 percent.
    c. 35 percent.
    d. 50 percent.

    b., Medium, Page 160

40. The _____ approach to valuing a business assumes that a dollar earned in the future is worth less than that same dollar is today.
    a. balance sheet
    b. capitalized earnings
    c. adjusted balance sheet
    d. discounted future earnings

d., Medium, Page 160

41. Which of the following valuation techniques is best suited for determining the value of service businesses?
    a. discounted future earnings approach
    b. balance sheet technique
    c. adjusted balance sheet technique
    d. excess earnings approach

a., Medium, Page 161

42. Which of the following is a disadvantage of the market approach to valuing a business?
    a. necessary comparisons between publicly-traded and privately-owned companies
    b. unrepresentative earnings estimates
    c. difficulty in finding similar companies for comparison
    d. All of the above.

d., Medium, Page 162

43. Which of the following is a drawback of the market approach of evaluation?
    a. It does not consider current earnings.
    b. It may underrepresent earnings.
    c. Its reliability depends on the forecasts of future earnings.
    d. It overemphasizes the value of goodwill.

b., Medium, Page 162

44. You are considering purchasing Babcock Office Supply. You estimate that the company's earnings next year will be $67,400. You have found three similar companies whose stock is publicly traded. Their P/E ratios are 6.8, 7.4, and 7.1. Using the market approach, you estimate Babcock Office Supply to be worth:
    a. $478,540.
    b. $9,493.
    c. $67,400.
    d. $498,760.

a., Difficult, Page 162

45. The _____ approach to valuing a business uses the price-earnings ratios of similar businesses to establish the value of a company.
    a. balance sheet
    b. capitalized earnings
    c. discounted future earnings
    d. market

    d., Medium, Page 162

46. A company's P/E ratio is:
    a. the price of one share of its common stock divided by its earnings per share.
    b. its profits per share divided by its equity per share.
    c. its profits per share divided by its excess cash flow per share.
    d. None of the above.

    a., Easy, Page 162

47. Which of the following strategies would **not** be suitable for an entrepreneur who wants to surrender control of the company gradually?
    a. forming a family limited partnership
    b. restructuring the company
    c. straight business sale
    d. using a two-step sale

    c., Medium, Page 164

48 A(n) _____ allows owners to "cash out" by selling their companies to their employees as gradually or as quickly as they choose.
    a. two-step sale
    b. controlled sale
    c. company restructuring
    d. ESOP

    d., Easy, Page 166

49. _____ gives owners the security of a sales contract but permits them to stay at the "helm" for several years.
    a. The two-step sale
    b. A controlled sale
    c. Company restructuring
    d. An ESOP

    a., Easy, Page 166

50. An ESOP:
    a. allows an owner to transfer all or part of his company to the employees as gradually or as quickly as he chooses.
    b. works best in companies where pre-tax profits exceed $100,000.
    c. is not beneficial to companies with fewer than 15 to 20 employees.
    d. All of the above.

    d., Medium, Page 166

True/False Questions:

51. The due diligence process in analyzing and evaluating an existing business can be just as time consuming as the development of a comprehensive business plan for a start-up.

    True, Easy, Page 140

52. With an existing business, the new owner can depend on employees to help him make money while he is learning the business.

    True, Easy, Page 140

53. A principal advantage of buying an existing business is the purchaser's ability to rely on the previous owner's experience.

    True, Easy, Page 141

54. For a new owner of an existing business, physical facilities and equipment costs are very similar to what would have been spent on a startup with all new facilities and equipment.

    False, Medium, Page 141

55. When buying a business, an entrepreneur can usually purchase equipment and fixtures at prices well below their book value.

    True, Medium, Page 141

56. An entrepreneur should never purchase a business that is losing money.

    False, Easy, Page 142

57. A new owner of an existing business can generally introduce change and innovation almost as easily as if the company were a new business because employees and customers expect change in business practice when there is a change in ownership.

    False, Medium, Page 143

58. Accounts receivable are rarely worth face value and should be "aged" when evaluating a company's assets.

    True, Easy, Page 143

59. The reason a businessman should conduct a self-audit of his skills, abilities, and interests is to help him focus on those businesses that will best "fit" him.

True, Easy, Page 144

60. The business acquisition process should begin with the search for potential companies to acquire.

False, Medium, Page 144

61. The hidden market of companies that might be for sale but are not advertised as such is one of the richest sources of top-quality businesses to purchase.

True, Easy, Page 145

62. Financing the purchase of an existing business usually is easier than financing the startup of a new one.

True, Medium, Page 146

63. When evaluating a business as a potential candidate for purchase, an entrepreneur should determine the real reason the current owner wants to sell.

True, Easy, Page 147

64. The most common reasons that owners of small businesses give for selling are the intensity of competition and an inability to raise sufficient cash to continue to grow.

False, Medium, Page 148

65. Before purchasing an existing business, an entrepreneur should analyze both its existing and its potential customers.

True, Easy, Page 150

66. If a business has a lien against any of its assets at the time of the sale, the buyer must assume them and is financially responsible for them.

True, Medium, Page 151

67. A prospective buyer should have an attorney thoroughly investigate all of the assets for sale in a business and their lien status before buying any business.

True, Easy, Page 151

68. One way for a business buyer to avoid being surprised by liens against the assets she buys is to include a clause in the sales contract stating that any liability not shown on the balance sheet at the time of the sale remains the responsibility of the seller.

True, Medium, Page 151

69. By meeting the criteria of a bulk transfer, a business buyer acquires free and clear title to the assets purchased, which are not subject to prior claims from the seller's creditors.

True, Medium, Page 151

70. When a buyer purchases an existing business, she may "inherit" liability for damages and injuries caused by products the company has manufactured or sold in the past.

True, Medium, Page 152

71. A due-on-sale clause allows an entrepreneur buying a business to "assume" the seller's loan (usually at a lower interest rate).

False, Medium, Page 152

72. A due-on-sale clause requires a buyer to pay the full amount of the remaining balance on a loan or to finance the balance at prevailing interest rates.

True Easy, Page 152

73. A due-on-sale clause in a loan contract prohibits the buyer of a business from assuming a seller's loan even though it may carry a lower interest rate.

True, Medium, Page 152

74. If the corporation, rather than the business seller, signs a restrictive covenant, the seller may not be bound by its terms.

True, Medium, Page 152

75. A restrictive covenant prohibits the seller of an existing business from opening a competitive business within a specific time period and geographic area of the existing one.

True, Easy, Page 152

76. Ralph buys a software business from Waldo in Columbus, Ohio. As part of the deal, Waldo signs a covenant not to compete by opening another software business anywhere in Ohio for the rest of his life. Such a covenant would be enforceable.

False, Medium, Page 152

77. A business buyer can be held liable in product liability lawsuits for unsafe products that cause damage or injuries to customers even though they were made prior to the business purchase.

True, Medium, Page 153

78. Potential buyers should examine income statements, balance sheets, and income tax returns for the past three to five years.

True, Medium, Page 153

79. Many business owners show low profits in their businesses intentionally to lower their tax bills.

   True, Easy, Page 153

80. Because so many business owners take money from their companies' sales without reporting it as income, a business buyer should expect to pay for undocumented, "phantom" profits when buying an existing business.

   False, Medium, Page 153

81. The practice of taking money from sales without reporting it as income is called sliding.

   False, Easy, Page 153

82. Many buyers assume that if profits are adequate, there will be sufficient cash to pay all of the bills and fund an attractive salary for themselves, but that is not necessarily the case.

   True, Medium, Page 154

83. A nondisclosure document is an agreement between a business buyer and a seller that requires the buyer to maintain strict confidentiality of all records, documents, and information he receives during the parties' negotiations.

   True, Easy, Page 155

84. A letter of intent is a nonbinding document stating that a business buyer and a seller have reached a sufficient "meeting of the minds" to justify the time and the expense of negotiating a final agreement.

   True, Easy, Page 155

85. If the owner of an existing business refuses to disclose the company's financial records, an entrepreneur who is considering buying it should walk away from the deal.

   True, Easy, Page 155

86. The balance sheet technique is one of the most commonly used methods of evaluating an existing business, although it over-simplifies the valuation process because it values a company only on the basis of its net worth.

   True, Easy, Page 156

87. When an entrepreneur purchases an existing business, she essentially is purchasing its future profit potential.

   True, Medium, Page 156

88. Most small businesses have market values that exceed their book value.

   True, Medium, Page 156

89. The most meaningful method of determining the value of an existing business's inventory is its book value.

False, Medium, Page 156

90. Business evaluation based on balance sheet methods offers one key advantage: it considers the future earning potential of the business.

False, Easy, Page 156

91. The adjusted balance sheet method of valuing a business changes the book value of net worth to reflect its actual market value.

True, Medium, Page 156

92. Neither the balance sheet method nor the adjusted balance sheet method of valuing a business considers the future earning power of the business.

True, Medium, Page 158

93. Goodwill is the difference between an established successful business and one that has yet to prove itself.

True, Easy, Page 159

94. Goodwill is an intangible asset that the business buyer cannot depreciate or amortize for tax purposes.

False, Medium, Page 159

95. The rate of return used to value a business is composed of the basic, risk-free return, an inflation premium, and the risk allowance for investing in the particular business.

True, Medium, Page 159

96. The discounted future earnings approach to valuing an existing business involves estimating the company's net income for several years into the future and then discounting those future earnings back to their present value.

True, Easy, Page 160

97. According to the discounted future earnings technique, a dollar earned in the future is worth more than a dollar earned today.

False, Medium, Page 160

98. A business buyer should build his or her own pro forma income statement from an existing firm's accounting records and compare it to the same statement provided by the owner.

True, Easy, Page 160

99. Under the capitalized earnings approach to business valuation, firms with lower risk factors are more valuable than those with higher risk factors.

True, Easy, Page 160

100. Under the capitalized earnings approach to business valuation, firms with higher risk factors are more valuable than those with lower risk factors.

False, Medium, Page 160

101. Under the capitalized earnings approach to valuing an existing business, most normal-risk businesses use of rate-of-return factor ranging from 25 to 30 percent.

True, Medium, Page 160

102. The reliability of the discounted future earnings approach to valuing a business depends on making accurate forecasts of future earnings and on choosing a realistic present value rate.

True, Medium, Page 161

103. The best method for determining a business' worth is the discounted future earnings approach.

False, Medium, Page 161

104. A disadvantage of the market approach to valuing a business is the difficulty of finding similar companies for comparison.

True, Medium, Page 162

105. Next to picking the right buyer, planning the structure of a business sale is one of the most important decisions a seller can make.

True, Easy, Page 164

106. Owners who do not want to sell a business outright, but want to stay around for a while or surrender control gradually can use a restructuring strategy.

True, Medium, Page 165

107. Although selling the business outright is the cleanest exit path for an entrepreneur, it may have negative tax consequences, and it often excludes the option of "staying on" and exiting gradually.

True, Medium, Page 165

108. The country that tops the list of nations buying U.S. companies is Japan.

False, Medium, Page 166

109. To use an ESOP successfully, a company should have pre-tax profits of at least $100,000 and a payroll exceeding $500,000 a year.

   True, Difficult, Page 166

110. The Five Ps of Negotiating the Purchase of a Business include preparation, poise, persuasiveness, persistence, and patience.

   True, Medium, Page 169

Essay Questions:

111. Briefly describe the advantages and the disadvantages of buying an existing business.

   Advantages may include:
   increased likelihood of success
   established customer base
   supplier relationships
   set up business system
   equipment installed and productive capacity is known
   inventory in place and financing in place
   location established
   employees established
   previous owner experience base
   easier financing
   may be a bargain

   Disadvantages may include:
   may be losing money
   previous owner may have created ill will
   employees inherited with the business may not be suitable
   business location may have become unsatisfactory
   equipment and facilities may be obsolete or inefficient
   change and innovation are difficult to implement
   inventory may be outdated or obsolete
   accounts receivable may be worth less than face value
   business may be overpriced
   Page 140

112. What is "goodwill"? Is it possible to inherit "ill will" from an existing business?

   Goodwill is an intangible asset. It is based on the company's reputation and ability to attract customers. Yes, it is possible to inherit ill will. Customers aren't always aware when a business changes hands, nor are previous poor business practices easily forgiven.
   Page 142

113. Briefly discuss the five steps in acquiring a business.

   Analyze your skills, abilities, and interests to determine what kind(s) of businesses you should consider. Think about what you expect to get out of a business, what size company you want to buy, what location you prefer, etc.

Prepare a list of potential candidates. Search not only the obvious sources, but also the hidden market of companies that may be for sale but are not advertised as such. This might include business brokers, bankers, accountants, industry contacts, networking, trade associations, etc.

Investigate and evaluate the best one. Consider the strengths and weaknesses of the candidates, their profitability, customer base, physical condition, competition, etc.

Explore financing options. Consider approaching the seller for financial assistance. Also, consider traditional sources.

Ensure a smooth transition. Communicate openly with employees. Consider asking the seller to serve as a consultant until the transition is complete.
Page 144

114. Your friend Susan is considering purchasing an existing business. How would you explain to her what due diligence is, why it is important, and the critical areas of it?

The due diligence process in analyzing and evaluating an existing business may be just as time consuming as the development of a comprehensive business plan for a start-up company. It is also just as crucial. It is important to verify all the facts and figures provided to you by the seller. It is also important in determining the potential for success.

The five critical areas include:

- Why does the owner really want to sell the business? His stated reason may not be the real one. Is he trying to hide anything from you?
- What is the physical condition of the business? Carefully evaluate the assets to determine their value. Consider the location and physical facility's appearance.
- What is the potential for the company's products or services? Complete a thorough market analysis to develop an accurate and realistic sales forecast. Evaluate industry trends.
- What legal aspects should you consider? Liens, bulk transfers, contract assignments, covenants not to compete, ongoing legal liabilities, and product liability lawsuits should all be considered.
- Is the business financially sound? Remember that any investment in a company should produce a reasonable salary for her, an attractive return on the money she invests, and enough to cover the amount she must borrow to make the purchase. Carefully review past sales, operating expenses, and profits, as well as the assets used to generate those profits. Analyze income statements, balance sheets, and income tax returns for the past three to five years, as well as cash flow documents.

Page 147

115. Explain the steps in the acquisition process.

See Figure 5.1

1) Identify and approach candidate

2) Sign non-disclosure document
3) Sign letter of intent
4) Buyer's due diligence investigation
5) Draft Purchase Agreement
6) Close the final deal
7) Begin the transition
Page 155

116. Is there a "best method" for determining the value of a business? Why? How should a prospective buyer go about establishing the value of a business?

No. Valuation is partly an art and partly a science. Establishing a reasonable price for a privately held business is difficult due to a wide variety of factors that influence its value: the nature of the business itself, its position in the market or industry, the outlook for the market or industry, the company's financial status, its earning capacity, any intangible assets it may own (e.g., patents, trademarks, copyrights), the value of other similar publicly held companies, and many other factors. The wisest approach is to compute a company's value using several techniques and then to choose the one that makes the most sense.
Page 156

117. Briefly summarize the mechanics of each of the methods for valuing an existing business: balance sheet technique, adjusted balance sheet technique, excess earnings method, capitalized earnings method, discounted future earnings method, and the market approach.

- Balance Sheet Assets = Liabilities + Owner's Equity
- Balance sheet Adjusted to reflect Fair Market Value
- Earnings Approach Net Worth + Intangible Value
- Capitalized Earnings Net Income – owner's salary divided by ROR similar risk investment
- Discounted Future Earnings Weighted Average of 5 years use optimistic + most likely + pessimistic divided by +4 6
- Market Approach uses price/earnings ratios of similar businesses – once an average p/e ratio is found from as many businesses as possible – it is then multiplied by the private company's estimated earnings

Page 156 – Table 5.4

118. Explain five strategies business owners can use to exit their businesses.

- Straight Business Sale
- Forming a Family Limited Partnership
- Sell a Controlling Interest
- Restructure Company
- Sell to an International Buyer
- Use a Two-Step Method sale
- Establish an Employee (ESOP)

Page 164

119.   Explain what the buyer and the seller of a business are each looking for in the negotiation process.

The seller is looking to:
- Get the highest price possible for the business.
- Sever all responsibility for the company's liabilities.
- Avoid unreasonable contract terms that might limit his future opportunities.
- Maximize the cash he gets from the deal.
- Minimize the tax burden from the sale.
- Make sure the buyer will be able to make all future payments.

The buyer seeks to:
- Get the business at the lowest possible price.
- Negotiate favorable payment terms, preferably over time.
- Get assurances that he is buying the business he thinks he is getting.
- Avoid putting the seller in a position to open a competing business.
- Minimize the amount of cash paid up front.

Page 167

120.   What factors influence the negotiation process between a business buyer and a seller?

- How strong is the seller's desire to sell?
- Will the seller help with financing?
- What terms does the buyer suggest? Which terms are most important to him?
- Is it urgent that the seller close the deal quickly?
- What deal structure best suits your needs?
- What are the consequences for both parties?
- Will the seller sign a restrictive covenant?
- Is the seller willing to stay on with the company for a time as a consultant?
- What general economic conditions exist in the industry at the time of the sale?

Page 168

121.   Explain the "5 Ps" of the negotiation process.

- Preparation – examining the needs of both parties and all relevant factors affecting the business and sale

- Persuasiveness – know what your most important positions are, articulate them, and offer support for your position

- Poise – remaining calm and never raising your voice or losing your temper

- Patience – don't be in such a hurry to close the deal that you give up much of what you hoped to get

- Persistence – don't give up at the first sign of resistance

Page 169

Chapter 5
Buying an Existing Business
Mini-Cases

Case 5-1: What's It Worth?

Lauren Holcombe has wanted to open her own clothing store since she was in high school. Her career interest and dynamic personality enabled her to get a part-time job at a small women's clothing shop in her home town after school. When Lauren enrolled in the state university to major in retail management, she got a part-time job in the ladies' clothing section of a prestigious department store in the city. Lauren's supervisor was impressed with her business acumen and her congenial personality. "Lauren is one of the best workers we've ever had in this department. She's very bright, quite attractive, and very outgoing. Lauren is eager to learn anything she can about the business; she's always asking questions!"

During Lauren's senior year in college, her Aunt Bessie died and left her an inheritance totaling nearly $300,000. "I'll miss dear old Aunt Bessie, but have I got plans for my inheritance! Now, I'll be able to run my own clothing store just like I've always dreamed." Lauren immediately began planning to launch her business venture, but progress was slow. During a trip to her home town over the Christmas break, Lauren discovered that a well-established ladies' clothing shop was up for sale. The shop was well-known and quite successful, but the owner, Kathleen Todd, was quitting to retire in Tahiti. Lauren contacted Ms. Todd to discuss the sale of the business.

Ms. Todd hired a company to conduct an independent appraisal of the business, which concluded that tangible assets were $230,000 and assumable liabilities were $18,000. The appraisal estimated net profit for the next year to be $73,000 before deducting any managerial salaries. Lauren expects to draw $20,000 in salary since she believes this is the salary she could expect when working for someone else. Lauren estimates that a reasonable rate of return on an investment of similar risk is 25 percent. Ms. Todd has set a value of $85,000 for intangibles such as goodwill, and is asking $297,000 for the business.

1. Using the capitalized earnings method, calculate the value of the business.

$$\text{Value} = \frac{\text{Net profit (after deducting managerial salary)}}{\text{Rate of return on investment of similar risk}}$$

$$= \frac{73,800 - 20,000}{25} = \$215,200)$$

2. Based on the excess earnings approach, what do you expect the business to be worth?

Tangible net worth ($230,000-$18,000)	$212,000	
Opportunity cost:		
Salary		$20,000
Investment ($212,000 x.25)		53,000
Total opportunity costs		$73,000
Estimated net profit	$73,800	
Extra earning power($73,800-73,000)=	800	

Value of intangibles (3 x $800)   <u>$ 2,400</u>
Total Value $214,400

3. Given the following earnings estimates, compute the value of the business using the discounted future earnings technique.

Number of Years into the Future	Pessimistic	Most Likely	Optimistic
1	$62,000	$73,800	$75,000
2	$65,000	$75,000	$77,000
3	$68,000	$77,000	$79,000
4	$71,000	$79,000	$80,000
5	$73,000	$80,000	$82,000

	Average Earnings	x PV Factor	= PV of Earnings
Year 1	$72,033	.8000	$ 57,626
Year 2	$73,667	.6400	$ 47,147
Year 3	$75,833	.5120	$ 38,826
Year 4	$77,833	.4096	$ 31,880
Year 5	$79,167	.3277	$ 25,941
Total		$201,429	

Estimate of cash flow stream beyond 6 years:
$79,167 \times \dfrac{1}{25} = \$316,668$

$316,688 x .2621 = $83,013
Total Value = $284,433

4. Is Ms. Todd's asking price reasonable? How much should Lauren offer Ms. Todd at the beginning of the negotiation process?

P/E Ratios   3.98
                      3.64   Average $= \dfrac{11.18}{3} = 3.73$
                    <u>3.56</u>
Total   11.18
Value = $73,800 x 3.73 = $275,274

Ms. Todd's asking price of $297,000 seems to be high. Lauren should offer Ms. Todd a price below the $297,000 to allow some room for bargaining.

Case 5-2: Building Supply

Recently, you decided to purchase a local building supply store. The business has passed the initial screening test and you are ready to being discussing prices with the present owner. An independent appraisal has calculated the tangible net worth of the business to be $175,000. You determine the rate of return on an investment of similar risk to be 25 percent. You plan to draw a salary of $19,000. Your CPA estimates the net profit of the business (before your salary is deducted) to be $75,000. The present owner has selected a goodwill value of $65,000, and is asking $240,000 for the business.

5.   Based on the balance sheet method, what do you calculate the business to be worth?

   Value = $175,000

6.   Based on the capitalized earnings method, what do you calculate the business to be worth?

   Value = $\frac{\$75,000-\$19,000}{.25}$ = $224.000

7.   Based on the excess earnings approach, what do you calculate the business to be worth?

   Adjusted tangible net worth $175,000
   Opportunity costs:
                  Investment $175,000 x .25=$43,750
                  Salary $19,000
                  Total opportunity costs $62,750
   Extra earnings power=$75,000 – 62,750=$12,250
   Value of intangibles:
   $12,250 x 3*=   36,750
      or
   $12,250 x 4*=   49,000
   Total value= $211,750
                                              Or
                                      $224,000
   *Students may use a years-of-profit figure of 3 or 4

8.   You have found two similar businesses whose stock is publicly traded on the OTC market. Their price-earnings ratios are 3.19 and 2.91. Using these two firms as a benchmark, what do you estimate the business to be worth using the market approach?

   Average P/E ratio = 3.05
   Value = $75,000 x 3.05 = $228,750

9.   Given the following earnings estimates, compute the value of the business.

Number of Years into the Future	Pessimistic	Most Likely	Optimistic
1	$62,000	$75,000	$80,000
2	$68,000	$78,000	$82,000
3	$72,000	$82,000	$85,000
4	$78,000	$86,000	$89,000
5	$85,000	$89,000	$91,000

(Weighted)

Year	Average Earnings	x PV Factor	= PV of Earnings
1	$73,667	.8000	$58,933
2	77,000	.6400	49,280
3	80,833	.5120	41,387
4	85,167	.4096	34,884
5	88,667	.3277	29,054
Total			$213,539

Estimate of cash flow stream beyond 6 years:
$88,667 x 1/.25 = $354,667
$354,667 x .2621 = $92,974
Total value = $213,539 + 92,974 = $306,513

10. How much would you offer the present owner at the beginning of the negotiation process?

Students' responses will be different, but their initial offer price should be below the asking price of $240,000.

Chapter 6   **Building a Powerful Marketing Plan**

Multiple Choice Questions:

1. _____ is the process of creating and delivering desired goods and services to customers and involves all of the activities associated with winning and retaining loyal customers.
   a. Marketing
   b. Personal selling
   c. Promotion
   d. Customer service

   a., Easy, Page 174

2. For an entrepreneur, a business plan:
   a. is of relatively little importance due to the dynamic nature of the marketplace.
   b. is synonymous with the marketing plan.
   c. tends to stress how the entrepreneur will operate rather than detailing what he/she wants to accomplish.
   d. contains both a marketing plan and a financial plan.

   d., Medium, Page 174

3. The focus of a small company's marketing plan is:
   a. preparing accurate financial forecasts.
   b. the customer.
   c. describing how its products or services are superior to those of competitors.
   d. the competition.

   b., Easy, Page 174

4. Successful marketing requires a business owner to:
   a. understand what her target customers' needs, demands, and wants are before her competitor can.
   b. offer customers products and services that will satisfy their needs, demands, and wants.
   c. provide customers with service, convenience, and value so that they will keep coming back.
   d. All of the above.

   d., Easy, Page 174

5. Warren Cassell, owner of Just Books, a very small book store, makes special orders for customers at no extra charge, provides free gift-wrapping, conducts out-of-print book searches, offers autographed copies of books, hosts "Meet the Author" breakfasts, and publishes a newsletter for book lovers. By offering his customers lots of "extras" they don't get at larger bookstores, Cassell has won a growing base of loyal customers. Cassell is relying on which marketing strategy?
   a. demographic marketing
   b. transaction selling
   c. individualized marketing
   d. guerrilla marketing

   d., Medium, Page 174

6. Small businesses can compete with larger rivals with bigger budgets by employing unconventional, low-cost creative techniques known as:
   a. market research.
   b. astonishing customer service.
   c. guerrilla marketing techniques.
   d. psychographics.

   c., Easy, Page 174

7. The foundation of every business is:
   a. its products and services.
   b. satisfying the customer.
   c. doing whatever it takes to earn a profit.
   d. operating in a socially responsible manner.

   b., Medium, Page 175

8. Which of the following is **not** one of the objectives a guerrilla marketing plan should accomplish?
   a. Determine customer needs and wants through market research.
   b. Determine how the company will be able to serve all customers.
   c. Analyze the firm's competitive advantages and build a marketing strategy around them.
   d. Create a marketing mix that meets customer needs and wants.

   b., Medium, Page 175

9. Which of the following statements concerning a company's target market is **false**?
   a. Marketing experts contend that the greatest marketing mistake small companies make is failing to clearly define the target market to be served.
   b. A "shotgun approach" to marketing--trying to appeal to everyone rather than to only a small market segment--is the most effective way to compete with large companies and their bigger marketing budgets.
   c. Small companies are usually better suited to pinpointing target markets that their larger rivals overlook or consider too small to be attractive.
   d. Most successful small businesses have well-defined portraits of the customers they are trying to attract.

   b., Difficult, Page 175

10. Most marketing experts contend that the greatest marketing mistake small businesses make is:
    a. failing to identify the target market.
    b. spending too little on advertising.
    c. underpricing their products and services.
    d. spending too little on quality improvement.

    a., Medium, Page 175

11. Which of the following is **not** part of a marketing plan?
    a. Determining customer needs and wants through market research
    b. Pinpointing the specific target markets the small company will serve
    c. Determining the most efficient way to produce a product and then finding a way to sell it
    d. Creating a marketing mix that meets customer needs and wants

    c., Medium, Page 175

12. Studies of shifting patterns in age, income, education, race, and other population characteristics are the subject of:
    a. psychographics.
    b. demographics.
    c. sociographics.
    d. paleontology.

    b., Easy, Page 177

13. Demographic patterns indicate that by 2050, the population of Caucasians will shrink to 53 percent of the nation's population from 72 percent in 2000, but the populations of other groups such as _____ and _____ will climb rapidly.
    a. African-Americans; Hispanic Americans
    b. Hispanic Americans; Asian Americans
    c. Asian Americans; Native Americans
    d. Native Americans; Hispanic Americans

    b., Medium, Page 177

14. Which of the following statements concerning marketing research is **false**?
    a. Market research is the vehicle for gathering the information that serves as the foundation for the company's marketing plan, helps avoid costly marketing mistakes, and can uncover unmet customer needs the business can serve.
    b. Market research involves systematically collecting, analyzing, and interpreting data pertaining to the small company's market, customers, and competitors.
    c. Small companies are at a distinct disadvantage compared to larger ones when conducting market research since it is so expensive.
    d. Actually, all of the above are **true** statements.

    c., Medium, Page 177

15. One of the worst—and most common—mistakes entrepreneurs make is:
    a. assuming that a market exists for their product or service.
    b. taking too much time to conduct planning and research.
    c. conducting informal research.
    d. conducting on-line research, which is too impersonal and doesn't yield accurate information.

    a., Medium, Page 178

16. Which of the following techniques does marketing consultant Faith Popcorn recommend to small business owners interested in tracking market trends?
    a. Hire a top 10 market research firm to track trends for you.
    b. Watch what the large corporations in your industry are doing.
    c. Read as many current publications as possible.
    d. Talk with 2 to 3 people at random each week to hear what they're buying and why.

    c., Medium, Page 178

17. Which of the following is **not** one of the techniques recommended by marketing consultant Faith Popcorn as a way to monitor trends in the marketplace?
    a. Watch the top 10 TV shows and movies.
    b. Talk to at least 150 customers a year about what they are buying and why.
    c. Read as many current publications as possible
    d. Pay attention to what your parents and grandparents buy and how they make their purchase decisions, as history always repeats itself.

    d., Medium, Page 178

18. Your friend has decided to conduct market research to assist in making informed decisions for his small business. What should you recommend as the first step in the market research process?
    a. Collect data.
    b. Define the objective.
    c. Design the research.
    d. Determine the relevant information.

    b., Easy, Page 179

19. An individualized (one-to-one) marketing campaign requires business owners to:
    a. collect information on their customers, linking their identities to their transactions.
    b. calculate the long-term value of their customers so they know which ones are most desirable and most profitable.
    c. practice "just-in-time marketing" by knowing what their customers' buying cycle is and time their marketing efforts to coincide with it.
    d. All of the above.

    d., Medium, Page 180

20. Which of the following is **not** a secondary source of market research data?
    a. Census data
    b. Trade publications
    c. Focus groups
    d. Magazines

    c., Easy, Page 181

21. Which of the following is **not** a primary market research source?
    a. Customer surveys
    b. Focus groups
    c. Daily transactions
    d. Actually, all of the above **are** sources of primary market research.

    d., Medium, Page 181

22. Which of the following features allows a small company to utilize relationship marketing successfully?
    a. Close contact with its customers
    b. Personal attention to its customers
    c. Emphasis on superior service for its customers
    d. All of the above.

    d., Easy, Page 182

23. One "natural" advantage small businesses have over large businesses, which can be a significant competitive advantage, is:
    a. relationship marketing.
    b. their ability to conduct market research.
    c. their lower costs.
    d. their ability to serve many highly diverse target markets.

    a., Medium, Page 182

24. Juan wants to calculate the sales revenue his company would lose by measuring the percentage of customers who would leave because of poor service. He wants to measure the company's _____.
    a. rain checks
    b. risk capital
    c. customer risk
    d. revenue at risk

    d., Easy, Page 184

25. The marketing approach that is most effective today for a small business is:
    a. mass marketing.
    b. market segmentation.
    c. niche marketing.
    d. individualized (one-to-one) marketing.

    c., Medium, Page 185

26. In relationship marketing, the _____ level of customer involvement is characterized by the attitude "There's a customer out there." However, managers and employees know little about the company's customers.
    a. Level 1 Customer Awareness
    b. Level 2 Customer Sensitivity
    c. Level 3 Customer Alignment
    d. Level 4 Customer Partnership

    a., Medium, Page 185

27. In relationship marketing, the _____ level of customer involvement is characterized by managers and employees who seek customer feedback through surveys, focus groups, interviews, and visits. Managers and employees understand the customer's central role in the business.
    a. Level 1 Customer Awareness
    b. Level 2 Customer Sensitivity
    c. Level 3 Customer Alignment
    d. Level 4 Customer Partnership

    c., Medium, Page 185

28. When a company has refined its customer service attitude from mere technique to an all encompassing part of its culture and managers and employees focus on building lasting relationships with customers, it has reached which level of customer involvement?
    a. Level 1 Customer Awareness
    b. Level 2 Customer Sensitivity
    c. Level 3 Customer Alignment
    d. Level 4 Customer Partnership

    d., Medium, Page 185

29. When managers and employees understand the central role of the customer and spend considerable time talking to them and about them, a company is at which level of customer involvement?
    a. Level 1 Customer Awareness
    b. Level 2 Customer Sensitivity
    c. Level 3 Customer Alignment
    d. Level 4 Customer Partnership

    c., Medium, Page 185

30. A marketing concept designed to draw customers into a store by creating a kaleidoscope of sights, sounds, smells, and activities, all designed to entertain—and of course, sell, is:
    a. entertailing.
    b. entertaining.
    c. retailing.
    d. None of the above

    a., Easy, Page 187

31.   Which of the following was **not** identified as one of the guerrilla marketing principles in your text?
       a.   Strive to be like everyone else so that your company "fits in."
       b.   Create an identity for your business.
       c.   Connect with customers on an emotional level.
       d.   Don't just sell—entertain.

       a., Medium, Page 188

32.   A recent study by the consulting firm Bain & Company found that companies that retain just 5 percent more customers experience profit increases of at least _____.
       a.   5 percent
       b.   25 percent
       c.   50 percent
       d.   75 percent

       c., Difficult, Page 191

33.   In your training program, you stress to all new employees the importance of customer satisfaction, citing the fact that _____ percent of the average company's sales come from present customers.
       a.   30
       b.   50
       c.   70
       d.   90

       c., Difficult, Page 191

34.   The typical business loses ____ percent of its customers each year.
       a.   20
       b.   30
       c.   45
       d.   70

       a., Difficult, Page 191

35.   The majority of customers who stop patronizing a particular store do so because:
       a.   its prices are too high.
       b.   its quality is too low.
       c.   an indifferent employee treated them poorly.
       d.   it failed to advertise enough.

       c., Medium, Page 191

36. ___ percent of dissatisfied customers never complain about rude or discourteous service but ___ percent will not buy from that business again.
    a. 10; 55
    b. 26; 75
    c. 45; 67
    d. 96; 91

    d., Difficult, Page 191

37. Attracting a new customer costs ____ as much as keeping an existing one.
    a. twice
    b. five times
    c. half
    d. three-fourths

    b., Difficult, Page 191

38. Companies with a customer focus typically ask their customers all but which of the following questions?
    a. What are we doing right?
    b. What have we done wrong?
    c. What can we do in the future?
    d. What have our competitors done wrong?

    d., Medium, Page 192

39. The worst catastrophe to befall any business would be to:
    a. encourage customers to complain and have employees give management feedback on the complaints.
    b. have great advertising and poor quality products.
    c. spend an excessive amount of money attracting new customers.
    d. have a great product and an inaccessible location.

    b., Medium, Page 192

40. Which of the following is **not** a suggestion of a means of focusing on the customer?
    a. Discourage customer complaints.
    b. Get total commitment to superior customer service from top managers.
    c. Carefully select and train everyone who will deal with the customer.
    d. Actually, all of the above **are** suggested as a means of focusing on the customer.

    a., Medium, Page 193

41. Which of the following is a way to improve customer service?
    a. Encourage customers to complain.
    b. Ask employees for feedback on improving customer service.
    c. Develop a service theme that communicates the importance of customer service in the company.
    d. All of the above.

    d., Easy, Page 193

42. The Total Quality Management (TQM) concept:
    a. strives to achieve quality not just in the product or service itself, but in every aspect of the business and its relationship with the customer.
    b. relies on quality inspections through an army of quality control inspectors.
    c. focuses on reducing the time it takes to fulfill a customer's request for a product.
    d. None of the above.

    a., Easy, Page 193

43. Which of the following factors do American consumers rank as the top component of quality?
    a. low price
    b. reliability
    c. ease of use
    d. durability

    b., Medium, Page 193

44. Companies with strong reputations for quality follow certain guidelines, such as:
    a. establishing long-term relationships with suppliers.
    b. fostering individual effort and pride of workmanship.
    c. securing employees' commitment to the quality philosophy; it is not important to secure top management's full support, as the employees are the ones who work more closely with the products and the customers.
    d. All of the above.

    a., Medium, Page 194

45. Your ETDBW ("Easy To Do Business With") index is based on customer convenience factors, including which of the following?
    a. Is your business located near your customers, and does it provide easy access?
    b. Are your business hours suitable to your customers?
    c. Are your employees trained to handle business transactions quickly, efficiently, and politely?
    d. All of the above.

    d., Easy, Page 195

46. Small businesses are able to maintain a leadership role in innovation by:
    a. using their size, flexibility, and speed to their advantage.
    b. spending much more money on R&D than larger companies do.
    c. foreseeing trends better and far enough in advance that they can spread innovation costs over several years.
    d. making better use of technology than large companies.

    a., Medium, Page 196

47. One recent study of consumer behavior found that _____ percent of customers buy for reasons other than price.
    a. 10
    b. 33
    c. 50
    d. 73

d., Difficult, Page 196

48. Numerous surveys have concluded that the most important element of service is:
    a. the personal touch.
    b. convenient business hours.
    c. speedy transactions.
    d. innovative product design.

a., Easy, Page 197

49. What can a company do to achieve stellar customer service and satisfaction?
    a. Listen to customers with the help of suggestion boxes, focus groups, surveys, and other tools.
    b. Define what "superior service" means so that customers and employees know exactly what to expect and what to provide.
    c. Hire friendly, courteous sales and service representatives.
    d. All of the above.

d., Easy, Page 197

50. The key ingredient in the superior customer service equation is:
    a. state-of-the-art equipment.
    b. standards and measurements of customer service.
    c. the support of managers.
    d. friendly, courteous, well-trained people delivering customer service.

d., Medium, Page 198

51. Recent studies by the National Science Foundation concluded that linking pay to performance:
    a. had no effect on employees' motivation and productivity.
    b. caused employees' motivation and productivity to fall by as much as 29 percent.
    c. caused employees' motivation and productivity to climb by as much as 5 percent.
    d. caused employees' motivation and productivity to climb by as much as 63 percent.

d., Medium, Page 199

52. Time compression management (TCM) involves:
    a. speeding new products to market.
    b. reducing the administrative time required to fill an order.
    c. shortening customer response time in manufacturing and delivery.
    d. All of the above.

d., Easy, Page 201

53. Which of the following is **not** a suggestion for using time compression management (TCM) to turn speed into a competitive advantage?
    a. Instill speed in the company's culture.
    b. Use technology to find shortcuts wherever possible.
    c. Pay workers more if they do their jobs the same way -- only faster.
    d. Set aggressive goals for time reduction and stick to them.

    c., Difficult, Page 201

54. To attract potential customers, a World Wide Web site should be:
    a. easy to navigate.
    b. interactive.
    c. inviting, offering more than a "laundry list" of items for sale.
    d. All of the above.

    d., Easy, Page 203

55. The "typical" World Wide Web user is:
    a. young.
    b. educated.
    c. wealthy.
    d. All of the above.

    d., Easy, Page 203

56. Which of the following is **not** an element of the marketing mix?
    a. Product
    b. Place
    c. Profit
    d. Promotion

    c., Easy, Page 204

57. Profits normally reach their peak in the _____ stage of the product life cycle, while sales normally reach their peak in the _____ stage of the product life cycle.
    a. growth and acceptance; maturity
    b. maturity and competition; market saturation
    c. growth and acceptance; market saturation
    d. introduction; growth

    b., Difficult, Page 205

58. The typical product's life cycle lasts _____ years, but the length of that cycle appears to be _____.
    a. 1 to 2; increasing
    b. 4 to 6; increasing
    c. 10 to 14; shrinking
    d. 15 to 20; shrinking

    c., Difficult, Page 205

59. The most common channel of distribution for consumer goods is:
    a. manufacturer ---> consumer.
    b. manufacturer ---> retailer ---> consumer.
    c. manufacturer ---> wholesaler ---> retailer ---> consumer.
    d. manufacturer ---> broker ---> consumer.

    c., Medium, Page 206

60. The right price for a product or service depends on three main factors. Which of the following is **not** one of the main three factors?
    a. Cost structure
    b. What the market will bear
    c. Desired image the company wants to create in its customer's minds
    d. Competitors' prices

    d., Medium, Page 207

True/False Questions:

61. Too many business plans describe in great detail what an entrepreneur intends to accomplish and pay little, if any, attention to the strategies to achieve those targets.

    True, Medium, Page 174

62. A business plan is a written statement of what an entrepreneur plans to accomplish in both quantitative and qualitative terms and how she plans to accomplish it.

    True, Easy, Page 174

63. By using guerrilla marketing strategies—unconventional, low-cost, creative techniques—small companies can get as much "bang" for their marketing bucks as their larger rivals.

    True, Easy, Page 174

64. Because they lack the size and financial resources of their larger competitors, small companies are powerless when it comes to developing effective marketing strategies.

    False, Easy, Page 174

65. A marketing plan should identify a small company's target customers and describe how the business will attract and keep them.

    True, Easy, Page 175

66. A "shotgun approach" to marketing is the small business' secret to competing successfully with larger rivals and their bigger marketing budgets.

    False, Medium, Page 175

67. An effective marketing program depends on a clear, concise definition of the firm's target market.

   True, Easy, Page 175

68. Most marketing experts contend that the greatest marketing mistake small businesses make is failing to clearly define their target market.

   True, Medium, Page 175

69. The specific group of customers at whom a company aims its goods and services is its target market.

   True, Easy, Page 175

70. The company's target customer should permeate the entire business, from the merchandise purchased to the layout and decor of the store.

   True, Easy, Page 175

71. The increasing diversity of our population is creating a marketing "threat" to small businesses because they can't profitably serve small niches.

   False, Medium, Page 176

72. Small companies that spot demographic trends and act on them early can gain a distinctive edge in the market.

   True, Easy, Page 177

73. Throughout the twenty-first century, minorities such as Hispanic Americans and Asian Americans will represent the slowest growing segments of the U.S. population.

   False, Easy, Page 177

74. Market research is a valuable tool for defining the firm's target market, its needs, and its potential profitability.

   True, Easy, Page 177

75. Watching the top ten TV shows, seeing the top ten movies, or listening to her children are all ways a small business owner could conduct market research.

   True, Easy, Page 178

76. To be useful, market research must be structured, formal, and highly sophisticated.

   False, Easy, Page 178

77. An individualized marketing strategy requires a business owner to collect data on individual customers and then to develop a marketing program designed specifically to appeal to their needs, tastes, and preferences.

True, Medium, Page 179

78. Small companies are at a definite disadvantage compared to larger ones when it comes to conducting market research since it is so expensive.

False, Medium, Page 179

79. Secondary research data is less time-consuming and less costly to gather than primary research data.

True, Easy, Page 181

80. Primary research data is less time-consuming and less costly to gather than secondary research data.

False, Easy, Page 181

81. The best way for small retailers to compete effectively with the giant "category killers" is to offer lower prices than their larger rivals.

False, Easy, Page 182

82. Relationship marketing involves developing and maintaining long-term relationships with customers so that they will keep coming back to make repeat purchases.

True, Easy, Page 182

83. A company has a competitive edge when customers perceive that its products or services are superior to those of competitors.

True, Easy, Page 182

84. In relationship marketing, the level of customer involvement in which a company makes its customers an all-encompassing part of its culture is "Customer Partnership."

True, Difficult, Page 185

85. When an employee in a business treats a customer poorly, that customer usually does not complain; however, she does tell her "horror story" about that business to at least nine other people.

True, Medium, Page 191

86.   Because about 20 percent of a typical company's customers account for about 80 percent of its sales, a business should focus its resources on keeping its best customers rather than trying to chase "fair weather" customers who will defect to any better deal that comes along.

      True, Medium, Page 191

87.   Because 70 percent of the average company's sales come from present customers, few can afford to alienate any customers.

      True, Medium, Page 191

88.   Most dissatisfied customers complain about rude or discourteous service to the owner or the manager.

      False, Medium, Page 191

89.   The typical business loses 20 percent of its customers each year.

      True, Difficult, Page 191

90.   If employees are committed to quality, management's commitment becomes unimportant.

      False, Medium, Page 191

91.   Providing low prices is the most effective way for a small business to attract and maintain a growing customer base.

      False, Medium, Page 192

92.   It takes much less money and time to keep existing customers than it does to attract new ones.

      True, Easy, Page 192

93.   It costs five times as much money and time to keep existing customers as it does to attract new ones.

      False, Medium, Page 192

94.   The best way to find out what customers really want and value is to ask them.

      True, Easy, Page 192

95.   Giving customers a chance to complain about a problem usually is fruitless; once a business makes a customer angry, he typically will not buy from that company again under any circumstances.

      False, Medium, Page 193

96. If given the chance to complain, 95 percent of customers will buy again when a business handles their complaints promptly and effectively.

True, Difficult, Page 193

97. Since front-line service workers are not able to predict the causes of customer complaints, managers must be the ones to identify potential customer service problems.

False, Medium, Page 193

98. One disadvantage of total quality management (TQM) is that its principles apply only to manufacturers.

False, Easy, Page 193

99. Total quality management (TQM) works best when it becomes an integral part of a small company's strategy and focuses on continuous improvement in the quality the company delivers to customers.

True, Easy, Page 194

100. The best way for a small business to ensure quality products is to use quality inspections.

False, Medium, Page 194

101. Several studies have found that customers rank convenience and easy access to goods and services at the top of their purchase criteria.

True, Medium, Page 194

102. Hours of operation, quick answering of phone calls and ease of use of credit cards are just three "measures" of a company's "ETDBW" index.

True, Medium, Page 195

103. Truly customer-oriented companies seek to go beyond customer satisfaction, striving for customer astonishment.

True, Easy, Page 197

104. The easiest and least expensive way to achieve customer satisfaction is through friendly, personal service.

True, Easy, Page 197

105. Companies known for their superior service devote from one to five percent of their employees' work hours to training.

True, Difficult, Page 198

106.   Most businesses currently selling their products and services on the World Wide Web are earning extremely high profits from their Web sites.

    False, Medium, Page 202

107.   The World Wide Web allows creative small business owners to make their companies look as big as their larger rivals.

    True, Easy, Page 202

108.   Small companies that have had the greatest success selling on the Web have marketing strategies that emphasize their existing strengths and core competencies.

    True, Easy, Page 203

109.   Just as in any marketing venture, the key to successful marketing on the World Wide Web is selling the right product or service at the right price to the right target audience.

    True, Easy, Page 203

110.   The four Ps of marketing are product, place, profit, and promotion.

    False, Easy, Page 203

111.   Marketing experts recommend introducing a new product only when the existing one is in the maturity stage of the product life cycle.

    False, Medium, Page 205

112.   Profits generally are low, or even negative, in the introductory stage of the product life cycle.

    True, Medium, Page 205

113.   The typical product's life cycle lasts four to six years.

    False, Medium, Page 205

114.   When products reach the decline stage of the product life cycle, they fail and become extinct.

    False, Medium, Page 205

115.   Sales and profits peak in the growth stage of the product life cycle.

    False, Medium, Page 205

116.   In the maturity stage of the product life cycle, sales volume continues to rise, but profit margins begin to fall as competitors enter the market.

    True, Medium, Page 205

117. For many small businesses, nonprice competition—focusing on factors other than price—is a more effective strategy than trying to beat larger competitors in a price war.

True, Easy, Page 207

118. Promotion is an important part of a small firm's marketing mix because it plays a significant role in creating the proper perception of a product or service in the customer's mind.

True, Easy, Page 207

119. Promotion, which involves both advertising and personal selling, should inform and persuade consumers.

True, Easy, Page 207

120. A marketing strategy results when a small business owner blends together the results of meaningful market research with a plan to develop a competitive advantage in a particular target market to develop a successful marketing mix.

True, Medium, Page 207

Essay Questions:

121. Why is it important for small business owners to define clearly its target market(s) as part of their marketing strategies?

   It is important that small businesses define the specific group of customers at whom the company aims its goods or services. Many companies try a "shotgun approach" to marketing, where the company fires marketing blasts at ever customer they see, hoping to capture some of them. Unfortunately, most small businesses do not have the deep pockets to continue this type of marketing approach. Small businesses must be more focused on the types of customers they want to target. Small firms are ideally suited to reaching market segments that their larger rivals overlook or consider too small to be profitable. A clear, concise target market allows a small business to be profitable.

   Page 175

122. Why is it important for small business owners to track demographic trends? How can small companies become effective trend trackers?

   Shifting patterns in age, income, education, race, and other population characteristics (demographics) will have a major impact on companies, their customers, and the way they do business with those customers.

   Small businesses can become effective trend trackers by staying close to their customer base and staying abreast of changes in their environment through various information sources. According to Faith Popcorn, possible sources of market information include current publications, top ten shows, top ten movies, and customers. **Page 177**

123. Your friend Maria is experiencing declining sales in the business she has owned and successfully operated for three years. She has asked for your guidance in determining the course(s) of action she should take. Your recommendation to her is to undertake a marketing research project. Briefly outline the steps involved in market research. She is concerned that market research will be too expensive and sophisticated for a small business such as hers. Is this true? Explain.

The steps in marketing research include:

- Define the objective—most crucial step; should be clear and concise; don't confuse a symptom with the true problem.

- Collect the data—gather secondary research and, if necessary, conduct primary research on your customers.

- Analyze and interpret the data—use judgment and common sense to determine what the facts you have uncovered actually mean

- Draw conclusions and act—decide how to use the information in the business; what is the appropriate action to take?

No, market research does not have to be expensive and sophisticated to be valuable. For example, for most business owners, information is often floating around. It can often be just a matter of asking customers, suppliers or collecting and organizing the data to make it valuable. This valuable information is often available for most small businesses. Not only is this type of information convenient, but the cost of obtaining it can be low as well. **Page 179**

124. Explain what is meant by relationship marketing or customer relationship management (CRM); compare and contrast CRM and transaction selling.

CRM involves developing, maintaining, and managing long-term relationships with customers so that they will want to keep coming back to make repeat purchases. This concept recognizes that customers have a lifetime value to a business and that keeping the best customers over time may be a company's greatest sustainable advantage. The customer becomes the center of a company's thinking, planning, and action.

Several differences between CRM and transaction selling include:

- Duration—With CRM, it is ongoing; with transaction selling, there is a distinct beginning and end, with a one-transaction only attitude.

- Driven by—CRM is driven by commitment and trust; transaction selling is driven by making profitable short-term transactions.

- Business plan implications—CRM concentrates on building a network of relationships with dependable suppliers and customers that will lead to long-term profitability; transaction selling seeks to maximize short-term profits; make the bottom line look good, whatever the long-term costs.

- Primary advantage—With CRM, an intimate knowledge of customers' needs, wants, and preferences developed over time; with transaction selling, cash in hand.

- Primary disadvantage—CRM depends on other partners in the web of relationships; transaction selling risks losing the sale if a competitor makes the customer a better offer.

(For the complete list of differences, refer to Table 6.1, Page 185.)
Page 182, 185

125. Describe what is meant by guerrilla marketing. What objectives should a guerrilla marketing plan accomplish? List at least five guerrilla marketing tactics your small business might be able to use successfully.

Guerrilla marketing involves using unconventional, low-cost, creative techniques in order to get more out of every marketing dollar.

The marketing plan has four objectives that include:

- Pinpoint the specific target market the small company will serve
- Determine customer needs and wants through market research
- Analyze the firm's competitive advantages and build a guerrilla marketing strategy around them
- Help create a marketing mix that meets customer needs and wants.

Examples of guerrilla marketing tactics include:

- Help organize and sponsor a service- or community-oriented project.
- Always be on the lookout for new niches to enter. Try to develop multiple niches.
- Offer to speak about your business, industry, product, or service to local organizations.
- Ask current customers for referrals.
- Offer customers gift certificates.
- Offer samples of your product to give to customers.
- Offer a 100 percent, money-back, no-hassles guarantee.
- Create a frequent-buyer program.
- Find unique ways to thank customers for their business—a note, a lunch, a gift basket, etc.
- Accept competitors' coupons.

(For a complete list, refer to Table 6.2, Page 186)
Page 175, 186

126. Describe why a small business might gain a competitive edge over its rivals by using: a focus on the customer, devotion to quality, paying attention to convenience, concentration on innovation, dedication to service, and emphasis on speed.

- Focusing on the customer develops and allows the small business to retain a close relationship, which fosters repeat purchases and positive referrals.

- Devotion to quality focuses on continuous improvement fostering trust and customer loyalty.
- Paying attention to convenience makes access easy to products and services, increasing sales.
- Concentration on innovation allows the company to stay abreast of new trends and opportunities that allows them to detect and act on new opportunities faster.
- Dedication to service can make customer astonishment a reality.
- Emphasis on speed can satisfy the time pressures of customers.

Page 191

127. Why is it important for a small business to keep existing customers satisfied? How can a company achieve such customer satisfaction?

It is important to retain existing customers because typically 70 percent of the average company's sales come from its present customers. Few businesses can afford to alienate shoppers. 80 percent of a company's sales typically come from the best 20 percent of its customers. It is also five times more costly to attract new customers than to retain existing ones.

Customer satisfaction can be achieved by giving your best customers incentives to return, encouraging them to complain, including employees in the feedback loop, calling customers by name, getting total commitment to superior customer service astonishment, carefully training everyone who comes into contact with customers, making your products easy to buy and access.

Page 191

128. Explain the concept of Total Quality Management. How is it different from the quality inspection of a final product just before being packaged?

TQM is a strategic objective an integral part of a company's strategy and culture. Quality not just in the product or service, but every aspect of the business and its relationship with the customer and continuous improvement in the quality delivered to the customer.

Total Quality Management is a philosophy of continuous improvement where cross-functional teams and employees contribute individually to product quality along the manufacturing process. It is different from the typical quality inspection in that quality is a component all along the way, not just at the time a product is inspected before packaging or shipment.

Page 193

129. What marketing potential does the World Wide Web offer small business owners?

The WWW offers a vast network connecting the world's computers and information sources. With its ability to display colorful graphics, sound, animation, and video as well as text, the web allows small businesses to equal or even surpass their larger rival's web presence. It offers small businesses a world-wide opportunity for marketing and distribution system access.

Page 201

130. Define the four P's of the marketing mix and explain the importance of each for a small business owner's marketing strategy.

- Product (and/or service)—essential for customer satisfaction. Market research will help determine the products/services that meet the needs and wants of customers.
- Place—method of distribution. Provides place utility. Growing in importance as customers expect greater service and convenience from businesses.
- Price—determined by your costs, what the market will bear, and your desired image. Also impacted by factors of non-price competition, such as free delivery, lengthy warranties, money-back guarantees, etc.
- Promotion—involves both advertising and personal selling. Goal is to inform and persuade consumers.

As the main elements of a marketing strategy, the four elements are self-reinforcing, and when coordinated, increase the sales appeal of a product or service.
Page 204

131. List and explain the stages in the product life cycle.

- Introductory stage – products are presented to potential customers. Generally, new products must break into existing markets and compete with established products. Costs are generally high and profits are low.
- Sales growth – consumers begin to buy in large enough numbers for sales to rise, with a potential for profits.
- Maturity – sales volume continues to rise, but profit margins peak and then begin to fall as competitors enter the market.
- Market Saturation – sales peak.
- Decline – the final stage in which sales drop and profits fall. A focus on product innovation and change, as well as the development of more stable products, versus fad merchandise will extend product life cycle.
Page 205

Chapter 6
Building a Powerful Marketing Plan
Mini-Cases

Case 6-1: Customers: Key to Success

Lloyd Dixon has owned and operated a small dress shop for the past three years. Each fashion season, Lloyd attends the apparel shows and he is always very impressed by the glamour and the hundreds of different manufacturers, all with the merchandise that they say will be this season's biggest sellers. Lloyd caters to an older market and baby boomers. He hopes to tap into the upscale market.

After his first year of operation, Lloyd recognized that some of his merchandise was not selling. The "inventory close-out sale" did rescue his investment in this merchandise but did not make him a profit or contribute much to his overhead. Lloyd knew that it was not reasonable to expect to sell everything you bought, but he was not sure exactly how much of his inventory was comprised of slow movers. Lloyd believed that when he went into business he knew what women wanted in dresses. He had always prided himself on having good taste. When he had the opportunity to open this store, he was confident that he could choose merchandise that would be well received. In the first three years of operations, sales have not met Lloyd's expectations.

1. How could Lloyd realistically create a competitive advantage by giving customer service a focus in his business?

    - Lloyd should consider asking his customers questions such as:
      What are we doing right?
      How can we do that even better?
      What have we done wrong?
      What can we do in the future?
    - He should ensure that the customers believe that he values their business. He should give his best customers incentives to return, encourage customers to complain, include employees in the feedback loop, call customers by name, get total commitment to superior customer service astonishment, carefully train everyone who comes into contact with customers, and make his products easy to buy and access.

2. Faith Popcorn offers several ways Lloyd Dixon could collect information about his customers and competitors. Explain at least five of those ways.

    - Lloyd should read current magazines, especially women's fashion magazines and industry trade publications to get a sense of what fashions, colors, styles, and designs are becoming popular – and which ones are not.
    - He should also watch the top ten TV shows and the top ten movies to see which styles they might inspire.
    - Lloyd should also spend time talking to his current customers and notice how they dress (perhaps even taking photos of their garments).
    - In addition, Lloyd could use census data and other sources such as the "Survey of Buying Power" to gather demographic statistics on his customers. To collect more specific data, he could conduct an in-depth survey of present customers using current sales records to compile a mailing list.

Case 6-2: TQM and TV in Omaha

Nobody who knew Marvin Tollison ever met a man who liked television better. In the Navy, he had the opportunity to learn a great deal about his trade. When he finished his tour of duty, Marvin opened a television repair shop back home in Omaha, Nebraska. Over the years the quality of his workmanship, his fair prices, and his general overall good nature made his business flourish. Marvin had a way of finding men and women like himself when expansion was needed.

Over 17 years, the business had grown from a one-man shop operating in his garage to a 38-employee television repair staff that was dispatched to customers by two-way truck radio. Over the years, the time between a customer's call and the television repairman getting to their home had increased to about two days because the repairmen were taking longer with each call. Call-backs, having to "rerepair" equipment, are up significantly. Marvin wasn't sure, but he thought some of his customers were going elsewhere for service.

1. Can Marvin use TQM to develop a competitive edge? If so, what would you recommend he do?

    Yes, in fact, if Marvin doesn't improve the quality of his company's repair service soon, he'll soon be out of business.

    Marvin should start tracking key measures of quality in his company – repair time, number of "re-repairs," number of complaints, and others listen to them, to learn what they say about quality problems. Are they too rushed to provide good service? Do they lack proper tools and equipment? Do they need additional training?

    Marvin should create a system of rewards (financial or otherwise) for employees who perform quality work. He should track manner of quality and post results for all to see. Above all, he should avoid the tendency to try to identify employees who are causing the quality problems just so he can punish them.

    Marvin should empower his employees and involve them in designing a new and improved system for improving the company's quality.

2. How can Marvin develop "stellar" customer service?

    Once the company's quality improves, Marvin should be able to offer additional services that his customers would appreciate, such as guarantees, overnight repairs, pick-up and delivery services, and a host of other "value-added" services.

Chapter 7   E-Commerce and the Entrepreneur

Multiple Choice Questions:

1. Which type of products and/or services, are best suited for selling on the Web?
    a. High-volume, low-margin
    b. High-volume, high-margin
    c. Low-volume, low-margin
    d. Low-volume, high-margin

    a., Medium, Page 214

2. Online shopping currently accounts for _____% of total retail sales in the United States.
    a. 4.5
    b. 10.5
    c. 25.5
    d. 30.5

    a., Difficult, Page 214

3. Online sales are growing by _____ percent a year, much faster than the _____ percent growth of off-line sales.
    a. 10 to 20; 4
    b. 60 to 70; 20
    c. 50; 4.5
    d. 30 to 40; 4

    d., Difficult, Page 214

4. All of the following represent benefits of selling on the Web **except**:
    a. Opportunity to increase revenues
    b. Power to educate and inform
    c. Ability to remain open 24 hours a day
    d. Ability to advertise in a cheaper media form

    d., Easy, Page 214

5. What is the greatest benefit for small businesses that have a website?
    a. New customers
    b. Increased sales outside the United States
    c. Reduced unit costs
    d. Increased profits

    a., Medium, Page 215

6. The Web is one of the most efficient ways of reaching both new and existing customers. Properly promoted, a Web site can:
   a. reduce a company's cost of generating sales leads.
   b. provide customer support.
   c. distribute marketing materials.
   d. All of the above.

   d., Easy, Page 215

7. Which of the following is an important issue that business owners should consider before launching an e-commerce effort?
   a. How to develop long-term relationships with customers
   b. How to exploit the interconnectivity and the opportunities it creates to transform relationships with its suppliers, customers and external stakeholders.
   c. How to measure the success of its Web-based sales effort
   d. All of the above.

   d., Easy, Page 217

8. To avoid unpleasant surprises in launching an e-commerce effort an entrepreneur should:
   a. test her web site with real customers to make sure it is easy to navigate.
   b. avoid being talked into establishing a privacy policy.
   c. cancel all current advertisements in other media.
   d. not try to out-guess her customers, and handle order fulfillment as orders come in.

   a., Medium, Page 217

9. Entrepreneurs should make sure they don't fall victim to any of the e-commerce myths. Which of the following is NOT one of those myths?
   a. Setting up a business on the Web is easy and inexpensive.
   b. If I launch a site, customers will flock to it.
   c. Making money on the Web is easy.
   d. Privacy is an important issue on the Web.

   d., Easy, Page 218

10. A study by Jupiter Communications found that __% of Web customers distrust Web sites.
    a. 25
    b. 42
    c. 64
    d. 87

    c., Difficult, Page 220

11. The most important part of any e-commerce effort is:
    a. technology.
    b. the ability to understand the underlying business.
    c. to develop a workable business model.
    d. B and C only.

    d., Medium, Page 220

12. The entrepreneurs who are proving to be the most successful in e-commerce are those who know how:
     a. their industries work inside and out.
     b. technology works.
     c. to turn a profit.
     d. to effectively finance their e-commerce effort.

     a., Medium, Page 220

13. Before a Web site can become the foundation for a successful e-business:
     a. the technology must be right.
     b. it should be previewed by a Web designer.
     c. it must be created with the target audience in mind.
     d. the physical store front must be established.

     c., Medium, Page 221

14. The most common reasons for leaving a site without purchasing include which of the following?
     a. Shipping charges were too high.
     b. Site did not look trustworthy.
     c. Customers could not find the items they were looking for.
     d. All of the above.

     d., Easy, Page 221

15. Which of the following is NOT a common reason customers leave web sites before checking out?
     a. Shipping charges were too high.
     b. Privacy policy was not posted.
     c. Shopping cart was too hard to find.
     d. Site did not look trustworthy.

     b., Medium, Page 221

16. There is plenty of room for improvement in customer service on the Web. Research by BizRate.com found that _____ percent of web shoppers who actually fill their online shopping carts become frustrated, and leave the site before checking out.
     a. 10
     b. 25
     c. 50
     d. 75

     d., , Medium, Page 221

17. The most significant ways on-line companies can bolster customer service include all of the following **except**:
    a. create a well-staffed and well-trained customer response team.
    b. offer a simple return policy.
    c. provide an easy order tracking process.
    d. make financing available.

    d., Easy, Page 221

18. Unfortunately e-mail takes a very low priority at many e-commerce businesses. A recent study by Jupiter Communications found that 42 percent of business Web sites took longer than _____ to reply to e-mail inquiries, never replied at all, or simply were not accessible by e-mail.
    a. three days
    b. five days
    c. seven days
    d. ten days

    b., Medium, Page 221

19. Although e-commerce can lower many costs of doing business, it still requires:
    a. a professional web designer's input.
    b. a basic infrastructure in the distribution channel to process orders, maintain inventory, fill orders, and handle customer service.
    c. a brick-and-mortar-store presence.
    d. None of the above.

    b., Medium, Page 222

20. The greatest opportunities for e-commerce lie in:
    a. the retail sector.
    b. on-line business-to-business transactions.
    c. the service sector.
    d. high-volume, high-margin consumer goods.

    b., Medium, Page 223

21. The major disadvantages of this approach to e-commerce are the individual store's lack of prominence, and the lack of control the entrepreneur has over the site.
    a. On-line Shopping Malls
    b. Storefront-Building Services
    c. Internet Service Providers
    d. Building a Website In-House

    a., Easy, Page 225

22.	The primary advantages of on-line shopping malls are:
	a.	their simplicity and low cost.
	b.	their willingness to handle a limited number of transactions for free.
	c.	their ability to customize individual storefronts
	d.	their ability to effectively promote each resident business.

	a., Medium, Page 225

23.	All of the following approaches to e-commerce fall into the under $10,000 category **except**:
	a.	On-line Shopping Malls
	b.	Storefront-Building Services
	c.	Internet Service Providers
	d.	Building a Website In-House

	d., Medium, Page 227

24.	Strategies for successful e-commerce efforts should include all of the following **except**:
	a.	focusing on a niche market
	b.	developing a community of customers
	c.	attracting visitors by giving away "freebies"
	d.	adding value to recipients by sending spam e-mail to them

	d., Easy, Page 228

25.	Experts advise keeping an on-line newsletter short—no more than about _____ words should be used.
	a.	250
	b.	400
	c.	600
	d.	750

	c., Difficult, Page 229

26.	Customers will typically welcome well-constructed permission e-mail that directs them to company sites for information or special deals, unlike unsolicited and universally despised e-mail known as:
	a.	spam.
	b.	electronic flyers.
	c.	voice mail.
	d.	clipboards.

	a., Easy, Page 230

27. Visitors begin to evaluate the credibility of a Web site as soon as they arrive. Which of the following does **not** help develop credibility?
    a. Posting a privacy policy.
    b. Citing reference sources.
    c. Presenting fair and objective information.
    d. Avoiding the promotion of brand names.

    d., Easy, Page 230

28. If building name recognition is one of the keys to success on the Web, how can small companies with their limited resources hope to compete?
    a. Form a strategic alliance with larger companies.
    b. Register with many of the major search engines.
    c. Barter services with professional Web designers
    d. Create huge websites with all the "bells" and "Whistles."

    a., Medium, Page 230

29 Businesses selling less well-known brands should:
    a. reduce prices.
    b. offer freebies.
    c. use customer testimonials and endorsements.
    d. All of the above.

    c., Medium, Page 230

30. What percent of Web users speak English?
    a. 21
    b. 43
    c. 65
    d. 81

    b., Difficult, Page 231

31. When creating a web site, the goal is to create a design:
    a. in which customers see themselves when they visit.
    b. that is flashy.
    c. in which customers cannot relate.
    d. None of the above.

    a., Easy, Page 233

32. Perhaps the best domain name is one that:
    a. customers can easily guess if they know the company's name.
    b. is very complex to stop competitors from copying it.
    c. sounds very much like a larger competitor's name.
    d. does not use the company's initials

    a., Medium, Page 234

33.   The ideal domain name should be:
        a.   short.
        b.   memorable.
        c.   easy to spell.
        d.   All of the above.

d., Easy, Page 234

34.   What percent of web surfers use search engines to locate the business or site they are seeking?
        a.   35
        b.   55
        c.   77
        d.   89

c., Difficult, Page 235

35.   All of the following are effective ways to encourage customers to return to a site **except**:
        a.   offer "Frequent Buyer" programs.
        b.   give away items with the company's logo.
        c.   advertise with pop-ups.
        d.   reward them with special services.

c., Medium, Page 236

36.   To launch a successful Web site, business owners should consider:
        a.   a simple design.
        b.   that to stand out on the Web, the logic is that a site really has to sparkle.
        c.   all the "bells" and "whistles" technology can provide.
        d.   that flash makes a Web site better.

a., Medium, Page 236

37.   Catchy graphics and photographs are important to customers, but designers must choose them carefully. A specific Web site design tip is to:
        a.   Use a number of different colors and design patterns.
        b.   Avoid graphics.
        c.   Make the site a challenge to navigate.
        d.   Incorporate meaningful content and information.

d., Medium, Page 236

38.   A successful Web site should include all of the following characteristics **except**:
        a.   an (FAQ) section.
        b.   continuous automated music.
        c.   updated and timely information.
        d.   readable font sizes.

b., Easy, Page 238

39.   Responsible online merchants should make sure shipping and handling charges are:
        a.   reasonable.
        b.   displayed early in the buying process.
        c.   easy to find.
        d.   All of the above.

        d., Easy, Page 238

40.   The simplest method for tracking web results is:
        a.   a counter.
        b.   log-analysis software.
        c.   a viral site.
        d.   a sticky site.

        a., Easy, Page 240

41.   A _____ is one that catches the website visitor's attention and makes him/her stay
        at the site.
        a.   a counter
        b.   log-analysis software
        c.   a viral site
        d.   a sticky site

        d., Easy, Page 240

42.   Recording every page, graphic, audio clip, or photograph that visitors access is identified
        by:
        a.   a counter.
        b.   log-analysis software.
        c.   a viral site.
        d.   a sticky site.

        b., Easy, Page 240

43.   Which of the following was **not** identified as a tracking method that owners of e-
        businesses might use?
        a.   Browsing
        b.   Collaborative filtering
        c.   Profiling
        d.   Artificial intelligence

        a., Medium, Page 240

44.   According to the Pew Internet & American Life Project, ___ percent of Internet users say
        they worry about online privacy.
        a.   36
        b.   54
        c.   71
        d.   86

        d., Difficult, Page 241

45. To minimize the likelihood of invasion by hackers, e-commerce companies rely on several tools, including:
    a. virus detection software.
    b. intrusion detection software.
    c. firewalls.
    d. All of the above.

    d., Easy, Page 242

46. A combination of hardware and software that allows employees to have access to the Internet but keeps unauthorized users from entering the company's network is called:
    a. virus detection software.
    b. intrusion detection software.
    c. a firewall.
    d. None of the above.

    c., Easy, Page 242

47. The security software that can trace a hacker's location is identified by which of the following?
    a. Virus detection software
    b. Intrusion detection software
    c. A firewall
    d. A viral site

    b., Easy, Page 242

48. Web sites have two conflicting goals regarding security. The first is to establish a presence on the Web so that customers from across the globe can have access to its site, and the second is:
    a. to maintain a data base system of customer information and preferences.
    b. to have a system in place to prosecute hackers.
    c. to maintain a high level of security so that the business, its site, and the information it collects are safe from hackers and intruders intent on doing harm.
    d. to develop an in-house payment processing system.

    c., Medium, Page 242

49. A valuable method of preventing online fraud is to:
    a. ask customers for their card verification value.
    b. not accept credit cards.
    c. run background checks on customers.
    d. All of the above.

    a., Medium, Page 243

50.   Research firm GarterG2 says that one out of every ___ internet transactions is an attempted fraud.
       a.   10
       b.   20
       c.   30
       d.   40

       b., Difficult, Page 243

True/False Questions:

51.   E-commerce is replacing traditional retailing.

       False, Easy, Page 213

52.   One study by Ernst & Young found that 64 percent of Internet users research products on-line before buying them.

       True, Difficult, Page 213

53.   Online sales are growing by 30 to 40 percent a year, which is much faster than the 4 percent growth-rate of offline sales.

       True, Medium, Page 214

54.   More than half of all retail sales occur after 6 p.m.

       True, Medium, Page 214

55.   Women and members of Generation Y do not particularly crave product information before they make a purchase.

       False, Medium, Page 215

56.   The Web is one of the most efficient ways of reaching both new and existing customers.

       True, Easy, Page 215

57.   The Web typically lacks the ability to lower the cost of doing business.

       False, Easy, Page 215

58.   Seventy-seven percent of small business owners who have not taken their businesses online say that their products are not suitable for sale on the Web, while another 37 percent say that they do not see any benefits to selling online.

       True, Medium, Page 216

59.   For many entrepreneurs, the key barrier to not using the Web as a business tool is that they do not see any benefits to selling online.

False, Medium, Page 216

60.   Business owners who are not at least considering creating a Web presence are putting their companies at risk.

True, Easy, Page 216

61.   Before planning a Web site, business owners should address such issues as promotional strategies and maintenance.

True, Easy, Page 217

62.   Doing business on the Web takes less time and energy than most entrepreneurs think.

False, Medium, Page 217

63.   Any company that wants to succeed in the years ahead must make technology and the Internet part of its core competence, according to an experienced venture capitalist.

True, Easy, Page 217

64.   Measuring the success of its Web-based sales is not essential because customer tastes and preferences are always changing.

False, Easy, Page 217

65.   Setting up a business on the Web is easy and inexpensive.

False, Easy, Page 218

66.   Most small businesses set up their websites as "electronic flyers".

True, Easy, Page 218

67.   Electronic flyer websites lack the capacity for true electronic commerce; however, they do provide a company with another way of reaching both new and existing customers.

True, Medium, Page 218

68.   Listing a site with a popular Web search engine will guarantee that surfing customers will find your site.

False, Easy, Page 219

69.   Virtual shop owners using banner ads have no reason to buy ads in traditional advertising media.

False, Easy, Page 219

70. Making money on the Web is easy.

   False, Easy, Page 219

71. Businesses that publish privacy policies and then adhere to them build trust among their customers, an important facet of doing business on the Web.

   True, Easy, Page 219

72. One of the surest ways to alienate online customers is to abuse the information collected from them by selling it to third parties or by spamming them with unwanted solicitations.

   True, Easy, Page 219

73. The most important part of any e-commerce effort is technology.

   False, Medium, Page 220

74. A study by Jupiter Communications found that 64 percent of Web users distrust Web sites.

   True, Medium, Page 220

75. E-Commerce requires focusing on technology first and then determining how the technology fits the business idea.

   False, Medium, Page 220

76. Before your web site can become the foundation of a successful e-business, you must create it with your target audience in mind.

   True, Easy, Page 221

77. The concept of a traditional marketing strategy is not necessary in building a successful e-business.

   False, Easy, Page 221

78. On the Web, service is not as important as it is in a traditional retail environment.

   False, Easy, Page 221

79. E-mail takes a very low priority at many e-businesses.

   True, Medium, Page 221

80. Flash makes a Web site better.

   False, Medium, Page 221

81. Establishing a policy of responding to all customer e-mails within 24 hours and sending customers order and shipping confirmations and "thank you for your order" e-mails are not very important to enhancing online customer service.

False, Easy, Page 221

82. Web-based companies should not be concerned with supply-chain management, warehouses, or typical customer service policies.

False, Easy, Page 222

83. Although e-tailers avoid the major problems that managing inventory presents, they lose control over delivery times and service quality.

True, Medium, Page 223

84. E-Commerce will cause brick-and-mortar retail stores to disappear.

False, Easy, Page 223

85. The greatest opportunities for e-commerce lie in the retail sector.

False, Difficult, Page 223

86. An important factor of e-commerce is speed.

True, Easy, Page 225

87. It is better to avoid delays in going online by simply getting your site up and running, and then fixing it, tweaking it, and updating it to meet changing customer demands, rather than taking so much time trying to create the perfect on-line store at first attempt.

True, Medium, Page 225

88. The simplest way entrepreneurs can get their businesses on-line is by renting space for their products in on-line shopping malls.

True, Medium, Page 225

89. The major disadvantages of using an online shopping mall are an individual store's lack of prominence and the lack of control entrepreneurs have over their sites.

True, Medium, Page 225

90. The major disadvantage of storefront-building services is that most of their sites have a "cookie-cutter" appearance because they rely on a limited number of templates to create store sites.

True, Medium, Page 225

91. Storefront-building services, building a Web site in-house, and on-line shopping malls are options for entrepreneurs to develop an e-business for under $10,000.

   False, Medium, Page 225

92. The primary benefit of hiring a professional Web designer to build a business Web site is the unlimited ability to customize a site.

   True, Easy, Page 227

93. Launching an e-business is very different from launching a traditional off-line company.

   False, Medium, Page 228

94. How a company integrates the Web into its overall business strategy determines how successful it ultimately will become.

   True, Easy, Page 228

95. Rather than try to compete head-to-head with the dominant players on the Web who have almost unlimited resources and recognition, entrepreneurs should consider focusing on serving a market niche.

   True, Easy, Page 228

96. A marketing niche can be defined by geography, customer profile, product, product usage, and many other ways.

   True, Easy, Page 228

97. A method of increasing customer loyalty and establishing better relationships is to develop a community of customers with similar interests who can use chat rooms, message boards, guest books, etc.

   True, Easy, Page 229

98. You should never offer your customers "freebies" unless they are truly valuable and expensive; otherwise, you will earn a negative reputation among your customers.

   False, Medium, Page 229

99. Most customers welcome well-constructed permission e-mail that directs them to a company's site for information or special deals; however, they usually do not appreciate spam.

   True, Easy, Page 230

100. One of the simplest ways to establish credibility with customers is to use brand names they know and trust.

   True, Easy, Page 230

101. A method small businesses might use to achieve more of the brand and name recognition that larger, more established companies have is to form strategic alliances with bigger companies.

    True, Easy, Page 230

102. Almost 75 percent of Internet users live within the United States.

    False, Difficult, Page 231

103. Before launching into the design of their Web sites, entrepreneurs must develop a clear picture of their target customers.

    True, Easy, Page 233

104. The more innovative your domain and name, the better.

    False, Medium, Page 234

105. Establish hyperlinks with different product types to ensure you cover a variety of different customers.

    False, Medium, Page 236

106. The better websites avoid clutter, include a menu bar for easier navigation, include a FAQ section, and are careful about typos, formatting, font sizes, and colors.

    True, Easy, Page 237

107. Responsible online merchants should keep shipping and handling charges reasonable, but do not need to show them early on in the check out process.

    False, Medium, Page 238

108. Virus detection software, intrusion detection software, and a firewall are tools that minimize the likelihood of invasion by hackers, and eliminate your responsibility for damages they inflict.

    False, Medium, Page 242

109. Experts estimate that one of every 20 Internet transactions is an attempted fraud.

    True, Difficult, Page 243

110. An important way to prevent online credit card fraud is to ask customers not only for their card number and expiration date, but also for the three digit number above the signature panel on the back of the credit card—the card verification value.

    True, Medium, Page 243

Essay Questions:

111.   How significant are the Internet and a Web site presence to small businesses of the twenty-first century? How have they transformed the way we do business?

Although e-commerce will not replace traditional retailing, no retailer, from the smallest corner store to industry giants, can afford to ignore the impact of the World Wide Web. It is connecting customers and suppliers in a way that is creating a new industrial order.

In this fast paced world of e-commerce, size no longer matters as much as speed and flexibility. Pricing is no longer a simple chore. The Internet allows companies to collect more information on consumers and gives shoppers an unlimited source of information and the ability to track their merchandise from ordering to delivery date. The Web operates with the speed of light, anywhere in the world, 24 hours a day.
Page 213

112.   After years of being an entrepreneur, Wynn has come to you for help in establishing his first web site. He has expressed a desire to have a site with all the "bells and whistles" he can get. What should your advice to him be? Which other five factors should he consider before launching an e-commerce site?

Keeping up with technology does not necessarily mean, "more is better." In developing a website, the primary focus should be a simple design, easy navigation, and quick download. Avoid busy clutter ("bells and whistles") and provide meaningful information in a secure environment. A successful Website plan should include promotional and advertising support.

The (5) factors to be considered include:

- How a company exploits the Web's interconnectivity and the opportunities it creates to transform relationships with its suppliers and vendors, its customers, and other external stakeholders is crucial to its success.

- Web success requires a company to develop a plan for integrating the Web into its overall strategy. The plan should address issues such as site design and maintenance, creating and managing a brand name, marketing and promotional strategies, sales, and customer service.

- Developing deep, lasting relationships with customers takes on even greater importance on the Web. Attracting customers on the Web costs money, and companies must be able to retain their online customers to make their Websites profitable.

- Creating a meaningful presence on the Web requires an ongoing investment of resources—time, money, energy, and talent. Establishing an attractive Website, brimming with catchy photographs of products, is only the beginning.

- Measuring the success of its Web-based sales effort is essential to customers whose tastes, needs, and preferences are always changing.
Page 213

113.   Identify the benefits of selling on the Web.

- The opportunity to increase revenue
- The ability to expand their reach into global markets
- The ability to remain open 24 hours a day, seven days a week
- The capacity to use the Web's interactive nature to enhance customer service
- The power to educate and to inform
- The ability to lower the cost of doing business
- The ability to spot new business opportunities and to capitalize on them
- The ability to grow faster
- The power to track sales results

Page 214

114.   Identify the 12 myths of e-commerce.

- Setting up a business on the web is easy and inexpensive.
- If I launch a site, customers will flock to it.
- Making money on the web is easy.
- Privacy is not an important issue on the Web.
- The most important part of any e-commerce effort is technology.
- Strategy? I don't need a strategy to sell on the Web! Just give me a Web site, and the rest will take care of itself.
- On the Web, customer service is not as important as it is in a traditional retail store.
- Flash makes a Web site better.
- It's what's up front that counts.
- E-commerce will cause brick-and-mortar retail stores to disappear.

Page 218

115.   Identify the five basic approaches available to entrepreneurs for launching an e-commerce effort. What are the advantages, the disadvantages, and the costs associated with each one?

- On-line shopping malls, under $10,000, are the simplest way to get a business on-line by renting space for products. Disadvantages are an individual store's lack of prominence and a lack of control over the site.

- Storefront building services, also under $10,000, includes Web hosting services, credit card handling services, order fulfillment, and order tracking. Weak points are a "cookie cutter" look and a limit to the number of products they handle for the base price.

- Internet service providers (ISP) and application service providers (ASP), also under $10,000, offer the ability to create a customized on-line store. The entrepreneur needs basic HTML language skills. Special software is required with ISPs and rented with ASPs.

- Hiring professionals to design a custom site will cost approximately $10,000 to $30,000. The primary benefit is the unlimited ability to customize and control an individual site. The major disadvantage is cost.

- Building a site in-house gives ultimate control; however, costs of developing and maintaining the site can be extremely expensive (can run $250,000 to $500,000) and time consuming.

Page 225

116. Identify the guidelines for building a successful Web strategy for a small e-company.

- Consider focusing on a niche in the market.
- Develop a community of customers.
- Attract visitors by giving away "freebies."
- Make creative use of e-mail, but avoid becoming a "spammer."
- Make sure your Web site says "credibility."
- Consider forming strategic alliances.
- Make the most of the Web's global reach.
- Promote your Web site online and off-line.

Page 228

117. Identify and briefly explain five of the design characteristics that contribute to a successful Web page.

- Understand your target customer.
- Select a domain name consistent with the image you want to create for your company, and register it. The ideal domain name should be short, memorable, indicative of a company's business or business name, and easy to spell.
- The page should be easy to find.
- Give customers want they want.
- Build loyalty by giving online customers a reason to return to your Web site.
- Establish hyperlinks with other businesses, preferably those selling products or services that complement yours.
- Include an e-mail option and a telephone number in your site.
- Give shoppers the ability to track their orders on-line.
- Offer Web shoppers a special all their own.
- Follow a simple design for your Web page. Specific tips include: avoid clutter, avoid slow downloading of huge graphics, include a menu bar at the top, make the site easy to navigate, incorporate meaningful content, include FAQs; identify privacy and return policies, avoid fancy typeface, do not misspell words, don't use small fonts on busy backgrounds, use contrasting colors, and be careful with frames. Test the site on different monitors and Web browsers.
- Assure customers that their on-line transactions are secure. Use proper security software and encryption devices.
- Post shipping and handling charges up front.
- Keep your site updated.
- Consider hiring a professional to design your site, but don't give him/her free reign.

Page 233

Chapter 7
E-Commerce and the Entrepreneur
Mini-Case

Case 7-1: Marketing a Nonprofit - Virtual Opportunities

New Wave Chance Youth Club is a local youth organization supported solely by the donations of individuals and the local church community. Its co-founders, Valerie and Kristen, are considering launching a website to promote upcoming events and raise money for a new gym. Their good friend Paul has volunteered to develop a website, which they feel will help promote their efforts.

1.   How might a web site benefit the youth club?

- An opportunity to increase donations
- An opportunity to expand their fund raising efforts into a larger market.
- Ability to remain open 24 hours a day, seven days a week.
- Capacity to use the Web's interactive nature to enhance the services the club offers.
- The power to educate and to inform.
- The ability to lower fund raising costs.
- The ability to spot and capitalize on new opportunities
- The possibility to generate reports and track results

Note: Students should be able to apply the benefits of selling on the web to this non-profit situation.

2.   The building fund manager, Mr. Grover, has been overwhelmed by the generosity of the community and numerous requests to donate supplies. Describe how the Web site may be able to help him organize the donation requests and determine the type and quality of the building supplies?

Posting a list of requirements the organization will need on the Web site, as well as the quality of donations needed, will assist Grover in organizing and keeping track of a great deal of information. It will also save a considerable amount of time in determining which donations to accept and what supplies will still be needed. Any donations not used could be sold via a silent auction to raise other needed funds.

3.   What other type of activities should New Wave Chance implement to support the success of the new Web site?

According to Myth 2, "If I launch a site, customers will flock to it." To avoid developing a website that no one knows about or can find, New Wave Chance should print its Web URL on everything it publishes. It should distribute flyers and newsletters to schools and local organizations in the community, and send out press releases with the URL.

Students should be able to apply the basic e-commerce suggestions for designing a Killer website:

- Understand your target customer.
- Select a domain name that is consistent with the image you want to create for your company, and register it. The ideal domain name should be short, memorable, indicative of a company's business or business name, and easy to spell.
- The page should be easy to find.
- Give customers want they want.
- Build loyalty by giving online customers a reason to return to your Web site.
- Establish hyperlinks with other businesses, preferably those selling products or services that complement yours.
- Include an e-mail option and a telephone number in your site.
- Give shoppers the ability to track their orders on-line.
- Offer Web shoppers a special all their own.
- Follow a simple design for your Web page. Specific tips include: avoid clutter, avoid slow downloading of huge graphics, include a menu bar at the top, make the site easy to navigate, incorporate meaningful content, include FAQs; identify privacy and return policies, avoid fancy typeface, do not misspell words, don't use small fonts on busy backgrounds, use contrasting colors, and be careful with frames. Test the site on different monitors and Web browsers.
- Assure customers that their on-line transactions are secure. Use proper security software and encryption devices.
- Post shipping and handling charges up front.
- Keep your site updated.
- Consider hiring a professional to design your site, but don't give him/her free reign.

Chapter 8   Integrative Marketing Communications and Pricing Strategies

Multiple Choice Questions:

1.   Which of the following statements is **not** true?
      a. Marketing communications is not just an expense; it is an investment in your company's future.
      b. Advertising and promotion can increase sales, improve your company's image, and persuade customers to buy your goods and services.
      c. Although a large budget is required for building an effective marketing communications campaign, it is money well spent.
      d. None of the above.

      c., Medium, Page 248

2.   The first step in creating an advertising plan is:
      a. analyzing the firm's target customers.
      b. defining the purpose of the marketing communications program by creating specific, measurable objectives.
      c. developing a "unique selling position."
      d. creating the advertising message.

      b., Medium, Page 248

3.   Which of the following statements about a unique selling proposition (USP) is **false**?
      a. A unique selling proposition is a key customer benefit of a product or service that sets it apart from its competition.
      b. In some cases, the most powerful USPs are the intangible or psychological benefits a product or service offers customers.
      c. Every ad should be designed to communicate as many USPs as possible, at least 8 or 10, so that the advertiser gets the most from each advertising dollar spent.
      d. Building an ad around a USP spells out for customers the specific benefit they get if they buy the product or service.

      c., Medium, Page 249

4.   Which of the following is **not** one of the Five Fundamentals of a Successful Advertisement?
      a. It should attract attention.
      b. It should emphasize a key benefit of the product or service to the customer.
      c. It should communicate the company's USP and back it up with facts, statistics, and testimonials.
      d. It should motivate customers to consider taking action the next chance they have.

      d., Easy, Page 251

5.   Marcie, a young woman just beginning a design business, decides to offer a free seminar to community residents called "Home Design 101." The local newspaper writes an article about the upcoming seminar and includes a brief sketch of Marcie's business. Marcie is using which promotional technique?
     a.   Publicity
     b.   Personal selling
     c.   Advertising
     d.   Transaction selling

     a., Medium, Page 252

6.   Which of the following is **not** one of the suggestions for a small company to get the most promotional impact from the sponsorship of an event?
     a.   Sponsorships are most effective when they are part of a coordinated advertising effort; therefore, be sure your advertising campaign includes other efforts as well.
     b.   Look for an event that is appropriate for your company and its products and services.
     c.   Research the event and the organization hosting it before agreeing to become a sponsor.
     d.   Try to align yourself with several other companies in your industry as co-sponsors; this will make it easier for you in the long run and will still give you same the results you are seeking.

     d., Medium, Page 254

7.   Assume that you recently reviewed the profile of top salespeople and are training new salespeople for your company. Which of the following are **not** recommendations you should make to them?
     a.   Concentrate on customers with the greatest sales potential.
     b.   Consider yourself a problem solver rather than just a vendor. Ask "How can I be a valuable resource for my customers?"
     c.   Empathize with your customers and look at the situation from their perspective.
     d.   Use an indirect approach, rather than getting right to the point with the customers.

     d., Medium, Page 255

8.   Which of the following is/are true regarding types of objectives a sales representative should set before making a sales call?
     a.   The visionary objective is the most reasonable outcome expected from the meeting.
     b.   The minimum objective is the very least the salesperson will leave with.
     c.   The primary objective is the most optimistic outcome of the meeting.
     d.   All of the above.

     b., Medium, Page 256

9.   Which of the following is **not** a recommended part of the personal selling process?
   a.   Establish a rapport with the prospect since customers seldom buy from salespeople they dislike or distrust.
   b.   Demonstrate, explain, and show the features and benefits of the product or service and point out how it meets the prospect's needs or solves his problems.
   c.   Discourage the prospect from making any objections during the sales pitch, preventing the experience from taking on negative overtones.
   d.   Close the sale by asking for the order.

c., Medium, Page 256

10.   Which of the following questions should a small business owner ask before choosing an advertising medium?
   a.   Who are my target customers and what are their characteristics?
   b.   What media do my competitors use?
   c.   What does the advertising medium cost?
   d.   All of the above.

d., Easy, Page 257

11.   The top three media accounting for the largest percentages of advertising expenditures by U. S. businesses include all but which of the following?
   a.   television
   b.   radio
   c.   newspapers
   d.   direct mail

c., Medium, Page 258

12.   Word-of-mouth advertising is perhaps the _____ form of advertising.
   a.   most expensive
   b.   most effective
   c.   least expensive
   d.   B and C above.

d., Easy, Page 258

13.   Which one of the following is **not** a characteristic of newspaper ads?
   a.   Low absolute cost
   b.   Reach people in all economic classes
   c.   Long life expectancy
   d.   Flexible

c., Medium, Page 259

14. Which of the following statements about newspaper ads is **false**?
    a. Newspaper ads typically produce relatively quick responses.
    b. Because newspapers become outdated so quickly, their ads tend to be short-lived.
    c. Because the ratio of advertising to news content is so low in newspapers, advertisements are more prominent to potential customers.
    d. Newspaper circulation as a percentage of U.S. households has dropped in recent years.

    c., Medium, Page 259

15. Which of the following is **not** an advantage of radio advertising?
    a. No need for repetition of radio ads.
    b. Ads can be changed quickly and have short closing times.
    c. Ads can be targeted to a specific market by choosing the proper station.
    d. None of the above.

    a., Medium, Page 260

16. Which of the following times would typically be considered radio "prime time"?
    a. Noon to 4 p.m. and 8 p.m. to midnight
    b. 6 a.m. to 10 a.m. and 4 p.m. to 7 p.m.
    c. 8 a.m. to noon and 6 p.m. to 10 p.m.
    d. 10 a.m. to 4 p.m. and midnight to 6 a.m.

    b., Easy, Page 260

17. Which of the following is **not** an advantage offered by magazines and magazine ads?
    a. Long life spans
    b. Multiple readership
    c. High quality ad reproduction
    d. Short closing times

    d., Medium, Page 263

18. Direct mail ads' **greatest** strength is their:
    a. low relative costs.
    b. long life spans.
    c. ability to target a specific audience to receive a particular advertising message.
    d. multiple exposures.

    c., Medium, Page 263

19. The key to the success of direct mail advertising is:
    a. designing the right envelope.
    b. the accuracy of the customer mailing list.
    c. creative use of color and photographs in the mailing.
    d. using key words such as "free," "hurry," and "savings."

    b., Medium, Page 264

20. Which of the following is **not** true regarding Web advertising?
    a. The primary disadvantage of banner ads is that Web users can easily ignore them.
    b. Cookies are small programs that attach to users' computers when they visit certain Web sites; they track the locations users visit while in the site and use this information to send pop-up ads.
    c. Full-page ads are those that download to Web users' screens before they can access certain Web sites.
    d. A disadvantage of e-mail promotions and advertising messages is that, unlike print ads, they cannot be tested prior to use to ensure maximum impact.

    d., Medium, Page 267

21. Which of the following is **not** a characteristic of outdoor ads?
    a. High exposure
    b. Broad reach
    c. Prominence
    d. Brief exposure

    c., Medium, Page 267

22. Which of the following is a **disadvantage** of transit advertising?
    a. Limited coverage
    b. High cost
    c. The inability to target specific audiences
    d. Minimum ad exposure over a period of time

    c., Difficult, Page 269

23. Directories have several **disadvantages**, which include:
    a. poor selectivity of the target audience.
    b. very high cost.
    c. their listings are sometimes obsolete.
    d. a short life.

    c., Medium, Page 269

24. A hardware store giving customers nail aprons and yardsticks emblazoned with its name, address, phone number, logo, and slogan is using which advertising medium?
    a. Point-of-purchase ads
    b. Cooperative advertising
    c. Specialty advertising
    d. Shared ads

    c., Easy, Page 270

25. To make the most out of a trade show, a business owner should:
    a. staff the booth with knowledgeable salespeople.
    b. communicate with key potential customers **before** the show by inviting them to stop by the company's booth.
    c. follow up promptly on all sales leads from the show.
    d. All of the above.

    d., Easy, Page 270

26. Research shows that consumers make ___% of their buying decisions at the point of sale.
    a. 3/4
    b. 2/3
    c. 1/2
    d. 8

    b., Difficult, Page 271

27. Under the _____ method of establishing an advertising budget, the owner sees advertising as a luxury—an expense rather than an investment—and only allocates funds after all other budget items have been financed.
    a. what-is-affordable
    b. matching competitors
    c. percentage of sales
    d. objective-and-task

    a., Easy, Page 272

28. The most commonly used method of establishing an advertising budget for a small business is:
    a. a percentage of sales.
    b. spending what competitors spend.
    c. objective-and-task method.
    d. what is affordable.

    a., Easy, Page 273

29. The _____ method of establishing an advertising budget is the most difficult, most recommended, and least used.
    a. what-is-affordable
    b. matching competitors
    c. percentage of sales
    d. objective-and-task

    d., Easy, Page 274

30. Which of the following methods can small business owners use to stretch their advertising budgets to get the most from what they spend?
    a. Cooperative advertising
    b. Shared advertising
    c. Public relations
    d. All of the above.

    d., Easy, Page 274

31. What should a small business owner avoid if he wants to get the most from his advertising dollar?
    a. Repeat ads that have been successful.
    b. Use identical ads in different media.
    c. Concentrate advertising during times when customers are least likely to buy in order to boost sales.
    d. Hire "freelance" ad copywriters, designers, artists, and others.

    c., Medium, Page 275

32. When Timex designs a set of newspaper ads promoting its watches and then makes them available at no cost to jewelers selling its watches so they can add their names, addresses, and phone numbers, it is using _____ advertising.
    a. institutional
    b. generic
    c. cooperative
    d. shared

    c., Medium, Page 275

33. A successful public relations technique used by local businesses to sponsor and promote fundraising activities of nonprofit groups while raising its own visibility in the community is called:
    a. cooperative advertising.
    b. shared advertising.
    c. cause marketing.
    d. integrated marketing.

    c., Easy, Page 276

34. Which of the following statements about price is **false**?
    a. Price measures what the customer must exchange to obtain goods and services in the marketplace.
    b. Target market, business image, and price are closely related.
    c. For most goods and services, there is an acceptable price range and not just a single "ideal price."
    d. None of the above.

    d., Medium, Page 276

35. The acceptable price range of a product or service is the area between the _____ defined by customers in the market and the _____ established by the company's cost structure.
    a. price floor; price ceiling
    b. image; quality
    c. price ceiling; price floor
    d. price floor; value

    c., Medium, Page 278

36. The final price a business owner sets within the acceptable price range depends on:
    a. the cost of the product or service.
    b. the desired "image" he wants to create in the customer's mind.
    c. the maximum price customers are willing to pay.
    d. All of the above.

    d., Easy, Page 278

37. Which of the following statements concerning the impact of competition on a small company's prices is **true**?
    a. When setting prices, a business owner must either match or beat competitors' prices on similar products or services.
    b. Because federal laws prohibit the practice as an unfair trade practice, business owners should not monitor their rivals' prices on identical items.
    c. When going up against larger, more powerful rivals, small firms should consider using nonprice competition as a way to differentiate their products or services rather than head-to-head price competition.
    d. All of the above.

    c., Medium, Page 278

38. The "ideal price" for a product:
    a. is high enough to cover costs and to generate a profit.
    b. is low enough to produce adequate sales volume.
    c. today may be different from the "ideal price" tomorrow.
    d. All of the above.

    d., Medium, Page 279

39. When pricing a new product, a small business owner should strive to always satisfy which three objectives?
    a. product acceptance, maintaining market share, and earning a profit.
    b. quick acceptance, extensive distribution, and quickly recovering costs.
    c. recovering initial development costs, recovering initial promotional costs, and discouraging competition.
    d. discouraging competition, recovering development costs, and developing a prestige image.

    a., Medium, Page 279

40. Gateway 2000 is a computer manufacturer that strives to constantly lower its costs so that it can cut the prices on its popular line of personal computers ahead of its competitors. Gateway 2000 is pursuing a _____ pricing strategy.
    a. skimming
    b. sliding-down-the-demand-curve
    c. penetration
    d. lender

    b., Medium, Page 280

41. XYZ, Inc., spent a tremendous amount of time and money developing a unique new product. In order to re-coup some of the high R & D costs, they will likely use which pricing strategy?
    a. Skimming
    b. Penetration
    c. Sliding-down-the-demand-curve
    d. Discount

    a., Medium, Page 280

42. _____ pricing strategies work best in markets where no "elite" segments exist or in highly competitive markets where similar products are trying to gain a foothold.
    a. Skimming
    b. Sliding-down-the-demand-curve
    c. Odd
    d. Penetration

    d., Medium, Page 280

43. CD Connection sells popular CDs at three price levels: $11, $14, and $17. This illustrates which of the following pricing techniques?
    a. Odd pricing
    b. Leader pricing
    c. Price lining
    d. Suggested retail pricing

    c., Medium, Page 280

44. Your local grocery store uses a pricing technique known as_____ on a weekly basis, in which they mark down the price of several popular items—sometimes well below their normal price—in an effort to increase customer traffic and to boost sales of other items.
    a. Odd pricing
    b. Leader pricing
    c. Price lining
    d. Suggested retail pricing

    b., Easy, Page 281

45. _____ is the difference between the cost of a product or service and its selling price.
   a. Markup
   b. Break-even price
   c. Contribution margin
   d. Absorption costing

a., Easy, Page 282

46. The Blouse Barn buys white, pinpoint oxford blouses at $14 each and sells them at $30 each. The Blouse Barn's percentage (of cost) markup is:
   a. 46.7%.
   b. 87.5%.
   c. 53.3%.
   d. 114.3%.

d., Easy, Page 282

47. The Blouse Barn buys white, pinpoint oxford blouses at $14 each and sells them at $30 each. The Blouse Barn's percentage (of retail price) markup is:
   a. 46.7%.
   b. 87.5%.
   c. 53.3%.
   d. 114.3%.

c., Easy, Page 282

48. The Sound Shop buys a popular programmable telephone from a supplier for $12.19. If the desired markup of retail price on the telephone is 35 percent, the retail price should be:
   a. $34.83.
   b. $18.75.
   c. $16.46.
   d. $20.11.

c., Medium, Page 283

49. Which of the following is/are true regarding cost-plus pricing?
   a. It encourages the manufacturer to operate efficiently.
   b. It fails to consider competitors' prices appropriately.
   c. It fails to guarantee the manufacturer a desired profit margin.
   d. Only A and C.

b., Difficult, Page 284

50. A reliable cost accounting system is necessary for accurate pricing. The traditional method of product costing, where the costs of direct materials, direct labor, and factory overhead are included in a finished product's total cost is called _____ costing.
     a. absorption
     b. break-even
     c. direct
     d. variable

     a., Easy, Page 284

51. _____ tells what portion of the total revenues remains after covering variable costs to contribute toward meeting fixed expenses and earning a profit.
     a. The full absorption statement
     b. The break-even selling price
     c. The contribution percentage
     d. Cost-plus pricing

     c., Medium, Page 285

52. Pandecker, Inc. estimates the variable costs of producing one unit to be $11.26. The company plans to produce 26,500 units. The fixed costs the company expects to incur are $82,770. What is Pandecker's break-even selling price?
     a. $14.38
     b. $35.17
     c. $11.26
     d. $3.12

     a., Medium, Page 286

53. Pandecker, Inc. estimates the variable costs of producing one unit to be $11.26. The company plans to produce 26,500 units. The fixed costs the company expects to incur are $82,770. If Pandecker's profit target is $75,000, what price should it charge?
     a. $14.38
     b. $35.17
     c. $17.21
     d. $11.26

     c., Medium, Page 286

54. Which of the following is/are **not** true regarding pricing for service firms?
     a. A service firm must establish a price based on the materials used to provide the service, the labor employed, an allowance for overhead, and a profit.
     b. Most service firms base their prices on an hourly rate—usually actual hours, but sometimes standard hours are used.
     c. For most service firms, labor and profit comprise the largest portion of the cost of the service.
     d. None of the above.

     c., Medium, Page 287

55. Customers use credit cards to pay for _____ out of every $100 spent on consumable goods and services.
    a. $16
    b. $28
    c. $42
    d. $63

b., Medium, Page 288

56. The normal fee that a credit service charges for using the system is __ percent of total credit card charges.
    a. 1 - 6
    b. 7 - 10
    c. 8 - 9
    d. 1/2 - 1

a., Medium, Page 288

57. It has been reported that the use of credit cards increases the _____ of customer spending.
    a. probability
    b. speed
    c. magnitude
    d. All of the above.

d., Medium, Page 288

58. The use of credit cards by consumers:
    a. has little real impact on sales.
    b. broadens a small company's customer base.
    c. costs businesses nothing and adds significantly to their sales.
    d. has no impact on pricing decisions.

b., Medium, Page 288

59. Which of the following businesses would be most likely to offer installment credit to its customers?
    a. A retailer of major appliances
    b. A convenience store
    c. A printer
    d. A clothing retailer

a., Easy, Page 289

60. A customer who purchases a television from Ace Appliance Store and pays for it in 36 monthly payments is most likely using:
    a. trade credit.
    b. charge account credit.
    c. installment credit.
    d. debit card credit.

c., Easy, Page 289

True/False Questions:

61. As advertising options, advertising clutter, and skeptical consumers have increased; developing an effective advertising campaign has become more of a challenge for business.

    True, Easy, Page 248

62. The first step in establishing an advertising plan is to establish specific, measurable objectives for the advertising program.

    True, Easy, Page 248

63. Advertising is an expense a small business owner should undertake only when the company's budget permits; it is a "leftover" expense.

    False, Easy, Page 248

64. A unique selling proposition (USP) is a key customer benefit of a product or service that aligns a small business with its competitors.

    False, Medium, Page 249

65. Building an advertisement around a unique selling proposition (USP) spells out for customers the specific benefits they get if they buy the product or service.

    True, Easy, Page 249

66. Publicity is any commercial news covered by the media that boosts sales but for which the small business does not pay.

    True, Easy, Page 252

67. Although sponsorships and specialty events can attract a great deal of interest, they do little to leave a lasting impression of the company in the customer's mind.

    False, Medium, Page 253

68. Good sales representatives know that once a prospect raises an objection, it is time to stop selling and come back later when the prospect is in a better frame of mind.

    False, Medium, Page 255

69. Top salespeople tend to use an indirect approach to selling, taking their time before they make a "sales pitch" to their customers.

    False, Medium Page 255

70 Susan decided to start including testimonials about her product from satisfied users during the close of her sales presentation; this is a good idea.

    True, Easy, Page 256

71. The "right" advertising message sent via the "wrong" advertising medium will not increase sales.

   True, Easy, Page 256

72. John believes that he should employ the same advertising media as his competitors to increase the likelihood of advertising success; this is a good idea for most small business owners.

   False, Medium, Page 257

73. The advertising medium that accounts for the greatest portion of advertising expenditures is television.

   True, Medium, Page 258

74. Newspapers advertising offers flexibility, broad coverage in the firm's trading area, and usually quick customer responses.

   True, Easy, Page 259

75. Given current readership rates and trends, newspaper ads would be most effective in reaching young people.

   False, Easy, Page 260

76. Radio ads require repeated broadcasting in order to be effective; one time exposures typically don't work.

   True, Easy, Page 260

77. In radio advertising, 30-second ads are the most common.

   False, Medium, Page 260

78. The primary benefit of television ads is their ability to demonstrate a good or service in a graphic, vivid manner.

   True, Easy, Page 261

79. When designing an effective television commercial, a small business owner should focus her message on a single, important benefit to the customer rather than trying to cram as much as possible into the ad.

   True, Medium, Page 262

80. Magazines have a shorter closing time than newspapers, making them timely and highly flexible.

   False, Medium, Page 259

81.   Even the best direct mail ad will fail if sent to the wrong audience; the key to the success of a direct mailing campaign is the accuracy of the customer list.

True, Easy, Page 263

82.   Direct mail ads on computer disks and CDs are more likely to catch and hold a customer's attention than traditional "paper" ads.

True, Easy, Page 263

83.   Direct mail ads typically produce quick results; in most cases, the ad will generate sales within three or four days after it is received.

True, Medium, Page 264

84.   The World Wide Web's full motion, color, and sound capacity make it an ideal medium for businesses to demonstrate their products and services.

True, Easy, Page 264

85.   Banner ads are small rectangular ads that reside on websites and are judged using the click-through rate.

True, Easy, Page 264

86.   Cookies are small programs that attach to users' computers when they visit certain Web sites that may be used by the company to track your Web browsing patterns, interests, etc.

True, Medium, Page 266

87.   When designing an outdoor ad, the small business owner must remember that "more" is better and put as much information as possible in the ad.

False, Easy, Page 267

88.   To be effective, an outdoor ad should use short copy, simple design, and large illustrations; simplicity and brevity are the keys to designing an effective outdoor ad.

True, Easy, Page 267

89.   Transit ads offer the advantages of wide coverage and low costs for advertising messages.

True, Medium, Page 269

90.   Directories are an important advertising medium for reaching those customers who have already made the purchase decision and are looking for the product or service.

True, Easy, Page 269

91. One disadvantage of ads placed in directories is their short life span.

   False, Medium, Page 269

92. To get maximum benefit out of a trade show, a small business owner should contact key potential customers before the show by sending them invitations to drop by the company's booth, for example.

   True, Medium, Page 269

93. A major advantage of trade shows is their ability to provide a pre-selected audience of potential customers.

   True, Easy, Page 269

94. Specialty advertising, such as gifts with the company's name and address printed on them, works best as a supplement to other forms of advertising.

   True, Medium, Page 270

95. Specialty advertising gives small businesses an opportunity to fine tune or personalize their advertising to specific customers.

   True, Easy, Page 270

96. Research suggests that consumers make about 20 percent of all buying decisions at the point of sale.

   False, Difficult, Page 271

97. Self service stores such as supermarkets are especially well-suited for point-of-purchase ads.

   True, Easy, Page 271

98. Under the "what is affordable method" of establishing an advertising budget, advertising is viewed as an investment which produces sales and profits in the future.

   False, Medium, Page 272

99. The "what is affordable" method relates the advertising budget to the advertising objective.

   False, Medium, Page 272

100. The objective-and-task method is the easiest and most used technique for establishing an advertising budget.

   False, Medium, Page 274

101. The normal cooperative advertising plan involves a united advertising effort by a group of small businessmen in related businesses.

   False, Easy, Page 275

102. In cooperative advertising, a manufacturer shares the cost of advertising with small retailers if they feature the manufacturer's products in their ads.

   True, Easy, Page 275

103. Most small business owners take advantage of manufacturers' cooperative advertising programs.

   False, Medium, Page 275

104. Cause marketing involves local businesses sponsoring and promoting fundraising activities of nonprofit groups and charities.

   True, Easy, Page 276

105. Price is a measure of what the customer must exchange to obtain goods and services, and is an indicator of value to the customer.

   True, Easy, Page 276

106. The prices a small business charges influence its image in the marketplace.

   True, Easy, Page 276

107. The desired image for the business, the target market the owner is trying to reach, and the prices she charges are all closely related to one another.

   True, Easy, Page 277

108. To avoid major pricing mistakes, business owners should comparison shop their rivals' prices, especially on identical products.

   True, Medium, Page 277

109. Without the advantage of a unique business image, a small business must match local competitors' prices or risk losing sales and customers.

   True, Medium, Page 277

110. The most common pricing mistake small business owners make is setting the price for the products and services they sell too high.

   False, Medium, Page 277

111. The most effective technique by which small companies can gain a competitive edge over their larger rivals is to charge lower prices for the goods and services they sell.

   False, Easy, Page 278

112. For most products, there is an acceptable price range, not a single ideal price.

   True, Easy, Page 278

113. Penetration pricing is a short-term pricing strategy that achieves high profits quickly.

   False, Medium, Page 280

114. If a company wants quick acceptance and extensive distribution when introducing a new product into a highly competitive market with a large number of similar products, penetration pricing is the best strategy.

   True, Medium, Page 280

115. A penetration pricing strategy is designed to recover a company's development and promotional cost of a new product very quickly.

   False, Medium, Page 280

116. A skimming price strategy is used to introduce relatively low-priced goods into a market where no "elite" segment exists.

   False, Medium, Page 280

117. A skimming pricing strategy sets a relatively high price for a product to appeal to the segment of the market that is not sensitive to price.

   True, Medium, Page 280

118. Sliding down the demand curve is a short-term pricing strategy that assumes that competition will eventually emerge and the price will be lowered.

   True, Medium, Page 280

119. James decides to price his products in his small hardware store with ".95," thinking that customers will perceive a price of $9.95 is much lower than a price of $10. This is an example of odd pricing.

   True, Medium, Page 280

120. Price lining occurs when a small company raises the price of all of its goods by the same percentage to cover operating expenses.

   False, Medium, Page 280

121. It is much easier to lower a product's price once it is on the market than to increase it after its introduction.

    True, Easy, Page 280

122. Leader pricing is a technique in which a small company marks down the price of a popular item below its normal price in an attempt to increase customer traffic and to boost sales of other items.

    True, Easy, Page 281

123. Under FOB factory terms, the customer pays all shipping costs.

    True, Medium, Page 281

124. The manufacturer's suggested price takes into account the small firm's cost structure and its competitive situation.

    False, Easy, Page 282

125. The manufacturer's suggested retail prices may create an undesirable image for the small firm.

    True, Medium, Page 282

126. A manufacturer can force a small business to charge the "manufacturer's suggested retail price."

    False, Medium, Page 282

127. When a small business owner doesn't want to make a pricing decision, he can use a suggested retail pricing strategy.

    True, Easy, Page 282

128. The best pricing strategy for a small business owner to follow is to charge the manufacturer's suggested retail price.

    False, Easy, Page 282

129. Markup is the difference between the cost of a product or service and its selling price.

    True, Easy, Page 282

130. Below-market pricing strategies can be risky for small companies because they require businesses to constantly achieve high sales volume to remain competitive.

    True, Medium, Page 284

131. Even though cost-plus pricing is simple, it does not encourage a small business to use its resources efficiently.

   True, Medium, Page 284

132. For setting prices, full absorption financial statements are much more useful to the small business owner than are direct cost statements.

   False, Medium, Page 284

133. Direct (variable) costing includes in the unit cost of a product only those costs that vary with the quantity of units produced.

   True, Easy, Page 284

134. For most service firms, labor and profit comprise the greatest portion of the cost of the service.

   False, Medium, Page 287

135. Approximately 70 percent of the adult U.S. population uses credit cards to make purchases.

   True, Medium, Page 287

136. The use of a credit card by small business customers costs the small business from 1 to 6 percent of the price of the product.

   True, Medium, Page 288

137. The use of credit cards increases the probability, speed, and magnitude of customer spending.

   True, Medium, Page 288

138. Because installment credit absorbs a company's cash, many small businesses rely on financial institutions to provide it for their customers.

   True, Easy, Page 289

139. One advantage of installment loans for a small business is that the business owner retains a security interest in the item sold as collateral on the loan.

   True, Medium, Page 289

140. A small business must carefully assess its own cash position before offering trade credit to its customers.

   True, Easy, Page 290

Essay Questions:

141.   One small business owner says, "My business is so small, I really can't afford to advertise."
What would you say to the business owner? Do you agree with him? Explain.

Students will most likely not agree. Small business owners often believe that to be
effective, advertising and promotion requires mega-buck spending. Advertising for the
small business doesn't have to be complex or expensive. When done correctly, it is an
investment. Without a steady advertising and promotional campaign, a small business's
customer base would soon dry up. Advertising can be an effective means of increasing
sales by informing customers of the business, its products and services; by improving the
image of the firm and its products; or by persuading customers to purchase.
Page 248

142.   What is a Unique Selling Proposition? How can a small business identify a USP? Why is
it important to do so?

A USP is a key customer benefit of a product or service that sets it apart from its
competition. To be effective, it must be something unique that the competition does not
have. The best way to identify a USP is to describe the primary benefit your product or
service offers customers and then to list other secondary benefits it provides. Sometimes
the most powerful USPs are the intangible or psychological benefits a product or service
offers customers. Not developing a USP leads to "me too" advertising that cries out "buy
from us" without offering customers any compelling reason to do so.
Page 249

143.   Discuss the steps involved in developing an advertising plan. What questions should he
address?

The first step in creating an advertising plan is to develop specific, measurable objectives
for the program. Then, the owner must analyze the firm and its customers to focus on a
specific advertising target most efficiently. Finally, the owner designs an advertising
message and chooses the media for transmitting it.

The questions to ask are:

An entrepreneur should address the following questions in order to best focus its
communications efforts:

*   What business am I in?
*   What image do I want to project?
*   Who are my target customers and what are their characteristics?
*   Through which can they best be reached?
*   What do my customers *really* purchase from me?
*   What benefits can the customer derive from my goods or services?
*   How can I prove those benefits to my target customers?
*   What sets my company, products, or services apart from the competition?
*   How do I want to position my company in the market?
*   What advertising approach do my competitors take?
    Page 249

144. Explain the three elements of promotion: publicity, personal selling, and advertising.

- Publicity—any commercial news covered by the media that boosts sales but for which the small business does not pay.

- Personal selling—the personal contact between sales people and potential customers resulting from sales efforts.

- Advertising—any sales presentation that is non-personal in nature and is paid for by an identified sponsor.

Page 250

145. What questions should a business owner consider when selecting the appropriate advertising media?

- How large is my firm's trading area? Determines the range the advertising medium must cover.
- Who are my target customers and what are their characteristics? Knowing who to target and what their common needs are can help in determining the kinds of messages sent and how they are sent.
- Which media are my target customers most likely to watch, listen to, or read? Not all media have the same audience.
- What budget limitations do I face? Cost factors must be considered for each media type according to circulation and reach to the proper target market.
- What media do my competitors use? Find out why they use it.
- How important is repetition and continuity of my advertising message? Reach and frequency are important concepts and must be considered when determining how many times an ad needs to be run. Sending out different messages, can confuse customers and interfere with establishing a consistent image.
- What does the advertising medium cost? A sharp entrepreneur should be aware of the full ranges of pricing offered. For example, contract pricing, off peak-hours pricing etc…

Page 257

146. Your small firm is considering using newspaper and magazines for an advertising campaign. Explain the differences between them, emphasizing their advantages and disadvantages.

Advertising Mediums	Advantages	Disadvantages
Newspapers	*selected geographical coverage *flexibility *timeliness *communication potential *prompt responses	*wasted readership *reproduction limitations *lack of prominence *short ad life
Magazines	*long life spans *multiple readership *target marketing *ad quality	*costs *long closing time *lack of prominence

Newspapers are extremely popular and particularly useful in covering a small geographical area that has varied demographic characteristics. Even though they have a short life span, they are very flexible, and in some cases ads can be updated right up to press time. As a low-cost communication tool, newspapers typically produce prompt responses.

Magazines have the capacity to reach a greater number of specifically targeted individuals and have a relatively long life span. The average magazine has readership of 3.9 adults. Reproduction quality results in a strong visual presentation; however, they are expensive and require long closing times.

Page 259, 263

147.   Discuss the advantages and disadvantages of radio and television as advertising vehicles. Is one better than the other? Why or why not?

Advertising Mediums	Advantages	Disadvantages
Radio	*universal infiltration *market segmentation *flexibility and timeliness *friendliness	*poor listening *need for repetition *limited message
Television	*broad coverage *visual advantage *flexibility *design and assistance	*brief exposure *costs

Each type of media is best suited for different target markets, products or services, industry types or company image strategies. Radio permits advertisers to appeal to specific audiences over large geographical areas. By choosing a particular station, day and time, a marketer can reach almost any target market. Radio ads contain vocal subtleties, which also help to convey messages. Although consumers don't always listen to all the actual ads, it is still very cost efficient.

Television appeals to all the senses using color, imagery and sound to convey an advertiser's message. It normally provides a "shot gun" approach for the small business message and except for some local programming, can be quite costly.

Page 260-261

148.   Explain the four methods of establishing an advertising budget.

- What is Affordable—Management spends whatever it can afford on advertising; whatever is left over.
- Matching competitors—The approach is to match the advertising expenditures of the firm's competitors either in a flat dollar amount or as a percentage of sales.
- Percentage of sales—The most commonly used method because of its simplicity. It relates advertising expenditures to actual sales results.
- Objective-and-task—The most difficult and least used technique, however advertising expenditures are linked to specific objectives.

Page 272

149. What recommendations would you give a small business owner who must advertise big on a small budget?

With a little creativity and a dose of ingenuity, small business owners can stretch their advertising dollars and make the most of what they spend. Several useful techniques to do this include cooperative advertising, shared advertising, and publicity.

In cooperative advertising, a manufacturing company shares the cost of advertising with a small retailer if the retailer features its products in those ads. Both the manufacturer and the retailer get more advertising per dollar by sharing expenses.

In shared advertising, a group of similar businesses forms a syndicate to produce generic ads that allow the individual businesses to dub in local information. The technique is especially useful for small businesses that sell relatively standardized products or services such as legal assistance, autos, and furniture. Because the small firms in the syndicate pool their funds, the result usually is higher quality ads and significantly lower production costs.

Publicity or public relations is a thoughtful process of gaining positive recognition about the business or its products or services through writing interesting and newsworthy articles about what the business is doing or plans to do. Publicity is any commercial news covered by the media that is positive in nature, with the distinct possibility that it will increase recognition of the firm or its products. Publicity, unlike advertising, is free. In addition to being free, publicity has great power to influence an interested reader because it is viewed as more objective than advertising.

Other cost-saving suggestions for advertising expenditures include the following:

- Repeat ads that have been successful. In addition to reducing the cost of ad preparation, this may create a consistent image in a small firm's advertising program.

- Use identical ads in different media. If a billboard has been an effective advertising tool, an owner should consider converting it to a newspaper or magazine ad or a direct mail flier.

- Hire independent copywriters, graphic designers, photographers, and other media specialists.

- Many small businesses that cannot afford a full-time advertising staff buy their advertising services a la carte. They work directly with independent specialists and usually receive high-quality work that compares favorably to that of advertising agencies without paying a fee for overhead.

- Concentrate advertising during times when customers are most likely to buy. Some small business owners make the mistake of spreading an already small advertising budget evenly—and thinly—over a 12-month period.
  Page 274, 252

150. Name and explain the three basic pricing strategies a small business owner has in establishing a new product's price.

Three basic strategies to choose from in establishing the new product's price include:

- Penetration: set price just above total unit cost to develop a wedge in the market and quickly achieve a high volume of sales.

- Skimming: set a higher-than-normal price in an effort to quickly recover the initial developmental and promotional costs of the product.

- Sliding-Down-the-Demand-Curve: set product price high, but with technological advancement, the firm can lower costs quickly and reduce the product's price sooner than competition can.

When introducing a new product, the owner should try to satisfy three objectives:

- Getting the product accepted
- Maintaining market share as competition grows
- Earning a profit

Page 279

151. There are at least eight different pricing strategies for established goods and services. Explain four of those strategies and under what conditions a business owner should use them.

- Odd pricing: establish prices that end in odd numbers with the belief that merchandise selling with an odd ending number ($12.95) is cheaper than an item evenly priced ($13.00).

- Price lining: manager stocks merchandise in several different price ranges, or price lines. Each category of merchandise contains items that are similar in appearance, quality, cost, performance, or other features making it less complicated for the customer.

- Leader pricing: small retailer marks down the customary price of a popular item in an attempt to attract more customers.

- Geographical pricing:

    - Zone pricing: small company sells merchandise at different prices to customers located in different territories.

    - Delivered pricing: the firm charges all of its customers the same price regardless of their location, even though the cost of selling or transporting merchandise varies making it possible to charge the same price to all customers regardless of geographical location.

- FOB-Factory: company sells its merchandise to customers on the condition that they pay all shipping costs. Also called FOB Origin. This is also important when determining liability and insurance issues.

- Opportunistic pricing: when products or services are in short supply, people are willing to pay more. This may backfire because customers may see this as price-gouging.

- Discounts: reduction in the price of stale, outdated, damaged, or slow-moving merchandise.

- Multiple pricing: offers customers discounts if they purchase in quantity.

- Suggested Retail prices: accepting the manufacturer's suggested price does not take into consideration the small firm's cost structure, image or competitive situation. It makes pricing less complicated.

Page 280

152.   Explain the difference between absorption costing and variable(or direct) costing. Which one is more useful when establishing prices? Why?

Full absorption costing is the traditional method of product costing. It "absorbs" the cost of direct materials, direct labor, plus a portion of fixed and variable factory overhead into each unit manufactured. It is not very helpful in setting prices because it confuses the true relationships among price, volume, and costs by including fixed expenses in unit-cost computations.

Direct costing includes only those costs of production that vary directly with the volume of production. Fixed overhead expenses are considered to be expenses of the period; thus, constant unit cost for the product regardless of the production level. The result is a clear picture of the price-costs-volume relationship.

Page 284

153.   Explain the different kinds of credit a small business can offer its customers and the impact each has on pricing.

- Credit cards—businesses should consider the 1- 6 percent of the purchase price they will pay as a fee for their service.

- Installment credit—is financed over time and often requires small business owners to turn to local banks and credit unions. If they have the financial strength to carry their "own paper," it can be a major source of interest income, which technically can subsidizes prices.

- Trade credit—or customer charge accounts can be a drain on small business cash reserves.

Page 288

154. Explain the advantages and the disadvantages of a small business accepting credit cards for customer purchases.

When small businesses offer customers credit, they receive several benefits such as: increases probability, speed, and magnitude of customer spending; customers give higher service ratings; in some cases, the business retains the title of the merchandise until it is paid in full; the interest received on the loans is often greater than the original amount paid for the item.

However, there are costs incurred as well. The main cost when issuing credit to customers is that credit cards are not free to businesses. Typically, small businesses must pay one to six percent of the total credit card charges for the use of the system.
Page 288

Chapter 7
Advertising and Pricing for Profit
Mini-Cases

Case 7-1: "Dr. Boogy Calling"

"I don't know if my customers listen to Dr. Boogy in the morning on their way to work." Bob Wentworth was concerned over where to spend his advertising budget and was talking with one of his younger and brighter employees.

"Everybody listens to Dr. Boogy. He is the final word on what's happening," replied Frank. "Frank, I appreciate your opinion, but I am not sure that you are an example of our customers." "Be serious, Mr. Wentworth. In today's world, I am about as typical as you can get. Trust me on this. The audience for Dr. Boogy's morning show covers the city from border to border."

Bob Wentworth knew that he was naive about advertising and was even more out-of-step with this younger generation, but he was very concerned about the image of his business. Prior to now, all advertising was limited to newspapers. Bob knew that radio could reach large numbers and there was no question that the Dr. Boogy radio program had the largest audience in the city. Bob was still concerned. Would advertising on the Dr. Boogy radio show reach the right markets for Wentworth Mortuary?

1. From what you know about radio advertising, how would you respond to Bob Wentworth?

    Clearly, "Dr. Boogy's" morning radio show does not reach the target for Wentworth Mortuary. In addition, an ad on such a show would hardly convey the image the mortuary wishes to create among its potential customers. Perhaps a "tamer" radio show with a greater portion of older listeners would be more appropriate for Wentworth's advertisement.

2. If Bob Wentworth owned a shoe store, would your advice be different? Why?

    An ad for a shoe store would be more appropriate for Dr. Boogy's morning show. But, again, Wentworth should compare his customer profile of Dr. Boogy's show and those of other radio programs.

Case 7-2: Pricing for Profit

Miller Manufacturing, Inc. produces electronic components for television circuitry. Variable costs comprise 67 percent of the product's selling price. The variable costs of producing a component include:

Direct material	$1.83/unit
Direct labor	$6.72/unit
Variable factory overhead	$ .86/unit

Vicki Miller, President, expects to produce 80,000 electronic components and to incur $280,000 of fixed costs.

1. If Miller desires a profit of $120,000, what price should she set?

$$\frac{\$120,000 + (80,000 \times \$9.41/\text{unit}) + \$280,000}{80,000 \text{ units}} = \$14.41/\text{unit}$$

2. What is Miller Manufacturing's break-even price?

$$\frac{0 + (80,000 \text{ units} \times \$9.41/\text{unit}) + \$280,000}{80,000 \text{ units}} = \$12.91/\text{unit}$$

3. What is the minimum price that Miller Manufacturing would sell its electrical components for?

Minimum price: $ 1.83/unit
6.72/unit
.86/unit
$9.41 per unit

Case 7-3: The Pen is Mightier Than the Sword, But the Word Processor Beats Both

Upon her retirement, after working at the university for 35 years, Betty Woodall opened an editorial service for both faculty and townspeople. Known for years as the best editorial assistant at the university, Betty purchased the latest state-of-the-art word processor for her business. Her home was within walking distance of both the university and the town. Her office was in her basement. "With my low overhead and my high-speed word processor, I can move this work along at top-notch speed." Betty was all set to start. Now she needed to make the community aware of her new service.

1. How can Betty use her reputation for quality work to promote her new business?

   Betty's promotion should emphasize her 35 years of experience in producing editorial services and her outstanding reputation for producing quality work.

2. Who will be the target market for her editorial services and how can this group best be reached?

   The two primary target customers will be faculty and students. She should rely on ads in campus newspapers and newsletters, ads on the campus radio station, and on posters and signs located throughout the campus. She might ask permission to place flyers in faculty members' campus mailboxes. Direct mailings to students could be another practical advertising medium. She might also consider offering free seminars on writing tips. These may very well offer new leads.

3.   How would you promote the opening of the business?

Betty should begin her promotion by making sure the faculty members for whom she performed editorial services know of her new business. As mentioned above, she should rely on ads in campus newspapers and newsletters, ads on the campus radio station, and on posters and signs located throughout the campus. She might ask permission to place flyers in faculty members' campus mailboxes. Direct mailings to students could be another practical advertising medium. She might also consider offering free seminars on writing tips. These may offer significant potential to jump-start her new business.

Case 7-4: The Banner versus The Bulletin

Lawnmowers Unlimited was a new business in town. After working for 10 years in a factory job, Harry Owens decided it was time to be his own boss. Harry had taken courses at the local community college for the past two years and was ready for the grand opening. When it came to advertising, Harry thought it would be valuable to put a major ad in one of the two local newspapers, the Banner or the Bulletin. He could not afford a full page ad in both, and Harry did not want to have only a half-page ad, so it was obvious that the choice was one paper or the other. Harry called both newspapers and the next day a sales representative from each visited Harry to sell the merits of their newspapers.

The Banner had evidence that its circulation was 29,000, and its full-page ad cost $1,600. The Bulletin's circulation was only 20,000 but the cost for a comparable ad was only $1,000. Harry was undecided after talking with both sales representatives, so be began to conduct an informational survey to determine which of his potential customers read either or both papers. Early in the morning on two consecutive days, Harry went around the neighborhood from which he hoped to draw customers. Each day he would stop the newspaper delivery people and ask how many papers they delivered each day and what territory they served. From this research, Harry concluded that 36 percent of his potential customers read the Banner while 25 percent read the Bulletin.

Based on the data supplied by the two newspaper sales representatives and the survey Harry conducted, which newspaper should Harry use for his ad?

	The Banner	The Bulletin
Cost of ad	$ 1,600	$ 1,000
Circulation	29,000	20,000
Potential customers	36%	25%
Cost per potential customer reached	10,440	5,000
	$\frac{1,600}{\$10,440} = .153$	$\frac{1,000}{\$5,000} = .200$

Based on the cost per potential customer reached, Harry would be better off with The Banner.

Case 7-5: Weir's Painting Contractors

Bobby Weir, president of Weir's Painting Contractors, has noticed that profits have been declining, and he suspects that the problem may be the price of his services. This small contractor estimates that last year he and his crew spent 10,200 hours providing painting services. Variable costs were $29,000 and fixed costs totaled $47,000. Bobby expects a net profit of 14 percent on sales.

1. Assume that Weir's jobs typically require varied quantities of paint and other materials. If materials were $18,000 of the firm's variable costs, what should Weir's price per hour be?

    Cost per hour = $11,000 + $47,000 = $58,000/10,200 hours = $5.69/hour

    Price per hour = $5.69/hour x (1/.86) = $6.61/hour plus materials
    $\qquad\qquad\qquad$ 1 - .14 =.86

2. What should Weir's price per hour be?

    Cost per hour = $29,000 + $47,000 = $76,000/10,200 hours = $7.45/hour
    Price per hour = $7.45/hour x(1/.86) = $8.66/hour
    $\qquad\qquad\qquad$ 1 - .14 = .86

Case 7-6: The Price is Right?

"It is obvious what women want; I can't imagine why someone never thought of it before. What good is it to be rich if you have to stay around the house all day waiting for service representatives or doing paperwork?" Penny Matthews decided she would take those responsibilities off the backs of the well-to do women of Tucson, Arizona. "My business will arrange for all the services you need around the home (lawns mowed, plumbing, carpets cleaned, televisions repaired, pools cleaned, everything). My clients will be free to enjoy their lives without worrying about their houses. We will also arrange for parties to be completely catered. In addition, if you wish, we will pay all your bills and reconcile your bank statement. A life without the irritations of domestic hassles; that's our service."
Penny was explaining the idea to her close friend and banker, Wallace Trevillian. "You have definitely thought about this for some time and put months of work into its planning," said Wallace. "What do you plan to charge for these services?"

"That's a good question, Wallace. I haven't thought about it."

How would Penny Matthews go about determining how to price the services her business plans to offer?

This case addresses the issue of establishing a price for a service. Penny could charge clients for her services on the basis of an hourly fee developed from estimates of materials used, labor employed, an allowance for overhead, and a profit. She must estimate the total cost per productive hour. Next, she can compute the hourly price:

Price Total per hour =	Total cost per productive hour	X	$\dfrac{1.00}{(1.00 - \text{net profit target as \% of sales})}$

Finally, Penny might adjust this price to reflect the proper image of her service.

Chapter 9   **Managing Cash Flow**

Multiple Choice Questions:

1. Proper cash management permits a business owner to:
    a. adequately meet the cash demands of the business.
    b. avoid retaining unnecessarily large cash balances.
    c. stretch the profit-generating power of each dollar the business owns.
    d. All of the above.

    d., Easy, Page 294

2. _____ is the most important yet least productive asset that a small business owns.
    a. Profit
    b. Cash
    c. Inventory
    d. Accounts receivable

    b., Medium, Page 294

3. Which of the following statements concerning cash management is **false**?
    a. Cash is the most important yet least productive asset a small business owns.
    b. Young companies tend to be "cash sponges," soaking up every available dollar of cash.
    c. Because they generate large amounts of cash quickly, fast-growing businesses are least likely to experience shortages.
    d. None of the above.

    c., Medium, Page 294

4. The first step in managing cash more effectively is:
    a. having an adequate cash reserve for emergency expenditures.
    b. rapid payment of accounts payable.
    c. speeding up payment of accounts receivable.
    d. understanding the company's cash flow cycle.

    d., Medium, Page 295

5. Which of the following measures a company's liquidity and its ability to pay its bills and other financial obligations on time?
    a. Cash budget
    b. Cash flow
    c. Cash management
    d. All of the above.

    b., Easy, Page 297

6.   _____ typically lead(s) sales; _____ typically lag(s) sales.
      a.   Production; receivables
      b.   Collections; purchases
      c.   Receipts; production
      d.   Purchases; collections

d., Medium, Page 298

7.   A cash budget reveals important clues about how well a company_____.
      a.   balances its accounts receivable and accounts payable
      b.   controls inventory
      c.   finances its growth
      d.   All of the above.

d., Easy, Page 298

8.   A firm's cash budget:
      a.   should be prepared on a monthly basis for at least one year in advance.
      b.   should cover a longer planning horizon when a firm's pattern is highly variable.
      c.   must cover all seasonal fluctuations.
      d.   Only A and C above.

d., Medium, Page298

9.   A cash budget:
      a.   is based on the cash method of accounting.
      b.   is a "cash map," showing the amount and the timing of cash flowing into and out of the business over a given period of time.
      c.   will never be completely accurate since it is based on forecasts.
      d.   All of the above.

d., Medium, Page 298

10.   Which of the following is **not** a step in creating a cash budget?
      a.   Determining an adequate minimum cash balance
      b.   Forecasting profits
      c.   Forecasting cash receipts
      d.   Forecasting cash disbursements

b., Medium, Page 299

11. On March 10, a business owner receives an invoice from a supplier for $416.27 with "net 30" credit terms marked on it. On April 7, the owner writes the supplier a check for $416.27 and mails it. When would this cash disbursement show up on the company's cash budget?
    a. March 10
    b. March 30
    c. April 7
    d. April 10

    c., Medium, Page 299

12. Jane is arguing with Joan about how much cash their small retail outlet needs on hand as they prepare their cash budget. Jane feels that with the Christmas season coming up, their busiest time, they need more cash handy. Joan feels they don't because their sales volume will be up significantly. Jane and Joan are discussing which step of the cash budgeting process?
    a. Determining an adequate minimum cash balance
    b. Forecasting sales
    c. Forecasting cash receipts
    d. Forecasting cash disbursements

    a., Medium, Page 299

13. A cash budget is only as accurate as the _____ forecast from which it is derived.
    a. profit
    b. receivables
    c. income
    d. sales

    d., Easy, Page 300

14. What factors can drastically affect a company's cash flow?
    a. increased competition
    b. economic swings
    c. normal seasonal variations
    d. All of the above.

    d., Easy, Page 300

15. Which of the following would be a potential source of information for preparing a sales forecast?
    a. past records
    b. trade associations and the Chamber of Commerce
    c. similar firms
    d. All of the above.

    d., Easy, Page 301

16. When a firm sells goods or services on credit, the owner needs to remember that for cash budgeting purposes:
    a. the sale may be immediately posted as if it has been collected.
    b. the sale should be recorded in the month it was made.
    c. she must account for a delay between the sale and the actual collection of the proceeds.
    d. such a transaction counts as a cash disbursement.

    c., Medium, Page 302

17. It is recommended that new business owners estimate cash disbursements as best he can and then add on another _____.
    a. 3-4%
    b. 5-10%
    c. 10-25%
    d. 25-35%

    c., Difficult, Page 305

18. When estimating the firm's end-of-month cash balance, the owner should first:
    a. determine the cash balance at the beginning of the month.
    b. add up total cash receipts and subtract cash on hand.
    c. review the accounts receivable.
    d. make a daily list of cash disbursements.

    a., Medium, Page 306

19. One recent study showed that only about _____ percent of small businesses used formal techniques such as cash budgets to track their cash balances.
    a. 16
    b. 26
    c. 36
    d. 46

    c., Difficult, Page 306

20. The fact that the cash budget illustrates the flow of cash in a business helps the owner to:
    a. accelerate accounts payable payments.
    b. get a seasonal line of credit rather than an annual line of credit.
    c. slow accounts receivable payments.
    d. track the effects of depreciation and bad debts.

    b., Difficult, Page 306

21. By planning cash needs ahead of time, a small business is able to achieve all but which of the following?
    a. Make the most efficient use of available cash
    b. Provide the opportunity to forego quantity and cash discounts
    c. Finance seasonal business needs
    d. Provide funds for expansion

    b., Medium, Page 306

22. The "big three" of cash management include:
    a. accounts receivable, overhead, and inventory.
    b. accounts payable, accounts receivable, and taxes.
    c. accounts receivable, accounts payable, and inventory.
    d. accounts receivable, prices, and expenses.

    c., Medium, Page 307

23. Experts estimate that _____ percent of industrial and wholesale sales are on credit, while _____ percent of retail sales are on credit.
    a. 20; 40
    b. 40; 20
    c. 60; 30
    d. 90, 40

    d., Difficult, Page 307

24. Small businesses selling on credit find that:
    a. it is relatively inexpensive and simple.
    b. it is expensive, requires a great deal of effort, and is risky.
    c. it is essentially borrowing money from the customer.
    d. many can get by without selling on credit because their business customers don't expect to use credit.

    b., Medium, Page 307

25. One study indicated that only about _____ of small companies protected themselves by checking customers' credit.
    a. 1/4
    b. 40 percent
    c. 1/3
    d. 10 percent

    c., Difficult, Page 309

26. An important source of credit information that collects information on small businesses that other reporting services ignore is:
    a. National Association of Credit Management.
    b. TRW.
    c. Dun & Bradstreet.
    d. National Association of Small Business Owners.

    a., Easy, Page 309

27. The cost to check a potential customer's credit at a reporting service typically ranges from:
    a. $1 to $5.
    b. $15 to $85.
    c. $100 to $150.
    d. $500 to $750.

    b., Difficult, Page 309

28. To encourage credit customers to pay invoices promptly, a business owner should:
    a. ensure that all invoices are clear, accurate, and timely.
    b. state clearly a description of the goods or services purchased and an account number.
    c. include a telephone number and a contact person in case the customer has a question or a dispute.
    d. All of the above.

    d., Easy, Page 309

29. When a small business is writing off more than ____ percent of its sales as bad debts, it needs to tighten its credit and collection policies.
    a. 3
    b. 5
    c. 10
    d. 25

    b., Difficult, Page 309

30. Once a small business has established a firm written credit policy and communicated it, the next step in building an effective credit policy is to:
    a. send invoices promptly.
    b. determine what percentage of sales are being written off as bad debt.
    c. create a simple credit application.
    d. create a "tracking file" of events.

    a., Medium, Page 309

31. Once a credit account becomes past due, a small business owner should:
    a. wait patiently; the customer will most likely pay the bill sooner or later.
    b. turn the account over to a collection agency the day it becomes past due.
    c. send a "second notice" letter requesting immediate payment.
    d. call the "deadbeat" in the middle of the night and make harassing and threatening remarks until he pays.

    c., Medium, Page 309

32. A collection agency typically takes ___% of the amounts they collect on past due accounts.
    a. 5 to 10
    b. 10 to 20
    c. 25 to 50
    d. 75 to 90

    c., Medium, Page 310

33. According to the American Collector's Association, _____% of accounts more than 90 days delinquent will be paid voluntarily.
    a. 5
    b. 20
    c. 45
    d. 65

    a., Difficult, Page 310

34. The Fair Debt Collection Practices Act prohibits business owners from:
    a. harassing people who are past due.
    b. sending invoices the same day product is shipped.
    c. hiring debt collection attorneys.
    d. referring past due bills to collection agencies.

    a., Easy, Page 310

35. A small business owner could accelerate accounts receivable by:
    a. having customers mail printed orders to him.
    b. sending or faxing invoices the day of shipment.
    c. slowing their own accounts payable.
    d. depositing customer checks and credit card receipts weekly.

    b., Medium, Page 310

36. In the typical company, ____% of its customers generate ____% of its accounts receivable.
    a. 60; 80
    b. 50; 50
    c. 20; 80
    d. 10; 20

    c., Easy, Page 310

37. An arrangement in which customers mail their payments on account to a post office box which the company's bank monitors, collects payments, and immediately deposits them into the firm's account is called a(n):
    a. collection board.
    b. lockbox.
    c. electronic funds transfer system.
    d. cash box.

    b., Easy, Page 312

38. Patel Industries recently filled an order from one of its customers, Oxmoor Gardens, a small garden supply store. Oxmoor's owner, Jan McBride, recently received an invoice from Patel for $1,278.64 with selling terms of "2/10, net 30." Which of the following statements is **true**?
    a. The selling terms indicate that Oxmoor must pay 2 percent of the invoice by the 10th day of the month with the balance due in 30 days.
    b. The selling terms are offering Oxmoor a 2 percent discount if the bill is paid within 10 days; otherwise the full amount of the invoice is due in 30 days.
    c. The selling terms indicate that the full amount of the invoice is due within 30 days and Oxmoor will be subject to a 2 percent finance charge for every 10 days that the bill is past due.
    d. The selling terms indicate that Oxmoor has not yet qualified for a quantity discount and must pay the full amount of the invoice within 30 days.

    b., Medium, Page 313

39. Efficient cash managers:
    a. disregard trade discounts because of their hidden costs.
    b. avoid the use of credit cards to stretch their firm's cash balances.
    c. set up a payment calendar in order to both pay on time and take advantage of cash discounts for early payment.
    d. use expressions like "the check is in the mail" to mollify creditors when short on cash.

    c., Medium, Page 313

40. Only about ____ percent of a typical business' inventory turns over quickly.
    a. 20
    b. 40
    c. 60
    d. 80

    a., Medium, Page 315

41. Which of the following is true about inventory management for the small business owner?
    a. Most small business owners have turned to technology and computer spreadsheets to achieve maximum efficiency in managing it.
    b. Inventory is the largest capital investment for most businesses but few owners use any formal means for managing it.
    c. Inventory is generally very liquid and can be easily mortgaged to a bank for immediate cash if needed.
    d. Inventory yields a return of about 25% for manufacturing firms but nothing for service companies.

    b., Medium, Page 315

42. Which of the following inventory management techniques would help a business owner make the best use of her company's cash?
    a. Avoid overbuying inventory.
    b. Schedule inventory deliveries at the latest possible date.
    c. Purchase goods from the fastest suppliers who can meet quality standards to keep inventory levels low.
    d. All of the above.

    d., Easy, Page 315

43. Exchanging goods and services for other goods and services, or _____, is an effective way for a small business to conserve cash.
    a. leasing
    b. bartering
    c. arbitraging
    d. credit sales

    b., Easy, Page 316

44. It is estimated that approximately _____ companies, most of them small, engage in barter exchanges every year.
    a. 50,000
    b. 100,000
    c. 200,000
    d. 500,000

    a., Difficult, Page 316

45. The real benefit of barter for the entrepreneur is that:
    a. it is essentially without cost to the business owner.
    b. it is considered a depreciable item for tax purposes rather than as income.
    c. it saves the small business owner between $100,000 and $150,000 a year on the average.
    d. it is "paid" for at the wholesale cost of doing business, yet it is credited at the retail price.

    d., Difficult, Page 316

46. Barter offers business owners the benefit of:
    a. buying materials, equipment, and supplies without spending valuable cash on them.
    b. transforming slow-moving inventory into much-needed goods and services.
    c. "paying" for goods and services at wholesale cost and getting credit for retail price.
    d. All of the above.

    d., Medium, Page 316

47. Which of the following is an effective way to trim overhead?
    a. When able, buy instead of leasing.
    b. Hire more full-time employees; reduce the number of part-timers.
    c. Eliminate zero-based budgeting.
    d. Negotiate fixed loan payments to coincide with company cash flow.

    d., Difficult, Page 317

48. Which of the following statements concerning leasing is true?
    a. Leasing is an "off-the-balance-sheet" method of financing assets.
    b. Although total lease payments for an asset are greater than those on a conventional loan, most leases do not require large capital outlays as down payments.
    c. Leasing gives business owners access to equipment even when they cannot borrow the money to buy it.
    d. All of the above.

    d., Medium, Page 317

49. According to a recent survey, approximately _____ percent of U.S. companies use leasing as a cash management strategy.
    a. 35
    b. 50
    c. 73
    d. 88

    c., Difficult, Page 317

50. When investing surplus cash, the small business owner's key objectives should be:
    a. high yields.
    b. current income.
    c. liquidity and safety.
    d. long term yield.

    c., Medium, Page 320

True/False Questions:

51. Cash is the most important yet least productive asset a small business owns.

    True, Medium, Page 294

52. Developing a cash forecast is essential for new businesses because early profit levels usually do not generate sufficient cash to keep the company afloat.

    True, Easy, Page 294

53. A common cause of business failures is that owners neglect to forecast how much cash their companies will need until they reach the point of generating positive cash flow.

    True, Easy, Page 294

54. The objectives of cash management are to adequately meet the cash demands of the business, to avoid retaining unnecessarily large cash balances, and to stretch the profit-generating power of each dollar the business owns.

    True, Easy, Page 294

55. It is likely that young companies and rapidly growing companies will experience cash flow difficulties.

    True, Medium, Page 294

56. The shorter a company's cash flow cycle, the more likely it is to encounter a cash crisis.

    False, Medium, Page 295

57. Compiling the total cash on hand, bank balance, summary of the day's sales, summary of the day's cash receipts, and a summary of accounts receivables collections into monthly summaries provides the basis for making reliable cash forecasts.

    True, Medium, Page 296

58. A highly profitable business is a highly liquid business.

    False, Medium, Page 297

59. A small company's cash balance is the difference between total revenue and total expenses.

False, Easy, Page 297

60. Profit is the difference between a company's total revenue and its total expenses.

True, Easy, Page 297

61. The goal of cash management is to maintain as much cash as possible on hand to meet any unexpected circumstances that might arise.

False, Medium, Page 298

62. A cash budget allows a small business owner to anticipate cash shortages and cash surpluses and gives him time to handle, or even avoid, approaching problems.

True, Easy, Page 298

63. Typically, small business owners should prepare a projected weekly cash budget for at least six months and quarterly estimates for the remainder of the year, being careful to cover all seasonal sales fluctuations.

False, Medium, Page 298

64. A small business whose sales are highly variable (i.e., "seasonal") should use a short cash planning horizon.

True, Medium, Page 298

65. The primary problem with cash management tools is that they are too complex and time consuming for small business owners to use practically.

False, Medium, Page 298

66. In a cash budget, credit sales to customers are recorded at the time the sale is made.

False, Medium, Page 299

67. Depreciation and debt expenses are often left off the cash budget but need to be included to accurately forecast cash requirements for running the business.

False, Medium, Page 299

68. The cash budget is nothing more than a forecast of the firm's cash inflows and outflows for a specific time period, and it will never be completely accurate.

True, Medium, Page 299

69. The first step in preparing a cash budget is to forecast sales.

     False, Medium, Page 299

70. The most reliable method of determining an adequate minimum cash balance is using estimates of similar businesses from trade literature.

     False, Medium, Page 299

71. A small firm's minimum cash balance should be two times its average weekly sales.

     False, Medium, Page 299

72. A small company's ideal minimum cash balance is one month's sales.

     False, Medium, Page 299

73. Because the heart of the cash budget is the sales forecast, the cash budget is only as accurate as the sales forecast on which it is based.

     True, Medium, Page 300

74. Since even the best sales forecast will be wrong, the small business owner should prepare three forecasts—optimistic, pessimistic, and most likely.

     True, Medium, Page 301

75. Difficulty in collecting accounts receivable is the primary cause of cash flow problems, according to small business owners.

     True, Medium, Page 303

76. The longer an accounts receivable is outstanding, the lower its probability of collection.

     True, Easy, Page 303

77. The key factor in forecasting cash disbursements for a cash budget is to record them in the month when they are incurred, not when they are paid.

     False, Medium, Page 303

78. For cash planning purposes, it is better to underestimate cash disbursements than to overestimate them.

     False, Easy, Page 305

79. Seasonal sales patterns cause cash balances to fluctuate dramatically, creating the need for cash forecasts.

    True, Medium, Page 306

80. To manage cash efficiently, business owners should strive to accelerate their accounts payable and stretch out their accounts receivable.

    False, Medium, Page 307

81. Most small businesses conduct a thorough credit investigation before selling to a new customer.

    False, Medium, Page 307

82. Forty percent of industrial and wholesale sales are on credit, and 90 percent of retail sales are on account.

    False, Medium, Page 307

83. A sale to a customer is not really a sale until the business owner actually collects the money from it.

    True, Easy, Page 307

84. The first line of defense against bad debt losses is to have a financial institution extend loans to credit-seeking customers.

    False, Medium, Page 309

85. One effective technique for improving cash management is to establish a firm credit policy in writing and let customers know in advance what it is.

    True, Easy, Page 309

86. Some businesses use cycle billing, in which a company bills a portion of its credit customers each day of the month to smooth out uneven cash receipts.

    True, Easy, Page 309

87. As soon as an account receivable becomes past due, a business owner should turn it over to a collection agency.

    False, Easy, Page 309

88. If an account receivable becomes past due, the best strategy is simply to wait; statistics show that customers eventually pay their bills if business owners don't bother them with repeated collection attempts.

   False, Medium, Page 309

89. Small business owners should not press customers for payment of their past due accounts for fear of losing them as customers altogether.

   False, Easy, Page 309

90. A small business owner should concentrate her collection efforts on the top 20 percent of her company's customers since they typically account for 80 percent of all accounts receivable.

   True, Medium, Page 310

91. A security agreement is a contract in which a business selling an asset on credit gets a security interest in that asset, protecting its legal rights in case the buyer fails to pay.

   True, Easy, Page 312

92. Proper cash management techniques call for a small business owner to pay invoices as soon as he receives them.

   False, Medium, Page 312

93. Efficient cash managers set up a payment calendar each month, which allows them to pay their bills on time and to take advantage of cash discounts for early payment.

   True, Easy, Page 313

94. A basic principle of cash management is verifying all invoices before paying them.

   True, Easy, Page 313

95. A cash discount offers a price reduction if the owner pays an invoice on time.

   False, Easy, Page 313

96. Small business owners generally should not take advantage of cash discounts vendors offer, choosing instead to maintain control of their cash for as long as possible.

   False, Medium, Page 313

97. It is considered unethical for small business owners to regulate payments to their companies' advantage.

   False, Medium, Page 313

98. Because inventory is not a liquid asset, cash invested there is tied up and cannot be used for other purposes.

   True, Medium, Page 315

99. A typical manufacturing company pays 40-50 percent of the value of the inventory for the cost of borrowed money, warehouse space, materials handling, staff, lift-truck expenses, and fixed costs.

   False, Difficult, Page 315

100. Only about 20 percent of a typical business's inventory turns over quickly.

   True, Medium, Page 315

101. Roughly 80 percent of the typical business' inventory turns over quickly.

   False, Medium, Page 315

102. It is much wiser to carry too little inventory rather than too much because there are no costs associated with carrying too little inventory.

   False, Medium, Page 315

103. Bartering, exchanging goods and services for other goods and services, is an effective way for small business owners to conserve cash.

   True, Easy, Page 316

104. Bartering is an opportunity to transform slow-moving inventory into much-needed products and services.

   True, Easy, Page 316

105. The real benefit to a business owner engaging in barter is the ability to "pay" for goods and services at her wholesale cost and to get credit for the retail price.

   True, Medium, Page 316

106. Most business owners should avoid leasing as a cash management strategy because it requires large capital outlays as down payments, and total lease payments typically are greater than those for conventional loans.

   False, Medium, Page 317

107. Important advantages of leasing include the flexibility of the lease agreement and protection against obsolescence.

   True, Medium, Page 317

108. When a small business encounters a sales slowdown, the first thing the owner should do is cut marketing and advertising expenditures to conserve cash.

False, Easy, Page 317

109. Many banks allow entrepreneurs to schedule their loan payments to fit their company's cash flow cycles.

True, Medium, Page 318

110. Changing your firm's shipping terms from "F.O.B. buyer" to "F.O.B. seller" can improve your cash flow, as it switches the cost of shipping from you to your buyer.

True, Medium, Page 318

111. Rather than build the current year's budget on increases from the previous year's budget, zero-based budgeting starts from a budget of zero and evaluates the necessity of every item.

True, Easy, Page 318

112. Companies lose billions of dollars each year due to employee theft.

True, Easy, Page 318

113. In order to deter employee theft, it is best to separate cash management duties between at least two different employees.

True, Easy, Page 318

114. When trying to prevent employee theft, business owners should create a "police state" environment and trust no one.

False, Easy, Page 318

115. Because small business owners often rely on informal procedures for managing cash, they are most likely to become victims of embezzlement and fraud by their employees.

True, Easy, Page 318

116. Revising business plans annually forces owners to focus on managing the business more effectively.

True, Easy, Page 319

117. Small business managers need not be concerned about investing surplus cash since small amounts of cash sitting around for a few days or weeks are not worth investing.

False, Easy, Page 320

118. When investing surplus cash, the small business owner should seek the highest returns possible on the money.

    False, Medium, Page 320

119. When investing surplus cash, an owner's primary objective should be on the safety and liquidity of the investments.

    True, Easy, Page 320

120. A sweep account automatically "sweeps" all funds in a company's checking account above a predetermined minimum into an interest-bearing account, enabling it to keep otherwise idle cash invested until it is needed to cover checks.

    False, Easy, Page 320

Essay Questions:

121. Why is cash a unique asset? What are the advantages of efficient cash management?

    Cash is the most important yet least productive asset that a small business owns. A business must have enough cash to meet its obligations, or it will go bankrupt. Creditors, employees, and lenders expect to be paid on time, and cash is the required medium of exchange. Cash is the lifeblood of any small business.

    Proper cash management permits the owner to adequately meet the cash demands of the business, to avoid retaining unnecessarily large cash balances, and to stretch the profit-generating power of each dollar the business owns. Also, more businesses fail for lack of cash than for lack of profit.
    Page 294

122. Your friend Jake owns a business that is achieving phenomenal growth. Explain why it is said that: "Fast-growing companies are most likely to experience cash shortages."

    Many successful, growing, and profitable businesses fail because they become insolvent; they do not have adequate cash to meet the needs of a growing business with a booming sales volume. If a company's sales are up, its owner must also hire more employees, expand plant capacity, increase the sales force, build inventory, and incur other drains on the firm's cash supply. During rapid growth, cash collections often fall behind, compounding the problem. Inventory and receivables often increase faster than profits can fund them.
    Pages 294-295

123. The profits your small business is generating are high; however, you never seem to have enough cash to pay your bills on time. Are cash and profit the same thing? Why or why not?

    Cash and profit are not the same thing. Cash is the money (the actual receipt of money) that flows through the business in a continuous cycle. It is the money that is free and readily available to use in the business. Profit is the difference between the company's total revenue and total expenses. It is the net increase over a period of time in capital

cycled through the business, and it tells how effectively the firm is being managed. A business cannot spend profits or pay bills with profits; these require cash. Businesses sometimes fail not because they are not making a profit, but because they simply run out of cash.
Page 297

124. What are the basic steps in preparing a cash budget? Which forecast is the "heart" of the cash budget?

   Five basic steps to preparing a cash budget include:

   - Determining an adequate minimum cash balance – some suggest it should be at least one-fourth of a firm's current debts. Be sure to account for seasonal fluctuations and add extra for "cushion." The most reliable method involves past operating records.
   - Forecasting sales – which ultimately are transformed into cash receipts and cash disbursements. Be careful not to be excessively optimistic; consider economic swings, increased competition, fluctuations in demand, normal seasonal variations, and other factors that can have a dramatic effect on sales. A cash budget is only as accurate as the sales forecast from which it is derived.
   - Forecasting cash receipts – includes accounting for the delay between the sale and the actual collection of the proceeds. To predict accurately the firm's cash receipts, the owner must analyze the accounts receivable to determine the collection pattern.
   - Forecasting cash disbursements – many cash payments are fixed amounts due on specified dates. The key is to record them in the month in which they will be paid, not when the obligation is incurred.
   - Determining the end-of-month cash balance – add total cash receipts to, and subtract total cash disbursements from, the beginning cash balance for the month. The cash balance at the end of a month becomes the beginning balance for the following month.

   The heart of the cash budget is the sales forecast. As mentioned above, a cash budget is only as accurate as the sales forecast from which it was derived.
   Page 298

125. How are sales forecasts developed for an established business? A new business enterprise?

   For an established business, a sales forecast can be derived from past sales data, using quantitative techniques like linear or multiple regression, time series analysis, and others. The business owner must be aware that economic swings, increased competition, fluctuations in demand, normal seasonal variations, and other factors that can have a dramatic effect on sales.

   The task of forecasting sales for the new firm is more difficult, but not impossible. The founder of a new business might rely on similar firms and their first year sales patterns, published statistics, market surveys, and experts' opinions to derive a sales forecast. The local Chamber of Commerce and trade associations may be able to provide helpful statistics. Marketing research using census data, government statistics, polls, surveys, etc., is also a potential source of data for forecasting sales.
   Page 300

126. Identify the "big three" of cash management. As a small business consultant, what would you recommend your clients do to control the "big three" more effectively?

The "big three" primary causes of cash flow problems are accounts receivable, accounts payable, and inventory.

Selling on credit is a common practice in business. It is essential that business owners establish a workable credit policy before granting credit. It should include: a detailed credit application and a firm written credit policy issued to every customer in advance. Other techniques for accelerating accounts receivable include: send invoices promptly, indicate due date and late payment penalties, and track results of collection efforts.

Although a firm should try to accelerate its receivables, it should strive to stretch out its payables as long as possible without damaging its credit rating. Businesses should always verify invoices before paying them and should strongly consider taking advantage of cash discount opportunities offered by their vendors. Wise use of credit cards may also be considered.

Because inventory is a significant investment for many small businesses, it can create a severe strain on cash flow. Inventory should be carefully managed to reduce the possibilities of carrying the wrong type, too much, or failing to meet customer demand/stock-outs. Scheduling inventory deliveries at the latest possible date will prevent premature cash distributions.
Page 307

127. What steps can a small business owner take to minimize bad debt losses?

A credit policy that is too lenient can destroy a business's cash flow, attracting nothing but slow paying or "deadbeat" customers. However, extending a carefully designed credit policy to customers can boost sales and cash flow.

How to establish a credit and collection policy:

- Screen customers carefully by requiring that they submit a detailed credit application.
- Establish a firm written credit policy and let every customer know in advance the company's credit terms.
- Send invoices promptly.
- When an account becomes overdue, take immediate action.

Steps to encourage prompt payment of invoices:

- Ensure that all invoices are clear, accurate, and timely.
- State clearly a description of the goods or services purchased and an account number.
- Ensure that prices on invoices agree with price quotations on purchase orders or contracts.
- Highlight the terms of sale (e.g. "net 30") on all invoices and reinforce them.

- Include a telephone number and a contact person in your organization in case the customer has a question or a dispute.

Page 307

128. What steps can a small business owner take to avoid the cash "crunch"?

Techniques that allow small business owners to get the maximum benefit from their companies' pool of available cash include:

- Barter: the exchange of goods and services for other goods and services rather than for cash, is an effective way to conserve cash. The owner can get the goods and services he needs <u>without</u> having to spend valuable cash. He gets credit for the retail value of the goods or services, but the real cost to him is less, depending on the gross profit margin. In addition, the owner may be able to collect otherwise uncollectible accounts.

- Trim overhead costs: high overhead expenses can strain a small firm's cash supply. Ways to trim overhead costs include:

  - Periodically, evaluate expenses.
  - When practical, lease instead of buy.
  - Avoid nonessential outlays.
  - Negotiate fixed loan payments to coincide with your company's cash flow cycle.
  - Buy used or reconditioned equipment, especially if it is "behind-the-scenes" machinery.
  - Hire part-time employees and freelance specialists whenever possible.
  - Control employee advances and loans.
  - Establish an internal security and control system.
  - Develop a system to battle check fraud.
  - Change your shipping terms.
  - Switch to zero-based budgeting.

- Be on the lookout for employee theft.

- Keep your business plan current: keep your business plan up-to-date with annual revisions.

- Invest surplus cash: if a small business has a surplus of cash, a significant amount can be earned by investing to improve cash flow.

Page 315

Chapter 9
Managing Cash Flow
Mini-Cases

Case 9-1: Golden Company

1. From the information below, prepare a monthly cash budget for the next quarter (October-December) for the Golden Company.

	October	November	December
Sales	$750,000	$800,000	$900,000
Manufacturing costs	450,000	480,000	540,000
Operating expenses	225,000	240,000	270,000
Capital expenditures	-------	60,000	------

Golden Company expects 25 percent of its sales to be in cash, and of the accounts receivable, 705 will be collected within the next month. Depreciation, insurance, and property taxes comprise $25,000 of monthly manufacturing costs and $10,000 of the operating expenses. Insurance and property taxes are paid in February, June, and September. The rest of the manufacturing costs and operating expenses will be paid off, one-half in the month incurred and the rest in the following month. The current assets on October 1 are made up of:

*   Cash, $70,000
*   Marketable securities, $50,000
*   Accounts receivable, $600,000 ($450,000 from September, $150,000 from August) and current liabilities include a 90-day note for $60,000 at 9% due October 18
*   Accounts payable for $200,000 for September manufacturing expenses
*   Accrued liabilities of $100,000 for September operating expenses

Dividends of $1,000 should be received in November. An income tax payment of $50,000 will be made in November. The firm's minimum cash balance is $20,000.

CASH BUDGET—GOLDEN COMPANY

	August	September	October	November	December
Sales			$750,000	$800,000	$900,000
Credit Sales	150,000	450,000	562,500	600,000	675,000
Cash Receipts					
Collections					
1st Month - 70%			$315,000	$393,750	$420,000
2nd Month - 25%			37,500	112,500	140,625
Cash Sales			187,500	200,000	225,000
Dividends Received			0	1,000	0
Other			0	0	0
Total Cash Receipts			$540,000	$707,250	$785,625

Cash Disbursements

Manufacturing Costs - 1/2	$212,500	$227,500	$257,500
Manufacturing Costs - 1/2	200,000	212,500	227,500
Operating Costs - 1/2	120,000	115,000	130,000
Operating Costs - 1/2	100,000	120,000	115,000
Note Payable	60,900	0	0
Capital Expenditure	0	60,000	0
Tax Payment	0	50,000	0
Other	0	0	0
Total Cash Disbursements	$693,400	$785,000	$730,000

EOM Balance

Beginning Cash	$70,000	$20,000	$20,000
Cash Receipts	540,000	707,250	785,625
Cash Disbursements	693,400	785,000	730,000
EOM Balance	($83,400)	($57,750)	$75,625
Repay	0	104,262	183,528
Borrow	103,400	182,012	127,903
Final EOM Balance	$20,000	$20,000	$20,000

Calculations:

Oct 18 notes payable: 60,000 principal + 60,000 x .09 x ¼ of a year = 61,350

Manufacturing costs:
Because depreciation (a non-cash expense) is a component of mftg costs and because insurance and property taxes (cash expenses, which are included on a cash budget) are paid only in February, June, and September, we must subtract out $25,000 of monthly mftg costs as follows:
October 475,000-25,000 = 450,000
November 520,000-25,000 = 495,000
December 575,000-25,000= 550,000

Now we can show the actual cash outflow of these expenses, which is 50% in current month and 50% in the following month:

October: 450,000/2 = 225,000 PLUS the half from September, 200,000 accounts payable. So cash outflow for mftg in October are 225,000 + 200,000 = 425,000.

November: 495,000/2 = 247,500 PLUS the half from October, 225,000. So cash outflow for mftg expenses for November are 247,500 + 225,000 = 472,500.

And so on...

Case 9-2: The Laurens Corporation

In past years, Sue Salgado, owner of the Laurens Corporation, has been plagued by unexpected cash flow problems. Her banker, worried about her lack of cash flow management, has suggested that Sue create a cash budget for the upcoming quarter. Sue does this, using the following information:

	October	November	December
Sales	$800,000	$900,000	$950,000
Manufacturing Costs	475,000	520,000	575,000
Operational Expenses	250,000	270,000	290,000
Capital Expenditures	20,000	70,000	------

Laurens Corporation expects 35 percent of its sales to be in cash, and that of the accounts receivable, 70% will be collected within the next month, and 25 percent in the second month after sale. Depreciation, insurance, and property taxes comprise $25,000 of monthly manufacturing costs and $12,000 of operating expenses. Insurance and property taxes are paid in February, June and September. One-half of the remaining manufacturing costs and operating expenses will be paid in the month in which incurred, and the rest in the following month. As of October 1, the following facts are relevant:

- Current assets consist of $50,000 in cash, $50,000 in securities
- Credit sales for August and September were $500,000 and $450,000 respectively
- The firm has a line of credit with a local bank at 18 percent APR, and loan is due the following month
- Accounts payable of $200,000 for September manufacturing expenses
- Accrued liabilities of $100,000 for September operating expenses

Dividends of $1,000 should be received in November. An income tax payment of $20,000 will be made in November. The firm's minimum cash balance is $10,000.

From the information given, prepare a monthly cash budget for the next quarter (October - December) for the Laurens Corporation.

CASH BUDGET—LAURENS CORPORATION

	August	September	October	November	December
Sales			$800,000	$900,000	$950,000
Credit Sales	$500,000	$450,000	520,000	585,000	617,500
Collections			315,000	364,000	409,500
1st month after sale					
2nd month after sale			125,000	112,500	130,000
Cash sales			280,000	315,000	332,500
Dividends received				____	1,000
Total Cash Receipts			$720,000	$792,500	$872,000
Manufacturing Costs			225,000	247,500	275,000
			200,000	225,000	247,500
Operating Costs			119,000	129,000	139,000
			100,000	119,000	129,000
Notes Payable				61,350	
Capital Expenditures				20,000	70,000
Income tax payments				____	0,000
Total Cash Disbursements			$725,350	$810,500	$790,500

387

Cash-Beginning of month	50,000	44,650	26,650
+ Cash Receipts	720,000	792,500	872,000
- Cash Receipts	725,350	810,500	790,500
Cash-End of month	44,650	26,650	108,150
Borrowing (repayment)	___	0	
Cash-End of month	$44,650	$26,650	$108,150

Laurens Corporation's cash balance never dips below the minimum cash balance so the firm does not need to borrow on its line of credit.

Case 9-3: Rent-A-Nerd Computer Consultants

The owners of Rent-A-Nerd Computer Consultants have prepared the following cash budget for the upcoming quarter:

	Month 1	Month 2	Month 3
Cash Receipts:			
Total Sales	$42,650	$45,500	$47,000
Credit Sales	25,590	27,300	28,200
Collections:			
10 percent same month	2,559	2,730	2,820
80 percent next month	19,941	20,472	21,840
8 percent following month	1,864	1,994	2,048
Cash Sales	17,060	18,200	18,800
Total Cash Receipts			
Cash Disbursements:			
Purchases	$32,404	$33,267	$35,490
Wages/Salaries	4,212	4,897	5,126
Rent/Utilities	1,865	1,910	2,250
Other	2,400	3,750	6,105
Total Cash Disbursements			
End of Month Balance:			
Beginning Cash	$ 4,750		
Cash Receipts			
Cash Disbursement			

EOM Balance			
Borrow			
Repay			

FINAL EOM BALANCE
1.   How much would Rent-A-Nerd have to borrow if its desired minimum cash balance is

$4,000?
a. $2,224 in Month 3.
b.   Nothing. Rent-A-Nerd's end of the month cash balance is below $4,000.
c. $2,598 in Month 3.
d. $20,771 in Month 3.

c.

2.   Total cash receipts for months 1, 2 and 3 are
a. $42,650, $45,400, $47,000.
b. $25,590, $27,300, $28,200.
c. $68,240, $72,800, $75,200.
d. $41,424, $43,396, $45,508.

d.

3.   The end-of-the-month balances for months 1, 2, and 3 are
a. $5,293, $4,865, $1,402.
b. $6,519, $8,195, $6,224.
c.   -$10,541, -$12,524, -$16,771.
d. $32,109, $61,085, $87,314.

a.

Chapter 10   **Creating a Successful Financial Plan**

<u>**Multiple Choice Questions:**</u>

1.   In order to reach profit objectives, entrepreneurs must be aware of their firms':
       a.   current ratio.
       b.   overall financial position.
       c.   changes in financial status.
       d.   B & C only.

       d., Easy, Page 324

2.   The _____ shows what assets the business owns and what claims creditors and owners
       have against those assets, and is built on the basic accounting equation: Assets =
       Liabilities + Owner's Equity.
       a.   income statement
       b.   sources and uses of funds statement
       c.   balance sheet
       d.   cash budget

       c., Easy, Page 324

3.   _____ are those items of value the business owns; _____ are those things the business
       owes.
       a.   Assets; liabilities
       b.   Liabilities; assets
       c.   Ratios; equities
       d.   Equities; liabilities

       a., Easy, Page 324

4.   The first section of a balance sheet lists:
       a.   assets.
       b.   liabilities.
       c.   claims creditors have against the firm's assets payable within one year.
       d.   the owner's equity in terms of initial capital invested and retained earnings.

       a., Easy, Page 324

5.   Which of the following items would **not** be listed as a current asset in a company's
       financial reports?
       a.   Cash
       b.   Accounts receivable
       c.   Fixtures
       d.   Inventory

       c., Medium, Page 324

6. The _____ represents a "snapshot" of a business, showing an estimate of its value on a given date, while the _____ is a "moving picture" of the firm's profitability over time.
    a. balance sheet; income statement
    b. income statement; balance sheet
    c. statement of cash flows; income statement
    d. balance sheet; statement of cash flows

    a., Medium, Page 324

7. Cost of goods sold is located on which financial statement?
    a. income statement
    b. balance sheet
    c. statement of cash flows
    d. All of the above.

    a., Medium, Page 325

8. Which of the following is **not** true regarding the components of the income statement?
    a. Cost of goods sold represents the total cost, excluding shipping, of the merchandise sold during the accounting period.
    b. Gross profit margin is calculated by dividing gross profit by net sales revenue.
    c. Operating expenses include those costs that contribute directly to the manufacture and distribution of goods.
    d. A and B above.

    a., Difficult, Page 325

9. The statement of cash flows:
    a. compares costs and expenses against firm's net profits.
    b. is built on the basic accounting equation: Assets = Liabilities + Capital.
    c. shows what assets the business owns and what claims creditors and owners have against those assets.
    d. shows changes in working capital by listing sources and uses of funds.

    d., Medium, Page 327

10. On a company's statement of cash flows, depreciation is:
    a. the difference between the total sources available to the owner and the total uses of those assets.
    b. listed as a source of funds because it is a non-cash expense, deducted as a cost of doing business.
    c. the owner's total investment at the company's inception plus retained earnings.
    d. creditors' total claims against the firm's assets.

    b., Medium, Page 327

11. Which of the following associations is **correct**?
    a. balance sheet - cost of goods sold
    b. income statement - owner's equity
    c. current assets - inventory
    d. long-term liabilities - accounts payable

    c., Medium, Page 324

12. Creating projected (pro forma) financial statements would allow a business owner to answer which of the following questions?
    a. What profit can any business expect to achieve?
    b. What sales level must any business reach if our targeted profit is X dollars?
    c. What fixed and variable expenses can any business expect to incur at our targeted sales level?
    d. All of the above.

    d., Easy, Page 328

13. On a projected income statement, a business owner's target income is:
    a. the sum of a reasonable salary for the time spent running the business and a normal return on the amount invested in it.
    b. the income at which the company's total revenues and its total expenses are equal.
    c. the income that will produce a 10 percent return on the owner's financial investment in the business.
    d. the income that the owner could earn working for someone else.

    a., Medium, Page 329

14. You are to prepare a projected income statement for a proposed business venture. Your desired income is $28,000 and you have the following published statistics:
    Costs of goods sold = 56.9 percent of net sales
    Operating expenses = 37.1 percent of net sales
    Gross profit margin = 43.1 percent of net sales

    Net sales on your pro forma "P & L" (income statement) would be:
    a. $491,228.
    b. $500,000.
    c. $466,667.
    d. None of the above.

    c., Medium, Page 329

15. Gaither Mack is preparing projected financial statements to include in the business plan he is preparing for the launch of a specialty retail store. Using published financial statistics, Mack finds that the typical net profit margin for a store like his is 7.3 percent. If Mack's target income for his first year of operation is $32,000, what level of sales must he achieve to reach it?
    a. $438,356
    b. $233,600
    c. $2,966,400
    d. Cannot be determined from the information given

    a., Medium, Page 329

16. Typically, in a start-up firm, salaries are not the best use of cash; a guideline is for the owner to draw a salary that is about _____ to ___% below the market rate for a similar position.
    a. 5-10
    b. 10-20
    c. 20-25
    d. 25-30

    d., Difficult, Page 330

17. A business should provide the owner with a reasonable rate of return on:
    a. the time she invests in the business.
    b. the money she invests in the business.
    c. the capital she borrows from the bank.
    d. A and B only.

    d., Easy, Page 330

18. Michelle Becker's target income in her business for the upcoming year is $78,500. The company's gross profit margin averages 32.6 percent of sales, and its total operating expenses run 24.7 percent of sales. To achieve her target income, sales of Michelle's company should be:
    a. $148,773.
    b. $993,671.
    c. $317,814.
    d. $1,271,348.

    b., Medium, Page 330

19. A technique that allows the small business owner to perform financial analysis by understanding the relationship between two accounting elements is called:
    a. creating the pro forma.
    b. budgeting.
    c. break-even analysis.
    d. ratio analysis.

    d., Easy, Page 334

20. Analyzing financial ratios could alert a business owner to which of these problems?
    a. excessive inventory
    b. overextending credit
    c. too much debt
    d. All of the above.

    d., Easy, Page 334

21. _____ ratios tell whether or not the small company will be able to meet its short-term obligations.
    a. Leverage
    b. Profitability
    c. Liquidity
    d. Operating

    c., Easy, Page 335

22. Which of the following is **not** a liquidity ratio?
    a. current ratio
    b. total asset turnover ratio
    c. quick ratio
    d. None of the above.

    b., Easy, Page 335

23. The ____ ratio is a measure of the small company's ability to pay current debts from current assets and is the liquidity ratio most commonly used as a measure of short-term solvency.
    a. quick
    b. debt-to-net worth
    c. current
    d. debt-to-assets

    c., Easy, Page 335

24. Financial analysts suggest that a small business should maintain a current ratio of at least:
    a. 1:1.
    b. 2:1.
    c. 3:1.
    d. 4:1.

    b., Medium, Page 335

25. The _____ ratio is a conservative measure of a firm's liquidity and shows the extent to which a firm's most liquid assets cover its current liabilities.
    a. current
    b. quick
    c. turnover
    d. net profit

    b., Easy, Page 335

26. Bettina has just calculated her company's current ratio. To calculate the quick ratio, she should:
    a. subtract current liabilities from current assets before dividing by total liabilities.
    b. subtract total liabilities from current assets before dividing by current liabilities.
    c. subtract inventory from current assets before dividing by current liabilities.
    d. subtract depreciation expense from current assets before dividing by current liabilities.

    c., Medium, Page 335

27. When a company is forced into liquidation, owners are most likely to incur a loss when selling:
    a. accounts receivable.
    b. inventory.
    c. marketable securities.
    d. real estate.

    b., Medium, Page 336

28. _____ ratios measure the extent to which an entrepreneur relies on debt capital rather than equity capital to finance a business.
    a. Liquidity
    b. Leverage
    c. Operating
    d. Profitability

    b., Easy, Page 336

29. The _____ ratio measures the percentage of total assets financed by a small company's creditors compared to its owners.
    a. debt
    b. times-interest-earned
    c. net sales to total assets
    d. total asset turnover

    a., Easy, Page 336

30. A high debt ratio:
    a. means that creditors provide a large percentage of the company's total financing.
    b. gives a small business more borrowing capacity.
    c. decreases the chances that creditors will lose money if the business is liquidated.
    d. represents a lower risk to potential lenders and creditors.

    a., Medium, Page 336

31. Which ratio would best give an owner an indication that the business is undercapitalized?
    a. Debt-to-net worth
    b. Net sales to total assets
    c. Average inventory turnover
    d. Quick

    a., Easy, Page 337

32. The higher the _____ ratio, the lower the degree of protection afforded creditors, and the closer creditors' interest approaches the owner's interest.
    a. debt-to-net worth
    b. quick
    c. asset turnover
    d. current

    a., Easy, Page 337

33. _____ is one indication that a small business may be undercapitalized.
    a. A current ratio below 1:1.
    b. A quick ratio above 2:1.
    c. A debt-to-net worth ratio above 1:1.
    d. A net sales-to-working capital ratio equal to 3:1.

    c., Medium, Page 337

34. The _____ ratio tells how many times the company's earnings cover the interest payments on the debt it is carrying.
    a. debt
    b. debt-to-net worth
    c. times-interest-earned
    d. net sales-to-working capital

    c., Easy, Page 337

35. _____ ratios help a business owner evaluate the company's performance and indicate how effectively the business employs its resources.
    a. Liquidity
    b. Leverage
    c. Operating
    d. Profitability

    c., Easy, Page 338

36. The average inventory turnover ratio:
    a. measures the number of times a company's inventory is sold out during the accounting period.
    b. tells a business owner whether she is managing the company's inventory properly.
    c. tells a business owner how fast the merchandise is moving through the business.
    d. All of the above.

    d., Easy, Page 338

37. Sarah's Smart Shop has an inventory turnover ratio of 3 times per year and an average inventory of $156,000. If Sarah could manage her inventory better and increase the number of turnovers to the industry average of 6 times per year, what average inventory would she need to generate the same level of sales?
    a. $78,000
    b. $52,000
    c. $468,000
    d. $312,000

a., Medium, Page 338

38. Which of the following combinations of ratios would indicate that a company is financially mismanaged and is not a good credit risk?
    a. high liquidity; high leverage
    b. low liquidity; high leverage
    c. high liquidity; low leverage
    d. low liquidity; low leverage

b., Medium, Page 339

39. For the most meaningful interpretation, the small business owner should compare his firm's average collection period to:
    a. the average for the industry.
    b. his firm's credit terms.
    c. the universal standard of 25 days.
    d. A & B only.

d., Medium, Page 340

40. A business that turns over its receivables 5.9 times a year would have an average collection period of about:
    a. 30 days.
    b. 2/10, net 30.
    c. 71 days.
    d. 62 days.

d., Medium, Page 340

41. If the accounting period is one year with credit sales totaling $2,500,000 and accounts receivable totaling $200,000, what is the average collection period ratio?
    a. 29.2 days
    b. 365 days
    c. 119.3 days
    d. Cannot be determined

a., Difficult, Page 340

42. A business with a payables turnover ratio of 10.4 times a year would have an average payable period of about:
    a. 3 days.
    b. 30 days.
    c. 35 days.
    d. 62 days.

    c., Easy, Page 341

43. An excessively high average payable period ratio:
    a. suggests that the company is making the best use of its available cash balance.
    b. indicates that the company is doing a poor job of collecting its accounts receivable.
    c. indicates the presence of a significant amount of past-due accounts payable.
    d. suggests that the company is highly liquid.

    c., Medium, Page 341

44. The _____ ratio measures a company's ability to generate sales in relation to its assets.
    a. net sales-to-working capital
    b. net sales to total assets
    c. average collection period
    d. average inventory turnover

    b., Easy, Page 341

45. Which ratio would be most helpful to a business owner trying to make sure that he maintains a sufficient amount of working capital to nourish his company's expansion?
    a. net sales to total assets
    b. net sales to working capital
    c. net profit on sales
    d. net profit to equity

    b., Easy, Page 342

46. _____ ratios indicate how efficiently the small firm is being managed.
    a. Liquidity
    b. Profitability
    c. Leverage
    d. Operating

    b., Easy, Page 343

47. The _____ ratio shows the portion of each sales dollar remaining after deducting all expenses.
    a. net profit on sales
    b. net profit to equity
    c. net sales to total assets
    d. net sales to working capital

    a., Easy, Page 343

48. The _____ ratio measures the owner's rate of return on the investment in the business.
    a. net profit to equity
    b. net profit on sales
    c. quick profit
    d. net sales to working capital

    a., Easy, Page 343

49. The break-even point:
    a. occurs where a company's total revenue equals its total expenses.
    b. is the point at which a company neither earns a profit nor incurs a loss.
    c. tells a business owner the minimum level of activity needed to keep her company in operation.
    d. All of the above.

    d., Easy, Page 350

50. Which of the following is an assumption of break-even analysis?
    a. Fixed expenses remain constant for all levels of sales volume.
    b. Variable expenses change in direct proportion to changes in sales volume.
    c. Changes in sales volume have no effect on unit sales price.
    d. All of the above.

    d., Easy, Page 355

Refer to the following information to answer Questions 51-52 regarding Anita Lupino:

Anita Lupino is planning to open her own toy and game shop. She has conducted a great deal of research at the local library, contacted the industry trade association, and has set up a meeting with a consultant at the SBDC next week. Before she goes to the SBDC, she wants to sketch out an estimated income statement. She gets the following data from RMA's Annual Statement Studies:

Costs of goods sold	57.3 percent of net sales
Operating expenses	32.9 percent of net sales
Gross profit	42.7 percent of net sales

51. If Anita's research suggests that she can expect net sales of $475,000, what net profit could she expect?
    a. $202,825
    b. $46,550
    c. $69,350
    d. $156,275

    b., Medium, Page 329

52.   If Anita's net profit target is $32,000, what level of net sales must she achieve?
        a. $74,941
        b. $97,264
        c. $326,531
        d. $219,178

        c., Medium, Page 329

Refer to the following information to answer Questions 53-55 regarding Port Royal:
        Net sales = $927,641
        Gross profit = $301,483
        Net profit = $48,457
        Total assets = $203,869
        Total liabilities = $74,325

53.   Port Royal's debt-to-net worth ratio is:
        a. 0.36:1.
        b. 0.08:1.
        c. 1.57:1.
        d. 0.57:1.

        d., Medium, Page 337

54.   Port Royal's profit margin on sales is _____ percent.
        a. 5.2
        b. 32.5
        c. 16.1
        d. 8.0

        a., Medium, Page 343

55.   Port Royal's net profit-to-equity ratio is ____ percent.
        a. 23.8
        b. 37.4
        c. 16.1
        d. 232.7

        b., Medium, Page 344

Refer to the following information to answer Questions 56-57 about Alhambra Meters, Inc.:
        Alhambra Meters, Inc. reported net sales of $874,916 and a net profit of $74,563 on its
        most recent income statement. The company's balance sheet shows total assets of $342,742
        and total liabilities of $88,367.

56.   What is Alhambra's net profit margin?
        a. 8.5 percent
        b. 1.91:1
        c. 21.8 percent
        d. 29.3 percent

        a., Medium, Page 343

57. What is Alhambra's return on net worth ratio?
    a. 8.5 percent
    b. 1.91:1
    c. 21.8 percent
    d. 29.3 percent

d., Medium, Page 344

58. Refer to the following information:

	Smith Office Supply	Industry Mean
Current ratio	2.3	1.8
Quick ratio	.4	.8
Average inventory turnover	2.0	3.9
Net sales-to-working capital	4.0	7.8
Debt-to-net worth ratio	3.0	1.7
Net profit to equity ratio	40.1 percent	22.2 percent

Which of the following statements is most likely **false**?
    a. Smith relies on inventory fairly heavily to meet its debt obligations.
    b. Smith is sufficiently capitalized.
    c. Smith's sales are inadequate.
    d. Smith's prices may be too high and/or the inventory too "stale."

b., Medium, Page 343

Refer to the following to answer Questions 59-61 regarding Gunther's Gum Emporium:

Gunther's Gum Emporium expects net sales of $2,396,919 for the upcoming year, with variable expenses totaling $1,813,443 and fixed expenses of $412,190.

59. If Gunther's net profit target for the year is $190,000, what sales level must he achieve?
    a. $2,473,796
    b. $1,876,324
    c. $5,667,009
    d. None of the above.

a., Medium, Page 353

60. Gunther's Gum Emporium expects net sales of $2,396,919 for the upcoming year, with variable expenses totaling $1,813,443 and fixed expenses of $412,190.

What is Gunther's break-even point?
    a. $1,876,324
    b. $1,693,276
    c. $5,667,009
    d. Insufficient information given to determine

b., Medium, Page 352

61. Using break-even analysis, what is Gunther's contribution margin?
     a. 4 percent
     b. 32 percent
     c. 24 percent
     d. 12 percent

     c., Medium, Page 352

Refer to the following Break-even Chart to answer Questions 62-65:

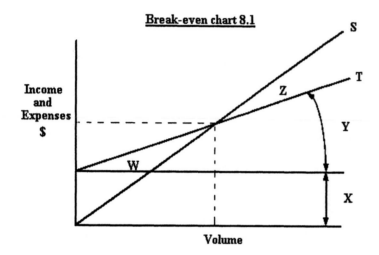

62. Line T is the _____ line, while Line S is the _____ line.
     a. total revenue; total expense
     b. total expense; total revenue
     c. fixed cost; variable cost
     a. variable cost; fixed cost

     b., Medium, Page 354

63. The area labeled _____ represents the firm's fixed expenses, while _____ represents its variable expenses.
     a. Z; W
     b. X; Y
     c. Y; X
     d. W; Z

     b., Medium, Page 355

64. The area labeled _____ is the "profit area."
     a. W
     b. X
     c. Y
     d. Z

     d., Medium, Page 355

65. The area labeled _____ is the "loss area."
    a. W
    b. X
    c. Y
    d. Z

    a., Medium, Page 355

True/False Questions:

66. According to one study, only 11 percent of small business owners analyzed their financial statements as part of the managerial planning process, and another study found that one-third of all entrepreneurs run their companies without any kind of financial plan.

    True, Medium, Page 324

67. The income statement is based on the fundamental accounting equation: Assets = Liabilities + Owner's Equity.

    False, Easy, Page 324

68. Assets represent what a business owns, while liabilities represent the claims creditors have against a company's assets.

    True, Easy, Page 324

69. The balance sheet provides owners with an estimate of the firm's worth for a specific moment in time, while the income statement presents a "moving picture" of its profitability over a period of time.

    True, Medium, Page 324

70. On the income statement, the cost of goods sold represents the total cost, excluding shipping, of the merchandise sold during the year.

    False, Medium, Page 325

71. To determine net profit, the owner records sales revenue for the year and subtracts liabilities.

    False, Easy, Page 325

72. Service companies spend the greatest percentage of their sales revenue on cost of goods sold.

    False, Easy, Page 325

73. Comparing a company's current income statement to those of prior accounting periods rarely reveals valuable information about key trends.

False, Easy, Page 326

74. Almost fifty percent of small businesses become profitable within zero to twelve months.

True, Difficult, Page 327

75. The difference between the total sources of funds and the total uses of funds represents the increase or decrease in a firm's working capital.

True, Easy, Page 327

76. The most common mistake entrepreneurs make when preparing pro forma (projected) financial statements for their companies is being overly pessimistic in their financial plans.

False, Easy, Page 328

77. Pro forma financial statements show a company's most recent financial position.

False, Medium, Page 328

78. On a projected income statement, a business owner's target income is the sum of a reasonable salary for the time spent running the business and a normal return on the amount the owner has invested in it.

True, Medium, Page 329

79. In start-up firms, one guideline is for the owner to draw a salary 25-30 percent below the market rate for a similar position.

True, Medium, Page 330

80. Concerning how much cash to have at startup, one rule of thumb is to have enough to cover operating expenses (less depreciation) for two inventory turnover periods.

False, Medium, Page 331

81. Ratio analysis allows a business owner to identify potential problem areas in her business before they become business-threatening crises.

True, Easy, Page 333

82. Ratio analysis is a useful managerial tool that can help business owners maintain financial control over their businesses, but it is of no use to a business owner trying to obtain a bank loan.

False, Medium, Page 334

83. Liquidity ratios such as the current ratio and the quick ratio, tell whether a small business will be able to meet its short-term obligations as they come due.

True, Easy, Page 335

84. A current ratio of 2.4:1 means that a small company has $2.40 in current liabilities for every $1 has in current assets.

False, Medium, Page 335

85. A high current ratio guarantees that the small firm's assets are being used in the most profitable manner.

False, Difficult, Page 335

86. Generally, the higher the current ratio, the stronger the small firm's financial position.

True, Medium, Page 335

87. Most firms calculate their quick assets by subtracting the value of their inventory from their current asset total.

True, Medium, Page 335

88. A quick ratio of more than 1:1 suggests that a small company is overly dependent on inventory and future sales to satisfy its short-term debt.

False, Difficult, Page 336

89. Operating ratios measure the extent to which an entrepreneur relies on debt capital rather than equity capital to finance the business.

False, Easy, Page 336

90. Leverage ratios measure the financing supplied by the firm's owner against that supplied by his creditors.

True, Easy, Page 336

91. Small businesses with high leverage ratios are more vulnerable to economic downturns, but they have greater potential for large profits.

True, Difficult, Page 336

92. The small business with a high debt to net worth ratio has more borrowing capacity than a firm with a low ratio.

False, Difficult, Page 337

93. As a company's debt to net worth ratio approaches 1:1, its creditors' interest in that business approaches that of the owners.

   True, Medium, Page 337

94. A company with a low debt to net worth ratio has less capacity to borrow than a company with a high debt to net worth ratio.

   False, Medium, Page 337

95. The times-interest-earned ratio tells how many times the company's earnings cover the interest payments on the debt it is carrying.

   True, Medium, Page 337

96. A company with a times-interest earned ratio that is well above the industry average would likely have difficulty making the interest payments on its loans, as creditors would see that it was overextended in its debts.

   False, Difficult, Page 337

97. Creditors often look for a times interest earned ratio of at least 4:1 to 6:1 before pronouncing a company a good credit risk.

   True, Medium, Page 337

98. Taking on debt destroys a business; therefore, small business owners should avoid it at all costs.

   False, Medium, Page 338

99. Liquidity ratios help a business owner evaluate a small company's performance and indicate how effectively it employs its resources.

   False, Easy, Page 338

100. The average inventory turnover ratio measures the number of times a company's inventory is sold out during the accounting period.

   True, Easy, Page 338

101. An inventory turnover ratio above the industry average suggests that a business is overstocked with obsolete, stale, overpriced, or unpopular merchandise.

   False, Medium, Page 340

102. A high inventory turnover ratio relative to the industry average could mean that a business has too little inventory and is experiencing stockouts.

   True, Medium, Page 340

103. A company's average collection period ratio tells the average number of days it takes to collect its accounts receivable.

   True, Easy, Page 340

104. Generally, the higher the small firm's average collection period ratio, the greater the chance of bad debt losses.

   True, Medium, Page 340

105. Slow accounts receivable are a real danger to a small business because they often lead to cash crises.

   True, Medium, Page 341

106. If a company's average payable period ratio is significantly lower than the credit terms vendors offer, it may be a sign that the company is not using its cash most effectively.

   True, Medium, Page 341

107. An excessively high average payable period ratio indicates the possibility of the presence of a significant amount of past-due accounts payable.

   True, Medium, Page 341

108. Although sound cash management principles call for a business owner to keep her cash as long as possible, slowing accounts payable too drastically can severely damage a company's credit rating.

   True, Easy, Page 341

109. A net sales to working capital ratio of 6.25:1 means that for every dollar in working capital $6.25 is generated in sales.

   True, Medium, Page 342

110. The net profit on sales ratio measures the owner's rate of return on the investment in the business.

   False, Medium, Page 343

111. The net profit to equity ratio reports the percentage of the owners' investment in the business that is being returned through profits annually.

   True, Easy, Page 343

112. Ratio analysis provides an owner with a "snapshot" of the company's financial picture at a single instant; therefore, she should track these ratios over time, looking for trends that otherwise might go undetected.

   True, Easy, Page 350

113. The break-even point is the level of operation at which a business neither earns a profit nor incurs a loss, and lets the business owner know the minimum level of activity required to keep the firm in operation.

True, Medium, Page 350

114. Fixed expenses are those that do not vary with changes in the volume of sales, but do vary with production.

False, Medium, Page 352

115. On a break-even chart, the break-even point occurs at the intersection of the fixed expense line and the total revenue line.

False, Medium, Page 355

Essay Questions:

116. Explain the three basic financial reports that a small business uses in building a financial plan: the balance sheet, the income statement and the statement of cash flows. What information is contained in each, and of what value is it to the small business owner?

A. Balance sheet: takes a "snapshot" of a business, providing owners with an estimate of its worth on a given date. It is built on the fundamental accounting equation Assets = Liabilities + Owner's Equity and provides a baseline from which to measure future changes in assets, liability and equity.

Components include: Assets (Current and Long Term), Liabilities (Current and Long term), and Owner's Equity.

B. Income statement: compares expenses against revenue over a certain period of time to show the firm's net profit (or loss). It is a "moving picture" of the firm's profit over a period of time and provides "the bottom line" figure for the small business owner. It is also known as the Profit and Loss Statement or P & L.

Components include various categories of Revenues and Expenses.

C. Statement of cash flows: shows the changes in the firm's working capital since the beginning of the year by listing the sources of funds and the use of these funds. Although many small business owners never create them, IRS, creditors, investors and new owners may require them when investigating the changes in a firm's working capital.

Components include categories of Sources and Uses of Funds.

Page 324

117. Define what a pro forma financial statement is. What are the two types a small business owner uses, and how are they created?

Pro forma statements are vital elements in a small business financial plan. They estimate the firm's future profitability and overall financial condition. These statements help the owner determine the funds required to launch the business and sustain it. The basic pro forma financial statements are:

The Income Statement

Most entrepreneurs select a target income and build a pro forma income statement from the bottom up. The target income includes a reasonable salary and a normal return on the amount invested in the firm. The owner computes target sales from his target income by:

$$\text{Net Sales} = \frac{\text{Target Income}}{\text{Net profit margin (as a \% of net sales)}}$$

Next, using published statistics, the owner computes the remaining entries by multiplying the proper statistic by the net sales figure. After the owner determines that the targeted net sales figure is reasonable, expenses are listed accordingly.

The Balance Sheet

Creating a pro forma balance sheet begins with a statement of assets. One rule of thumb suggests that the company's cash balance should cover its operating expenses (less depreciation, a noncash expense) for one inventory turnover period.

The method of determining the firm's cash requirement is:

$$\text{Cash requirement} = \frac{\text{Cash expenses}}{\text{Average inventory turnover}}$$

The inventory level is computed from published statistics and the cost of goods sold figure from the income statement:

$$\text{Inventory level} = \frac{\text{Cost of goods sold}}{\text{Average inventory level}}$$

To complete the projected balance sheet, the owner must record the firm's other assets, and liabilities, the claims against its assets. Using the accounting equation of Assets = Liabilities + Owner Equity, calculates the final component—Owner's Equity.
Page 328

118. Explain what ratio analysis is. Name the four categories of ratios and describe the type of information each group provides the small business owner.

Ratios help measure the small firm's performance and can point out potential problem areas before they become business crises. They use accounts from both the balance sheet and income statement and provide relevant information to the overall financial plan. One way to use ratios is to compare those of the small business to other businesses in the same industry through a number of published industry averages and standards. It is also helpful for the owner to analyze the firm's financial ratios over time. The four categories are:

Liquidity ratios – tell whether a firm will be able to meet its short-term financial obligations as they come due. These ratios can forewarn a business owner of impending cash flow problems. A firm with a solid liquidity is able to pay bills on time and take advantage of attractive opportunities as they arrive.

Leverage ratios – measure the financing supplied by the firm's owners against that supplied by its creditors. The ratios are a gauge of the depth of a firm's debt. These ratios show the extent to which a business relies on debt capital (rather than equity) to finance operating expenses, capital expenditures, and expansion costs. In a sense, they measure the degree of financial risk in a company. Generally small businesses with low leverage ratios are affected less by economic downturns, but the returns are lower during economic booms. Firms with higher ratios are more vulnerable during economic downturns because of their debt loads, but have a greater potential for large profits in economic booms.

Operating ratios – evaluate a firm's overall performance and indicate how effectively the business employs its resources. The more effectively its resources are used, the less capital a small business will require.

Profitability ratios – indicate how efficiently a small business is being managed. These ratios provide information on the company's bottom line—how successfully the firm is using its available resources to generate a profit.
Page 333

119. List ten key ratios outlined in the text and explain the type of information they provide the small business owner.

Students should select from the following Twelve Key Ratios:

- Current ratio--firm's ability to pay current debts out of current assets. Rule of thumb = 2:1

- Quick ratio--extent to which firm's most liquid assets cover its current liabilities. Rule of thumb - 1:1

- Debt ratio--measure the financing supplied by business owners and that supplied by business creditors.

- Debt-to-net-worth ratio--compares what the business owes to what it "owns."

- Times interest earned--a measure of the firm's ability to make the interest payments on its debt.

- Average inventory turnover ratio--measures the average number of times its inventory is "turned over" during the year.

- Average collection period ratio--tells the average number of days it takes to collect accounts receivable.

- Average payable period ratio--tells the average number of days it takes a company to pay its accounts payable.

- Net sales to total assets ratio--a general measure of firm's ability to generate sales in relation to its assets.

- Net sales to working capital ratio--measures how much in sales the business generates for every dollar of working capital.

- Net profit on sales ratio--measures firm's profit per dollar of sales.

- Net profit to equity ratio--measures owner's rate of return on investment (ROI).

Page 347

120. Why is it important for an entrepreneur, about to launch a business, to perform a breakeven analysis? Describe the steps in calculating it.

Breakeven analysis is important because it helps the entrepreneur understand what sales volume he/she must achieve to "break even" –neither earning a profit nor incurring a loss. It shows the minimum level of sales required to stay in business and what minimum level of sales is required to cover expenses. The formula can be adapted to figure the minimum level of sales needed to support a certain profit margin or dollar amount.

The steps in calculating Break-even include:

A. Determining variable and fixed expenses:

   1. Fixed expenses—costs that do not vary with changes in the volume of sales or production.

   2. Variable expenses—costs that vary directly with changes in the volume of sales or production.

B. Steps in calculating the breakeven point:

   Step 1: Determine the expenses the business can expect to incur.

   Step 2: Categorize the expenses estimated in step 1 into fixed expenses and variable expenses.

   Step 3: Calculate the ratio of variable expenses to net sales.

   Step 4: Compute the breakeven point by inserting this information into the following formula:

   $$\text{Breakeven sales (\$)} = \frac{\text{total fixed costs}}{\text{contribution margin expressed as a percentage of sales}}$$

C.   Including Desired Net Income in Breakeven Analysis:

Sales ($) = $\dfrac{\text{total fixed expenses} + \text{desired net income}}{\text{contribution margin expressed as a percentage of sales}}$

D.   Breakeven Point in Units:

Breakeven volume = $\dfrac{\text{total fixed costs}}{\text{sales price per unit} - \text{variable cost per unit}}$

Page 350

121.   Explain the procedure for constructing a graph that visually portrays the firm's break-even point (the point where revenues equal expenses).

- Step 1: On the horizontal axis, mark a scale measuring sales volume in dollars (or in units sold or some other measure of volume).
- Step 2: On the vertical axis, mark a scale measuring income and expenses in dollars.
- Step 3: Draw a fixed expense line intersecting the vertical axis at the proper dollar level parallel to the horizontal axis. The area between this line and the horizontal axis represents the firm's fixed expenses.
- Step 4: Draw a total expense line that slopes upward beginning at the point where the fixed cost line intersects the vertical axis. The precise location of the total expenses line is determined by plotting the total cost incurred at a particular sales volume. The total cost for a given sales level is determined by:

Total expenses = Fixed expenses + Variable expenses expressed as a % of sales x Sales level

- Step 5: Beginning at the graph's origin, draw a 45-degree line showing where total sales volume equals total income.
- Step 6: Locate the break-even point by finding the intersection of the total expense line and the revenue line. If the company operates at a sales volume to the left of the break-even point, it will incur a loss because the expense line is higher than the revenue line. On the other hand, if the firm operates at a sales volume to the right of the break-even point, it will earn a profit because the revenue line lies above the expense line.

Page 352

122.   What are the advantages and the disadvantages of using break-even analysis?

Advantages of break-even analysis include:

Being a key component in a sound financial plan. By analyzing costs and expenses in this manner, an entrepreneur can calculate the minimum level of activity required to keep the firm in operation. These techniques can then be refined to project the sales needed to generate the desired profit. It is a simple useful screening device. Business owners can also employ nonlinear break-even analysis using a graphical approach.

Disadvantages include:

Having certain limitations such as being too simple to use as a final screening device because it ignores the importance of cash flows. Also, the accuracy of the analysis depends on the accuracy of the revenue and expense estimates, and the basic assumptions pertaining to break-even analysis may not be realistic for some businesses. These assumptions include: that fixed expenses remain constant for all levels of sales volume; variable expenses change in direct proportion to changes in sales volume; and changes in sales volume have no effect on unit sales price.
Page 355

Chapter 10
Creating a Successful Financial Plan
Mini-Cases

Case 10-1: Bowden Brake Service (Part A)

Jim Bowden, owner of Bowden Brake Service, is planning to expand his six-year old brake service to include tune-ups and tire services. Based on budget estimates for the upcoming year, Jim expects net sales to be $825,000 with a cost of goods sold of $530,000 and total operating expenses of $210,000. From the budget, Jim computes fixed expenses to be $168,000, while variable expenses (including cost of goods sold) are $572,000. Jim is worried that the new cost structure may damage his ability to produce a profit, so he wants to perform a quick break-even analysis for the upcoming year.

1. Prepare an outline for Jim describing the components he should include in the business plan when requesting a loan.

    Jim's business plan should include: a cover letter, resumes of the owners, company history, general business summary, business strategy, a description of the firm's products and services, marketing strategy, a plan of operation, financial data, and a loan proposal.

2. If Jim were to reduce his fixed costs by 10 percent by reducing a middle management position, what benefit would that be to him and the company? What would his new contribution margin be?

    By reducing his fixed costs, Jim improves his contribution margin.
    If fixed costs are reduced by 10%
    Then: $572,000 x 90% = $514,800
    Calculate New Contribution Margin
    $\frac{\$514,800}{\$825,800} = .62$
    1 - .62 = .38, or 38%

    Since middle managers are normally salaried employees, which constitutes a fixed cost, it is easy to see why middle management positions have been significantly reduced in recent years.

3.   Help Jim compute the break-even point for his brake service.

Contribution margin = 1 = $\dfrac{\$572,000}{\$825,000}$ = 1 = .6933 = .3067

Break-even sales = $168,000 = $\dfrac{\$547,767}{.3067}$

Case 10-2: Bowden Brake Service (Part B)

One day while you are in Bowden Brake Service getting your brakes repaired, Jim storms into his office, slamming doors and shouting about the local financial institutions. After a few minutes of building your courage, you approach Jim and ask him what the problem is. He shouts, "It's the financial institutions in this town! Not one of them will lend me the money I need to expand my business. They all said I needed to take a closer look at my financial position before I consider expanding. One of them said something about ratio analysis. I know a lot about cars and brakes, but what is ratio analysis?"
You tell Jim you'll perform a ratio analysis for the business if he gives you a free brake job. Jim provides you with the following financial statements.

Bowden Brake Service
Income Statement
Year Ended 31 December 2000

Net sales		$780,000
Costs of goods sold:		
Beginning inventory	$104,000	
Purchases	526,480	
Goods available for sale	$630,480	
Ending inventory	134,400	
Costs of goods sold		493,080
Gross margin		$283,920
Operating expenses:		
Rent	24,000	
Insurance	5,250	
Advertising	6,000	
Travel	2,500	
Interest	72,750	
Taxes (property, etc.)	2,500	
Salaries & admin. expenses	97,000	
Utilities	12,500	
Supplies	1,360	
Total operating expenses		$223,860
Net profit		$ 60,060

Bowden Brake Service
Balance Sheet
31 December 2001

Assets

Current assets:

Cash		$20,000
Accounts receivable	10,000	
Notes receivable	5,000	
Inventory		<u>134,400</u>
Total current assets		$169,400

Fixed assets:

Land		$147,000
Machinery	$ 73,000	
Equipment	160,800	
Less accumulated depreciation	<u>30,200</u>	203,600
Total fixed assets		<u>350,600</u>
Total assets		$520,000

Liabilities & Owner's Equity

Current liabilities:

Accounts payable	$40,500
Notes payable	20,200
Accrued salaries payable	<u>4,300</u>
Total current liabilities:	$65,000

Long-term liabilities	
Long-term loan	325,000
Owner's equity, Jim Bowden	<u>130,000</u>
Total liabilities and net worth	$520,000

1. Refer to the income statement and balance sheet. Prepare a ratio analysis for Bowden Brake Service. Also, using the following industry statistics for firms like Jim's, explain and interpret what these ratios mean.

Current ratio	1:4:1
Quick ratio	0:7:1
Debt ratio	1:8:1
Debt-to-net worth ratio	1:9:1
Average inventory turnover	N/A
Average collection period	21.22 days
Net sales-to-total assets	2.8 percent
Net sales-to-working capital	17.2 percent
Net profit on sales	9.0 percent
Net profit to equity	22.2 percent

Current ratio = $\frac{\$169,400}{\$65,000}$ = 2.61

Bowden has $2.61 in current assets for every $1 in current liabilities. This surpasses both the 2:1 "rule of thumb" and the 1.4 industry median.

Quick ratio = $\underline{\$169,000} = \$134,400 = .54$
$\qquad\qquad\quad \$65,000$

Bowden has .54 in quick assets for every $1 in current liabilities.
This is below both the 1:1 rule of thumb and the .7. Bowden apparently relies heavily on inventory to help satisfy its short-term debt.

Debt ratio = $\underline{\$65,000 + \$325,000} = .75$
$\qquad\qquad\quad \$520,000$

Compared to the industry median of 1.80, Bowden is not overburdened with debt.

Debt to net worth ratio = $\underline{\$65,000} = \$325,000 = 3.0$
$\qquad\qquad\qquad\qquad \$130,000$

Creditors have contributed three times as much to the business as Jim Bowden. Creditors are likely to see Bowden as being "borrowed up," especially since the industry median is 1.90.

Average inventory = $\qquad \underline{\$496,080} \qquad = 4.16$
$\qquad\qquad\qquad \$104,000 = \$134,000$

Bowden turns over its inventory about 4.16 times per year. A comparison is difficult since industry figures are unavailable.

Average collection period ratio = $\underline{365\ days}$
$\qquad\qquad\qquad\qquad\qquad \underline{\$780,000} = 7.02$
$\qquad\qquad\qquad\qquad\qquad \$ 15,000$

Bowden's accounts and notes receivable are outstanding for an average of 7.02 days, while the industry median is 21.22 days.

Net sales to total assets ratio = $\underline{\$780,000} \quad = \ 1.5$
$\qquad\qquad\qquad\qquad\qquad \$520,000$

Bowden generates $1.5 in sales for every $1 in total assets. The industry median is 2.8. Bowden is not producing enough sales in relation to its asset size.

Net sales to working capital ratio = $\qquad \underline{\$780,000} \qquad = \ 7.47$
$\qquad\qquad\qquad\qquad\qquad\quad \$169,900 - \$69,000$

Bowden is not using working capital efficiently to produce sales. The industry median is 17.2; Bowden must boost sales.

Net profit on sales ratio = $\underline{\$\ 60,060} \ = \ .077$
$\qquad\qquad\qquad\qquad \$780,000$

Each dollar of sales yields 7.7 cents in profit for Bowden, below the industry median of 9.0 cents.

Net profit to equity ratio = $\underline{\$\ 60,000} \ = \ .462$
$\qquad\qquad\qquad\qquad \$130,000$

Bowden's rate of return on his investments in the business is 46.2 percent, well above the industry median of 22.2 percent. This reflects Bowden's low investment in the business.

2.   Were the bankers correct? Do you think Jim should expand the business?

Bowden needs to increase sales, and expanding the business could help; but, Jim may have a problem obtaining a loan since creditors have provided three times as much capital as he has. Also, Jim seems to rely on inventory to meet short-term debt. Still, with a sound business plan explaining how the additional funds would be used, Jim could probably obtain the financing he needs.

Case 10-3: Birmingham's Stereo Shop

Birmingham's Stereo Shop expects net sales of $280,000 in the upcoming year, with a cost of goods sold of $173,600 and total expenses of $76,200. Birmingham expects variable expenses (including cost of goods sold) to be $195,700 and fixed expenses to be $54,100.

1. What level of sales would Birmingham's have to achieve if it wanted to make a $25,000 profit?

    Sales needed to make $25,000 profit:

    $$\text{Sales} = \frac{\$25,000 + \$54,100}{.3011} = \$262,703$$

2. Construct a break-even chart for Birmingham's.

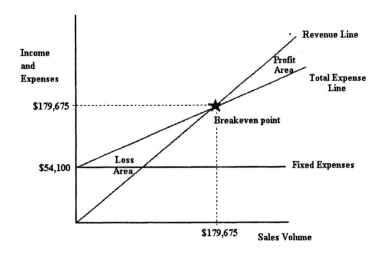

3. Compute a break-even point in dollars.

    $$\text{Contribution margin} = 1 - \frac{\$195,700}{\$280,000} = 1 - .6989 = .3011$$

    $$\text{Break-even point} = \frac{\$54,100}{.3011} = \$179,675$$

Case 10-4: Calculating the Break-even Point

A small manufacturer plans to sell tents for $120 each. The variable cost for each tent is $90. Fixed costs for the process are estimated to be $36,000. How many tents must the company sell to break-even?

Suppose that the manufacturer desires a profit of $9,000 on this process. How many units must be sold?

Price/unit   = $120
Variable cost/unit   = $90
Fixed cost   = $36,000

Sales required to earn a $9,000 profit:

Contribution Margin   = $120 - $90 = $30

Break-even Units = $\dfrac{\$36,000}{\$30}$ = 1,200 Units

Use breakeven formula and add desired profit:

Break-even Units   = $\dfrac{\$9,000 + 36,000}{\$120 - \$90}$ = 1,500 tents
plus desired profit

Case 10-5: A Projected Income Statement

You want to start your own retail furniture store, and you have already gathered a great deal of information on location, layout, form of ownership, business failure rates, etc.

In applying for a loan, you notice that a project income statement is required. Your problem is to complete this projected "P&L," given a desired income of $23,000 and the following published statistics. Show and clearly label all work!

Cost of goods sold   60.3 percent of net sales
Operating expenses   36.4 percent of net sales
Gross profit margin   39.7 percent of net sales

If a market survey indicates that your firm's sales would be $620,000, what net profit would you expect to earn?

First find Net Profit Margin Percentage

Sales	100 percent
- CGS	60.3 percent
Gross Profit Margin	39.7 percent
- Operating Expenses	36.4 percent
Net Profit Margin	3.3 percent

So... if Net sales = $696,970
Then Net Profit is...$696,970 x 3.3% = $23,000

Net Profit can also be calculated by using dollar values:

Sales	$696,970	100%
-CGS	420,273	60.3%
Gross Profit	276,697	39.7%
- Operating Expenses	253,697	36.4%
Net Profit	$ 23,000	3.3%

Note: percentages are approximate due to rounding errors.

Case 10-6: Crazy Harry's

The following is a pro forma income statement for Crazy Harry's.

Sales		$96,000
Cost of goods sold		46,240
Gross profit		$49,760
Fixed expenses		
Rent	$ 2,400	
Insurance	3,000	
Salaries	16,500	
Taxes	1,100	
Miscellaneous fixed expenses	900	
Total fixed expenses		$23,900
Variable expenses		
Wages	$11,200	
Advertising	5,700	
Benefits	2,800	
Other variable expenses	1,120	
Total variable expenses		$20,080
Net profit		$ 5,040

1.   Calculate Harry's break-even point.

Break-even point:
Variable costs = $46,240 + $20,080 = $66,320
Contribution margin = 1 - $66,320 = 1 - .6908 = .3092
            $96,000
Break-even sales point = $23,900 = $77,296
            .3092

2.   Create a break-even chart for Harry.

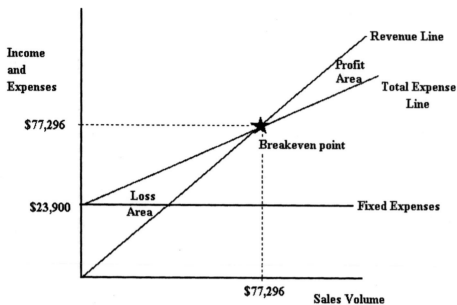

3.   If Harry's profit target is $15,000, what level of sales must be achieved?

Sales required to earn a $15,000 profit:

$$Sales = \frac{\$15,000 + \$23,900}{.3092} = \$125,808$$

Case 10-7: Sharps and Flats

Anthony Gray has been interested in music since he was old enough to sit at the piano. He literally grew up with music, and he used his talent to earn his way through college. Anthony has grown tired of his job at a large music house in Houston and is seriously considering moving back to his hometown in Massachusetts to open his own small music shop. In researching this venture, Anthony notices that he must include a projected income statement in his loan application. Use the following statistics from Robert Morris Associates' Annual Statement Studies to answer the following question(s).

Net sales	100.0 percent
Cost of sales	59.9 percent
Gross profit	40.1 percent
Operating expenses	31.2 percent
Net profit (before taxes)	8.9 percent

1.   Suppose that a market survey indicates that Anthony's proposed business is likely to generate only $190,000 in sales. What net profit should Anthony expect to earn?

If expected sales are $190,000
Anthony's expected profit is:
$190,000 x .089 = $16,910

2.   Using Anthony's target income of $23,000, construct a pro forma income statement for Anthony's proposed music shop.

Net sales	$258,427
Cost of goods sold	254,798
Gross profit	103,629
Operating expenses	80,629
Net profit (before taxes)	$ 23,000

To compute net sales: $\frac{\$23,000}{.089} = \$258,427$

Chapter 11   **Crafting a Winning Business Plan**

<u>**Multiple Choice Questions:**</u>

1. A business plan is a written summary of:
    a. an entrepreneur's proposed business venture.
    b. a business venture's operational, financial, and marketing details.
    c. the skills and abilities of a business venture's managers.
    d. All of the above.

    d., Easy, Page 359

2. A business plan:
    a. is a valuable managerial tool that helps an entrepreneur focus on developing a course for the business in the future.
    b. is a valuable tool for convincing lenders or investors to put money into the business.
    c. forces an entrepreneur to think a business idea through, considering both its positive and its negative aspects.
    d. All of the above.

    d., Easy, Page 359

3. A solid business plan:
    a. forces potential entrepreneurs to look at their business idea in the harsh light of reality.
    b. requires a potential entrepreneur to assess the venture's chances of success more objectively.
    c. helps prove to outsiders such as potential lenders and investors that a business idea can be successful.
    d. All of the above.

    d., Easy, Page 359

4. The primary purpose of a business plan is to:
    a. attract lenders and investors.
    b. enable an entrepreneur to take her company public.
    c. guide a company by charting its future course and devising a strategy for success.
    d. meet SEC and other legal requirements designed to protect lenders and investors.

    c., Medium, Page 359

5. The second essential purpose for creating a business plan is:
    a. to guide the operation of the company by charting its future course and devising a strategy for following it.
    b. to attract lenders and investors.
    c. to file with the SEC before making a public stock offering.
    d. to attract potential managers and employees to run the new venture.

    b., Medium, Page 359

6. Potential investors tend to believe that if an entrepreneur can't develop a good plan,
    a. he is probably the action-oriented sort of person they need running a business.
    b. he needs to hire a consultant to write the plan for him.
    c. he probably lacks the discipline to run a business.
    d. he is just like the majority of entrepreneurs and will probably do quite well.

c., Medium, Page 361

7. Before putting their money into a business idea, potential lenders and investors:
    a. look for entrepreneurs who have evaluated the risk in the business venture realistically and have a strategy for addressing it.
    b. want proof that the business will become profitable.
    c. want proof that the business will produce a reasonable return on their investment.
    d. All of the above.

d., Easy, Page 361

8. Which of the following is **not** true according to the "two-thirds rule?"
    a. Only two-thirds of entrepreneurs with a sound and viable business venture will find financial backing.
    b. Entrepreneurs who do get financing for their business will get only two-thirds of the capital they initially requested.
    c. Entrepreneurs who do get financing for their businesses will find that it takes them two-thirds longer to get it than they anticipated.
    d. Only two-thirds of entrepreneurs will take the time to prepare a business plan.

d., Medium, Page 361

9. _____ is an entrepreneur's best insurance against launching a business destined to fail or mismanaging a potentially successful company.
    a. Bankrolling the business with plenty of startup capital
    b. Creating a solid business plan
    c. Spending lots of money on marketing and advertising
    d. Hiring a team of accountants and attorneys as advisors

b., Medium, Page 361

10. To get external financing, an entrepreneur's plan must pass the _____ tests with potential lenders and investors.
    a. reality, competitive, and value
    b. competitive, profitability, and value
    c. value, reality, and profitability
    d. None of the above.

d., Medium, Page 360

11. The _____ test that a business plan must pass in order to attract financing from lenders and investors involves proving that a business venture offers a high probability of repayment or an attractive rate of return.
    a. reality
    b. competitive
    c. value
    d. profitability

    c., Medium, Page 360

12. The _____ test that a business plan must pass in order to attract financing from lenders and investors involves proving that a market for the company's product or service actually does exist and that the company actually can build it for the cost estimates included in the plan.
    a. reality
    b. competitive
    c. value
    d. profitability

    a., Medium, Page 360

13. The value test that a business plan must pass in order to attract financing from lenders and investors involves proving:
    a. that the company can gain a competitive advantage over its key competitors.
    b. that the business venture will provide lenders and investors a high probability of repayment or an attractive rate of return.
    c. that a market for the company's product or service actually does exist and that the company can actually build it for the cost estimates included in the plan.
    d. that the industry in which the business will compete is growing faster than the overall economy and has room for more competitors.

    b., Medium, Page 360

14. The competitive test that a business plan must pass in order to attract financing from lenders and investors involves proving:
    a. that the company can gain a competitive advantage over its key competitors.
    b. that the business venture will provide lenders and investors a high probability of repayment or an attractive rate of return.
    c. that a market for the company's product or service actually does exist and that the company can actually build it for the cost estimates included in the plan.
    d. that the industry in which the business will compete is growing faster than the overall economy and has room for more competitors.

    a., Medium, Page 360

15. The reality test that a business plan must pass in order to attract financing from lenders and investors involves proving:
    a. that the company can gain a competitive advantage over its key competitors.
    b. that the business venture will provide lenders and investors a high probability of repayment or an attractive rate of return.
    c. that a market for the company's product or service actually does exist and that the company can actually build it for the cost estimates included in the plan.
    d. that the industry in which the business will compete is growing faster than the overall economy and has room for more competitors.

c., Medium, Page 360

16. Which of the following is **not** true regarding the process of building a business plan:
    a. It is not very valuable when compared with the final plan itself.
    b. It allows an entrepreneur to replace "I thinks" with more "I knows" and to make mistakes on paper, which is cheaper than making them in reality.
    c. It reduces the risk and uncertainty of launching a company by teaching the entrepreneur to do it the right way.
    d. It requires an entrepreneur to subject his idea to an objective, critical evaluation.

a., Medium, Page 360

17. Which of the following is true about the preparation of a business plan?
    a. The format should follow a "cookie-cutter" approach to ensure uniformity and consistency with others and to promote ease of understanding.
    b. The elements of the plan may be standard, but the content should reflect the unique aspects of the business and the excitement of the entrepreneur.
    c. The plan should cover every standard element in great detail and be at least 100 pages long to prove to potential lenders and investors that the entrepreneur has studied the business and the market opportunity.
    d. Entrepreneur should avoid seeking the advice of professionals, such as accountants, business professors, and attorneys.

b., Medium, Page 361

18. Ideally, a business plan should range from _____ pages in length.
    a. 10 to 20
    b. 25 to 50
    c. 40 to 75
    d. 50 to 100

b., Medium, Page 362

19. The executive summary section of the business plan:
    a. is the last section of the plan but should be the first part written.
    b. should be no more than 8 or 10 pages long.
    c. should summarize the essence of the plan in a capsulated form and should capture the reader's attention.
    d. All of the above.

c., Medium, Page 362

20. The _____ serves as the thesis statement for the entire business plan.
    a. executive summary
    b. mission statement
    c. company history
    d. marketing strategy

    b., Medium, Page 362

21. The company history section of the business plan typically includes:
    a. significant financial and operational events.
    b. highlights of the key goals and objectives the company has accomplished in the past.
    c. a brief description of when and how the company was formed and how it has evolved over time.
    d. All of the above.

    d., Medium, Page 362

22. The _____ highlights significant financial and operational events in the company's life and should concentrate on the company's accomplishments.
    a. executive summary
    b. company history
    c. business and industry profile
    d. marketing strategy

    b., Medium, Page 362

23. The _____ , also known as the "elevator pitch," is written last, but is included as the first part of the business plan; it should summarize all the relevant points in about two pages.
    a. loan proposal
    b. business history
    c. business profile
    d. executive summary

    d., Easy, Page 362

24. The executive summary section of the business plan:
    a. should be a concise summary of the business venture.
    b. should be no more than two pages long.
    c. must capture the reader's attention and entice her to read the rest of the plan.
    d. All of the above.

    d., Easy, Page 362

25. _____ are broad, long-range statements of what a company plans to achieve in the future that guide its overall direction and addresses the question, "Why am I in business?"
    a. Goals
    b. Strategies
    c. Objectives
    d. Key performance factors

    a., Easy, Page 363

26. The _____ acquaints lenders and investors with the nature of the business and the general goals and objectives of the company.
    a. executive summary
    b. company history
    c. business and industry profile
    d. marketing strategy

    c., Medium, Page 363

27. _____ are short-term, specific targets which are attainable, measurable, and controllable.
    a. Objectives
    b. Policies
    c. Goals
    d. Standard operating procedures

    a., Easy, Page 363

28. Issues such as market size, growth trends, ease of market entry and exit, the presence of cyclical or seasonal sales trends, and the competitive dynamics of an industry appear in the _____ section of the business plan.
    a. executive summary
    b. company history
    c. business and industry profile
    d. marketing strategy

    c., Medium, Page 363

29. Which of the following would be included in the description of the product or service section of the business plan?
    a. The position of the product in the product life cycle
    b. A summary of any patents, copyrights, or trademarks protecting the product or service
    c. A description of the features and the benefits customers get by purchasing the company's products or services
    d. All of the above.

    d., Easy, Page 364

30. A _____ is a descriptive fact about a product or service; a _____ is what the customer gains from that characteristic.
    a. feature; benefit
    b. feature; trait
    c. benefit; feature
    d. benefit; trait

    a., Easy, 364

31. What is the lesson to be learned about writing a business plan from Leo Burnett's statement, "Don't tell people how good you make the goods; tell them how good your goods make them"?
    a. The plan should emphasize the **features** of the company's products and services rather than their **benefits**.
    b. The plan should describe how the business will transform tangible product or service features into important but often intangible customer benefits.
    c. The plan should recognize that advertising is a waste of money for startup companies.
    d. The plan should focus on developing sales in a niche rather than across an entire industry.

    b., Medium, Page 364

Refer to the following information to answer questions 32 to 34:

Describing her company's revolutionary design for a bottle cap, Kyoto says, "It has a special locking mechanism that you know is engaged when a red panel is showing through this little window on top of the cap. If you want to keep unauthorized hands - for instance, those of children - from opening the bottle, you engage the locking mechanism. Unlike other childproof caps, however, this design does not frustrate adults who might have arthritis and elderly people whose grip may not be as strong as it once was." Removing the cap from the bottle in no time with just a few turns, Kyoto says, "They can open the cap quite easily by disengaging the locking mechanism this way...see? You get the safety of a childproof cap without the problems most adults have getting them off!"

32. The special locking mechanism on Kyoto's new cap is a _____ of the product.
    a. feature
    b. unique selling proposition
    c. benefit
    d. All of the above.

    a., Medium, Page 364

33. The fact that with Kyoto's new cap "you get the safety of a childproof cap without the problems most adults have getting them off" is a _____ of the product.
    a. feature
    b. trait
    c. benefit
    d. All of the above.

    c., Medium, Page 364

34. Which of the following would be considered a **benefit** of Kyoto's new cap?
    a. The special locking mechanism
    b. The red panel showing through the little window on top of the cap signaling that the locking mechanism is engaged
    c. The fact that you get the safety of a childproof cap without the problems most adults have getting them off
    d. All of the above.

    c., Medium, Page 364

35. In the business strategy section of the business plan, the entrepreneur should explain to investors:
    a. significant financial and operational events in the life of the company.
    b. how she intends to accomplish the company's goals and objectives.
    c. the nature and characteristics of the target market.
    d. All of the above.

    b., Medium, Page 364

36. Which of the following questions will probably **not** be addressed in the marketing strategy section of the business plan?
    a. Who are my target customers, what are their characteristics, and how many are in my company's trading area?
    b. What, why, and when do my target customers buy?
    c. What exit policy do I have in place for my investors?
    d. How should I seek to position my company in its market(s)?

    c., Medium, Page 365

37. An explanation of how the product will be distributed is contained within the _____ section of the business plan.
    a. description of the product line
    b. marketing strategy
    c. competitive analysis
    d. business strategy

    b., Easy, Page 365

38. Defining the company's target market, its characteristics, and its potential is part of which element of the business plan?
    a. Description of the product or service
    b. Marketing strategy
    c. Competitor analysis
    d. Business and industry profile

    b., Easy, Page 365

39. Proving that a profitable market exists involves:
    a. proving that customers in the marketplace need or want the good or service and are willing to pay for it.
    b. documenting claims about market size and growth rates with as much factual information as possible.
    c. making claims such as "This market is so big that if we get just 1 percent of it, we'll be profitable within 6 months."
    d. A and B only.

    d., Easy, Page 365

40. When formulating a marketing strategy, small companies usually are most successful when they:
  a. try to be "everything to everybody."
  b. focus on a particular market niche where they can excel at meeting customers' needs and wants.
  c. compete with their larger rivals on the basis on price.
  d. discover what the market leader is doing and pursue a "me-too" strategy that imitates the leader.

  b., Medium, Page 365

41. The focus of the competitor analysis section of the business plan is on:
  a. demonstrating the existence of the market for your product.
  b. showing that your experienced management team is better than your competitors'.
  c. demonstrating your company's advantage over competitors.
  d. describing your overall product line.

  c., Easy, Page 368

42. The plan of operation of the company within the business plan should detail:
  a. the experience of the management team.
  b. the production process for the product being sold.
  c. plans for keeping the important officers in place with the company.
  d. All of the above.

  c., Medium, Page 369

43. The organization chart is described in which section of the business plan?
  a. The plan of operation
  b. The resumes of the officers/owners
  c. The business strategy
  d. The executive summary

  a., Medium, Page 369

44. The form of ownership under which a company is organized appears in which section of the business plan?
  a. Marketing strategy
  b. Business strategy
  c. Plan of operation
  d. Mission statement

  c., Medium, Page 369

45. When creating financial forecasts in a business plan for a proposed venture, an entrepreneur should:
    a. be sure that all forecasts are realistic.
    b. list all previous loans which are in default.
    c. avoid including a statement of the assumptions on which financial projections are based.
    d. All of the above.

a., Medium, Page 369

46. The loan proposal section of a business plan should include all but which of the following?
    a. A general request for funds without stating a specific dollar amount
    b. A repayment schedule and exit strategy
    c. A timetable for implementing the plan
    d. The purpose of the financing

a., Medium, Page 370

47. Which of the following statements about the preparation of a business plan is/are **not** true?
    a. Grammatical and spelling errors in a business plan don't really count since potential lenders and investors judge the quality of a plan by its content.
    b. The business plan should be "crisp," long enough to say what it should but not so long that it is a chore to read.
    c. Always include cash flow projections for the venture, in addition to projected income statements and balance sheets.
    d. Always tell the truth.

a., Easy, Page 370

48. Carly will be presenting her business plan to potential lenders and investors soon. Which of the following is **not** one of the suggested helpful tips for presenting the business plan?
    a. She should demonstrate enthusiasm for the venture but avoid becoming overemotional about it.
    b. She should use visual aids to make it easier for people to follow her presentation.
    c. She should avoid getting caught up in too much detail in early meetings with potential lenders and investors.
    d. She should use a great deal of technological jargon to impress the audience with her knowledge.

d., Medium, Page 371

49. After presenting her business plan to a group of potential lenders and investors, an entrepreneur should:
    a. sit back and wait to hear from those who might be interested in the venture.
    b. conduct credit checks on all potential lenders and investors.
    c. take a proactive approach by following up with every potential lender and investor to whom she makes a presentation.
    d. None of the above.

c., Medium, Page 372

50. The most common reason cited by banks for rejecting small business loans is:
    a. poor credit history.
    b. undercapitalization and too much debt.
    c. lack of collateral.
    d. insufficient cash flow or poor profitability.

    b., Medium, Page 373

True/False Questions:

51. A business plan is a written summary of an entrepreneur's proposed venture, its operational and financial details, its marketing opportunities and strategy, and its managers' skills and abilities.

    True, Easy, Page 359

52. A recent survey of small companies found that only 14 percent had created an annual written business plan and that 60 percent had no written plans of any type.

    True, Difficult, Page 359

53. The primary purpose of building a business plan is to raise capital.

    False, Medium, Page 359

54. A well-prepared business plan forces an entrepreneur to assess the venture's chances of success more objectively.

    True, Easy, Page 359

55. To get external financing, an entrepreneur's business plan must pass the reality test, the competitive test, and the value test with potential lenders and investors.

    True, Medium, Page 360

56. The competitive test that a business plan must pass in order to attract financing for lenders and investors involves proving to them that the venture offers a high probability of repayment or an attractive rate of return.

    False, Difficult, Page 360

57. The reality test that a business plan must pass in order to attract financing from lenders and investors involves proving that a market for the company's product or service actually does exist, and that the company actually can build it for the cost estimates in the plan.

    True, Easy, Page 360

58. The value test that a business must pass in order to attract financing from lenders and investors involves proving to them that the venture offers a high probability of repayment or an attractive rate of return.

    True, Medium, Page 360

59. Sometimes a potential small business owner finds, while developing a business plan, that the business won't succeed; at least, it was before he committed significant resources to the venture.

    True, Medium, Page 360

60. The real value in preparing a business plan is not so much in the plan itself as it is in the process the entrepreneur goes through to create the plan.

    True, Medium, Page 360

61. The "two-thirds rule" says that only two-thirds of the entrepreneurs with a sound new business venture will get financing, that they will get only two-thirds of what they need, and that it will take them two-thirds longer to get it than they anticipated.

    True, Medium, Page 361

62. Potential lenders and investors believe that an entrepreneur who lacks the discipline to develop a good business plan likely lacks the discipline to run a business.

    True, Easy, Page 361

63. Because the entrepreneur is the driving force behind a business idea, she should also be the driving force behind the business plan.

    True, Easy, Page 361

64. Before presenting a business plan to potential lenders and investors, an entrepreneur must be well informed and well prepared.

    True, Easy, Page 361

65. Although building a business plan does not guarantee an entrepreneur's success, it does increase her chances of succeeding in business.

    True, Easy, Page 361

66. A business plan should contain certain basic elements, but it should also be tailored to the individual company by emphasizing its particular personality and reflecting the entrepreneur's excitement for the business opportunity.

    True, Easy, Page 361

67. The most effective business plans follow the "cookie cutter approach," following the standard format most preferred by lenders and investors.

False, Medium, Page 361

68. The ideal business plan should be at least 100 pages long to prove to potential lenders and investors that the entrepreneur has studied the business and the market opportunity sufficiently.

False, Medium, Page 361

69. The executive summary serves as the thesis statement for the entire business plan.

False, Difficult, Page 362

70. The executive summary of a business plan should summarize all of the relevant points of the proposed venture and should be concise—no more than two pages.

True, Medium, Page 362

71. The executive summary of a business plan should highlight significant financial and operational events.

False, Medium, Page 362

72. The company's mission statement expresses in words the entrepreneur's vision for what her company is and what it is to become.

True, Easy, Page 362

73. In the business and industry profile section of the business plan, the entrepreneur should provide information on the size of the market, growth trends, and the relative economic and competitive strength of the industry's major players.

True, Medium, Page 363

74. The business and industry profile section of the business plan should cover existing and anticipated profitability of firms in the targeted market segment and any significant entry or exit of firms.

True, Medium, Page 363

75. In a business plan, both company goals and objectives should relate to the company's mission.

True, Easy, Page 363

76. Objectives are short-term, specific targets that the small company plans to accomplish.

True, Easy, Page 363

77. To be meaningful, an objective must include a time frame for achievement.

   True, Medium, Page 363

78. The business strategy section of the business plan addresses the question of **how** the entrepreneur plans to achieve the mission, goals, and objectives he has established for his business venture.

   True, Easy, Page 364

79. An important theme of the business strategy section of the business plan is what makes the owner's company original in the eyes of its target customers.

   True, Medium, Page 364

80. The safest strategy for an entrepreneur launching a new business to follow is a "me-too" strategy—copying products, services, and the images of already successful businesses.

   False, Medium, Page 364

81. The section of the business plan that describes the company's products or services should focus on how a business will transform the tangible features of its products or services into important but often intangible customer benefits.

   True, Medium, Page 364

82. A benefit is a descriptive fact about a product or service; a feature is what the customer gains from that product or service benefit.

   False, Easy, Page 364

83. When describing their products and services in their business plans, entrepreneurs must remember that customers buy the benefits from products and services, not the features.

   True, Medium, Page 364

84. An important goal of the "marketing strategy" section of the business plan is to prove that there is a real market for the proposed good or service.

   True, Medium, Page 365

85. Defining the company's target market and its buying potential is one of the most important and most challenging parts of building a business plan.

   True, Medium, Page 365

86. Identifying a specific target market is not an essential part of creating a solid business plan for a small company.

   False, Easy, Page 367

87. The wise entrepreneur will indicate that there is no real competition for his new business venture, thereby increasing the likelihood that he will gain more interested investors.

False, Easy, Page 368

88. A business plan that fails to assess a company's competitors realistically makes the entrepreneur appear to be poorly prepared.

True, Easy, Page 368

89. Because gathering information on competitors' products or services, strategies, and market share is so difficult, most lenders and investors see the competitor analysis section of the business plan as optional.

False, Medium, Page 368

90. The business plan should include the resumes of anyone with more than a 5 percent ownership interest in the company.

False, Medium, Page 368

91. The most important factor in the success of a business venture is the quality of its management, and financial officers and investors weigh heavily the ability and experience of the firm's managers in their financing decisions.

True, Medium, Page 368

92. Lenders and investors prefer experienced managers when they consider financing a business venture.

True, Easy, Page 368

93. The plan of operation section of the business plan should address how the business plans to retain key managers and employees.

True, Medium, Page 369

94. The business plan should include an existing firm's past three years of financial statements as well as its projected statements.

True, Medium, Page 369

95. Essential pieces of information for potential lenders and investors include the assumptions the entrepreneur uses to derive the financial forecasts and projections in the business plan.

True, Easy, Page 369

96. An entrepreneur should prepare a single set of "most likely" financial forecasts for one year into the future as part of the business plan.

False, Medium, Page 369

97. To make her business plan more attractive, an entrepreneur should include an exit strategy as a way to "cash out" for investors.

True, Easy, Page 370

98. Cash flow projections are not an essential part of a business plan as long as the entrepreneur provides accurate forecasts of the venture's profits.

False, Medium, Page 369

99. The loan proposal portion of the business plan should include a realistic timetable for repayment or for investors to exit.

True, Medium, Page 370

100. Entrepreneurs should artificially inflate the amount of a loan request and expect the loan officer to "talk them down."

False, Easy, Page 370

101. A lender's primary concern in granting a loan is reassurance that the applicant will repay it, whereas an investor's primary concern is earning a satisfactory rate of return.

True, Medium, Page 370

102. The entrepreneur's request for funds in the business plan should be specific and detailed.

True, Medium, Page 370

103. Spelling and grammatical errors in a business plan don't really matter; potential lenders and investors look past them at the **content** of the plan.

False, Easy, Page 370

104. Potential lenders and investors expect entrepreneurs to exaggerate the truth in their business plans, so telling the truth in the plan is really not important.

False, Medium, Page 370

105. A table of contents that allows lenders to navigate a business plan easily is an important element of any business plan.

True, Easy, Page 370

106. The quality of the entrepreneur's business plan determines the first impression potential lenders and investors have of the company.

True, Easy, Page 370

107. After presenting her business plan to a group of potential lenders and investors, an entrepreneur should sit back and wait to hear from those who might be interested in the venture.

   False, Medium, Page 372

108. When presenting his business plan to a group of potential lenders and investors, an entrepreneur should cover every detail in the plan, striving to answer every question his audience might have.

   False, Medium, Page 372

109. The most common reasons banks give for rejecting small business loan applications are undercapitalization and too much debt.

   True, Medium, Page 373

110. The most common reason banks give for rejecting small business loan applications is the entrepreneur's poor credit history.

   False, Medium, Page 373

111. The "C" of the 5 C's of Credit that is synonymous with cash flow is capital.

   False, Medium, Page 373

112. The majority of loans from banks make to small business startups are unsecured loans.

   False, Medium, Page 374

113. Most loans banks make to startup businesses are secured not by collateral but by the character of the entrepreneur.

   False, Difficult, Page 374

114. The entrepreneur's "character" (even though it is an intangible factor) and the quality of the presentation are important factors in evaluating a loan proposal.

   True, Medium, Page 374

115. The higher a small business scores on the 5 C's of credit, the greater its chances will be of receiving a loan.

   True, Easy, Page 375

Essay Questions:

116. Explain at least two functions or purposes of preparing a business plan.

   There are a number of reasons an entrepreneur should develop a business plan. First and most importantly, the business plan serves as a guide to company operations by charting its future course and devising a strategy for following it. It plans a battery of tools to help the entrepreneur lead the company and it provides direction for managers and employees. It gives everyone a target to shoot for and it provides a yardstick for measuring the actual performance against those targets.

A second function of the business plan is to attract lenders and investors. A quality business plan will assure potential lenders and investors that the business venture will be able to repay loans and produce an attractive rate of return. Building the business plan requires that the entrepreneur evaluate his or her business realistically and objectively.

Sometimes, the greatest service a business plan provides an entrepreneur is the realization that it just won't work. This benefits the entrepreneur if he or she is able to make this determination prior to committing extensive resources to the venture. In other cases, it reveals important problems to overcome before launching the business.

The real value in preparing a business plan is not so much in the plan itself as it is in the process an entrepreneur goes through to create the plan. What he or she learns about the company, its target market, its financial requirements, competition, and other factors can be essential to making the venture a success. In other words, developing a business plan reduces the risk and uncertainty in launching a company by allowing the entrepreneur to make mistakes on paper rather than in reality and to learn to do things the right way.
Page 359

117. To get external financing, an entrepreneur's plan must pass three tests with potential lenders and investors. List and briefly explain all three.

- Reality Test—You must prove that a market for your product or service really does exist. Focuses on industry attractiveness, market niches, potential customers, market size, degree of competition, and similar factors. These factors point to the potential for a strong demand for the business idea.
- Competitive Test—Evaluate your company's relative position to its key competitors. How do your company's strengths and weaknesses compare to those of the competition?
- Value Test—You must prove to potential lenders and investors that your business offers a high probability of repayment or an attractive rate of return.

Page 360

118. "Sometimes the greatest service a business plan provides an entrepreneur is the realization that the business venture just won't succeed." Explain this statement.

The business plan is the entrepreneur's best insurance against launching a business destined to fail or mismanaging a potentially successful business. Creating a plan also forces him/her to consider both the positive and negative aspects of the business, and to subject these ideas to a reality test. This process allows the entrepreneur to replace the "I thinks" with more "I knows. To expose flaws and make mistakes on paper is much cheaper than committing significant resources to a business. It reduces the risk and uncertainty in launching a business by teaching the entrepreneur to do it the right way.
Page 360

119. You have been asked to explain the basic elements of a sound business plan to your friend, who is considering beginning a new business. What elements should you recommend he include in his business plan?

Although a business plan should be tailored to fit company needs, it should include these basic components:

- Executive summary—concise summary of all the relevant points of the business venture; brief synopsis of the entire plan; must catch the reader's attention.
- Mission statement—expresses the vision for what the company is and what it is to become; broad expression of company's purpose and direction.
- Company history—highlights significant financial and operational events in the company's life; describes formation, evolution, and vision for the future.
- Business and industry profile—acquaints potential lenders and investors with the industry in which the company operates; includes summary of goals and objectives.
- Business strategy—explain how you can meet and beat the competition; addresses the question of how to accomplish your goals and objectives.
- Description of products/services—describe product line, product's position in the product life cycle, and any patents, trademarks, or copyrights; define features and benefits of products or services.
- Marketing strategy—prove that there is a real market for the proposed good or service; describe target market and positioning, advertising, distribution, and pricing.
- Competitor analysis—compare your strengths and weaknesses with those of your competition, images in the marketplace, level of success, etc.
- Description of the management team—describe qualifications of business officers, key directors, and any person with at least 20 percent ownership in the company; lenders and investors prefer experienced managers when making funding decisions.
- Plan of operation—construct organization chart; explain steps taken to encourage important officers to remain with the company.
- Forecasted or pro forma financial statements—include financial statements from the past three years (if an existing business) and pro forma for the next year (existing or new), including statement of cash flows; should develop realistic forecasts and a statement of the assumptions on which the financial projections are based.
- Loan or investment proposal—state the purpose of the financing, the amount requested, and either the plans for repayment (lenders) or an attractive exit strategy (investors).

Page 361

120. Explain the concept of a company's mission. What are goals? Objectives? How are the three concepts related?

- A mission statement expresses in words an entrepreneur's vision of what the company is and what it become. It is the broadest expression of the company's purpose and defines the direction in which it will move.
- Goals are broad statements of what a company plans to achieve. They guide its overall direction and define the basis of its business.
- Objectives are short-term, specific performance targets that are attainable, measurable, and controllable.
- Every objective should reflect some general business goal and include a technique for measuring progress towards its accomplishment. To be meaningful, an

objective must have a time frame for achievement. Both goals and objectives should relate to the company's mission statement.

Page 362-363

121. The marketing strategy section is a vital part of any business plan. What issues should it address?

- Who are my target customers and what are their demographics?
- Where do they live, work, and shop?
- How many potential customers are in my trading area?
- Why do they buy and what needs/wants drive their purchase decisions?
- How can my business meet those needs/wants better than my competitors? Knowing my customers needs, wants, and habits, what should be the basis for differentiating my business in their minds?

Page 365

122. The financial plan within a business plan is of interest to potential lenders and investors. Explain the contents of this section and describe what potential lenders and investors look for.

For an existing business, lenders and investors use past financial statements to judge the health of the company and its ability to repay the loan and generate adequate returns. Ideally these statements should be audited or at least reviewed by a certified public accountant. Pro forma income statements, balance sheets and cash flow statements for the coming year and at least three more accounting periods should also be prepared—covering pessimistic, most likely and optimistic estimates. A breakeven and ratio analysis should also be done.

It is also important to include a statement of assumptions on which these financial projections were based because potential lenders and investors will view them as being more credible than a single set of overly optimistic figures. Lenders and investors also look for honest, realistic forecasts and compare them to industry standards.

Page 369

123. What tips would you offer an entrepreneur who is scheduled to present her business plan to a group of potential lenders and investors in one week?

- As with all presentations, entrepreneurs should be informed and well-prepared beforehand. The following tips might also be helpful:
- Demonstrate enthusiasm, but don't be overemotional.
- "Hook" investors quickly with an up-front explanation of the new venture, its opportunities, and the anticipated benefits to them.
- Use visual aids.
- Hit the highlights; leave details to questions and future meetings.
- Avoid the use of technological terms.
- Close by reinforcing the nature of the opportunity and relating benefits to investors.
- Be prepared for questions.
- Follow up with every investor you make a presentation to.

Page 371

124. When making a loan to a small business, bankers tend to look for the 5 Cs. List and explain each of the 5 Cs of credit.

Bankers score the small business in terms of the five Cs. The greater the score, the higher probability that the small business will receive the loan.

- Capital—A small business must have a stable capital base before a bank will grant a loan. The most common reasons that banks give for rejecting loans are undercapitalization or too much debt. The bank expects the small business to have an equity base of investment by the owner(s) that will help support the venture during times of financial stress.
- Capacity—The bank must be convinced that the small business has sufficient cash flow to meet its regular financial obligations and to repay the bank loan. The bank expects the applicant to pass the test for liquidity, especially for short-term loans.
- Collateral—Collateral is the bank's security for repayment of the loan. If the company defaults on the loan, the bank has the right to sell the collateral and use the proceeds to satisfy the loan. Banks view the owner's willingness to pledge collateral (personal or business assets) as an indication of dedication to making the venture successful.
- Character—The loan officer's evaluation of the owner's character (honesty, competence, polish, determination, intelligence, and ability) play a critical role in the banker's decision. The applicant can possibly enhance the officer's view of his character with a thorough business plan and polished presentation.
- Conditions—The banks consider potential growth in the market, competition, location, form of ownership, loan purpose, and the state of the overall economy before making a decision on the loan. The owner should provide relevant information pertaining to these factors in the business plan.

Page 372

Chapter 10
Crafting a Winning Business Plan
Mini-Case

Case 10-1: The Need For A Plan

Twenty-three year-old Shirley Halperin had just been kicked off the staff of her college newspaper, when she launched Smug magazine with just $1,700 in personal savings, $7,000 in donations, and a $10,000 loan, co-signed by her father Eli Halperin who helped her get a line of credit.

The ten-issues-a-year publication is targeted at music fans in the 16-to-30-year-old age group with well-written stories "about musicians that matter plus bands you haven't even heard of yet," says Halperin. It covers the alternative-music scene between the musical meccas of New York City and Philadelphia. Her enthusiasm for her subject has spilled over to the writers, editors, designers and photographers who now total 30, and continue to contribute without pay. They donate their talents for such incentives as by-lines, photo credits, college internships, job experience, free tickets to concerts, free CD's, and other things. Halperin cuts costs whenever possible and her frugality enables her to keep start-up costs low she runs Smug out of her Gramercy Park apartment with two roommates.

Smug charges $1,000 per ad. Competitive publications like Village Voice, Spin, and the Aquarian Weekly charge between $7,000-$29,700 for a similar ad. Halperin says that her budget ads are designed specifically for smaller bands with a regional following that haven't hit the big time yet. "It doesn't make sense for baby bands to advertise in the bigger publications until awareness of them rises," she says.

In less than 18 months, Smug's circulation went from 5,000 to 20,000, its readership expanded to 60,000 and advertising revenues climbed from zero to $15,000 per month. After publishing its fourth issue, *Smug* beat out its larger, more established competitors to win a prestigious local music award. Readers rave about the quality of the magazine's writing, its design and photography; however, Smug's continued success is not guaranteed. Half of all magazines fail the first year, and those that don't take five years to breakeven. If Smug succeeds, it can look forward to attractive profit margins of between 15-30 percent.

Halperin is very good at knowing what music people are listening to and what people want to read about; however, she is quick to admit that finance is not one of her strong points. Another concern is cash flow; at the end of its first year, $7,500 of Smug's and $70,000 in revenues were still in accounts receivables. Although she started Smug without a business plan, she now realizes she needs one to raise the $500,000 necessary to take the magazine "to the next level." She needs the money to upgrade the newsprint to semi-glossy paper stock, and most importantly, to pay her staff. She wants the plan to reflect her business philosophy: "Every year circulation should go up, your pages should go up, and your ad revenues should go up."

Questions:

1.   Write a memo to Shirley Halperin explaining what topics she should include in her business plan.

     In their memos, the students should somewhat incorporate the uniqueness of each business plan as well as the importance of Ms. Halperin's personal input into the process. Suggested topics should include the following elements:

     Executive Summary
     Mission Statement
     Company History
     Business and Industry Profile
     Business Strategy
     Description of Products/Service
     Marketing Strategy
     Competitor Analysis
     Description of Management Team
     Plan of Operation
     Forecasted or Pro Forma Financial Statements
     Loan of Investment Proposal

2.   What advice would you offer Halperin when she begins to use her business plan to locate capital?

     The students should stress the importance of having the business plan as "perfect as possible" when she uses the business plan to obtain capital. It is also important that students understand the importance of a business plan that is aesthetically pleasing and free from errors—the plan should have the look of a polished professional presentation parcel that details the company's past, present, and future goals. The following guidelines should be recommended as Ms. Halperin tries to locate potential investors for her enterprise:

Be enthusiastic, not emotional
Gain investors attention up front
Use creative visual aides
Hit the highlights
Don't get too technical
Close by reinforcing
Be prepared for questions
Follow up with each potential investor

In addition to the "showmanship" necessary for a good presentation, Ms. Halperin needs to have solid information concerning the 5 C's of credit, as this will ultimately be used to judge her worthiness for the necessary loan.

3. If Shirley Halperin approached you as a potential investor, what questions would you ask her? Explain. Would your answer change the content of the memo in question #1 above? If so, how?

Several concerns should be addressed by the students. For example: how will the transition from an all volunteer staff with low advertising rates and minimal overhead be made smoothly to "the next level?" How is Ms. Halperin qualified to go to the "next level?" Why are accounts rewarded at $7,500? How does this impact the magazine currently? Are Ms. Halperin's growth projections feasible? If so, how? Has she conducted any type of market research to support her beliefs? These questions should all be covered by the suggestions for topics in # 1.

Source: Adapted from Alessandra Bianchi, "What's Love Got to Do With It?" Inc., May 1996, pp. 77-85. Essentials of Entrepreneurship and Small Business Management 2nd Edition

Chapter 9   Managing Cash Flow

Multiple Choice Questions:

1.   Proper cash management permits a business owner to:
      a. adequately meet the cash demands of the business.
      b. avoid retaining unnecessarily large cash balances.
      c. stretch the profit-generating power of each dollar the business owns.
      d. All of the above.

      d., Easy, Page 294

2.   _____ is the most important yet least productive asset that a small business owns.
      a. Profit
      b. Cash
      c. Inventory
      d. Accounts receivable

      b., Medium, Page 294

3.   Which of the following statements concerning cash management is **false**?
      a. Cash is the most important yet least productive asset a small business owns.
      b. Young companies tend to be "cash sponges," soaking up every available dollar of cash.
      c. Because they generate large amounts of cash quickly, fast-growing businesses are least likely to experience shortages.
      d. None of the above.

      c., Medium, Page 294

4.   The first step in managing cash more effectively is:
      a. having an adequate cash reserve for emergency expenditures.
      b. rapid payment of accounts payable.
      c. speeding up payment of accounts receivable.
      d. understanding the company's cash flow cycle.

      d., Medium, Page 295

5.   Which of the following measures a company's liquidity and its ability to pay its bills and other financial obligations on time?
      a. Cash budget
      b. Cash flow
      c. Cash management
      d. All of the above.

      b., Easy, Page 297

6.   _____ typically lead(s) sales; _____ typically lag(s) sales.
      a.   Production; receivables
      b.   Collections; purchases
      c.   Receipts; production
      d.   Purchases; collections

      d., Medium, Page 298

7.   A cash budget reveals important clues about how well a company_____.
      a.   balances its accounts receivable and accounts payable
      b.   controls inventory
      c.   finances its growth
      d.   All of the above.

      d., Easy, Page 298

8.   A firm's cash budget:
      a.   should be prepared on a monthly basis for at least one year in advance.
      b.   should cover a longer planning horizon when a firm's pattern is highly variable.
      c.   must cover all seasonal fluctuations.
      d.   Only A and C above.

      d., Medium, Page298

9.   A cash budget:
      a.   is based on the cash method of accounting.
      b.   is a "cash map," showing the amount and the timing of cash flowing into and out of the business over a given period of time.
      c.   will never be completely accurate since it is based on forecasts.
      d.   All of the above.

      d., Medium, Page 298

10.   Which of the following is **not** a step in creating a cash budget?
      a.   Determining an adequate minimum cash balance
      b.   Forecasting profits
      c.   Forecasting cash receipts
      d.   Forecasting cash disbursements

      b., Medium, Page 299

11. On March 10, a business owner receives an invoice from a supplier for $416.27 with "net 30" credit terms marked on it. On April 7, the owner writes the supplier a check for $416.27 and mails it. When would this cash disbursement show up on the company's cash budget?
    a. March 10
    b. March 30
    c. April 7
    d. April 10

c., Medium, Page 299

12. Jane is arguing with Joan about how much cash their small retail outlet needs on hand as they prepare their cash budget. Jane feels that with the Christmas season coming up, their busiest time, they need more cash handy. Joan feels they don't because their sales volume will be up significantly. Jane and Joan are discussing which step of the cash budgeting process?
    a. Determining an adequate minimum cash balance
    b. Forecasting sales
    c. Forecasting cash receipts
    d. Forecasting cash disbursements

a., Medium, Page 299

13. A cash budget is only as accurate as the _____ forecast from which it is derived.
    a. profit
    b. receivables
    c. income
    d. sales

d., Easy, Page 300

14. What factors can drastically affect a company's cash flow?
    a. increased competition
    b. economic swings
    c. normal seasonal variations
    d. All of the above.

d., Easy, Page 300

15. Which of the following would be a potential source of information for preparing a sales forecast?
    a. past records
    b. trade associations and the Chamber of Commerce
    c. similar firms
    d. All of the above.

d., Easy, Page 301

16. When a firm sells goods or services on credit, the owner needs to remember that for cash budgeting purposes:
    a. the sale may be immediately posted as if it has been collected.
    b. the sale should be recorded in the month it was made.
    c. she must account for a delay between the sale and the actual collection of the proceeds.
    d. such a transaction counts as a cash disbursement.

    c., Medium, Page 302

17. It is recommended that new business owners estimate cash disbursements as best he can and then add on another _____.
    a. 3-4%
    b. 5-10%
    c. 10-25%
    d. 25-35%

    c., Difficult, Page 305

18. When estimating the firm's end-of-month cash balance, the owner should first:
    a. determine the cash balance at the beginning of the month.
    b. add up total cash receipts and subtract cash on hand.
    c. review the accounts receivable.
    d. make a daily list of cash disbursements.

    a., Medium, Page 306

19. One recent study showed that only about _____ percent of small businesses used formal techniques such as cash budgets to track their cash balances.
    a. 16
    b. 26
    c. 36
    d. 46

    c., Difficult, Page 306

20. The fact that the cash budget illustrates the flow of cash in a business helps the owner to:
    a. accelerate accounts payable payments.
    b. get a seasonal line of credit rather than an annual line of credit.
    c. slow accounts receivable payments.
    d. track the effects of depreciation and bad debts.

    b., Difficult, Page 306

21. By planning cash needs ahead of time, a small business is able to achieve all but which of the following?
    a. Make the most efficient use of available cash
    b. Provide the opportunity to forego quantity and cash discounts
    c. Finance seasonal business needs
    d. Provide funds for expansion

    b., Medium, Page 306

22. The "big three" of cash management include:
    a. accounts receivable, overhead, and inventory.
    b. accounts payable, accounts receivable, and taxes.
    c. accounts receivable, accounts payable, and inventory.
    d. accounts receivable, prices, and expenses.

    c., Medium, Page 307

23. Experts estimate that _____ percent of industrial and wholesale sales are on credit, while _____ percent of retail sales are on credit.
    a. 20; 40
    b. 40; 20
    c. 60; 30
    d. 90, 40

    d., Difficult, Page 307

24. Small businesses selling on credit find that:
    a. it is relatively inexpensive and simple.
    b. it is expensive, requires a great deal of effort, and is risky.
    c. it is essentially borrowing money from the customer.
    d. many can get by without selling on credit because their business customers don't expect to use credit.

    b., Medium, Page 307

25. One study indicated that only about _____ of small companies protected themselves by checking customers' credit.
    a. 1/4
    b. 40 percent
    c. 1/3
    d. 10 percent

    c., Difficult, Page 309

26. An important source of credit information that collects information on small businesses that other reporting services ignore is:
    a. National Association of Credit Management.
    b. TRW.
    c. Dun & Bradstreet.
    d. National Association of Small Business Owners.

    a., Easy, Page 309

27. The cost to check a potential customer's credit at a reporting service typically ranges from:
    a. $1 to $5.
    b. $15 to $85.
    c. $100 to $150.
    d. $500 to $750.

    b., Difficult, Page 309

28. To encourage credit customers to pay invoices promptly, a business owner should:
    a. ensure that all invoices are clear, accurate, and timely.
    b. state clearly a description of the goods or services purchased and an account number.
    c. include a telephone number and a contact person in case the customer has a question or a dispute.
    d. All of the above.

    d., Easy, Page 309

29. When a small business is writing off more than _____ percent of its sales as bad debts, it needs to tighten its credit and collection policies.
    a. 3
    b. 5
    c. 10
    d. 25

    b., Difficult, Page 309

30. Once a small business has established a firm written credit policy and communicated it, the next step in building an effective credit policy is to:
    a. send invoices promptly.
    b. determine what percentage of sales are being written off as bad debt.
    c. create a simple credit application.
    d. create a "tracking file" of events.

    a., Medium, Page 309

31. Once a credit account becomes past due, a small business owner should:
    a. wait patiently; the customer will most likely pay the bill sooner or later.
    b. turn the account over to a collection agency the day it becomes past due.
    c. send a "second notice" letter requesting immediate payment.
    d. call the "deadbeat" in the middle of the night and make harassing and threatening remarks until he pays.

    c., Medium, Page 309

32. A collection agency typically takes ___% of the amounts they collect on past due accounts.
    a. 5 to 10
    b. 10 to 20
    c. 25 to 50
    d. 75 to 90

    c., Medium, Page 310

33. According to the American Collector's Association, _____% of accounts more than 90 days delinquent will be paid voluntarily.
    a. 5
    b. 20
    c. 45
    d. 65

    a., Difficult, Page 310

34. The Fair Debt Collection Practices Act prohibits business owners from:
    a. harassing people who are past due.
    b. sending invoices the same day product is shipped.
    c. hiring debt collection attorneys.
    d. referring past due bills to collection agencies.

    a., Easy, Page 310

35. A small business owner could accelerate accounts receivable by:
    a. having customers mail printed orders to him.
    b. sending or faxing invoices the day of shipment.
    c. slowing their own accounts payable.
    d. depositing customer checks and credit card receipts weekly.

    b., Medium, Page 310

36. In the typical company, ____% of its customers generate ____% of its accounts receivable.
    a. 60; 80
    b. 50; 50
    c. 20; 80
    d. 10; 20

    c., Easy, Page 310

37. An arrangement in which customers mail their payments on account to a post office box which the company's bank monitors, collects payments, and immediately deposits them into the firm's account is called a(n):
    a. collection board.
    b. lockbox.
    c. electronic funds transfer system.
    d. cash box.

    b., Easy, Page 312

38. Patel Industries recently filled an order from one of its customers, Oxmoor Gardens, a small garden supply store. Oxmoor's owner, Jan McBride, recently received an invoice from Patel for $1,278.64 with selling terms of "2/10, net 30." Which of the following statements is **true**?
    a. The selling terms indicate that Oxmoor must pay 2 percent of the invoice by the 10th day of the month with the balance due in 30 days.
    b. The selling terms are offering Oxmoor a 2 percent discount if the bill is paid within 10 days; otherwise the full amount of the invoice is due in 30 days.
    c. The selling terms indicate that the full amount of the invoice is due within 30 days and Oxmoor will be subject to a 2 percent finance charge for every 10 days that the bill is past due.
    d. The selling terms indicate that Oxmoor has not yet qualified for a quantity discount and must pay the full amount of the invoice within 30 days.

    b., Medium, Page 313

39. Efficient cash managers:
    a. disregard trade discounts because of their hidden costs.
    b. avoid the use of credit cards to stretch their firm's cash balances.
    c. set up a payment calendar in order to both pay on time and take advantage of cash discounts for early payment.
    d. use expressions like "the check is in the mail" to mollify creditors when short on cash.

    c., Medium, Page 313

40. Only about ____ percent of a typical business' inventory turns over quickly.
    a. 20
    b. 40
    c. 60
    d. 80

    a., Medium, Page 315

41. Which of the following is true about inventory management for the small business owner?
    a. Most small business owners have turned to technology and computer spreadsheets to achieve maximum efficiency in managing it.
    b. Inventory is the largest capital investment for most businesses but few owners use any formal means for managing it.
    c. Inventory is generally very liquid and can be easily mortgaged to a bank for immediate cash if needed.
    d. Inventory yields a return of about 25% for manufacturing firms but nothing for service companies.

    b., Medium, Page 315

42. Which of the following inventory management techniques would help a business owner make the best use of her company's cash?
    a. Avoid overbuying inventory.
    b. Schedule inventory deliveries at the latest possible date.
    c. Purchase goods from the fastest suppliers who can meet quality standards to keep inventory levels low.
    d. All of the above.

    d., Easy, Page 315

43. Exchanging goods and services for other goods and services, or _____, is an effective way for a small business to conserve cash.
    a. leasing
    b. bartering
    c. arbitraging
    d. credit sales

    b., Easy, Page 316

44. It is estimated that approximately _____ companies, most of them small, engage in barter exchanges every year.
    a. 50,000
    b. 100,000
    c. 200,000
    d. 500,000

    a., Difficult, Page 316

45. The real benefit of barter for the entrepreneur is that:
    a. it is essentially without cost to the business owner.
    b. it is considered a depreciable item for tax purposes rather than as income.
    c. it saves the small business owner between $100,000 and $150,000 a year on the average.
    d. it is "paid" for at the wholesale cost of doing business, yet it is credited at the retail price.

    d., Difficult, Page 316

46. Barter offers business owners the benefit of:
    a. buying materials, equipment, and supplies without spending valuable cash on them.
    b. transforming slow-moving inventory into much-needed goods and services.
    c. "paying" for goods and services at wholesale cost and getting credit for retail price.
    d. All of the above.

    d., Medium, Page 316

47. Which of the following is an effective way to trim overhead?
    a. When able, buy instead of leasing.
    b. Hire more full-time employees; reduce the number of part-timers.
    c. Eliminate zero-based budgeting.
    d. Negotiate fixed loan payments to coincide with company cash flow.

    d., Difficult, Page 317

48. Which of the following statements concerning leasing is true?
    a. Leasing is an "off-the-balance-sheet" method of financing assets.
    b. Although total lease payments for an asset are greater than those on a conventional loan, most leases do not require large capital outlays as down payments.
    c. Leasing gives business owners access to equipment even when they cannot borrow the money to buy it.
    d. All of the above.

    d., Medium, Page 317

49. According to a recent survey, approximately _____ percent of U.S. companies use leasing as a cash management strategy.
    a. 35
    b. 50
    c. 73
    d. 88

    c., Difficult, Page 317

50. When investing surplus cash, the small business owner's key objectives should be:
    a. high yields.
    b. current income.
    c. liquidity and safety.
    d. long term yield.

    c., Medium, Page 320

True/False Questions:

51. Cash is the most important yet least productive asset a small business owns.

    True, Medium, Page 294

52. Developing a cash forecast is essential for new businesses because early profit levels usually do not generate sufficient cash to keep the company afloat.

    True, Easy, Page 294

53. A common cause of business failures is that owners neglect to forecast how much cash their companies will need until they reach the point of generating positive cash flow.

    True, Easy, Page 294

54. The objectives of cash management are to adequately meet the cash demands of the business, to avoid retaining unnecessarily large cash balances, and to stretch the profit-generating power of each dollar the business owns.

    True, Easy, Page 294

55. It is likely that young companies and rapidly growing companies will experience cash flow difficulties.

    True, Medium, Page 294

56. The shorter a company's cash flow cycle, the more likely it is to encounter a cash crisis.

    False, Medium, Page 295

57. Compiling the total cash on hand, bank balance, summary of the day's sales, summary of the day's cash receipts, and a summary of accounts receivables collections into monthly summaries provides the basis for making reliable cash forecasts.

    True, Medium, Page 296

58. A highly profitable business is a highly liquid business.

    False, Medium, Page 297

59. A small company's cash balance is the difference between total revenue and total expenses.

   False, Easy, Page 297

60. Profit is the difference between a company's total revenue and its total expenses.

   True, Easy, Page 297

61. The goal of cash management is to maintain as much cash as possible on hand to meet any unexpected circumstances that might arise.

   False, Medium, Page 298

62. A cash budget allows a small business owner to anticipate cash shortages and cash surpluses and gives him time to handle, or even avoid, approaching problems.

   True, Easy, Page 298

63. Typically, small business owners should prepare a projected weekly cash budget for at least six months and quarterly estimates for the remainder of the year, being careful to cover all seasonal sales fluctuations.

   False, Medium, Page 298

64. A small business whose sales are highly variable (i.e., "seasonal") should use a short cash planning horizon.

   True, Medium, Page 298

65. The primary problem with cash management tools is that they are too complex and time consuming for small business owners to use practically.

   False, Medium, Page 298

66. In a cash budget, credit sales to customers are recorded at the time the sale is made.

   False, Medium, Page 299

67. Depreciation and debt expenses are often left off the cash budget but need to be included to accurately forecast cash requirements for running the business.

   False, Medium, Page 299

68. The cash budget is nothing more than a forecast of the firm's cash inflows and outflows for a specific time period, and it will never be completely accurate.

   True, Medium, Page 299

69. The first step in preparing a cash budget is to forecast sales.

   False, Medium, Page 299

70. The most reliable method of determining an adequate minimum cash balance is using estimates of similar businesses from trade literature.

   False, Medium, Page 299

71. A small firm's minimum cash balance should be two times its average weekly sales.

   False, Medium, Page 299

72. A small company's ideal minimum cash balance is one month's sales.

   False, Medium, Page 299

73. Because the heart of the cash budget is the sales forecast, the cash budget is only as accurate as the sales forecast on which it is based.

   True, Medium, Page 300

74. Since even the best sales forecast will be wrong, the small business owner should prepare three forecasts—optimistic, pessimistic, and most likely.

   True, Medium, Page 301

75. Difficulty in collecting accounts receivable is the primary cause of cash flow problems, according to small business owners.

   True, Medium, Page 303

76. The longer an accounts receivable is outstanding, the lower its probability of collection.

   True, Easy, Page 303

77. The key factor in forecasting cash disbursements for a cash budget is to record them in the month when they are incurred, not when they are paid.

   False, Medium, Page 303

78. For cash planning purposes, it is better to underestimate cash disbursements than to overestimate them.

   False, Easy, Page 305

79.	Seasonal sales patterns cause cash balances to fluctuate dramatically, creating the need for cash forecasts.

	True, Medium, Page 306

80.	To manage cash efficiently, business owners should strive to accelerate their accounts payable and stretch out their accounts receivable.

	False, Medium, Page 307

81.	Most small businesses conduct a thorough credit investigation before selling to a new customer.

	False, Medium, Page 307

82.	Forty percent of industrial and wholesale sales are on credit, and 90 percent of retail sales are on account.

	False, Medium, Page 307

83.	A sale to a customer is not really a sale until the business owner actually collects the money from it.

	True, Easy, Page 307

84.	The first line of defense against bad debt losses is to have a financial institution extend loans to credit-seeking customers.

	False, Medium, Page 309

85.	One effective technique for improving cash management is to establish a firm credit policy in writing and let customers know in advance what it is.

	True, Easy, Page 309

86.	Some businesses use cycle billing, in which a company bills a portion of its credit customers each day of the month to smooth out uneven cash receipts.

	True, Easy, Page 309

87.	As soon as an account receivable becomes past due, a business owner should turn it over to a collection agency.

	False, Easy, Page 309

88. If an account receivable becomes past due, the best strategy is simply to wait; statistics show that customers eventually pay their bills if business owners don't bother them with repeated collection attempts.

   False, Medium, Page 309

89. Small business owners should not press customers for payment of their past due accounts for fear of losing them as customers altogether.

   False, Easy, Page 309

90. A small business owner should concentrate her collection efforts on the top 20 percent of her company's customers since they typically account for 80 percent of all accounts receivable.

   True, Medium, Page 310

91. A security agreement is a contract in which a business selling an asset on credit gets a security interest in that asset, protecting its legal rights in case the buyer fails to pay.

   True, Easy, Page 312

92. Proper cash management techniques call for a small business owner to pay invoices as soon as he receives them.

   False, Medium, Page 312

93. Efficient cash managers set up a payment calendar each month, which allows them to pay their bills on time and to take advantage of cash discounts for early payment.

   True, Easy, Page 313

94. A basic principle of cash management is verifying all invoices before paying them.

   True, Easy, Page 313

95. A cash discount offers a price reduction if the owner pays an invoice on time.

   False, Easy, Page 313

96. Small business owners generally should not take advantage of cash discounts vendors offer, choosing instead to maintain control of their cash for as long as possible.

   False, Medium, Page 313

97. It is considered unethical for small business owners to regulate payments to their companies' advantage.

   False, Medium, Page 313

98. Because inventory is not a liquid asset, cash invested there is tied up and cannot be used for other purposes.

True, Medium, Page 315

99. A typical manufacturing company pays 40-50 percent of the value of the inventory for the cost of borrowed money, warehouse space, materials handling, staff, lift-truck expenses, and fixed costs.

False, Difficult, Page 315

100. Only about 20 percent of a typical business's inventory turns over quickly.

True, Medium, Page 315

101. Roughly 80 percent of the typical business' inventory turns over quickly.

False, Medium, Page 315

102. It is much wiser to carry too little inventory rather than too much because there are no costs associated with carrying too little inventory.

False, Medium, Page 315

103. Bartering, exchanging goods and services for other goods and services, is an effective way for small business owners to conserve cash.

True, Easy, Page 316

104. Bartering is an opportunity to transform slow-moving inventory into much-needed products and services.

True, Easy, Page 316

105. The real benefit to a business owner engaging in barter is the ability to "pay" for goods and services at her wholesale cost and to get credit for the retail price.

True, Medium, Page 316

106. Most business owners should avoid leasing as a cash management strategy because it requires large capital outlays as down payments, and total lease payments typically are greater than those for conventional loans.

False, Medium, Page 317

107. Important advantages of leasing include the flexibility of the lease agreement and protection against obsolescence.

True, Medium, Page 317

108. When a small business encounters a sales slowdown, the first thing the owner should do is cut marketing and advertising expenditures to conserve cash.

    False, Easy, Page 317

109. Many banks allow entrepreneurs to schedule their loan payments to fit their company's cash flow cycles.

    True, Medium, Page 318

110. Changing your firm's shipping terms from "F.O.B. buyer" to "F.O.B. seller" can improve your cash flow, as it switches the cost of shipping from you to your buyer.

    True, Medium, Page 318

111. Rather than build the current year's budget on increases from the previous year's budget, zero-based budgeting starts from a budget of zero and evaluates the necessity of every item.

    True, Easy, Page 318

112. Companies lose billions of dollars each year due to employee theft.

    True, Easy, Page 318

113. In order to deter employee theft, it is best to separate cash management duties between at least two different employees.

    True, Easy, Page 318

114. When trying to prevent employee theft, business owners should create a "police state" environment and trust no one.

    False, Easy, Page 318

115. Because small business owners often rely on informal procedures for managing cash, they are most likely to become victims of embezzlement and fraud by their employees.

    True, Easy, Page 318

116. Revising business plans annually forces owners to focus on managing the business more effectively.

    True, Easy, Page 319

117. Small business managers need not be concerned about investing surplus cash since small amounts of cash sitting around for a few days or weeks are not worth investing.

    False, Easy, Page 320

118. When investing surplus cash, the small business owner should seek the highest returns possible on the money.

   False, Medium, Page 320

119. When investing surplus cash, an owner's primary objective should be on the safety and liquidity of the investments.

   True, Easy, Page 320

120. A sweep account automatically "sweeps" all funds in a company's checking account above a predetermined minimum into an interest-bearing account, enabling it to keep otherwise idle cash invested until it is needed to cover checks.

   False, Easy, Page 320

Essay Questions:

121. Why is cash a unique asset? What are the advantages of efficient cash management?

   Cash is the most important yet least productive asset that a small business owns. A business must have enough cash to meet its obligations, or it will go bankrupt. Creditors, employees, and lenders expect to be paid on time, and cash is the required medium of exchange. Cash is the lifeblood of any small business.

   Proper cash management permits the owner to adequately meet the cash demands of the business, to avoid retaining unnecessarily large cash balances, and to stretch the profit-generating power of each dollar the business owns. Also, more businesses fail for lack of cash than for lack of profit.
   Page 294

122. Your friend Jake owns a business that is achieving phenomenal growth. Explain why it is said that: "Fast-growing companies are most likely to experience cash shortages."

   Many successful, growing, and profitable businesses fail because they become insolvent; they do not have adequate cash to meet the needs of a growing business with a booming sales volume. If a company's sales are up, its owner must also hire more employees, expand plant capacity, increase the sales force, build inventory, and incur other drains on the firm's cash supply. During rapid growth, cash collections often fall behind, compounding the problem. Inventory and receivables often increase faster than profits can fund them.
   Pages 294-295

123. The profits your small business is generating are high; however, you never seem to have enough cash to pay your bills on time. Are cash and profit the same thing? Why or why not?

   Cash and profit are not the same thing. Cash is the money (the actual receipt of money) that flows through the business in a continuous cycle. It is the money that is free and readily available to use in the business. Profit is the difference between the company's total revenue and total expenses. It is the net increase over a period of time in capital

cycled through the business, and it tells how effectively the firm is being managed. A business cannot spend profits or pay bills with profits; these require cash. Businesses sometimes fail not because they are not making a profit, but because they simply run out of cash.
Page 297

124. What are the basic steps in preparing a cash budget? Which forecast is the "heart" of the cash budget?

Five basic steps to preparing a cash budget include:

- Determining an adequate minimum cash balance – some suggest it should be at least one-fourth of a firm's current debts. Be sure to account for seasonal fluctuations and add extra for "cushion." The most reliable method involves past operating records.
- Forecasting sales – which ultimately are transformed into cash receipts and cash disbursements. Be careful not to be excessively optimistic; consider economic swings, increased competition, fluctuations in demand, normal seasonal variations, and other factors that can have a dramatic effect on sales. A cash budget is only as accurate as the sales forecast from which it is derived.
- Forecasting cash receipts – includes accounting for the delay between the sale and the actual collection of the proceeds. To predict accurately the firm's cash receipts, the owner must analyze the accounts receivable to determine the collection pattern.
- Forecasting cash disbursements – many cash payments are fixed amounts due on specified dates. The key is to record them in the month in which they will be paid, not when the obligation is incurred.
- Determining the end-of-month cash balance – add total cash receipts to, and subtract total cash disbursements from, the beginning cash balance for the month. The cash balance at the end of a month becomes the beginning balance for the following month.

The heart of the cash budget is the sales forecast. As mentioned above, a cash budget is only as accurate as the sales forecast from which it was derived.
Page 298

125. How are sales forecasts developed for an established business? A new business enterprise?

For an established business, a sales forecast can be derived from past sales data, using quantitative techniques like linear or multiple regression, time series analysis, and others. The business owner must be aware that economic swings, increased competition, fluctuations in demand, normal seasonal variations, and other factors that can have a dramatic effect on sales.

The task of forecasting sales for the new firm is more difficult, but not impossible. The founder of a new business might rely on similar firms and their first year sales patterns, published statistics, market surveys, and experts' opinions to derive a sales forecast. The local Chamber of Commerce and trade associations may be able to provide helpful statistics. Marketing research using census data, government statistics, polls, surveys, etc., is also a potential source of data for forecasting sales.
Page 300

126. Identify the "big three" of cash management. As a small business consultant, what would you recommend your clients do to control the "big three" more effectively?

The "big three" primary causes of cash flow problems are accounts receivable, accounts payable, and inventory.

Selling on credit is a common practice in business. It is essential that business owners establish a workable credit policy before granting credit. It should include: a detailed credit application and a firm written credit policy issued to every customer in advance. Other techniques for accelerating accounts receivable include: send invoices promptly, indicate due date and late payment penalties, and track results of collection efforts.

Although a firm should try to accelerate its receivables, it should strive to stretch out its payables as long as possible without damaging its credit rating. Businesses should always verify invoices before paying them and should strongly consider taking advantage of cash discount opportunities offered by their vendors. Wise use of credit cards may also be considered.

Because inventory is a significant investment for many small businesses, it can create a severe strain on cash flow. Inventory should be carefully managed to reduce the possibilities of carrying the wrong type, too much, or failing to meet customer demand/stock-outs. Scheduling inventory deliveries at the latest possible date will prevent premature cash distributions.
Page 307

127. What steps can a small business owner take to minimize bad debt losses?

A credit policy that is too lenient can destroy a business's cash flow, attracting nothing but slow paying or "deadbeat" customers. However, extending a carefully designed credit policy to customers can boost sales and cash flow.

How to establish a credit and collection policy:

- Screen customers carefully by requiring that they submit a detailed credit application.
- Establish a firm written credit policy and let every customer know in advance the company's credit terms.
- Send invoices promptly.
- When an account becomes overdue, take immediate action.

Steps to encourage prompt payment of invoices:

- Ensure that all invoices are clear, accurate, and timely.
- State clearly a description of the goods or services purchased and an account number.
- Ensure that prices on invoices agree with price quotations on purchase orders or contracts.
- Highlight the terms of sale (e.g. "net 30") on all invoices and reinforce them.

- Include a telephone number and a contact person in your organization in case the customer has a question or a dispute.

Page 307

128. What steps can a small business owner take to avoid the cash "crunch"?

Techniques that allow small business owners to get the maximum benefit from their companies' pool of available cash include:

- Barter: the exchange of goods and services for other goods and services rather than for cash, is an effective way to conserve cash. The owner can get the goods and services he needs <u>without</u> having to spend valuable cash. He gets credit for the retail value of the goods or services, but the real cost to him is less, depending on the gross profit margin. In addition, the owner may be able to collect otherwise uncollectible accounts.

- Trim overhead costs: high overhead expenses can strain a small firm's cash supply. Ways to trim overhead costs include:

  - Periodically, evaluate expenses.
  - When practical, lease instead of buy.
  - Avoid nonessential outlays.
  - Negotiate fixed loan payments to coincide with your company's cash flow cycle.
  - Buy used or reconditioned equipment, especially if it is "behind-the-scenes" machinery.
  - Hire part-time employees and freelance specialists whenever possible.
  - Control employee advances and loans.
  - Establish an internal security and control system.
  - Develop a system to battle check fraud.
  - Change your shipping terms.
  - Switch to zero-based budgeting.

- Be on the lookout for employee theft.

- Keep your business plan current: keep your business plan up-to-date with annual revisions.

- Invest surplus cash: if a small business has a surplus of cash, a significant amount can be earned by investing to improve cash flow.

Page 315

Chapter 9
Managing Cash Flow
Mini-Cases

Case 9-1: Golden Company

1.   From the information below, prepare a monthly cash budget for the next quarter (October-December) for the Golden Company.

	October	November	December
Sales	$750,000	$800,000	$900,000
Manufacturing costs	450,000	480,000	540,000
Operating expenses	225,000	240,000	270,000
Capital expenditures	-------	60,000	------

Golden Company expects 25 percent of its sales to be in cash, and of the accounts receivable, 705 will be collected within the next month. Depreciation, insurance, and property taxes comprise $25,000 of monthly manufacturing costs and $10,000 of the operating expenses. Insurance and property taxes are paid in February, June, and September. The rest of the manufacturing costs and operating expenses will be paid off, one-half in the month incurred and the rest in the following month. The current assets on October 1 are made up of:

- Cash, $70,000
- Marketable securities, $50,000
- Accounts receivable, $600,000 ($450,000 from September, $150,000 from August) and current liabilities include a 90-day note for $60,000 at 9% due October 18
- Accounts payable for $200,000 for September manufacturing expenses
- Accrued liabilities of $100,000 for September operating expenses

Dividends of $1,000 should be received in November. An income tax payment of $50,000 will be made in November. The firm's minimum cash balance is $20,000.

CASH BUDGET—GOLDEN COMPANY

	August	September	October	November	December
Sales			$750,000	$800,000	$900,000
Credit Sales	150,000	450,000	562,500	600,000	675,000
Cash Receipts					
Collections					
1st Month - 70%			$315,000	$393,750	$420,000
2nd Month - 25%			37,500	112,500	140,625
Cash Sales			187,500	200,000	225,000
Dividends Received			0	1,000	0
Other			0	0	0
Total Cash Receipts			$540,000	$707,250	$785,625

Cash Disbursements

Manufacturing Costs - 1/2	$212,500	$227,500	$257,500
Manufacturing Costs - 1/2	200,000	212,500	227,500
Operating Costs - 1/2	120,000	115,000	130,000
Operating Costs - 1/2	100,000	120,000	115,000
Note Payable	60,900	0	0
Capital Expenditure	0	60,000	0
Tax Payment	0	50,000	0
Other	0	0	0
Total Cash Disbursements	$693,400	$785,000	$730,000

EOM Balance

Beginning Cash	$70,000	$20,000	$20,000
Cash Receipts	540,000	707,250	785,625
Cash Disbursements	693,400	785,000	730,000
EOM Balance	($83,400)	($57,750)	$75,625
Repay	0	104,262	183,528
Borrow	103,400	182,012	127,903
Final EOM Balance	$20,000	$20,000	$20,000

Calculations:

Oct 18 notes payable: 60,000 principal + 60,000 x .09 x ¼ of a year = 61,350

Manufacturing costs:

Because depreciation (a non-cash expense) is a component of mftg costs and because insurance and property taxes (cash expenses, which are included on a cash budget) are paid only in February, June, and September, we must subtract out $25,000 of monthly mftg costs as follows:
October 475,000-25,000 = 450,000
November 520,000-25,000 = 495,000
December 575,000-25,000= 550,000

Now we can show the actual cash outflow of these expenses, which is 50% in current month and 50% in the following month:

October: 450,000/2 = 225,000 PLUS the half from September, 200,000 accounts payable. So cash outflow for mftg in October are 225,000 + 200,000 = 425,000.

November: 495,000/2 = 247,500 PLUS the half from October, 225,000. So cash outflow for mftg expenses for November are 247,500 + 225,000 = 472,500.

And so on...

Case 9-2: The Laurens Corporation

In past years, Sue Salgado, owner of the Laurens Corporation, has been plagued by unexpected cash flow problems. Her banker, worried about her lack of cash flow management, has suggested that Sue create a cash budget for the upcoming quarter. Sue does this, using the following information:

	October	November	December
Sales	$800,000	$900,000	$950,000
Manufacturing Costs	475,000	520,000	575,000
Operational Expenses	250,000	270,000	290,000
Capital Expenditures	20,000	70,000	------

Laurens Corporation expects 35 percent of its sales to be in cash, and that of the accounts receivable, 70% will be collected within the next month, and 25 percent in the second month after sale. Depreciation, insurance, and property taxes comprise $25,000 of monthly manufacturing costs and $12,000 of operating expenses. Insurance and property taxes are paid in February, June and September. One-half of the remaining manufacturing costs and operating expenses will be paid in the month in which incurred, and the rest in the following month. As of October 1, the following facts are relevant:

- Current assets consist of $50,000 in cash, $50,000 in securities
- Credit sales for August and September were $500,000 and $450,000 respectively
- The firm has a line of credit with a local bank at 18 percent APR, and loan is due the following month
- Accounts payable of $200,000 for September manufacturing expenses
- Accrued liabilities of $100,000 for September operating expenses

Dividends of $1,000 should be received in November. An income tax payment of $20,000 will be made in November. The firm's minimum cash balance is $10,000.

From the information given, prepare a monthly cash budget for the next quarter (October - December) for the Laurens Corporation.

CASH BUDGET—LAURENS CORPORATION

	August	September	October	November	December
Sales			$800,000	$900,000	$950,000
Credit Sales	$500,000	$450,000	520,000	585,000	617,500
Collections			315,000	364,000	409,500
1st month after sale					
2nd month after sale			125,000	112,500	130,000
Cash sales			280,000	315,000	332,500
Dividends received				____	1,000
Total Cash Receipts			$720,000	$792,500	$872,000
Manufacturing Costs			225,000	247,500	275,000
			200,000	225,000	247,500
Operating Costs			119,000	129,000	139,000
			100,000	119,000	129,000
Notes Payable				61,350	
Capital Expenditures				20,000	70,000
Income tax payments				____	0,000
Total Cash Disbursements			$725,350	$810,500	$790,500

Cash-Beginning of month	50,000	44,650	26,650
+ Cash Receipts	720,000	792,500	872,000
- Cash Receipts	725,350	810,500	790,500
Cash-End of month	44,650	26,650	108,150
Borrowing (repayment)	___	0	
Cash-End of month	$44,650	$26,650	$108,150

Laurens Corporation's cash balance never dips below the minimum cash balance so the firm does not need to borrow on its line of credit.

Case 9-3: Rent-A-Nerd Computer Consultants

The owners of Rent-A-Nerd Computer Consultants have prepared the following cash budget for the upcoming quarter:

	Month 1	Month 2	Month 3
Cash Receipts:			
Total Sales	$42,650	$45,500	$47,000
Credit Sales	25,590	27,300	28,200
Collections:			
10 percent same month	2,559	2,730	2,820
80 percent next month	19,941	20,472	21,840
8 percent following month	1,864	1,994	2,048
Cash Sales	17,060	18,200	18,800
Total Cash Receipts			
Cash Disbursements:			
Purchases	$32,404	$33,267	$35,490
Wages/Salaries	4,212	4,897	5,126
Rent/Utilities	1,865	1,910	2,250
Other	2,400	3,750	6,105
Total Cash Disbursements			
End of Month Balance:			
Beginning Cash	$ 4,750		
Cash Receipts			
Cash Disbursement			

EOM Balance
Borrow
Repay

FINAL EOM BALANCE

1. How much would Rent-A-Nerd have to borrow if its desired minimum cash balance is $4,000?
   a. $2,224 in Month 3.
   b. Nothing. Rent-A-Nerd's end of the month cash balance is below $4,000.
   c. $2,598 in Month 3.
   d. $20,771 in Month 3.

   c.

2. Total cash receipts for months 1, 2 and 3 are
   a. $42,650, $45,400, $47,000.
   b. $25,590, $27,300, $28,200.
   c. $68,240, $72,800, $75,200.
   d. $41,424, $43,396, $45,508.

   d.

3. The end-of-the-month balances for months 1, 2, and 3 are
   a. $5,293, $4,865, $1,402.
   b. $6,519, $8,195, $6,224.
   c. -$10,541, -$12,524, -$16,771.
   d. $32,109, $61,085, $87,314.

   a.

Chapter 10   Creating a Successful Financial Plan

Multiple Choice Questions:

1.   In order to reach profit objectives, entrepreneurs must be aware of their firms':
     a.   current ratio.
     b.   overall financial position.
     c.   changes in financial status.
     d.   B & C only.

     d., Easy, Page 324

2.   The _____ shows what assets the business owns and what claims creditors and owners have against those assets, and is built on the basic accounting equation: Assets = Liabilities + Owner's Equity.
     a.   income statement
     b.   sources and uses of funds statement
     c.   balance sheet
     d.   cash budget

     c., Easy, Page 324

3.   _____ are those items of value the business owns; _____ are those things the business owes.
     a.   Assets; liabilities
     b.   Liabilities; assets
     c.   Ratios; equities
     d.   Equities; liabilities

     a., Easy, Page 324

4.   The first section of a balance sheet lists:
     a.   assets.
     b.   liabilities.
     c.   claims creditors have against the firm's assets payable within one year.
     d.   the owner's equity in terms of initial capital invested and retained earnings.

     a., Easy, Page 324

5.   Which of the following items would **not** be listed as a current asset in a company's financial reports?
     a.   Cash
     b.   Accounts receivable
     c.   Fixtures
     d.   Inventory

     c., Medium, Page 324

6. The _____ represents a "snapshot" of a business, showing an estimate of its value on a given date, while the _____ is a "moving picture" of the firm's profitability over time.
    a. balance sheet; income statement
    b. income statement; balance sheet
    c. statement of cash flows; income statement
    d. balance sheet; statement of cash flows

    a., Medium, Page 324

7. Cost of goods sold is located on which financial statement?
    a. income statement
    b. balance sheet
    c. statement of cash flows
    d. All of the above.

    a., Medium, Page 325

8. Which of the following is **not** true regarding the components of the income statement?
    a. Cost of goods sold represents the total cost, excluding shipping, of the merchandise sold during the accounting period.
    b. Gross profit margin is calculated by dividing gross profit by net sales revenue.
    c. Operating expenses include those costs that contribute directly to the manufacture and distribution of goods.
    d. A and B above.

    a., Difficult, Page 325

9. The statement of cash flows:
    a. compares costs and expenses against firm's net profits.
    b. is built on the basic accounting equation: Assets = Liabilities + Capital.
    c. shows what assets the business owns and what claims creditors and owners have against those assets.
    d. shows changes in working capital by listing sources and uses of funds.

    d., Medium, Page 327

10. On a company's statement of cash flows, depreciation is:
    a. the difference between the total sources available to the owner and the total uses of those assets.
    b. listed as a source of funds because it is a non-cash expense, deducted as a cost of doing business.
    c. the owner's total investment at the company's inception plus retained earnings.
    d. creditors' total claims against the firm's assets.

    b., Medium, Page 327

11. Which of the following associations is **correct?**
    a. balance sheet - cost of goods sold
    b. income statement - owner's equity
    c. current assets - inventory
    d. long-term liabilities - accounts payable

    c., Medium, Page 324

12. Creating projected (pro forma) financial statements would allow a business owner to answer which of the following questions?
    a. What profit can any business expect to achieve?
    b. What sales level must any business reach if our targeted profit is X dollars?
    c. What fixed and variable expenses can any business expect to incur at our targeted sales level?
    d. All of the above.

    d., Easy, Page 328

13. On a projected income statement, a business owner's target income is:
    a. the sum of a reasonable salary for the time spent running the business and a normal return on the amount invested in it.
    b. the income at which the company's total revenues and its total expenses are equal.
    c. the income that will produce a 10 percent return on the owner's financial investment in the business.
    d. the income that the owner could earn working for someone else.

    a., Medium, Page 329

14. You are to prepare a projected income statement for a proposed business venture. Your desired income is $28,000 and you have the following published statistics:
    Costs of goods sold = 56.9 percent of net sales
    Operating expenses = 37.1 percent of net sales
    Gross profit margin = 43.1 percent of net sales

    Net sales on your pro forma "P & L" (income statement) would be:
    a. $491,228.
    b. $500,000.
    c. $466,667.
    d. None of the above.

    c., Medium, Page 329

15. Gaither Mack is preparing projected financial statements to include in the business plan he is preparing for the launch of a specialty retail store. Using published financial statistics, Mack finds that the typical net profit margin for a store like his is 7.3 percent. If Mack's target income for his first year of operation is $32,000, what level of sales must he achieve to reach it?
    a. $438,356
    b. $233,600
    c. $2,966,400
    d. Cannot be determined from the information given

    a., Medium, Page 329

16. Typically, in a start-up firm, salaries are not the best use of cash; a guideline is for the owner to draw a salary that is about ____ to ___% below the market rate for a similar position.
    a. 5-10
    b. 10-20
    c. 20-25
    d. 25-30

    d., Difficult, Page 330

17. A business should provide the owner with a reasonable rate of return on:
    a. the time she invests in the business.
    b. the money she invests in the business.
    c. the capital she borrows from the bank.
    d. A and B only.

    d., Easy, Page 330

18. Michelle Becker's target income in her business for the upcoming year is $78,500. The company's gross profit margin averages 32.6 percent of sales, and its total operating expenses run 24.7 percent of sales. To achieve her target income, sales of Michelle's company should be:
    a. $148,773.
    b. $993,671.
    c. $317,814.
    d. $1,271,348.

    b., Medium, Page 330

19. A technique that allows the small business owner to perform financial analysis by understanding the relationship between two accounting elements is called:
    a. creating the pro forma.
    b. budgeting.
    c. break-even analysis.
    d. ratio analysis.

    d., Easy, Page 334

20. Analyzing financial ratios could alert a business owner to which of these problems?
    a. excessive inventory
    b. overextending credit
    c. too much debt
    d. All of the above.

    d., Easy, Page 334

21. _____ ratios tell whether or not the small company will be able to meet its short-term obligations.
    a. Leverage
    b. Profitability
    c. Liquidity
    d. Operating

    c., Easy, Page 335

22. Which of the following is **not** a liquidity ratio?
    a. current ratio
    b. total asset turnover ratio
    c. quick ratio
    d. None of the above.

    b., Easy, Page 335

23. The ____ ratio is a measure of the small company's ability to pay current debts from current assets and is the liquidity ratio most commonly used as a measure of short-term solvency.
    a. quick
    b. debt-to-net worth
    c. current
    d. debt-to-assets

    c., Easy, Page 335

24. Financial analysts suggest that a small business should maintain a current ratio of at least:
    a. 1:1.
    b. 2:1.
    c. 3:1.
    d. 4:1.

    b., Medium, Page 335

25. The _____ ratio is a conservative measure of a firm's liquidity and shows the extent to which a firm's most liquid assets cover its current liabilities.
    a. current
    b. quick
    c. turnover
    d. net profit

    b., Easy, Page 335

26. Bettina has just calculated her company's current ratio. To calculate the quick ratio, she should:
    a. subtract current liabilities from current assets before dividing by total liabilities.
    b. subtract total liabilities from current assets before dividing by current liabilities.
    c. subtract inventory from current assets before dividing by current liabilities.
    d. subtract depreciation expense from current assets before dividing by current liabilities.

    c., Medium, Page 335

27. When a company is forced into liquidation, owners are most likely to incur a loss when selling:
    a. accounts receivable.
    b. inventory.
    c. marketable securities.
    d. real estate.

    b., Medium, Page 336

28. _____ ratios measure the extent to which an entrepreneur relies on debt capital rather than equity capital to finance a business.
    a. Liquidity
    b. Leverage
    c. Operating
    d. Profitability

    b., Easy, Page 336

29. The _____ ratio measures the percentage of total assets financed by a small company's creditors compared to its owners.
    a. debt
    b. times-interest-earned
    c. net sales to total assets
    d. total asset turnover

    a., Easy, Page 336

30. A high debt ratio:
    a. means that creditors provide a large percentage of the company's total financing.
    b. gives a small business more borrowing capacity.
    c. decreases the chances that creditors will lose money if the business is liquidated.
    d. represents a lower risk to potential lenders and creditors.

    a., Medium, Page 336

31. Which ratio would best give an owner an indication that the business is undercapitalized?
    a. Debt-to-net worth
    b. Net sales to total assets
    c. Average inventory turnover
    d. Quick

    a., Easy, Page 337

32. The higher the ____ ratio, the lower the degree of protection afforded creditors, and the closer creditors' interest approaches the owner's interest.
   a. debt-to-net worth
   b. quick
   c. asset turnover
   d. current

   a., Easy, Page 337

33. _____ is one indication that a small business may be undercapitalized.
   a. A current ratio below 1:1.
   b. A quick ratio above 2:1.
   c. A debt-to-net worth ratio above 1:1.
   d. A net sales-to-working capital ratio equal to 3:1.

   c., Medium, Page 337

34. The _____ ratio tells how many times the company's earnings cover the interest payments on the debt it is carrying.
   a. debt
   b. debt-to-net worth
   c. times-interest-earned
   d. net sales-to-working capital

   c., Easy, Page 337

35. _____ ratios help a business owner evaluate the company's performance and indicate how effectively the business employs its resources.
   a. Liquidity
   b. Leverage
   c. Operating
   d. Profitability

   c., Easy, Page 338

36. The average inventory turnover ratio:
   a. measures the number of times a company's inventory is sold out during the accounting period.
   b. tells a business owner whether she is managing the company's inventory properly.
   c. tells a business owner how fast the merchandise is moving through the business.
   d. All of the above.

   d., Easy, Page 338

37. Sarah's Smart Shop has an inventory turnover ratio of 3 times per year and an average inventory of $156,000. If Sarah could manage her inventory better and increase the number of turnovers to the industry average of 6 times per year, what average inventory would she need to generate the same level of sales?
    a. $78,000
    b. $52,000
    c. $468,000
    d. $312,000

    a., Medium, Page 338

38. Which of the following combinations of ratios would indicate that a company is financially mismanaged and is not a good credit risk?
    a. high liquidity; high leverage
    b. low liquidity; high leverage
    c. high liquidity; low leverage
    d. low liquidity; low leverage

    b., Medium, Page 339

39. For the most meaningful interpretation, the small business owner should compare his firm's average collection period to:
    a. the average for the industry.
    b. his firm's credit terms.
    c. the universal standard of 25 days.
    d. A & B only.

    d., Medium, Page 340

40. A business that turns over its receivables 5.9 times a year would have an average collection period of about:
    a. 30 days.
    b. 2/10, net 30.
    c. 71 days.
    d. 62 days.

    d., Medium, Page 340

41. If the accounting period is one year with credit sales totaling $2,500,000 and accounts receivable totaling $200,000, what is the average collection period ratio?
    a. 29.2 days
    b. 365 days
    c. 119.3 days
    d. Cannot be determined

    a., Difficult, Page 340

42.   A business with a payables turnover ratio of 10.4 times a year would have an average payable period of about:
      a.   3 days.
      b.   30 days.
      c.   35 days.
      d.   62 days.

      c., Easy, Page 341

43.   An excessively high average payable period ratio:
      a.   suggests that the company is making the best use of its available cash balance.
      b.   indicates that the company is doing a poor job of collecting its accounts receivable.
      c.   indicates the presence of a significant amount of past-due accounts payable.
      d.   suggests that the company is highly liquid.

      c., Medium, Page 341

44.   The _____ ratio measures a company's ability to generate sales in relation to its assets.
      a.   net sales-to-working capital
      b.   net sales to total assets
      c.   average collection period
      d.   average inventory turnover

      b., Easy, Page 341

45.   Which ratio would be most helpful to a business owner trying to make sure that he maintains a sufficient amount of working capital to nourish his company's expansion?
      a.   net sales to total assets
      b.   net sales to working capital
      c.   net profit on sales
      d.   net profit to equity

      b., Easy, Page 342

46.   _____ ratios indicate how efficiently the small firm is being managed.
      a.   Liquidity
      b.   Profitability
      c.   Leverage
      d.   Operating

      b., Easy, Page 343

47.   The _____ ratio shows the portion of each sales dollar remaining after deducting all expenses.
      a.   net profit on sales
      b.   net profit to equity
      c.   net sales to total assets
      d.   net sales to working capital

      a., Easy, Page 343

48. The ____ ratio measures the owner's rate of return on the investment in the business.
    a. net profit to equity
    b. net profit on sales
    c. quick profit
    d. net sales to working capital

    a., Easy, Page 343

49. The break-even point:
    a. occurs where a company's total revenue equals its total expenses.
    b. is the point at which a company neither earns a profit nor incurs a loss.
    c. tells a business owner the minimum level of activity needed to keep her company in operation.
    d. All of the above.

    d., Easy, Page 350

50. Which of the following is an assumption of break-even analysis?
    a. Fixed expenses remain constant for all levels of sales volume.
    b. Variable expenses change in direct proportion to changes in sales volume.
    c. Changes in sales volume have no effect on unit sales price.
    d. All of the above.

    d., Easy, Page 355

Refer to the following information to answer Questions 51-52 regarding Anita Lupino:

Anita Lupino is planning to open her own toy and game shop. She has conducted a great deal of research at the local library, contacted the industry trade association, and has set up a meeting with a consultant at the SBDC next week. Before she goes to the SBDC, she wants to sketch out an estimated income statement. She gets the following data from RMA's Annual Statement Studies:

Costs of goods sold	57.3 percent of net sales
Operating expenses	32.9 percent of net sales
Gross profit	42.7 percent of net sales

51. If Anita's research suggests that she can expect net sales of $475,000, what net profit could she expect?
    a. $202,825
    b. $46,550
    c. $69,350
    d. $156,275

    b., Medium, Page 329

52. If Anita's net profit target is $32,000, what level of net sales must she achieve?
    a. $74,941
    b. $97,264
    c. $326,531
    d. $219,178

c., Medium, Page 329

Refer to the following information to answer Questions 53-55 regarding Port Royal:
     Net sales = $927,641
     Gross profit = $301,483
     Net profit = $48,457
     Total assets = $203,869
     Total liabilities = $74,325

53. Port Royal's debt-to-net worth ratio is:
    a. 0.36:1.
    b. 0.08:1.
    c. 1.57:1.
    d. 0.57:1.

d., Medium, Page 337

54. Port Royal's profit margin on sales is _____ percent.
    a. 5.2
    b. 32.5
    c. 16.1
    d. 8.0

a., Medium, Page 343

55. Port Royal's net profit-to-equity ratio is ____ percent.
    a. 23.8
    b. 37.4
    c. 16.1
    d. 232.7

b., Medium, Page 344

Refer to the following information to answer Questions 56-57 about Alhambra Meters, Inc.:
     Alhambra Meters, Inc. reported net sales of $874,916 and a net profit of $74,563 on its
     most recent income statement. The company's balance sheet shows total assets of $342,742
     and total liabilities of $88,367.

56. What is Alhambra's net profit margin?
    a. 8.5 percent
    b. 1.91:1
    c. 21.8 percent
    d. 29.3 percent

a., Medium, Page 343

57. What is Alhambra's return on net worth ratio?
    a. 8.5 percent
    b. 1.91:1
    c. 21.8 percent
    d. 29.3 percent

d., Medium, Page 344

58. Refer to the following information:

	Smith Office Supply	Industry Mean
Current ratio	2.3	1.8
Quick ratio	.4	.8
Average inventory turnover	2.0	3.9
Net sales-to-working capital	4.0	7.8
Debt-to-net worth ratio	3.0	1.7
Net profit to equity ratio	40.1 percent	22.2 percent

Which of the following statements is most likely **false**?
    a. Smith relies on inventory fairly heavily to meet its debt obligations.
    b. Smith is sufficiently capitalized.
    c. Smith's sales are inadequate.
    d. Smith's prices may be too high and/or the inventory too "stale."

b., Medium, Page 343

Refer to the following to answer Questions 59-61 regarding Gunther's Gum Emporium:

Gunther's Gum Emporium expects net sales of $2,396,919 for the upcoming year, with variable expenses totaling $1,813,443 and fixed expenses of $412,190.

59. If Gunther's net profit target for the year is $190,000, what sales level must he achieve?
    a. $2,473,796
    b. $1,876,324
    c. $5,667,009
    d. None of the above.

a., Medium, Page 353

60. Gunther's Gum Emporium expects net sales of $2,396,919 for the upcoming year, with variable expenses totaling $1,813,443 and fixed expenses of $412,190.

What is Gunther's break-even point?
    a. $1,876,324
    b. $1,693,276
    c. $5,667,009
    d. Insufficient information given to determine

b., Medium, Page 352

61.   Using break-even analysis, what is Gunther's contribution margin?
       a.   4 percent
       b.   32 percent
       c.   24 percent
       d.   12 percent

       c., Medium, Page 352

Refer to the following Break-even Chart to answer Questions 62-65:

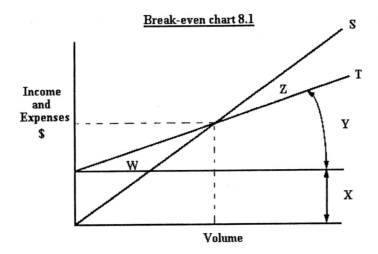

62.   Line T is the _____ line, while Line S is the _____ line.
       a.   total revenue; total expense
       b.   total expense; total revenue
       c.   fixed cost; variable cost
       a.   variable cost; fixed cost

       b., Medium, Page 354

63.   The area labeled _____ represents the firm's fixed expenses, while _____ represents its
       variable expenses.
       a.   Z; W
       b.   X; Y
       c.   Y; X
       d.   W; Z

       b., Medium, Page 355

64.   The area labeled ____ is the "profit area."
       a.   W
       b.   X
       c.   Y
       d.   Z

       d., Medium, Page 355

65. The area labeled _____ is the "loss area."
    a. W
    b. X
    c. Y
    d. Z

    a., Medium, Page 355

True/False Questions:

66. According to one study, only 11 percent of small business owners analyzed their financial statements as part of the managerial planning process, and another study found that one-third of all entrepreneurs run their companies without any kind of financial plan.

    True, Medium, Page 324

67. The income statement is based on the fundamental accounting equation: Assets = Liabilities + Owner's Equity.

    False, Easy, Page 324

68. Assets represent what a business owns, while liabilities represent the claims creditors have against a company's assets.

    True, Easy, Page 324

69. The balance sheet provides owners with an estimate of the firm's worth for a specific moment in time, while the income statement presents a "moving picture" of its profitability over a period of time.

    True, Medium, Page 324

70. On the income statement, the cost of goods sold represents the total cost, excluding shipping, of the merchandise sold during the year.

    False, Medium, Page 325

71. To determine net profit, the owner records sales revenue for the year and subtracts liabilities.

    False, Easy, Page 325

72. Service companies spend the greatest percentage of their sales revenue on cost of goods sold.

    False, Easy, Page 325

73. Comparing a company's current income statement to those of prior accounting periods rarely reveals valuable information about key trends.

False, Easy, Page 326

74. Almost fifty percent of small businesses become profitable within zero to twelve months.

True, Difficult, Page 327

75. The difference between the total sources of funds and the total uses of funds represents the increase or decrease in a firm's working capital.

True, Easy, Page 327

76. The most common mistake entrepreneurs make when preparing pro forma (projected) financial statements for their companies is being overly pessimistic in their financial plans.

False, Easy, Page 328

77. Pro forma financial statements show a company's most recent financial position.

False, Medium, Page 328

78. On a projected income statement, a business owner's target income is the sum of a reasonable salary for the time spent running the business and a normal return on the amount the owner has invested in it.

True, Medium, Page 329

79. In start-up firms, one guideline is for the owner to draw a salary 25-30 percent below the market rate for a similar position.

True, Medium, Page 330

80. Concerning how much cash to have at startup, one rule of thumb is to have enough to cover operating expenses (less depreciation) for two inventory turnover periods.

False, Medium, Page 331

81. Ratio analysis allows a business owner to identify potential problem areas in her business before they become business-threatening crises.

True, Easy, Page 333

82. Ratio analysis is a useful managerial tool that can help business owners maintain financial control over their businesses, but it is of no use to a business owner trying to obtain a bank loan.

False, Medium, Page 334

83. Liquidity ratios such as the current ratio and the quick ratio, tell whether a small business will be able to meet its short-term obligations as they come due.

True, Easy, Page 335

84. A current ratio of 2.4:1 means that a small company has $2.40 in current liabilities for every $1 has in current assets.

False, Medium, Page 335

85. A high current ratio guarantees that the small firm's assets are being used in the most profitable manner.

False, Difficult, Page 335

86. Generally, the higher the current ratio, the stronger the small firm's financial position.

True, Medium, Page 335

87. Most firms calculate their quick assets by subtracting the value of their inventory from their current asset total.

True, Medium, Page 335

88. A quick ratio of more than 1:1 suggests that a small company is overly dependent on inventory and future sales to satisfy its short-term debt.

False, Difficult, Page 336

89. Operating ratios measure the extent to which an entrepreneur relies on debt capital rather than equity capital to finance the business.

False, Easy, Page 336

90. Leverage ratios measure the financing supplied by the firm's owner against that supplied by his creditors.

True, Easy, Page 336

91. Small businesses with high leverage ratios are more vulnerable to economic downturns, but they have greater potential for large profits.

True, Difficult, Page 336

92. The small business with a high debt to net worth ratio has more borrowing capacity than a firm with a low ratio.

False, Difficult, Page 337

93. As a company's debt to net worth ratio approaches 1:1, its creditors' interest in that business approaches that of the owners.

   True, Medium, Page 337

94. A company with a low debt to net worth ratio has less capacity to borrow than a company with a high debt to net worth ratio.

   False, Medium, Page 337

95. The times-interest-earned ratio tells how many times the company's earnings cover the interest payments on the debt it is carrying.

   True, Medium, Page 337

96. A company with a times-interest earned ratio that is well above the industry average would likely have difficulty making the interest payments on its loans, as creditors would see that it was overextended in its debts.

   False, Difficult, Page 337

97. Creditors often look for a times interest earned ratio of at least 4:1 to 6:1 before pronouncing a company a good credit risk.

   True, Medium, Page 337

98. Taking on debt destroys a business; therefore, small business owners should avoid it at all costs.

   False, Medium, Page 338

99. Liquidity ratios help a business owner evaluate a small company's performance and indicate how effectively it employs its resources.

   False, Easy, Page 338

100. The average inventory turnover ratio measures the number of times a company's inventory is sold out during the accounting period.

   True, Easy, Page 338

101. An inventory turnover ratio above the industry average suggests that a business is overstocked with obsolete, stale, overpriced, or unpopular merchandise.

   False, Medium, Page 340

102. A high inventory turnover ratio relative to the industry average could mean that a business has too little inventory and is experiencing stockouts.

   True, Medium, Page 340

103. A company's average collection period ratio tells the average number of days it takes to collect its accounts receivable.

    True, Easy, Page 340

104. Generally, the higher the small firm's average collection period ratio, the greater the chance of bad debt losses.

    True, Medium, Page 340

105. Slow accounts receivable are a real danger to a small business because they often lead to cash crises.

    True, Medium, Page 341

106. If a company's average payable period ratio is significantly lower than the credit terms vendors offer, it may be a sign that the company is not using its cash most effectively.

    True, Medium, Page 341

107. An excessively high average payable period ratio indicates the possibility of the presence of a significant amount of past-due accounts payable.

    True, Medium, Page 341

108. Although sound cash management principles call for a business owner to keep her cash as long as possible, slowing accounts payable too drastically can severely damage a company's credit rating.

    True, Easy, Page 341

109. A net sales to working capital ratio of 6.25:1 means that for every dollar in working capital $6.25 is generated in sales.

    True, Medium, Page 342

110. The net profit on sales ratio measures the owner's rate of return on the investment in the business.

    False, Medium, Page 343

111. The net profit to equity ratio reports the percentage of the owners' investment in the business that is being returned through profits annually.

    True, Easy, Page 343

112. Ratio analysis provides an owner with a "snapshot" of the company's financial picture at a single instant; therefore, she should track these ratios over time, looking for trends that otherwise might go undetected.

    True, Easy, Page 350

113. The break-even point is the level of operation at which a business neither earns a profit nor incurs a loss, and lets the business owner know the minimum level of activity required to keep the firm in operation.

     True, Medium, Page 350

114. Fixed expenses are those that do not vary with changes in the volume of sales, but do vary with production.

     False, Medium, Page 352

115. On a break-even chart, the break-even point occurs at the intersection of the fixed expense line and the total revenue line.

     False, Medium, Page 355

Essay Questions:

116. Explain the three basic financial reports that a small business uses in building a financial plan: the balance sheet, the income statement and the statement of cash flows. What information is contained in each, and of what value is it to the small business owner?

     A.   Balance sheet: takes a "snapshot" of a business, providing owners with an estimate of its worth on a given date. It is built on the fundamental accounting equation Assets = Liabilities + Owner's Equity and provides a baseline from which to measure future changes in assets, liability and equity.

           Components include: Assets (Current and Long Term), Liabilities (Current and Long term), and Owner's Equity.

     B.   Income statement: compares expenses against revenue over a certain period of time to show the firm's net profit (or loss). It is a "moving picture" of the firm's profit over a period of time and provides "the bottom line" figure for the small business owner. It is also known as the Profit and Loss Statement or P & L.

           Components include various categories of Revenues and Expenses.

     C.   Statement of cash flows: shows the changes in the firm's working capital since the beginning of the year by listing the sources of funds and the use of these funds. Although many small business owners never create them, IRS, creditors, investors and new owners may require them when investigating the changes in a firm's working capital.

           Components include categories of Sources and Uses of Funds.
     Page 324

117. Define what a pro forma financial statement is. What are the two types a small business owner uses, and how are they created?

Pro forma statements are vital elements in a small business financial plan. They estimate the firm's future profitability and overall financial condition. These statements help the owner determine the funds required to launch the business and sustain it. The basic pro forma financial statements are:

<u>The Income Statement</u>

Most entrepreneurs select a target income and build a pro forma income statement from the bottom up. The target income includes a reasonable salary and a normal return on the amount invested in the firm. The owner computes target sales from his target income by:

$$\text{Net Sales} = \frac{\text{Target Income}}{\text{Net profit margin (as a \% of net sales)}}$$

Next, using published statistics, the owner computes the remaining entries by multiplying the proper statistic by the net sales figure. After the owner determines that the targeted net sales figure is reasonable, expenses are listed accordingly.

<u>The Balance Sheet</u>

Creating a pro forma balance sheet begins with a statement of assets. One rule of thumb suggests that the company's cash balance should cover its operating expenses (less depreciation, a noncash expense) for one inventory turnover period.

The method of determining the firm's cash requirement is:

$$\text{Cash requirement} = \frac{\text{Cash expenses}}{\text{Average inventory turnover}}$$

The inventory level is computed from published statistics and the cost of goods sold figure from the income statement:

$$\text{Inventory level} = \frac{\text{Cost of goods sold}}{\text{Average inventory level}}$$

To complete the projected balance sheet, the owner must record the firm's other assets, and liabilities, the claims against its assets. Using the accounting equation of Assets = Liabilities + Owner Equity, calculates the final component—Owner's Equity.
Page 328

118. Explain what ratio analysis is. Name the four categories of ratios and describe the type of information each group provides the small business owner.

Ratios help measure the small firm's performance and can point out potential problem areas before they become business crises. They use accounts from both the balance sheet and income statement and provide relevant information to the overall financial plan. One way to use ratios is to compare those of the small business to other businesses in the same industry through a number of published industry averages and standards. It is also helpful for the owner to analyze the firm's financial ratios over time. The four categories are:

Liquidity ratios – tell whether a firm will be able to meet its short-term financial obligations as they come due. These ratios can forewarn a business owner of impending cash flow problems. A firm with a solid liquidity is able to pay bills on time and take advantage of attractive opportunities as they arrive.

Leverage ratios – measure the financing supplied by the firm's owners against that supplied by its creditors. The ratios are a gauge of the depth of a firm's debt. These ratios show the extent to which a business relies on debt capital (rather than equity) to finance operating expenses, capital expenditures, and expansion costs. In a sense, they measure the degree of financial risk in a company. Generally small businesses with low leverage ratios are affected less by economic downturns, but the returns are lower during economic booms. Firms with higher ratios are more vulnerable during economic downturns because of their debt loads, but have a greater potential for large profits in economic booms.

Operating ratios – evaluate a firm's overall performance and indicate how effectively the business employs its resources. The more effectively its resources are used, the less capital a small business will require.

Profitability ratios – indicate how efficiently a small business is being managed. These ratios provide information on the company's bottom line—how successfully the firm is using its available resources to generate a profit.
Page 333

119. List ten key ratios outlined in the text and explain the type of information they provide the small business owner.

Students should select from the following Twelve Key Ratios:

- Current ratio--firm's ability to pay current debts out of current assets. Rule of thumb = 2:1

- Quick ratio--extent to which firm's most liquid assets cover its current liabilities. Rule of thumb - 1:1

- Debt ratio--measure the financing supplied by business owners and that supplied by business creditors.

- Debt-to-net-worth ratio--compares what the business owes to what it "owns."

- Times interest earned--a measure of the firm's ability to make the interest payments on its debt.

- Average inventory turnover ratio--measures the average number of times its inventory is "turned over" during the year.

- Average collection period ratio--tells the average number of days it takes to collect accounts receivable.

- Average payable period ratio--tells the average number of days it takes a company to pay its accounts payable.

- Net sales to total assets ratio--a general measure of firm's ability to generate sales in relation to its assets.

- Net sales to working capital ratio--measures how much in sales the business generates for every dollar of working capital.

- Net profit on sales ratio--measures firm's profit per dollar of sales.

- Net profit to equity ratio--measures owner's rate of return on investment (ROI).

Page 347

120. Why is it important for an entrepreneur, about to launch a business, to perform a breakeven analysis? Describe the steps in calculating it.

Breakeven analysis is important because it helps the entrepreneur understand what sales volume he/she must achieve to "break even" –neither earning a profit nor incurring a loss. It shows the minimum level of sales required to stay in business and what minimum level of sales is required to cover expenses. The formula can be adapted to figure the minimum level of sales needed to support a certain profit margin or dollar amount.

The steps in calculating Break-even include:

A. Determining variable and fixed expenses:

1. Fixed expenses—costs that do not vary with changes in the volume of sales or production.

2. Variable expenses—costs that vary directly with changes in the volume of sales or production.

B. Steps in calculating the breakeven point:

Step 1: Determine the expenses the business can expect to incur.

Step 2: Categorize the expenses estimated in step 1 into fixed expenses and variable expenses.

Step 3: Calculate the ratio of variable expenses to net sales.

Step 4: Compute the breakeven point by inserting this information into the following formula:

$$\text{Breakeven sales (\$)} = \frac{\text{total fixed costs}}{\text{contribution margin expressed as a percentage of sales}}$$

C.   Including Desired Net Income in Breakeven Analysis:

Sales ($) = $\dfrac{\text{total fixed expenses} + \text{desired net income}}{\text{contribution margin expressed as a percentage of sales}}$

D.   Breakeven Point in Units:

Breakeven volume = $\dfrac{\text{total fixed costs}}{\text{sales price per unit - variable cost per unit}}$

Page 350

121.   Explain the procedure for constructing a graph that visually portrays the firm's break-even point (the point where revenues equal expenses).

- Step 1: On the horizontal axis, mark a scale measuring sales volume in dollars (or in units sold or some other measure of volume).
- Step 2: On the vertical axis, mark a scale measuring income and expenses in dollars.
- Step 3: Draw a fixed expense line intersecting the vertical axis at the proper dollar level parallel to the horizontal axis. The area between this line and the horizontal axis represents the firm's fixed expenses.
- Step 4: Draw a total expense line that slopes upward beginning at the point where the fixed cost line intersects the vertical axis. The precise location of the total expenses line is determined by plotting the total cost incurred at a particular sales volume. The total cost for a given sales level is determined by:

Total expenses = Fixed expenses + Variable expenses expressed as a % of sales x Sales level

- Step 5: Beginning at the graph's origin, draw a 45-degree line showing where total sales volume equals total income.
- Step 6: Locate the break-even point by finding the intersection of the total expense line and the revenue line. If the company operates at a sales volume to the left of the break-even point, it will incur a loss because the expense line is higher than the revenue line. On the other hand, if the firm operates at a sales volume to the right of the break-even point, it will earn a profit because the revenue line lies above the expense line.

Page 352

122.   What are the advantages and the disadvantages of using break-even analysis?

Advantages of break-even analysis include:

Being a key component in a sound financial plan. By analyzing costs and expenses in this manner, an entrepreneur can calculate the minimum level of activity required to keep the firm in operation. These techniques can then be refined to project the sales needed to generate the desired profit. It is a simple useful screening device. Business owners can also employ nonlinear break-even analysis using a graphical approach.

Disadvantages include:

Having certain limitations such as being too simple to use as a final screening device because it ignores the importance of cash flows. Also, the accuracy of the analysis depends on the accuracy of the revenue and expense estimates, and the basic assumptions pertaining to break-even analysis may not be realistic for some businesses. These assumptions include: that fixed expenses remain constant for all levels of sales volume; variable expenses change in direct proportion to changes in sales volume; and changes in sales volume have no effect on unit sales price.
Page 355

Chapter 10
Creating a Successful Financial Plan
Mini-Cases

Case 10-1: Bowden Brake Service (Part A)

Jim Bowden, owner of Bowden Brake Service, is planning to expand his six-year old brake service to include tune-ups and tire services. Based on budget estimates for the upcoming year, Jim expects net sales to be $825,000 with a cost of goods sold of $530,000 and total operating expenses of $210,000. From the budget, Jim computes fixed expenses to be $168,000, while variable expenses (including cost of goods sold) are $572,000. Jim is worried that the new cost structure may damage his ability to produce a profit, so he wants to perform a quick break-even analysis for the upcoming year.

1. Prepare an outline for Jim describing the components he should include in the business plan when requesting a loan.

    Jim's business plan should include: a cover letter, resumes of the owners, company history, general business summary, business strategy, a description of the firm's products and services, marketing strategy, a plan of operation, financial data, and a loan proposal.

2. If Jim were to reduce his fixed costs by 10 percent by reducing a middle management position, what benefit would that be to him and the company? What would his new contribution margin be?

    By reducing his fixed costs, Jim improves his contribution margin.
    If fixed costs are reduced by 10%
    Then: $572,000 x 90% = $514,800
    Calculate New Contribution Margin
    $$\frac{\$514,800}{\$825,800} = .62$$
    1 - .62 = .38, or 38%

Since middle managers are normally salaried employees, which constitutes a fixed cost, it is easy to see why middle management positions have been significantly reduced in recent years.

3. Help Jim compute the break-even point for his brake service.

Contribution margin $= 1 = \dfrac{\$572,000}{\$825,000} = 1 = .6933 = .3067$

Break-even sales $= \$168,000 = \dfrac{\$547,767}{.3067}$

Case 10-2: Bowden Brake Service (Part B)

One day while you are in Bowden Brake Service getting your brakes repaired, Jim storms into his office, slamming doors and shouting about the local financial institutions. After a few minutes of building your courage, you approach Jim and ask him what the problem is. He shouts, "It's the financial institutions in this town! Not one of them will lend me the money I need to expand my business. They all said I needed to take a closer look at my financial position before I consider expanding. One of them said something about ratio analysis. I know a lot about cars and brakes, but what is ratio analysis?"
You tell Jim you'll perform a ratio analysis for the business if he gives you a free brake job. Jim provides you with the following financial statements.

Bowden Brake Service
Income Statement
Year Ended 31 December 2000

Net sales		$780,000
Costs of goods sold:		
Beginning inventory	$104,000	
Purchases	526,480	
Goods available for sale	$630,480	
Ending inventory	134,400	
Costs of goods sold		493,080
Gross margin		$283,920
Operating expenses:		
Rent	24,000	
Insurance	5,250	
Advertising	6,000	
Travel	2,500	
Interest	72,750	
Taxes (property, etc.)	2,500	
Salaries & admin. expenses	97,000	
Utilities	12,500	
Supplies	1,360	
Total operating expenses		$223,860
Net profit		$ 60,060

Bowden Brake Service
Balance Sheet
31 December 2001

Assets

Current assets:		
Cash		$20,000
Accounts receivable	10,000	
Notes receivable	5,000	
Inventory		134,400
Total current assets		$169,400
Fixed assets:		
Land		$147,000
Machinery	$ 73,000	
Equipment	160,800	
Less accumulated depreciation	30,200	203,600
Total fixed assets		350,600
Total assets		$520,000

Liabilities & Owner's Equity

Current liabilities:	
Accounts payable	$40,500
Notes payable	20,200
Accrued salaries payable	4,300
Total current liabilities:	$65,000
Long-term liabilities	
Long-term loan	325,000
Owner's equity, Jim Bowden	130,000
Total liabilities and net worth	$520,000

1. Refer to the income statement and balance sheet. Prepare a ratio analysis for Bowden Brake Service. Also, using the following industry statistics for firms like Jim's, explain and interpret what these ratios mean.

Current ratio	1:4:1
Quick ratio	0:7:1
Debt ratio	1:8:1
Debt-to-net worth ratio	1:9:1
Average inventory turnover	N/A
Average collection period	21.22 days
Net sales-to-total assets	2.8 percent
Net sales-to-working capital	17.2 percent
Net profit on sales	9.0 percent
Net profit to equity	22.2 percent

Current ratio = $\dfrac{\$169,400}{\$65,000}$ = 2.61

Bowden has $2.61 in current assets for every $1 in current liabilities. This surpasses both the 2:1 "rule of thumb" and the 1.4 industry median.

Quick ratio = $\dfrac{\$169,000}{\$65,000}$ = $134,400 = .54

Bowden has .54 in quick assets for every $1 in current liabilities.
This is below both the 1:1 rule of thumb and the .7. Bowden apparently relies heavily on inventory to help satisfy its short-term debt.

Debt ratio = $\dfrac{\$65,000 + \$325,000}{\$520,000}$ = .75

Compared to the industry median of 1.80, Bowden is not overburdened with debt.

Debt to net worth ratio = $\dfrac{\$65,000}{\$130,000}$ = $325,000 = 3.0

Creditors have contributed three times as much to the business as Jim Bowden. Creditors are likely to see Bowden as being "borrowed up," especially since the industry median is 1.90.

Average inventory = $\dfrac{\$496,080}{\$104,000}$ = $134,000 = 4.16

Bowden turns over its inventory about 4.16 times per year. A comparison is difficult since industry figures are unavailable.

Average collection period ratio = $\dfrac{365 \text{ days}}{\$780,000}$ = 7.02
$15,000

Bowden's accounts and notes receivable are outstanding for an average of 7.02 days, while the industry median is 21.22 days.

Net sales to total assets ratio = $\dfrac{\$780,000}{\$520,000}$ = 1.5

Bowden generates $1.5 in sales for every $1 in total assets. The industry median is 2.8. Bowden is not producing enough sales in relation to its asset size.

Net sales to working capital ratio = $\dfrac{\$780,000}{\$169,900 - \$69,000}$ = 7.47

Bowden is not using working capital efficiently to produce sales. The industry median is 17.2; Bowden must boost sales.

Net profit on sales ratio = $\dfrac{\$60,060}{\$780,000}$ = .077

Each dollar of sales yields 7.7 cents in profit for Bowden, below the industry median of 9.0 cents.

Net profit to equity ratio = $\dfrac{\$60,000}{\$130,000}$ = .462

Bowden's rate of return on his investments in the business is 46.2 percent, well above the industry median of 22.2 percent. This reflects Bowden's low investment in the business.

2.   Were the bankers correct? Do you think Jim should expand the business?

Bowden needs to increase sales, and expanding the business could help; but, Jim may have a problem obtaining a loan since creditors have provided three times as much capital as he has. Also, Jim seems to rely on inventory to meet short-term debt. Still, with a sound business plan explaining how the additional funds would be used, Jim could probably obtain the financing he needs.

Case 10-3: Birmingham's Stereo Shop

Birmingham's Stereo Shop expects net sales of $280,000 in the upcoming year, with a cost of goods sold of $173,600 and total expenses of $76,200. Birmingham expects variable expenses (including cost of goods sold) to be $195,700 and fixed expenses to be $54,100.

1. What level of sales would Birmingham's have to achieve if it wanted to make a $25,000 profit?

    Sales needed to make $25,000 profit:

    $$\text{Sales} = \frac{\$25,000 + \$54,100}{.3011} = \$262,703$$

2. Construct a break-even chart for Birmingham's.

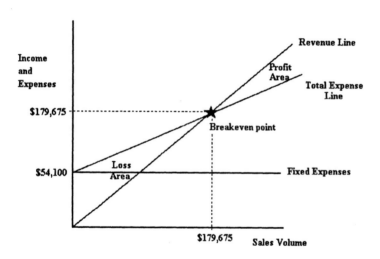

3. Compute a break-even point in dollars.

    $$\text{Contribution margin} = 1 - \frac{\$195,700}{\$280,000} = 1 - .6989 = .3011$$

    $$\text{Break-even point} = \frac{\$54,100}{.3011} = \$179,675$$

Case 10-4: Calculating the Break-even Point

A small manufacturer plans to sell tents for $120 each. The variable cost for each tent is $90. Fixed costs for the process are estimated to be $36,000. How many tents must the company sell to break-even?

Suppose that the manufacturer desires a profit of $9,000 on this process. How many units must be sold?

Price/unit	= $120
Variable cost/unit	= $90
Fixed cost	= $36,000

Sales required to earn a $9,000 profit:

Contribution Margin   = $120 - $90 = $30

Break-even Units = $\dfrac{\$36,000}{\$30}$ = 1,200 Units

Use breakeven formula and add desired profit:

Break-even Units   = $\dfrac{\$9,000 + 36,000}{\$120 - \$90}$ = 1,500 tents
plus desired profit

Case 10-5: A Projected Income Statement

You want to start your own retail furniture store, and you have already gathered a great deal of information on location, layout, form of ownership, business failure rates, etc.

In applying for a loan, you notice that a project income statement is required. Your problem is to complete this projected "P&L," given a desired income of $23,000 and the following published statistics. Show and clearly label all work!

Cost of goods sold	60.3 percent of net sales
Operating expenses	36.4 percent of net sales
Gross profit margin	39.7 percent of net sales

If a market survey indicates that your firm's sales would be $620,000, what net profit would you expect to earn?

First find Net Profit Margin Percentage

Sales	100 percent
- CGS	60.3 percent
Gross Profit Margin	39.7 percent
- Operating Expenses	36.4 percent
Net Profit Margin	3.3 percent

So... if Net sales = $696,970
Then Net Profit is...$696,970 x 3.3% = $23,000

Net Profit can also be calculated by using dollar values:

Sales	$696,970	100%
-CGS	420,273	60.3%
Gross Profit	276,697	39.7%
- Operating Expenses	253,697	36.4%
Net Profit	$ 23,000	3.3%

Note: percentages are approximate due to rounding errors.

Case 10-6: Crazy Harry's

The following is a pro forma income statement for Crazy Harry's.

Sales		$96,000
Cost of goods sold		46,240
Gross profit		$49,760
Fixed expenses		
Rent	$ 2,400	
Insurance	3,000	
Salaries	16,500	
Taxes	1,100	
Miscellaneous fixed expenses	900	
Total fixed expenses		$23,900
Variable expenses		
Wages	$11,200	
Advertising	5,700	
Benefits	2,800	
Other variable expenses	1,120	
Total variable expenses		$20,080
Net profit		$ 5,040

1. Calculate Harry's break-even point.

Break-even point:
Variable costs = $46,240 + $20,080 = $66,320
Contribution margin = $1 - \frac{\$66,320}{\$96,000} = 1 - .6908 = .3092$
Break-even sales point = $\frac{\$23,900}{.3092} = \$77,296$

2.   Create a break-even chart for Harry.

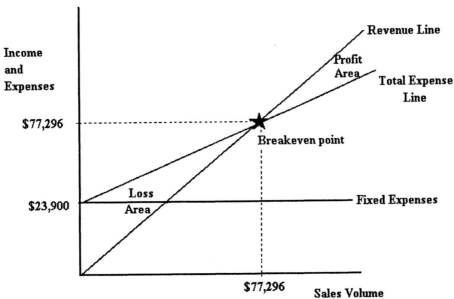

3.   If Harry's profit target is $15,000, what level of sales must be achieved?

Sales required to earn a $15,000 profit:

$$\text{Sales} = \frac{\$15,000 + \$23,900}{.3092} = \$125,808$$

Case 10-7: Sharps and Flats

Anthony Gray has been interested in music since he was old enough to sit at the piano. He literally grew up with music, and he used his talent to earn his way through college. Anthony has grown tired of his job at a large music house in Houston and is seriously considering moving back to his hometown in Massachusetts to open his own small music shop. In researching this venture, Anthony notices that he must include a projected income statement in his loan application. Use the following statistics from Robert Morris Associates' Annual Statement Studies to answer the following question(s).

Net sales	100.0 percent
Cost of sales	59.9 percent
Gross profit	40.1 percent
Operating expenses	31.2 percent
Net profit (before taxes)	8.9 percent

1. Suppose that a market survey indicates that Anthony's proposed business is likely to generate only $190,000 in sales. What net profit should Anthony expect to earn?

    If expected sales are $190,000
    Anthony's expected profit is:
    $190,000 x .089 = $16,910

2. Using Anthony's target income of $23,000, construct a pro forma income statement for Anthony's proposed music shop.

Net sales	$258,427
Cost of goods sold	254,798
Gross profit	103,629
Operating expenses	80,629
Net profit (before taxes)	$ 23,000

    To compute net sales: $\dfrac{\$23,000}{.089} = \$258,427$

Chapter 11   Crafting a Winning Business Plan

Multiple Choice Questions:

1. A business plan is a written summary of:
    a. an entrepreneur's proposed business venture.
    b. a business venture's operational, financial, and marketing details.
    c. the skills and abilities of a business venture's managers.
    d. All of the above.

    d., Easy, Page 359

2. A business plan:
    a. is a valuable managerial tool that helps an entrepreneur focus on developing a course for the business in the future.
    b. is a valuable tool for convincing lenders or investors to put money into the business.
    c. forces an entrepreneur to think a business idea through, considering both its positive and its negative aspects.
    d. All of the above.

    d., Easy, Page 359

3. A solid business plan:
    a. forces potential entrepreneurs to look at their business idea in the harsh light of reality.
    b. requires a potential entrepreneur to assess the venture's chances of success more objectively.
    c. helps prove to outsiders such as potential lenders and investors that a business idea can be successful.
    d. All of the above.

    d., Easy, Page 359

4. The primary purpose of a business plan is to:
    a. attract lenders and investors.
    b. enable an entrepreneur to take her company public.
    c. guide a company by charting its future course and devising a strategy for success.
    d. meet SEC and other legal requirements designed to protect lenders and investors.

    c., Medium, Page 359

5. The second essential purpose for creating a business plan is:
    a. to guide the operation of the company by charting its future course and devising a strategy for following it.
    b. to attract lenders and investors.
    c. to file with the SEC before making a public stock offering.
    d. to attract potential managers and employees to run the new venture.

    b., Medium, Page 359

6. Potential investors tend to believe that if an entrepreneur can't develop a good plan,
    a. he is probably the action-oriented sort of person they need running a business.
    b. he needs to hire a consultant to write the plan for him.
    c. he probably lacks the discipline to run a business.
    d. he is just like the majority of entrepreneurs and will probably do quite well.

    c., Medium, Page 361

7. Before putting their money into a business idea, potential lenders and investors:
    a. look for entrepreneurs who have evaluated the risk in the business venture realistically and have a strategy for addressing it.
    b. want proof that the business will become profitable.
    c. want proof that the business will produce a reasonable return on their investment.
    d. All of the above.

    d., Easy, Page 361

8. Which of the following is **not** true according to the "two-thirds rule?"
    a. Only two-thirds of entrepreneurs with a sound and viable business venture will find financial backing.
    b. Entrepreneurs who do get financing for their business will get only two-thirds of the capital they initially requested.
    c. Entrepreneurs who do get financing for their businesses will find that it takes them two-thirds longer to get it than they anticipated.
    d. Only two-thirds of entrepreneurs will take the time to prepare a business plan.

    d., Medium, Page 361

9. _____ is an entrepreneur's best insurance against launching a business destined to fail or mismanaging a potentially successful company.
    a. Bankrolling the business with plenty of startup capital
    b. Creating a solid business plan
    c. Spending lots of money on marketing and advertising
    d. Hiring a team of accountants and attorneys as advisors

    b., Medium, Page 361

10. To get external financing, an entrepreneur's plan must pass the _____ tests with potential lenders and investors.
    a. reality, competitive, and value
    b. competitive, profitability, and value
    c. value, reality, and profitability
    d. None of the above.

    d., Medium, Page 360

11.   The _____ test that a business plan must pass in order to attract financing from lenders and investors involves proving that a business venture offers a high probability of repayment or an attractive rate of return.
       a.   reality
       b.   competitive
       c.   value
       d.   profitability

       c., Medium, Page 360

12.   The _____ test that a business plan must pass in order to attract financing from lenders and investors involves proving that a market for the company's product or service actually does exist and that the company actually can build it for the cost estimates included in the plan.
       a.   reality
       b.   competitive
       c.   value
       d.   profitability

       a., Medium, Page 360

13.   The value test that a business plan must pass in order to attract financing from lenders and investors involves proving:
       a.   that the company can gain a competitive advantage over its key competitors.
       b.   that the business venture will provide lenders and investors a high probability of repayment or an attractive rate of return.
       c.   that a market for the company's product or service actually does exist and that the company can actually build it for the cost estimates included in the plan.
       d.   that the industry in which the business will compete is growing faster than the overall economy and has room for more competitors.

       b., Medium, Page 360

14.   The competitive test that a business plan must pass in order to attract financing from lenders and investors involves proving:
       a.   that the company can gain a competitive advantage over its key competitors.
       b.   that the business venture will provide lenders and investors a high probability of repayment or an attractive rate of return.
       c.   that a market for the company's product or service actually does exist and that the company can actually build it for the cost estimates included in the plan.
       d.   that the industry in which the business will compete is growing faster than the overall economy and has room for more competitors.

       a., Medium, Page 360

15. The reality test that a business plan must pass in order to attract financing from lenders and investors involves proving:
    a. that the company can gain a competitive advantage over its key competitors.
    b. that the business venture will provide lenders and investors a high probability of repayment or an attractive rate of return.
    c. that a market for the company's product or service actually does exist and that the company can actually build it for the cost estimates included in the plan.
    d. that the industry in which the business will compete is growing faster than the overall economy and has room for more competitors.

c., Medium, Page 360

16. Which of the following is **not** true regarding the process of building a business plan:
    a. It is not very valuable when compared with the final plan itself.
    b. It allows an entrepreneur to replace "I thinks" with more "I knows" and to make mistakes on paper, which is cheaper than making them in reality.
    c. It reduces the risk and uncertainty of launching a company by teaching the entrepreneur to do it the right way.
    d. It requires an entrepreneur to subject his idea to an objective, critical evaluation.

a., Medium, Page 360

17. Which of the following is true about the preparation of a business plan?
    a. The format should follow a "cookie-cutter" approach to ensure uniformity and consistency with others and to promote ease of understanding.
    b. The elements of the plan may be standard, but the content should reflect the unique aspects of the business and the excitement of the entrepreneur.
    c. The plan should cover every standard element in great detail and be at least 100 pages long to prove to potential lenders and investors that the entrepreneur has studied the business and the market opportunity.
    d. Entrepreneur should avoid seeking the advice of professionals, such as accountants, business professors, and attorneys.

b., Medium, Page 361

18. Ideally, a business plan should range from _____ pages in length.
    a. 10 to 20
    b. 25 to 50
    c. 40 to 75
    d. 50 to 100

b., Medium, Page 362

19. The executive summary section of the business plan:
    a. is the last section of the plan but should be the first part written.
    b. should be no more than 8 or 10 pages long.
    c. should summarize the essence of the plan in a capsulated form and should capture the reader's attention.
    d. All of the above.

c., Medium, Page 362

20. The _____ serves as the thesis statement for the entire business plan.
    a. executive summary
    b. mission statement
    c. company history
    d. marketing strategy

    b., Medium, Page 362

21. The company history section of the business plan typically includes:
    a. significant financial and operational events.
    b. highlights of the key goals and objectives the company has accomplished in the past.
    c. a brief description of when and how the company was formed and how it has evolved over time.
    d. All of the above.

    d., Medium, Page 362

22. The _____ highlights significant financial and operational events in the company's life and should concentrate on the company's accomplishments.
    a. executive summary
    b. company history
    c. business and industry profile
    d. marketing strategy

    b., Medium, Page 362

23. The _____ , also known as the "elevator pitch," is written last, but is included as the first part of the business plan; it should summarize all the relevant points in about two pages.
    a. loan proposal
    b. business history
    c. business profile
    d. executive summary

    d., Easy, Page 362

24. The executive summary section of the business plan:
    a. should be a concise summary of the business venture.
    b. should be no more than two pages long.
    c. must capture the reader's attention and entice her to read the rest of the plan.
    d. All of the above.

    d., Easy, Page 362

25. _____ are broad, long-range statements of what a company plans to achieve in the future that guide its overall direction and addresses the question, "Why am I in business?"
    a. Goals
    b. Strategies
    c. Objectives
    d. Key performance factors

    a., Easy, Page 363

26. The _____ acquaints lenders and investors with the nature of the business and the general goals and objectives of the company.
    a. executive summary
    b. company history
    c. business and industry profile
    d. marketing strategy

    c., Medium, Page 363

27. _____ are short-term, specific targets which are attainable, measurable, and controllable.
    a. Objectives
    b. Policies
    c. Goals
    d. Standard operating procedures

    a., Easy, Page 363

28. Issues such as market size, growth trends, ease of market entry and exit, the presence of cyclical or seasonal sales trends, and the competitive dynamics of an industry appear in the _____ section of the business plan.
    a. executive summary
    b. company history
    c. business and industry profile
    d. marketing strategy

    c., Medium, Page 363

29. Which of the following would be included in the description of the product or service section of the business plan?
    a. The position of the product in the product life cycle
    b. A summary of any patents, copyrights, or trademarks protecting the product or service
    c. A description of the features and the benefits customers get by purchasing the company's products or services
    d. All of the above.

    d., Easy, Page 364

30. A _____ is a descriptive fact about a product or service; a _____ is what the customer gains from that characteristic.
    a. feature; benefit
    b. feature; trait
    c. benefit; feature
    d. benefit; trait

    a., Easy, 364

31. What is the lesson to be learned about writing a business plan from Leo Burnett's statement, "Don't tell people how good you make the goods; tell them how good your goods make them"?
    a. The plan should emphasize the **features** of the company's products and services rather than their **benefits**.
    b. The plan should describe how the business will transform tangible product or service features into important but often intangible customer benefits.
    c. The plan should recognize that advertising is a waste of money for startup companies.
    d. The plan should focus on developing sales in a niche rather than across an entire industry.

    b., Medium, Page 364

Refer to the following information to answer questions 32 to 34:

Describing her company's revolutionary design for a bottle cap, Kyoto says, "It has a special locking mechanism that you know is engaged when a red panel is showing through this little window on top of the cap. If you want to keep unauthorized hands - for instance, those of children - from opening the bottle, you engage the locking mechanism. Unlike other childproof caps, however, this design does not frustrate adults who might have arthritis and elderly people whose grip may not be as strong as it once was." Removing the cap from the bottle in no time with just a few turns, Kyoto says, "They can open the cap quite easily by disengaging the locking mechanism this way...see? You get the safety of a childproof cap without the problems most adults have getting them off!"

32. The special locking mechanism on Kyoto's new cap is a _____ of the product.
    a. feature
    b. unique selling proposition
    c. benefit
    d. All of the above.

    a., Medium, Page 364

33. The fact that with Kyoto's new cap "you get the safety of a childproof cap without the problems most adults have getting them off" is a _____ of the product.
    a. feature
    b. trait
    c. benefit
    d. All of the above.

    c., Medium, Page 364

34. Which of the following would be considered a **benefit** of Kyoto's new cap?
    a. The special locking mechanism
    b. The red panel showing through the little window on top of the cap signaling that the locking mechanism is engaged
    c. The fact that you get the safety of a childproof cap without the problems most adults have getting them off
    d. All of the above.

    c., Medium, Page 364

35. In the business strategy section of the business plan, the entrepreneur should explain to investors:
    a. significant financial and operational events in the life of the company.
    b. how she intends to accomplish the company's goals and objectives.
    c. the nature and characteristics of the target market.
    d. All of the above.

    b., Medium, Page 364

36. Which of the following questions will probably **not** be addressed in the marketing strategy section of the business plan?
    a. Who are my target customers, what are their characteristics, and how many are in my company's trading area?
    b. What, why, and when do my target customers buy?
    c. What exit policy do I have in place for my investors?
    d. How should I seek to position my company in its market(s)?

    c., Medium, Page 365

37. An explanation of how the product will be distributed is contained within the _____ section of the business plan.
    a. description of the product line
    b. marketing strategy
    c. competitive analysis
    d. business strategy

    b., Easy, Page 365

38. Defining the company's target market, its characteristics, and its potential is part of which element of the business plan?
    a. Description of the product or service
    b. Marketing strategy
    c. Competitor analysis
    d. Business and industry profile

    b., Easy, Page 365

39. Proving that a profitable market exists involves:
    a. proving that customers in the marketplace need or want the good or service and are willing to pay for it.
    b. documenting claims about market size and growth rates with as much factual information as possible.
    c. making claims such as "This market is so big that if we get just 1 percent of it, we'll be profitable within 6 months."
    d. A and B only.

    d., Easy, Page 365

40. When formulating a marketing strategy, small companies usually are most successful when they:
    a. try to be "everything to everybody."
    b. focus on a particular market niche where they can excel at meeting customers' needs and wants.
    c. compete with their larger rivals on the basis on price.
    d. discover what the market leader is doing and pursue a "me-too" strategy that imitates the leader.

    b., Medium, Page 365

41. The focus of the competitor analysis section of the business plan is on:
    a. demonstrating the existence of the market for your product.
    b. showing that your experienced management team is better than your competitors'.
    c. demonstrating your company's advantage over competitors.
    d. describing your overall product line.

    c., Easy, Page 368

42. The plan of operation of the company within the business plan should detail:
    a. the experience of the management team.
    b. the production process for the product being sold.
    c. plans for keeping the important officers in place with the company.
    d. All of the above.

    c., Medium, Page 369

43. The organization chart is described in which section of the business plan?
    a. The plan of operation
    b. The resumes of the officers/owners
    c. The business strategy
    d. The executive summary

    a., Medium, Page 369

44. The form of ownership under which a company is organized appears in which section of the business plan?
    a. Marketing strategy
    b. Business strategy
    c. Plan of operation
    d. Mission statement

    c., Medium, Page 369

45. When creating financial forecasts in a business plan for a proposed venture, an entrepreneur should:
    a. be sure that all forecasts are realistic.
    b. list all previous loans which are in default.
    c. avoid including a statement of the assumptions on which financial projections are based.
    d. All of the above.

    a., Medium, Page 369

46. The loan proposal section of a business plan should include all but which of the following?
    a. A general request for funds without stating a specific dollar amount
    b. A repayment schedule and exit strategy
    c. A timetable for implementing the plan
    d. The purpose of the financing

    a., Medium, Page 370

47. Which of the following statements about the preparation of a business plan is/are **not** true?
    a. Grammatical and spelling errors in a business plan don't really count since potential lenders and investors judge the quality of a plan by its content.
    b. The business plan should be "crisp," long enough to say what it should but not so long that it is a chore to read.
    c. Always include cash flow projections for the venture, in addition to projected income statements and balance sheets.
    d. Always tell the truth.

    a., Easy, Page 370

48. Carly will be presenting her business plan to potential lenders and investors soon. Which of the following is **not** one of the suggested helpful tips for presenting the business plan?
    a. She should demonstrate enthusiasm for the venture but avoid becoming overemotional about it.
    b. She should use visual aids to make it easier for people to follow her presentation.
    c. She should avoid getting caught up in too much detail in early meetings with potential lenders and investors.
    d. She should use a great deal of technological jargon to impress the audience with her knowledge.

    d., Medium, Page 371

49. After presenting her business plan to a group of potential lenders and investors, an entrepreneur should:
    a. sit back and wait to hear from those who might be interested in the venture.
    b. conduct credit checks on all potential lenders and investors.
    c. take a proactive approach by following up with every potential lender and investor to whom she makes a presentation.
    d. None of the above.

    c., Medium, Page 372

50. The most common reason cited by banks for rejecting small business loans is:
     a. poor credit history.
     b. undercapitalization and too much debt.
     c. lack of collateral.
     d. insufficient cash flow or poor profitability.

     b., Medium, Page 373

True/False Questions:

51. A business plan is a written summary of an entrepreneur's proposed venture, its operational and financial details, its marketing opportunities and strategy, and its managers' skills and abilities.

     True, Easy, Page 359

52. A recent survey of small companies found that only 14 percent had created an annual written business plan and that 60 percent had no written plans of any type.

     True, Difficult, Page 359

53. The primary purpose of building a business plan is to raise capital.

     False, Medium, Page 359

54. A well-prepared business plan forces an entrepreneur to assess the venture's chances of success more objectively.

     True, Easy, Page 359

55. To get external financing, an entrepreneur's business plan must pass the reality test, the competitive test, and the value test with potential lenders and investors.

     True, Medium, Page 360

56. The competitive test that a business plan must pass in order to attract financing for lenders and investors involves proving to them that the venture offers a high probability of repayment or an attractive rate of return.

     False, Difficult, Page 360

57. The reality test that a business plan must pass in order to attract financing from lenders and investors involves proving that a market for the company's product or service actually does exist, and that the company actually can build it for the cost estimates in the plan.

     True, Easy, Page 360

58. The value test that a business must pass in order to attract financing from lenders and investors involves proving to them that the venture offers a high probability of repayment or an attractive rate of return.

True, Medium, Page 360

59. Sometimes a potential small business owner finds, while developing a business plan, that the business won't succeed; at least, it was before he committed significant resources to the venture.

True, Medium, Page 360

60. The real value in preparing a business plan is not so much in the plan itself as it is in the process the entrepreneur goes through to create the plan.

True, Medium, Page 360

61. The "two-thirds rule" says that only two-thirds of the entrepreneurs with a sound new business venture will get financing, that they will get only two-thirds of what they need, and that it will take them two-thirds longer to get it than they anticipated.

True, Medium, Page 361

62. Potential lenders and investors believe that an entrepreneur who lacks the discipline to develop a good business plan likely lacks the discipline to run a business.

True, Easy, Page 361

63. Because the entrepreneur is the driving force behind a business idea, she should also be the driving force behind the business plan.

True, Easy, Page 361

64. Before presenting a business plan to potential lenders and investors, an entrepreneur must be well informed and well prepared.

True, Easy, Page 361

65. Although building a business plan does not guarantee an entrepreneur's success, it does increase her chances of succeeding in business.

True, Easy, Page 361

66. A business plan should contain certain basic elements, but it should also be tailored to the individual company by emphasizing its particular personality and reflecting the entrepreneur's excitement for the business opportunity.

True, Easy, Page 361

67. The most effective business plans follow the "cookie cutter approach," following the standard format most preferred by lenders and investors.

   False, Medium, Page 361

68. The ideal business plan should be at least 100 pages long to prove to potential lenders and investors that the entrepreneur has studied the business and the market opportunity sufficiently.

   False, Medium, Page 361

69. The executive summary serves as the thesis statement for the entire business plan.

   False, Difficult, Page 362

70. The executive summary of a business plan should summarize all of the relevant points of the proposed venture and should be concise—no more than two pages.

   True, Medium, Page 362

71. The executive summary of a business plan should highlight significant financial and operational events.

   False, Medium, Page 362

72. The company's mission statement expresses in words the entrepreneur's vision for what her company is and what it is to become.

   True, Easy, Page 362

73. In the business and industry profile section of the business plan, the entrepreneur should provide information on the size of the market, growth trends, and the relative economic and competitive strength of the industry's major players.

   True, Medium, Page 363

74. The business and industry profile section of the business plan should cover existing and anticipated profitability of firms in the targeted market segment and any significant entry or exit of firms.

   True, Medium, Page 363

75. In a business plan, both company goals and objectives should relate to the company's mission.

   True, Easy, Page 363

76. Objectives are short-term, specific targets that the small company plans to accomplish.

   True, Easy, Page 363

77.   To be meaningful, an objective must include a time frame for achievement.

True, Medium, Page 363

78.   The business strategy section of the business plan addresses the question of **how** the entrepreneur plans to achieve the mission, goals, and objectives he has established for his business venture.

True, Easy, Page 364

79.   An important theme of the business strategy section of the business plan is what makes the owner's company original in the eyes of its target customers.

True, Medium, Page 364

80.   The safest strategy for an entrepreneur launching a new business to follow is a "me-too" strategy—copying products, services, and the images of already successful businesses.

False, Medium, Page 364

81.   The section of the business plan that describes the company's products or services should focus on how a business will transform the tangible features of its products or services into important but often intangible customer benefits.

True, Medium, Page 364

82.   A benefit is a descriptive fact about a product or service; a feature is what the customer gains from that product or service benefit.

False, Easy, Page 364

83.   When describing their products and services in their business plans, entrepreneurs must remember that customers buy the benefits from products and services, not the features.

True, Medium, Page 364

84.   An important goal of the "marketing strategy" section of the business plan is to prove that there is a real market for the proposed good or service.

True, Medium, Page 365

85.   Defining the company's target market and its buying potential is one of the most important and most challenging parts of building a business plan.

True, Medium, Page 365

86.   Identifying a specific target market is not an essential part of creating a solid business plan for a small company.

False, Easy, Page 367

87. The wise entrepreneur will indicate that there is no real competition for his new business venture, thereby increasing the likelihood that he will gain more interested investors.

   False, Easy, Page 368

88. A business plan that fails to assess a company's competitors realistically makes the entrepreneur appear to be poorly prepared.

   True, Easy, Page 368

89. Because gathering information on competitors' products or services, strategies, and market share is so difficult, most lenders and investors see the competitor analysis section of the business plan as optional.

   False, Medium, Page 368

90. The business plan should include the resumes of anyone with more than a 5 percent ownership interest in the company.

   False, Medium, Page 368

91. The most important factor in the success of a business venture is the quality of its management, and financial officers and investors weigh heavily the ability and experience of the firm's managers in their financing decisions.

   True, Medium, Page 368

92. Lenders and investors prefer experienced managers when they consider financing a business venture.

   True, Easy, Page 368

93. The plan of operation section of the business plan should address how the business plans to retain key managers and employees.

   True, Medium, Page 369

94. The business plan should include an existing firm's past three years of financial statements as well as its projected statements.

   True, Medium, Page 369

95. Essential pieces of information for potential lenders and investors include the assumptions the entrepreneur uses to derive the financial forecasts and projections in the business plan.

   True, Easy, Page 369

96. An entrepreneur should prepare a single set of "most likely" financial forecasts for one year into the future as part of the business plan.

   False, Medium, Page 369

97. To make her business plan more attractive, an entrepreneur should include an exit strategy as a way to "cash out" for investors.

True, Easy, Page 370

98. Cash flow projections are not an essential part of a business plan as long as the entrepreneur provides accurate forecasts of the venture's profits.

False, Medium, Page 369

99. The loan proposal portion of the business plan should include a realistic timetable for repayment or for investors to exit.

True, Medium, Page 370

100. Entrepreneurs should artificially inflate the amount of a loan request and expect the loan officer to "talk them down."

False, Easy, Page 370

101. A lender's primary concern in granting a loan is reassurance that the applicant will repay it, whereas an investor's primary concern is earning a satisfactory rate of return.

True, Medium, Page 370

102. The entrepreneur's request for funds in the business plan should be specific and detailed.

True, Medium, Page 370

103. Spelling and grammatical errors in a business plan don't really matter; potential lenders and investors look past them at the **content** of the plan.

False, Easy, Page 370

104. Potential lenders and investors expect entrepreneurs to exaggerate the truth in their business plans, so telling the truth in the plan is really not important.

False, Medium, Page 370

105. A table of contents that allows lenders to navigate a business plan easily is an important element of any business plan.

True, Easy, Page 370

106. The quality of the entrepreneur's business plan determines the first impression potential lenders and investors have of the company.

True, Easy, Page 370

107. After presenting her business plan to a group of potential lenders and investors, an entrepreneur should sit back and wait to hear from those who might be interested in the venture.

      False, Medium, Page 372

108. When presenting his business plan to a group of potential lenders and investors, an entrepreneur should cover every detail in the plan, striving to answer every question his audience might have.

      False, Medium, Page 372

109. The most common reasons banks give for rejecting small business loan applications are undercapitalization and too much debt.

      True, Medium, Page 373

110. The most common reason banks give for rejecting small business loan applications is the entrepreneur's poor credit history.

      False, Medium, Page 373

111. The "C" of the 5 C's of Credit that is synonymous with cash flow is capital.

      False, Medium, Page 373

112. The majority of loans from banks make to small business startups are unsecured loans.

      False, Medium, Page 374

113. Most loans banks make to startup businesses are secured not by collateral but by the character of the entrepreneur.

      False, Difficult, Page 374

114. The entrepreneur's "character" (even though it is an intangible factor) and the quality of the presentation are important factors in evaluating a loan proposal.

      True, Medium, Page 374

115. The higher a small business scores on the 5 C's of credit, the greater its chances will be of receiving a loan.

      True, Easy, Page 375

Essay Questions:

116. Explain at least two functions or purposes of preparing a business plan.

      There are a number of reasons an entrepreneur should develop a business plan. First and most importantly, the business plan serves as a guide to company operations by charting its future course and devising a strategy for following it. It plans a battery of tools to help the entrepreneur lead the company and it provides direction for managers and employees. It gives everyone a target to shoot for and it provides a yardstick for measuring the actual performance against those targets.

A second function of the business plan is to attract lenders and investors. A quality business plan will assure potential lenders and investors that the business venture will be able to repay loans and produce an attractive rate of return. Building the business plan requires that the entrepreneur evaluate his or her business realistically and objectively.

Sometimes, the greatest service a business plan provides an entrepreneur is the realization that it just won't work. This benefits the entrepreneur if he or she is able to make this determination prior to committing extensive resources to the venture. In other cases, it reveals important problems to overcome before launching the business.

The real value in preparing a business plan is not so much in the plan itself as it is in the process an entrepreneur goes through to create the plan. What he or she learns about the company, its target market, its financial requirements, competition, and other factors can be essential to making the venture a success. In other words, developing a business plan reduces the risk and uncertainty in launching a company by allowing the entrepreneur to make mistakes on paper rather than in reality and to learn to do things the right way.
Page 359

117. To get external financing, an entrepreneur's plan must pass three tests with potential lenders and investors. List and briefly explain all three.

- Reality Test—You must prove that a market for your product or service really does exist. Focuses on industry attractiveness, market niches, potential customers, market size, degree of competition, and similar factors. These factors point to the potential for a strong demand for the business idea.
- Competitive Test—Evaluate your company's relative position to its key competitors. How do your company's strengths and weaknesses compare to those of the competition?
- Value Test—You must prove to potential lenders and investors that your business offers a high probability of repayment or an attractive rate of return.

Page 360

118. "Sometimes the greatest service a business plan provides an entrepreneur is the realization that the business venture just won't succeed." Explain this statement.

The business plan is the entrepreneur's best insurance against launching a business destined to fail or mismanaging a potentially successful business. Creating a plan also forces him/her to consider both the positive and negative aspects of the business, and to subject these ideas to a reality test. This process allows the entrepreneur to replace the "I thinks" with more "I knows. To expose flaws and make mistakes on paper is much cheaper than committing significant resources to a business. It reduces the risk and uncertainty in launching a business by teaching the entrepreneur to do it the right way.
Page 360

119. You have been asked to explain the basic elements of a sound business plan to your friend, who is considering beginning a new business. What elements should you recommend he include in his business plan?

Although a business plan should be tailored to fit company needs, it should include these basic components:

- Executive summary—concise summary of all the relevant points of the business venture; brief synopsis of the entire plan; must catch the reader's attention.
- Mission statement—expresses the vision for what the company is and what it is to become; broad expression of company's purpose and direction.
- Company history—highlights significant financial and operational events in the company's life; describes formation, evolution, and vision for the future.
- Business and industry profile—acquaints potential lenders and investors with the industry in which the company operates; includes summary of goals and objectives.
- Business strategy—explain how you can meet and beat the competition; addresses the question of how to accomplish your goals and objectives.
- Description of products/services—describe product line, product's position in the product life cycle, and any patents, trademarks, or copyrights; define features and benefits of products or services.
- Marketing strategy—prove that there is a real market for the proposed good or service; describe target market and positioning, advertising, distribution, and pricing.
- Competitor analysis—compare your strengths and weaknesses with those of your competition, images in the marketplace, level of success, etc.
- Description of the management team—describe qualifications of business officers, key directors, and any person with at least 20 percent ownership in the company; lenders and investors prefer experienced managers when making funding decisions.
- Plan of operation—construct organization chart; explain steps taken to encourage important officers to remain with the company.
- Forecasted or pro forma financial statements—include financial statements from the past three years (if an existing business) and pro forma for the next year (existing or new), including statement of cash flows; should develop realistic forecasts and a statement of the assumptions on which the financial projections are based.
- Loan or investment proposal—state the purpose of the financing, the amount requested, and either the plans for repayment (lenders) or an attractive exit strategy (investors).

Page 361

120. Explain the concept of a company's mission. What are goals? Objectives? How are the three concepts related?

- A mission statement expresses in words an entrepreneur's vision of what the company is and what it become. It is the broadest expression of the company's purpose and defines the direction in which it will move.
- Goals are broad statements of what a company plans to achieve. They guide its overall direction and define the basis of its business.
- Objectives are short-term, specific performance targets that are attainable, measurable, and controllable.
- Every objective should reflect some general business goal and include a technique for measuring progress towards its accomplishment. To be meaningful, an

objective must have a time frame for achievement. Both goals and objectives should relate to the company's mission statement.
Page 362-363

121. The marketing strategy section is a vital part of any business plan. What issues should it address?

- Who are my target customers and what are their demographics?
- Where do they live, work, and shop?
- How many potential customers are in my trading area?
- Why do they buy and what needs/wants drive their purchase decisions?
- How can my business meet those needs/wants better than my competitors? Knowing my customers needs, wants, and habits, what should be the basis for differentiating my business in their minds?

Page 365

122. The financial plan within a business plan is of interest to potential lenders and investors. Explain the contents of this section and describe what potential lenders and investors look for.

For an existing business, lenders and investors use past financial statements to judge the health of the company and its ability to repay the loan and generate adequate returns. Ideally these statements should be audited or at least reviewed by a certified public accountant. Pro forma income statements, balance sheets and cash flow statements for the coming year and at least three more accounting periods should also be prepared—covering pessimistic, most likely and optimistic estimates. A breakeven and ratio analysis should also be done.

It is also important to include a statement of assumptions on which these financial projections were based because potential lenders and investors will view them as being more credible than a single set of overly optimistic figures. Lenders and investors also look for honest, realistic forecasts and compare them to industry standards.
Page 369

123. What tips would you offer an entrepreneur who is scheduled to present her business plan to a group of potential lenders and investors in one week?

- As with all presentations, entrepreneurs should be informed and well-prepared beforehand. The following tips might also be helpful:
- Demonstrate enthusiasm, but don't be overemotional.
- "Hook" investors quickly with an up-front explanation of the new venture, its opportunities, and the anticipated benefits to them.
- Use visual aids.
- Hit the highlights; leave details to questions and future meetings.
- Avoid the use of technological terms.
- Close by reinforcing the nature of the opportunity and relating benefits to investors.
- Be prepared for questions.
- Follow up with every investor you make a presentation to.

Page 371

124. When making a loan to a small business, bankers tend to look for the 5 Cs. List and explain each of the 5 Cs of credit.

Bankers score the small business in terms of the five Cs. The greater the score, the higher probability that the small business will receive the loan.

- Capital—A small business must have a stable capital base before a bank will grant a loan. The most common reasons that banks give for rejecting loans are undercapitalization or too much debt. The bank expects the small business to have an equity base of investment by the owner(s) that will help support the venture during times of financial stress.
- Capacity—The bank must be convinced that the small business has sufficient cash flow to meet its regular financial obligations and to repay the bank loan. The bank expects the applicant to pass the test for liquidity, especially for short-term loans.
- Collateral—Collateral is the bank's security for repayment of the loan. If the company defaults on the loan, the bank has the right to sell the collateral and use the proceeds to satisfy the loan. Banks view the owner's willingness to pledge collateral (personal or business assets) as an indication of dedication to making the venture successful.
- Character—The loan officer's evaluation of the owner's character (honesty, competence, polish, determination, intelligence, and ability)play a critical role in the banker's decision. The applicant can possibly enhance the officer's view of his character with a thorough business plan and polished presentation.
- Conditions—The banks consider potential growth in the market, competition, location, form of ownership, loan purpose, and the state of the overall economy before making a decision on the loan. The owner should provide relevant information pertaining to these factors in the business plan.

Page 372

Chapter 10
Crafting a Winning Business Plan
Mini-Case

Case 10-1: The Need For A Plan

Twenty-three year-old Shirley Halperin had just been kicked off the staff of her college newspaper, when she launched Smug magazine with just $1,700 in personal savings, $7,000 in donations, and a $10,000 loan, co-signed by her father Eli Halperin who helped her get a line of credit.

The ten-issues-a-year publication is targeted at music fans in the 16-to-30-year-old age group with well-written stories "about musicians that matter plus bands you haven't even heard of yet," says Halperin. It covers the alternative-music scene between the musical meccas of New York City and Philadelphia. Her enthusiasm for her subject has spilled over to the writers, editors, designers and photographers who now total 30, and continue to contribute without pay. They donate their talents for such incentives as by-lines, photo credits, college internships, job experience, free tickets to concerts, free CD's, and other things. Halperin cuts costs whenever possible and her frugality enables her to keep start-up costs low she runs Smug out of her Gramercy Park apartment with two roommates.

Smug charges $1,000 per ad. Competitive publications like Village Voice, Spin, and the Aquarian Weekly charge between $7,000-$29,700 for a similar ad. Halperin says that her budget ads are designed specifically for smaller bands with a regional following that haven't hit the big time yet. "It doesn't make sense for baby bands to advertise in the bigger publications until awareness of them rises," she says.

In less than 18 months, Smug's circulation went from 5,000 to 20,000, its readership expanded to 60,000 and advertising revenues climbed from zero to $15,000 per month. After publishing its fourth issue, Smug beat out its larger, more established competitors to win a prestigious local music award. Readers rave about the quality of the magazine's writing, its design and photography; however, Smug's continued success is not guaranteed. Half of all magazines fail the first year, and those that don't take five years to breakeven. If Smug succeeds, it can look forward to attractive profit margins of between 15-30 percent.

Halperin is very good at knowing what music people are listening to and what people want to read about; however, she is quick to admit that finance is not one of her strong points. Another concern is cash flow; at the end of its first year, $7,500 of Smug's and $70,000 in revenues were still in accounts receivables. Although she started Smug without a business plan, she now realizes she needs one to raise the $500,000 necessary to take the magazine "to the next level." She needs the money to upgrade the newsprint to semi-glossy paper stock, and most importantly, to pay her staff. She wants the plan to reflect her business philosophy: "Every year circulation should go up, your pages should go up, and your ad revenues should go up."

Questions:

1. Write a memo to Shirley Halperin explaining what topics she should include in her business plan.

    In their memos, the students should somewhat incorporate the uniqueness of each business plan as well as the importance of Ms. Halperin's personal input into the process. Suggested topics should include the following elements:

    Executive Summary
    Mission Statement
    Company History
    Business and Industry Profile
    Business Strategy
    Description of Products/Service
    Marketing Strategy
    Competitor Analysis
    Description of Management Team
    Plan of Operation
    Forecasted or Pro Forma Financial Statements
    Loan of Investment Proposal

2. What advice would you offer Halperin when she begins to use her business plan to locate capital?

    The students should stress the importance of having the business plan as "perfect as possible" when she uses the business plan to obtain capital. It is also important that students understand the importance of a business plan that is aesthetically pleasing and free from errors—the plan should have the look of a polished professional presentation parcel that details the company's past, present, and future goals. The following guidelines should be recommended as Ms. Halperin tries to locate potential investors for her enterprise:

Be enthusiastic, not emotional
Gain investors attention up front
Use creative visual aides
Hit the highlights
Don't get too technical
Close by reinforcing
Be prepared for questions
Follow up with each potential investor

In addition to the "showmanship" necessary for a good presentation, Ms. Halperin needs to have solid information concerning the 5 C's of credit, as this will ultimately be used to judge her worthiness for the necessary loan.

3.   If Shirley Halperin approached you as a potential investor, what questions would you ask her? Explain. Would your answer change the content of the memo in question #1 above? If so, how?

Several concerns should be addressed by the students. For example: how will the transition from an all volunteer staff with low advertising rates and minimal overhead be made smoothly to "the next level?" How is Ms. Halperin qualified to go to the "next level?" Why are accounts rewarded at $7,500? How does this impact the magazine currently? Are Ms. Halperin's growth projections feasible? If so, how? Has she conducted any type of market research to support her beliefs? These questions should all be covered by the suggestions for topics in # 1.

Source: Adapted from Alessandra Bianchi, "What's Love Got to Do With It?" Inc., May 1996, pp. 77-85. Essentials of Entrepreneurship and Small Business Management 2nd Edition

Chapter 12 Sources of Financing: Equity and Debt

Multiple Choice Questions:

1. When searching for capital to launch their companies, entrepreneurs should remember several "secrets" to successful financing. Which of the following is **not** one of those?
    a. Choosing the right sources of capital can be just as important as choosing the right form of ownership or the right location.
    b. The money is out there, but the key is knowing where to look.
    c. Creativity counts when searching for financing.
    d. Raising money shouldn't take very long; therefore, if it doesn't come quickly, it probably won't at all.

    d., Easy, Page 382

2. Unlike entrepreneurs of the past, today's entrepreneurs:
    a. are finding more government interest and funding for business startups than in the past decade.
    b. find fewer closed doors as small business startups have become less risky.
    c. have to piece their capital together from several sources.
    d. are spending a smaller percentage of their time raising capital for their businesses.

    c., Medium, Page 383

3. Most entrepreneurs are seeking _____ to launch their businesses.
    a. less than $5,000
    b. less than $100,000
    c. less than $500,000
    d. less than $1,000,000

    b., Difficult, Page 383

4. Which of the following represents capital?
    a. Inventory
    b. Equipment and machinery
    c. Cash
    d. All of the above.

    d., Easy, Page 383

5. _____ capital is used to purchase a company's permanent assets such as land, buildings, and equipment.
    a. Working
    b. Fixed
    c. Growth
    d. Stable

    b., Easy, Page 383

6. Susan borrows money from a bank to build up her inventory supply for the upcoming season, her busiest of the year. At the end of the season, she repays the money she borrowed. This entrepreneur was using _____ capital.
    a. fixed
    b. growth
    c. working
    d. robust

c., Medium, Page 383

7. Which of the following is not likely to be a use of working capital?
    a. Buy inventory
    b. Increase plant size
    c. Finance credit sales
    d. Pay wages and salaries

b., Medium, Page 383

8. The primary advantage of equity capital is:
    a. its lower interest rate.
    b. that it is readily available to a large number of entrepreneurs from a variety of lenders.
    c. that it does not have to be repaid like a loan does.
    d. that it does not appear on a company's balance sheet.

c., Medium, Page 384

9. The primary disadvantage of equity capital is that the entrepreneur:
    a. must repay it at some point with interest.
    b. must give up some, perhaps most, of the ownership in the business to outsiders.
    c. experiences the disadvantage of the risk/return tradeoff in the form of higher interest rates.
    d. B and C above.

b., Difficult, Page 384

10. Entrepreneurs are most likely to give up more equity in their businesses in the _____ phase of their companies than in any other.
    a. startup
    b. product development
    c. product testing
    d. product shipping

a., Medium, Page 384

11. The first place an entrepreneur should look for startup capital is:
    a. a bank.
    b. a venture capitalist.
    c. the Small Business Administration.
    d. his own savings.

d., Easy, Page 385

12. The largest single source of external equity capital for small businesses is:
    a. angels.
    b. venture capitalists.
    c. Small Business Administration loans.
    d. the stock market; i.e., "going public."

    a., Medium, Page 386

13. When looking for an angel, the key is:
    a. networking.
    b. waiting until you need the money.
    c. looking across industries.
    d. using computer matches.

    a., Medium, Page 386

14. Which of the following is **not** a characteristic of a typical angel investor?
    a. Investing money locally
    b. Purchasing majority ownership in the company
    c. Investing in the startup phase of the company
    d. Willing to wait seven years or more to cash out an investment

    b., Medium, Page 386

15. A/An _____ is a private, for-profit organization that purchases equity positions in young businesses that will potentially produce returns of 300 to 500 percent over five to seven years.
    a. commercial bank
    b. venture capital company
    c. angel
    d. SB-1 filing

    b., Easy, Page 389

16. The average venture capital firm screens about _____ investment proposals each year and ultimately invests in _____ of them.
    a. 10,000; 100 to 125
    b. 1,200; 3 to 6
    c. 5,000; 6 to 10
    d. 500; 80 to 90

    b., Difficult, Page 391

17. Although there is no limit on the amount of stock it can buy, a typical venture capital firm will purchase _____ percent of the ownership in a small firm.
    a. 10-20
    b. 20-40
    c. 50-60
    d. 80-90

    b., Difficult, Page 391

18. When evaluating a company as a potential investment target, venture capitalists look for all but which of the following?
    a. a competent management team
    b. potential for high returns
    c. convenient and profitable exit strategy
    d. stable industry

d., Medium, Page 391

19. Venture capitalists look for _____ as the most important ingredient in the success of any business.
    a. innovation
    b. a growth industry
    c. a competitive edge
    d. competent management

d., Medium, Page 391

20. Investment bankers who underwrite public stock offerings typically look for all but which of the following characteristics in a small company?
    a. a strong record of earnings
    b. a solid position in a stable market
    c. consistently high growth rates
    d. a sound management team with experience and a strong board of directors

b., Medium, Page 393

21. Less than _____ percent of all U.S. companies are publicly held corporations.
    a. 1
    b. 5
    c. 10
    d. 12

a., Difficult, Page 393

22. The biggest benefit of a public stock offering is:
    a. the capital infusion the company receives.
    b. the ability to use its stock to acquire other companies.
    c. a listing on a stock exchange.
    d. the ability to use its stock to attract and retain key managers and employees.

a., Medium, Page 394

23. To the entrepreneur who founded the company, the biggest disadvantage of making a public stock offering is the:
    a. dilution of her ownership interest and potential for loss of control.
    b. diminished corporate image.
    c. loss of key employees to competitors.
    d. reporting to the Securities and Exchange Commission.

a., Medium, Page 395

24. For the typical small company, the cost of a public stock offering is approximately ____ percent of the capital raised.
    a. 4
    b. 12
    c. 30
    d. 50

    b., Difficult, Page 395

25. The largest cost in a public stock offering is:
    a. printing expenses.
    b. filing fees with the SEC.
    c. the underwriter's commission.
    d. legal fees.

    c., Medium, Page 396

26. In an initial public offering, the underwriter (or investment banker):
    a. serves as an advisor and helps prepare the company's registration statement for the SEC.
    b. determines the price of the shares issued in the offering.
    c. sells the company's stock through an underwriting syndicate of other investment bankers it develops.
    d. All of the above.

    d., Medium, Page 397

27. The single most important ingredient in making a successful public offering is:
    a. choosing a capable underwriter.
    b. negotiating a favorable letter of intent.
    c. preparing a suitable registration statement.
    d. filing Regulation D with the SEC.

    a., Medium, Page 397

28. The document outlining the details of the agreement between the entrepreneur and the stock underwriter is called:
    a. Regulation D.
    b. a "blue sky" agreement.
    c. the letter of intent.
    d. the registration statement.

    c., Easy, Page 397

29. The "wait to go effective" is the time period when:
    a. the SEC registration statement is being prepared.
    b. the underwriter decides what Regulation to file under.
    c. the firm prices the stock for the offering.
    d. the company is waiting for SEC approval after filing the registration statement.

    d., Medium, Page 398

30. The formal underwriting agreement between the company and the underwriter is signed:
    a. on the last day before the registration statement becomes effective.
    b. when the statement of registration is filed.
    c. during the road show.
    d. at the time of the letter of intent.

    a., Medium, Page 398

31. Typically, the entire process of going public takes _____ , but it can take much longer if the issuing company is not properly prepared for the process.
    a. 30 days
    b. one year
    c. 60 to 180 days
    d. two weeks

    c., Medium, Page 398

32. The goal of the SEC's Regulation S-B is:
    a. to discourage small companies from trying to "go public."
    b. to make it easier for the SEC to detect companies whose stock would be bad investments for consumers.
    c. to open the doors to capital markets to smaller companies by cutting the paperwork and the costs normally required to make a public offering.
    d. to make the standards for making a public stock offering more stringent.

    c., Medium, Page 398

33. To be eligible for the simplified registration process under Regulation S-B, a company must:
    a. be based in either the United States or Canada.
    b. have revenues of less than $25 million.
    c. have outstanding securities of less than $25 million.
    d. All of the above.

    d., Difficult, Page 399

34. The standardized 50-question fill-in-the-blank registration statement that an entrepreneur uses when making a Small Company Offering Registration (SCOR) public stock offering serves as:
    a. a registration statement for the SEC.
    b. a prospectus for potential investors.
    c. a state securities offering registration.
    d. All of the above.

    d., Medium, Page 399

35. The maximum number of shares a company can sell under a SCOR is:
    a. 200,000.
    b. 10,000.
    c. 100,000.
    d. 1,000,000.

    a., Difficult, Page 399

36. Which of the following kinds of securities can an entrepreneur sell through a Small Company Offering Registration (SCOR)?
    a. common stock
    b. preferred stock
    c. convertible preferred stock
    d. All of the above.

    d., Medium, Page 399

37. The capital ceiling on a SCOR issue is:
    a. $100,000.
    b. $500,000.
    c. $1,000,000.
    d. $10,000,000.

    c., Difficult, Page 400

38. A SCOR filing has a number of advantages to it, such as the fact that:
    a. partnerships can use it.
    b. it is recognized in every state.
    c. a company may raise between $3 and $5 million per year.
    d. there is no requirement for an audited financial statement if the offering is under $500,000.

    d., Difficult, Page 400

39. Which of the following is **not** an advantage of a Small Company Offering Registration (SCOR)?
    a. access to a huge pool of equity financing without the expense of full registration with the SEC
    b. the ability to raise up to $1 million in a one-year period
    c. the ability to make the offering in several states at once
    d. the ability to market the offering through advertisements and to sell to investors with no restrictions and no minimums

    d., Difficult, Page 400

40. Which of the following is a disadvantage of making a public stock offering through a Small Company Offering Registration (SCOR)?
    a. Every state in which the offering is made must approve it.
    b. A limited secondary market for the securities may limit investors' interest in the offering.
    c. A company can raise no more than $1 million in a 12-month period.
    d. All of the above.

d., Medium, Page 400

41. In a Regulation D stock offering, the company:
    a. sells its shares directly to private investors.
    b. makes a private placement without actually "going public."
    c. does not have to register its shares with the SEC.
    d. All of the above.

d., Medium, Page 400

42. To qualify for a Rule 147 (Intrastate) public stock offering, a company must _____ in the state in which it makes this offering.
    a. be incorporated and maintain its executive offices
    b. derive 80 percent of its revenue
    c. use 80 percent of the offering proceeds for business
    d. All of the above.

d., Medium, Page 400

43. Because of the risk/return tradeoff, small businesses that borrow money repay it with interest at the:
    a. prime interest rate.
    b. prime interest rate minus a few percentage points.
    c. prime interest rate plus a few percentage points.
    d. lender's cost of capital.

c., Medium, Page 403

44. For small businesses, _____ are the very heart of the financial market, providing the greatest number and variety of loans to small companies.
    a. commercial banks
    b. factors
    c. commercial finance companies
    d. credit unions

a., Easy, Page 404

45. Studies suggest that _____ banks are most likely to lend money to small businesses.
    a. small
    b. large regional
    c. very large national
    d. foreign

    a., Medium, Page 404

46. A recent SBA study found that commercial banks provide over _____ percent of the credit available to small businesses.
    a. 22
    b. 40
    c. 60
    d. 80

    c., Medium, Page 404

47. Before making a loan to a business startup, banks prefer to see:
    a. sufficient cash flow generated by the business.
    b. ample collateral for the loan amount.
    c. an SBA guarantee to insure the loan.
    d. All of the above.

    d., Easy, Page 404

48. The most common type of commercial bank loan granted to small businesses is:
    a. the short-term loan.
    b. the line of credit agreement.
    c. floor planning.
    d. the unsecured term loan.

    a., Medium, Page 404

49. A _____ is an agreement with a bank that allows a small business to borrow up to a predetermined specified amount during the year without making an application each time.
    a. term loan
    b. factor
    c. line of credit
    d. floor plan

    c., Easy, Page 405

50. Banks typically limit a company's line of credit to:
    a. $10,000.
    b. 50 percent of the value of its inventory.
    c. 40 to 50 percent of its present working capital.
    d. 80 percent of its net worth.

    c., Difficult, Page 405

51. The Tanning Parlor is in the middle of the busy season. Owner Sunny Bright has hired extra help and encountered some unexpected repairs that have left her short of operating capital. What type of financing would Sunny most likely use in this situation?
    a. a line of credit
    b. floor planning
    c. a discounted installment contract
    d. trade credit

a, Medium, Page 405

52. _____ is a method of financing frequently used by retailers of "big ticket items" such as autos.
    a. Discounted installment contracts
    b. Trade credit
    c. Installment loans
    d. Floor planning

d., Easy, Page 405

53. When financing a business's purchase of equipment, a bank usually lends ____ percent of the equipment's value in return for a security interest in the equipment.
    a. 20 to 30
    b. 40 to 55
    c. 60 to 80
    d. 85 to 100

c., Medium, Page 405

54. When financing a small company's purchase of real estate, a bank typically will lend up to _____ percent of the property's value and will allow lengthier repayment schedules.
    a. 20 to 30
    b. 45 to 50
    c. 60 to 70
    d. 75 to 80

d., Medium, Page 405

55. The Boat and Ski Shop, a small retail boat shop, would most likely rely on which of the following methods to finance its inventory?
    a. Discounted installment contracts
    b. Floor planning
    c. Installment loans
    d. Trade credit

b., Medium, Page 405

56. A term loan:
    a. is typically unsecured.
    b. may contain restrictions or covenants.
    c. is based on past operating history and a firm's high probability of repayment.
    d. All of the above.

    d., Medium, Page 406

57. The most common method used by commercial finance companies to provide credit to small businesses is:
    a. asset-based.
    b. insurance based.
    c. unsecured lines of credit or "character loans."
    d. profitability-based.

    a., Medium, Page 406

58. Asset-based borrowing permits small businesses:
    a. to borrow up to 100 percent of the value of their inventory or their accounts receivable for the money they need for long-term goals.
    b. to use normally unproductive assets such as accounts receivable and inventory.
    c. to obtain loans more easily but with less borrowing power than using unsecured lines of credit.
    d. access to a source of funds ideally suited for long-term financing needs.

    b., Medium, Page 406

59. In asset-based borrowing, the _____ is the percentage of an asset's value that a lender will lend.
    a. prime rate
    b. margin rate
    c. advance rate
    d. discounted rate

    c., Easy, Page 407

60. Which of the following is **not** an asset-based financing technique?

    a. Discounting accounts receivable
    b. Inventory financing
    c. Term loan
    d. None of the above.

    c., Medium, Page 407

61. A company pledging its inventory, accounts receivables, or fixtures as collateral for a loan is using:
    a. floor planning.
    b. asset-based financing.
    c. trade credit.
    d. margin loan.

    b., Easy, Page 407

62. In discounted accounts receivable financing, a small business can typically borrow an amount equal to _____ percent of its receivables it pledges as collateral.
    a. 10 - 25
    b. 35 - 50
    c. 55 - 80
    d. 80 - 95

    c., Medium, Page 407

63. In inventory financing, a small business can typically borrow an amount equal to ____ percent of the inventory it pledges as collateral.
    a. no more than 50
    b. 70 to 80
    c. 85 to 90
    d. 90 to 100

    a., Medium, Page 407

64. When a small business is refused a loan because it is not profitable and deemed a poor credit risk, the owner can usually turn to _____ as a source of short-term funds.
    a. venture capital companies
    b. trade credit
    c. stock brokers
    d. loans from insurance companies

    b., Medium, Page 408

65. The owner of a small retail shop who needs to finance the purchase of display cases most likely would use which method of financing?
    a. Trade credit from equipment suppliers
    b. Discounted installment contract
    c. Floor planning
    d. Unsecured term loan

    a., Medium, Page 408

66. Janis Reardon is in the process of launching a craft shop. Her biggest supplier, Lothrop's Craft Supply, agrees to sell her the inventory she needs to stock her store on a delayed payment schedule. Janis is using what type of financing?
    a. Line of credit
    b. Floor planning
    c. Trade credit
    d. Asset-based borrowing

c., Easy, Page 408

67. The loans from commercial finance companies to small businesses:
    a. tend to be for smaller amounts than those from commercial banks, and at lower interest rates.
    b. are based on the strength of the small companies' earning power.
    c. tend to be at lower interest rates than those from commercial banks and are much harder to qualify for.
    d. are often similar to the types of loans commercial banks offer, but commercial finance loans usually carry higher interest rates.

d., Medium, Page 408

68. Savings and loan associations typically specialize in loans for:
    a. equipment.
    b. inventory.
    c. real property.
    d. accounts receivable.

c., Easy, Page 409

69. The most common types of financing commercial finance companies provide to small businesses are:
    a. accounts receivable financing and floor planning.
    b. floor planning and inventory loans.
    c. accounts receivable financing and inventory loans.
    d. inventory loans and unsecured term loans.

c., Medium, Page 409

70. A margin loan:
    a. is one made by a commercial bank to a small business whose financial performance is marginal.
    b. carries much higher rates because the collateral supporting it is so risky.
    c. is a loan from an entrepreneur's stockbroker that uses the entrepreneur's investment portfolio as collateral for the loan.
    d. must be repaid within 60 days or is considered to be in default.

c., Easy, Page 409

71. A loan from a stockbroker based on the stocks and bonds in the customer's portfolio:
    a. tends to be at a higher rate than a bank but easier to obtain.
    b. can be "called" for payment in a matter of hours or days.
    c. is for a maximum of $50,000.
    d. has a fixed repayment schedule and must be paid within 90 days.

b., Medium, Page 409

72. If the value of the borrower's collateral drops, a stockbroker can make a _____, requiring the borrower to provide more collateral for. his margin loan.
    a. broker's margin
    b. margin call
    c. broker's call
    d. None of the above.

b., Easy, Page 409

73. Insurance companies typically make two types of loans:
    a. policy loans and mortgage loans.
    b. asset-based inventory and discounted accounts receivable.
    c. short-term and policy loans.
    d. mortgage loans and unsecured loans.

a., Medium, Page 410

74. Which of the following life insurance policies would **not** enable an entrepreneur to borrow against it?
    a. whole life
    b. universal life
    c. term life
    d. variable life

c., Medium, Page 410

75. A(n) _____ is a private nonprofit financial institution that will make small loans to its members for the purpose of starting a business.
    a. SBIC
    b. private placement
    c. credit union
    d. insurance company

c., Easy, Page 410

76. A popular form of debt financing with large companies, a sort of corporate "IOU," which is becoming more accessible to a growing number of small companies, is:
    a. stockbroker-based loans.
    b. bonds.
    c. commercial bank loans.
    d. SBICs.

b., Easy, Page 410

77. A _____ is a hybrid between a conventional loan and a bond; at its heart it is a bond, but its terms are tailored to the borrower's individual needs, as a loan would be.
    a. private placement
    b. industrial revenue bond
    c. 504 loan
    d. zero coupon bond

    a., Easy, Page 411

78. Private placements of debt offer all but which of the following advantages?
    a. variable interest rates
    b. longer maturity times than most bank loans
    c. more willing to finance deals for fledgling small companies
    d. Actually, all of the above **are** advantages of private placements.

    a., Medium, Page 411

79. Which of the following is a characteristic of a typical private placement of debt?
    a. It carries a variable interest rate.
    b. Its maturity is shorter than most bank loans.
    c. Because of the higher risk, more restrictions are imposed on the borrower than with a comparable bank loan.
    d. It operates much like a bond, but its terms are tailored to the borrower's individual needs, as a loan would be.

    d., Medium, Page 411

80. SBICs:
    a. were chartered by the SBA to help startup companies find private financing from commercial banks and finance companies.
    b. provide short-term debt-based capital to small businesses through the sale of the debt to private investors.
    c. cannot invest in or lend money to a business for more than five years.
    d. were created by the Small Business Investment Act to use a combination of private and federal guaranteed debt to provide long-term capital to small businesses.

    d., Medium, Page 411

81. SBICs:
    a. tend to prefer later round financing over funding raw start-ups.
    b. can provide both debt and equity capital to small businesses.
    c. are prohibited from obtaining a controlling interest in the companies in which they invest.
    d. All of the above.

    d., Medium, Page 411

82. A(n) _____ makes only intermediate and long-term SBA guaranteed loans. It specializes in loans many banks would not consider.
    a. small business investment company
    b. local development company
    c. small business lending company
    d. SSBIC

    c., Easy, Page 412

83. A federally sponsored program which offers loan guarantees to create and expand businesses in areas with below-average income and high unemployment is called:
    a. the Small Business Administration.
    b. the Economic Development Administration.
    c. SBIC.
    d. U.S. Department of Agriculture's Rural Business Co-op Service.

    b., Easy, Page 412

84. Grants to small businesses made to strengthen the local economy in cities and towns that are considered economically distressed are made by:
    a. the Department of Housing and Urban Development.
    b. a local development company.
    c. US Department of Agriculture's Rural Business Co-op services
    d. the Economic Development Administration.

    a., Easy, Page 413

85. Malcolm wants to start a business in the prosperous little town of Grove City, a rural town of 10,000 about 65 miles from Pittsburgh, Pennsylvania. His business will create 25 manufacturing jobs. What federal agency would most likely be interested in guaranteeing a bank loan for Malcolm?
    a. The Department of Housing and Urban Development.
    b. A local development company
    c. US Department of Agriculture's Rural Business Co-op Service
    d. The Economic Development Administration

    c., Medium, Page 413

86. When a bank makes enough SBA-guaranteed loans to become a _____ lender, the SBA promises a faster turnaround time for the loan decision—typically 3 to 10 business days.
    a. preferred
    b. qualified
    c. certified
    d. LDC

    c., Easy, Page 415

87. When a bank proves the quality of its loan decisions to the SBA and becomes a _____ lender, the bank makes the final lending decision itself, subject to SBA review.
    a. preferred
    b. qualified
    c. certified
    d. LDC

    a., Easy, Page 415

88. Which of the following is **not** true regarding the SBA Low Doc Loan Program?
    a. It was created to help reduce the paperwork requirements involved in SBA loans.
    b. It allows small businesses to use a simple one-page application for all loan applications and has cut response time to these loans significantly.
    c. To qualify for a Low Doc loan, a company must have average sales below $5 million during the previous three years and employ fewer than 100 people.
    d. These loans may only be used for the purchase of fixed assets.

    d., Medium, Page 416

89. The majority of loans provided by the SBA are:
    a. direct.
    b. preferred.
    c. guaranteed.
    d. asset-based.

    c., Easy, Page 416

90. The average duration of an SBA loan is_____, while the mean loan amount is _____.
    a. 5 years; $95,000.
    b. 7 years; $135,500.
    c. 12 years; $232,500.
    d. 19 years; $450,000.

    c., Medium, Page 417

91. The average interest rates on SBA-guaranteed loans is:
    a. prime-minus-2-percent.
    b. 2 percent.
    c. prime-plus-2-percent.
    d. 7 percent.

    c., Medium, Page 417

92. Under the SBA's Certified Development Company Program, the entrepreneur provides ___ percent of the project's cost, the CDC puts up ___ percent, and the participating bank provides ___ percent.
    a.   10; 40; 50
    b.   40; 10; 50
    c.   50; 10; 50
    d.   0; 90; 10

    a., Difficult, Page 417

93. Which of the following restrictions does the SBA impose on a Section 504 CDC loan?
    a.   For every $35,000 the CDC loans, the project must create at least one new job or achieve a public policy goal.
    b.   Machinery and equipment financed must have a useful life of at least 10 years.
    c.   The borrower must be a "small business" and must not have a tangible net worth in excess of $7 million and a net income in excess of $2.5 million for the preceding two years.
    d.   All of the above.

    d., Difficult, Page 417

94. _____ were created by the SBA to provide loans under $35,000 that are normally shunned by banks.
    a.   Microloans
    b.   Preferred loans
    c.   Seasonal line of credit
    d.   Disaster loans

    a., Medium, Page 418

95. Small businesses devastated by floods, earthquakes, fires, and other maladies would seek assistance through which SBA loan program?
    a.   Calamity
    b.   Catastrophic
    c.   Disaster
    d.   SBIR

    c., Easy, Page 419

96. Under which state program are loans designed to encourage lending institutions to make loans to businesses that do not qualify for traditional financing?
    a.   capital access program
    b.   SBA7(A)
    c.   community development
    d.   None of the above.

    a., Easy, Page 419

97. Factors typically discount ____ percent of the face value of a company's accounts receivable.
    a. 5 - 40
    b. 10 - 20
    c. 60 - 95
    d. 95 - 100

    a., Difficult, Page 420

98. Selling the small company's accounts receivable outright to another business is called:
    a. collateral.
    b. factoring.
    c. trade credit.
    d. a line of credit.

    b., Easy, Page 420

99. Factoring:
    a. is a more expensive method of financing than borrowing from a bank.
    b. places the risk of uncollected accounts receivable on the small business owner.
    c. is best used as a long-term source of capital.
    d. is a type of trade credit.

    a., Medium, Page 420

100. A small business that uses factoring:
    a. pledges its accounts receivable as collateral to obtain a loan from a financial institution.
    b. relies on a third party consultant to apply for SBA-guaranteed loans.
    c. sells its accounts receivable to a third party to get the capital it needs.
    d. borrows money from lenders by offering them the option to convert the loan into stock in the company.

    c., Easy, Page 420

True/False Questions:

101. The World Wide Web offers entrepreneurs, especially those looking for relatively small amounts of money, the opportunity to discover sources of funds that they otherwise might miss.

    True, Easy, Page 382

102. Rather than piecing together their startup capital from multiple sources as they have in the past, entrepreneurs now are relying on a single source of funding.

    False, Medium, Page 383

103. Rather than relying primarily on a single source of funds as they have in the past, entrepreneurs today must piece together their capital from multiple sources, a method known as layered financing.

   True, Easy, Page 383

104. In startup companies, raising capital can easily consume as much as one-half of the entrepreneur's time and take many months to complete.

   True, Easy, Page 383

105. Capital is any form of wealth employed to produce more wealth.

   True, Easy, Page 383

106. Most entrepreneurs seeking money to launch their businesses need more than $100,000 in startup capital.

   False, Medium, Page 383

107. The creator of a computer software program and the originator of a small manufacturing process would likely have the same capital requirements.

   False, Easy, Page 383

108. A small company needs fixed capital to purchase its permanent assets.

   True, Medium, Page 383

109. Lenders of fixed capital expect the assets purchased to increase the borrowing firm's efficiency, profitability, and cash flows.

   True, Medium, Page 383

110. Working capital is the financing used to purchase a business's permanent assets such as buildings, land, and equipment.

   False, Easy, Page 383

111. Working capital is not related to the seasonal fluctuations of a business but is needed when a company is expanding.

   False, Medium, Page 383

112. A company that is experiencing rapid expansion has similar capital requirements as those of a fledgling business.

   True, Medium, Page 384

113. While equity capital represents the personal investment of the owner(s) of a business and does not have to be repaid, debt capital is a liability that must be repaid with interest in the future.

     True, Easy, Page 384

114. Entrepreneurs are most likely to give up more equity in their businesses in the startup phase than in any other.

     True, Medium, Page 384

115. Most small businesses that borrow money pay the prime interest rate minus one or two percentage points due to the risk/return tradeoff.

     False, Medium, Page 384

116. Unlike equity financing, debt financing does not require an entrepreneur to dilute her ownership interest in the company.

     True, Medium, Page 385

117. After an entrepreneur invests his own money for startup, he will typically seek additional financing from friends and family next.

     True, Easy, Page 385

118. Unlike venture capital firms and most other institutional investors, angels typically invest in businesses in their earliest phases, providing the seed capital needed to get the business going.

     True, Medium, Page 386

119. If an entrepreneur needs a relatively small amount of money to launch a company, angels are a primary source of funds.

     True, Easy, Page 387

120. Angels are **not** a good source of financing for entrepreneurs seeking relatively small amounts of money, as they typically do not make investments of less than $1 million.

     False, Medium, Page 387

121. Networking is one of the best ways to find angels, who usually prefer to invest in local businesses operating in industries they know something about.

     True, Easy, Page 387

122. One of the disadvantages of angels is that they are typically not willing to wait more than three years to cash out their investments.

     False, Medium, Page 387

123. Private investors, or angels, seek 60 to 75 percent annual return-on-investment, which is much higher than those of professional venture capitalists, and tend to take a 51 percent + share of the business.

False, Difficult, Page 387

124. Private investors look to earn the return on their investments in a business through the increased value of the business, not through dividends and interest.

True, Medium, Page 387

125. An option for acquiring equity capital is for the entrepreneur to take on partner(s); however, it is important that he consider the impact of giving up some personal control over operations and of sharing profits with others.

True, Easy, Page 388

126. Foreign corporations invest in U.S. small businesses through strategic partnerships in order to gain access to new technology, new products, and U.S. markets.

True, Medium, Page 388

127. A typical venture capital firm seeks investments in the $20,000 to $50,000 range and annual returns of 35-50 percent over three to five years.

False, Medium, Page 389

128. Venture capital companies reject 90 percent of the proposals they receive because they don't meet the firms' investment criteria.

True, Medium, Page 391

129. Venture capital companies invest only in companies in the startup phase.

False, Medium, Page 391

130. Venture capital firms rarely take an active role in managing the business in which they invest.

False, Medium, Page 391

131. Two factors that make a deal attractive to venture capitalists include high returns and a convenient and profitable exit strategy.

True, Medium, Page 391

132. The most important ingredient that venture capitalists look for in judging the potential success of a small business is a competent management team.

True, Medium, Page 391

133. In an initial public offering, a company raises capital by selling shares of its stock to the general public for the first time.

   True, Easy, Page 393

134. A public stock sale is an effective method of raising large amounts of capital, but it can be an expensive and time-consuming process filled with regulatory nightmares.

   True, Easy, Page 393

135. It is extremely difficult for a startup company with no track record of success to raise money with a public stock offering.

   True, Easy, Page 393

136. Few companies with less than $20 million in annual sales manage to go public successfully.

   True, Difficult, Page 393

137. The biggest benefit of a public stock offering is the capital infusion the company receives.

   True, Easy, Page 394

138. Only about half of the companies that attempt a public stock offering ever complete the process.

   False, Difficult, Page 395

139. Publicly held companies must file periodic reports with the Securities and Exchange Commission.

   True, Easy, Page 395

140. For the typical small company, the cost of a public offering is around 30 percent of the capital raised.

   False, Difficult, Page 395

141. The largest cost to a company making a public offering is the underwriter's commission.

   True, Easy, Page 396

142. One risk a small company runs when it is preparing to make an initial public offering (IPO) is that the stock market may be in a decline, making the IPO less attractive or impossible.

   True, Easy, Page 396

143. Since their stock offerings are small, most entrepreneurs are able to take their companies public without the assistance of accountants, attorneys, and underwriters.

   False, Medium, Page 397

144. The single most important ingredient in making a successful initial public offering is selecting a capable underwriter to manage the process.

   True, Medium, Page 397

145. The typical letter of intent states that the underwriter of a stock issue is not bound to the offering until it is executed, usually the day before or the day of the offering.

   True, Medium, Page 397

146. A company involved in an initial public offering may sell its shares of stock before the effective date of the offering as long as the investors are accredited.

   False, Medium, Page 398

147. The purpose of the road show coordinated by the underwriter of an initial public offering (IPO) is to promote interest in the IPO among potential syndicate members.

   True, Easy, Page 398

148. Not only must a company meet SEC requirements for a public offering, but it also must meet securities laws in all states in which the issue is sold.

   True, Medium, Page 398

149. The goal of regulation S-B's simplified registration process is to make it easier for small companies to go public by cutting the paperwork and the costs of raising capital.

   True, Medium, Page 399

150. Making a public stock offering through the Small Company Offering Registration (SCOR) is easier and less expensive than a traditional public offering, with typical costs being less than half and only minimal notification to the SEC required.

   True, Medium, Page 399

151. The capital ceiling on a Small Company Offering Registration (SCOR) is $1 million (except in Texas, where there is no limit), and the price of each share must be at least $5.

   True, Medium, Page 399

152. Entrepreneurs using a Small Company Offering Registration (SCOR) can advertise their companies' stock offerings and can sell them directly to any investor with no restrictions and no minimums.

   True, Medium, Page 399

153. In a Rule 147 (intrastate) offering, a company may only sell its shares to investors in the state in which it is incorporated and does business.

   True, Medium, Page 401

154. Because small businesses typically borrow small amounts of money, they pay interest rates below the "prime rate."

    False, Easy, Page 403

155. Commercial banks are lenders of last resort for small businesses.

    False, Easy, Page 404

156. Banks tend to be very conservative in their lending practices and prefer to make loans to established small businesses rather than to high-risk business startups.

    True, Easy, Page 404

157. Banks prefer to make loans to business startups because although the risk level is higher, the potential returns are also much higher.

    False, Easy, Page 404

158. A line of credit is a form of financing employed by sellers of big-ticket items such as cars, boats, and furniture, which the retailers pledge as collateral against the loan.

    False, Easy, Page 405

159. A boat retailer would most likely use a line of credit to finance the purchase of her inventory.

    False, Medium, Page 405

160. A business owner does not pay interest on a floor-planned item in inventory until it is sold.

    False, Medium, Page 405

161. Commercial banks are primarily lenders of short-term capital to small businesses, although they will make certain intermediate and long-term loans, normally requiring the loan to be secured by collateral.

    True, Easy, Page 405

162. When financing a small company's purchase of real estate, a bank typically will lend up to 75 to 80 percent of the property's value and will allow repayment schedules of 10 to 30 years.

    True, Medium, Page 405

163. Asset-based borrowing enables a small company to borrow money by pledging otherwise idle assets such as accounts receivable and inventory.

    True, Easy, Page 406

164. The most common form of secured credit is accounts receivable financing in which businesses can usually borrow an amount equal to 55-80 percent of its receivables.

True, Medium, Page 407

165. Typically, a lender is willing to lend a small business owner 100 percent of the value of accounts receivable pledged as collateral.

False, Easy, Page 407

166. Inventory-only deals are the easiest form of asset-based financing to obtain because banks like to have "tangible" assets backing a loan.

False, Medium, Page 407

167. Asset-based loans are an expensive method of financing because of the cost of originating and maintaining them and the higher risk involved.

True, Medium, Page 408

168. If banks refuse to lend money to a startup business, the owner usually cannot convince his vendors and suppliers to extend trade credit to him either.

False, Medium, Page 408

169. Vendors and suppliers often are willing to finance a small business owner's purchase of goods for 30 to 60 days, interest free, which is usually easier for small businesses than obtaining a bank loan.

True, Medium, Page 408

170. In an installment loan for equipment, the loan's amortization schedule would coincide with the equipment's useful life.

True, Easy, Page 408

171. Commercial finance companies are willing to take more risk in making loans than commercial banks, but they also charge a higher interest rate.

True, Easy, Page 408

172. The majority of the loans a commercial finance company makes are unsecured by collateral.

False, Medium, Page 408

173. Savings and loan associations specialize in loans for the purchase of inventory and for working capital.

False, Easy, Page 409

174. In a typical commercial or industrial loan, a savings and loan association will lend up to 80 percent of the real property's value with a repayment schedule of up to 30 years.

    True, Easy, Page 409

175. Loans from stockbrokers carry higher interest rates since the collateral—stocks and bonds in the borrower's portfolio—involve a high level of risk.

    False, Easy, Page 409

176. On a margin loan, if the value of the borrower's investment portfolio drops, the broker can make a margin call, requiring the borrower to provide more cash or securities as collateral, within a matter of days or even hours.

    True, Medium, Page 409

177. Insurance companies offer two basic types of loans: policy loans and mortgage loans.

    True, Easy, Page 410

178. Lending practices at credit unions are very much like those at banks, but credit unions usually are willing to make smaller loans and will loan only to their members.

    True, Medium, Page 410

179. Even the smallest businesses find it easy to sell bonds as a source of capital.

    False, Medium, Page 410

180. Companies issuing bonds to raise capital must follow the same regulations that govern businesses making public stock offerings.

    True, Medium, Page 410

181. Private placement debt is a hybrid between a conventional loan and a bond.

    True, Easy, Page 411

182. SBICs, privately owned financial institutions that are licensed and regulated by the SBA, provide both debt and equity financing to small businesses.

    True, Medium, Page 411

183. SSBICs provide financing to small businesses that are at least 51 percent owned by minorities or socially or economically disadvantaged people.

    True, Medium, Page 411

184. SBIC financing would be attractive to an entrepreneur whose primary concern is maintaining majority ownership in her business, as SBICs are prohibited from obtaining a controlling interest in the companies in which they invest.

True, Medium, Page 412

185. Small Business Lending Companies (SBLCs) make only intermediate and long-term SBA-guaranteed loans that many banks would not consider.

True, Medium, Page 412

186. The Economic Development Administration offers loan guarantees to create new businesses in economically depressed areas with below-average incomes and high unemployment rates.

True, Easy, Page 412

187. The U.S. Department of Agricultures Rural Business Co-op Service provides financial assistance to businesses that create non-farm employment opportunities in rural areas.

True, Easy, Page 413

188. To speed up loan processing times, an entrepreneur seeking an SBA loan guarantee should work with a bank that is either a certified (CLP) or a preferred (PLP) lender.

True, Easy, Page 415

189. To reduce the paperwork required and speed up its loan application process, the SBA has instituted the Low Doc Loan Program, which allows small businesses to use a simple one-page application, cutting response time significantly.

True, Medium, Page 416

190. Businesses can use Low Doc loans for working capital, machinery, equipment, and real estate.

True, Medium, Page 416

191. In most SBA loans, the SBA does not actually lend any money; it merely guarantees a bank repayment of a portion of the loan the bank makes in case the borrower defaults.

True, Easy, Page 416

192. When the SBA makes a loan guarantee, banks are willing to consider riskier deals that they normally would refuse.

True, Medium, Page 416

193. In an SBA loan guarantee, the SBA determines the loan terms, including the interest rate, which is usually set at or below market rate.

False, Medium, Page 416

194. The longer loan terms of SBA loans are ideally suited for young, cash-strapped companies.

True, Easy, Page 417

195. The average interest rate on SBA-guaranteed loans is prime-minus-2-percent.

False, Medium, Page 417

196. The SBA's Section 504 Certified Development Company Program (CDC), which provides long-term, fixed-asset financing, is designed to encourage small businesses to expand their facilities and to create jobs.

True, Medium, Page 417

197. The average loan in the SBA's Microloan Program is $100,000 with a three-year repayment term.

False, Medium, Page 418

198. Loans made under the SBA's Disaster Loan Program carry below-market interest rates and are designed to provide assistance to small businesses that have been the victims of a variety of disasters, such as hurricanes, floods, earthquakes, and tornadoes, as well as the terrorist attacks of September 11, 2001.

True, Easy, Page 419

199. Under factoring deals "with recourse," the small business owner bears the risk of uncollected accounts receivable; under factoring deals "without recourse," the factor bears the loss.

True, Medium, Page 420

200. Leasing is **not** an effective method for entrepreneurs to reduce the long-term capital requirements of their businesses.

False, Medium, Page 420

Essay Questions:

201. Define capital, describe the three basic types of capital small businesses require, and give an example of how each is used.

Capital is any form of wealth employed to produce more wealth and consists of:

- Fixed Capital—Capital used to purchase a company's permanent or fixed assets. Examples include buildings, land, and equipment.

- Working Capital—Capital used as the business's temporary funds and to support the normal short-term operations. Examples include accounts receivable financing, inventory purchases, and seasonal cash demands.
- Growth Capital—Capital used to expand an existing business or to change its primary direction. Needs include increasing plant size, expanding sales and production workforce, and buying additional equipment.

Page 383

202. Explain the difference between equity capital and debt capital. What advantages and disadvantages characterize each?

- Equity financing—represents the personal investment of the owner(s) of the business. The primary advantage of this type of financing is that is does not have to be repaid with interest. The primary disadvantage is that an owner has to share ownership and may lose a great deal of control of the venture, especially if equity capital is being raised in early start-up stages.
- Debt financing—involves the funds that the small business owner borrows and must repay with interest. Lenders of debt capital are more numerous than investors of equity capital; however, loans may be more difficult to obtain. The primary advantage of debt capital is that it does not normally remove ownership from the small business owner. Its primary disadvantages are that the debt must be carried as a liability on the balance sheet, and must be repaid with very costly interest payments at some point in the future.

Page 384

203. Your text describes eight common sources of equity capital. Outline and briefly describe five.

- The owner's personal savings are the most common source of equity financing.
- If the owner lacks sufficient funds, most turn next to family and friends for the needed capital.

Entrepreneurs can also turn to:

- Angels are wealthy private investors, often entrepreneurs themselves, who invest in business start-ups in exchange for equity stakes in the company.
- Partners who can share in operational control, equity and profits
- Corporate Venture Capital is large companies that provide capital as well as, shared expertise, distribution channels, marketing know-how, and introductions to important suppliers or clients
- Venture Capital Companies are private, for-profit organizations that purchase equity positions in young businesses they believe have high growth and high profit potential.
- Public Stock Offerings (IPO)
- Direct Public Offering (DPO) or Simplified Registrations and Exemptions

Page 384

204. Sarah's aunt and cousin have offered to provide some financial assistance for her new business. Should an entrepreneur turn to friends and family members for money to launch a company? Why or why not? If so, under what conditions?

During the last decade, the financial industry has been through difficult times with resulting credit crunches. Therefore, banks have tightened their lending criteria, venture capitalists have become more conservative, private investors have grown more cautious, and the issuing of public stock remains viable for only a select few businesses with good track records. Because of their relationship with the founder, friends and family are more likely to invest. Often, they are more patient and less meddlesome in the business affairs and say, "pay us back when you can." Therefore, this is an excellent source of "seed" money.

Unfortunately, however, unrealistic expectations or misunderstood risks have destroyed many relationships. To avoid such problems, the entrepreneur should honestly present the investment opportunity and the nature of the risks involved to reduce the possibility of alienating friends and family members if the business fails. It is a good idea to treat financial assistance from friends and family as you would that from others—a business deal.
Page 385

205. Angels fill an important role in equity financing of a small business. Discuss their role, their typical profile, and how to find an angel.

Angels are wealthy investors, often entrepreneurs themselves, who invest in business start-ups in exchange for equity stakes in the companies. They represent the largest single source of external equity capital for small businesses. The typical angel invests in companies in the start-up or infant growth stage. He usually invests in local companies in a clearly defined niche with market potential, a competitive advantage, and qualified managers. The real challenge lies in finding angels—the primary way to locate angels is networking through friends, attorneys, investment institutions, business associations, and other business owners.
Page 386

206. Venture capital companies are an important source of equity funding for small businesses. Discuss their policies, ownership control, and investment preferences regarding funding small businesses.

Venture capital companies are for-profit organizations that purchase equity positions in young businesses they believe have high-growth and-profit potential, producing annual returns of 300-500 percent over five to seven years. The screening process of venture capital firms is extremely stringent. These companies rely heavily on their gut instinct, but they do tend to look for small businesses that have competent management, a competitive edge, and exist in a growth industry.

Typically, venture capital companies invest in high-tech industries such as computer software, medical care, biotechnology, and communications, but any company with extraordinary growth potential can possibly attract venture capital. Most venture capitalists prefer to purchase 20-40 percent of a business through common stock or convertible preferred stock; however, they may buy 70 percent or more of a company's stock, leaving its founders with a minority share. Although venture capitalists prefer to let the founding team of managers employ its skill to operate the business, they usually join the boards of directors and/or send in some new management to protect their investment. Also, since venture capital companies are becoming so popular and large, many are choosing to focus their investments in "niches."

Venture capital firms differ from private investors in terms of return on investment. Whereas angels require 20-50 percent ROI, venture capitalists shoot for 60-75 percent. Also, angels usually take less than 50 percent ownership control of the business, and venture capital companies base the ownership decision on the individual stability of the firm and the risk involved in the investment.
Page 389

207. What is an (IPO)? What type of companies should go public? Outline the advantages and disadvantages of and IPO. Also, outline the steps a company should follow in taking a company public.

An Initial Public Offering (IPO) is how a company raises capital by selling shares of its stock to the general public for the first time.

Companies attempting an (IPO) should have: a strong record of earnings, a consistently high growth rate, a three to five year record of audited financial statements, a solid position in a rapidly growing market, a sound management team, and a strong board of directors.

Advantages include:

- Ability to raise large amounts of capital
- Improved corporate image
- Improved access to future financing
- Attracting and retaining key employees
- Using stock for acquisitions
- Listing on a stock exchange

Disadvantages include:

- Dilution of founder's ownership
- Loss of control
- Loss of privacy
- Reporting to the SEC
- Filing expenses
- Accountability to shareholders
- Pressure for short-term performance
- Timing

The key steps in taking a company public include:

- Choose the Underwriter
- Negotiate a Letter of Intent
- Prepare the Registration Statement
- File with the SEC

- Wait to Go Effective
- Meet State Requirements

Page 393

208. Explain the role that commercial banks play in financing small businesses. What kinds of loans do banks offer small companies?

Commercial banks provide the greatest number and variety of loans to small companies. One study by the Small Business Administration concluded that commercial banks provide 64% of the credit available to small businesses. Banks tend to be conservative in their lending practices and prefer to make loans to established small businesses rather than high-risk start-ups. They also focus on a company's capacity to create positive cash flows.

Short-Term Loans, the most common type of commercial loan, are extended for less than one year. They consist of the following types:
- Commercial Loans—Basic short-term loan that is usually repaid as a lump sum within three to six months and is unsecured.
- Lines of Credit—A short-term loan with a pre-set limit which provides cash flow for day-to-day operations. It is usually extended for one year and is secured by collateral. There are seasonal lines of credit to finance such needs as inventory or accounts receivable. Sustained growth lines of credit are designed to finance rapidly growing companies' cash flow needs over a longer period of time.
- Floor Planning—This is a form of financing frequently employed by retailers of "big ticket items" that are easily distinguishable from one another (usually by serial number).

Intermediate and Long-Term Loans are extended for one year or longer are normally used to increase fixed- and growth-capital balances. Loan repayments are usually made monthly or quarterly. One of the most common types is an installment loan.
Page 404

209. What is asset-based borrowing? Explain the two major types of asset based borrowing, including the pros and cons of each.

Asset-based lenders, which are normally smaller commercial banks, commercial finance companies, or specialty lenders, allow small businesses to borrow money by pledging otherwise idle assets such as accounts receivable, inventory, or purchase orders as collateral. Cash-poor but asset-rich small companies can use normally unproductive assets such as accounts receivable, inventory, fixtures, and purchase orders to finance growth and the cash crises that normally accompany it. The amount a small business can borrow is determined by the advance rate, a percentage of the assets' determined value, which is often discounted. Asset based lending is a powerful tool. A small business can borrow an amount significantly larger than it normally could without pledging these assets; however, still typically only 55 to 80 percent of the value of the receivables. It is a more costly method of financing, because of origination and monitoring fees. Rates can run from two to three points above the prime rate.

The most common form of secured credit is accounts receivable financing. Under this arrangement a small business pledges its accounts receivables. The lender does not accept past due receivables. Inventory financing is secured by inventory in the form of

raw materials, work in progress, and finished goods. Usually, lenders are willing to lend only a portion of the value of the inventory—typically no more than 50 percent.
Page 406

210. Explain the differences in the lending practices of commercial banks, commercial finance companies, and savings and loans associations.

- Commercial Banks—provide the greatest number and variety of loans to small businesses.
  Banks tend to be conservative in their lending practices and prefer to make loans to established businesses rather than high-risk startups. Banks are interested in a company's track record. They also want proof of stability. Banks like to see sufficient cash flow to repay the loan, ample collateral to secure it, or the Small Business Administration guarantee to ensure it. Studies suggest that small banks with assets of under $300 million in assets, are most likely to lend to small businesses.
- Commercial finance companies—are willing to tolerate more risk than banks. They rely more on obtaining a security interest in some type of collateral and are less interested in future financial projections. They provide similar loans to small businesses; however, they charge a higher rate of interest, usually at least prime plus 4 percent. Their most common loans are asset-based, accounts receivable and inventory financing with rates as high as 20 to 30 percent, including fees.
- Savings and Loans Associations—specialize in loans for real property, including commercial and industrial properties. S&L's will lend up to 89% of the value and allow a 30-year repayment schedule. They hesitate lending for specialized buildings or industries and rely on future profit projections for repayment.

Pages 404, 408-409

211. What is trade credit? How important is it as a source of debt financing to small firms? What role does it play in "bootstrapping?" What are some other bootstrapping techniques?

Trade credit revolves around getting vendors to extend credit in the form of delayed payments, usually 30, 60, or 90 days interest free. It is an extremely important source of small business financing, especially when small businesses are seen as a high risk by commercial banks.

Firms can generate internal methods of financing through bootstrapping which encompasses trade credit, factoring, leasing rather than purchasing equipment, using credit cards, and managing the business frugally.

Factors are financial institutions that buy business' accounts receivable at a discount. Under deals arranged "with recourse," the small business owner retains the responsibility for customers who fail to pay their accounts. The business owner must take back these unpaid invoices. Under deals arranged "with recourse," the owner is relieved of the responsibility for collecting unpaid invoices. The factoring company bears the loss if the accounts are not collected. Factoring is a more expensive type of financing than loans from either banks or commercial finance companies, but for businesses that cannot qualify for those loans, factoring may be the only choice.

Small businesses can lease virtually any kind of asset—from office space and telephones to computers and heavy equipment. Leasing allows the small business owner to use the assets without tying up valuable capital for an extended period of time, which improves his cash flow.

Credit cards are quick and convenient; however, entrepreneurs should be careful about depending on them for significant amounts of financing.
Page 408, 419

212. Briefly describe the two basic types of loans offered by insurance companies.

   - Policy loans—are extended on the basis of the amount of money paid through premiums into the insurance policy. It takes about two years for an insurance policy to accumulate enough cash surrender value to justify a loan against it. An entrepreneur may borrow up to 95% of the policy value, interest is paid annually and repayment may be deferred indefinitely.
   - Mortgage loans—on a long-term basis on real property worth a minimum of $500,000. They are based primarily on the real property being purchased and finance between 75-80% of the real estate's value. The normal repayment schedule is 25-30 years.

Page 410

213. Explain how a typical SBA Loan guarantee works. What interest rates do these loans normally carry?

The SBA has several loan programs designed to help finance both startup and existing businesses that cannot qualify for traditional loans because of their thin asset base or their high risk of failure. The SBA works with local lenders to offer a variety of loan programs. The SBA does not actually lend any money; it merely acts as an insurer, guaranteeing the lender a certain amount of repayment in case the borrower defaults on the loan.
Contrary to popular beliefs, SBA loans do not carry special interest rate deals. The lender determines the terms and rate set within SBA limits. The average rate on an SBA loan is prime plus 2 percent, compared with prime plus 1 for conventional banks. The SBA also assesses a one-time fee of 3.875 for all loan guarantees. The most common loan is the 7(A) loan guarantee.
Page 416

Chapter 12
Sources of Financing: Debt and Equity
Mini-Cases

Case 12-1: "Where do I go now...?

Christine Hernandez is in the process of launching a restaurant. Christine has never owned her own restaurant before, but she has worked for two of the best restaurants in town. Starting out as a hostess, Christine developed a special knack for the business and quickly worked her way up to the job of manager. Her 18 years of experience have given her a solid foundation for running her own restaurant.

Christine has worked with a counselor at a nearby Small Business Development Center and a counselor from the Service Corps of Retired Executives to prepare a business plan. She asked two other consultants and an accountant to review the plan and incorporated their suggestions into the finished product. When Christine took her plan to her bank, however, the bank turned down her loan request of $165,000, citing the venture as "too risky, given the failure rate of restaurants." The bank acknowledged her experience as "a major asset," but said that it "could not expose itself to such risks in its portfolio." Christine heard the same story from three other banks.

Christine is confident in her ability to manage her own restaurant successfully, and she is determined to get the financing she needs to launch it.

1.   What might Christine do to convince a bank to lend her the money she needs to launch her company?

     Christine has discovered the disadvantage of approaching banks for loans to finance startup ventures: They are typically very conservative in their lending practices. Unless she finds a bank targeting small businesses as its primary customers, she's likely to get the same response from other bankers.

     Christine should consider equity sources such as friends and family members, partners, and private investors (angels). However, raising equity capital will require her to give up some of the ownership in her business, something she may not be willing to do.

2.   Review the various loan programs under the Small Business Administration designed to help finance businesses like Christine's. Which of these programs would most likely help Christine get the capital she needs?

     Christine should seek out a bank that is an SBA preferred lender to explore the possibility of getting a loan guarantee under the SBA's 7(a) loan program. With her experience in the business and a solid business plan, she would stand a good chance of getting the financing she seeks.

3.   What other sources of capital would you suggest that Christine explore?

     Other sources of debt capital are another possibility. Christine could approach her stockbroker if she has an investment portfolio, her insurance company (for a policy loan), friends and relatives (careful!), a state agency, or the SBA. Since she's already been turned down by four banks, Christine may be able to quality for an SBA loan guarantee, especially given her experience in the restaurant business.

Case 12-2: Bowden Brake Service

Jim Bowden has been operating his business for some time now and thinks it's time to grow and expand. To compute the cost of expanding his existing business, Jim Bowden makes the following estimates:

Adjacent lot	$ 40,000
Metal prefab building	25,000
Hydraulic lifts	15,000
Tools and equipment	9,000
Parts and inventory	5,000
Additional operating expenses	55,000
Total	$149,000

1.   Classify Jim's expansion estimates into the three categories of capital: (a) fixed capital requirements, (b) working capital requirements, and (c) growth capital requirements.

Fixed capital requirements:	
adjacent lot	$40,000
Metal prefab building	25,000
Hydraulic lifts	15,000
Total	$80,000
Working capital requirements:	
Tools and equipment	$ 9,000
Parts and inventory	5,000
Total	$14,000
Growth capital requirements:	
Additional operating expenses	$55,000

2.   Explain to Jim the possible (and realistic) sources of capital for expansion. Where would you recommend that he go for the funds he needs? Why?

To meet his fixed capital requirements, Jim should approach banks, savings and loan association, insurance companies, and the SBA. It is doubtful that venture capitalists would be interested in an investment in a brake repair business. Jim may be able to find equity financing in the form of a partner or a wealthy angel.

Jim could seek working capital at banks, savings and loan associations, the SBA, and suppliers.

Chapter 13 Choosing The Right Location and Layout

Multiple Choice Questions:

1. The **first** phase of determining where to locate a business is:
    a. choosing a state in which the business owner wants to live.
    b. determining which city has the demographics that best fit the business.
    c. conducting a specific site analysis.
    d. determining which regions of the country are experiencing growth.

    d., Medium, Page 426

2. Entrepreneurs using the Census Bureau's World Wide Web site to evaluate potential locations have access to which of the following information about the residents in those locations?
    a. income levels
    b. age distributions
    c. occupational data
    d. All of the above.

    d., Easy, Page 427

3. Which of the following information is **not** available from Census data?
    a. Education levels
    b. Income levels
    c. Expenditures on dining out
    d. Occupational data

    c., Easy, Page 427

4. Which of the following information is available from U.S. Census data?
    a. The value of the homes in an area
    b. The number of rooms in the homes in an area
    c. Number of vehicles owned
    d. All of the above.

    d., Medium, Page 427

5. _____, published annually, provides a detailed breakdown of population, retail sales, spendable income, and other characteristics for census regions, states, metropolitan areas, counties, and cities. It also includes analyses of changes in metro markets, descriptions of newspaper and TV markets, and summaries of sales of certain merchandise.
    a. Sales and Marketing Management's Survey of Buying Power
    b. The Commercial Atlas and Marketing Guide
    c. The Zip Code Atlas and Market Planner
    d. A Researcher's Guide to the 1990 Census

    a., Medium, Page 428

6. A publication that reports on more than 128,000 places in the United States, many of which are not available through census data, and includes eleven economic indicators for major markets is:
    a. The Topological Integrated Geographic Encoding Referencing.
    b. The Commercial Atlas and Marketing Guide.
    c. The Zip Code Atlas and Market Planner.
    d. Sales and Marketing Management's Survey of Buying Power.

    b., Medium, Page 428

7. A Geographic Information System (GIS):
    a. is a software package combining the ability to draw detailed maps with the power to search through databases.
    b. helps entrepreneurs discover important trends and characteristics in the population that otherwise might go unnoticed.
    c. can be an incredibly powerful tool for determining the ideal location based on specific criteria the entrepreneur establishes.
    d. All of the above.

    d., Easy, Page 428

8. TIGER:
    a. is a software package combining the ability to draw detailed maps with the power to search through databases.
    b. breaks down the population, retail sales, etc. by census region.
    c. contains the names of every street in the country and detailed block statistics for 345 urban areas.
    d. All of the above.

    c., Medium, Page 429

9. When choosing a state in which to locate, one must evaluate which of the following?
    a. the general business climate
    b. the state's business laws, regulations, and taxes
    c. tax incentives and/or investment credits
    d. All of the above.

    d., Easy, Page 429

10. A glass manufacturer that requires an extremely pure, very fine type of sand in its production process would be most concerned with which location criterion?
    a. business climate
    b. proximity to raw materials
    c. a demographic profile of the local market
    d. wage rates

    b., Medium, Page 429

11. When the cost of transporting finished goods to market is high relative to their value, the key location criterion is:
    a. low rental or lease rates.
    b. proximity to raw materials.
    c. proximity to markets.
    d. zoning regulations.

    c., Easy, Page 429

12. When would a business choose to locate near the source of the raw material?
    a. The company requires an important raw material that is difficult to transport.
    b. The company requires an important raw material that is expensive to transport.
    c. The company keeps its inventory of an important raw material low to keep costs down and counts on quick deliveries from suppliers.
    d. All of the above.

    d., Easy, Page 429

13. If a small business owner wanted detailed census information broken down into areas as small as a city block, she would refer to:
    a. TIGER.
    b. Population and Housing Characteristics for Census Tracts and Block Numbering Areas.
    c. Summary Population and Housing Characteristics.
    d. The Survey of Buying Power.

    a., Medium, Page 429

14. When examining a state's available labor force, the potential business owner needs to know:
    a. the state's labor relations history.
    b. the demographics of the target customers.
    c. both the number and education of the available workforce.
    d. the proximity of its customers.

    c., Medium, Page 430

15. A labor force that has technical training would be most important to a:
    a. clothing store.
    b. restaurant.
    c. skiing equipment specialty store.
    d. computer company.

    d., Easy, Page 430

16.   Which of the following characteristics for selecting a city would be of greatest interest to a retail store selling fine china and collectibles?
       a.   public services
       b.   transportation
       c.   zoning
       d.   population characteristics

       d., Easy, Page 431

17.   _____ is a system that divides a county or city into small cells or districts to control the use of land, buildings, and sites.
       a.   An enterprise zone
       b.   Zoning
       c.   Apportioning
       d.   Redistricting

       b., Easy, Page 433

18.   The purpose of zoning regulations is to:
       a.   restrict the growth of businesses.
       b.   contain similar types of activities in suitable locations.
       c.   help new businesses "incubate" in their startup period.
       d.   build the traffic volume for retail and service businesses.

       b., Medium, Page 434

19.   The Census Bureau has divided the United States into _____ Metropolitan Statistical Areas (MSAs) on which it provides a multitude of statistical reports.
       a.   74
       b.   146
       c.   255
       d.   619

       c., Difficult, Page 435

20.   The average census tract contains about _____ people.
       a.   500 to 1,000
       b.   4,000 to 5,000
       c.   8,000 to 10,000
       d.   80,000 to 100,000

       b., Difficult, Page 435

21.   **Moving from largest to smallest**, which of the following is the correct sequence for the Census Bureau's divisions of the United States?
       a.   Metropolitan Statistical Areas (MSAs); census tracts; block statistics
       b.   census tracts; MSAs; block statistics
       c.   block statistics; MSAs; census tracts
       d.   MSAs; block statistics; census tracts

       a., Medium, Page 435

22. The region from which a business can expect to draw its customers over a reasonable time span is called its:
    a. enterprise zone.
    b. zoning area.
    c. trade area.
    d. retail draw.

    c., Easy, Page 435

23. The primary variable(s) that influence(s) the scope of a trade area is/are:
    a. the character of the transportation network.
    b. the nature of competing businesses.
    c. the type and size of the business operation.
    d. the racial and political barriers in the local community.

    c., Medium, Page 435

24. Nature's Way, a health food store, has just opened in a popular neighborhood shopping center next to Silver's Gym, a physical fitness center catering to both men and women. Nature's Way is relying on which location principle?
    a. piggybacking
    b. retail consistency
    c. retail compatibility
    d. zoning

    c., Easy, Page 436

25. The index of retail saturation:
    a. is retail expenditures times retail facilities divided by the number of customers.
    b. is the ratio of a trading area's sales potential to its sales capacity.
    c. evaluates both the number of customers and the intensity of competition in a trading area.
    d. B and C above.

    d., Medium, Page 436

Refer to the following information to answer Questions 26-28:

An entrepreneur considering two sites for a men and boys' shop determines that he needs sales of $158 per square foot to be profitable. Site #1 has 13,500 potential customers who spend an average of $160.20 per year on men and boys' wear. Two competitors occupy 14,200 square feet of space. Site #2 has 10,800 potential customers spending an average of $152.10 per year on men and boys' wear. One competitor has 10,000 square feet.

26. The index of retail saturation for site #1 is:
    a. $150.21.
    b. $168.51.
    c. $152.30.
    d. $166.19.

    b., Medium, Page 436

27. The index of retail saturation for site #2 is:
a. $164.27.
b. $140.83.
c. $170.64.
d. $146.30.

a., Medium, Page 436

28. Based on the above calculations, what is the entrepreneur's best option?
a. He should choose site #1.
b. He should choose site #2.
c. Neither site meets minimum criteria of $158 per square foot.
d. Either site will work well since both meet minimum criteria of $158 per square foot.

a., Medium, Page 436

29. Shopping malls typically average _____ parking spaces per 1,000 square feet of shopping while a typical central business district offers _____ spaces per 1,000 square feet of shopping space.
a. 20; 1
b. 3; 6
c. 5; 3.5
d. 3; 8

c., Medium, Page 438

30. Carmen is starting a childcare center. One location, a former "biker bar," closed after a murder in the bar and is near a neighborhood where there are many single parents. What city site selection factor might give Carmen problems with her childcare center?
a. Transportation
b. Police and fire protection
c. The reputation of the location
d. Compatibility with the community

c., Medium, Page 438

31. Ben was doing more business than his store could handle. Because there were stores on each side of his location, he had to open a second store. This expense cut into profits and didn't really double his business. Ben had neglected to keep which site selection criteria in mind?
a. What is the proximity of the business to the market?
b. Can customers find the business? Is it visible?
c. Is there adequate parking?
d. Does the site have room for future expansion?

d., Easy, Page 438

32. Mary's successful clothing store was located on the back edge of the parking lot of a large mall. She didn't have to pay mall rents since she wasn't part of the mall, but drew a lot of customers who parked at the mall and then noticed her store. The mall developers built a movie theater on the part of the parking lot directly in front of Mary's store, basically hiding her from most mall customers. After about six months, Mary's business dropped off so much she had to move. What retailer site selection criterion forced Mary to move?
    a. Proximity of competitors
    b. Visibility
    c. Adequate parking
    d. Room for expansion

    b., Medium, Page 438

33. According to the International Council of Shopping Centers, which of the following locations offers the **lowest** lease rate per square foot on average?
    a. central business district locations
    b. regional malls
    c. shopping centers
    d. None of the above.

    c., Medium, Page 439

34. According to the International Council of Shopping Centers, the average cost to lease space in a central business district location is _____ per square foot, a shopping center is about _____ per square foot, and a regional mall is _____ per square foot.
    a. $15; $20 - $40; $43
    b. $20 - $40; $15; $43
    c. $43; $15; $20 - $40
    d. $43; $20 - $40; $15

    c., Difficult, Page 439

35. The central business district (CBD):
    a. is the traditional center of town.
    b. in many cities experienced decay in years past as customers began shopping more frequently at malls and shopping centers, but are now going through revitalization programs.
    c. attracts customers from the entire trading area of the city.
    d. All of the above.

    d., Medium, Page 439

36. Which of the following is an **advantage** of locating in a central business district?
    a. Low rent
    b. Easy and abundant parking
    c. The ability to attract customers from the entire trading area
    d. Moderate to low levels of competition

    c., Medium, Page 439

37. Which of the following are disadvantages of locating in a central business district?
     a. intense competition
     b. high rental rates
     c. traffic congestion and inadequate parking facilities
     d. All of the above.

     d., Easy, Page 439

38. A ____ contains from 12 to 50 stores and serves a population of 40,000 to 150,000 people.
     a. neighborhood shopping center
     b. community shopping center
     c. regional shopping mall
     d. central business district

     b., Medium, Page 440

39. A _____ combines the drawing strength of a large regional mall with the convenience of a neighborhood shopping center.
     a. power center
     b. community shopping center
     c. central business district
     d. strip mall

     a., Easy, Page 440

40. The _____ serves a large trading area (10 to 15 miles or more), contains from 50 to 100 stores, and draws customers from a population that lives within 20- to 40-minutes driving time.
     a. neighborhood shopping center
     b. community shopping center
     c. regional shopping mall
     d. central business district

     c., Medium, Page 440

41. The typical _____ is relatively small, contains from 3 to 12 stores, and serves a population that lives within a 10-minute drive.
     a. neighborhood shopping center
     b. community shopping center
     c. regional shopping mall
     d. central business district

     a., Medium, Page 440

42. Which of the following is an important consideration for an entrepreneur evaluating a shopping mall or center location?
    a. In terms of customer demographics, is the mall or center a good fit for my products or services? How much foot traffic and vehicle traffic does the mall or center generate?
    b. Who are the other tenants? The anchor tenants? Is there a good fit for my products and services?
    c. What are the mall's or center's vacancy and turnover rates?
    d. All of the above.

d., Easy, Page 440

43. A type of business that does well when located near competition is:
    a. one that has a unique product line, dissimilar to that of its competitors.
    b. one that carries products for which customers comparison shop.
    c. one whose location is part of its trademark.
    d. None of the above.

b., Medium, Page 441

44. Which of the following is the **greatest** advantage of operating a home-based business?
    a. The ability to save money by avoiding business startup taxes.
    b. The exemption that home-based businesses receive from local zoning laws.
    c. The low cost of setting up and operating the business.
    d. The ability to claim all household expenses as business deductions for tax purposes.

c., Medium, Page 441

45. Which of the following is **not** true of home-based businesses?
    a. Home-based businesses represent the fastest-growing segment of the U. S. economy.
    b. The biggest benefit of operating a business from home typically is its low cost.
    c. Home-based retail businesses represent the fastest-growing segment of all home-based businesses.
    d. None of the above.

c., Medium, Page 441

46. Which of the following is a potential **disadvantage** of a home-based business?
    a. Frequent interruptions of work
    b. Feelings of isolation
    c. Problems with zoning laws from running a business
    d. All of the above.

d., Easy, Page 442

47. Jan and Detmar Wolcinski live in a cozy house in a beautiful old neighborhood. When they bought the 152-year old house in which they live, they began remodeling it with one goal in mind: opening a bed and breakfast inn. The Chadwick Inn has exceeded the Wolcinski's expectations in its first year of operation, but now some neighbors are starting to complain about the increased traffic in their neighborhood and the late hours some of the Inn's guests keep. The Wolcinski's greatest challenge in the near future is most likely:
    a. convincing the local historical preservation board that the modifications they made to the house are in keeping with its historical character.
    b. zoning laws prohibiting commercial businesses in residentially zoned area.
    c. major hotel chains opening competing "bed and breakfast" hotels on adjacent lots.
    d. encroaching shopping centers and malls that push up real estate prices.

    b., Medium, Page 442

48. _____ offer new businesses the protection of low-cost locations and a multitude of support services in an attempt to improve the companies' chances of success.
    a. Research parks
    b. Incubators
    c. Industrial parks
    d. Discount malls

    b., Easy, Page 444

49. Incubator facilities are established in order to:
    a. revitalize central business districts.
    b. enhance economic development and diversify the local economy.
    c. centralize types of businesses and provide tax breaks to those businesses.
    d. reuse old military bases and abandoned structures in economically depressed areas of a city.

    b., Medium, Page 444

50. The most common sponsors of business incubators are:
    a. colleges and universities.
    b. government agencies.
    c. private investment groups.
    d. public/private partnerships.

    b., Medium, Page 444

51. Most business incubator residents are engaged in which businesses?
    a. heavy manufacturing
    b. light manufacturing, service, or technology-related fields
    c. mixed retail and restaurant business
    d. heavy manufacturing, food preparation and service

    b., Medium, Page 444

52. Which of the following do incubators offer their tenants?
    a. Flexible rental space at below-market rates
    b. Larger trading areas
    c. Exemptions from zoning regulations
    d. Lower, or an exemption from, state and city taxes

    a., Medium, Page 444

53. Which of the following do most incubators offer their tenants?
    a. Conference rooms/meeting facilities
    b. Business services on a shared-cost basis
    c. Management consulting services
    d. All of the above.

    a., Easy, Page 444

54. Firms that graduate from incubators have a _____ percent **survival** rate.
    a. 34
    b. 50
    c. 67
    d. 87

    d., Difficult, Page 444

55. _____ is the logical arrangement of the physical facilities in a business that contributes to efficient operations, increased productivity, and higher sales.
    a. The Index of Retail Saturation
    b. Layout
    c. Logistics
    d. The Sales Conversion Index

    b., Easy, Page 445

56. When evaluating existing buildings, retailers:
    a. need to find the lowest cost per square foot possible due to the need for maximum display space.
    b. should locate in store space previously occupied by a similar type of business.
    c. should recognize that the store's appearance and layout create an image for the customers of the business.
    d. can discount the interior appearance of the building if it has a strong exterior appeal.

    c., Medium, Page 446

57. To ensure that a building will accommodate expansion plans, a new business should:
    a. plan space requirements for one to two years into the future and update the plans every six months.
    b. build, buy, or lease facilities that are 50-100 percent too big for their current operations.
    c. buy or lease facilities that had the same type of business in them previously.
    d. always build a new facility.

a., Moderate, Page 446

58. Which of the following statements concerning layout is **true**?
    a. A company's physical facilities send important messages to potential customers about its "personality."
    b. The physical appearance of a building provides customers with their first impressions of a business.
    c. Communicating the right signals through a business' layout and physical facilities is an important step in creating a competitive edge over rivals.
    d. All of the above.

d., Easy, Page 446

59. Entrances should invite entry. The way to accomplish this is to:
    a. have wide entryways and attractive displays set back from the doorway that can lure customers into the store.
    b. offer discounts.
    c. have displays as close to the entry of the store as possible.
    d. have a big sign to attract customers.

a., Medium, Page 447

60. Under the Americans with Disabilities Act, a newly constructed:
    a. building must have elevators if they are three stories or higher.
    b. retail store must have checkout aisles wide enough to accommodate wheelchairs (36 inches).
    c. restaurant must make five percent of its tables accessible to wheelchair-bound patrons.
    d. All of the above.

d., Medium, Page 447

61. The Justice Department estimates that more than 20 percent of the cases customers have filed under the Americans with Disabilities Act involved changes the business owners could have made at a cost of:
    a. $0.
    b. $250.
    c. $1,000.
    d. $8,000.

a., Medium, Page 447

62. The Americans with Disabilities Act of 1990 requires that:
    a. all buildings be remodeled to accommodate any disabled customer or employee.
    b. all businesses must accommodate all disabled customers or job candidates, regardless of the cost to the business.
    c. businesses must make their facilities available to physically challenged customers and employees.
    d. All of the above.

    c., Medium, Page 447

63. The Americans with Disabilities Act:
    a. protects disabled employees, job candidates, and customers.
    b. does not apply to small businesses with fewer than 100 employees.
    c. requires companies to hire any disabled worker who applies for a job and then find a way to fit the job requirements to that worker's abilities.
    d. All of the above.

    a., Medium, Page 447

64. To be effective, a business sign should:
    a. be large enough for passersby to read from a distance.
    b. contain a message that is short, simple, and clear.
    c. be properly illuminated so that it is legible both day and night.
    d. All of the above.

    d., Easy, Page 448

65. Which of the following is **not** a characteristic of an effective business sign?
    a. Includes a message that is short, simple, and clear
    b. Is illuminated so that it is readable both day and night
    c. Uses complementary color schemes and ornate typefaces
    d. Is well maintained

    c., Medium, Page 448

66. The science of adapting work and working conditions to complement employees' strengths and to suit customers' needs is called:
    a. physiology.
    b. ergonomics.
    c. formology.
    d. kinesiology.

    b., Easy, Page 448

67. Which of the following is an example of ergonomics?
    a. Evaluating the climate-control needs of the work environment
    b. Assessing the lighting needs and the acoustics of a business office
    c. Considering the proper height of desks, chairs, etc., when designing a work station
    d. All of the above.

    d., Easy, Page 448

68. When designing the layout of a store, office, or plant, a business owner's primary focus is usually on _____; however, it should be on _____.
   a. minimizing costs; maximizing security
   b. enhancing workers' productivity; minimizing costs
   c. increasing sales; customer accessibility
   d. minimizing costs; minimizing injuries and enhancing employees' productivity

   d., Medium, Page 449

69. One extensive study concluded that changes in office design have a direct impact on workers':
   a. performance.
   b. job satisfaction.
   c. ease of communication.
   d. All of the above.

   d., Easy, Page 449

70. When considering the functional and attractive aspects of walls and ceilings in a retail store, the small business owner should:
   a. paint ceilings a dark color to conserve energy.
   b. strive for a light and bright interior.
   c. avoid all wall coverings because of their expense.
   d. emphasize function over attractiveness.

   b., Medium, Page 450

71. An effective retail layout should:
   a. pull customers into the store.
   b. make it easy for customers to locate the merchandise they are looking for.
   c. take customers past displays of items they might buy on impulse.
   d. All of the above.

   d., Easy, Page 452

72. Products with the highest markup should be placed:
   a. so as to pull customers into the store.
   b. in prime selling space.
   c. near the front of the store.
   d. anywhere since they draw their own customers.

   b., Medium, Page 452

73. A(n) _____ layout arranges displays in a rectangular fashion with parallel aisles. It is a formal, efficient layout that controls the traffic flow through the store.
   a. free-form
   b. grid
   c. angled
   d. boutique

   b., Easy, Page 452

74. Self-service stores, grocery stores, and discount stores are best suited to a _____ layout.
    a. free-form
    b. boutique
    c. angled
    d. grid

    d., Medium, Page 452

75. A store that uses a grid layout is:
    a. using lights in ceiling grids for extra emphasis.
    b. a sports store specializing in football equipment.
    c. using a simple access, rectangular arrangement with parallel aisles
    d. encouraging shoppers to shop longer and increasing impulse purchases.

    c., Medium, Page 452

76. A(n) _____ layout has the advantage of creating a relaxed, friendly shopping atmosphere encouraging shoppers to linger and increasing the number of impulse purchases.
    a. free-form
    b. grid
    c. angled
    d. boutique

    a., Easy, Page 452

77. A(n) _____ layout divides a store into a series of individual shopping areas, each with its own theme. This layout can create a distinctive image for a business.
    a. free-form
    b. grid
    c. angled
    d. boutique

    d., Easy, Page 454

78. The boutique layout is commonly used in:
    a. supermarkets.
    b. self-service stores.
    c. department stores.
    d. stores with a high number of impulse goods.

    c., Medium, Page 454

79. What is the 40-30-20-10 rule in retailing?
    a. A way of figuring who your best and worst customers are
    b. A formula for calculating the ratio of expenditures on signage, displays, advertising, and interior decorating
    c. An expression of the decline of the value of store space as you move front to back in the store
    d. The percentage of customers who move straight into a store, go right, go left, leave before fully entering

    c., Medium, Page 455

80. The most valuable space in a store is the:
    a. nonselling space.
    b. main entry-level space.
    c. space at the back of the store.
    d. left-side, entry level space.

    b., Medium, Page 455

81. Which of the following statements concerning store layout is **true**?
    a. The farther an area is from the store's entrance, the greater its value.
    b. Most shoppers turn left upon entering a store and move around it in a clockwise fashion.
    c. Only about one-fourth of a store's customers will go more than halfway into a store.
    d. The second quarter of the store is worth 1/2 of the front quarter.

    c., Medium, Page 455

82. When the typical shopper enters a store, (s)he turns _____ and moves around it in a _____ fashion.
    a. left; clockwise
    b. right; clockwise
    c. left; counterclockwise
    d. right; counterclockwise

    d., Medium, Page 455

83. Which of the following sections of a retail store would be most valuable?
    a. Third floor
    b. Intersection of two secondary aisles
    c. The front right corner of the store
    d. The front left corner of the store

    c., Medium, Page 455

84. Manufacturing layout decisions take into consideration:
    a. customer buying behavior, the types of product sold, and the physical dimensions of the building.
    b. the status of the building: built, bought, or leased, and the type of product sold.
    c. the product, the process, the space availability within the facility, ergonomic considerations, and key economic considerations.
    d. the employees, the customer, and the mechanical process used to produce the product.

c., Medium, Page 456

85. The manufacturing layout that arranges workers and equipment according to sequence of operation and is best suited for highly standardized or mass-produced products, such as automobiles, is called:
    a. process layout.
    b. fixed-position layout.
    c. function layout.
    d. product layout.

d., Easy, Page 457

86. A product layout has the disadvantage of:
    a. a high fixed investment in specialized equipment.
    b. the highest materials costs with lower productivity.
    c. being harder to schedule and monitor.
    d. dividing the work area into separate operations that are highly independent with a duplication of equipment.

a., Difficult, Page 457

87. The manufacturing layout that groups workers and equipment, according to the general function performed, and that works best with short production runs or when there are considerable variations in the finished product, is called
    a. process layout.
    b. fixed-position layout.
    c. function layout.
    d. product layout.

a., Easy, Page 457

88. A process layout would be best suited to:
    a. an automobile assembly plant.
    b. an oil refinery.
    c. a manufacturer of handmade metal gifts.
    d. a textbook publishing plant.

c., Medium, Page 457

89. For manufacturing, productivity is important; therefore, layout plays a major role. Product layout is arranged to allow:
    a. high volume output.
    b. lower material and handling costs.
    c. output of highly standardized products.
    d. All of the above.

    d., Medium, Page 457

90. Disadvantage(s) of a product layout can be:
    a. monotony.
    b. interdependence of all operations.
    c. duplication of equipment.
    d. All of the above.

    d., Medium, Page 457

91. When manufacturing large bulky products, it is sometimes necessary to bring the materials to a specific spot and do the assembly in one place. This type of layout is known as a:
    a. process layout.
    b. fixed-position layout.
    c. function layout.
    d. product layout.

    b., Easy, Page 458

92. A good manufacturing layout requires all but which of the following?
    a. flow/process study
    b. easy adjustment to changing conditions
    c. good housekeeping
    d. an assembly line

    d., Medium, Page 458

93. The decision to buy a facility means that the small business owner:
    a. needs the same outline of facility requirements as she would if building.
    b. has greater mobility than leasing because it is easier to sell property than break a lease.
    c. will have a smaller initial capital outlay than leasing because the building will collateralize the construction loan, while a lease requires a large down payment.
    d. is limited in the amount and number of changes that can be made in the building.

    a., Difficult, Page 459

94.   Which of the following is a disadvantage of leasing?
   a.   The lessee must renew a commercial lease at least once before moving or pay a penalty.
   b.   The business owner is not free to remodel a leased building at her own discretion.
   c.   Lease expenses are not tax deductible as business expenses.
   d.   Permanent modifications a lessee makes to a building must be removed if the lessee leaves the building.

   b., Medium, Page 460

95.   The major advantage of leasing is:
   a.   there is no large initial cash outlay required.
   b.   unlimited ability to remodel.
   c.   more favorable consideration by lenders when seeking startup capital.
   d.   not needing a facility's requirement plan or layout plan.

   a., Medium, Page 460

True/False Questions:

96.   By collecting a wealth of data on possible locations, an entrepreneur will find that the location decision is made for him.

   False, Medium, Page 426

97.   The key to finding a suitable location is identifying the characteristics that can give a company a competitive edge and then searching out potential sites that meet those criteria.

   True, Medium, Page 426

98.   The first phase in selecting a location is determining what regions of the country are experiencing substantial growth.

   True, Easy, Page 426

99.   When conducting a regional evaluation, one of the first places an entrepreneur should turn for information is the U.S. Census Bureau.

   True, Easy, Page 427

100.   Published annually, The Survey of Buying Power, provides a detailed breakdown of population, retail sales, spendable income, etc., for various census regions, states, etc.

   True, Medium, Page 428

101.   Geographic Information Systems are powerful software programs that allow entrepreneurs to pinpoint the ideal location for their businesses.

   True, Easy, Page 428

102. <u>The Zip Code Atlas and Market Planner</u> provides detailed information on sales, spendable income, etc., by census region, county, and city.

     False, Medium, Page 428

103. When the cost of transporting a product is high relative to its value, locating close to the market a manufacturer plans to serve is critical.

     True, Medium, Page 429

104. The U.S. Census Department's "TIGER" file is a computerized map of the entire United States that gives entrepreneurs the power to pinpoint existing and potential customers.

     True, Medium, Page 429

105. Proximity to needed raw materials is critically important for a service firm.

     False, Easy, Page 429

106. When analyzing the labor supply, a small business is concerned only with the level of education and training of the labor force in the area.

     False, Easy, Page 430

107. When choosing a location, a small business owner should match the characteristics of the labor force her company requires with the characteristics of an area's available labor pool.

     True, Easy, Page 430

108. Knowing the type of labor a business needs and preparing job descriptions and job specifications in advance will help a business owner determine whether or not there is a good match with the available labor pool.

     True, Easy, Page 430

109. The most important factor when evaluating the labor supply in an area is its prevailing wage rate.

     False, Medium, Page 430

110. By studying the demographics of a proposed location, a small business owner can determine how well it matches the market for the owner's product or service.

     True, Easy, Page 431

111. Local laws, zoning regulations, and building codes can affect the location to be chosen, depending on the type of business and its particular requirements.

     True, Easy, Page 433

112. Increased traffic flow can be beneficial to similar businesses located in close proximity to one another e.g., auto dealers or antique shops.

    True, Medium, Page 433

113. For some retailers, locating near competitors makes sense because similar businesses located near one another can increase traffic flow to all.

    True, Medium, Page 433

114. Zoning is a system for mixing types of business and industrial activities in order to make maximum efficient use of the area.

    False, Medium, Page 434

115. Zoning is a system that divides a city or country into small cells or districts to control the use of land, buildings, and sites.

    True, Easy, Page 434

116. The average census tract contains about 100,000 people.

    False, Medium, Page 435

117. Few decisions are as important for retailers as the choice of a location.

    True, Medium, Page 435

118. One element of the location decision common to all businesses is the need to locate where customers want to do business.

    True, Easy, Page 435

119. Criteria for a "good location" are universal and apply to all types of small businesses.

    False, Medium, Page 435

120. Generally, the larger a retail store and the greater its selection, the broader its trade area.

    True, Easy, Page 435

121. The Index of Retail Saturation (IRS) is a measure of the potential sales per square foot of store space for a given product in a specific trading area.

    True, Easy, Page 436

122. Clever business owners choose their location with an eye on the surrounding mix of businesses.

    True, Easy, Page 436

123. To calculate the IRS, a retailer needs to know the number of customers in the area, the retail expenditures for his product, and the total square feet of space allocated to selling his kind of product in the trading area.

    True, Medium, Page 436

124. To calculate the IRS, a retailer needs to know the number of customers, the number of competitors, and the total square feet of space allocated to selling his kind of product in the trading area.

    False, Medium, Page 436

125. Retail compatibility describes the benefits a company receives by locating near other businesses selling complementary products and services.

    True, Easy, Page 436

126. To ensure ready access to raw materials and to customers, a manufacturer should consider the quality of an area's transportation network when choosing a location.

    True, Easy, Page 437

127. A company's trade area can be influenced by intangible factors, such as physical, racial, and political barriers.

    True, Medium, Page 437

128. One of the key factors in choosing a location for a convenience store is finding a location with high traffic volume and easy accessibility.

    True, Easy, Page 438

129. On average, the typical central business district has more parking spaces per square foot of shopping space than the typical shopping mall.

    False, Easy, Page 438

130. Choosing a location in which many other businesses have failed can create a negative image, even for a "new" business.

    True, Easy, Page 438

131. A location that has housed several businesses that have failed within the past few years is likely to have a bad reputation and a negative image.

    True, Easy, Page 438

132. Because they are centrally located, central business district locations offer business owners the ability to attract customers from the entire trading area of the city.

    True, Medium, Page 439

133. Many central business districts suffer from intense competition, high rental rates, traffic congestion, and inadequate parking facilities.

    True, Medium, Page 439

134. According to the International Council of Shopping Centers, the average cost to lease space in a shopping center is about $40 per square foot.

    False, Difficult, Page 439

135. According to the International Council of Shopping Centers, the average cost to lease space in a regional shopping mall runs from $20 to $40 per square foot.

    True, Difficult, Page 439

136. A community shopping center contains from three to twelve stores and serves a population that lives within a 10-minute drive.

    False, Medium, Page 440

137. Shopping centers are always a wise location for a small business owner to choose.

    False, Easy, Page 440

138. The typical neighborhood shopping center contains from 3 to 12 stores and serves a population that lives within a 10-minute drive.

    True, Medium, Page 440

139. A regional shopping mall serves a large trading area (10 to 15 miles or more), contains from 50 to 100 stores, and draws customers from a population that lives within 20 to 40 minutes driving time.

    True, Medium, Page 440

140. A power center combines the drawing strength of a large regional mall with the convenience of a neighborhood shopping center.

    True, Easy, Page 440

141. For a service company that goes into its customers' homes to perform its service, the choice to locate in the entrepreneur's home is a poor one.

    False, Easy, Page 441

142. The ideal location for a retail business is in the entrepreneur's home.

    False, Medium, Page 441

143. Retailers should be careful not to locate near anyone in direct competition with them.

    False, Medium, Page 441

144. If a business sells merchandise for which customers typically do a good deal of comparison shopping, it should choose a location as far away from competitors as possible.

    False, Medium, Page 441

145. A recent study found that 52 percent of all small companies are home-based.

    True, Medium, Page 441

146. Many home-based entrepreneurs whose businesses are successful run into problems with zoning laws as they run businesses from locations in areas that are zoned "residential."

    True, Medium, Page 442

147. Empowerment zones are specially designated areas in or near a U. S. customs port of entry that allows resident companies to import materials and components from foreign countries; assemble, process, manufacture, or package them; ad then ship the finished product while either reducing or eliminating tariffs and duties.

    False, Medium, Page 444

148. An "incubator" is a facility that offers low rental rates and permits startup small businesses to share resources.

    True, Easy, Page 444

149. The primary reason for establishing a business incubator is to enhance economic development in an area and to diversify the local economy.

    True, Medium, Page 444

150. Common sponsors of incubators include government agencies and colleges and universities.

    True, Medium, Page 444

151. Graduates from business incubators have a much higher success rate than the typical small business.

    True, Medium, Page 444

152. Layout is the logical arrangement of the physical facilities in a business that contribute to efficient operations, increased productivity, and higher sales.

    True, Easy, Page 444

153. Developing a layout plan really is not essential unless an entrepreneur is able to build a new building to house the business.

    False, Medium, Page 445

154. A store's external appearance plays only an insignificant role in identifying its "personality" or image to customers.

    False, Medium, Page 446

155. The rules of the Americans with Disabilities Act protecting customers are designed to ensure that disabled customers have equal access to a company's goods and services.

    True, Easy, Page 447

156. Any company with 15 or more employees and any buildings occupied after January 25, 1993, must comply with the Americans with Disabilities Act.

    True, Medium, Page 447

157. Studies show that complying with the Americans with Disabilities Act (ADA) requires businesses to spend an average of almost $17,000 to bring their buildings up to ADA standards.

    False, Medium, Page 447

158. The Justice Department estimates that more than 20 percent of the cases customers have filed under the Americans with Disabilities Act involved changes the business owners would have made at no cost.

    True, Medium, Page 447

159. Most small companies that invest in making their locations accessible to all customers under the Americans with Disabilities Act qualify for a tax credit.

    True, Medium, Page 447

160. In some cities and towns, local regulations impose restrictions on the size, location, height, and construction materials used in business signs.

    True, Easy, Page 448

161. Signs are one of the most expensive and least effective ways of communicating with customers available to small businesses.

    False, Easy, Page 448

162. Ergonomics, the science of adapting work and the work environment to complement employees' strengths and to suit customers' needs, in an integral part of a successful layout.

True, Easy, Page 449

163. When planning store, office, or plant layouts, business owners usually focus on minimizing costs when what they should focus on is minimizing injuries and enhancing employees' productivity.

True, Medium, Page 449

164. When designing the layout of a store, office, or plant, a business owner's primary focus should be minimizing costs.

False, Medium, Page 449

165. Office design has little impact on workers' job performance, job satisfaction, and ease of communication.

False, Medium, Page 449

166. Lighting is often an inexpensive investment for improving employee performance and the overall appearance of the business.

True, Easy, Page 450

167. Retailers design their layouts with the goal of maximizing sales revenue while manufacturers see layout as an opportunity to increase efficiency and productivity and to lower costs.

True, Medium, Page 450

168. Studies have found that between 65 and 70 percent of all buying decisions are made once a customer enters a store and that 68 percent of the items bought on major shopping trips were impulse purchases.

True, Difficult, Page 452

169. In a retail layout, impulse and convenience goods should be located near the front of the store.

True, Easy, Page 452

170. Well-designed floor displays are critical to a retailer's success.

True, Easy, Page 452

171. Proper layout of any retail facility requires the owner's observation and understanding of customers' buying habits.

    True, Easy, Page 452

172. Prime selling space should be reserved for items that are slow sellers so that customers will notice them.

    False, Medium, Page 452

173. Observing customer behavior in a retail store can help a business owner identify "hot spots" where merchandise sells briskly and "cold spots" where it may sit indefinitely.

    True, Easy, Page 452

174. Prime selling space should be reserved for items that carry the highest markups.

    True, Medium, Page 452

175. A grid layout is a formal layout that arranges displays in rectangular fashion so that aisles are parallel, allowing better control of traffic flow through the store.

    True, Medium, Page 452

176. A primary advantage of a free-form layout is the relaxed, friendly shopping atmosphere it creates, which encourages customers to shop longer and increases the number of impulse purchases they make.

    True, Medium, Page 452

177. The boutique layout divides a store into a series of individual shopping areas, each with its own theme, similar to building a series of specialty shops into a single store.

    True, Medium, Page 454

178. The wise small retailer separates selling and nonselling activities; she does not waste valuable selling space with nonselling activities.

    True, Medium, Page 454

179. In small stores, every portion of the interior space is of equal value in generating sales.

    False, Easy, Page 454

180. The majority of a store's customers go more than halfway into the store.

    False, Medium, Page 455

181. Space values increase as their distance from the main entry-level floor increases.

    False, Easy, Page 455

182. The decline in value of store space from front to back of the shop is expressed in the 40-30-20-10 rule.

True, Medium, Page 455

183. Creating a proper layout is important for retail operations, but not for manufacturers since manufacturing layout principles offer very little opportunity to improve efficiency or to increase productivity.

False, Easy, Page 456

184. Process layouts are used where the process flows in a straight line to enable high volume output.

False, Medium, Page 457

185. Product layouts have the advantage of maximum flexibility to do a customer's work and to enhance job satisfaction among employees.

False, Medium, Page 457

186. A significant advantage of product layout is that the company will not have duplication of machinery and equipment.

False, Medium, Page 457

187. The design of a product layout requires the fitting of equipment and workstations needed in the available facilities in the correct sequence.

True, Medium, Page 457

188. Aircraft assembly plants and shipyards typify the fixed position layout.

True, Medium, Page 458

189. Buying a building has the advantage of ensuring a positive return on your investment since commercial real estate always appreciates its value.

False, Easy, Page 459

190. One disadvantage of owning the building which houses a business is that the owner may feel tied to one location.

True, Easy, Page 459

191. A disadvantage of leasing is that the business does not get a tax break since lease expenses are not tax deductible.

False, Medium, Page 460

192. Leasing is an option that small businesses that are short on cash should consider.

    True, Easy, Page 460

Essay Questions:

193. Discuss the various sources of information available to the small business owner for deciding in which region of the country to locate her business.

    In evaluating a region for site selection, entrepreneurs should evaluate the general demographic characteristics of the population in Government publications, census information, and statistical data. In evaluating a region for site selection, entrepreneurs should evaluate the general demographic characteristics of the population. Government publications, census information, and statistical data are useful sources of this information. The U.S. Census Bureau sources: U.S. Statistical Abstract, County and City Data Book and the WWW site (http://www.census.gov/). Other sources of demographic data include:

    - Sales and Marketing Management's Survey of Buying Power
    - Editor and Publisher Market Guide
    - The American Marketplace
    - Demographic and Spending Patterns
    - Rand McNally's Commercial Atlas and Marketing Guide
    - Zip Code Atlas and Market Planner

    Many entrepreneurs combine map drawing and database management capabilities (GIS). GIS street files originate in the U. S. Census Department's TIGER (Topographically Integrated Geographic Encoding Referencing). Universities and the Small Business Administration Small Business Development Centers also provide numerous sources of information.
    Page 426

194. Identify and explain five of the seven criteria a small business owner should consider when selecting the state in which to locate her business.

    - Proximity to Markets – locating close to markets is critical in reducing distribution costs, staying competitive and making it easy for customers to access products and services.
    - Proximity to Needed Raw Materials – the value of product and service components, their material costs, transportation costs, and their function all interact in determining how close a business needs to be to its source of supplies.
    - Wage Rates – wages can vary significantly from state to state affecting a company's cost of doing business.
    - Labor Supply Needs – two factors should be considered: the number of workers available in the area and their level of education
    - Business Climate – includes whether a city/state regulates restrictions on the way a company can operate, imposes inventory taxes, implements laws that prohibit certain business activities on Sundays "blue laws," and whether or not a state provides support programs or financial assistance.

- Tax Rates – location selection must consider: state income taxes, payroll taxes sales taxes, property taxes, and any specialized taxes on the operations of their business.
- Internet Access – speedy and reliable service is increasingly more important. DSL and T1 line availability is essential for a high tech company and those engaging in e-commerce.

Page 429

195. Identify and briefly discuss the nine factors an entrepreneur should consider when selecting the city in which to locate her business.

   - Population Trends – and demographics; growth trends, family size, age distribution, education, income levels, religion, race, nationality, gender. Match the market to your products or services.
   - Competition – Locate near or away from competitors? Evaluate the number and strengths/weaknesses of competitors.
   - Clustering – Some cities have characteristics that attract certain industries, and, as a result, companies tend to cluster there.
   - Compatibility with the community – Company's image must fit in with the character of a town and the needs and wants of its residents.
   - Local laws and regulations – Government regulations affect many aspects of a company's operation, from acquiring business licenses and building permits to erecting business signs and dumping trash.
   - Transportation networks – Quality and availability of various transportation options; availability of loading and unloading zones.
   - Police and fire protection – If these services are not adequate and crime rates are high, the cost of the company's business insurance will reflect that.
   - Cost of utilities and public services – Seek a municipality that provides all utility services, street maintenance, etc., at a reasonable cost.
   - Quality of life – Comfortable weather, cultural events, museums, outdoor activities, concerts, restaurants, interesting nightlife, etc; not only attractive to an entrepreneur, but can also make recruiting employees much easier.

Page 431

196. List and explain the main location criteria for retail and service businesses.

   - Trade area size – the region from which the business can expect to draw customers over a reasonable time span. The following environmental factors influence trading area size:

      - Retail compatibility – Shoppers tend to be drawn to clusters of related businesses.
      - Degree of competition – size, location, and activity of competing businesses.
      - Index of retail saturation – measures the level of saturation in an area; ratio of a trading area's sales potential for a particular product or service to its sales capacity.
      - Transportation network – highways, roads, and public service routes that presently exist or are planned. If customers find it

inconvenient to get to a location, the store's trading area is reduced.

- Physical, racial, or emotional barriers – parks, rivers, lakes, high crime areas; clusters of people sharing a common culture and language; fear.
- Political barriers – county, city, or state laws; tax structure; licenses and fees.

- Customer traffic – the business must be able to generate sufficient sales to surpass its break-even point, and that requires an ample volume of customer traffic going past its doors.

- Adequate parking – If customers cannot find convenient and safe parking, they are not likely to stop in the area.

- Reputation – of the previous owner or the fact that several businesses have failed in that location (creates negative image in customers' minds).

- Room for expansion – flexible enough to provide for expansion if success warrants it.

- Visibility – makes it easy for customers to find your business and to make purchases.

Page 435

197. List and discuss the six basic areas where retail and service business can locate. What are their advantages and disadvantages?

- Central Business Districts (CBDs) – the traditional center of town. Advantages include the ability to attract customers from the entire trading area and benefiting from the customer traffic generated by other stores in the district. Disadvantages may include intense competition, high rental rates, traffic congestion, and inadequate parking facilities.
- Neighborhood Locations – locating near residential areas relies heavily on the local trading areas for business. Most grocery stores are within a five-mile radius of their customers. An advantage is relatively low rents and operating costs.
- Shopping Centers and Malls – there are four types and each have separate requirements: Neighborhood Shopping Centers (3-12 stores within a 10 mile drive), Community Shopping Centers (12-50 stores from 40-150 thousand people), Regional Shopping Malls (50-100 stores needs an excess of 150,000 people living within 20-40 minute drive), Power Centers (80% need to be anchor stores).
- Near Competitors – high price items and those products and services that customers prefer to comparison shop, typically benefit from locating near competitors or retail outlets offering complementary offerings. Potential disadvantage of market saturation, with one store cannibalizing sales from another, making it difficult to succeed.
- Outlying Areas – generally not advisable unless the business can distinguish itself from competitors.

- Home-based Businesses – 24 million, almost 52% of all small businesses, and the fastest growing segment. The biggest benefit is the low cost of set up and operations. The disadvantages include: interruptions, isolation, and neighborhood and zoning regulations.

Page 439

198. What is a business incubator? What can an incubator offer an entrepreneur just starting out?

A business incubator is an organization that combines low-cost, flexible rental space with a multitude of support services (secretarial services, meeting rooms, fax machine, telephone systems etc…) for its small business residents. Its goal is to nurture young companies during the volatile start-up period and to help them survive until they are strong enough to go out on their own. Incubators have entry requirements and expectations for graduation. After graduation into the business world, these businesses have a higher success rate (87%) than independent small businesses.

Page 444

199. Briefly explain the fundamental considerations in evaluating an existing building as a location. Utilize the explanation of zoning laws, ergonomics and the Americans with Disabilities Act in your explanation.

Zoning is a system that divides a city or county into small cells or districts to control the use of the land, buildings, and sites. Its purpose is to contain similar activities in suitable locations. Each city has its own ordinances that place restrictions on certain types of business activity altogether. Because of this, entrepreneurs must be familiar with all necessary ordinances in cities where they are considering a building location.

The Americans with Disabilities Act requires practically all businesses to make their facilities available to physically challenged customers and employees. In addition, the law requires businesses with 15 employees or more, to accommodate physically challenged people in their hiring practices. The law requires business owners to remove architectural and communication barriers when "readily achievable." Although the law allows for a good deal of flexibility in retrofitting existing structures, buildings that are occupied after January 25, 1993, must comply with all aspects of the law.

Ergonomics, the science of adapting work and the work environment to complement employees' strengths and to suit customers' needs, is an integral part of a successful design. An ergonomically designed workplace can improve workers' productivity significantly and decrease days lost due to injuries and accidents.

Page 447

200. Briefly describe the three basic layout options available to retailers. Generally comment on the most and least valuable areas in a retail store.

The three basic layouts are: Grid, which arranges displays in a rectangular fashion with parallel aisles that control traffic pattern. Free Form is less formal and is primarily designed to relax and encourage customers to purchase impulse items. The Boutique layout divides the stores into separate shopping areas with separate themes.

Depending on the type of store you have and its type of product or service offering, the interior space plays an important part in the site's ability to generate sale revenue.

Typically, the farther away an area is from the entrance, the lower its value. Impulse items with higher mark ups should be placed close to the check out counters—with regard to security issues. Another consideration is that most American shoppers turn to the right entering a store and move around it counterclockwise. Selling areas on the main level contribute a greater portion to sales than either basement or higher levels because they offer greater exposure to the customer. Items located on primary walkways should be assigned a higher share of rental costs and should contribute a higher portion to sales than those displays located along secondary aisles. Retailers must also remember to separate the selling and non-selling areas of a store. Although non-selling activities are important, they should not take up valuable selling space.
Page 452

201. Identify and describe the goal/purpose of the three basic types of manufacturing layouts.

   - Product Layouts consist of an unbroken flow from raw material input or customer arrival to finished goods to customer's departure. This layout is best suited for rigid-flow, high-volume, continuous or mass-production operations, or when service or product is highly standardized. Products are routed along the same fixed path and are usually scheduled by a production rate. This layout does lower material handling costs, simplify tasks, and reduce the amounts in work-in-process inventory, but is characterized by its inflexibility, monotony of job tasks, high investment in specialized equipment, and heavy interdependence of all operations.
   - Process Layouts group workers or equipment according to the general function that they perform. They are most applicable when production runs are short, when demand varies, when the costs of holding finished goods inventory are high, or when the service or product is customized.
   - Fixed Position Layouts are similar to product layouts, but due to bulk or weight, the final product is assembled in one spot.

   Page 457

202. What are the pros and cons an entrepreneur should consider before making the decision to build, buy, or lease a business location?

Decision to Build:

Advantages:	Constructing a new building lets the entrepreneur ultimately design and build a facility that matches perfectly with her needs. Often times, new buildings create an image of a modern, efficient, and top quality business. New buildings can be constructed with the most modern features, in effect reducing total costs over time.
Disadvantages:	The major disadvantage concerns the high initial outlay of capital. The high initial fixed expenses must be weighed against the facility's capability to attract additional sales revenue and reduce operating costs. Another disadvantage revolves around the lack of mobility. If the building is not located in an ideal spot, it is very difficult to alleviate the problem.

Decision to Buy:

Advantages:	Buying an existing building typically has a lower cost than constructing a new building, and the owner will know how much monthly payments will

be. Plus the entrepreneur has the opportunity to remodel the building to fit her exact needs.

Disadvantages: The initial cost to purchase the existing building can be a drain on finances. Again as mentioned above, the lack of mobility is a concern.

<u>Decision to Lease:</u>

Advantages: The major advantage of leasing is that it requires no large initial investment. Firms short on cash find leasing as their primary option. Another plus is that the small business owner has mobility to her advantage.

Disadvantages: One major disadvantage is that the property owner may choose not to renew the lease. If the business is successful, then relocating may be costly and decrease the number of regular customers. Another disadvantage is that, in most cases, the small business is very limited on remodeling. In addition, all permanent modifications of the structure become the property of the owner.

Page 459

Chapter 13
Choosing The Right Location and Layout
Mini-Cases

<u>Case 13-1: Hungarian Heaven</u>

Mike Pontya has operated a neighborhood restaurant in Cleveland for over 30 years. Mike is planning to move to Arizona because of his health, and has put the business up for sale. The restaurant, which caters to the local trade, is well known in the Hungarian community of Cleveland as having the best authentic Hungarian food in town, but it is not in a traditional restaurant district. The restaurant has parking for 10 cars. Most customers park on the street. In the past this wasn't a problem as there was a great deal of walk-in business from the neighborhood. Now, however, a new four-lane highway passes by the front door of the restaurant. There is a stoplight on the corner the restaurant is on to improve access to the highway for drivers emerging from the neighborhood. The flight to the suburbs has taken a heavy toll on the neighborhood. However, the restaurant is still doing well financially.

Terry and Judy Kozma are brother and sister who share a love for cooking and a desire to be in the restaurant business. All of their relatives have encouraged them to quit their jobs and buy the restaurant. Terry and Judy were reared two blocks from the restaurant, and both worked part-time for Mike Pontya while in college.

1. What site analysis criteria are relevant to Terry and Judy's evaluation of the restaurant's location?

   Although no entrepreneur has a crystal ball for peering into the future to evaluate the long-run value of a site, he can observe general trends. While the restaurant is well established and is financially successful now, Terry and Judy must be concerned about the number of potential customers moving away from the old neighborhood. Restaurants such as these must be close to their clientele, and it appears that Hungarian Heaven's customer base is steadily dwindling.

2. What are the advantages and disadvantages of the restaurant's current location?

Advantages:	Disadvantages:

- well-known in the community
- reputation for good Hungarian food
- new four-lane highway
- limited parking space
- traffic light that improves access
- restaurant is doing well financially
- established business with goodwill
	- location is not in the
	  traditional restaurant district
	- potential for increased traffic
	  in future
	- flight to suburbs may be the
	  robbing the restaurant its
	  customer base
	- uncertain future of location's
	  suitability

Case 13-2: "It's a Great Location for a Bar"

Fred Stanford has just completed bartenders' school in Los Angeles and is ready to build a life for himself. Sunday's paper has an ad in the business opportunities section for a bar in Mesa Verde, Colorado. Fred has heard that the West is a high growth area and the quality of life in Colorado is very good. Fred's best friend, Carl, begins to ask Fred some questions about his new idea. "To begin with, Fred, where is Mesa Verde, Colorado?"

Fred decides to call the telephone number in the ad and is put in touch with Ansel King, a business broker located in Pueblo, Colorado. When asked where in Colorado Mesa Verde was, Ansel was prompt to point out that it was only 35 miles from Pueblo on the Interstate and has a population of nearly ten thousand. "Fred, this town is a great location for a bar, and I have just the kind of deal for a young man like you looking to get started."

1. What city-related factors does Fred need to consider when evaluating this community as a location for a bar?

   Fred should look at the city's population trends and composition, its laws and regulations (especially those affecting bars), the nature and the extent of competition, the city's attitude toward bars (compatibility with the community), and the public services the city offers.

2. What publications could Fred use to investigate whether or not this is a good region for this bar?

   This case study offers students a chance to establish a procedure for analyzing a potential business location. It appears that Fred may be choosing a location by chance instead of by careful analysis. The basic approach is: the region of the country, the state in the region, the city in the state, the neighborhood in the city; and the specific site in the neighborhood. A demographic analysis of the area is a good place to begin.

Case 13-3: Custom Cars, Inc.

Al and Helen Wise have a love affair with cars. After collecting and restoring cars for a number of years, they decide to form their own "kit car" company. This type of company sells "kits" to people who want to build their own functioning replicas of famous or collectable cars. About 60 percent of their business is selling the kits, 10 percent is conducting classes and seminars on assembling the kits, and the remaining 30 percent is actually building the cars for the customers.

Their business has three distinct manufacturing issues. The production of the car kits, the assembly of the custom cars for owners who want them but don't have the time to do the work themselves, and the "assembling and selling" training seminars on how to put the cars together.

1.   Explain which manufacturing layout would be best for each of the three manufacturing issues the Wises face.

        Kit production: probably the most efficient layout for kit production would be either the product layout or the process layout. Custom car assembly: Again, the best layouts for the Wises to consider are the product layout and the process layout. Training seminars: a "hands-on" classroom would be ideal here so that customers can practice what they learn. The Wises should consider including video equipment in their layout to improve their teaching flexibility.

2.   Compare and contrast the three layout options.

        •   Product Layouts consist of an unbroken flow from raw material input or customer arrival to finished goods to customer's departure. This layout is best suited for rigid-flow, high-volume, continuous or mass-production operations, or when service or product is highly standardized. Products are routed along the same fixed path and are usually scheduled by a production rate. This layout does lower material handling costs, simplify tasks, and reduce the amounts in work-in-process inventory, but is characterized by its inflexibility, monotony of job tasks, high investment in specialized equipment, and heavy interdependence of all operations.
        •   Process Layouts group workers or equipment according to the general function that they perform. They are most applicable when production runs are short, when demand varies, when the costs of holding finished goods inventory are high, or when the service or product is customized.
        •   Fixed Position Layouts are similar to product layouts, but due to bulk or weight, the final product is assembled in one spot.

Case 13-4: "We're Moving On Up"

Mike and Earl Moore, owners of College Men's Unlimited, have just signed a five-year lease in the new College Town Mall. The new mall is ideally located for their business - a short walk from campus and only two blocks from downtown. The far side of the mall is bounded by the most prestigious homes in the city. It will be opening in five weeks and Mike and Earl are lucky to have such a prime spot. Ray Thomas, their banker, called them last Wednesday with word that the store, which had agreed to take the space they just leased, had canceled. Eighteen months ago when the mall had put this location up for lease, they were not in financial condition to make a commitment. In the last 18 months, however, business has been exceptional. The city has grown and the college has experienced expanded enrollments. By next Monday morning, Mike and Earl must provide the mall developer with a complete layout for their new store so the developer can assign an emergency work crew to complete the store for the grand opening.

College Men's Unlimited is a full-line men's store offering middle-to-upper-quality traditional men's wearing apparel. The present location is an old two-story house that Mike and Earl converted into their combination business and living area. The house has 4,000 square feet of area, 3,600 being used for the store, and the rest for a three-room apartment. The new store has a 30-foot front and is 70 feet deep. The mall developer is willing to put up walls for storage and office space wherever they wish.

1. What other considerations should be included in the layout?

This case asks the student to develop the layout for a men's clothing store to be located in a mall location. While student responses will vary, certain general principles should emerge.

- Separate selling and nonselling activities.
- Locate shopping and specialty goods at the rear of the store.
- Place impulse items in high exposure areas.
- Store should be well lighted; track lighting could be used to accent clothing and displays.
- Pastel colors that do not clash with the merchandise would be wise.
- A free-form layout, which offers an informal atmosphere should be used.
- The layout should be spacious and uncluttered.
- Those items accounting for the greatest portion of sales volume should be located in the most valuable selling space.
- An angled storefront might invite shoppers to enter the store.

2. Assuming that the new store space is 2,100 square feet (30' x 70'), and that the shape is rectangular, draw a layout for the new men's store. What merchandise should be placed where? What size office space and storage is needed? Where should counters be placed?

While student responses will vary, here is one suggested layout.

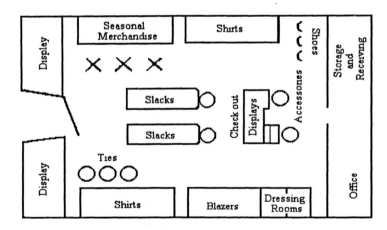

Case Study 27 Figure

Chapter 14   **The Global Aspects of Entrepreneurship**

Multiple Choice Questions:

1. Becoming a global entrepreneur requires:
    a. constant innovation
    b. maintaining a high level of quality and constantly improving it
    c. being sensitive to foreign customers' unique requirements and adopting a more respectful attitude toward foreign habits and customs.
    d. All of the above.

    d., Easy, Page 465

2. For a small business, expanding into international markets:
    a. guarantees its success in the marketplace.
    b. makes it a member of GATT automatically.
    c. helps it grow faster and survive competition better.
    d. leads to business failure for companies under $100 million in annual revenue.

    c., Medium, Page 465

3. Small businesses that take the plunge into global business can expect all but which of the following to occur?
    a. Higher quality levels
    b. Higher manufacturing costs
    c. An increase in sales and profits
    d. Extension of their products' life cycles

    b., Medium, Page 465

4. The first obstacle an entrepreneur must overcome on the way to creating a truly global business is:
    a. finding a joint venture partner.
    b. learning to think globally.
    c. locating motivated, multilingual managers for overseas assignments.
    d. finding overseas distributors for the company's products.

    b., Easy, Page 465

5. All of these are steps small companies follow when they begin conducting global business on the Web **except**:
    a. connecting to email.
    b. building a globally accessible Web site.
    c. setting up links to related company websites.
    d. using the Web to conduct international market research.

    c., Medium, Page 467

6.   Which of the following statements is/are true regarding export management companies?
   a.   Most are merchant intermediaries that work on a buy-and-sell arrangement with domestic small companies.
   b.   They provide small businesses with a low-cost, efficient, independent, international marketing department.
   c.   Many specialize in particular products or product lines and offer services ranging from market research and advice or patent protection to arranging financing and handling shipping.
   d.   All of the above.

d., Easy, Page 468

7.   An export trading company:
   a.   is a business that buys and sells products in many countries, either in its own name or as an agent for its buyer-seller clients.
   b.   typically offer a wide range of services such as exporting, shipping, storing, distributing, and others to their clients.
   c.   is formed by an agreement by which a licenser gives a foreign licensee the right to use a patent, trademark, copyright, technology, and products in return for a percentage of the licensee's sales or profits.
   d.   A and C above.

d., Easy, Page 468

8.   A resident buying office is:
   a.   a business that buys and sells products in many countries, either in its own name or as an agent for its buyer-seller clients.
   b.   a government-owned or business-owned facility set up in a foreign country to buy products that are made there.
   c.   a firm in an overseas distribution network selling noncompetitive products made by other firms.
   d.   formed by an agreement where a licenser gives a foreign licensee the right to use a patent, trademark, copyright, technology, and products in return for a percentage of the licensee's sales or profits.

b., Medium, Page 468

9.   Which of the following trade intermediaries lowers the risk of exporting for a small business?
   a.   export management companies
   b.   export trading companies
   c.   resident buying offices
   d.   All of the above.

d., Easy, Page 468

10. _____ act as international sales representatives in a limited number of markets for various noncompeting domestic companies, typically operating on a commission basis.
    a. Manufacturer's export agents
    b. Export merchants
    c. Resident buying offices
    d. Foreign distributors

    a., Easy, Page 468

11. _____ are domestic wholesalers who do business in foreign markets, buying goods from domestic companies and selling them in foreign markets, often handling competing lines.
    a. Resident buying offices
    b. Export trading companies
    c. Foreign distributors
    d. Export merchants

    d., Easy, Page 468

12. Foreign distributors offer small businesses which of the following benefits?
    a. A detailed knowledge of the local markets in which they sell.
    b. The ability to cover a foreign sales territory thoroughly.
    c. The ability to handle all of the marketing, distribution, and service functions in foreign markets.
    d. All of the above.

    d., Easy, Page 469

13. The most important ingredient in the recipe for a successful joint venture is:
    a. targeting the right country in which to sell.
    b. getting government approval and avoiding antitrust charges.
    c. choosing the right partner.
    d. splitting costs and profits equally.

    c., Medium, Page 469

14. In a(n) _____, two or more U.S. small businesses form an alliance for the purpose of exporting their goods and services. The companies get antitrust immunity and share responsibility for the business equally.
    a. foreign joint venture
    b. trade intermediary
    c. domestic joint venture
    d. export management company

    c., Easy, Page 469

15. In a(n) _____, a domestic small business forms an alliance with a company in the target nation for the purpose of exporting to that market.
    a. foreign joint venture
    b. trade intermediary
    c. domestic joint venture
    d. export management company

    a., Easy, Page 469

16. Which of the following is a common problem in joint ventures?
    a. Incompatible management styles among partners.
    b. Failure of partners to establish common goals.
    c. Failure of partners to carefully determine each party's contributions and responsibilities, distribution of earnings, etc.
    d. All of the above.

    d., Easy, Page 470

17. Many joint ventures fail because the parties involved neglected to:
    a. select a partner who shares their company's values.
    b. spell out in writing exactly how the venture will work and who has decision-making authority.
    c. select a partner whose skills are different from, but compatible with, their own.
    d. All of the above.

    d., Easy, Page 470

18. Foreign licensing has its greatest potential in the licensing of:
    a. products.
    b. intangibles, such as technology, copyrights, and trademarks.
    c. goods.
    d. franchises.

    b., Medium, Page 471

19. If a business owner can't afford to invest in foreign facilities and doesn't have time to learn the foreign market, but is willing to give someone else the right to make and market her product for a fee and royalties, her best bet for entering the foreign market is:
    a. a foreign management company.
    b. joint venturing.
    c. foreign licensing.
    d. international franchising.

    c., Medium, Page 471

20. Foreign licensing is:
    a. required when a business buys and sells products in many countries, either in its own name or as an agent for its buyer-seller clients.
    b. a government-owned or business-owned facility set up in a foreign country to buy products that are made there.
    c. the use by one firm (the carrier) of its overseas distribution network to sell noncompetitive products made by other firms (riders).
    d. an agreement in which a licenser gives a licensee in another country the right to use that licenser's patent, trademark, copyright, technology, and products in return for a percentage of the licensee's sales or profits.

    d., Easy, Page 471

21. Domino's Pizza and McDonald's operating in Japan and Europe are examples of:
    a. foreign management companies.
    b. joint venturing.
    c. foreign licensing.
    d. international franchising.

    d., Easy, Page 471

22. In international franchising, _____ is the primary market for U.S. franchisers, followed by _____ and _____.
    a. Japan; Mexico and Canada
    b. Russia; Japan and Canada
    c. Canada; Japan and Europe
    d. Europe; Canada and Mexico

    c., Medium, Page 471

23. _____ is a transaction in which a company selling goods and services in a foreign market agrees to help promote investment and trade in that country.
    a. Countertrading
    b. Bartering
    c. Foreign licensing
    d. Exporting

    a., Easy, Page 471

24. The drawbacks of countertrading include which of the following?
    a. Countertrade transactions can be complicated, cumbersome, and time consuming.
    b. Countertrade transactions can increase the chances that a company will get stuck with merchandise it cannot move.
    c. Countertrade transactions can lead to unpleasant surprises concerning the quantity and quality of products required in the countertrade.
    d. All of the above.

    d., Medium, Page 472

25. _____, the exchange of goods and services for other goods and services, is one way of trading with countries that lack convertible currency.
    a. Counter trading
    b. Bartering
    c. Foreign licensing
    d. Exporting

    b., Easy, Page 472

26. Which of the following is/are often used by companies exporting to countries that lack a convertible currency?
    a. Counter trading.
    b. Indirect exporting.
    c. Bartering.
    d. A and C only.

    d., Medium, Page 472

27. Nance Technologies, Inc., has agreed to sell some of its computers to a company in Bascovina, a country whose currency is worthless outside its own borders. As part of the agreement, Nance will sell the foreign customer its computers in exchange for a specified number of tons of coffee, a major export of Bascovina. Nance has already arranged to sell the coffee to a major processor for a set price in U.S. dollars. Nance has engaged in:
    a. bartering.
    b. foreign licensing.
    c. exporting.
    d. countertrading.

    a., Medium, Page 472

28. What percentage of small businesses export to only one country?
    a. one-fourth
    b. two-thirds
    c. one-half
    d. one-third

    b., Medium, Page 472

29. The biggest barrier facing companies that have never exported is:
    a. finding the financing to launch an export program.
    b. not knowing where or how to start.
    c. locating a trade intermediary to represent them in foreign markets.
    d. winning government approval to begin selling in foreign markets.

    b., Medium, Page 472

30. The first two stops on an entrepreneur's agenda for going global should include:
    a. U.S. Department of Commerce.
    b. International Trade Administration.
    c. A and B above.
    d. B and the Small Business Administration.

    c., Medium, Page 473

31. Among major industrialized nations, the U.S. government spends _____ to promote exports.
    a. the least per capita
    b. the most per capita
    c. more than average
    d. none of the above

    a., Medium, Page 474

32. A _____ is an agreement between an exporter's bank and the foreign buyer's bank that guarantees payment to the exporter for a specific shipment of goods.
    a. bank draft
    b. letter of credit
    c. repurchase agreement
    d. trade acceptance

    b., Easy, Page 475

33. A _____ is a document an exporter draws on a foreign buyer, requiring the buyer to pay the face amount either on sight or on a specified date once the goods are shipped.
    a. bank draft
    b. letter of credit
    c. repurchase agreement
    d. trade acceptance

    a., Easy, Page 476

34. Which of the following is **not** one of the three major advantages to establishing an international location?
    a. lower production costs
    b. need for smaller staff
    c. lower marketing costs
    d. development of an intimate knowledge of customer preferences

    b., Medium, Page 477

35. Which of the following is a **domestic** barrier to small business exporting?
    a. The attitude, "I'm too small to export."
    b. A lack of information about how to get started in exporting.
    c. A lack of export financing for small companies.
    d. All of the above.

    d., Medium, Page 478

36. Malcolm won a contract to provide nuts, bolts, and washers to a small African country's military. Unfortunately, neither his bankers nor venture capitalists would provide the loans needed to buy the material to produce the order. The bank didn't do international loans. Which barrier to international trade is Malcolm experiencing?
   a. Financing
   b. Information
   c. Cultural
   d. Attitude

   a., Easy, Page 478

37. John wants to expand into the foreign markets, but he can't convince his partners. They believe that international markets are the domain of large corporations. John is facing which barrier to international trade?
   a. Financing
   b. Political
   c. Cultural
   d. Attitude

   d., Easy, Page 478

38. A tariff is:
   a. a law that government uses to regulate products that are imported into the country.
   b. the maximum amount of a product that can be imported or exported.
   c. a prohibition or suspension of foreign trade of specific imports or exports.
   d. a duty, or tax, that a government puts on products that are imported into the country.

   d., Easy, Page 478

39. The small country of Bascovina wanted to protect its infant basket industry and imposed a 400 percent tariff on all imported baskets. The high tariff dropped the bottom out of imported basket sales, and imports of baskets stops. Why did this happen?
   a. The citizens realized that because the government imposed the tariff, imported basket purchases were undesirable.
   b. The tariff reduced the price of imported baskets and consumers felt that because of the low prices, the baskets were of low quality and stopped their purchases.
   c. The tariff barred all shipments of baskets to Bascovina.
   d. The tariff makes the price of imported baskets so high that they are not competitive.

   d., Medium, Page 478

40. A quota is:
   a. a duty or tax that a government puts on products that are imported into the country.
   b. the maximum amount of a product that can be imported into a country.
   c. a prohibition or suspension of foreign trade of specific imports or exports.
   d. a law that a government uses to regulate products that are imported into the country.

   b., Medium, Page 478

41. _____ is the practice of selling substantial quantities of a product in a foreign market at prices that are below either the home-market price or below the full cost of producing it.
    a. Exporting
    b. Bartering
    c. Dumping
    d. Price discrimination

c., Easy, Page 479

42. An embargo is:
    a. a duty, or tax, that a government puts on products that are imported into the country.
    b. the maximum amount of a product that can be imported or exported.
    c. a prohibition or suspension of foreign trade of specific imports or exports.
    d. a law that a government uses to regulate products that are imported into the country.

c., Medium, Page 479

43. An American executive went to a foreign country to sign a business contract. While there, he found that there were numerous complex government regulations his company needed to meet before closing the deal. This executive was experiencing which barrier to international trade?
    a. Tariff
    b. Political
    c. Cultural
    d. Domestic

b., Easy, Page 479

44. Business owners new to international business are sometimes shocked:
    a. by the wide range of labor costs they encounter.
    b. that practices common in the United States, such as overtime, women workers, and employee benefits, are restricted, disfavored, or forbidden in other cultures.
    c. that what appear to be "bargain" labor rates turn out to be excessively high after accounting for the quality of the labor force and the benefits their governments mandate.
    d. All of the above.

d., Medium, Page 479

45. An American executive went to a Middle Eastern country to sign an oil contract. Before the contract was signed, the American and the Arab official met for tea. Relaxing, the American put his feet up on a table. The official became angry and left the room. Later it was found that showing the soles of shoes was a serious insult. This represents which barrier to international trade?
    a. Tactical
    b. Political
    c. Strategic
    d. Cultural

d., Easy, Page 480

46.   As of 2003, the World Trade Organization had 146 member countries that represent over
       _____ of all world trade.
       a.   97 percent
       b.   39 percent
       c.   76 percent
       d.   52 percent

       a., Difficult, Page 481

47.   The North American Free Trade Agreement:
       a.   brought South America, Mexico, the U.S., and Canada together as one market.
       b.   eliminated all tariffs among member nations, effective immediately, and raised them to
            nonmembers.
       c.   mostly benefits the trading relationship between Canada and the U.S..
       d.   created a unified market of 400 million people and $6.5 trillion in goods and services.

       d., Medium, Page 482

48.   The North American Free Trade Agreement (NAFTA) created a free trade area among:
       a.   Canada, Mexico, and the United States.
       b.   Japan, Mexico, and Canada
       c.   Mexico, Japan, and the United States
       d.   None of the above.

       a., Medium, Page 482

49.   The North American Free Trade Agreement has which of the following provisions?
       a.   The immediate elimination of all tariff and quota barriers on all goods
       b.   The elimination of nontariff barriers by 2008
       c.   A lowering of safety and air quality standards
       d.   The formation of a North American Trade Organization

       b., Medium, Page 483

50.   Which of the following is a guideline for becoming a successful international competitor?
       a.   Make yourself at home in all of the world's key markets—North America, Europe, and
            Asia.
       b.   Become familiar with foreign customs and languages.
       c.   Consider using partners and joint ventures to break into foreign markets you cannot
            penetrate on your own.
       d.   All of the above.

       d., Easy, Page 483

True/False Questions:

51.   Only about one-third of the world's purchasing power lies outside the borders of the United
       States.

       False, Medium, Page 464

52. As the trend toward increased globalization continues, successful companies must consider themselves businesses without borders.

    True, Easy, Page 464

53. In industries with high levels of fixed costs, one of the drawbacks of expanding into global markets is increased manufacturing costs.

    False, Medium, Page 465

54. Success in the global economy requires constant innovation, high quality, and flexibility.

    True, Easy, Page 465

55. Small companies that take the plunge into global business can extend their products' life cycles, raise their quality levels, and increase sales and profits.

    True, Medium, Page 465

56 Learning to think globally may be the first—and most threatening—obstacle an entrepreneur must overcome on the way to creating a truly global business.

    True, Medium, Page 465

57. Some of the strategic options entrepreneurs have when deciding to go global include the World Wide Web, joint ventures, and franchising.

    True, Easy, Page 466

58. Entreprenuers can use the Web to generate sales leads by researching customers and market characteristics in other countries.

    True, Easy, Page 467

59. Most export management companies are merchant intermediaries that work on a buy-and-sell arrangement with domestic small companies, providing small businesses with a low-cost, efficient, independent, international marketing department.

    True, Easy, Page 468

60. While export management companies tend to focus on exporting, export trading companies usually perform both import and export trades across many countries' borders.

    True, Medium, Page 468

61. Export trading companies are government-owned operations established in countries around the world (including the United States) for the purpose of buying goods there.

    False, Easy, Page 468

62. Unlike an EMC or an ETC, manufacturers' export agents act as international sales representatives in a limited number of markets for various noncompeting domestic companies, typically operating on a commission basis.

   True, Medium, Page 468

63. Most export merchants buy goods, often competing lines, from many domestic companies and then sell them in foreign markets.

   True, Medium, Page 468

64. Selling to a resident buying office is just like selling to domestic customers since the buying office handles all of the details of exporting the products.

   True, Medium, Page 468

65. Foreign distributors offer exporting small businesses the benefit of knowledge of the local markets in which they sell, the ability to cover a foreign sales territory thoroughly, and the ability to handle all of the marketing, distribution, and service functions in foreign markets.

   True, Medium, Page 469

66. Most small businesses getting started in conducting global business do not need the services of trade intermediaries because "going global" has become so easy that even the smallest businesses can do it alone.

   False, Medium, Page 469

67. In a domestic joint venture, a domestic company forms an alliance with a company in the target nation.

   False, Easy, Page 469

68. When two small businesses in the target nation form an alliance, they have formed a foreign joint venture.

   False, Medium, Page 469

69. Some foreign countries place limitations on joint ventures with host companies within their borders, e.g., by requiring the host company to own at least 51 percent of the venture.

   True, Easy, Page 469

70. One reason joint ventures fail is because entrepreneurs did not select a partner who shares their company's values and standards of conduct.

   True, Easy, Page 470

71. Foreign licensing is when a business buys and sells products in many countries, either in its own name, or as an agent for its buyer-seller clients.

    False, Medium, Page 471

72. Foreign licensing is a relatively simple way for even the most inexperienced business owner to extend his reach into global markets.

    True, Medium, Page 471

73. Before engaging in foreign licensing, a business owner should secure patent trademark and copyright protection.

    True, Easy, Page 471

74. The licensing potential for intangibles, such as technology, trademarks, etc., is often greater than the licensing opportunities for products.

    True, Medium, Page 471

75. As the domestic market for franchises has become increasingly saturated with outlets, the number of franchisers attracted to foreign markets has grown.

    True, Easy, Page 471

76. Although franchising is a popular way to do business in the United States, it is not a popular strategy in international markets.

    False, Medium, Page 471

77. Although franchise outlets operate throughout the world, the primary market for U.S. franchisers is Europe.

    False, Medium, Page 471

78. One reason for McDonald's success in foreign markets is its decision to stick to exactly the same menu in every country that it offers in the United States.

    False, Medium, Page 471

79. A countertrade is a transaction in which a company selling goods and services in a foreign country agrees to help promote investment and trade in that country.

    True, Easy, Page 471

80. If a country's currency is not convertible into any other currency, companies exporting to that country usually engage in either countertrading or bartering.

    True, Medium, Page 472

81. Successful bartering is easier than countertrade but requires finding a business with complementary needs.

   True, Medium, Page 472

82. The biggest barrier facing companies that have never exported is not knowing where or how to start.

   True, Medium, Page 472

83. The first and most difficult step to exporting for the small business is breaking the psychological barrier, "My company is too small to export."

   True, Easy, Page 472

84. Even the smallest businesses have the potential to export.

   True, Easy, Page 472

85. Researching potential export markets is a waste of time and resources for small business owners; the best way to find export opportunities is to travel abroad and sell.

   False, Easy, Page 472

86. The U.S. Department of Commerce and the International Trade Administration have the market research available for locating that best target markets for a particular company and specific customers in those markets.

   True, Medium, Page 473

87. Lack of export financing remains a significant barrier to small businesses selling in foreign markets.

   True, Easy, Page 474

88. Among major industrialized nations, the United States spends the greatest amount per capita to promote exports.

   False, Medium, Page 474

89. Collecting foreign accounts is usually less complex than collecting domestic ones.

   False, Easy, Page 475

90. A letter of credit is an agreement between an exporter's bank and a foreign buyer's bank that guarantees payment to the exporter for a specific shipment of goods.

   True, Easy, Page 475

91. Many small companies are forming foreign sales corporations (FSCs) to take advantage of a tax benefit that is designed to stimulate exports.

True, Medium, Page 476

92. Most small businesses begin their global ventures by establishing international locations.

False, Medium, Page 477

93. The key to success in international markets is choosing the correct target market and designing a strategy to reach it.

True, Easy, Page 478

94. The three biggest domestic barriers to exporting facing small businesses are attitude, information, and financing.

True, Medium, Page 478

95. A tariff is a limit on the amount of a product imported into a country.

False, Easy, Page 478

96. The government of Palmeria placed a high import tariff on steel from Dano. Dano's steel is higher in quality and cheaper. Palmeria's actions result in higher prices for their consumers.

True, Medium, Page 478

97. A quota is a limit on the amount of certain products imported into a country, while an embargo is a total ban on imports of certain products.

True, Easy, Page 478

98. Dumping involves selling large quantities of a product in a foreign market below cost.

True, Easy, Page 479

99. Selling large quantities of a product in a foreign market below cost is the best way for a small company to begin its export program.

False, Medium, Page 479

100. To prove a charge of dumping under the U.S. Antidumping Act, a company must prove that a foreign company's prices on a product are lower here than in the home country and that U.S. companies are directly harmed.

True, Medium, Page 479

101. The only cultural barrier an American small business manager must overcome when conducting business internationally is the language gap.

False, Easy, Page 479

102. Learning the habits and the customs of the cultures in which they do business is essential for small business managers trying to go global.

True, Easy, Page 480

103. American business people can be on their best American behavior and go overseas and offend the locals. This is, in part, due to the fact that business customs that are acceptable or even expected in one country may be taboo in another.

True, Easy, Page 480

104. Fortunately for U.S. business owners, American customs and habits have become the standard for proper business behavior around the world.

False, Medium, Page 480

105. A free trade area is an association of countries that have agreed to knock down trade barriers—both tariff and nontariff—among partner nations.

True, Easy, Page 482

106. NAFTA is an agreement between the U.S., Canada, Mexico, Argentina, and Chile, forming a free trade area among these countries.

False, Medium, Page 482

107. While the WTO had 146 member countries in 2003, which represent over 97 percent of all world trade, the market formed by NAFTA has more than 400 million people and an annual output of $6.5 trillion in goods and services.

True, Medium, Page 482

108. NAFTA includes provisions reducing tariff and nontariff barriers and toughening health and safety standards.

True, Medium, Page 483

109. An important guideline for companies wanting to successfully compete internationally is to appeal to the similarities within the various regions in which you operate, but recognize the differences in their specific cultures.

True, Medium, Page 483

110. An important guideline for companies wanting to successfully compete internationally is to familiarize yourself with foreign customs, languages, and cultures, including their lifestyles, values, customs, and business practices.

True, Medium, Page 483

Essay Questions:

111. Explain why it is important to "go global." What benefits can companies that take the plunge into global business expect?

Small businesses can no longer consider themselves to be domestic companies if they truly want to compete. Political, social, cultural, and economic forces are driving small businesses into international markets. Powerful, affordable technology increases access to information on conducting global business, and the growing independence of the world economies makes it easier for companies of all sizes to engage in international trade.

Since the global market offers more niches, the flexibility and speed of a small business can become a competitive advantage. Advantages of going global include:

- Offsetting sales declines in the domestic market
- Increasing sales and profits
- Extending their products' life cycles
- Lowering manufacturing costs
- Improving competitive position and enhancing reputation
- Raising quality levels
- Becoming more customer-oriented.

Page 464-465

112. Outline the eight strategies for "going global" available to the small business owner.

- Launching a World Wide Web site—Small businesses should follow a three-step approach to conducting global business on the Web. Step 1 – connect to e-mail, Step 2 – connect to and conduct international market research, Step 3 – build a global Web site.

- Relying on trade intermediaries—Rather than create an export program "from scratch," small companies can rely on trade intermediaries for assistance - Export Management companies (EMC), Export Trading Companies (ETC), Manufacturers Export agents (MEA), Export Merchants, Resident Buying Offices, and overseas distributors all provide a variety of services for a fee. Typically, at least $50,000 in sales is required to make their fees affordable.

- Joint ventures—In a domestic joint venture, two or more U.S. small businesses form an alliance for the purpose of exporting their goods and services abroad, which typically lowers their individual risk. Special anti-trust immunity is typically requested, allowing them to cooperate freely. In a foreign joint venture, a domestic small business forms an alliance with a company in the target nation.

- Foreign licensing—Small companies can license businesses in other nations to use their patents, copyrights, trademarks, technology, processes, or products in return for royalty payments from sales. Risks include losing control or the possibility of creating a competitor.

- International franchising—International outlets provide new sales to boost lagging sales and saturated U.S. markets. Most franchises have found they need to modify their normally standardized products for foreign tastes. Entrepreneurs have the backing of a large organization and need help in understanding different markets.

- Countertrading and bartering—When a target nation's currency is worthless outside its borders, companies often turn to barter—the exchange of goods and services for other goods and services.

- Exporting—Even the tiniest and least experienced entrepreneurs have the potential to export. The biggest barrier is not knowing where or how to start.

- Establishing international locations—Setting up an international office can require a significant investment.

Pages 466-477

113. One of the eight strategies a company uses to "go global" includes the use of trade intermediaries. Identify the six types of trade intermediaries and explain why a small business owner might use each one.

- Export Management Companies (EMCs)—EMCs are merchant intermediaries that provide small businesses with a low-cost, efficient, independent international marketing department. Their focus is on exporting, and they typically do not handle competing firms.

- Export Trading Companies (ETCs)—ETCs are businesses that buy and sell products in a number of countries and offer a wide variety of services—exporting, importing, shipping, storing, and distributing—to their clients who may be competitors. They focus on long-term relationships.

- Manufacturer's Export Agents (MEAs)—MEAs are businesses that act as international sales representatives in a limited number of markets for various non-competing domestic companies. They are commissioned based and focus on short-term commitments.

- Export Merchants—Export merchants are domestic wholesalers who buy goods from many domestic manufacturers and then market them in foreign markets. Most export merchants specialize in particular industries and often carry competing lines.

- Resident Buying Offices—A government- or privately-owned operation established in a country for the purpose of buying goods from businesses there. The buying office handles all the details of exporting.

- Foreign Distributors—Domestic small companies export their products to foreign distributors who handle all of the marketing, distribution, and service functions in the foreign country. They offer exporting small businesses the benefits of knowledge in their local markets, the ability to cover a given territory thoroughly, and prompt sales and service support.

Page 468-469

114. What advantages do taking on a partner in a joint venture offer a small business in an international business opportunity? Disadvantages?

Domestic joint venture—two or more U.S. small businesses form an alliance for the purpose of exporting their goods and services abroad.
Foreign joint venture—a domestic small business forms an alliance with a company in the target nation.
Advantages of international joint venture:
- Penetrate protected markets.
- Lower production costs.
- Share risks and high R&D costs.
- Gain access to marketing and distribution channels.
Disadvantages of international joint venture:
- Failure of the venture.
- Relationships that sour.
- Becoming overly dependent on the partner.

Pages 469-471

115. What strategies for trade can businesses use when exporting to countries whose currencies are not convertible to other currencies? What are the disadvantages?

Countertrade is a transaction in which a company selling goods and services in a foreign country agrees to help promote investment and trade in that country, even though profits cannot be taken in the form of currency exchange. Countertrading transactions can be complicated, cumbersome, and time consuming. They also increase the chances that a company will get stuck with useless merchandise that it cannot move. They can also lead to surprises in the quantity and quality of products required in the counter trade. Bartering is the exchange for goods and services for other goods and services. Usually the traded goods are sold to a third party for cash. Barter transactions require finding a business with complementary needs, but they are much simpler than countertrading.

Pages 471-472

116. List and briefly explain the steps an entrepreneur should follow to establish an export program.

The following steps provide guidance to an entrepreneur on how to establish an exporting program:

1. Recognize that even the tiniest companies and least experienced entrepreneurs have the potential to export. The size of the firm has nothing to do with the demand for its products. If the products meet the needs of global customers, there is a potential to export.

2. Analyze your product or service. Is it special? New? Unique? High quality? Priced favorably because of lower costs or exchange rates? In which countries would there be sufficient demand for it?

3. Analyze your commitment. Are you willing to devote the time and energy to develop export markets? Does your company have the necessary resources? Export start-ups can take from six to eight months (or longer), but entering foreign markets isn't as tough as most entrepreneurs think.

4. Research markets and pick your target. Before investing in a costly sales trip abroad, entrepreneurs should make a trip to the local library or the nearest branch of the Department of Commerce. Exporters can choose from a multitude of guides, manuals, books, newsletters, videos, and other resources to help them research potential markets. Armed with research, small business owners can avoid wasting a lot of time and money on markets with limited potential for their products and can concentrate on those with the greatest promise. Research shows export entrepreneurs whether they need to modify their existing products and services to suit the tastes and preferences of their foreign target customers. Sometimes foreign customers' lifestyles, housing needs, body size, and cultures require exporters to make alterations in their product lines. Such modifications can sometimes spell the difference between success and failure in the global market.

5. Develop a distribution strategy. Should you use an export middleperson or sell directly to foreign customers? Small companies just entering international markets may prefer to rely on export middlepersons to break new ground.

6. Find your customer. Small businesses can rely on a host of export specialists to help them track down foreign customers. The U.S. Department of Commerce and the International Trade Administration should be the first stops on an entrepreneur's agenda for going global. These agencies have the market research available for locating the best target markets for a particular company and specific customers in those markets. They also have knowledgeable staff specialists experienced in the details of global trade and in the intricacies of foreign cultures.

7. Find financing. One of the biggest barriers to small business exports is lack of financing. Access to adequate financing is a crucial ingredient in a successful export program because the cost of generating foreign sales often is higher and collection cycles are longer than in domestic markets. The trouble is that bankers and other sources of capital don't always understand the intricacies of international sales and view financing them as excessively risky. Also, among major industrialized nations, the U.S. government spent the least per capita to promote exports.
Several federal, state, and private programs are operating to fill this export financing void, however.

8. Ship your goods. Export novices usually rely on international freight forwarders and custom-house agents – experienced specialists in overseas shipping – for help in navigating the bureaucratic morass of packaging requirements and paperwork demanded by customs. These specialists, also known as transport architects, are to

exporters what travel agents are to passengers and normally charge relatively small fees for a valuable service. They move shipments of all sizes to destinations all over the world efficiently, saving entrepreneurs many headaches.

9. Collect your money. Collecting foreign accounts can be more complex than collecting domestic ones, but by picking their customers carefully and checking their credit references closely, entrepreneurs can minimize bad-debt losses. Financing foreign sales often involves special credit arrangements such as letters of credit and bank (or documentary) drafts.

Page 472

117. Identify and discuss the domestic barriers to trade.

Three major domestic barriers to international trade are common:

- Attitude of "I'm too small to export"—The first step to building an export program is recognizing that the opportunity to export exists.
- Lack of Information—Entrepreneurs should thoroughly research the possibility of going global and use every possible resource available to them—government and private organizations' international exporting and marketing information—in order to make valid decisions. Also, companies must be willing to make the necessary adjustments to their products and services, promotional campaigns, packaging, and sales techniques in foreign markets.
- Lack of Available Financing—Many entrepreneurs cite lack of financing as a major barrier to international trade. Before embarking on an export program, entrepreneurs should have available financing lined up.

Page 478

118. Identify and discuss the international barriers to trade.

International barriers include the following:
- Tariffs—a tax, or duty, that a government imposes on goods and services imported into that country. Imposing tariffs raises the price of the imported goods – making them less attractive to consumers – and protects the makers of comparable domestic product and services.

- Quotas—a limit on the amount of a product imported into a country, which helps to protect domestic markets by limiting opportunities for foreign competitors.

- Embargoes—a total ban on imports of certain products, which helps to protect domestic markets by keeping foreign competitors out.

- Dumping—selling large quantities of them in foreign countries below cost. Under the U.S. Antidumping Act, a company must prove that the foreign company's prices are lower here than in the home country and that U.S. companies are directly harmed.

Page 478-479

119. Describe the other barriers to trade, including political, business, and cultural:

- Political barriers—Although many U.S. business owners complain of excessive government regulation in the United States, they are often astounded by the complex web of governmental and legal regulations and barriers they encounter in foreign countries. Companies doing business in politically risky lands face the very real dangers of government takeovers of private property; attempts at coups to overthrow ruling parties; kidnapping, bombings, and other violent acts against businesses and their employees; and other threatening events. Their investments of millions of dollars may evaporate overnight in the wake of a government coup or the passage of a law nationalizing an industry (giving control of an entire industry to the government).

- Business barriers—American companies doing business internationally quickly learn that business practices and regulations in foreign lands can be quite different from those in the United States. Simply duplicating the practices they have adopted (and have used successfully) in the domestic market and using them in foreign markets is not always a good idea. Perhaps the biggest shock comes in the area of human resources management, where international managers discover that practices common in the United States, such as overtime, women workers, and employee benefits are restricted, disfavored, or forbidden in other cultures. Business owners new to international business sometimes are shocked at the wide range of labor costs they encounter and the accompanying wide range of skilled labor available. In some countries, what appear to be "bargain" labor rates turn out to be excessively high after accounting for the quality of the labor force and the benefits their governments mandate. In many nations, labor unions are present in almost every company, yet they play a very different role from the unions in the United States. Although management-union relations are not as hostile as in the United States and strikes are not as common, unions can greatly complicate a company's ability to compete effectively.

- Cultural barriers—The culture of a nation includes the beliefs, values, view, and mores that its inhabitants have. Differences in cultures among nations create another barrier to international trade. The diversity of languages, business philosophies, practices, and traditions make international trade more complex than selling to the business down the street. The assumption that the American way of doing things is universal is false. Many international business deals fail because businesspersons do not understand the importance of valuing diversity, or being sensitive and respectful to different ways of doing business. Entrepreneurs who want to be successful in international markets must understand the culture in which they plan to do business and adapt their business styles and their products to suit that culture.

Page 479

Chapter 14
Global Aspects of Entrepreneurship
Mini-Case

Case 14-1: The Grass is Really Greener

It's not usual for city people to be concerned about plants or grass—they see so little of them. But Martha Goldman has been interested in these things since her first biology course back in Brooklyn, New York. Martha won all the awards in the science fairs and eventually was the recipient of a scholarship to college. She chose to major in botany and became fascinated with the creation of hybrid plants and grasses. Martha was also concerned about the problem of hunger around the world. She knew that improved plants and grains increased the productivity of American agriculture, and hoped that someday, she would find a way to play a small part in reducing world hunger.

After college, with the help of her dad, she opened a small wholesale greenhouse. The business was a modest success and allowed Martha to experiment with new growing methods. Two years ago, Martha's research paid off. She had been working on developing a fast-growing grass that needed less water. One of the experiments produced a grass that seemed to have real potential. She tested it with a local cattle rancher. All tests so far have shown that the new hybrid grass is better for feeding cattle. Martha may have realized her dream—a grass that will grow better in parts of the world that could not previously support cattle. High protein beef cattle may now be able to thrive in parts of the world where previously it was not possible.

How should Martha proceed to determine the best way to export her new grass seed?

It appears that Martha's product has definite potential. Now, she must target specific export markets, develop an export marketing strategy, and then implement it. Initially, she should target one or two "prime" markets using the wealth of published data from the U.S. Department of Commerce. Martha should explore many of the developing nations in arid regions. She should seek advice and assistance from Export Trading Companies and Export Management Companies. She should also contact the International Trade Association and conduct searches on the World Wide Web to determine which markets could be best to target first. (See Table 14.1 in the text for more international trade resources.) Martha should focus on locating dependable foreign distributors and invoice all sales in U.S. dollars.

Chapter 15 Leading the Growing Company and Planning for Management Succession

Multiple Choice Questions:

1. _____ is the process of influencing and inspiring others to work to achieve a common goal and then giving them the power and the freedom to achieve it.
   a. Management
   b. Organizing
   c. Leadership
   d. Coordination

   c., Easy, Page 487

2. Leadership:
   a. is essential to a company's success.
   b. is not an easy skill to learn.
   c. involves influencing and inspiring others to work to achieve a common goal and then giving them the power and the freedom to achieve it.
   d. All of the above.

   d., Easy, Page 487

3. Which of the following pairs describing leadership (first column) and management (second column) is **not** correct?

	Leadership	**Management**
a.	comes first	comes second
b.	deals with people	deals with things
c.	involves doing things right	involves doing the right things
d.	Actually, all of the above **are** correct.	

   c., Medium, Page 487

4. Which of the following is **not** a behavior typically exhibited by effective leaders?
   a. Define and constantly reinforce the vision they have for the company.
   b. Respect and support their employees.
   c. Require employees to gather necessary resources to complete their tasks; they will be more likely to "feel ownership" than if you did it for them.
   d. Create an environment in which people have the motivation, the training, and the freedom to achieve the goals they have set.

   c., Easy, Page 488

5.   Which of the following is **not** one of the four vital tasks small business leaders must perform?
     a.   Hire the right employees and constantly improve their skills.
     b.   Build an organizational culture and structure that allow both workers and the company to reach their potential.
     c.   Motivate workers to higher levels of performance.
     d.   Don't plan to "pass the torch" to the next generation of leadership; everything changes so quickly that the next generation is going to have challenges and opportunities you know nothing about.

d., Easy, Page 489

6.   Which of the following is true regarding hiring mistakes?
     a.   Hiring mistakes are very expensive.
     b.   One study concluded that an employee hired into a typical entry-level position who quits after six months costs a company about $17,000 in salary, benefits, and training; the indirect costs are seven times that figure, which brings the total cost of the "bad hire" to $136,000.
     c.   Small businesses are most likely to make hiring mistakes because they lack the human resources experts and the disciplined hiring procedures large companies have.
     d.   All of the above.

d., Medium, Page 491

7.   One study concluded that an employee hired into a typical entry-level position who quits after six months, costs a company approximately _____ in salary, benefits, and training.
     a. $8,500
     b. $13,000
     c. $17,000
     d. $22,500

c., Medium, Page 491

8.   Small companies are most likely to make hiring mistakes for all but which of the following reasons?
     a.   They lack the human resources experts that larger companies have.
     b.   Their hiring process is too formal and its results often unpredictable.
     c.   They lack the disciplined hiring procedures that larger companies have.
     d.   They rarely take the time to create job descriptions and job specifications.

b., Medium, Page 491

9.   Which of the following is **not** one of suggested guidelines for small business managers to avoid making costly hiring mistakes?
     a.   Elevate recruiting to a strategic position in the company.
     b.   Create practical job descriptions and job specifications.
     c.   Plan and conduct an effective interview.
     d.   Avoid checking references; no one is going to tell you anything anyway.

d., Medium, Page 491

10.   Which of the following techniques would you **not** recommend to a company desiring a stronger recruiting strategy?
    a.   Look inside the company first; a promotion from within policy serves as an incentive for existing workers to upgrade their skills.
    b.   Encourage employee referrals; reward employees for successful referrals.
    c.   Ensure that your recruitment efforts are known—whether in traditional media, the Internet, or on college campuses.
    d.   Steer clear of retired workers; they don't have anything to offer.

    d., Easy, Page 491

11.   A _____ is the process by which a company determines the duties and the nature of the jobs to be filled and the skills and experience required of the people who are to fill them.
    a.   job analysis
    b.   job description
    c.   job specification
    d.   management audit

    a., Easy, Page 493

12.   Luisa, the director of human resources, is discussing the duties and responsibilities of a new position and its working conditions with Delmar, the manager over the position. Luisa and Delmar are discussing a:
    a.   job description.
    b.   management audit.
    c.   job specification.
    d.   job analysis.

    a., Easy, Page 493

13.   Burt is applying for a position as a staff accountant. The job specification for the position might list all of the following items **except:**
    a.   BBA in Accounting.
    b.   3 years of experience.
    c.   prepare daily sales reports.
    d.   knowledge of Quickbooks.

    c., Medium, Page 493

14.   A _____ identifies the duties and responsibilities of a position and its working conditions, while a _____ identifies the qualifications required of the job candidate in terms of skills, education, and experience needed.
    a.   job specification; job description
    b.   job description; job specification
    c.   job analysis; job specification
    d.   job analysis; job description

    a., Medium, Page 493

15. The _____, published by the Department of Labor, lists more than 20,000 job titles and descriptions and serves as a useful tool for getting a small business owner started when writing job descriptions.
    a. Title IX Handbook
    b. Team Handbook
    c. Job Listing Directory
    d. Dictionary of Occupational Titles

    d., Medium, Page 493

16. Which of the following types of questions should a business owner ask a candidate in a job interview?
    a. questions calling for "yes or no" answers
    b. questions about the candidate's religious beliefs
    c. questions based on on-the-job scenarios that require open-ended answers
    d. questions about the candidate's physical traits, characteristics, and family life

    c., Medium, Page 494

17. Which of the following is **not** a recommended guideline for developing questions to ask candidates in job interviews?
    a. Develop a series of core questions and ask them of every candidate.
    b. Ask only questions calling for "yes or no" answers to avoid any controversy regarding the   direction the job interview took; this way, you have better control of the situation.
    c. Create hypothetical situations candidates would likely encounter on the job and ask how they would handle them.
    d. Ask candidates to describe a recent success and a recent failure and how they dealt with them.

    b., Medium, Page 494

18. Which of the following is **not** one of the phases of an effective job interview?
    a. Breaking the ice
    b. Performing random drug tests
    c. Selling the candidate on the company
    d. Asking questions

    b., Easy, Page 495

19. The interviewer's **primary** responsibility in a job interview is to:
    a. put candidates under as much stress as possible and observe how they handle it.
    b. listen.
    c. try to catch candidates in the lies they tell.
    d. do whatever it takes to convince candidates that the company is a great place to work.

    b., Medium, Page 495

20. Effective interviewers spend about ____ percent of the interview talking and ___ percent listening.
    a. 25; 75
    b. 50; 50
    c. 75; 25
    d. 90; 10

    a., Medium, Page 495

21. Successful interviewers always listen for these in an interview to see whether or not it matches the candidate's words. This interviewer is referring to the candidate's:
    a. work experience.
    b. job-related skills.
    c. nonverbal clues or body language.
    d. nervousness.

    c., Medium, Page 495

22. Which government agency is responsible for enforcing employment laws?
    a. The Fair Labor Standards Commission
    b. The National Labor Relations Board
    c. The Equal Employment Opportunity Commission
    d. The Justice Department

    c., Medium, Page 495

23. If a job candidate files charges of employment discrimination against a company, the burden of proof in the case falls on:
    a. the employer to prove that all pre-employment questions are job-related and nondiscriminatory.
    b. the candidate to prove that some pre-employment questions and actions were discriminatory.
    c. the Equal Employment Opportunity Commission representing the job candidate in the lawsuit.
    d. None of the above.

    a., Medium, Page 495

24. In the final phase of an interview:
    a. the employer tries to "sell" her company to desirable candidates.
    b. the interviewer gives the job candidates the opportunity to ask questions about the company, the job, or other issues.
    c. the interviewer tells the candidate what happens next in the selection process.
    d. All of the above.

    d., Medium, Page 496

25. According to the Society for Human Resource Management, more than _____ of candidates either exaggerated or falsified information about their previous employment on their resumes.
     a. one-third
     b. three-fourths
     c. half
     d. two-thirds

     c., Medium, Page 496

26. _____ is the distinctive, unwritten code of conduct that governs the behavior, attitudes, relationships, and style of an organization.
     a. Organizational structure
     b. Company culture
     c. Hierarchy of command
     d. Formal organization

     b., Easy, Page 496

27. Company culture has a powerful impact on:
     a. the way people work together in a business.
     b. how people in a company do their jobs.
     c. how people in a company treat their customers.
     d. All of the above.

     c., Easy, Page 496

28. Which of the following statements about a company's culture is **false?**
     a. Company culture manifests itself in a variety of ways from how workers dress and act to the language they use.
     b. As a company grows larger, its culture tends to remain constant.
     c. Culture arises from an entrepreneur's consistent and relentless pursuit of a set of core values that everyone in the company can believe in.
     d. All of the above.

     b., Medium, Page 496

29. A company's culture manifests itself in:
     a. how workers dress.
     b. the language workers use.
     c. the way workers behave.
     d. All of the above.

     d., Easy, Page 496

30. Which of the following questions would be **illegal** in a job interview?
     a. "Have you ever been arrested?"
     b. "Are you a U.S. citizen?"
     c. "Do you have any physical or mental disabilities that would interfere with your doing this job?"
     d. All of the above.

d., Medium, Page 497

31. Which of the following questions would be **legal** in a job interview?
     a. "Do you have any children or are you planning to have children?"
     b. "Do you have any physical or mental disabilities that would interfere with your doing this job?"
     c. "Is there any limit to your ability to work overtime or to travel?"
     d. "What contraceptive practices do you employ?"

c., Medium, Page 497

32. Successful organizational culture supports exceptional performance and is compatible with the firm's stated values and beliefs. Which of the following does **not** illustrate this concept?
     a. Respect for work and life balance
     b. A sense of purpose and a sense of fun
     c. Honesty and integrity
     d. Autocratic management

d., Easy, Page 499

33. According to recent studies, which of the following is/are true regarding the differences between small companies and their larger rivals?
     a. Large companies' inability to react quickly is a major barrier to their growth.
     b. Small companies focus on expanding their existing product and service lines, while large companies concentrate more on creating new ones.
     c. Large companies follow a "clean slate" approach to market research and technology while small companies are hesitant to change research and technology that has worked in the past.
     d. Actually all of the above **are** true.

a., Difficult, Page 503

34. Under the _____ management style, entrepreneurs run a one-man or one-woman show, doing everything themselves because their primary concern is with the quality of the products or services they produce.
     a. Craftsman
     b. Classic
     c. Coordinator
     d. Big-team venture

a., Easy, Page 503

35. The biggest **disadvantage** of the Craftsman management style is:
    a. the entrepreneur's inability to control the key aspects of the business.
    b. that the entrepreneur must do everything in the business.
    c. the limitations it puts on a company's ability to grow.
    d. the quality problems it creates for the company.

c., Difficult, Page 503

36. Under the Classic management style, an entrepreneur:
    a. insists on tight supervision.
    b. constantly monitors employees' work.
    c. performs all critical tasks herself.
    d. All of the above.

d., Easy, Page 503

37. Which of the following is **not** a characteristic of the Coordinator management style?
    a. It gives an entrepreneur the ability to build a fairly large company with very few employees.
    b. The company's success is highly dependent on its suppliers and their ability to produce quality products and services in a timely fashion.
    c. The company is called a virtual corporation because it is actually quite "hollow" since the entrepreneur farms out a large portion of the work to other companies.
    d. The entrepreneur's tendency is to "micromanage" every aspect of the business rather than spending her time focusing on those tasks that are most important and most productive for the company.

d., Medium, Page 504

38. Under the _____ management style, the entrepreneur shifts to a team-based approach, delegating authority to key employees but retaining the final decision-making authority.
    a. Classic
    b. Coordinator
    c. Entrepreneur-plus-employee team
    d. Big-team venture

c., Easy, Page 504

39. Under the _____ management style, an entrepreneur shares managerial responsibilities with at least one other person rather than choosing to manage the company alone.
    a. Classic
    b. Coordinator
    c. Small partnership
    d. Entrepreneur-plus-employee team

c., Easy, Page 504

40. Which of the following management styles typically emerges over time as a company grows and as workload demands and responsibilities increase?
    a. The Craftsman
    b. The Classic
    c. The Big-team venture
    d. The Coordinator

    c., Medium, Page 504

41. Self-directed work teams:
    a. are made up of workers from different functional areas of a company who work together as a unit—largely without supervision.
    b. make decisions and perform tasks that once belonged only to managers.
    c. dramatically change the nature of managers' work in a company.
    d. All of the above.

    d., Easy, Page 505

42. Which of the following is **not** part of a manager's role in a company using self-directed work teams?
    a. coaching
    b. facilitating
    c. bossing
    d. empowering

    c., Easy, Page 505

43. In which of the following companies would a team-based management style be **least** effective?
    a. a small manufacturer of gas grills
    b. a real estate office
    c. an advertising agency
    d. Actually, team-based management would be equally effective in all of the above.

    b., Medium, Page 505

44. Companies using team-based management effectively report all of the following **except**:
    a. gains in quality and increased customer satisfaction.
    b. improved employee motivation and morale.
    c. higher costs.
    d. Actually, they typically report all of the above.

    d., Medium, Page 505

45.   When utilizing a team-based management approach, a manager should **not:**
       a.   pay team members based solely on their individual performances.
       b.   expect employees to become effective team players without training in team dynamics
            and the team processes.
       c.   place a poorly performing employee on a team, expecting team members to improve
            his performance.
       d.   All of the above.

d., Medium, Page 505

46.   To ensure a team's success, managers should:
       a.   form teams around the natural work flow in a company and give them specific tasks to
            accomplish.
       b.   involve team members in determining how their performance will be measured.
       c.   make sure that the teams are appropriate for the company, the nature of the work, and
            the task to be accomplished.
       d.   All of the above.

d., Medium, Page 506

47.   _____ is the degree of effort an employee exerts to accomplish a task; it shows up as
       excitement about work.
       a.   Empowerment
       b.   Motivation
       c.   Job enrichment
       d.   Job enlargement

b., Easy, Page 506

48.   The "startup" phase of team development is characterized by:
       a.   high expectations but unclear goals and roles among team members.
       b.   roadblocks and frustrations as team members discover the time and effort required for
            the team to be successful.
       c.   resetting goals and roles as team members learn, and a growing sense of cooperation
            and trust among team members.
       d.   involvement, openness, true teamwork, and a commitment among team members to
            accomplish the task at hand.

a., Medium, Page 507

49.   The "performance" phase of team development is characterized by:
       a.   high expectations but unclear goals and roles among team members.
       b.   roadblocks and frustrations as team members discover the time and effort required for
            the team to be successful.
       c.   resetting goals and roles as team members learn, and a growing sense of cooperation
            and trust among team members.
       d.   involvement, openness, true teamwork, and a commitment among team members to
            accomplish the task at hand.

d., Medium, Page 507

50. The "realigning expectations" phase of team development is characterized by:
    a. high expectations but unclear goals and roles among team members.
    b. roadblocks and frustrations as team members discover the time and effort required for the team to be successful.
    c. resetting goals and roles as team members learn and a sense of cooperation and trust among team members.
    d. involvement, openness, and true teamwork and a commitment among team members to accomplish the task at hand.

    c., Medium, Page 507

51. The "reality strikes" phase of team development is characterized by:
    a. high expectations but unclear goals and roles among team members.
    b. roadblocks and frustrations as team members discover the time and effort required for the team to be successful.
    c. resetting goals and roles as team members learn and a sense of cooperation and trust among team members.
    d. involvement, openness, and true teamwork and a commitment among team members to accomplish the task at hand.

    b., Medium, Page 507

52. _____ involves giving workers at every level of the organization the power, the freedom, and the responsibility to control their own work, to make decisions, and to take action to meet the company's objectives.
    a. Empowerment
    b. Motivation
    c. Job simplification
    d. Job rotation

    a., Easy, Page 507

53. Typical benefits of empowerment include all but which of the following?
    a. significant productivity gains
    b. quality improvements
    c. more satisfied customers and employees
    d. Actually, all of the above **are** typical benefits of empowerment.

    d., Easy, Page 507

54. Empowerment works best when a business owner:
    a. is confident enough to give workers all the authority and responsibility they can handle.
    b. plays the role of coach and facilitator, not the role of meddlesome boss.
    c. trusts workers to do their jobs
    d. All of the above.

    d., Easy, Page 508

55. A Japanese study found that workers "in the trenches" knew _____ percent of the problems in a company; supervisors knew _____ percent; and top managers knew _____ percent.
    a. 4; 74; 100
    b. 24; 68; 95
    c. 95; 68; 24
    d. 100; 74; 4

    d., Difficult, Page 508

56. Under open-book management, employees:
    a. seek and learn to understand a company's financial statements and other critical numbers measuring its performance.
    b. learn that a significant part of their job is making sure the company's critical numbers move in the right direction.
    c. have a direct stake in the company's success through profit-sharing, ESOPs, or performance-based bonuses.
    d. All of the above.

    d., Medium, Page 508

57. Experts estimate that when a company moves from traditional management to empowerment, about _____ percent of its workforce will eagerly choose empowerment because it is something they have been wanting to do all of their work lives, and they will lose about _____ percent—those who will be impossible to change.
    a. 5; 20
    b. 20; 5
    c. 50; 10
    d. 75; 25

    b., Difficult, Page 508

58. _____ involves breaking a job down into its simplest form and standardizing each task.
    a. Job simplification
    b. Job enlargement
    c. Job rotation
    d. Job enrichment

    a., Easy, Page 509

59. The classic auto assembly line is based on which job design principle?
    a. Job enlargement
    b. Job enrichment
    c. Job simplification
    d. Job rotation

    c., Medium, Page 509

60. The _____ design strategy adds more tasks to a job to broaden its scope.
    a. job simplification
    b. job enlargement
    c. job enrichment
    d. job rotation

    b., Easy, Page 509

61. The _____ design strategy involves cross-training workers so they can move from one job in the company to others, giving them a greater number and variety of tasks to perform.
    a. job simplification
    b. job enlargement
    c. job enrichment
    d. job rotation

    d., Easy, Page 509

62. The _____ design strategy involves building motivators into a job by increasing the planning, decision-making, organizing, and controlling functions workers perform.
    a. job simplification
    b. job enlargement
    c. job enrichment
    d. job rotation

    c., Easy, Page 509

63. In job enrichment, _____ is the degree to which a job requires a variety of different skills, talents, and activities from the worker.
    a. skill variety
    b. task identity
    c. task significance
    d. autonomy

    a., Easy, Page 509

64. In job enrichment, _____ is the degree to which a job gives a worker the freedom, independence, and discretion in planning and performing tasks.
    a. task identity
    b. task significance
    c. autonomy
    d. feedback

    c., Easy, Page 510

65. In job enrichment, _____ is the degree to which a job gives the worker direct, timely information about the quality of his performance.
    a. task identity
    b. task significance
    c. autonomy
    d. feedback

    d., Easy, Page 510

66. In job enrichment, _____ is the degree to which a job substantially influences the lives or work of others—employees or final customers.
    a. skill variety
    b. task identity
    c. task significance
    d. autonomy

    c., Easy, Page 510

67. In job enrichment, _____ is the degree to which a job allows a worker to complete a whole or identifiable piece of work.
    a. skill variety
    b. task identity
    c. task significance
    d. autonomy

    b., Easy, Page 510

68. Cora arrived at work at 7 am today, and she will get off at 4 pm so that she can watch her son's soccer game. Her office mate, Emma, is not a "morning person" and usually arrives at the office at 10 am and gets off at 7 pm. Their company uses:
    a. job sharing.
    b. flextime.
    c. flexplace.
    d. job enrichment.

    b., Easy, Page 510

69. Arturo, a sales representative for a small manufacturer, works out of an office in his home, using his laptop computer, a fax machine, and a beeper to communicate with the home office, which is located in a city 58 miles away. Arturo actually goes to the main office, on average, once every 10 to 14 days. His company is using which work arrangement?
    a. job sharing
    b. flextime
    c. flexplace
    d. job enrichment

    c., Easy, Page 511

70. Maria is excited about the new opportunity her company has offered her—she will be able to work from her home office while she spends time with her newborn son. This is possible because of the implementation of:
    a. telecommuting.
    b. hoteling.
    c. job sharing.
    d. job rotation.

    a., Easy, Page 511

71. Growing in popularity, _____ allows employees who spend most of their time away from the office, to use the same office space at different times.
    a. telecommuting
    b. hoteling
    c. job sharing
    d. job rotation

    b., Easy, Page 512

72. As a motivator, money:
    a. is the best motivator a business owner can use.
    b. is the most effective motivator for younger, "Generation X" workers.
    c. is only a short-term motivator, losing its impact over time.
    d. All of the above.

    c., Medium, Page 512

73. The first step in the feedback loop is:
    a. deciding what to measure.
    b. deciding how to measure.
    c. comparing actual results with standards.
    d. taking action to improve performance.

    a., Medium, Page 517

74. Every business is characterized by a set of numbers that are crucial to its success, called _____, that include sales, profits, profit margins, cash flow, and other standard financial measures.
    a. profitability ratios
    b. critical numbers
    c. motivational measures
    d. productivity

    b., Easy, Page 517

75. _____ is the extent to which a measurement device or technique produces consistent results over time, while _____ is the extent to which a measuring device or technique actually measures what it is intended to measure and how well it measures that factor.
    a. Reliability; Validity
    b. Validity; Reliability
    c. Robustness; Significance
    d. Significance; Reliability

    a., Medium, Page 518

76. Which of the following is a goal of performance appraisal programs?
    a. To give employees feedback on how they are doing their jobs.
    b. To give a business owner and an employee the opportunity to create a plan for developing the employee's skills and improving his performance.
    c. To establish a basis for determining promotions and salary increases.
    d. All of the above.

    d., Easy, Page 518

77. In an effective performance appraisal session, a manager should spend about ____ percent of the time discussing the employee's past performance and ____ percent of the time developing goals, objectives, and a plan for the future.
    a. 20; 80
    b. 40; 60
    c. 60; 40
    d. 80; 20

    a., Medium, Page 519

78. Which of the following is a potential disadvantage of peer appraisals?
    a. Potential retaliation against coworkers who criticize
    b. Possibility that appraisals will be reduced to popularity contests
    c. Workers who refuse to offer any criticism because they feel uncomfortable evaluating others
    d. All of the above.

    d., Medium, Page 520

79. About _____ of the Fortune 500 companies are family businesses.
    a. one-third
    b. one-quarter
    c. one-half
    d. one in ten

    a., Medium, Page 520

80. Regarding management succession of family businesses:
    a. 70 percent of first-generation businesses fail to survive into the second generation.
    b. Only 12 percent make it to the third generation.
    c. Only 3 percent make it to the fourth generation and beyond.
    d. All of the above.

d., Difficult, Page 520

81. Almost __ percent of business founders intend to pass theirs on to their children; however, only __ percent have created a formal management succession plan.
    a. 81; 25
    b. 90; 65
    c. 75; 50
    d. 60; 10

a., Difficult, Page 520

82. When building your management succession "survival kit,"
    a. never assume your children want to take control of the business.
    b. keep your succession choice a secret to avoid conflict among other family members.
    c. remember that entrepreneurial skills and desire are largely hereditary.
    d. you may assume your children want to take control of the business.

a., Medium, Page 520

83. When transferring power in a management succession, the small business owner should do **all but which** of the following?
    a. Tell the successor where all the critical documents are—wills, trusts, insurance policies, etc.
    b. Provide the successor with a list of advisers, people who have given you good advice in the past.
    c. Be open to learn from as well as to teach the successor.
    d. Transfer power quickly and step back, letting the successor run the business completely without any advice or interference by the owner.

d., Medium, Page 521

84. During the transfer of power, how should the owner deal with company problems and mistakes the successor makes?
    a. Use them as a means for teaching.
    b. Step in and fix them herself, to prevent damage to the company.
    c. Explain how the owner would have handled it and insist it be done that way in the future.
    d. Use them as an opportunity to maintain control for as long as possible.

a., Medium, Page 522

85. A business founder relying on a lifetime gifting strategy to minimize the taxes on the estate she is passing on to her son can give him a maximum gift of _____ in company stock each year, tax exempt.
   a. $5,000
   b. $10,000
   c. $25,000
   d. $100,000

   b., Medium, Page 523

86. In a Grantor-Retained Annuity Trust (GRAT),
   a. there is an attempt to minimize taxes on a family by creating two classes of stock—preferred stock whose value is locked in and common stock whose value reflects the market value of the business.
   b. a business owner can pass on up to $10,000 annually which is exempt from federal gift taxes.
   c. the grantor retains the voting power and interest income from the stock in the trust for up to ten years before the business goes to the beneficiaries.
   d. the surviving owner or heir of a family business has the right to purchase the stock of the deceased owner at a price established by a predetermined formula.

   c., Medium, Page 523

87. In a Grantor-Retained Annuity Trust (GRAT):
   a. the grantor could put company stock in an irrevocable trust lasting for up to 10 years.
   b. the grantor retains the voting power and interest income from the stock in the trust.
   c. the company stock transfers to the beneficiaries at the end of the trust and is taxed at its discounted present value.
   d. All of the above.

   d., Medium, Page 523

88. A(n) _____ is the most basic type of trust, which allows a business owner to put up to $1.3 million into trust, naming his spouse as the beneficiary upon his death. The spouse receives the income from the trust throughout her life, but the principal in the trust goes to the couple's heirs free of estate taxes upon the spouse's death.
   a. grantor-retained annuity trust
   b. family limited partnership
   c. bypass trust
   d. estate freeze

   c., Medium, Page 523

89.   A(n) _____ attempts to minimize taxes on a family business passed from one generation to the next by creating two classes of stock—one for the parents (preferred voting stock), whose value is locked in, and another for the children (nonvoting common stock), whose value reflects the market value of the business.
a.   grantor-retained annuity trust
b.   estate freeze
c.   bypass trust
d.   buy/sell agreement

b., Medium, Page 524

True/False Questions:

90.   Both leadership and management are essential to a small company's success, but leadership comes first.

True, Easy, Page 487

91.   Leadership deals with doing things right; management deals with doing the right things.

False, Medium, Page 487

92.   Although a small business manager must assume a wide range of ideas, tasks, and responsibilities, none is more important than the role of leader.

True, Medium, Page 487

93.   Management and leadership are essentially the same.

False, Medium, Page 487

94.   Leadership is an easy skill to learn.

False, Easy, Page 487

95.   Leadership gets a small business going; management keeps it going.

True, Medium, Page 487

96.   If their companies are to grow and reach their potential, entrepreneurs must learn to be effective leaders.

True, Easy, Page 487

97.   Because their companies are small, entrepreneurs need not develop the leadership skills managers in larger companies need.

False, Easy, Page 487

98. Today's workforce responds best to a leadership style based on instilling fear and intimidation.

False, Easy, Page 487

99. Effective leaders make sure that workers have both the tangible and the intangible resources they need to do their jobs well.

True, Easy, Page 488

100. A strong leader does not share aspects of her company's financial health, its future plans, or her vision for it with employees.

False, Medium, Page 488

101. Effective leaders know they must punish workers who take risks and fail so that other workers don't make the same mistakes.

False, Easy, Page 488

102. Effective leaders know that what they do is more important than what they say because they set the example for their employees.

True, Easy, Page 488

103. Effective leaders recognize that money is not the only reward that motivates workers.

True, Easy, Page 488

104. An organizational leader's job seldom changes.

False, Easy, Page 489

105. Every new employee a business owner hires determines the heights to which the company can climb or the depths to which it will plunge.

True, Easy, Page 490

106. "Bad hires" are incredibly expensive, and no organization, especially a small one, can afford too many of them.

True, Easy, Page 490

107. Business owners must recognize that what they do before they start interviewing candidates for a position determines to a great extent how successful they will be in the hiring process.

True, Easy, Page 491

108. One study concluded that an employee hired into a typical entry-level position who quits after six months costs a company about $17,000 in salary, benefits, and training.

   True, Medium, Page 491

109. Companies desiring to improve their recruitment efforts are finding that the Internet offers tremendous reach at a relatively low cost and is very effective.

   True, Medium, Page 492

110. The Dictionary of Occupational Titles, a listing of more than 20,000 job titles and descriptions, is a useful tool for getting a small business owner started when writing job descriptions.

   True, Medium, Page 493

111. Information gathered during a job analysis provides the foundation for creating job descriptions and job specifications.

   True, Medium, Page 493

112. A job analysis describes what the job is, what its duties and responsibilities are, and what work conditions are involved.

   False, Easy, Page 493

113. A job description sets forth a job's duties and responsibilities; a job specification translates these duties into the qualifications needed for that job.

   True, Easy, Page 493

114. The job specification outlines the duties and responsibilities of a job and its working conditions while the job description outlines the characteristics—skills, education, experience—a person needs to fill a job.

   False, Medium, Page 493

115. Small companies are least likely to make hiring mistakes because most owners have developed clearly defined job specifications and job descriptions.

   False, Medium, Page 493

116. To give the interviewing process more consistency, a business owner should develop a series of core questions and ask them of every candidate.

   True, Medium, Page 494

117. Interviewers should avoid asking job candidates questions based on hypothetical on-the-job scenarios and how the candidate would handle them because the Equal Employment Opportunity Commission considers such questions to be illegal.

    False, Medium, Page 494

118. The most effective job interviews are unplanned, unstructured interactions between the small business owner and the job applicant.

    False, Medium, Page 494

119. Effective interviewers ignore candidates' nonverbal clues ("body language") in interviews because they know that most candidates are so nervous that their nonverbal communication is meaningless.

    False, Medium, Page 495

120. Effective interviewers skip the breaking the ice phase of a job interview and immediately start asking candidates tough questions so they can see how the candidates respond under stress.

    False, Medium, Page 495

121. Effective interviewers spend about 75 percent of the interview talking and about 25 percent listening.

    False, Easy, Page 495

122. In the breaking the ice phase of the interview process, skilled interviewers often use the job description to explain the nature of the job and the company's culture to candidates.

    True, Medium, Page 495

123. An effective job interview contains three phases: breaking the ice, asking questions, and selling the candidate on the company.

    True, Medium, Page 495

124. The Equal Employment Opportunity Commission (EEOC) supplies employers with a list of questions it considers illegal in interviews.

    False, Medium, Page 495

125. The final phase of the job interview begins by allowing the candidate to ask questions about the company, the job, or other issues.

    True, Medium, Page 496

126. In addition to contacting the references a job applicant provides, experienced employers also call an applicant's previous employers to attempt to get a clear picture of the applicant's job performance, character, and work habits.

   True, Medium, Page 496

127. According to the American Association for Personnel Administrators, approximately 10 percent of all resumes and applications contain at least one major fabrication.

   False, Medium, Page 496

128. Small business owners should take the time to check every candidate's references.

   True, Easy, Page 496

129. Company culture is the essence of "the way we do things around here" and often originates with the founder.

   True, Easy, Page 496

130. Company culture is the distinctive, unwritten code of conduct that governs the behavior, attitudes, relationships, and style of an organization.

   True, Easy, Page 496

131. Asking a job candidate in an interview if she is a U.S. citizen is legal.

   False, Medium, Page 497

132. Asking a job candidate in an interview if she is HIV-positive is illegal because it is a violation of the Americans with Disabilities Act.

   True, Medium, Page 497

133. Growth requires changes in a company's management style, organizational strategy, and methods of operations.

   True, Easy, Page 502

134. As companies grow larger, their cultures tend to remain the same.

   False, Medium, Page 502

135. Studies show that large companies focus on creating new product and service lines while small companies concentrate more on expanding their existing lines.

   False, Medium, Page 503

136. Studies comparing large companies to small ones have found that large companies' inability to react quickly is a major barrier to their growth.

   True, Easy, Page 503

137. The biggest disadvantage of the craftsman management style is the limitations it puts on a company's ability to produce quality products and services.

   False, Medium, Page 503

138. A cabinetmaker who works alone to make custom-built cabinets for a group of wealthy customers is using the craftsman management style in his business.

   True, Medium, Page 503

139. An entrepreneur using the classic management style insists on tight supervision, constantly monitors employees' work, and performs all critical tasks herself.

   True, Medium, Page 503

140. In the classic management style, entrepreneurs run a one-man show, doing everything themselves because their primary concern is with the quality of the products or services they produce.

   False, Medium, Page 503

141. Entrepreneurs using the classic management style do not feel comfortable delegating the power and authority to make decisions to others, preferring instead to keep a tight rein on the business and everyone who works there.

   True, Medium, Page 503

142. The best management style for a small company is the classic management style.

   False, Easy, Page 503

143. Under the coordinator management style, the company is actually quite "hollow" because the entrepreneur farms out a large portion of the work to other companies and then manages all of the activities from headquarters.

   True, Medium, Page 504

144. Delegating authority and power to key workers requires a manager to realize that there are several ways to accomplish a task and that employees will make mistakes.

   True, Easy, Page 504

145. Under the coordinator management style, an entrepreneur brings other people into the company but does not delegate any significant authority to them, choosing instead to "watch over everything" herself.

False, Medium, Page 504

146. The entrepreneur-plus-employee team management style gives a business the power to grow beyond the scope of the manager-only style.

True, Medium, Page 504

147. In many ways, team-based management is best suited for small companies.

True, Medium, Page 505

148. Under a team-based management style, managers must make at least part of team members' pay dependent on team performance.

True, Easy, Page 505

149. One of the major benefits of switching from a traditional management style to a team-based one is that workers don't need any special training; they already know how to be team members.

False, Medium, Page 505

150. Companies that use team-based management effectively report significant gains in quality and employee morale, but they also report higher costs and lower productivity.

False, Medium, Page 505

151. In a team-based work environment, managers take on the role of "coaches" who empower those around them to make decisions affecting their work and share information with workers.

True, Easy, Page 505

152. The best way for a manager to handle a poorly performing employee is to assign him to a team so that team members can improve his performance.

False, Medium, Page 505

153. The goal of team-based management and the self-directed work teams resulting from it is to get people in a company working together to serve customers better.

True, Medium, Page 505

154. In a company built around self-directed work teams, managers delegate a few simple decisions and tasks to teams, but the managers retain the power to make all really important decisions since they are better trained to do so.

    False, Medium, Page 505

155. Empowerment challenges workers to make the most of their creativity, imagination, knowledge, and skills.

    True, Easy, Page 507

156. Empowerment is the degree of effort an employee exerts to accomplish a task; it shows up as excitement about work.

    False, Easy, Page 507

157. Empowering employees requires a different style of management and leadership from that of the traditional manager.

    True, Easy, Page 507

158. Managers should avoid sharing power and information with their subordinates because it weakens the managers' authority and influence.

    False, Easy, Page 507

159. Once they see the benefits it offers them, every worker in a company typically wants to be empowered.

    False, Medium, Page 508

160. Successfully empowering employees requires a business owner to continuously upgrade workers' skills.

    True, Easy, Page 508

161. The best way to build employees' confidence is to supervise their projects closely.

    False, Easy, Page 508

162. Under open-book management, a business owner gives employees access to all of the company's records, except its financial records and statements.

    False, Medium, Page 508

163. An assembly line is based on the principle of job simplification.

    True, Easy, Page 509

164. Job enlargement is based on the premise that the best way to design a job is to break it down into its simplest form and to standardize each task.

False, Easy, Page 509

165. The principle of job enlargement is to make a job more varied and to allow employees to perform a more complete unit of work by broadening its scope.

True, Medium, Page 509

166. Job enrichment increases the planning, decision making, organizing, and control functions in a job.

True, Medium, Page 509

167. The concept of empowering employees is based on the principle of job enrichment.

True, Medium, Page 509

168. To enrich employees' jobs, a business owner must build five core characteristics into them: skill variety, task identity, task significance, autonomy, and feedback.

True, Medium, Page 509

169. In job enrichment, task identity is the degree to which a job substantially influences the lives or the work of others, employees or final customers.

False, Medium, Page 510

170. Flextime is a work arrangement in which two or more people share the same 40-hour-a-week job.

False, Easy, Page 510

171. Companies using flextime schedules often experience lower levels of tardiness and absenteeism.

True, Medium, Page 510

172. Flexplace is a work arrangement in which employees work at a place other than the traditional office, such as a satellite branch closer to their homes or, in many cases, at home.

True, Easy, Page 511

173. Telecommuting employees reap benefits such as flexibility and reduced commuting times and expenses.

True, Easy, Page 511

174. By linking employees' compensation directly to the company's financial performance, a business owner increases the likelihood that workers will achieve performance targets that are in their best interest and in the company's best interest.

True, Easy, Page 512

175. Money can be a powerful short-term motivational tool, but it usually does not have a lasting motivational effect.

True, Easy, Page 512

176. Younger workers, especially "Generation Xers," respond best to monetary rewards rather than to intangible rewards such as praise and recognition.

False, Medium, Page 513

177. Although they are very inexpensive from a business owner's perspective, motivators such as praise, recognition, feedback, job security, and others are not very effective at encouraging workers to achieve higher levels of performance.

False, Easy, Page 513

178. The key to using rewards to motivate employees involves tailoring them to the needs and characteristics of the workers.

True, Easy, Page 513

179. In the future, managers will rely more on nonmonetary rewards such as praise, recognition, game tickets, dinners, and others to create a work environment where employees take pride in their work, enjoy it, are challenged by it, and get excited about it.

True, Medium, Page 515

180. One characteristic successful people have in common is that they never set goals and objectives for themselves, choosing instead to take advantage of whatever opportunities pop up before them.

False, Medium, Page 517

181. The goal of the feedback loop is to find those employees whose performances are below standard and to punish them.

False, Medium, Page 518

182. Reliability is the extent to which a measurement device or technique provides consistent measurements of a factor over time.

True, Easy, Page 518

183. Validity is the extent to which a measuring device or technique actually measures what it is intended to measure and how well it measures that factor.

    True, Easy, Page 518

184. One of the most common methods of providing feedback on employee performance is through performance appraisals.

    True, Easy, Page 518

185. The biggest complaint concerning performance appraisals is that they happen periodically, typically just once a year.

    True, Easy, Page 518

186. The focus of a performance appraisal session should be on correcting what an employee has done wrong.

    False, Easy, Page 518

187. To conduct a meaningful performance appraisal, a manager should keep a record of the critical incidents, both positive and negative, of an employee's performance.

    True, Easy, Page 519

188. One of the most common complaints employees have about the performance appraisal process is that managers' comments are too general to be of any value in improving their performances.

    True, Easy, Page 519

189. The best way to improve an employee's performance is to surprise him with a list of everything he has done wrong over the past year in the annual performance appraisal.

    False, Easy, Page 519

190. Ideally, managers should withhold negative feedback about employees' job performances until their annual performance appraisals so that they can cover it all at one time.

    False, Easy, Page 519

191. In an effective performance appraisal session, a manager should spend about 80 percent of the time discussing the employee's past performance and the remaining 20 percent developing goals, objectives, and a plan for the future.

    False, Medium, Page 519

192. Peer evaluations of an employee's performance tend to be less accurate and less valid than those of managers.

    False, Medium, Page 520

193. In performance appraisal systems, peer appraisals can be especially useful because an employee's coworkers see his on-the-job performance every day.

    True, Easy, Page 520

194. More than 90 percent of all U.S. businesses are family owned.

    True, Medium, Page 520

195. About one-third of *Fortune 500* companies are family owned.

    True, Medium, Page 520

196. The majority of first-generation family businesses do not survive into the second generation.

    True, Medium, Page 520

197. Most business founders intend to pass their companies on to their children, and have a formal management succession plan for doing so.

    False, Medium, Page 520

198. It is generally safe for a business founder to assume that his children will succeed him in managing the family business.

    False, Medium, Page 520

199. The oldest child is the best choice for a successor to manage a company.

    False, Easy, Page 520

200. A major advantage of family businesses is that there is always a guaranteed successor within the family whenever the owner decides to step down.

    False, Medium, Page 520

201. The preparation of a successor is a two-way process, showing the direction of the business and what led to its success, but also learning and listening.

    True, Easy, Page 521

202. For management succession to be successful, the process should start early in the successor's life.

    True, Easy, Page 522

203. The process of transferring power should be quick and absolute.

    False, Easy, Page 522

204. Once a business owner transfers power and control to her successor, she should not hesitate to step back into the business to fix problems when they occur.

    False, Medium, Page 522

205. One of the primary concerns of entrepreneurs transferring their businesses to the next generation is minimizing the tax bite of the transfer.

    True, Easy, Page 522

206. Without proper estate planning, the heirs to a successful business may be required to sell it just to pay the estate tax bill.

    True, Easy, Page 522

207. A buy/sell agreement allows the founder of the business to sell it outright to the successor and avoid taxation on the transfer.

    False, Medium, Page 523

208. The IRS permits annual gifts of up to $100,000 from a parent to each child per year to be exempt from federal gift taxes.

    False, Medium, Page 523

209. A trust is a contract between a grantor and a trustee, which shields all assets from any federal tax and permits the small business owner to pass on his business without incurring tax liabilities.

    False, Easy, Page 523

210. Creating a family limited partnership allows business-owning parents to transfer their company to their children (thus lowering their estate taxes) while still retaining control over it for themselves.

    True, Easy, Page 524

Essay Questions:

211. What is leadership? How does leadership differ from management?

    Leadership is the process of influencing and inspiring others to work to achieve a common goal and then giving them the power and the freedom to achieve it. Management and leadership are not the same; yet both are essential to a small company's success. Leadership without management is unbridled; management without leadership is uninspired. Leadership gets a small business going; management keeps it going. Leadership deals with people; management deals with things. Leadership deals with vision; management deals with logistics toward that vision. Leadership deals with doing the right things; management focuses on doing things right. Leadership comes first, then management, but both are necessary. **Page 487**

212. List at least ten of the fifteen behaviors effective leaders exhibit.

Effective leaders exhibit many of the following characteristics:

- Create a set of values and beliefs for employees and passionately pursue them.
- Define and then constantly reinforce the vision they have for the company.
- Respect and support their employees.
- Set the example for their employees.
- Create a climate of trust in the organization.
- Focus employees' efforts on challenging goals and keep them driving toward those goals.
- Provide the resources employees need to achieve their goals.
- Communicate with their employees.
- Value the diversity of their workers.
- Celebrate their workers' successes.
- Encourage creativity among their workers.
- Maintain a sense of humor.
- Create an environment in which people have the motivation, the training, and the freedom to achieve the goals they have set.
- Become a catalyst for change when change is needed.
- Keep their eyes on the horizon.

Page 488

213. To be effective, a small business leader must perform four vital tasks. List and briefly explain these four tasks.

- Hire the right employees and constantly improve their skills – Hiring mistakes are incredibly expensive, and there is no way to successfully compete without high-quality employees. Competition among businesses for quality workers is intense, and in order to assemble a quality workforce, the business owner must begin by investing the time and money necessary to achieve this goal at the beginning of the staffing process by developing a sound recruiting process. He must create practical job descriptions and job specifications, plan and conduct effective interviews, and carefully check references prior to making a hiring decision.
- Build an organizational culture and structure that allow both workers and the company to reach their potential – Culture is the distinctive, unwritten, informal code of conduct that governs a company's behavior, attitudes, relationships, and style. It is the essence of "the way we do things around here" and originates with the founder. It is critical to create a culture that supports a company's strategy. As a company grows, its structure typically evolves from a "one-man show" to relying more on a team approach to run the company.
- Motivate workers to higher levels of performance – Motivation is the degree of effort an employee exerts to accomplish a task; it shows up as excitement about work. Motivating workers to higher levels of performance is one of the most difficult and challenging tasks facing a small business owner. There are various job design strategies, reward and compensation systems, and performance appraisal methods that business owners can incorporate to improve motivation.
- Plan for "passing the torch" to the next generation of leadership – The best way to avoid conflicts over control of the business is for the founder to develop a formal management succession plan. It increases the probability of survival to the next

generation and eases the transition by reducing the tension and stress created by the "changing of the guard." Additionally, it allows business owners to minimize the impact of taxes on their businesses, their estates, and their successors' wealth.

Page 489

214. Assume the role of a consultant to a small business owner who is about to conduct a job interview for the first time. Identify the guidelines that will help him develop interview questions. Also, explain the three phases of an effective interview.

The guidelines for developing interview questions include:

- Develop a series of core questions and ask them of every candidate.
- Ask open-ended questions (including on-the-job "scenarios") rather than questions calling for "yes or no" answers.
- Create hypothetical situations candidates would be likely to encounter on the job and ask how they would handle them.
- Probe for specific examples in the candidate's past work experience that demonstrate the necessary traits and characteristics.
- Ask candidates to describe a recent success and a recent failure and how they dealt with them.

An effective interview consists of three phases:

- Breaking the ice – The first phase is used to set the interviewee and the interviewer at ease.
- Asking questions – In the second phase, the interviewer asks questions and listens to the candidate's responses and body language. Effective interviewers spend about 25% of the time talking and listen the remaining 75%.
- Selling the candidate on the company – In the final phase, the employer tries to sell the candidate on her company. Usually in this phase, the interviewee asks several questions about the company, the job, itself, and other relevant issues.

Page 494

215. List and describe the six different management styles entrepreneurs rely on to guide their companies as they grow. Identify the advantages and disadvantages of each.

- The Craftsman – In this case, the owner is in total control and responsible for all tasks. It is a one-man or one-woman show. Most often, this management style occurs in the start-up and early growth stages. This style includes minimum operating expenses; however, the entrepreneur must do everything—even the things (s)he dislike. It limits a company's ability to grow.
- The Classic – In this case, the owner begins to hire employees, but does not pass any significant authority to them. The owner still watches over everything. This style does provide more growth potential than the craftsman, but there are still limits to growth while the owner remains in tight control.
- The Coordinator – In this management style, the owner operates by outsourcing a large portion of the work and then coordinates all of the activities from "headquarters." This pushes the owner into a vulnerable position—dependent on suppliers, manufactures, etc. It does allow the entrepreneur to grow a fairly large company with very few employees.

- The Entrepreneur-plus-Employee Team – This style is the first shift into a team-based management approach. Here, the entrepreneur delegates authority to key employees, but retains the final decision making power. Delegation allows the owner to focus on more important tasks in growing the business.
- The Small Partnership – In this case, the owner realizes that there is an advantage of sharing responsibility for the company with others. This can be a very advantageous, but the loss of total control is also an issue.
- The Big-Team Venture – This approach is the broadest-based management style and usually occurs when the company grows larger. When the workload demands on a small number of partners exceed their time, ability, and energy, managers must expand the breadth of the management team's experience to handle the increasing level of responsibility that results from the sheer size of the company.

Page 503

216. List the suggested guidelines managers should follow to ensure teams' success.

- Make sure that teams are appropriate for the company and the nature of its work.
- Make sure that teams are appropriate for the task to be accomplished.
- Form teams around the natural work flow and give them specific tasks to accomplish.
- Provide adequate support and training for team members and leaders.
- Involve team members in determining how their performances will be measured, what will be measured, and when it will be measured.
- Make at least part of team members' pay dependent on team performance.

Page 506

217. Define motivation. Discuss the various motivational tools managers have at their disposal to encourage employees to reach higher levels of performance. What role does money play?

Motivation is the degree of effort an employee exerts to accomplish a task; it shows up as excitement about work. Motivating workers to higher levels of performance is one of the most difficult and challenging tasks facing a small business manager. Money may not always be the "best" motivator because its effect as a motivator is usually only short-term. It does not have a lasting effect on motivation. Small business managers can use praise, recognition, feedback, and inexpensive perks (free car wash; discounts; game tickets; restaurant gift certificates; movie coupons, etc.) to motivate their employees for the long-term. Empowerment, open-book management, and various job design concepts, such as job rotation, job enlargement, job enrichment, flextime, telecommuting, and job sharing, are also available. Generally, any concept that contributes to the employee's quality of life will motivate and create loyalty.
Page 506

218. Explain the differences among job simplification, job enlargement, job rotation, and job enrichment. Why should small business owners utilize these concepts?

- Job Simplification – In this type of job design, the work is broken down into its simplest form and then standardized into tasks. Job simplification evokes monotony and impersonal, unchallenging work. It allows small business owners and their employees to create specific job descriptions.
- Job Enlargement – In this type of job design, more tasks are added to a job in order to broaden its scope. The idea is to make the job more varied and to allow employees to perform a more complete unit of work.
- Job Rotation – This job design involves cross-training employees so that they can move form one job in the company to others. Job rotation, like the former, provides variety to workers and increases the skills and understanding of workers.
- Job Enrichment – This type of job design builds motivators into a job by increasing the planning, decision-making, organizing, and controlling functions that workers perform. The idea is to make every employee a manager, at least for his or her own particular job.

Page 509

219. What is performance appraisal, and what are the goals of performance appraisal? What are the most common mistakes managers make in performance appraisals? Why is feedback such an important part of the motivational process, and how does it fit with performance appraisals?

Performance appraisal is one of the most common methods of providing feedback on employee performance. During a performance appraisal, an employee's performance is evaluated against desire performance standards. The three primary goals of performance appraisal are to give employees feedback about how they are doing their jobs, to provide a business owner and an employee the opportunity to develop a plan for improving the employee's performance by enhancing his skills and abilities, and to establish a basis for determining promotions and salary increases.

Many managers make the mistake of conducting performance appraisals only once a year, which limits feedback. Managers have commonly made the mistake of forgetting the real purpose of performance appraisals—to encourage and help employees improve their performance, by letting the meeting become an uncomfortable confrontation. Also, employers should provide clear objectives to employees: be aware of employee performance, be prepared, and be honest and sincere in appraisals.

Business owners not only motivate employees; they must also focus their efforts on the right targets. The owner should develop specific measures that connect daily operational responsibilities. These benchmarks measure performance so that what gets measured, gets done. Managers should address problems when they occur rather than wait until the performance appraisal session. Continuous feedback, both positive and negative, is a much more effective way to improve employees' performances and to increase their motivation to produce.

Page 518

220. Why is developing a management succession plan so important to the founder of a family business? Identify and briefly describe the steps of a successful plan.

The best way to avoid conflicts over control of the business is for the founder to develop a formal management succession plan. It increases the probability of survival to the next generation and eases the transition by reducing the tension and stress created by the "changing of the guard." Additionally, it allows business owners to minimize the impact of taxes on their businesses, their estates, and their successors' wealth.

Planning for succession involves the following five steps:

- Step 1—Select the successor: Never assume that your children will want to take control of the family business. The successor does not have to be a family member. If it is a child, merit is a better standard to use than birth order.
- Step 2—Create a survival kit for the successor: Regularly visit with the successor about the key factors that have led to the success of the business; tie those key factors to performance and profitability; explain businesses strategies, values, and philosophies; document as much process knowledge as possible.
- Step 3—Groom the successor: Be an effective communicator and listener; establish reasonable expectations for the successor's performance; be patient and understand that the successor will make mistakes.
- Step 4—Promote an environment of trust and respect: Trust and respect on the part of the founder and others fuel the successor's desire to learn and excel and will help build his confidence; understand that this is a gradual process; there will be a greater likelihood that customers, creditors, suppliers, and staff members will gradually develop confidence in the successor.
- Step 5—Cope with the financial realities of estate and gift taxes: Structure the transition so as to minimize the impact of estate, gift, and inheritance taxes on family members and the business. Entrepreneurs who fail to consider the impact of these taxes may force their heirs to sell a successful business just to pay the estate's tax bill.

Page 520

221. List and briefly identify the five estate planning tools the owners of a family business should consider.

- Buy/sell agreement – a contract that co-owners often rely on to ensure the continuity of a business. It states that each agrees to buy the others out in case of the death or disability of one, which allows the heirs to "cash out" of the business, leaving control of the business in the hands of the remaining owners.
- Lifetime gifting – the owner of a successful business may transfer money to their children (or other recipients) from their estate throughout the parents' lives; currently, the maximum allowable per person per year that is exempt from federal gift taxes.
- Trust – a contract between a grantor (the company founder) and a trustee (generally a bank officer or attorney) in which the grantor gives to the trustee legal title to assets (e.g., stock in the company), which the trustee agrees to hold for the beneficiaries (children). The beneficiaries can receive income from the trust, or they can receive the property in the trust, or both, at some specified time. There

are several types of trusts, including a grantor-retained annuity trusts (GRAT) and a bypass trust.

- Estate freeze – minimizes estate taxes by having family members create two classes of stock for the business: (1) preferred voting stock for the parents and (2) nonvoting common stock for the children.
- Family limited partnership – allows business-owning parents to transfer their company to their children (thus lowering their estate taxes) while still retaining control over it for themselves. The parents retain the general partnership interest, and the children become the limited partners.

Page 523

Chapter 15
Leading the Growing Company and Planning for Management Succession
Mini-Cases

Case 15-1: Kansas Manufacturers and Assemblers

Rose Richardson always knew that if she could land a major order for her firm, she could prove its quality to the industry. Kansas Manufacturing and Assemblers was a job shop manufacturing and assembling operation specializing in fast turnaround projects for manufacturers with orders in excess of production capacity. Each job Rose's firm did was on special order.

In September, a major appliance manufacturer approached Rose and inquired about her ability and willingness to manufacture and assemble a new appliance. This order could mean a very substantial profit for the firm, as well as recognition throughout the industry. Rose was asked to undertake a project that would require a 100 percent assignment of the firm's personnel for seven months. In addition, any slight modification in design or material would require overtime. If this job went as most, changes could be expected. On this short notice, it would be impractical for Rose to hire additional personnel because it takes weeks, even months, to learn the necessary skills.

Rose faces an interesting dilemma: if she doesn't take the job, it may be years before another one of this magnitude comes along; but if she takes the job and then fails to deliver on time, or fails to meet the
quality specifications because of her overworked employees, her reputation will be hurt for years. Rose sees this opportunity as a crossroads in the firm's history, but knows that she must gain the full and unquestioned support of the employees, if the project is to be a success.

1. If you were Rose, how would you go about gaining the commitment of your employees to a project that will last a full seven months and will likely require each person to work overtime and weekends and to forgo vacations for the duration of the project?

   Rose must win the commitment of her employees to this project if her company is to complete it successfully. She should consider having a meeting with her entire workforce to explain the importance of the project and what it means to finish it on time. If the workers are willing to commit to the project, Rose might sponsor a celebration at which employees sign "pledge cards", dedicating themselves to completing the project on time. Of course, Rose should consider sharing some of the financial benefits from the project with her employees. She could link performance on the project to financial incentives. She should also establish intermediate objectives as "checkpoints" along the way to completing the project and offer rewards (financial or non-financial) to workers if they achieve them.

Case 15-2: Passing the Baton

Carol Wingard started a small jewelry manufacturing company when she was in her late 20s, and has worked hard to build it into a highly successful family business. Now, 40 years later, she was "ready to sit down and enjoy life." Seven family members, including her two sons, Ralph and Cooper, work in the business. Ralph, with 30 years of experience, and Cooper, with 22 years of experience, are both vice-presidents of the company.

Carol has always intended to pass the business on to her sons, who together own 20 percent of the company's stock. However, she has always been too busy running the business to put together a formal management succession plan. For the past decade, many of the employees have whispered among themselves about who would be named president if Mrs. Wingard stepped down and exactly what would happen to the business.

Now that she has decided to retire, Carol wants to begin developing a management succession plan.

1. Carol calls you and announces her plans to retire within a year. What advice would you offer her about a management succession plan?

   It's probably too late for Carol to develop a management succession plan. This is something she should have started at least 20 years ago. Since both Ralph and Cooper are actively involved in the business, Carol must name a successor soon. She should spend the next year coaching her successor, gradually handing over the reins of the business to him (or her, if neither Ralph nor Cooper is qualified).

2. What tools would you suggest to Carol to minimize the estate taxes involved in passing the business on to Ralph and Cooper? Explain the advantages and disadvantages of at least three choices and explain why you make the final recommendation that you do.

   By waiting so long, there's only so much Carol can do to minimize estate taxes. One option she should consider heavily is the estate freeze. Others include a buy/sell agreement (but at her age, insurance policies will be expensive) or even an ESOP. She will need the help of a capable attorney and a good accountant.

Case 15-3: The Pride of Vicksburg

Wallace Fry had been a lover of good food from the time he was a child. The only son of wealthy Southern parents, he spent hours with his mother watching her prepare meals for the family and friends. By the time Wallace was in high school, he had already won a number of awards for his original recipes. After leaving Vicksburg, Mississippi, to attend college in the Midwest, Wallace returned home to what must have been an unbelievable graduation present. His relatives purchased an old paddlewheel riverboat and had begun initial preparations to have it moored permanently at the foot of the Vicksburg landing on the Mississippi River. Wallace was presented with a 50 percent interest in the restaurant named "The Pride of Vicksburg."

The complete renovations and restoration of the beautiful old riverboat took an additional four months. Wallace was planning to have his new restaurant open for the spring tourist season. A number of regional magazines had already run feature stories on the project. With the opening one month away, Wallace decided it was time to staff the restaurant.

1.   Are job descriptions necessary in a restaurant?

Yes. Job descriptions form the foundation for providing quality food and service in a restaurant. They will help Wallace select the most qualified employees.

2.   Has Wallace waited too long to begin searching for employees?

Yes. Wallace has a tremendous amount of work to do in choosing qualified employees in one month. Selecting quality employees is especially important in the restaurant business since personal service is an integral part of the restaurant's image and ultimate success. Clearly, Wallace needs to develop job descriptions and specifications before he begins his search for personnel.

3.   Develop a list of interview questions to help Wallace select the right person for the following jobs:
   - Head chef
   - Wait staff
   - Dishwasher
   - Host/Hostess

The question lists students develop will be unique. However, the quality of their lists will be higher if they first work alone for a few minutes to develop questions, and then work in teams of two to five to brainstorm for other questions to add to their lists.

4.   What criteria should Wallace use in selecting employees?

Criteria Wallace should consider include: experience in the restaurant business, friendliness, personality ("outgoing" or not), "people-oriented," work ethic, honesty, appearance, attitude, and other factors.

5.   What would be the most effective way to recruit personnel for this type of business?

Sources of recruitment for Wallace include: employment agencies, cooking schools, "help wanted" ads in trade papers and newspapers, other restaurants, and referrals.

Case 15-4: Plumbers Don't Want Recognition

"If I ever went out to those guys and asked them if they wanted a little more recognition, they would laugh me out of the shop. People work for money." Norm Schultz had been a plumber himself for 18 years before he saved enough money to open a small plumbing contractor business. The men who worked for Norm knew what was expected of them—a fair day's work for a fair day's pay. "You don't need to tell a man that he is doing a good job; he is either doing the work or he is not working for me."

Norm's son-in-law was taking a management course at a local college. When Norm asked him what he was learning in class, he told him the management of people. Norm was very emphatic about managing the plumbers who worked for him. "Tell a man what you expect from him right

off. Watch to see if he does the job properly. Treat your people fairly and never cheat them."
Norm went on to tell his son-in-law that this was the way good managers did things. "Recognition
won't put bread on the table."

1.   Is Norm Schultz correct in his attitude about workers not wanting recognition?

      No. Norm is correct in saying that "Recognition won't put bread on the table," but he fails
      to see that recognition can be a primary source of motivation for many employees. Some
      workers strive for a "pat on the back" from the boss, and, in some cases, recognition can be
      just as important as money.

2.   What do you think about Norm Schultz's attitudes toward employees?

      While, "treat people fairly and never cheat them" is good advice, Norm could go one step
      further and become a more effective manager by offering praise and recognition more
      often.

3.   Would you like working for Norm? Why or why not?

      Most students probably would not like to work for Norm.

Video Guide

to Accompany

Essentials of Entrepreneurship and Small Business Management
4th Edition

by
Thomas W. Zimmerer
and
Norman M. Scarborough

To the Professor

This video guide accompanies ***Essentials of Entrepreneurship and Small Business Management, Fourth Edition*** and offers guidelines for using the twelve videos from ***Business Now***. Each video gives your students special insight into the exciting and challenging world of entrepreneurship. Students will see and hear entrepreneurs describe the challenges they faced as they worked to launch their businesses and the rewards of running their own companies.

Each video outline in this guide contains:

> ➤ The video segment's running time.

> ➤ The section of the book to which each video applies.

> ➤ The topic of the video segment.

> ➤ A synopsis of the video.

> ➤ Discussion questions designed to focus students' attention on the key concepts in the video and to link those concepts to those in the textbook.

> ➤ Suggested answers to the discussion questions for each video segment.

The discussion questions for each video segment are printed separately so that you can photocopy them as handouts for your students. Use them as either individual or group assignments. They are designed to help you stimulate meaningful class discussions using the videos as a starting point. The goal is to maximize student involvement and learning. We trust that you will enjoy using these outstanding videos as another important teaching tool in your classroom and that your students will learn many important lessons as they see first-hand what it takes to make a small business successful.

Norman M. Scarborough
Thomas W. Zimmerer

Table of Contents

938   *Video #5. Strike Holdings LLC.* Tóm Shannon, owner of Strike Holdings LLC, is putting a new spin on an old game: bowling. Shannon bought a run-down bowling alley, and, with a new marketing approach, has transformed it into a thriving business. By adding automatic scoring, day-glow balls, video screens, music, and an upscale menu, Shannon has turned his bowling alley into a hot spot for young professionals and others.

941   *Video #6:The Golf Network.* Entrepreneur Greg Matzel describes his online golf store, the centerpiece of which is a tee time reservation system that allows golfers to use the Internet to book tee times at more than 400 golf courses in 33 states.

944   *Video #7: Bay Partners.*   Bay Partners is a Cupertino, California-based venture capital firm that focuses on investments in promising technology companies. The partners explain the value that venture capitalists can bring to a growing small company in addition to the infusion of their capital investments.

947   *Video #8. MyTeam.com.* Years ago, professional sports teams took their games to the Internet. Now, Entrepreneur Elliot Katzman, cofounder of MyTeam.com, provides that same access to amateur athletes, their teams, their fans, and their communities for sports ranging from T-ball to adult-league softball. MyTeam.com allows people to create a Web page that includes player statistics, team schedules, league standings, and other information for their favorite amateur sports teams. The business proved to be so promising that venture capital firm Charles River Ventures has invested in MyTeam.com.

950   *Video #9: Crunch Fitness.* Crunch Fitness is a chain of very unique gyms located in major urban areas. Firemen and drag queens teach some of the aerobics classes at Crunch, and its cardio-belly-dancing classes (called "The Goddess Workout") are among its most popular.

953   *Video #10: Neema Clothing.* In 1991, Jim Ameen purchased a bankrupt company and transformed it into Neema Clothing, a powerhouse in the men's clothing industry. Ameen's strategy is to provide "great fit, great quality and great price" by purchasing quality fabrics at reasonable prices, controlling inventory, and speeding up the production and delivery cycle.

957   *Video #11: CESSI (Cherry Engineering Support Services Inc).* Fred Cherry founded CESSI after he returned from the Vietnam War, where he was disabled because of torture and injuries. He created a company that helps disabled employees make the most of their abilities. The company also practices what it preaches by hiring many disabled workers.

960   *Video #12: Second Gear Bicycles.* At age 14, Jason Upshaw was in trouble with the law and found himself in juvenile court. That's when he decided to turn his life around by launching his own business, Second Gear Bicycles, a bicycle sales and repair shop. The video focuses on Upshaw's sense of social responsibility; he gives back to his community by teaching a 25-hour bicycle repair course to kids in the area. Through his business, Upshaw has become a positive role model for the community's children.

963   Suggested Answers to Discussion Questions

Video #1
Joan Rivers Worldwide Enterprises

Length:
Introductory Video
Topics: Entrepreneurship and Small Business Management
Company Web Site: http://www.joanrivers.com/

Synopsis: This introductory video sets the stage for a course in entrepreneurship or small business management. Joan Rivers is more than a successful radio and television star, comedienne, and author; she is also a successful entrepreneur. Her company, Joan Rivers Worldwide Enterprises, sells $40 million worth of jewelry and beauty items a year, much of it through the television shopping network QVC. For the past decade, Rivers has been one of QVC's most popular vendors.

Like many entrepreneurs, Rivers has transformed something she loves into a successful business, and she has learned by trial and error along the way. She actually started her business in her dressing room at CBS, where between shows, she would sketch jewelry designs. Her attitude towards business is typical of many entrepreneurs. "Let's do it, let's try it, let's see," she says.

Joan Rivers Worldwide Enterprises
Discussion Questions

1. In what ways does Joan Rivers demonstrate the characteristics of the "typical entrepreneur"?

2. In the video, Joan Rivers says "Have 40 balloons up there, and if one doesn't pop, they'll say, 'She's brilliant. She had that idea.'" What they don't realize was that was one of a million ideas you've tried." How does Rivers' statement relate to the way most entrepreneurs view failure?

3. Joan Rivers says, "A lot of our business has come from 'Let's do it, let's try it, let's see." What does she mean? Do you think this attitude is typical of other entrepreneurs?

Video #2

TheWaggingTail.com

Length:
Section I: The Challenges and Rewards of Entrepreneurship
Topics: Entrepreneurship; technology; differentiation; customer service.
Company Web Site: http://www.thewaggingtail.com

Synopsis: This video tells the story of TheWaggingTail.com, a "doggy day care" business in the Tribeca section of New York founded by entrepreneur Keith Durst. Durst targets pet owners who treat their dogs like members of the family, and he uses technology to differentiate his business from regular kennels. Not only does the company pamper its canine customers but it also puts their owners' minds at ease. TheWaggingTail.com's "Doggy Cam" allows indulgent customers to tune in to the company's Web site to check on their pets while they are at work, traveling on business, or on vacation. Customers can also talk with one another on the company's chat line.

**TheWaggingTail.com
Discussion Questions**

4. Which characteristics of the "typical entrepreneur" does owner Keith Durst exhibit?

5. Describe TheWaggingTail.com's target customer.

6. What advantages does TheWaggingTail.com offer pet owners?

7. In what ways has Keith Durst differentiated his business from "ordinary" dog kennels?

5. What role does technology play in TheWaggingTail.com's success?

Video #3
Build-A-Bear Workshop

Length:
Book Section II: Building a Business Plan: Beginning Considerations
Topic: Strategic management; focus strategy; competitive advantage. (See "In the Footsteps of an Entrepreneur" on page 57 of the text for more details on this business.)
Company Web Site: http://www.buildabear.com

Synopsis: After spending 25 years in retail, Maxine Clark decided to launch her own business, one that is part retail and part interactive bear factory. A Build-A-Bear Workshop is *not* the average toy store. Here, customers work with Master Bear Builders to create their own stuffed animals —and their own special memories. After they finish creating their teddy bear creations, customers can dress them in the latest fashions in the Bear Wear department. In a high-tech world, Clark has created a highly successful high-touch business that appeals to kids of all ages.

Build-A-Bear Workshop
Discussion Questions

1. Which of the three business strategies described in Chapter 2 is Maxine Clark using? Explain.

2. In what ways has Clark set Build-A-Bear Workshop apart from the typical toy store?

3. Would the Build-A-Bear concept make a successful franchise? Explain.

4. Describe the sources of Build-A-Bear's competitive advantage.

Video #4
Zoots

Length:
Book Section III: Building the Business Plan: Marketing and Financial Matters
Topics: Marketing; customer service; convenience; competitive advantage; social responsibility.
Company Web Site: http://www.zoots.com

Synopsis: Zoots, a dry cleaning business, targets time-starved customers by offering them a multitude of options for getting their clothes cleaned, from 24-hour drop-off and pick-up to online scheduling. The company strives to deliver high quality service, reliability, and convenience. The company's Vice-President of Human Resources of says that Zoots' goal is to "provide the best possible experience for our customers." Zoots' Director of Operations explains that the company strives to "wow" its customers by exceeding their expectations of quality and convenience.

The video also addresses the company's sense of social responsibility. Zoots has developed a system that makes it easy for customers to donate clothing to Goodwill Industries.

Zoots
Discussion Questions

1. Describe Zoots' target customer.

2. The video never mentions Zoots prices or how they compare to competitors. How important do you think price is to the typical Zoots customer? Explain.

3. How has Zoots marketing strategy enabled the company to gain a competitive advantage over its rivals in the dry cleaning business?

4. Describe the opportunities and threats that Zoots faces as it grows.

Video #5
Strike Holdings LLC

Length:
Book Section IV: Small Business Marketing Strategies
Topics: Marketing; target market; advertising; innovation; competitive advantage.

Synopsis: Tom Shannon, owner of Strike Holdings LLC, is putting a new spin on an old game: bowling. Shannon bought a run-down bowling alley, and, with a new marketing approach, has transformed it into a thriving business. By adding automatic scoring, day-glow balls, video screens, music, and an upscale menu (including crab cakes and wraps), Shannon has turned his bowling alley into a hot spot for young professionals and others. Customers have responded so well to the new look and new features that Shannon has opened a second bowling alley in Washington, D.C. He says that "business is a lot about marketing."

Strike Holdings LLC
Discussion Questions

1. How has Tom Shannon created a competitive edge for Strike Holdings LLC?

2. In what ways has Shannon repackaged the simple game of bowling to appeal to his company's target customers? How successful has it been?

3. Given its marketing strategy, what opportunities and threats does Strike Holdings face?

Video #6

The Golf Network

Length:
Book Section IV: Small Business Marketing Strategies
Topics: E-commerce, marketing; target market; pricing; advertising; innovation.
Company Web Site: http://www.thegolfnetwork.com

Synopsis: In 1999, entrepreneur Greg Matzel took his golf superstore online, selling a wide variety of golf-related products –"everything for the golfer," says Matzel. The centerpiece of his new business, however, became the company's online tee time reservation system. Recognizing that golfers were becoming increasingly frustrated by the difficulties of getting on the courses they wanted to play when they wanted to play, Matzel launched TheGolfNetwork.com, which allows golfers to make online reservations for tee times at more than 400 golf courses in 33 states. On the company's Web site, golf enthusiasts also can learn about golf schools, driving ranges, golf vacations, real estate for sale on golf courses, and discounts on golf equipment.

TheGolfNetwork.com has more than 300,000 members using the system, and the company books about 2.5 million rounds a year, receiving a fee of $.75 to $1.50 per booking from the golf courses it serves. Advertisers are attracted to the company's Web site because of the attractive demographic profile of its golfing customers, whose average annual income exceeds $65,000

The Golf Network
Discussion Questions

4. How is Greg Matzel using the World Wide Web to create a competitive edge for The Golf Network?

5. Refer to "Strategies for E-Success" in Chapter 13 of your book (pages 389 to 393). Which of these strategies is Greg Metzel using? Explain.

6. Visit the Web site for The Golf Network at http://www.thegolfnework.com. What suggestions can you make for improving the Web site? (Hint: You may want to read "Designing a Killer Web Site" on pages 393 to 398 in your book.)

7. What recommendations can you make to Greg Matzel for advertising The Golf Network?

Video #7
Bay Partners

Length:
Book Section V: Putting the Plan to Work: Finding Financing
Topics: Sources of financing; venture capital.
Company Web Site: http://www.baypartners.com

Synopsis: Bay Partners is a 25-year-old venture capital firm whose mission is to "identify new technologies in networking, wireless, and software and invest in companies that leverage these innovations to create and lead new market opportunities." Although dozens of venture capital firms watched dot.com firms burn through billions of dollars of their money only to go bankrupt, Bay Partners avoided that problem by sticking to its mission. Bay Partners makes early stage investments in the $1 million to $10 million range, and the company focuses on small companies that have developed new technology that offers value to customers.

One partner in the firm addresses the negative reputation that venture capitalists have and argues that they seek to be "partners" with entrepreneurs in search of capital rather than "monsters." He says that venture capital firms invest in companies that need money and mentoring to execute their business plans. Every partner in the firm has business start-up experience and expertise in business. The partners explain that being a venture capitalist can be very stressful but also very rewarding. The video gives an overview of some of the most successful companies in Bay Partners' portfolio of investments.

Bay Partners
Discussion Questions

1. Bay Parnters' mission statement is to "identify new technologies in networking, wireless, and software and invest in companies that leverage these innovations to create and lead new market opportunities." How did sticking to their mission during the rise (and subsequent fall) of the dot.coms benefit the venture capital firm?

2. Explain the process by which venture capital firms screen small businesses candidates as possible investments.

3. What do venture capital firms such as Bay Partners look for when considering making an investment in a small company?

4. Describe the benefits a venture capital firm can provide a growing small business.

Video #8
MyTeam.com

Length:
Book Section V: Putting the Plan to Work: Finding Financing
Topics: Sources of financing; venture capital.
Company Web Site: http://www.myteam.com

Synopsis: Years ago, professional sports teams took their games to the Internet. Now, Entrepreneur Elliot Katzman, cofounder of MyTeam.com, provides that same access to amateur athletes, their teams, their fans, and their communities for sports ranging from T-ball to adult-league softball. MyTeam.com allows people to create a Web page that includes player statistics, team schedules, league standngs, and other information for their favorite amateur sports teams. Katzman says his goal is "to make the kids the stars."

The business proved to be so promising that venture capital firm Charles River Ventures has invested in MyTeam.com. Venture capitalist Ted Dintersmith says that MyTeam.com is appealing on many levels; the company has a very strong position in its market segment that offers tremendous value and a founder with a track record of success who has clear vision of what he wants to accomplish. The company has forged strategic alliances with several important organizations, including Little League Baseball, the Amateur Athletic Association, and the Youth Basketball Association. Also, former professional athletes Gary Carter, Bobby Orr, and M.L. Carr serve as advisors to MyTeam.com. What's next for the company? Katzman says he plans to allow his customers to broadcast their games over the Web.

MyTeam.com
Discussion Questions

1. Venture capitalist Ted Dintersmith says that MyTeam.com "is appealing on multiple dimensions." What are some of the characteristics of the company that make it unique and so appealing to professional investors?

2. What do venture capitalists look for when considering making an investment in a small company?

3. Describe several sources of financing that MyTeam.com might rely on to finance its growth.

Video #9
Crunch Fitness

Length:
Book Section VI: Location and Layout
Topics: Location; international business; differentiation
Company Web Address: http://www.crunch.com

Synopsis: About two out of every three new gym members drop out of their fitness regimes within just 90 days, but not at Crunch Fitness, where classes are anything but mundane. The atmosphere is high-energy and unlike other gyms because it seamlessly fuses fitness and entertainment. Here, firemen, hip-hoppers, and drag queens lead aerobics classes, and its cardio-belly-dancing classes (called "The Goddess Workout") are among its most popular. By locating in large urban areas such as Los Angeles, Atlanta, and New York, Crunch has carved out a profitable niche with its fast-pace and irreverent attitude. Crunch was founded in 1989 by Jim Solomon, who says that the company's strategy will work only in urban areas, where all 19 of the company's gyms are located. Average sales at a Crunch Fitness center exceed $5 million per year, compared to the industry average of between $1 and $1.5 million per year.

Crunch Fitness
Discussion Questions

1. CEO Jim Solomon says that Crunch locations will be successful only in major urban areas. Do you agree? Explain.

2. Visit the Crunch Web site at http://www.crunch.com to get a sense of the company's unique approach to the fitness market. Develop a list of factors that the company should consider when selecting a location for its new fitness centers.

3. Select a city you think would be suitable for locating a new Crunch Fitness
    center and use the resources on the Web site for your book
    (http://www.prenhall.com/scarborough) to research the demographics of that
    city. Offer convincing evidence that the city would be a profitable location for
    Crunch Fitness.

Video #10
Neema Clothing

Length:
Book Section VII: Managing a Small Business: Techniques for Enhancing Profitability
Topics: Purchasing; quality management; electronic data interchange; managing inventory.

Synopsis: In 1991, Jim Ameen purchased a bankrupt company and transformed it into Neema Clothing, a powerhouse in the men's clothing industry that turns out more than 1 million garments a year. With the rapid changes shaping the fashion industry, Neema must be extremely responsive to customers' changing tastes. The company's suits, sports coats, and separates are cut and sewn in the Far East and then shipped to U.S. retailers for sale under famous labels that include Bert Pulitzer, Haspel, Jeffrey Banks, and others. A key part of Ameen's strategy has been shortening production times and negotiating good deals on fabrics from textile makers. Neema also strives to provide "great fit, great quality and great price" by purchasing quality fabrics at reasonable prices, controlling inventory, and speeding up the production and delivery cycle. In fact, Neema's suits are made in just four to six weeks compared to the industry average of twelve weeks. Citing "a mentality of speed," Ameen says, "We have to find a way to turn (our inventory) quicker."

Neema's retail customers appreciate its electronic ordering (EDI) system, which allows the company to restock garments within just 48 to 72 hours. Recently, Neema has expanded its line with the purchase of upscale lines such as Haspel (worn by movie stars and presidents) and Halston. Ameen also is pursuing young, urban, customers by working with designer Karl Kani to create more fashion-forward garments. The company's success is evidenced by its impressive 30 percent annual growth rate in a mature industry.

Neema Clothing
Discussion Questions

1. How important is the purchasing function to Neema Clothing? Explain.

2. What advantages have an effective purchasing strategy and tight inventory control given Neema in the men's clothing industry?

3. What benefits does Neema's electronic data interchange (EDI) system produce for both itself and its customers?

Video #11
CESSI (Cherry Engineering Support Services Inc.)

Length:
Book Section VIII: Managing People: A Company's Most Valuable Resource
Topic: Leadership; managing people; motivation; disabilities; staffing; social responsibility.
Company Web Site: http://www.cessi.net/

Synopsis: Fred Cherry, a Navy pilot during the Vietnam War, was disabled as a result of torture and injuries sustained in the war. After returning to the United States, Cherry launched Cherry Engineering Support Services Inc. (CESSI), a company that helps disabled Americans make the most of their abilities. CESSI helps government agencies comply with the provisions of the Federal Rehabilitation Act and disabled people function as normally as possible in their jobs. Some 54 million Americans have disabilities.

The company also practices what it preaches, hiring many employees with disabilities. "We didn't hire them because they have disabilities, says a CESSI manager. "We hired them because they can do a good job and are doing a good job."

Reflecting on the success of his company, founder Fred Cherry says, "The goal of this company is to help. Yes, we make money. We have to make a living, but I love to see... the people who work for CESSI happy... and helping someone, especially people with disabilities."

CESSI (Cherry Engineering Support Services Inc.)
Discussion Questions

1. Why do disabled people have a difficult time finding employment?

2. How important are hiring decisions to the typical small business? Explain.

3. What can business owners do to minimize the likelihood of making hiring mistakes?

4. In the video, Fred Cherry says, "The goal of this company is to help. Yes, we make money. We have to make a living, but I love to see... the people who work for CESSI happy... and helping someone, especially people with disabilities." Is earning a profit incompatible with fulfilling a company's social responsibility? Explain.

Video #12
Second Gear Bicycles

Length: 5:31
Book Section IX: Legal Aspects of Entrepreneurship
Topic: Ethics and social responsibility.

Synopsis: Seven out of 10 high-school students say that want to start their own businesses. Jason Upshaw is a teenager who has done just that. At age 14, Upshaw was in trouble with the law and found himself in juvenile court. That's when he decided to turn his life around by launching his own business, Second Gear Bicycles, a bicycle sales and repair shop. Started in 1996 with bicycles and computers donated by Goodwill and money from Boston Youth Venture, Upshaw has succeeded. He also is giving back to his community by teaching a 25-hour bicycle repair course to kids in the area. Those who complete the course learn a new skill and earn a free bicycle. Through his business, Upshaw has become a positive role model for the community's children.

Second Gear Bicycles
Discussion Questions

1. What is social responsibility? Identify several areas in which a company has a responsibility to society.

2. How is Jason Upshaw demonstrating his company's social responsibility?

3. Should a company be able to "escape" its responsibility to society simply because it is small? Explain.

Suggested Answers to Discussion Questions

Video 1. Joan Rivers Worldwide Enterprises

1. In what ways does Joan Rivers demonstrate the characteristics of the "typical entrepreneur"?
   Joan Rivers personifies the typical entrepreneur in that she started her business very small, designing jewelry in between shows in her CBS dressing room. She also demonstrates the optimism and creativity so often seen among entrepreneurs as well as the determination so important to success. (Recall the story of her bumble bee pin.) Like many entrepreneurs, Rivers has taken something she enjoyed doing and has turned it into a successful business. She also is embracing technology to build her business by using the power of the Internet to reach her customers.

2. In the video, Joan Rivers says "Have 40 balloons up there, and if one doesn't pop, they'll say, 'She's brilliant. She had that idea.'" What they don't realize was that was one of a million ideas you've tried." How does Rivers' statement relate to the way most entrepreneurs view failure?
   Like every successful entrepreneur, Rivers keeps failure in proper perspective. She knows that not every idea or product she tries will succeed, but she also realizes that it often takes lots of ideas to find one or two highly successful ones. She is not afraid to fail! She sees failure as merely a stepping stone on the pathway to success.

3. Joan Rivers says, "A lot of our business has come from 'Let's do it, let's try it, let's see.'" What does she mean? Do you think this attitude is typical of other entrepreneurs?
   Creativity is one hallmark of entrepreneurship. Entrepreneurs tend to be people of action, and Rivers' attitude of "Let's do it, let's try it, let's see" is typical of many successful entrepreneurs throughout history. Her approach to business means that she will occasionally fail, but she is not about to let setbacks stop her from achieving her vision for her business.

Video 2: TheWaggingTail.com

1. Which characteristics of the "typical entrepreneur" does owner Keith Durst exhibit?
   Keith Durst exhibits many of the traits of entrepreneurs, including confidence in his ability to succeed, a high level of energy, a future orientation, flexibility, and tenacity. His innovative business also is proof of his creativity and vision.

2. Describe TheWaggingTail.com's target customer.
   The company's target customer is upscale customers who treat their pets as members of their families. These customers want to pamper their pets and to make sure they receive the best care.

3. What advantages does TheWaggingTail.com offer pet owners?
   The company's customers get the assurance that their pets are well cared for while their owners are away, allowing them to go about their lives without worrying that their pets are not getting proper care. The "Doggy Cam" also allows indulgent owners to check in on their pets during their absences.

4. In what ways has Keith Durst differentiated his business from "ordinary" dog kennels?
   TheWaggingTail.com is not the typical kennel. Here, dogs are pampered and played with in their owners' absences. Durst has captured a loyal base of customers by tapping into the needs of indulgent dog owners. Customers know that the only place their dogs get better care is at home!

5. What role does technology play in TheWaggingTail.com's success?
   The company's primary use of technology is the "Doggy Cam," which allows customers to check in on their pets on the World Wide Web from anywhere in the world! Allowing owners to see their pets while they are away gives them the knowledge that their pets are getting good care (and gives them great peace of mind), something that is extremely important to the company's target customers.

Video 3. Build-A-Bear Workshop

1. Which of the three business strategies described in Chapter 2 is Maxine Clark using? Explain.
    Clark is relying on a focus strategy for her company's success. Rather than attempting to serve the entire market, a company pursuing a focus strategy specializes in serving a specific target segment or niche. Build-A-Bear is focusing on a unique niche by allowing children of all ages to custom-build their own teddy bears!   Other examples from the text of companies following this strategy include Clown Shoes and Props, Border States Leatherworks, and Frank J. Zamboni and Company.

2. In what ways has Clark set Build-A-Bear Workshop apart from the typical toy store?
    Clark has differentiated her business from the typical toy store in numerous ways, from the company's name to the interactive nature of the product itself. She has tapped into everyone's love of a favorite teddy bear while engaging her customers in the process of actually creating their own toy bears. *Everything* in the store is designed to give the customer a unique and fun experience, much more than merely purchasing a toy.

3. Would the Build-A-Bear concept make a successful franchise? Explain.
    Yes, Build-A-Bear has all of the key factors for a successful franchise: A unique business concept, a profitable chain of stores, a registered trademark, a management team that is skilled and experienced in retail, an established name, and a business system that works.

4. Describe the sources of Build-A-Bear's competitive advantage.
    Most of Build-A-Bear's competitive advantage is based on the uniqueness of the company's approach to retail and the experiential, interactive relationship it creates with customers. As students will see in Chapter 7, Creating a Guerrilla Marketing Plan, shopping has lost its allure for many people and has become a chore. Those retail businesses that are most successful are those that engage their customers in an interactive experience. The approach is called entertailing, a blend of entertainment and retailing. Build-A-Bear does this extremely well.

Video 4. Zoots

1. Describe Zoots' target customer.
   Zoots' target customer is the busy professional person with relatively high disposable incomes and to whom convenience is more important than price. These customers are willing and able to pay extra for the convenience of home pickup and delivery, 24-hour pickup, and online scheduling of pickups and deliveries.

2. The video never mentions Zoots prices or how they compare to competitors. How important do you think price is to the typical Zoots customer? Explain. Although never mentioned specifically in the video, Zoots' prices are probably higher than those of competitors who offer less convenience. Offering the many extra services that Zoots does cost more, but company founders know that their target customers value convenience more than the lowest price and are willing to pay for that convenience.

3. How has Zoots marketing strategy enabled the company to gain a competitive advantage over its rivals in the dry cleaning business? Zoots offers far more than the typical dry cleaning business. In addition to providing a quality service, Zoots strives to offer customers the maximum amount of convenience. The company's goal is to "wow" its customers by exceeding their expectations of quality and convenience. That is how businesses win and keep a loyal base of customers.

4. Describe the opportunities and threats that Zoots faces as it grows. Competition is always a threat to a small business. A larger competitor with more resources may enter Zoots' market and try to win its customers away. Also, growth can present major challenges to a small business. Entrepreneurs who launch successful companies sometimes have trouble making the transition to the role of managers as their companies grow and their management needs change. Economic downturns, cash management problems, and other growing pains represent threats to small businesses such as Zoots.

The primary opportunity for Zoots is opening stores in new locations. The company appears to have its business and marketing concepts in place.

Expanding into other markets (but only the right ones!) with the same approach could accelerate the company's growth.

Video 5. Strike Holdings LLC

1. How has Tom Shannon created a competitive edge for Strike Holdings LLC?

   Shannon has taken an old game and has given it a new spin! He recognized that before he built his business, customers who wanted to bowl had to make sacrifices (e.g., dirty environment, poor food, dismal surroundings, and others). Shannon decided to create a bowling alley that would appeal to young professionals by creating a clean, fun, interesting, high-tech environment. Everything about the business, from the day-glow bowling balls and video screens to the automatic scoring and upscale menu, is designed to appeal to his target customers. Shannon's bowling alleys are *not* typical of the average bowling facilities in the industry.

2. In what ways has Shannon repackaged the simple game of bowling to appeal to his company's target customers? How successful has it been?

   In his alleys, Shannon has revamped the game of bowling by adding fun, interesting, and exciting features such as day-glow bowling balls, automatic scoring, video screens, a bright colorful (and clean) atmosphere, and an upscale menu. His goal is to combine his target customers' expectations of quality, service, and value with the entertainment aspects of bowling. His approach has been so successful that Shannon already has opened a second location in Washington, D.C.

3. Given its marketing strategy, what opportunities and threats does Strike Holdings face?

   The primary opportunity for Strike Holdings LLC is to continue to expand into other markets. (You might want to ask students what characteristics Shannon should look for as he selects new locations for his bowling alleys.) He could also expand into other types of entertainment.

The threats facing Strike Holdings LLC include the possibility that bowling will lose its popularity among customers and that expanding too rapidly could create internal problems for the company. Another threat is that a larger competitor with deeper pockets could enter the market and outspend Strike Holdings in terms of marketing and advertising. That is why a successful guerrilla marketing strategy is so important to small companies.

Video 6. The Golf Network

1. How is Greg Matzel using the World Wide Web to create a competitive edge
for The Golf Network?
In addition to selling "everything for the golfer," Matzel has built his
company's competitive edge on the foundation of the online tee time
reservation system that takes much of the hassle and frustration out of the
game for golfers. As the sport has grown in popularity, golfers increasingly
are having difficulty getting on the courses they want to play when they
want to play them. Matzel's answer was TheGolfNetwork.com, which
allows golfers to make online reservations for tee times at more than 400
golf courses in 33 states. Matzel has found a way to use the Web to offer
golfers a valuable service and to generate a profit for his company.

2. Refer to "Strategies for E-Success" in Chapter 13 of your book (pages 389 to
393). Which of these strategies is Greg Metzel using? Explain.
Matzel is using the following strategies for e-success: Focus on a niche in
the market, develop a community; make sure your Web site says
"credibility," and promote your site online and offline.

3. Visit the Web site for The Golf Network at http://www.thegolfnework.com.
What suggestions can you make for improving the Web site? (Hint: You
may want to read "Designing a Killer Web Site" on pages 393 to 398 in your
book.)
Students will offer a variety of answers here. The current site is an effective
one and follows a simple design so many students are likely to make
suggestions to improve the design.

4. What recommendations can you make to Greg Matzel for advertising The Golf Network?

Matzel should advertise his site as much as possible both online and offline. Every publication the company creates should have its Web address featured on it. The company's offline ads also should feature the Web address. Online, Matzel should consider registering his site with the top search engines so that it will appear at or near the top of their lists for users conducting golf-related searches. He should also consider establishing links to his company's site on the Web sites of all of the golf courses it serves. Because golfers tend to be more financially savvy than the average person, he should consider setting up link exchanges with financial services companies as well.

Video 7: Bay Partners

1. Bay Parnters' mission statement is to "identify new technologies in networking, wireless, and software and invest in companies that leverage these innovations to create and lead new market opportunities." How did sticking to their mission during the rise (and subsequent fall) of the dot.coms benefit the venture capital firm?

   One of the partners mentions that during the rise of the dot.coms it was tempting for the venture capital firm to stray from its mission and try to hit a home run by investing in hot dot.coms. He goes on to say that the company never could get the numbers to make sense. The partners stuck to their mission statement, investing in the businesses they know best, and it paid off for them. Many venture capital firms are still struggling to overcome the investments they made in failed dot.com companies.

2. Explain the process by which venture capital firms screen small businesses candidates as possible investments.

   Venture capital firms provide about 7 percent of all funding for private companies, investing billions of dollars in high potential businesses. Most venture capital firms seek investments in the $3 million to $10 million range, although Bay Partners will consider investments as low as $1 million. The screening process is extremely intense. Of the 1,200 proposals a typical venture capital firm receives in a year, it ends up making an investment in just three to six of them.

   Most prefer to purchase ownership in a business through common stock or convertible preferred stock. Most venture capitalists expect to gain one or more seats on a company's board of directors, and they often advise the management team as the company grows.

3. What do venture capital firms such as Bay Partners look for when considering making an investment in a small company?

   When considering an investment, venture capitalists look for a competent and skilled management team, a business with a sustainable competitive edge, a growth industry, a viable exit strategy (e.g. selling out to a larger business or an initial public offering), and a host of intangible factors.

4. Describe the benefits a venture capital firm can provide a growing small business.

Certainly the most obvious benefit venture capitalists offer a company is the infusion of much-needed capital to finance growth and expansion. However, as the partners in the video explain, they also bring to a company much more. The advice, counsel, mentoring, business experience, and contacts that venture capitalists have often prove to be a great help to growing businesses.

Video 8. MyTeam.com

1. Venture capitalist Ted Dintersmith says that MyTeam.com "is appealing on multiple dimensions." What are some of the characteristics of the company that make it unique and so appealing to professional investors?

   MyTeam.com is in a very strong position in its market segment and a has a founder with a track record of success who has clear vision of what he wants to accomplish. The company also has forged strategic alliances with several important organizations, including Little League Baseball, the Amateur Athletic Association, and the Youth Basketball Association. Also, former professional athletes Gary Carter, Bobby Orr, and M.L. Carr serve as advisors to MyTeam.com.

2. What do venture capitalists look for when considering making an investment in a small company?

   When considering an investment, venture capitalists look for a competent and skilled management team, a business with a sustainable competitive edge, a growth industry, a viable exit strategy (e.g. selling out to a larger business or an initial public offering), and a host of intangible factors.

3. Describe several sources of financing that MyTeam.com might rely on to finance its growth.

   MyTeam.com is established enough that it would qualify for a variety of bank loans. Many banks are hesitant to lend money to business start-ups, preferring to make loans to small companies with a track record of success. The company already has attracted financing from a venture capital firm, which opens the door for further investments from venture capitalists. The business is probably past the point of approaching private investors for financing. (They usually come in before venture capital firms do.) If the company sustains its growth, it may be able to make an initial public offering (IPO) or sell shares of its stock to a larger company.

Video 9. Crunch Fitness

1. CEO Jim Solomon says that Crunch locations will be successful only in major urban areas. Do you agree? Explain.
   Yes! Given its unique and sometimes provocative approach (e.g. its "cardio-striptease exercise class") to fitness, major metropolitan areas make the best locations for Crunch Fitness Centers. New York and Atlanta currently are the strongest markets for Crunch Fitness Centers, but the company has plans to expand its presence in Los Angeles and to open locations in Boston and other major metropolitan areas in the U.S.

2. Visit the Crunch Web site at http://www.crunch.com to get a sense of the company's unique approach to the fitness market. Develop a list of factors that the company should consider when selecting a location for its new fitness centers.
   Crunch must consider a variety of factors as it selects sites for new fitness centers, but its main criteria is a large population of young, upscale, urban customers. The intensity of the competition is always a consideration when choosing a location, but with Crunch's unusual approach to fitness, finding cities with large concentrations of its target customers is the primary factor.

3. Select a city you think would be suitable for locating a new Crunch Fitness center and use the resources on the Web site for your book (http://www.prenhall.com/scarborough) to research the demographics of that city. Offer convincing evidence that the city would be a profitable location for Crunch Fitness.
   Students will probably hone in on cities into which Crunch is planning to expand or has already expanded. Some of the best cities include Miami, Chicago, San Francisco, Dallas-Fort Worth, San Diego, and others. Demographic profiles should show a sizeable population of upscale young people.

Video 10. Neema Clothing

1. How important is the purchasing function to Neema Clothing? Explain.
   Purchasing is important to practically every firm, but it is especially
   important to Neema. As Jim Ameen mentions in the video, he must buy top
   quality fabrics at reasonable prices so he can keep Neema's inventory
   turnover ratio high. The old expression, "Goods well bought are goods half
   sold" applies to Neema.

2. What advantages have an effective purchasing strategy and tight inventory
   control given Neema in the men's clothing industry?
   Neema's purchasing strategy allows the company to purchase quality fabrics
   at reasonable prices, which enables it to sell its garments at reasonable prices
   and to generate a profit. Another advantage that Neema's purchasing
   strategy and tight inventory control has produced is the ability to deliver
   garments to retailers in just four to six weeks, compared to the industry
   average of twelve weeks.

3. What benefits does Neema's electronic data interchange (EDI) system
   produce for both itself and its customers?
   With the help of its electronic ordering (EDI) system, Neema's retail
   customers can have items restocked within just 48 to 72 hours. This speed
   and flexibility allows both Neema and its retail customers to keep their
   inventories turning quickly and to avoid the cash crises that often
   accompany slow turning inventories. EDI systems also cut order-processing
   costs well below paper-based systems.

Video 11. CESSI (Cherry Engineering Support Services Inc.)

1. Why do disabled people have a difficult time finding employment? Disabled people often have difficulty finding employment because of discrimination by employers in spite of all of the laws passed to protect them from discrimination. People who are not disabled often have misconceptions about what a disabled person can and cannot do. In addition, some business owners think that they will be required to make extensive and expensive modification in their workplaces to accommodate disabled workers. CESSI proves these beliefs wrong!

2. How important are hiring decisions to the typical small business? Explain. The hiring process is extremely crucial to small businesses. In a large business, a poor hiring decision creates problems but typically does not cripple the company's ability to compete. In a small business, however, a poor hiring decision can disrupt the entire business and its culture, making it difficult for the company to function smoothly. Every new hire a business owner makes determines the heights to which it the company can climb –or the depths to which it can plunge.

3. What can business owners do to minimize the likelihood of making hiring mistakes?
   To avoid costly hiring mistakes, business owners should:
   - Create practical job descriptions and job specifications.
   - Plan an effective interview that includes much more than simple "yes/no" questions.
   - Conduct an effective and legal interview, in which the candidate talks about 75 percent of the time.
   - Check *every* candidate's references. (According to the American Association for Personnel Administration, 25 percent of all résumés and applications contain at least one major fabrication.)
   - Conduct employment tests.
   - Make the job offer.

4. In the video, Fred Cherry says, "The goal of this company is to help. Yes, we make money. We have to make a living, but I love to see... the people who work for CESSI happy... and helping someone, especially people with

disabilities."   Is earning a profit incompatible with fulfilling a company's social responsibility? Explain.

No!!! In fact, a company's first responsibility is to earn a profit. Before a company can "do good" (i.e., live up to its social responsibility), it must first "do well" (i.e., earn a profit). A business that is not earning a profit and is struggling to survive will have an extremely difficult time giving back to society.

Video 12. Second Gear Bicycles

1. What is social responsibility? Identify several areas in which a company has a responsibility to society.
Social responsibility is the awareness by a company's managers of the social, environmental, political, human, and financial consequences their decisions and actions produce.

A company has a responsibility to society in several key areas, including the environment, its employees, its customers, its investors, and the local (and perhaps global) community.

2. How is Jason Upshaw demonstrating his company's social responsibility?
This young entrepreneur demonstrates a sense of his social responsibility by giving back to his local community. Upshaw teaches a free 25-hour course in bicycle repair to kids in his community, something that not only teaches them a new skill but for some gives a new lease on life. Upshaw also serves as a positive role model for the children in his community.

3. Should a company be able to "escape" its responsibility to society simply because it is small? Explain.
No. Every company, no matter how small, has a responsibility to society. Business owners must conduct their business dealings in an ethical manner and must live up to their social responsibility. Businesses of every size can find ways to contribute something positive to our society.

THE BUSINESS DISC
How to Start and Run a Small Business

The Business Disc is a sophisticated experiential learning and development simulation that leads students through the steps of planning and managing a small business. Part I of The Business Disc simulates the first six months of crucial decision making that leads to creating a business plan and forming a company. The students will first meet Harrison Field, "Harry," an accountant who will guide them through the program. Students will meet and gain insights and information from a banker, insurance agent, lawyer, realtor and many of Harry's former clients.

The students will be able to start and operate any type of business, service, retail or manufacturing. As they develop their business plan the following topics are covered in detail:

- Types of Businesses
- Organizational Structure
- Business Profile
- The Business Plan
- Personal Income Statement
- Location of Business
- Know the Competition
- Employees
- Job Description Form
- Work Hours Form
- Withholding Statement
- Taxes and Employee Benefits
- Productivity Estimates

- Payroll Record
- Review of Payroll Expenses
- Insurance
- Legal Advice
- How to Keep Records
- Concept of Cash Flow
- Cash Flow Statement
- Monthly Sales Projections
- Pricing
- Start up Costs
- Letter of Intent
- Depreciation
- The Bank Loan

Every decision made in Part figures into later events which occur in Part II.

Part II simulates the first twelve months of business operation. Learning opportunities continue as they have to deal with employee issues, community relations situations, late supply deliveries, strikes, community development issues, liability issues and much more. Additional information will come from advice from other small business owners, TV news shows, advertising and tax seminars. Events are based on decisions made in the planning stage and reactions to those events which happen within the first year of business operation.

Although the program can be run in class, it is most effective as an outside assignment. Students simply follow the End-of-Chapter Exercises in the *Essentials of Entrepreneurship and Small Business Management, 4/e.* They take the Entrepreneurial Attitude Survey during their first week and compare their attitudes to those of successful entrepreneurs. Then during the second week they will begin the actual program. In order to keep students on track it's recommended that they work through the program in sequential order and complete Part I around the mid point of the semester.

It's completely self-instructing and requires no preparation to begin using. Your expectations or requirements are flexible. You may want to require brief report where students can explain their experiences and what they got out of the simulation and why the made certain decisions. Or you may have them submit a printout of the Business Income Statement simply to verify that they have completed the program. Establishing "mileposts" throughout the semester – points by which students must have completed the various parts of the simulation – allows professors to use The Business Disc as the basis for meaningful classroom discussions. If you have students prepare a business plan as part of your class, The Business Disc is an excellent "warm-up exercise" that gets students oriented to the business planning process.

ORGANIZATION AND CONTENT OF THE BUSINESS DISC

The following headings are taken from the "Go To" Menu on THE BUSINESS DISC program. - The "Go To" feature is one of the handiest tools in THE BUSINESS DISC. The sub-menu is divided into four parts. Again this is a convenient way to return to earlier parts of the program or just explore. But, forewarn students NOT try to use this as a short cut to skip information on the CD. If they do, they will miss opportunities to make various decisions along the way and their data will become corrupted. As a result, an attempt, on the user's part, to save time will end up costing time since they'll have to return to the beginning and start over.

Introduction to The Business Disc - The user begins by meeting Harrison Fields, Harry, who will be the central thread and guide the user through the program. Here, Harry provides a general overview. Although Harry points out that the easiest way to go through the program is to have only one product or service, the entrepreneur will actually be able to identify up to five products or categories of products or services. During this early section, the user will go through a brief tutorial describing the function key shortcuts available. Then the user begins entering information into the Business Profile.

Slide show of example businesses - This section is used to help students generate ideas for types of businesses they might create as part of their assignment. It can be skipped by pressing the F12 function key. If you wish you may substitute pictures of businesses in your community. See the Tutorial on the Demonstration CD.

Harry explains: Kinds of Businesses - He basically points out that all businesses fall into one or more of the three basic business categories, retail, service and manufacturing.

Menu: More information on Kinds of Businesses - Here the user can meet with former clients of Harry's who will offer insights to things the entrepreneur should keep in mind. Such as advertising, distribution, quality control, the importance of keeping up with the latest technology, operational costs, the realities of self employment, inventory, pricing, competition, community recognition, importance of location and more.

Harry talks about: Organizational Structure - The basic structures dealt with in the program are sole proprietorship and partnerships. However, it is pointed out to the individual that professional guidance is extremely important in making the right choice between these, or Incorporation or Limited Liability Companies, or other options that might be available.

Menu: More information on Organizational Structure - Again former clients of Harry's offer some of the pros and cons of sole proprietorships and partnerships. Issues covered include, being the sole decision maker, liability issues, financing and more.
See the Banker - At this juncture the user is given the opportunity to see a banker if they

think they're ready. The banker asks for their business plan and when none is produced he fires off a series of questions for the unwitting user to answer: "What's the purpose of your business...how many employees will you have, who's your attorney, who's your accountant, are you renting a place of business or will you operate out of your home, what are your fixed expenses, what are your variable expenses, your start-up costs, Do you know what kind of cash flow you can expect for the first 12 months?"

Harry talks about: The Business Plan - The importance of the plan is emphasized whether a loan is needed or not. It helps one plan and be prepared for the otherwise unexpected. Harry gives an overview of the plan's typical content and the key parts are defined.

Personal Income Statement Parts I & II - Part I is listing of savings and other sources of income that may mitigate the need for a loan. Harry offers recommendations on estimating expenses and budgeting. The purpose of the Personal Income Statement is explained. Part II is really a summary of annual living expenses. This is used by the program to determine whether the banker accepts or rejects your request for a loan later on in the program.

Menu: Working at home vs. renting - A former client explains the pros and cons of working at home, such as the need for self-discipline, zoning issues, need for space and storage considerations. Or the user may meet a realtor who shows four general types of properties. The types covered are Urban Residential, Shopping Center, Downtown and Highway locations. Within these types there are almost two dozen properties to choose from – eight for each business type: service, manufacturing and retail. The exception is the combination of Shopping Center and Manufacturing. When a manufacturer picks Shopping Center an animation appears and explains why they wouldn't normally rent there.

Again a variety of issues are brought up for consideration such as community loyalty, zoning restrictions, customer traffic, window displays, business neighbors, visibility, and rental costs. Once a property is selected and a lease is signed the user may accept the rental fee shown or enter their own figures.

See Joe Delgado, attorney, concerning lease - After looking at the available properties, the realtor tries to pressure the entrepreneur into signing a lease without legal counsel. If the entrepreneur decides to see an attorney before signing he/she discovers several important points in the lease, such as it's duration and maintenance responsibility issues.

See TV talk show about starting a Business - Learning opportunities are provided throughout the program. In some cases, the user has the choice of taking advantage of them or not. Valuable information necessary for decision making later on is presented. The TV show covers key points about analyzing the competition such as determining exactly who the competition is by looking for ads in newspapers, trade journals, magazines and the yellow pages. Then visit the location, talk with customers find out what they like or dislike. Then determine how you can improve upon the competition.

Information in this section is valuable for decisions that have to be made in Part I and II.

Meet with Harry about hiring employees - Harry reviews some of the key responsibilities an employer faces when hiring employees, like setting hours, defining job descriptions and setting salaries.

Enter the # of employees you'll hire - The user may have from zero up to nine employees. If they have employees they are then taken to the Job Description Form and the Work Hours Form.

Harry discusses: Employees & Taxes - Here Harry discusses the need for a Federal Identification Number, and the various taxes and withholdings required, if you have employees. He points out that stiff penalties are levied if withholdings are not submitted when required. Then Harry reviews the required and optional benefits the employer must consider, like Social Security (FICA in the US) (the Canadian Pension Plan in Canada), F.U.T.A. (Federal Unemployment Tax in the US), (Unemployment Insurance in Canada). Finally the Optional Benefits, like sick leave, medical benefits, vacations and holidays are reviewed. The program sites that these usually average 16% of the total salary.

Withholding Statement Form - If users decide to have employees they have to enter the employee's marital status and number of dependents for each. Of course, they may have to just guess for the moment. This information is reflected in the payroll form.

Productivity Form - Users are able to enter up to 5 products or categories of products in the Productivity form. Users enter the number of units of products or services they expect to sell, make or perform per week, or per month, or per year. The program will fill in the other columns automatically. Note: if 1 were entered in the week column, the month column would display 4.35 since that is the average number of weeks per month.

Payroll Form - Again if there are employees, the salary is entered and the program calculates the taxes and other withholdings.

Appointment with your insurance agent - The user now meets with an insurance agent. Which scenarios they see are dependent on whether they are working at home or renting, whether or not they have employees and the type of business. Flood insurance happens to be one of the options as certain properties are in flood prone areas. Only the observant will note the clues in the pictures of the properties.

Harry talks about: Record Keeping - Beginning with an anecdote about a friend who had to sell his business because he failed to keep good records, Harry covers the need for a cash receipts journal, a cash disbursements journal, payroll forms, cash flow projections, and a business checkbook. And he also mentions the "umpteen" forms and documents necessary for taxes.

Enter local retail sales tax rate - If you selected a Retail business in the Business Profile

Harry comes back to explain that you have to get a license and when and how to submit the sales taxes you collect.

Harry discusses: Credit Records - He cites the negative aspects of giving credit and explains that when you do accept credit, you'll need records for Accounts Receivable and Accounts Payable. Then he discusses the need to set aside a specific, regular time for all business paperwork and planning. It's important to set up an efficient filing system and to retain the files for at least three years. Finally he encourages the user to think about what records he/she'd need to re-establish the business if disaster should strike...and to keep those records in a bank safety deposit box or at least a fire-proof safe.

Records needed - Here the user reviews what records they will need for a service business, a manufacturing business or a retail business depending upon the entry in the Business Profile. (See the "Go To" Menu where you can override the program and select which type of business records you wish to review.)

Practice: Record-keeping - Following this review, Harry offers an opportunity to practice the type of record-keeping the user just viewed. Harry makes the point that the records should be current and accurate.

Harry introduces: Cash-Flow Statement - He explains that it's cash or checks that pass through your fingers in the day-to-day operation of your business. He stresses the importance of keeping accurate monthly records of this cash flow. Terminology, such as Income or Receipts and Disbursements, is discussed Harry also reminds the user that cash flow disbursements are for on-going expenses, not one-time start up costs. The Start-up Costs are calculated later.

The user won't enter Receipts, Cost of Sales, Gross Profit, nor Net Profit into the Cash Flow form itself. The program will fill that in as it makes calculations based on information entered elsewhere in the program. The user will have to estimate disbursements for the entire year before she/he can set their price later on. Then the program will fill in the estimated Receipts, Gross Profit and Net Profit. During the simulation of business operation, the program will fill in everything in the actual columns as each month is completed.

Following this sequence, the user reviews a series of screens that define each of the cash flow entries.

Harry discusses: Monthly Sales Projections - Harry point out that no matter what kind of business you're in, no matter what product or service you're selling, you should try to predict your peak periods, your slow periods, and a general percentage of business you'll do each month.

Harry illustrates the concept with this scenario: "Let's say I manufacture candy. There are certain times of the year when I'll need to produce more candy than at other times, so I have to plan my production schedule accordingly. Holidays, special sales, the changing seasons can all affect my distributors' demands for my product. For example, we know candy will be in more demand around Halloween, Christmas, and, of course, Valentine's Day...I've got to make the candy in time to get it to market at the peak demand period. Now let's say you're a retailer. You sell the candy I've made. You probably won't order as much in the summer because it won't sell like it will in early February, before Valentine's Day. So you have to plan your inventory accordingly, and know that your cost of sales will be higher those months, but so will your income."

"Now, our friend Jones down the hall is into a service business; he runs a diet program business. So he knows that after people have eaten all that candy at Christmas and Valentine's Day his business can be booming – if he throws a little extra effort into advertising."

Monthly Sales Projections - In this section, the user estimates percentages of sales for each month for each product or service. The total must equal 100% so the program makes adjustments if the user estimates too high.

Entering Cost of Sales Estimates - The user can get a reminder on what the Cost of Sales is for Retail: Total paid for goods they will sell. For Manufacturing: Cost of raw materials. And for Service: Citing that service doesn't usually have these costs. However, one may wish to include several of the variable costs associated with sales and marketing of one's service. If they're not sure they should seek help and always review classifications with the help of a professional accountant. Following the optional review the user enters the estimated costs.

Party at the Matthews - Now for a big decision point. While working at home with Harry (on a Saturday night) two neighboring party goers enter the home in a boisterous manner. They discover that Harry and the user are working on the business plan and commence to offer anything but encouragement... "You know, I really think you should forget this foolishness. Opening your own business is sooo risky. There's no security, no guaranteed salary, and none of the fringe benefits that come with a real job. And you're going to risk your life's savings?! Don't you realize how complex it can be. There are employees, and their salaries, and more expenses than you can think of, with unexpected problems popping up all the time. And the competition is fierce. Do you realize what the failure rate is on new businesses? It's probably going to be years before you see any sort of profit. I dunna know ... I think you're making a big mistake." After these words of neighborly advice Harry points out that what they've said is true and leaves the user with the decision to "Continue with your dream of owning a business?"

Cash Flow Statement - Perhaps one of the biggest tasks for the user is to fill in the estimated disbursements for a calendar year. Since some of the amounts, like insurance, have already been decided, the program will fill those in automatically. Those amounts include, rent, taxes and wages/benefits. The actual column will be filled in during the one year simulation. Cost of sales for retail and manufacturing and some service business will be filled in already. But Receipts can't be filled in because we have yet to set pricing. *Tip: By entering an amount in the first column and clicking "Fill Right," non variable amounts can be entered for all 12 months.*

Note: How does the program calculate and fill in the fields I can't enter data into?

Insurance, Rent, Taxes and Wages & Benefits are simply "remembered" or copied, by the program, from decisions you made or the forms you entered data into earlier. Receipts and Cost of Sales are another matter.

Once all of your disbursements for the full year are completed you will leave the Cash Flow Statement. The program will then ask you to estimate your monthly sales projections. That is, what percentage of total annual sales do you anticipate for each month.

Then the program will ask you to estimate your cost of sales for each item or service. At that time the Cost of Sales row will get filled in by the program. It will take the total annual number of sales you expect for each item and apply the monthly sales projections you have made to arrive at the number of sales you expect each month. Then it will multiply the monthly number of sales times your estimated cost for EACH item or service. The resulting amount will automatically be placed in the Cost of Sales row of the Cash Flow Statement.

Similarly, you will then be asked to set your price for each product/service. Again the program will take the total annual number of sales you expect for each item and apply the monthly sales projections you have made to arrive at the number of sales you expect each month. Then it will multiply the monthly number of sales times your price for EACH item or service. The resulting amount will automatically be placed in the Receipts row of the Cash Flow Statement.

Gross Profit is simply the Receipts minus the Cost of Sales.

All of the disbursements are totaled by the program and subtracted from the Gross Profit. This will yield the Net Profit.

Harry on: Pricing - Harry now shows a step by step process for setting pricing. What he is illustrating is what the program will actually do for the user who only has to enter the price they want to charge for the product or service. Harry's formulas are contained in the Workbook for future reference.

Startup Costs - Harry guides the user through calculating the Startup Costs. They include Equipment, Furnishings, Licenses and Fees, Opening Promotion, Professional Fees, Security Deposit, Supplies and Telephone Installation and the first months' expenses. The first months' expenses include 3 months operating expenses (including cost of sales), 4 months of taxes and 2 months of owner's salary.

Owner's contribution to startup costs - Now the user enters the amount they can contribute toward startup costs. It must be at least 20% of the total and would assume an SBA guaranteed loan. They can use the Calculator in the "Tools" menu to estimate their monthly loan payment.

Letter of Intent - If, in fact, the user needs a loan, the program generates a simple Letter of Intent for the bank.

Harry talks about Depreciation - If the user has entered a dollar amount in equipment startup costs Harry "knows" they have some equipment and plays an animated video to explain one method of calculating depreciation.

Depreciation Form - Now the user has the opportunity to fill in the Depreciation Form while the procedure is still fresh in their minds.

See the banker concerning your loan - If a loan is required, the user now returns to the bank to find out if his request has been approved. If the Business Plan is in order, the banker offers congratulations and hands over the check. However, the banker will reject the loan application for each of the following reasons:

1) If the user has asked for more than 80% of the total capitalization needed.

2) If she/he is taking too large an amount for his/her salary (the policy is to take the total minimum expenses from the Personal Income Statement Part II and add no more than 10%).

3) If the user has not budgeted properly for advertising. The banker offers the user the chance to make the necessary adjustments and reapply or "chuck the whole thing."

The rules of Thumb for Advertising used are:

- In a Retail business one should budget 4% to 8% of sales for high priced items and 6% to 12% for standard priced items.

- For a Service business one should allow 5% to 8% of sales.

- A Manufacturing business should target their add budget to 2% to 4% of sales.

Congratulations!! Party with friends - Once the user's loan is approved Harry throws a party.

Part II: Your first year in business - Now the user begins the calendar year simulation of running the business. The starting month is January and cannot be changed to start in a different month.
Actual startup costs - The user now reviews the actual startup costs. They will be within a few percent of what was estimated unless the estimates were very high or low relative

to the norm.

Beginning of the Month - At the beginning of each month users will have the opportunity to hire employees (unless they already have nine, which is the maximum), to layoff employees, to adjust productivity or to change the price they charge for their products or services. In each case they will get the necessary information to help them make the change. For example, let's say they started with no employees. If they hire employees, they will now view all of the related scenes with Harry that they didn't see earlier. At the end of each month they will review receipts, disbursements and their business checking account. They will also have the option to receive comments from a counselor.

While they are going through Part II, they will run into a variety of situations. One can go through the simulation multiple times and have different experiences. They may have to deal with irate neighbors, unhappy employees, even potholes in the parking lot. They'll also have the chance to get helpful information from a TV Newscast or have the opportunity to attend an advertising seminar. There are many more possibilities. If they are in debt for more than two months the creditors will foreclose. They always have the option to find ways of getting additional cash, such as borrowing from friends and family, taking it from savings, etc.

If they make it to the end of the year they'll see Harry again for a financial analysis. He'll compare their assets to liabilities ratio. If they have done well, the assets should be about twice the liabilities. And their initial investment should have made more profit than it would have if left in a savings account. Based on this balance sheet, Harry offers either a hardy congratulation or some suggestions on things to do to improve their business. Either way, they made it through the year and now have a party with Harry and their fellow business owners.

Integrating the program with the course:

Although the program can be brought into the class it is most effective if students simply follow the End-of-Chapter Exercises in the textbook. They take the Entrepreneurial Attitude Survey during their first week and compare their attitudes to those of successful entrepreneurs. Then during the second week they will begin the actual program. In order to keep students on track it's recommended that they work through the program in sequential order and complete Part I around the mid point of the semester.

It's completely self instructing and requires no preparation to begin using. Your expectations or requirements are flexible. You may want to require brief report where students explain their experiences and what they got out of the simulation and why the made certain decisions. Or you may have them submit a printout of the Business Income Statement simply to verify that they completed the program. Establishing "mileposts" throughout the semester – points by which students must have completed the various parts of the simulation – allows professors to use The Business Disc as the basis for meaningful classroom discussions. If you have students prepare a business plan as part of your class, The Business Disc is an excellent "warm-up exercise" that gets students oriented to the business planning process.